THE

Selected

Letters

OF

CHARLES DICKENS

THE

Selected Letters

OF

CHARLES DICKENS

Edited by

JENNY HARTLEY

OXFORD
UNIVERSITY PRESS

OXFORD
UNIVERSITY PRESS

Great Clarendon Street, Oxford OX2 6DP

Oxford University Press is a department of the University of Oxford.
It furthers the University's objective of excellence in research, scholarship,
and education by publishing worldwide in

Oxford New York

Auckland Cape Town Dar es Salaam Hong Kong Karachi
Kuala Lumpur Madrid Melbourne Mexico City Nairobi
New Delhi Shanghai Taipei Toronto

With offices in

Argentina Austria Brazil Chile Czech Republic France Greece
Guatemala Hungary Italy Japan Poland Portugal Singapore
South Korea Switzerland Thailand Turkey Ukraine Vietnam

Oxford is a registered trade mark of Oxford University Press
in the UK and in certain other countries

Published in the United States
by Oxford University Press Inc., New York

First published 2012

British Library Cataloguing in Publication Data

Data available

Library of Congress Cataloging in Publication Data

Data available

Typeset by RefineCatch Limited, Bungay, Suffolk
Printed in Great Britain
on acid-free paper by
Clays Ltd, St Ives plc

ISBN 978–0–19–959141–1

10 9 8 7 6 5 4 3 2 1

Acknowledgements

This selection owes its existence to the Pilgrim Trustees, and I am grateful to Georgina Naylor at the Pilgrim Trust. The original Pilgrim Edition benefited from the generosity of the British Academy with funding, and from the subsequent adoption of the edition as an official research project. Mark Dickens has been supportive on behalf of the family. The illustration in the letter to Daniel Maclise of February 13 1840 is from the Henry W. and Albert A. Berg Collection of English and America Literature, The New York Public Library, Astor, Lennox and Tilden Foundations, reproduced by permission of Mark Dickens.

I am especially grateful to Michael Slater for his generous interest and unstinting support; and for his expert advice and judgement. It is a pleasure to record my thanks to him. The knowledge, assistance, and kindness of Angus Easson and Margaret Brown, both Pilgrim editors, have been invaluable. I would also like to thank Malcolm Andrews and David Paroissien; Joan Dicks and the Dickens Fellowship; Florian Schweizer at the Charles Dickens Museum, and Nick Hartley for his attentive and careful eye. At Oxford University Press, Jacqueline Baker has been the ideal editor. I am also grateful to Ariane Petit, Jackie Pritchard, and Fiona Vlemmiks for guiding the book expertly through to publication. It is a great privilege to have had the index made by Douglas Matthews.

The selection is respectfully dedicated to the editors, assistant editors, and associate editors of the British Academy Pilgrim Edition of *The Letters of Charles Dickens*.

Specimens of signatures

1. July 1832. *2.* November 1834. *3.* November 1835. *4.* March 1836.
5. October 1836. *6.* April 1837. *7.* March 1838. *8.* November 1839.
9. August 1840. *10.* January 1842. *11.* November 1842. *12.* April 1846.
13. June 1847. *14.* July 1861

Contents

Introduction

Had it been up to Dickens, this selection of his letters would not have appeared. He was himself a great destroyer of letters, especially towards the end of his life. 'Yesterday,' he wrote in September 1860, 'I burnt, in the field at Gad's Hill, the accumulated letters and papers of twenty years.'[1] He was, he said, 'shocked by the misuse of private letters of public men'.[2] On the other hand, he delighted in the 'affection' which he fostered between himself and his readers; he built on that close relationship in his public readings, and he dispatched reams of letters to his friend John Forster, knowing that he was to be his biographer. So perhaps he would have given a back-handed blessing to this selection.

Dickens claimed to receive 'three or four score letters every day'.[3] Answering them was a regular and lifelong commitment. He liked to reply promptly: 'I can't bear to leave anything unanswered';[4] but they could pile up. 'Yours is the thirty eighth in the batch. Forgive me!' he apologised to Jane Carlyle, 'but I have been so much engaged in another kind of Penmanship, that I have not answered a letter this fortnight.'[5] Letter-writing was an integral part of his writing life, and fortunately for us, the recipients of his letters did not share his habits of destruction. His early fame ensured that people kept the briefest of notes and the most unflattering rejection letters. As David Paroissien remarks, 'To receive a letter from him—even a perfunctory request to renew an order for a dozen bottles of sherry—was to take delivery of a gift.'[6]

The 14,000 surviving letters, addressed to 2,500 known correspondents and over 200 unknown correspondents, have been painstakingly collected, dated, annotated, and published between 1965 and 2002, in the magisterial twelve-volume Pilgrim Edition, from which this selection is taken. Some of the 14,000 are tantalizing ghosts: letters which exist only as a mention in another letter, or a fragment in a sale catalogue. Some are mere notes of acceptance, invitation, or refusal. Some run to many pages. 'In his letter-writing alone,' George Gissing judged, 'Dickens did a life's literary work.'[7] All bear the stamp of the Inimitable.

Letters give us a particular version of a life: the 'freshness of first impressions', as Forster characterizes Dickens's letters from America in 1842 when comparing them

---

[1] 4 Sept. 1860. All references to Dickens's letters in this Introduction are to the Pilgrim Edition.
[2] 20 Dec. 1864.
[3] 22 Oct. 1841.
[4] 1 May 1848.
[5] 27 Jan. 1844.
[6] ' "Faithfully Yours, Charles Dickens": The Epistolary Art of the Inimitable', in David Paroissien (ed.), *A Companion to Charles Dickens* (Oxford: Blackwell Publishing, 2008), 35.
[7] George Gissing, *Charles Dickens: A Critical Study* (London: Blackie and Son, 1898), 235.

with *American Notes*, the book Dickens later composed from the letters.[8] Forster maintained that 'The *personal narrative* of this famous visit to America is in the letters alone.' It was, though, just this narrative of the personal which Dickens was attempting to edit out with his bonfire. When his children protested, his justification was that letters are 'written in the heat of the moment'.[9] This is of course what we value his letters for today: that quality of life lived on the hoof (sometimes literally so for Dickens), which the letters bring us with such immediacy.

In reducing twelve volumes to one, and the 14,000 to 450, the main criterion is to show Dickens's range as a letter writer. Readers who enjoy his fiction, his journalism, and his travel writing will appreciate his gifts in this fourth genre. On display here, notably in this condensed version, is the epistolary as the genre of exuberance. We see at first hand his indefatigable labours as a magazine editor, his exasperation with business arrangements (not always to his credit), his close involvement with philanthropic projects, his responses to issues of the day such as public hangings, and his alertness as a traveller. We can feel the warmth of his friendships, the richness of his social life, and, throughout, his pleasure in writing, if only (and sometimes especially) to an audience of one. In this selection one letter represents many more. A good example is the mass of letters concerning amateur theatricals. Dickens took sole responsibility for all the organization, which meant choosing the plays, distributing parts, cajoling cast members, and arranging rehearsals; ordering costumes, props, and scenery; booking theatres, railway carriages, and hotel rooms. 'I write 100 letters a day, about these plays,' he grumbled about this self-inflicted chore. 'I am fully persuaded that an amateur manager has more correspondence than the Home Secretary.'[10]

Dickens is primarily known and loved as a novelist, so letters which relate to the fiction have priority in this selection. His letters to publishers and illustrators, his letters to and about originals of his characters, and comments on sales and reception (although he claimed not to read reviews): all these augment our sense of Dickens the novelist. His progress reports—usually to Forster, his close friend and lifelong literary sounding-board and confidant—bring his working methods into focus. So, for instance, just a fortnight after 'breaking my heart' over the end of *The Old Curiosity Shop*, he describes the beginnings of *Barnaby Rudge*:

I didn't stir out yesterday, but sat and *thought* all day; not writing a line; not so much as the cross of a t or the dot of an i. I imaged forth a good deal of Barnaby by keeping my mind steadily upon him; and am happy to say I have gone to work this morning in good twig, strong hope, and cheerful spirits.

Occasional sentences suggest the ebb and flow of creativity. He reports being 'in a perpetual scald and boil' with 'the great turning idea of the Bleak House story' in November 1852. Eight months later he is 'now going, tooth and nail, at Bleak House'. We can track *Little Dorrit* from birth-pang to triumphant conclusion, growing from

---

[8] Forster, 244.
[9] Gladys Storey, *Dickens and Daughter* (London: Frederick Muller, 1939), 106–7.
[10] 9 July 1847; 22 June 1848.

'motes of new books in the dirty air' in February 1855. As late as January 1856, when the first two numbers have appeared, he writes to Forster: 'Again I am beset by my former notions of a book whereof the whole story shall be on the top of the Great St. Bernard. As I accept and reject ideas for Little Dorrit, it perpetually comes back to me.' Progress could be slow. 'I have not been in a quick vein (which is not to be commanded),' he tells Angela Burdett Coutts in September. In January 1857 he describes his 'knitted brows now turning into cordage over Little Dorrit'; and finally in May he can rejoice to Wilkie Collins, 'Thank God, I *have* finished! On Saturday last, I wrote the two little words of three letters each.' In the autumn of 1865, after the trauma of the railway accident earlier that year, he was relieved to observe his creative powers still functioning well, as he told Forster about the next Christmas story and his creation of Sophie, Dr Marigold's adopted deaf and dumb daughter:

Tired with Our Mutual, I sat down to cast about for an idea, with a depressing notion that I was, for the moment, overworked. Suddenly, the little character that you will see, and all belonging to it, came flashing up in the most cheerful manner, and I had only to look on and leisurely describe it. [11]

It is tempting to read this single volume of letters as a Dickens novel, with its cast of characters and voices, its keenly described scenes and situations, and its abundance of wit and vitality. It has stories too: long-running plots of friendships and domestic relations, sometimes with dramatic reversals. The main character is, naturally, Dickens himself, decidedly the hero of his own life in this version. [12] We can follow his trajectory from the early years of success and high spirits, through the middle years of writing confidence, to the later compulsive restlessness. The change in the letters themselves, as they become less expansive, is part of the plot of the life, and underlines how much his life altered after 1858 and the marital break-up. His resolution 'to write as short letters as I can' [13] in the 1860s signals the more guarded and secretive Dickens of the last twelve years. Allusions to 'perpetually oscillating between Paris and London' and 'my present Mysterious Disappearance' [14] hint at the life he was leading with Ellen Ternan; his sense of entitlement to privacy grew commensurately with his need for it.

According to his daughter Mamie and his sister-in-law Georgina Hogarth, who edited the first collection of his letters, 'no man ever expressed *himself* more in his letters than Charles Dickens'. [15] But did he? Reviewers of that first collection argued over how revealing the letters were. [16] Later, George Bernard Shaw disputed Edgar Johnson's estimation of Dickens's 'shiningly high rank as a letter writer', calling

---

[11] To Forster, early Nov. 1865.

[12] Cf. *David Copperfield*, which begins: 'Whether I shall turn out to be the hero of my own life, or whether that station will be held by anybody else, these pages must show.'

[13] 25 Feb. 1864.   [14] 16 June 1863; 26 June 1864.

[15] *The Letters of Charles Dickens*, edited by his Sister-in-law and his Eldest Daughter, 3 vols. (London: Chapman & Hall, 1880–2), preface.

[16] See Philip Collins (ed.), *Dickens: The Critical Heritage* (London: Routledge, 1971), 589.

them 'roast beef and pudding letters, explaining that what he meant by this was that they were all concerned with things done, places visited, what people looked like and how they acted.'[17] This is unfair (Shaw did not have access to the range of letters which we have), but it is true that Dickens was not given to sustained introspection. There are, however, fleeting glimpses, such as his description of 'looking upon my mind . . . as a sort of capitally prepared and highly sensitive plate. And I said, without the least conceit (as Watkins [the photographer] might have said of a plate of his) "it really is a pleasure to work with you, you receive the impression so nicely".'[18] What the letters show us is Dickens the watcher of himself.[19] It is worth noting that many of his friends belonged to the observing professions: they were journalists, actors, painters. Dickens observes himself as a writer, as a reader of his own work, and as man of suffering. He comments on the writing of *Martin Chuzzlewit*: 'As to the way in which these characters have opened out, that is, to me, one of the most surprising processes of the mind in this sort of invention.'[20] He listens to himself reading. 'I got things out of the old Carol—effects I mean—so entirely new and so very strong, that I quite amazed myself and wondered where I was going next. I really listened to Mr Peggotty's narrative in Copperfield, with admiration.'[21] To Angela Burdett Coutts's companion, Hannah Brown, he confided in the troubled August of 1857: 'The vague unhappiness which tracks a life of constant aim and ever impels to some new aim in which it may be lost, is so curious to consider, that I observe it in myself sometimes, with as much curiosity as if I were another man.'

These glimpses are all the more valuable because of Dickens's reticence in life.[22] The man who could write eloquent letters of consolation to bereaved friends noted his difficulty in expressing himself face to face. Three years after the death of his friend Richard Watson he visited Rockingham Castle, the Watsons' home, where he and his amateur company had acted, and commented to Georgina:

Rockingham was inexpressibly sad. . . . Mrs. Watson asked me, in a strange manner, if I had been in the old Gallery upstairs? I said No, and she returned "Then do come!" So we walked up together, and she raised that great iron latch, and we went in, and the furniture was all piled in a great ghostly heap in the middle, and the carpet was up, and the curtains were down. She turned her head away and looked out of a window; and for the life of me I could not decide upon the delicacy or friendliness of making any allusion to her grief. Consequently I turned my head and looked out of another window, until she moved. Then we both came out together, silently and sadly.[23]

[17] *Letters from Charles Dickens to Angela Burdett-Coutts 1841–1865*, ed. Edgar Johnson (London: Jonathan Cape, 1953), 21–2.

[18] To William H. Wills, 24 Sept. 1858.

[19] This point is made by Rosemarie Bodenheimer, *Knowing Dickens* (Ithaca, NY: Cornell University Press, 2007), 207.

[20] To Forster, mid-Feb. 1843.

[21] To Wills, 4 Feb. 1863.

[22] 'He was most extraordinarily reticent for a man who was supposed to be so full of frankness and geniality,' his daughter Katey told George Bernard Shaw, preface to Pilgrim 1, xiv.

[23] 19 Dec. 1855.

Writing reflectively about himself did not come easily. An early attempt to keep a journal in 1838, the year after the death of his sister-in-law Mary Hogarth, foundered after a fortnight because 'I grow sad over this checking off of days, and can't do it.'[24] In 1842 he hinted that 'I may one of these days be induced to lay violent hands upon myself—in other words attempt my own life'.[25] Fourteen years later he told an enquirer, 'I may probably leave my own record of my life for the satisfaction of my children.'[26] But apart from the fragment given to Forster, which transmuted into David Copperfield's childhood, nothing autobiographical survives.

Dickens had, moreover, long cultivated a hedge for himself in his letters, through his recourse to the third-person persona. Most famously he is the Inimitable. This was the designation bestowed upon him by his old schoolteacher William Giles, with a silver snuff-box inscribed to 'The Inimitable Boz', midway through publication of The Pickwick Papers. Dickens took enthusiastically to being Inimitable; he would also refer to himself as 'the Sparkler of Albion' and 'the planet Dick', underlining his role as national treasure and irresistible force of nature. Third-person facetiousness could convey brilliant triumph: 'Dick with the heart of a lion dashed in bravely and made decidedly the best speech I ever heard him achieve.'[27] Other versions of himself include the comic hero beset by the disasters of household alterations, publishing arrangements, would-be authors, and impecunious relatives—his 'blood petitioners'.[28] He also liked to construct himself as put-upon and betrayed, and as what Rosemary Bodenheimer calls 'the Great Protester'.[29] As a young man he enjoyed inventing joke sign-offs: 'The Mask', 'Victoria', 'Anti Pusey', 'The Congreve of the 19th Century', 'Dick the Doomed', 'Philo Forecastle', and 'Pitchcock, Swabber, Trillington, & Dawberry'.[30] Writing to Forster in 1849 about yet more familial importunings, he signed himself 'Yours Despondently, | And Disgustedly, | Wilkins Micawber.'

Each one of Dickens's letters is a performance, finely calibrated to the nature of its recipient, as if he were talking to him or her. This may be why, even if the correspondent is not known personally to him, he needs a name to reply to. He tells 'Miss M.' that her letter is so 'agreeable' that it 'induces me to break through the rule I generally observe of never replying to a correspondent who writes to me anonymously, as I hold no one justified in adopting that most objectionable and stealthy form of address'.[31] Some of his most affectionate letters are addressed to his older male friends, such as the actor William Macready, whom he had idolized as a boy and still venerated, and the painter Clarkson Stanfield ('Stanny'), who had been in the navy, evoking echoes of Dickens's Portsmouth and Chatham childhood

[24] 15 Jan. 1838.
[25] 16 Feb. 1842.
[26] 4 Oct. 1856.
[27] 28 Feb. 1844.
[28] 4 Dec. 1843.
[29] Bodenheimer, Knowing Dickens, 23–9.
[30] 9 June 1843; 30 Jan. 1843; 26 May 1843; 13 June 1843; 28 Mar. 1846; 9 Jan 1844; 4 Apr. 1846, respectively. See John Bowen, Other Dickens: Pickwick to Chuzzlewit (Oxford: Oxford University Press, 2000), 39–40.
[31] 3 Apr. 1847.

days. Letters to the artist Daniel Maclise are more sprightly, maybe to cheer him up (he was prone to depression); letters to fellow-novelist Wilkie Collins express a racier persona. Letters to Forster confirm his reliance on him for editorial advice. 'I would give any money that it were possible to consult with you,' he wrote from Italy in the autumn of 1846, agonizing over the progress of his Christmas book. His daughter Katey wanted to burn the 137 letters to her mother, which she was entrusted to publish, 'to shew the world that Dickens once loved her',[32] because in Katey's opinion they showed 'exactly the reverse'. It is true that letters to Catherine's sister Georgina tend to be livelier, but until shortly before the separation in 1858, his letters to Catherine relax into affection, a life of common concerns and gossip, private jokes, and a fully shared domestic arena. But, for her too as for every one of his correspondents: whoever he is writing to, and however briefly, he always has to perform himself, even to a clock-mender or chimney-sweep. He loves to give advice, and he always knows best: to Macready on how to organize his theatre,[33] to Angela Burdett Coutts on interior décor,[34] and to Wilkie Collins on novel titles (he suggested twenty-six for *No Name*, all of which Collins rejected).[35] He could also advise on recipes for dog-food, beef tea, and salad-dressing,[36] and write in French or Italian. He was aware, though, that he could overdo it. 'I find I am getting inimitable, so I'll stop,' ends his account of a visit to the Paris morgue in January 1847.

What the letters give us, then, is not so much inner Dickens as Dickens in motion. Humphry House, the prime mover of the Pilgrim Edition, claimed that 'even for the ordinary reader the view of Dickens's personality could never be complete without seeing day after day the streaming energy of his correspondence in bulk and detail; a mere selection disguises all that.'[37] True, but it can give a taste of the pace and flavour, as we witness the novelist writing continually to tight (and sometimes multiple) deadlines. At the same time, he was for most of his working life also a diligent magazine editor who took great pains with his contributors. He could be sharp if he thought the writer had not taken his or her work seriously, generous and helpful if he thought they had. He would offer lengthy long-distance tutorials, master-classes, and 'hints' which 'take the course that my pen would take if the story were mine'.[38] Then there are the letters of the social worker in charge of every detail, the sociable man who preferred not to dine alone if possible, the loyal friend, and the committed if sometimes infuriated family man. Dickens was also one of our first modern celebrities, dealing with requests for autographs and locks of hair (yes to the former, no to the latter), as well as pleas to the author in mid-flow. 'I am inundated with imploring letters recommending poor little Nell to mercy.—Six yesterday, and

---

[32] Preface to Pilgrim i, xxiii. The letters are now in the British Library.

[33] 28 Dec. 1841.

[34] 1 Nov. 1854.

[35] 24 Jan. 1866.

[36] 7 Nov. 1865; 25 Sept. 1854; 21 Aug. 1868.

[37] Humphry House, 'A New Edition of Dickens's Letters', BBC, 14 Oct. 1951; repr. in *All in Due Time: The Collected Essays and Broadcast Talks of Humphry House* (London: Rupert Hart-Davis, 1955), 221–9.

[38] To Charles Hamilton Aidé, 29 Mar. 1869.

four today (it's not 12 o'Clock yet) already!' he exclaimed during the publication of *The Old Curiosity Shop* in November 1840. The letters also show his passion for such issues as the Yorkshire schools, and the fate of fallen women such as Little Em'ly.

All this extensive correspondence functioned not only to keep the frenetic mechanics of Dickens's working and social life in action. It was also a pleasure and a need. His customary long end-of-year letter to William de Cerjat (one of the circle of friends Dickens joined in Switzerland in 1846) gave him space to stand back and survey the past year. A letter to Forster could substitute for the conversation which Dickens craved. 'To tell what Venice is,' he wrote from there in 1844, 'I feel to be an impossibility. And here I sit alone, writing it: with nothing to urge me on, or goad me to that estimate, which, speaking of it to anyone I loved, and being spoken to in return, would lead me to form.'[39] Or it might act like therapy. After sitting with his dying sister Fanny, he described the scene at length to Forster, ending with the comment: 'I don't know why I write this before going to bed. I only know that in the very pity and grief of my heart, I feel as if it were doing something.'[40] Letter-writing could also sop up the surplus of writerly force which Dickens seems to have had, especially when young—he simply liked writing. It could help, as acting did, to vent what he called his 'superfluous energy'.[41] According to his son Henry, the letters testified to the 'keen enjoyment' his father got out of life,[42] and one source of this was letter-writing itself. 'One of the impressions left by the letters', Forster concluded—presumably while in the process of destroying them—'is that of the intensity and tenacity with which he recognized, realized, contemplated, cultivated, and thoroughly enjoyed, his own individuality in even its most trivial manifestations.'[43] Dickens was amused but probably not surprised to see that his 8-year-old son Sydney 'has for some time conducted a large imaginary correspondence with scores of people.'[44]

Dickens wrote all his letters himself. For most of his life he employed no secretary, apart from Georgina to handle the begging letters, and his assistant editor William H. Wills for his two magazines, *Household Words* and *All the Year Round*.[45] Dickens seems at times to have thought in the written word. Being confronted with illegible writing was one of his recurring nightmares.[46] The shorthand which he learned to such good effect early in life never left him (he taught Frank Stone's son Arthur, and his own son Henry). George Dolby, who managed his reading tours in the late 1860s, spotted

---

[39] 12 Nov. 1844.

[40] 5 July 1848.

[41] To Emily Jolly, 30 May 1857.

[42] Henry F. Dickens, *Memories of my Father* (London: Victor Gollancz, 1928), 31.

[43] Forster, 818.

[44] To Revd Matthew Gibson, 18 July 1855.

[45] For *AYR* there was a pro forma rejection letter in a facsimile of Dickens's hand, with the details of the rejected paper filled in by office staff. In the last decade of his life he received so many requests for readings that he had a reply printed; see 29 Nov. 1861.

[46] See e.g. 2 Mar. 1853; 10 June 1857.

Dickens thinking in shorthand: 'When listening to a speech he would (if interested) follow the speaker's words by an almost imperceptible action, as if taking down the speech in shorthand, that being, as he used to say, a habit contracted in the early part of his career.' [47]

The appearance of a letter mattered to Dickens, as did the process of writing it. He used a quill, and groaned when he had to 'write with a steelpen (which I can never use)'. [48] He preferred blue ink on blue paper. In addition to signing his letters, he also signed his name on the bottom left-hand corner of the envelope. [49] Percy Fitzgerald, one of the young writers Dickens befriended in the 1860s, recalled his 'practice of using a numerical *word* instead of a figure to mark the date of his letter. He adhered to it without fail to the day, literally, of his death.' Fitzgerald thought 'the *verbal* form of the numeral appealed to his eye as being the most emphatic form'. [50]

Dickens attached great importance to the 'famous flourish' of his signature, and often commented on it. Replying to a youthful 'Master Francis G Waugh', he wrote underneath his signature: 'Perhaps you'll wonder why I make that flourish. I don't know. I have not the least idea.' [51] He knew that it was a statement in itself, and the analogy he uses to the actor Thomas Serle acknowledges the theatricality of it. 'No room for the flourish. We must "suppose that"—as you say at Rehearsals.' [52] In his analysis of thirty signatures from 1825 to 1870, J. Holt Schooling acclaims them as 'recorded tracings of Dickens's nerve muscular action—of his *gesture*': our only evidence of Dickens's body in motion. Holt Schooling admires the vigour and 'well-controlled activity' of the signatures. He estimates that the curves in the flourish are sometimes 'equal of about a two-feet length of pen-stroke, a fact which indicates an extraordinary amount of personal energy'. He also notes that many private letters are unostentatiously signed 'CD'. The curlicues of the more public signature are the assertion of power over the reader. [53] It ended by becoming his trademark and brand guarantee. The 1867 Charles Dickens edition of his novels had his signature complete with flourish stamped on its covers in gold, to 'suggest to the Author's countrymen', wrote Dickens in the advertisement, 'his present watchfulness over his own Edition'. [54] More than a decade earlier Rigaud, the villain of *Little Dorrit*, had malignly parodied his creator's flourishing tendency when he signs the convent-hotel register, 'in a small complicated hand, ending with a long lean flourish, not unlike a lasso thrown at all the rest of the names'. [55]

[47] George Dolby, *Charles Dickens as I Knew Him: The Story of the Reading Tours in Great Britain and America 1866–1870* (London: T. Fisher Unwin, 1885), 274.

[48] 9 May 1870.

[49] Members of the National Philatelic Society suggest that this practice may hark back to the days of free franking privileges.

[50] Percy Fitzgerald, *Memories of Charles Dickens* (Bristol: J. W. Arrowsmith, 1913), foreword.

[51] 30 June 1858.

[52] 2 Jan. 1844.

[53] J. Holt Schooling, 'The Signatures of Charles Dickens (with Portraits)', *Strand Magazine*, 7 (1894), 80–9.

[54] See Slater, 558–9.

[55] *LD* bk. 2, ch. 1.

Handwriting is something Dickens always notices, whether he is complimenting Emile de la Rue for his 'elegantly small calligraphy',[56] teasing Angela Burdett Coutts for her illegibility, or joking about Mary Boyle's 'hand—twisted like the rustic work of which they make garden chairs'.[57] Dickens's own handwriting is interpreted by Fitzgerald as 'an extraordinary revelation of his character. It was so "prompt", so alert, finished and full of purpose and decision; legible also, but requiring familiarity and training to read.'[58] For Dickens, as for Fitzgerald, the hand stands for the person; your writing does not just express you, it is you. It hits him in the eye, it shakes hands with him. 'Your handwriting last night', he wrote to the Countess of Blessington, 'had as startling effect upon me as though you had sealed your note with one of your own eyes.'[59] 'Your handwriting came like the renewal of some old friendship', he wrote to Thomas Talfourd, 'and gladdened my eyes like the face of some old friend.'[60] Handwriting is often the handmaid of memory. 'When I read your handwriting', he told his old schoolteacher William Giles, 'I half believe I am a very small boy again; and you magnify, in my bewildered sight, into something awful, though not at all severe.'[61] To his first love Maria Beadnell, now contacting him after twenty years, he described the action of her handwriting on his memory at some length, clearly fascinated by the process.[62] For him, the boundaries between the process of writing and mental and bodily states are permeable. Blushing paper figures frequently: 'If blushes could be forwarded by the General Post this sheet of paper would be rose-coloured.'[63] Ink gets inside him: 'I may shed a good deal of ink in the next fortnight,' he comments on sitting down to the next number of *Dombey and Son*.[64]

Dickens sent and received so many letters partly because people could. This was the golden age of letter-writing, ushered in by the 'new and startling experiment of penny postage'.[65] Before 1840 correspondence could be an expensive luxury. Customarily the recipient would pay (to prepay could be construed as a slur on the recipient's solvency). When Dickens apologizes to Forster in 1837, 'I am afraid you will find this letter extremely dear at eightpence', he was referring to the average cost of a letter. This was determined by multiplying the number of sheets (including envelope, or 'cover') by the distance travelled.[66] But reform was on its way. By 1839 Dickens can call his placatory letter a 'Dove . . . on twopenny wings'; and by March 1840 he can refer to 'Taking advantage of the Penny Postage Act'. Hailed by its inventor Rowland Hill as 'a powerful engine of civilization', universal penny postage was a communications

---

[56] To Emile de la Rue, 1 Dec. 1853.   [57] To Spencer Lyttleton, 30 Mar. 1852.

[58] Fitzgerald, *Memories of Charles Dickens*, 223.

[59] 2 June 1831.

[60] 15 July 1838. See also to Macready, 14 Jan. 1853.

[61] 31 Oct. 1848. See also to Miss Oppenheim, 26 Jan. 1848.

[62] See below, 10 Feb. 1855.

[63] 2 Dec. 1837.

[64] 13 Aug. 1846.

[65] 'Mechanism of the Post-Office', *Quarterly Review*, July 1850.

[66] See Catherine J. Golden, *Posting It: The Victorian Revolution in Letter Writing* (Gainesville, Fla.: University Press of Florida, 2009), 4.

revolution. In its first year the number of letters sent tripled; by the 1860s it had increased by more than eight times.[67] There were between ten and twelve deliveries a day in England's major cities, the first at seven in the morning, the last at 8.30 in the evening. Londoners expected to receive a letter two or three hours after posting, and wrote letters to *The Times* complaining when a letter posted 'in the Gray's-inn post-office on Saturday, at half-past one o'clock, addressed to a person living close to Westminster Abbey, was not delivered until past nine o'clock the same evening'.[68]

The cheapness and speed suited Dickens perfectly, although letters sent to him abroad, and thus still costly, might be rather meanly received. 'I am afraid you must have been fishing for a compliment when you talk about the postage of your letters,' he wrote to his sister-in-law Georgina from Venice, 'so I shall punish you by saying that indeed it does come heavy and that I would propose, if you see no objection, to make your mind easy on that score by stopping it out of your quarter.'[69] But the operations of the new institution intrigued him. For the first issue of *Household Words* he collaborated with Wills on an article tracking three brightly coloured Valentine cards through the busy intricacies of the central Post Office at St Martin's-le-Grand. Taking due account of the staggering volume of postal traffic—'entirely . . . attributable to the penny system'—Dickens was predictably impressed by the military efficiency. His imagination was also engaged by the sorting rooms, 'those silent receptacles of countless millions of passionate words, for ever pouring through them like a Niagara of language, and leaving not a drop behind'.[70]

'Nobody ever notices postmen, somehow,' reflects Father Brown in G. K. Chesterton's story 'The Invisible Man'. Dickens was the exception: postmen feature in his letters as members of the cast of his daily life. In the throes of a new book, he is so 'horribly cross and surly' that 'even the Postman knocks at the door with a mild feebleness'.[71] When the postman's knock jars his New Year's Day hangover, 'I damned him from my heart.' But seeing whom the letter was from, 'I immediately blessed him—presented him with a Glass of Whisky—inquired after his family (they are all well)—and opened the despatch' from his American friend Cornelius Felton 'with a moist and oystery twinkle in my eye.'[72] Postmen form a comic obstacle chorus, whether it is the drunken postman in Italy, or 'the man with the postbag . . . swearing in the passage' on the Isle of Wight, or the 'demon Postman' of Finchley, who provokes 'bitter, bitter shame' in Dickens when his dog Timber fails to mate with the postman's bitch.[73] Dickens knew he relied on the post, and on the messenger networks provided by younger brothers ('my small secretary', 15-year-old

---

[67] Rowland Hill, 'Results of Postal Reform', in William Lewins, *Her Majesty's Mails: An Historical and Descriptive Account of the British Post-Office* (London: Sampson Low, 1864), appendix H, 347. See also M. J. Daunton, *Royal Mail: The Post Office since 1840* (London: Athlone Press, 1985).

[68] *The Times*, 8 May 1861.

[69] 25 Nov. 1853.

[70] 'Valentine's Day at the Post-Office', *HW*, 30 Mar. 1850.

[71] 12 Nov. 1842.

[72] 2 Jan. 1844.

[73] 9 Aug. 1844; 16 July 1849; 21 Mar. 1843.

Fred) and servants ('John waiting for the Post, with his mouth open, like a Post office in itself').[74] One of the first attractions of the house he has found in Boulogne, he tells Forster, is that 'the door is within ten minutes of the post office'.[75] His magazine supported the claims of postmen for higher wages;[76] his little son Henry rejoiced in the nickname of The Jollypostboy.

Dickens constantly lamented the burden of 'a correspondence which knows no cessation'.[77] His imagery favours the wet: inundation rather than rubbish-heap. 'In the midst of such a roaring sea of correspondence'; 'Up to the chin in a raging sea of correspondence'; 'I look out of a sea of letters', 'an overwhelming and unbroken stream'.[78] Considering the inroads necessarily made upon his time, these metaphorical tidal waves seem to relate to the frequent trope throughout Dickens's fiction, of the 'sea of Time' and the 'swift river' which 'bears us to the ocean' of death.[79] His correspondence includes thousands of replies to requests for charitable donations, for support in aid of good causes, or protest against outrages. While he would often offer help privately, 'any public mention of my name' was anathema to him, as he explained to a Unitarian minister. 'I have a great objection to being supposed to "patronize" anything or anybody.'[80] He described his house as 'inundated with begging letters'[81] and got crosser as he got older. 'My correspondents', he wrote in 1866, 'are of two classes. One class wants print; the other class wants money. Both are extremely lachrymose, and are surrounded by friends who hold them in unspeakable estimation, but somehow don't tangibly express it.'[82] So afflicted was he by the barrage that he made it the subject of a coruscating article for an early number of *Household Words*. 'The Begging-Letter Writer' is Dickens at his most vituperative about 'one of the most shameless frauds and impositions of this time'.[83]

But, for all his grumbles, Dickens never thought letters were not a good thing. If he had had more time he would have written even more. 'I walk about brimful of letters, facetious descriptions, touching morsels, and pathetic friendships,' he wrote in apology for a tardy reply. But 'the Post-Office is my rock ahead. My average number of letters that *must* be written every day, is, at the least, a dozen.'[84] He was pleased when the emigrants to Australia from Urania Cottage, the home for fallen women in Shepherd's Bush, asked for more writing paper. 'Some of them', he told Miss Coutts, 'may have nobody to write to; but the separation even from so much Earth that they have been used to, is a tremendous one, and the feeling that they

[74] 30 Nov. 1835; 21 Aug. 1850.
[75] 26 June 1853.
[76] 'Hear the Postman!' *AYR*, 13 July 1861.
[77] 12 Sept. 1867.
[78] 20 Nov. 1849; 19 Dec. 1861; 28 Nov. 1850; 16 Jan. 1850.
[79] See e.g. *TC* Fourth Quarter; *D&S* ch. 16.
[80] 30 Mar. 1850.
[81] 13 Aug. 1848.
[82] To the Marchioness of Downshire, 26 Sept. 1866.
[83] *HW*, 18 May 1850.
[84] 1 Sept. 1843.

can connect themselves with England by a few pothooks . . . is a not unwholesome one.'[85] The first issue of *Household Words* show-cased 'A Bundle of Emigrants' Letters', compiled from letters collected by emigration expert Caroline Chisholm. Dickens commended them as 'very affecting'. Inconsistently, he 'strongly urged' Sydney Smith's daughter to publish a selection of her late father's letters, 'which has great merit, and often presents him exactly as he used to be'.[86]

Reading and writing letters punctuate the rhythm of Dickens's day. His devotion to the genre crosses over to inspire the legions of letter writers who populate his fiction. At the head of this band must stand Mr Micawber, who 'never missed any possible opportunity of writing a letter', and whose 'enjoyment of his epistolary powers' matches his creator's. ' "Letters!" cried my aunt. "I believe he dreams in letters!" ' Dickens seems to be mocking his own propensity here; after all, would he not too, as Betsey Trotwood says of Mr Micawber, ' "write letters by the ream, if it was a capital offence!" '[87]

Dickens's correspondents range from Queen Victoria, through her adviser Arthur Helps, to the women on the streets of London whom he invited to join his rehabilitation scheme. He corresponded with other writers such as Carlyle, Tennyson, Thackeray, Browning, and George Eliot, although apart from Wilkie Collins they tend not to be in his close circle. As well as the 14,000 letters itemized by the Pilgrim Editors, there must have been many more. A box of letters to his daughter Katey was lost in a warehouse fire; letters to Augustus Egg vanished in the Blitz of the Second World War. What might be an extensive correspondence with Chauncy Hare Townshend has disappeared, probably at the hands of Dickens himself as Townshend's literary executor. Dickens was fond of Townshend and gave him the manuscript of *Great Expectations*, but now only minute traces of the correspondence survive. At least three further substantial collections were consigned to the flames. When Hablot K. Browne ('Phiz') was moving house he 'had a bonfire to lessen the lumber'; the granddaughters of two of Dickens's friends, Richard Barham and James Muspratt, also burnt 'large numbers of letters'. One of them cut off a signature for her autograph book and put everything else 'on the nursery fire'.[88] Not one of Dickens's letters to Ellen Ternan is known to us, although we can spot references to them in other letters. In a tiny redress of the balance, new letters continue to surface at the rate of about twenty a year.

Many of Dickens's letters survive in manuscript; the major and regrettable exception is his correspondence with John Forster. Most of this was destroyed after the publication of Forster's *The Life of Charles Dickens*, doubtless in deference to Dickens's anxieties about 'misuse'. It was, after all, Mr Bucket, the detective in *Bleak House*, who 'often sees damaging letters produced in evidence, and has occasion to reflect that it was a green thing to write them'.[89] As he stoked that infamous bonfire in

[85] 13 Mar. 1849.
[86] 3 Jan. 1855.
[87] *DC* chs. 36, 52, and 54.
[88] See prefaces to Pilgrim 1 and 5.
[89] *BH* ch. 53.

the autumn of 1860, Dickens was moved to exclaim: 'Would to God every letter I had ever written was on that pile.' His wish denied, to us is left these privileged insights into his life as it was lived from day to strenuous day. The letters in this selection are not just Dickens at work and leisure (although that scarcely seems the right word); they are also Dickens on Scotland, Paris, and Venice; Dickens on child exploitation, Ragged Schools, and soup kitchens; Dickens on the Great Exhibition, women smoking, and dresses for reformed prostitutes; Dickens on ravens, waistcoats, and recipes for punch; Dickens on mesmerism and dreams, and on terrible acting and wonderful children's birthday parties. More than all these, what these letters revive for us is the sheer energy of being Dickens.

Note on the Text

The British Academy Pilgrim Edition: The Letters of Charles Dickens (1965–2002), from which the text for this selection is taken, started to take shape in the late 1940s. Half a century in the making, it is the fruit of twelve editors, including associate and assistant editors. Their painstaking labour combines research, scholarship, and deep immersion in the period, together with the perseverance and ingenuity necessary to track letters down, and the detective work and skill to date them.

The Pilgrim Editors aimed to publish every known letter by Dickens, in as complete a form as possible. Earlier editors worked to different rules. John Forster, Dickens's close friend and first biographer, quoted from nearly a thousand letters to him from Dickens, and claimed that as many again 'had to be put aside'. For those he used he adopted a cut-and-paste technique, subsequently destroying both the discarded fragments and practically all the set-aside letters. The manuscript of his biography no longer exists, and fewer than 200 letters to Forster survive. In the judgement of the Pilgrim Editors, 'Wherever he could improve on his originals Forster apparently thought he had a right to do so.' Not unusual for his time, Forster's was what the later biographer Edgar Johnson characterized as 'a very cavalier attitude to all correspondence'. The first collection of Dickens's letters, by his sister-in-law Georgina Hogarth and daughter Mamie, also bore the marks of strong editorial practice. 'Too *entirely* personal to be suitable for publication' was the reason Georgina gave for rejecting a letter offered to them. Letters they chose were 'cut and condensed *remorselessly*'.[1] Subsequent editors presented letters to single correspondents such as Angela Burdett Coutts, W. H. Wills, John Leech, Thomas Beard, Clarkson Stanfield, and Mark Lemon. The Pilgrim Edition continues to grow, with newly surfacing letters published as Supplements in The Dickensian.

In this selection, the correspondence from the American trip in 1842 and Italy in 1844–5 is under-represented, because it was quarried by Dickens himself for American Notes and Pictures from Italy. All letters are reproduced from the Pilgrim Edition in the most complete version we have them. I have, however, sometimes cut letters to Forster, since they have already been cut and edited by Forster. The italicized explanatory passages in and heading letters to Forster have been extracted by Pilgrim editors from his biography. Throughout, Dickens's underlinings are reproduced as italics; double underlining as capital letters.

---

[1] See John Forster, The Life of Charles Dickens, 817; Edgar Johnson, 'The Art of Biography, An Interview with Edgar Johnson', conducted by Fred Kaplan, Dickens Studies Annual, 1980, 1–38; preface to Pilgrim 1. The preface to Pilgrim 1 also describes previous editorial practices, and the Pilgrim rules of transcription.

Finally, a note on the notes. They are, for the most part, much abbreviated versions of the Pilgrim notes. I have tried to keep them brief, in order to include as many letters as possible.

A CHRONOLOGY OF CHARLES DICKENS

Dickens's major fictions are indicated by bold type.

	Life	*Historical and Cultural Background*
1809	(13 June) John Dickens, a clerk in the Navy Pay Office, marries Elizabeth Barrow.	
1810	(28 Oct.) Frances Dickens ('Fanny') born.	
1811		Prince of Wales becomes Prince Regent. W. M. Thackeray born. Jane Austen, *Sense and Sensibility*
1812	(7 Feb.) Charles Dickens born at Mile End Terrace, Landport, Portsea (now 393 Old Commercial Road, Portsmouth).	Luddite riots. War between Britain and the United States. Napoleon's retreat from Moscow. Robert Browning and Edward Lear born. Lord Byron, *Childe Harold's Pilgrimage*, i and ii (completed 1818)
1813		Robert Southey becomes poet laureate. Napoleon defeated at Leipzig. Austen, *Pride and Prejudice*; Byron, *The Bride of Abydos*, *The Giaour*; P. B. Shelley, *Queen Mab*
1814	Birth (Mar.) and death (Sept.) of Alfred Allen Dickens.	Napoleon exiled to Elba. Austen, *Mansfield Park*; Sir Walter Scott, *Waverley*; William Wordsworth, *The Excursion*
1815	(1 Jan.) Dickens family moves to London.	Escape of Napoleon; Battle of Waterloo. Anthony Trollope born. Thomas Robert Malthus, *An Inquiry into Rent*; Scott, *Guy Mannering*
1816	(Apr.) Letitia Dickens born.	Charlotte Brontë born. Austen, *Emma*; S. T. Coleridge, *Christabel and Other Poems*; Thomas Love Peacock, *Headlong Hall*; Scott, *The Antiquary*, *Old Mortality*
1817	(Apr.) Dickens family settles in Chatham.	Jane Austen dies. Byron, *Manfred*; Coleridge, *Biographia Literaria*; John Keats, *Poems*; Robert Owen, *Report to the Committee on the Poor Law*; Scott, *Rob Roy*
1818		Emily Brontë born. Austen, *Northanger Abbey*, *Persuasion* (posth.); Keats, *Endymion*; Peacock, *Nightmare Abbey*; Scott, *The Heart of Midlothian*; Mary Shelley, *Frankenstein*

Life	*Historical and Cultural Background*
1819 (Sept.) Harriet Dickens born.	Princess Victoria born. Peterloo 'Massacre' (11 deaths). A. H. Clough, Marian Evans (George Eliot), Charles Kingsley, John Ruskin born. Byron, *Don Juan*, i–ii (continued till 1824); Scott, *The Bride of Lammermoor*; Wordsworth, *Peter Bell*, *The Waggoner*
1820 Frederick Dickens ('Fred') born.	Death of George III; accession of Prince Regent as George IV. Trial of Queen Caroline. Anne Brontë born. John Clare, *Poems, Descriptive of Rural Life*; Keats, *Lamia, Isabella, The Eve of St Agnes and Other Poems*; Malthus, *Principles of Political Economy*; Charles Robert Maturin, *Melmoth the Wanderer*; P. B. Shelley, *The Cenci, Prometheus Unbound*; Scott, *Ivanhoe*
1821 CD goes to school run by William Giles.	Greek War of Independence starts. Napoleon dies. Keats dies. Clare, *The Village Minstrel and Other Poems*; Thomas De Quincey, *Confessions of an English Opium Eater*; Pierce Egan, *Life in London*; Thomas Moore, *Irish Melodies*; Scott, *Kenilworth*; P. B. Shelley, *Adonais*; Southey, *A Vision of Judgement*
1822 (Mar.) Alfred Lamert Dickens born; Harriet Dickens dies. CD stays in Chatham when family moves to Camden Town, London; rejoins them later, but his education is discontinued.	Shelley dies. Matthew Arnold born. Byron, *The Vision of Judgement*
1823 (Dec.) Family moves to 4 Gower Street North, where Mrs Dickens fails in her attempt to run a school.	Building of present British Museum begins. Coventry Patmore born. Charles Lamb, *Essays of Elia*; Scott, *Quentin Durward*
1824 (late Jan. or early Feb.) CD sent to work at Jonathan Warren's blacking warehouse, Hungerford Stairs; (20 Feb.) John Dickens arrested and imprisoned for debt in the Marshalsea till 28 May; CD in lodgings; family moves to Somers Town.	National Gallery founded in London. Repeal of acts forbidding formation of trades unions. Byron dies. Wilkie Collins born. James Hogg, *The Private Memoirs and Confessions of a Justified Sinner*; Walter Savage Landor, *Imaginary Conversations* (completed 1829); Scott, *Redgauntlet*
1825 (9 Mar.) John Dickens retires from Navy Pay Office with a pension; (Mar./Apr.) CD leaves Warren's and recommences his schooling at Wellington House Academy.	Stockton–Darlington railway opens. Hazlitt, *Table-Talk, The Spirit of the Age*; Alessandro Manzoni, *I promessi sposi*

Life	Historical and Cultural Background
1826 John Dickens works as parliamentary correspondent for *The British Press*.	University College London and Royal Zoological Society founded. J. Fenimore Cooper, *The Last of the Mohicans*; Benjamin Disraeli, *Vivian Grey* (completed 1827); Mary Shelley, *The Last Man*
1827 (Mar.) Family evicted for non-payment of rates; CD becomes a solicitor's clerk; (Nov.) Augustus Dickens born.	Battle of Navarino. William Blake dies. Clare, *The Shepherd's Calendar*; De Quincey, 'On Murder Considered as One of the Fine Arts'
1828 John Dickens works as reporter for *The Morning Herald*.	Duke of Wellington PM. George Meredith, D. G. Rossetti, Leo Tolstoy born. Pierce Egan, *Finish to the Adventures of Tom, Jerry and Logic*
1829 CD works at Doctors' Commons as a shorthand reporter.	Catholic Emancipation Act; Robert Peel establishes Metropolitan Police.
1830 (8 Feb.) Admitted as reader to British Museum; (May) falls in love with Maria Beadnell.	George IV dies; William IV succeeds. Opening of Manchester–Liverpool Railway. July revolution in France; accession of Louis-Philippe as emperor. Greece independent. Hazlitt dies. Christina Rossetti born. William Cobbett, *Rural Rides*; Sir Charles Lyell, *Principles of Geology* (completed 1832); Alfred Tennyson, *Poems, Chiefly Lyrical*
1831 Composes poem 'The Bill of Fare'; starts work as reporter for *The Mirror of Parliament*.	Reform Bill. Major cholera epidemic. Michael Faraday's electro-magnetic current. Peacock, *Crotchet Castle*; Edgar Allan Poe, *Poems*; Stendhal, *Le rouge et le noir*
1832 Becomes parliamentary reporter on the *True Sun*.	Lord Grey PM. First Reform Act. Jeremy Bentham, Crabbe, Goethe, and Scott die. Charles Lutwidge Dodgson (Lewis Carroll) born. Goethe, *Faust*, ii; Mary Russell Mitford, *Our Village*; Tennyson, *Poems*; Frances Trollope, *Domestic Manners of the Americans*
1833 Concludes relationship with Maria Beadnell; first story, 'A Dinner at Poplar Walk' (later called 'Mr Minns and his Cousin'), published in *Monthly Magazine*.	First steamship crosses the Atlantic. Abolition of slavery in all British colonies (from Aug. 1834). Factory Act forbids employment of children under 9. First government grant for schools. Oxford Movement starts. Robert Browning, *Pauline*; John Henry Newman, 'Lead, Kindly Light' and (with others) the first *Tracts for the Times*

Life	*Historical and Cultural Background*
1834 (Jan.–Feb.) Six more stories appear in *Monthly Magazine*; (Aug.) meets Catherine Hogarth; becomes reporter on *The Morning Chronicle*, which publishes (Sept.–Dec.) first five 'Street Sketches'; (Dec.) moves to Furnival's Inn, Holborn.	Robert Owen's Grand National Trades Union. 'Tolpuddle Martyrs' transported to Australia. Lord Melbourne PM; then Peel. Workhouses set up under Poor Law Amendment Act. Coleridge, Lamb, and Malthus die. William Morris born. Balzac, *Eugénie Grandet*; Thomas Carlyle, *Sartor Resartus*; Harriet Martineau, *Illustrations of Political Economy*
1835 (?May) Engaged to Catherine Hogarth ('Kate'); publishes stories, sketches, and scenes in *Monthly Magazine*, *Evening Chronicle*, and *Bell's Life in London*.	Lord Melbourne PM. Municipal Corporations Act reforms local government. Cobbett and James Hogg die. Browning, *Paracelsus*; Alexis de Tocqueville, *La Démocratie en Amérique*
1836 (Feb.) Takes larger chambers in Furnival's Inn; (8 Feb.) **Sketches by Boz, First Series** published; (31 Mar.) first monthly number of **Pickwick Papers** issued; (2 Apr.) marries Catherine Hogarth; (June) publishes *Sunday Under Three Heads*; (Nov.) leaves the *Morning Chronicle*; (17 Dec.) **Sketches by Boz, Second Series**; (?Dec.) meets John Forster.	Beginning of Chartism. First London train (to Greenwich). Forms of telegraph used in England and America. Augustus Pugin's *Contrasts* advocates Gothic style of architecture. Browning, 'Porphyria's Lover'; Nicolai Gogol, *The Government Inspector*; Frederick Marryat, *Mr Midshipman Easy*
1837 (1 Jan.) First monthly number of *Bentley's Miscellany*, edited by CD, published; (6 Jan.) birth of first child, Charles ('Charley'); (31 Jan.) serialization of **Oliver Twist** begins in *Bentley's*; (3 Mar.) *Is She His Wife?* produced at the St James's; (Apr.) family moves to 48 Doughty Street; (7 May) sudden death of his sister-in-law, Mary Hogarth, at 17; CD suspends publication of **Pickwick Papers** and **Oliver Twist** for a month; (Aug.– Sept.) first family holiday in Broadstairs; (17 Nov.) **Pickwick Papers** published in one volume.	William IV dies; Queen Victoria succeeds. Carlyle, *The French Revolution*; Isaac Pitman, *Stenographic Short-Hand*; J. G. Lockhart, *Memoirs of the Life of Sir Walter Scott*

Life	Historical and Cultural Background
1838 (Jan.–Feb.) Visits Yorkshire schools with Hablot Browne ('Phiz'); (6 Mar.) second child, Mary ('Mamie'), born; (31 Mar.) monthly serialization of *Nicholas Nickleby* begins; (9 Nov.) *Oliver Twist* published in three volumes.	Isambard Kingdom Brunel's *Great Western* inaugurates regular steamship service between England and USA. London–Birmingham railway completed. Irish Poor Law. Anti-Corn Law League founded by Richard Cobden. People's Charter advocates universal suffrage. Carlyle, *Sartor Resartus*; John Ruskin, *The Poetry of Architecture*; R. S. Surtees, *Jorrocks's Jaunts and Jollities*; Wordsworth, *Sonnets*
1839 (31 Jan.) Resigns editorship of *Bentley's*; (23 Oct.) *Nicholas Nickleby* published in one volume; (29 Oct.) third child, Kate ('Katey'), born; (Dec.) family moves to 1 Devonshire Terrace, Regent's Park.	Opium War between Britain and China. Chartist riots. Louis Daguerre and W. H. Fox Talbot independently develop photography. Carlyle, *Chartism*; Darwin, *Journal of Researches into the Geology and Natural History of . . . Countries Visited by HMS Beagle*; Harriet Martineau, *Deerbrook*
1840 (4 Apr.) First weekly issue of *Master Humphrey's Clock* (also published monthly) in which *The Old Curiosity Shop* is serialized from 25 Apr.; (1 June) moves family to Broadstairs; (11 Oct.) returns to London; (15 Oct.) *Master Humphrey's Clock*, Vol. I published.	Queen Victoria marries Prince Albert. Maoris yield sovereignty of New Zealand to Queen Victoria by Treaty of Waitangi. Rowland Hill introduces penny postage. Fanny Burney dies.
1841 (8 Feb.) Fourth child, Walter, born; (6 and 13 Feb.) *The Old Curiosity Shop* concluded and *Barnaby Rudge* commenced in *Master Humphrey's Clock*; operated on for fistula (without anaesthetic). *Master Humphrey's Clock*, Vols. II and III published (Apr. and Dec.); one-volume editions of *The Old Curiosity Shop* and *Barnaby Rudge* published (15 Dec.).	Peel PM. Hong Kong and New Zealand proclaimed British. *Punch* founded. W. H. Ainsworth, *Old St Paul's*; Browning, *Pippa Passes*; Carlyle, *On Heroes, Hero-Worship, and the Heroic in History*; R. W. Emerson, *Essays*. Dion Boucicault's *London Assurance* acted
1842 (Jan.–June) CD and Catherine visit North America; (Aug.–Sept.) with family in Broadstairs; (Oct.–Nov.) visits Cornwall with Forster and others; (19 Oct.) *American Notes* published; (31 Dec.) first monthly number of *Martin Chuzzlewit* published.	End of wars with China and Afghanistan. Mines Act: no underground work by women or by children under 10. Chadwick report on sanitary condition of the working classes. Chartist riots. Copyright Act. Stendhal dies. Browning, *Dramatic Lyrics*; Gogol, *Dead Souls*; Thomas Babington Macaulay, *Lays of Ancient Rome*; Tennyson, *Poems*

Life	Historical and Cultural Background
1843	(19 Dec.) *A Christmas Carol* published.	British annexation of Sind and Natal. I. K. Brunel's *Great Britain*, the first ocean screwsteamer, launched. Southey dies; Wordsworth becomes poet laureate. Carlyle, *Past and Present*; Thomas Hood, 'Song of the Shirt'; Macaulay, *Essays*; J. S. Mill, *System of Logic*; Ruskin, *Modern Painters*, i (completed 1860)
1844	(15 Jan.) Fifth child, Francis, born; (16 July) takes family to Genoa; one-volume edition of *Martin Chuzzlewit* published; (30 Nov.–8 Dec.) returns to London to read *The Chimes* (published 16 Dec.) to his friends.	Factory Act restricts working hours of women and children. 'Rochdale Pioneers' found first co-operative society. Ragged School Union. William Barnes, *Poems of Rural Life in the Dorset Dialect*; E. B. Barrett, *Poems*; Disraeli, *Coningsby*; Dumas, *Les Trois Mousquetaires*; A. W. Kinglake, *Eöthen*
1845	Travels in Italy with Catherine before returning to London from Genoa; (20 Sept.) directs and acts in first performance of the Amateur Players, Ben Jonson's *Every Man In His Humour*; (28 Oct.) sixth child, Alfred, born; (20 Dec.) *The Cricket on the Hearth* published.	Disappearance of Sir John Franklin's expedition to find a North-West Passage from the Atlantic to the Pacific. War with Sikhs. 1845–9: potato famine in Ireland: 1 million die; 8 million emigrate. Thomas Hood and Sydney Smith die. Browning, *Dramatic Romances and Lyrics*; Disraeli, *Sybil*; Engels, *Condition of the Working Class in England*; Poe, *The Raven and Other Poems*, *Tales of Mystery and Imagination*
1846	(21 Jan.–9 Feb.) Edits *The Daily News*; (May) *Pictures from Italy* published; (31 May) leaves with family for Switzerland via the Rhine; (11 June) settles in Lausanne; (30 Sept.) monthly serialization of *Dombey and Son* commences; (16 Nov.) family moves to Paris; (Dec.) *The Battle of Life* published.	Corn Laws repealed; Peel resigns; Lord John Russell PM. Ether first used as a general anaesthetic. Robert Browning and Elizabeth Barrett marry secretly and leave for Italy. Balzac, *La Cousine Bette*; *Poems by Currer, Ellis and Acton Bell* (i.e. Charlotte, Emily, and Anne Brontë); Edward Lear, *Book of Nonsense*
1847	(28 Feb.) Returns from Paris; (18 Apr.) seventh child, Sydney, is born; (June–Sept.) with family at Broadstairs; (27–8 July) performs in Manchester and Liverpool with the Amateurs; (Nov.) Urania Cottage, Miss Coutts's 'Home for Homeless Women', in whose administration CD is involved, opened in Shepherd's Bush.	Factory Act limits working day for women and young persons to 10 hours. James Simpson discovers anaesthetic properties of chloroform. Louis Napoleon escapes to England from prison. A. Brontë, *Agnes Grey*; C. Brontë, *Jane Eyre*; E. Brontë, *Wuthering Heights*; Tennyson, *The Princess*. J. M. Morton's *Box and Cox* acted

	Life	*Historical and Cultural Background*
1848	(12 Apr.) One-volume edition of ***Dombey and Son*** published; (May–July) the Amateurs perform in London, Manchester, Liverpool, Birmingham, Edinburgh, and Glasgow; (2 Sept.) sister Fanny dies; (19 Dec.) ***The Haunted Man*** published.	Outbreak of cholera in London. Public Health Act. End of Chartist Movement. Pre-Raphaelite Brotherhood founded. 'The Year of Revolutions' in Europe. Louis Napoleon becomes President of France. Emily Brontë, Branwell Brontë die. A. Brontë, *The Tenant of Wildfell Hall*; Elizabeth Gaskell, *Mary Barton*; Marx and Engels, *Communist Manifesto*; J. S. Mill, *Principles of Political Economy*; Thackeray, *Vanity Fair*
1849	(16 Jan.) Eighth child, Henry ('Harry'), born; (30 Apr.) monthly serialization of ***David Copperfield*** begins; (July–Oct.) with family at Bonchurch, Isle of Wight.	Revolt against the British in Montreal. Punjab annexed. Rome proclaimed a republic; later taken by the French. Suppression of Communist riots in Paris. Californian gold rush. Anne Brontë, E. A. Poe die. C. Brontë, *Shirley*; Sir John Herschel, *Outlines of Astronomy*; Macaulay, *History of England*, i–ii (unfinished at his death, in 1859); Ruskin, *The Seven Lamps of Architecture*
1850	(30 Mar.) First issue of *Household Words*, a weekly journal edited and contributed to by CD; (16 Aug.) ninth child, Dora, born; (Aug.–Oct.) at Broadstairs; (15 Nov.) one-volume edition of ***David Copperfield*** published.	Restoration of Roman Catholic hierarchy in England. Factory Act: 60-hour week for women and young persons. Public Libraries Act. Dover–Calais telegraph cable laid. Balzac and Wordsworth die. Tennyson becomes Poet Laureate. E. B. Browning, 'Sonnets from the Portuguese', in *Poems*; Nathaniel Hawthorne, *The Scarlet Letter*; Tennyson, *In Memoriam A.H.H.*; Thackeray, *The History of Pendennis*; Wordsworth, *The Prelude* (posth.)
1851	(25 Jan.) *A Child's History of England* starts serialization in *Household Words*; (31 Mar.) John Dickens dies; (14 Apr.) Dora dies suddenly, aged 8 months; (May) directs and acts in Bulwer-Lytton's *Not So Bad as We Seem* before the Queen, in aid of the Guild of Literature and Art; (May–Oct.) last family holiday at Broadstairs; (Nov.) moves to Tavistock House.	Great Exhibition in the Crystal Palace, Hyde Park. Fall of French Second Republic. Gold found in Australia. George Borrow, *Lavengro*; Henry Mayhew, *London Labour and the London Poor*; Herman Melville, *Moby Dick*; George Meredith, *Poems*; Ruskin, *The King of the Golden River*, *The Stones of Venice*, i (completed 1853)

Life	*Historical and Cultural Background*
1852	(28 Feb.) Monthly serialization of *Bleak House* begins; (14 Apr.) birth of tenth child, Edward ('Plorn'); (Feb.–Sept.) provincial performances of *Not So Bad as We Seem*; (July–Oct.) family stays in Dover.	Lord Derby becomes PM; then Lord Aberdeen. Louis Napoleon proclaimed Emperor Napoleon III. 1852–6: David Livingstone crosses Africa. Tom Moore and the Duke of Wellington die. M. P. Roget, *Roget's Thesaurus of English Words and Phrases*; Harriet Beecher Stowe, *Uncle Tom's Cabin*; Thackeray, *Henry Esmond*
1853	(June–Oct.) Family stays in Boulogne; (12 Sept.) one-volume edition of *Bleak House* published; (Oct.–Dec.) in Switzerland and Italy with Wilkie Collins and Augustus Egg; (10 Dec.) *A Child's History of England* concluded in *Household Words*; (27–30 Dec.) gives public readings of *A Christmas Carol* and *The Cricket on the Hearth* in Birmingham.	Arnold, *Poems*; C. Brontë, *Villette*; Gaskell, *Ruth*, *Cranford*; Surtees, *Mr Sponge's Sporting Career*
1854	(28–30 Jan.) Visits Preston; (1 Apr.–12 Aug.) weekly serialization of *Hard Times* in *Household Words*; (June–Oct.) family stays in Boulogne; (7 Aug.) *Hard Times* published in one volume; (Dec.) reads *A Christmas Carol* in Reading, Sherborne, and Bradford.	Reform of the Civil Service. France and Britain join Turkey against Russia in the Crimean War; battles of Alma, Balaclava, Inkerman and siege of Sebastopol; Florence Nightingale goes to Scutari. Patmore, *The Angel in the House*, i (completed 1862); Tennyson, 'The Charge of the Light Brigade'; H. D. Thoreau, *Walden*
1855	(Feb.) Meets Maria Winter (née Beadnell) again; (27 Mar.) reads *A Christmas Carol* in Ashford, Kent; (June) directs and acts in Collins's *The Lighthouse* at Tavistock House; family stays in Folkestone, where CD reads *A Christmas Carol* on 5 Oct.; (15 Oct.) settles family in Paris; (1 Dec.) monthly serialization of *Little Dorrit* begins; (Dec.) reads *A Christmas Carol* at Peterborough and Sheffield.	Lord Palmerston PM. Newspaper tax abolished. *Daily Telegraph*, first London penny newspaper, founded. Fall of Sebastopol. 1855–6: G. J. Mendel discovers laws of heredity. Charlotte Brontë and Mary Russell Mitford die. R. Browning, *Men and Women*; Gaskell, *North and South*; Longfellow, *Hiawatha*; Tennyson, *Maud and Other Poems*; Thackeray, *The Newcomes*, *The Rose and the Ring*; A. Trollope, *The Warden*; Walt Whitman, *Leaves of Grass*
1856	(Mar.) Buys Gad's Hill Place, Kent; (29 Apr.) family returns from Paris; (June–Sept.) family stays in Boulogne.	End of Crimean War. Britain annexes Oudh; Sir Henry Bessemer patents his steel-making process. Synthetic colours invented. Henry Irving's first stage appearance. National Gallery founded in London. Mrs Craik (Dinah Maria Mulock), *John Halifax, Gentleman*; Flaubert, *Madame Bovary*

Life	Historical and Cultural Background
1857 (Jan.) Directs and acts in Collins's *The Frozen Deep* at Tavistock House; (13 Feb.) moves to Gad's Hill Place; (30 May) **Little Dorrit** published in one volume; Walter leaves for service with the East India Company; (June–July) visited by Hans Andersen; gives three public readings of **A Christmas Carol**; (July–Aug.) performances of *The Frozen Deep* in London and, with Ellen Ternan, her sister, and mother in the cast, in Manchester.	Divorce courts established in England. Arnold becomes professor of poetry at Oxford. Museum—later, the Victoria and Albert Museum—opened in South Kensington. Beginning of Indian Mutiny; siege and relief of Lucknow. Baudelaire, *Les Fleurs du mal*; C. Brontë, *The Professor* (posth.); E. B. Browning, *Aurora Leigh*; Gaskell, *The Life of Charlotte Brontë*; Hughes, *Tom Brown's Schooldays*; Livingstone, *Missionary Travels and Researches in South Africa*; A. Trollope, *Barchester Towers*
1858 (19 Jan.; 26 Mar; 15 Apr.) Reads *A Christmas Carol* for charity; (29 Apr.–22 July) series of 17 public readings; (May) separation from Catherine; (7 and 12 June) publishes 'personal' statement about it in *The Times* and *Household Words*; (Aug.) *Reprinted Pieces* published; (Aug.–Nov.) first provincial reading tour, extending to Ireland and Scotland (85 readings); (24 Dec.) first series of London Christmas readings begins.	Derby PM. Indian Mutiny suppressed; powers of East India Company transferred to the Crown. Queen Victoria proclaimed Empress of India. Launch of I. K. Brunel's *Great Eastern*. Darwin and A. R. Wallace give joint paper on evolution. R. M. Ballantyne, *The Coral Island*; Clough, *Amours de Voyage*; Eliot, *Scenes of Clerical Life*; A. Trollope, *Doctor Thorne*
1859 (30 Apr.) Begins to edit *All the Year Round* in which *A Tale of Two Cities* appears weekly till 26 November; (28 May) final number of *Household Words*; (Oct.) gives 14 readings on second provincial tour; (21 Nov.) *A Tale of Two Cities* published in one volume; (24 Dec.) begins series of three London Christmas readings.	Palmerston PM. Franco-Austrian War: Austrians defeated at Solferino. War of Italian Liberation. The abolitionist John Brown hanged for treason at Charlestown, Virginia. Thomas de Quincey, Leigh Hunt, and Lord Macaulay die. Darwin, *On the Origin of Species by Means of Natural Selection*; Eliot, *Adam Bede*; Edward FitzGerald, *Rubáiyát of Omar Khayyám*; J. S. Mill, *On Liberty*; Samuel Smiles, *Self-Help*; Tennyson, *Idylls of the King*
1860 (17 July) Katey marries Charles Collins; (27 July) CD's brother Alfred dies, at 38; (21 Aug.) sells Tavistock House; (Oct.) settles permanently at Gad's Hill; (1 Dec.) weekly serialization of **Great Expectations** begins in *All the Year Round*, continuing till 3 Aug. 1861.	Abraham Lincoln elected US president; Carolina secedes from the Union. Collins, *The Woman in White*; Eliot, *The Mill on the Floss*; Faraday, *Various Forces of Matter*. Boucicault's *The Colleen Bawn* acted

Life	*Historical and Cultural Background*
1861 (Mar.–Apr.) Series of 6 London readings; (6 July) **Great Expectations** published in three volumes; (Oct.–Jan. 1862) gives 46 readings on third provincial tour; (19 Nov.) Charley marries Elizabeth ('Bessie') Evans: CD refuses to be present.	Abolition of Paper Tax. Prince Albert dies. Victor Emmanuel becomes King of Italy. Serfdom abolished in Russia. Outbreak of American Civil War. E. B. Browning and A. H. Clough die. Mrs Isabella Mary Beeton, *Book of Household Management*; Eliot, *Silas Marner*; J. S. Mill, *Utilitarianism*; F. T. Palgrave, *The Golden Treasury*; Reade, *The Cloister and the Hearth*; A. Trollope, *Framley Parsonage*; Mrs Henry Wood, *East Lynne*
1862 (Feb.–May) Exchanges Gad's Hill Place for a house in London but also uses rooms at the office of *All the Year Round*; (Mar.–June) London readings; (June–Oct.) makes several visits to France; (Oct.) settles Mamie and her aunt, Georgina Hogarth, in Paris; (Dec.) returns to Gad's Hill for Christmas.	Famine among Lancashire cotton workers. Bismarck becomes Chancellor of Prussia. Thoreau dies. Mary Elizabeth Braddon, *Lady Audley's Secret*; Hugo, *Les Misérables*; Meredith, *Modern Love*; Christina Rossetti, *Goblin Market and Other Poems*; Herbert Spencer, *First Principles*; Turgenev, *Fathers and Sons*
1863 (Jan.) Gives 3 readings for charity at British Embassy in Paris; (Feb. and Aug.) makes further visits to France; (Mar.–May) London readings; (13 Sept.) Elizabeth Dickens dies; (31 Dec.) Walter dies in Calcutta, India, aged 22.	Beginning of work on London underground railway. Lincoln's Gettysburg Address; emancipation of US slaves. Thackeray and Frances Trollope die. Eliot, *Romola*; Margaret Oliphant, *Salem Chapel*
1864 (1 May) Monthly serialization of **Our Mutual Friend** begins; (27 June–6 July) probably in France; (Nov.) in France.	Karl Marx organizes first Socialist International in London. Louis Pasteur publishes his theory of germs as the cause of disease. International Red Cross founded. John Clare, W. S. Landor, R. S. Surtees, and Hawthorne die. Sheridan Le Fanu, *Uncle Silas*; Newman, *Apologia pro Vita Sua*; Tennyson, *Enoch Arden and Other Poems*; Trollope, *The Small House at Allington*, *Can You Forgive Her?*
1865 (Feb.–June) Three trips to France; (Feb.–Apr.) first attack of lameness from swollen left foot; (29 May) sees Alfred off to Australia; (9 June) returning from France with Ellen Ternan and her mother, is in fatal railway accident at Staplehurst, Kent; (Sept.) visit to France; (20 Oct.) **Our Mutual Friend** published in two volumes.	Russell PM. William Booth founds Christian Mission in Whitechapel, known from 1878 as the Salvation Army. Completion of transatlantic cable. End of American Civil War. Abraham Lincoln assassinated. Elizabeth Gaskell dies. Arnold, *Essays in Criticism, First Series*; Lewis Carroll, *Alice's Adventures in Wonderland*

Life	Historical and Cultural Background
1866 (Apr.–June) Readings in London and the provinces; (June) CD's brother Augustus Dickens dies in Chicago, aged 38.	Derby PM. Second Reform Bill. Fenians active in Ireland: Habeas Corpus suspended. Elizabeth Garrett opens dispensary for women. Dr T. J. Barnardo opens home for destitute children in London's East End. Peacock and John Keble die. Fyodor Dostoevsky, *Crime and Punishment*; Eliot, *Felix Holt, the Radical*; Gaskell, *Wives and Daughters* (posth., unfinished); Swinburne, *Poems and Ballads, First Series*
1867 (Jan.–May) Readings in England and Ireland; (Nov.) begins American reading tour in Boston; (Dec.) *No Thoroughfare*, written jointly with Collins, published in *All the Year Round*.	Fenian outrages in England. Second Reform Act. Factory Act. Joseph Lister practises antiseptic surgery. Building of Royal Albert Hall commenced. Arnold, 'Dover Beach', 'Thyrsis', in *New Poems*; Walter Bagehot, *The English Constitution*; Henrik Ibsen, *Peer Gynt*; Karl Marx, *Das Kapital*, i; Trollope, *The Last Chronicle of Barset*; Emile Zola, *Thérèse Raquin*
1868 (22 Apr.) Sails home from New York, having cancelled planned readings in the USA and Canada; (26 Sept.) Plorn sails to Australia to join Alfred; (Oct.) Harry enters Trinity College, Cambridge; CD begins Farewell Reading Tour; CD's brother Fred dies, aged 48.	Disraeli PM; Gladstone PM. Trades' Union Congress founded. Basutoland annexed. Louisa May Alcott, *Little Women*; Collins, *The Moonstone*; Queen Victoria, *Leaves from a Journal of Our Life in the Highlands*
1869 (5 Jan.) Introduces 'Sikes and Nancy' into his repertoire; (22 Apr.) serious illness forces CD to break off reading tour after 74 readings.	Girton College for Women founded. Suez Canal opened. Arnold, *Culture and Anarchy*; R. D. Blackmore, *Lorna Doone*; R. Browning, *The Ring and the Book*; J. S. Mill, *On the Subjection of Women*; Leo Tolstoy, *War and Peace*; Trollope, *Phineas Finn, He Knew He Was Right*; Paul Verlaine, *Fêtes galantes*
1870 (Jan.– Mar.) Farewell readings in London; (9 Mar.) received by Queen Victoria; (1 Apr.) first of six completed numbers of **The Mystery of Edwin Drood** issued; (9 June) dies, aged 58, following a cerebral haemorrhage, at Gad's Hill; (14 June) buried in Westminster Abbey.	Gladstone's Irish Land Act. Married Women's Property Act gives wives the right to their own earnings. Elementary Education Act for England and Wales. Outbreak of Franco-Prussian War: Napoleon III defeated and exiled; siege of Paris (till 1871). E. C. Brewer, *Dictionary of Phrase and Fable*; D. G. Rossetti, *Poems*

Abbreviations and symbols

AN	American Notes (1842)
ANB	American National Biography
AYR	All the Year Round (1859–70)
BH	Bleak House (1852–3)
BR	Barnaby Rudge (1841)
CC	A Christmas Carol (1843)
CD	Charles Dickens
D&S	Dombey and Son (1846–8)
DC	David Copperfield (1849–50)
ED	The Mystery of Edwin Drood (1870)
Forster	John Forster, The Life of Charles Dickens, ed. J. W. T. Ley (London, 1928)
GE	Great Expectations (1859–60)
HT	Hard Times (1854)
HW	Household Words (1850–9)
LD	Little Dorrit (1855–7)
MC	Martin Chuzzlewit (1843–4)
MHC	Master Humphrey's Clock (1840–1)
MS	manuscript
NN	Nicholas Nickleby (1838–9)
No.	Issue number of Dickens's serial publications
OCS	The Old Curiosity Shop (1840–1)
OED	Oxford English Dictionary
OMF	Our Mutual Friend (1864–5)
OT	Oliver Twist (1837–9)
Pilgrim	The British Academy Pilgrim Edition, The Letters of Charles Dickens, 12 vols., ed. Madeline House, Graham Storey, Kathleen Tillotson, et al. (Oxford, 1965–2002)
PP	The Pickwick Papers (1836–7)
SB	Sketches by Boz (1836)
Slater	Michael Slater, Charles Dickens (New Haven, 2009)
Speeches	The Speeches of Charles Dickens, ed. K. J. Fielding (Oxford, 1960)
TC	The Chimes (1844)
TTC	A Tale of Two Cities (1859)
V&A	Victoria & Albert Museum, London
[ ]	indicates conjectured, missing, or illegible words or dates
†	indicates an entry in the Oxford Dictionary of National Biography
|	indicates a separate line in the manuscript

To Owen Thomas,[1] [1825–6]

Tom

I am quite ashamed I have not returned your Leg[2] but you shall have it by Harry to morrow. If you would like to purchase my Clavis[3] you shall have it at a very *reduced price*. Cheaper in comparison than a Leg.

Yours &c
C DICKENS

PS. I suppose all this time you have had a *wooden* leg. I have weighed yours every saturday Night.

---

1 Owen Peregrine Thomas (1811–98), a day-boy with CD, 1824–6, at Wellington House Academy, Mornington Crescent, London NW; a model for Salem House in *DC*.
2 Probably school slang for a lexicon.
3 A Latin grammar book.

To Mary Anne Leigh,[1] [7 MARCH 1831]

21 George Street | Monday.

My dear Miss Leigh.

I have to apologize for not keeping my promise last night; but the fact is I was so exceedingly tired from my week's exertions that I slept on the Sofa the whole day. I therefore hope you will pardon my apparent rudeness, and that you will say as you often do "Ah Mr. Dickens it's quite excusable."

I called at Beadnells[2] *on purpose to fetch you* this Morning but you had just gone which vexed me very much as I had anticipated not only the pleasure of walking with you but also of picking that bone that we have to discuss which I will embrace the first opportunity of doing.

Just this Instant as I was scoring under the second line from the top I smeared the letter which I hope you will also excuse as I am in a hurry and as "he is such a writer"!

With Compliments to Mr. and Mrs. Leigh, | I remain
| (what shall I say) Yours truly?
CHARLES DICKENS

---

1 Mary Anne (Marianne) Leigh, friend of Maria Beadnell.
2 George Beadnell (1773–1862), clerk in Smith, Payne & Smith's bank, where his brother John was manager.

To Maria Beadnell,[1] [LATE 1831]

3 Belle Vue, Hampstead. | Wednesday Morning

My dear Maria.—(I fear I ought to say "Miss Beadnell" but I hope you will pardon my adhering to the manner in which I have been accustomed to address you.) I have taken the opputunity of returning your sister's Album[2] to write these few hurried lines for the purpose of saying that my Glover made some stupid mistake about your gloves, and I shall therefore be much obliged if you will have the kindness to inclose me one of those I had before in an envelope addressed to me here.—Pray do not think this wrong *under existing circumstances*. You need not fear the fact of your writing being known to any one here for I shall be very busy at home and alone all day tomorrow as my mother and sister will be in town. I have another favour to ask: it is that you will tell me when you think would be a good opputunity for me to bring the Gloves. I am most anxious indeed to see you as I wish much to speak to you particularly about the Annual.—Surely, surely you will not refuse so trivial a present: a mere common place trifle; a common present even among the merest "friends". Do not misunderstand me: I am not desirous by making presents or by doing any other act to influence your thoughts, wishes, or feelings in the slightest degree.—I do not think I do:—I cannot hope I ever shall: but let me entreat of you do not refuse so slight a token of regard from me.

I cannot unless you will grant me an opputunity speak to you either on this, or any other subject;—I hope and trust you will not refuse: consider how long it is since I have seen you.

Trusting you will excuse haste and most anxiously waiting to hear from you which I hope and trust I shall in the course of tomorrow.

I remain | My dear—Miss Beadnell | Ever Yours Sincerely

C.D.

I hope you will like the Lines. I do not *think* what I *write* you know.—I allude, particularly to the *last four Lines* of the *Third Verse*.

---

1 Maria Beadnell (1810–86), daughter of George Beadnell, and CD's first love. He met her in 1830; her parents were first tolerant and then disapproving. This is CD's first surviving letter to her, first published in appendix to Pilgrim 7.

2 Anne Beadnell's Album, in which he had just transcribed 'The Bill of Fare', a 360-line poem imitating Oliver Goldsmith's 'Retaliation', see Slater, 34.

To Thomas Beard,[1] 4 FEBRUARY [1832]

70 Margaret Street Cavendish Square | Saturday February 4th.

Dear Beard.

I intend keeping the Anniversary of my Birth Day, which occurs on Wednesday next the Eighth Instant,[2] by asking a chosen few to join in a friendly quadrille.

If you will make one of our family circle by seven O'Clock, or as early as the house[3] will allow you, it will give us the greatest pleasure to see you.

Believe me | Yours Truly
CHARLES DICKENS

1 Thomas Beard (1807–91), journalist. He joined the *Morning Herald c.*1832, where CD's father was working. In 1834 he moved to the *Morning Chronicle* and worked with CD. Their friendship lasted until CD's death.
2 CD's birthday was in fact on 7 Feb. He always enjoyed celebrating it; this is the first surviving invitation to one of his birthday parties.
3 The House of Commons; Beard was a parliamentary reporter.

To Henry Kolle,[1] [?APRIL–MAY 1832]

North End | Friday Evening.

My dear Kollie.

I have great pleasure in being enabled to assure you, that I shall be perfectly disengaged on Sunday next and shall expect you. I always rise out here, by Seven and therefore you may safely wend your way here before one if you can.

In reply to your enquiry respecting a *sizeable poney* I have also great satisfaction in being enabled to say that I can procure you a "oss" which I have had once or twice since I have been here. I am a poor judge of distance but I should certainly say that your legs would be off the ground when you are on his back. To look at the animal in question you would think (with the exception of Dog's Meat) there was no earthly purpose to which he could be applied but *when* you try him joking apart I will pledge my veracity he will beat any horse hired or private that you would see in a Morning's ride. I am his especial patron but on this occasion I will procure something smaller for myself. Pray come before One as I shall order them to be at the Door punctually at that hour, and we can mount, dismount & ride eight or ten miles without seeing a Soul the *Peasantry* excepted.

I suppose I must consider your "pilgrimage" as a sufficient excuse for your long absence, but I trust when the Shrine at which you pay your devotion is once more removed[2] you will shew yourself a little more frequently. The people at Cecil Street[3] put too much water in the hashes, lost the nutmeg grater, attended on me most miserably, dirtied the Table Cloths &c &c—and so (detesting petty miseries) I gave them warning, and have not yet fixed on "a local habitation and a name".[4]

Envying you your devotions notwithstanding the pilgrimage attendant thereon and wishing you every success and happiness I remain

> My dear Kollie | Yours most truly
> CHARLES DICKENS

Come Early
P.S. I shall depend on your staying all night. You shall have breakfast by half past seven next Morning as I must walk to town the very first thing. CD.

1 Henry Kolle (?1808–81), bank clerk. Became engaged to Maria Beadnell's elder sister Anne, and acted as go-between in CD's love affair with Maria.
2 i.e. when Anne Beadnell is next away from home.
3 Cecil Street, Strand, CD's temporary lodgings.
4 *A Midsummer Night's Dream*, v. i. 17.

To Maria Beadnell, 18 MARCH [1833][1]

18 Bentinck Street | March 18th

Dear Miss Beadnell
　　Your own feelings will enable you to imagine far better than any attempt of mine to describe the painful struggle it has cost me to make up my mind to adopt the course which I now take—a course than which nothing can be so directly opposed to my wishes and feelings but the necessity of which becomes daily more apparent to me. Our meetings of late have been little more than so many displays of heartless indifference on the one hand while on the other they have never failed to prove a fertile source of wretchedness and misery and seeing as I cannot fail to do that I have engaged in a pursuit which has long since been worse than hopeless and a further perseverance in which can only expose me to deserved ridicule I have made up my mind to return the little present I received from you sometime since (which I have always prized as I still do far beyond anything I ever possessed) and the other enclosed mementos of our past correspondence which I am sure it must be gratifying to you to receive as after our recent relative situations they are certainly better adapted for your custody than mine. Need I say that I have not the most remote idea of hurting your feelings by the few lines which I think it necessary to write with the accompanying little parcel? I must be the last person in the world who could entertain such an intention but I feel that this is neither a matter nor a time for cold deliberate calculating trifling. *My* feelings upon any subject more especially upon this must be to you a matter of very little moment still I *have* feelings in common with other people—perhaps as far as they relate to you they have been

as strong and as good as ever warmed the human heart,—and I do feel that it is mean and contemptible of me to keep by me one gift of yours or to preserve one single line or word of remembrance or affection from you. I therefore return them and I can only wish that I could as easily forget that I ever received them.

I have but one word more to say and I say it in my own vindication. The result of our past acquaintance is indeed a melancholy one to me. I have felt too long ever to lose the feeling of utter desolation and wretchedness which has succeeded our former correspondence. Thank God! I can claim for myself and feel that I deserve the merit of having ever throughout our intercourse acted fairly, intelligibly and honorably. Under kindness and encouragement one day and a total change of conduct the next I have ever been the same. I have ever acted without reserve. I have never held out encouragement which I knew I never meant; I have never indirectly sanctioned hopes which I well knew I did not intend to fulfil. I have never made a mock confidante to whom to entrust a garbled story for my own purposes, and I think I never should (though God knows I am not likely to have the opportunity) encourage one dangler as a useful shield for—an excellent set off against—others more fortunate and doubtless more deserving. I have done nothing that I could say would be very likely to hurt you. If (I can hardly believe it possible) I have said any thing which can have that effect I can only ask you to place yourself for a moment in my situation and you will find a much better excuse than I can possibly devise. A wish for your happiness altho' it comes from me may not be the worse for being sincere and heartfelt. Accept it as it is meant and believe that nothing will ever afford me more real delight than to hear that you the object of my first, and my last love, are happy. If you are as happy as I hope you may be, you will indeed possess every blessing that this World can afford.

C.D.

1 This letter is a copy, presumably by Maria, as she returned the original to CD. She does not seem to have followed his punctuation.

To Henry Kolle, [?15 APRIL 1833]

Bentinck St. | Monday Morning

My dear Kolle.

I received your note the other day and of course much regretted the absence of any Member of my company on the occasion of a Grand Rehearsal. You ask me whether I do not congratulate you.[1] I do most sincerely. If any one can be supposed to take a lively and real interest in such a case it is an old and mutual friend of both parties. Though perhaps I cannot lay claim to the title of an "old" friend I hope I may to that of a real one, and although unfortunately and unhappily for myself I have no *fellow feeling* with you[2]— no cause to sympathise with your past causes of annoyance, or your present prospects of happiness,—I am not the less disposed to offer my heartfelt congratulations to you because you are, or at all events will be what I never can—happy and contented; taking present grievances as happiness compared with former difficulties and looking cheerfully and steadily forward to a bright perspective of many happy years.

Now turning from feeling, and making one's self miserable & so on, may I ask you to spare one Evening this week for the purpose of doing your two pair of side Scenes?³ I would not ask you but I really have no other resource; the time is fast approaching and I am rather nervous. Will you write and tell me when you will come and when I may send for your Scene? Thursday is a Rehearsal of Clari⁴ with the Band & Friday week a dress Rehearsal. You shall have your Bills when I see you— an immense audience are invited, including many Judges.—Write me an answer to these queries *as soon as possible* pray. The family are busy, the *Corps dramatique* are all anxiety, the scenery is all completing rapidly, the machinery is finished, the Curtain hemmed, the Orchestra complete—and the manager *grimy.*

Believe me | My dear Kolle | Truly Yours
CHARLES DICKENS

1 On his engagement to Anne Beadnell.
2 CD's relations with Maria were now at their unhappiest.
3 Kolle was partly responsible for the scenery for the amateur theatricals.
4 *Clari; or, The Maid of Milan*, an opera in two acts by J. H. Payne, music by Henry R. Bishop, first performed 1823. Best known for its popular song 'Home, Sweet Home!'

*To Henry Austin,*¹ [SPRING 1833]

Sunday Morning | 8 O'Clock

Dear Henry.

If you are down at Strand Lane and hail "The Alert" any time until 9 we will send our boat off for you.²

Believe me | Truly Yours
CD.

1 Henry Austin (1811/12–61†), civil engineer with an interest in sanitary reform. Pupil of Robert Stephenson; he married CD's sister Letitia in 1837.
2 For trip by river to Greenwich.

To Maria Beadnell, [14 MAY 1833]

18 Bentinck Street | Tuesday Afternoon

I do feel Miss Beadnell after my former note to you that common delicacy and a proper feeling of consideration alike require that I should without a moment's delay inform you (as I did verbally yesterday) that I never by word or deed in the slightest manner directly or by implication made in any way a Confidante of Mary Ann Leigh, and never was I more surprised, never did I endure more heartfelt annoyance and vexation than to hear yesterday by chance that days even weeks ago she had made this observation—not having the slightest idea that she had done so of course it was out of my power to contradict it before. Situated as we have been once I have— laying out of consideration every idea of common honour not to say common honesty—too often thought of our earlier correspondence, and too often looked back to happy hopes the loss of which have made me the miserable reckless wretch I am, to breathe the slightest hint to any creature living of one single circumstance that ever passed between us—much less to *her.*

In replying to your last note I denied Mary Ann Leighs interference, and I did so hoping to spare you the pain of any recrimination with her. Her duplicity and disgusting falsehood however renders it quite unnecessary to conceal the part she has acted and I therefore have now no hesitation in saying that she quite unasked volunteered the information that *you* had made her a Confidante *of all that had ever passed between us without reserve.* In proof of which assertion she not only detailed facts which I undoubtedly thought she could have heard from none but yourself, but she also communicated many things which certainly never occurred at all, equally calculated to excite something even more than ordinary angry feelings.

On hearing this yesterday (and no consideration on earth shall induce me ever to forget or forgive Fanny's[1] not telling me of it before) my first impulse was to go to Clapton:[2] my next to prevent misrepresentation to write immediately. I thought on reflection, however that the most considerate and proper course would be to state to you exactly what I wish to do. I ask your consent previously for this reason— because it is possible that you may think that my writing a violent note would have the effect of exciting ill nature which had better be avoided. I candidly own that I am most anxious to write. I care as little for her malice as I do for her, but as you are a party who would perhaps be mixed up with her story I think it is proper to ask you whether you object to my sending the note which I have already written. I need hardly say that if it be sent at all it should be at once and I therefore hope to receive your decision tomorrow assuring you that I will abide by it whatever it be.

I will not detain you or intrude upon your attention by any more observations. I fear I could say little, calculated to interest or please you. I have no hopes to express no wishes to communicate. I am past the one and must not think of the other. Though surprised at such inconceivable duplicity I can express no pleasure at the discovery, for I have been so long used to inward wretchedness, and real, real, misery that it matters little very little to me what others may think of or what becomes of me.—I have to apologize for troubling you at all but I hope you will believe that a sense of respect for and deference to your feelings has elicited this note to which I have once again to beg your immediate answer.

CHARLES DICKENS

1 CD's sister.
2 Where Mary Anne Leigh lived.

To *Maria Beadnell*, [16 MAY 1833]

18 Bentinck Street | Thursday 4 o'Clock.

I cannot forbear replying to your note this moment received Miss Beadnell because you really seem to have made two mistakes. In the first place you do not exactly understand the nature of my feelings with regard to your alledged communications to M A L[1] and in the next you certainly totally and entirely misunderstand my feeling with regard to her—that you could suppose as you clearly do (that is to say if the subject is worth a thought to you) that I have ever really thought of M A L in any other than my old way you are mistaken. That she has for some reason and to suit her own purposes, of late thrown herself in my way I could plainly see and I know it was noticed by others.—For instance on the night of the play[2] after we went up stairs I could not get rid of her; God knows that I have no pleasure in speaking to her or any girl living, and never had—May I say that *you* have ever been the sole exception? "Kind words and winning looks" have done much much with me—but not from her—*unkind* words and *cold* looks however have done much much more— That I have been the subject of both from *you* as your will altered and your pleasure changed, *I* know well—and so I think must you. I have often said before and I say again I have borne more from you than I do believe any creature breathing ever bore from a woman before. The slightest hint however even now of change or transfer of feeling I cannot bear and do not deserve.

Again. I never supposed nor did this girl give me to understand that you ever breathed a syllable *against* me. It is quite a mistake on your part but knowing (and there cannot be a stronger proof of my disliking her) what she was knowing her admirable qualifications for a Confidante and recollecting what had passed between ourselves I was more than hurt more than annoyed at the bare idea of your confiding the tale to *her* of all people living. I reflected upon it. I coupled her communication with what I saw (with a jaundiced eye perhaps) of your own conduct; on the very last occasion of seeing you before writing that note I heard even among your own friends (and there was no Mary Ann present) I heard even among them remarks on your own conduct and pity—pity Good God—for my situation and I did think (you will pardon my saying it for I am describing my *then* feelings and not my *present*) that the same light butterfly feeling which prompted the one action could influence the other—Wretched aye almost broken hearted I wrote to you—(I have the note for you returned it, and even now I do think it was written "more in sorrow than in anger", and to my mind—I had almost said to your better judgment—it must appear to breathe anything but an unkind or bitter feeling)—You replied to the note. I wrote another and that at least was expressive of the same sentiments as I ever had felt and ever should feel towards you to my dying day. *That note you sent me back by hand wrapped in a small loose piece of paper without even the formality of an envelope and that note I wrote after receiving yours.* It is poor sport to trifle on a subject like this: I know what your feelings must have been and by them I regulated my conduct.

To return to the question of what is best to be done. I go to Kolle's at 10 oClock tomorrow Evening and I will inclose to you and give to him then a copy of the note which if I send any I *will* send to Marianne Leigh. I do not ask your *advice*. All I ask is whether you see any reason to *object*. You will perhaps inclose it after reading it, and say whether you object to it's going or not.

With regard to Fanny if she owed a duty to you she owed a greater one to me—and for this reason *because she knew* what Marianne Leigh had said of *you*; she heard from you what she had said of *me* and yet she had not the fairness the candour the feeling to let me know it—and if I were to live a hundred years I never would forgive it.

As to sending my last note back, pray do not consult *my* feelings but *your own*. Look at the note itself. Do you think it is unkind cold hasty or conciliatory? and deliberate? I shall—indeed I need—express no wish upon the subject. You will act as you think best. It is too late for me to attempt to influence your decision. I have said doubtless both in this and my former note much more than perhaps I ought or should have said had I attempted disguise or concealment to you and I have no doubt more than is agreeable to yourself. Towards *you* I never had and never can have an angry feeling. If you had ever felt for me one hundredth part of my feeling for you there would have been little cause of regret, little coldness little unkindness between us. My feeling on *one* subject was early roused it has been strong, and it will be lasting. I am in no mood to quarrel with any one for not entertaining similar sentiments and least of all Miss Beadnell with you. You will think of what I have said and act accordingly. Destitute as I am of hope or comfort I have borne much and I dare say can bear more

Yours
CHARLES DICKENS

1 Mary Anne Leigh.
2 *Clari*, performed 27 Apr.

To *Mary Anne Leigh,* [17 MAY 1833][1]

Dear Miss Leigh.

I am very happy to avail myself of the opportunity of inclosing your Album (which I regret to say want of a moment's time has quite prevented me writing in), to say a very few words relative to an observation made by you the other day to one of the Miss Beadnell's I believe; and which has only I regret to say just reached my ears quite accidentally. I should not have noticed it at all were it merely an idle gossiping remark for one is necessarily compelled to hear so many of them and they are usually so trifling and so ridiculous, that it would be mere waste of time to notice them in any way. The remark to which I allude however is one which if it had the slightest foundation in truth—would so strongly tend to implicate me as a dishonorable babbler, with little heart and less head, that in justice to myself I cannot refrain from adverting to it—You will at once perceive I allude to your giving them to understand (if not directly by implication) that I had made you my confidante, with respect to anything which may have passed between Maria B—and myself. Now passing over any remark which may have been artfully elicited from me in any unguarded moment, I can safely say, that I never made a confidante of any one. I am perfectly willing to admit that if I had wished to secure a confidante in whom candour, secrecy and kind honorable feeling were indispensable requisites I could have looked to no one better calculated for this office than yourself: but still the making you the depository of my feelings or secrets, is an honor I never presumed to expect and one which I certainly must beg most positively to decline—A proof of self denial in which so far as I learn from other avowed confidantes of yours, I am by no means singular.

I have not hesitated to speak plainly because I feel most strongly on this subject— The allegation—if it were not grossly untrue—I again say tending so materially to inculpate me, and the assertion itself having been made (so far as I can learn at least, for it has reached me in a very circuitous manner) certainly not in the most unaffected or delicate way.

I hope you will understand that in troubling you, I am not actuated by any absurd idea of self consequence. I am perfectly aware of my own unimportance, and it is solely because I am so; because I would much rather mismanage my own affairs, than have them ably conducted by the officious interference of any one, because I do think that your interposition in this instance however well intentioned, has been productive of as much mischief as it has been uncalled for; and because I am really and sincerely desirous, of sparing you the meanness and humiliation, of acting in the petty character of an unauthorized go-between, that I have been induced to write this note—for the length of which I beg you will accept my apology.

> I am, | Dear Miss Leigh | Yours &c
> CHARLES DICKENS

---

1 This is a copy of the note which was enclosed in the next letter to Maria.

To Maria Beadnell, [17 MAY 1833]

18 Bentinck Street | Friday

Agreeably to my promise I beg to Inclose you a copy of the note I propose to send to Marianne Leigh, which you will perhaps be so good as to return me (as I have no other copy from which to write the original) as soon as possible. I had intended to have made it more severe but perhaps upon the whole the inclosed will be sufficient. Until receiving any answer you may make to my last note I will not trouble you with any further observation. Of course you will at least on this point (I mean Marianne Leigh's note) say what you think without reserve and any course you may propose or any alteration you may suggest shall on my word and honor be instantly adopted. Should anything you may say (in returning her note) to *me* make me anxious to return any answer may I have your permission to forward it to you?

I find I have proceeded to the end of my note without even inserting your name. May I ask you to excuse the omission and to believe that I would gladly have addressed you in a very very different way?

CHARLES DICKENS

To Maria Beadnell, [19 MAY 1833]

18 Bentinck Street. | Sunday Morning.

Dear Miss Beadnell.

I am anxious to take the earliest opportunity of writing to you again, knowing that the opportunity of addressing you through Kolle—now my only means of communicating with you—will shortly be lost, and having your own permission to write to you—I am most desirous of forwarding a note which had I received such permission earlier, I can assure you you would have received 'ere this. Before proceeding to say a word upon the subject of my present note let me beg you to believe that your request to see Marianne Leigh's answer is rendered quite unnecessary by my previous determination to shew it you, which I shall do immediately on receiving it—that is to say if I receive any at all. If I know anything of her art or disposition however you are mistaken in supposing that her remarks will be directed against yourself. *I* shall be the mark at which all the anger and spleen will be directed—and I shall take it very quietly, for whatever she may say I shall positively decline to enter into any further controversy with *her.* I shall have no objection to break a lance paper or otherwise with any champion to whom she may please to entrust her cause but I will have no further correspondence or communication with her personally, or in writing. I have copied the note and done up the parcel which will go off by the first Clapton Coach tomorrow morning.—

And now to the object of my present note. I have considered and reconsidered the matter, and I have come to the unqualified determination that I will allow no feeling of pride no haughty dislike to making a conciliation to prevent my expressing it without reserve.—I will advert to nothing that has passed; I will not again seek to excuse any part I have acted or to justify it by any course you have ever pursued, I will revert to nothing that has ever passed between us; I will only openly and at once say that there is nothing I have more at heart, nothing I more sincerely and earnestly desire than to be reconciled to you.—It would be useless for me to repeat here what I have so often said before; it would be equally useless to look forward and state my hopes for the future—all that any one can do to raise himself by his own exertions and unceasing assiduity I have done, and will do. I have no guide by which to ascertain your present feelings and I have God knows no means of influencing them in my favor. I never have loved and I never can love any human creature breathing but yourself. We have had many differences, and we have lately been entirely separated. Absence however has not altered my feelings in the slightest degree, and the Love I now tender you is as pure, and as lasting as at any period of our former correspondence. I have now done all I can to remove our most unfortunate and to me most unhappy misunderstanding—The matter now of course rests solely with you, and you will decide as your own feelings and wishes direct you. I could say much for myself, and I could entreat a favourable consideration in my own behalf but I purposely abstain from doing so because it would be only a repetition of an oft told tale, and because I am sure that nothing I could say would have the effect of influencing your decision in any degree whatever. Need I say that to me it is a matter of vital import and the most intense anxiety?—I fear that the numerous claims which must necessarilly be made on your time and attention next week will prevent your answering this note within anything like the time which my impatience would name. Let me entreat you to consider your determination well whatever it be and let me implore you to communicate it to me as early as possible.—As I am anxious to convey this note into the City in time to get it delivered today I will at once conclude by begging you to believe me

Yours sincerely
CHARLES DICKENS

To Richard Earle,[1] 6 JUNE [1833]

18 Bentinck Street | Cavendish Square | Thursday June 6th.

Sir.

I trust you will pardon the very great liberty I take in troubling you with any application on my own behalf, but as you have been kind enough to express an opinion in favour of my abilities as a Reporter, and as you have had opportunities of perusing my Reports, and being enabled to judge of their accuracy &c I am induced to make a request of a strictly private nature—and I can only plead my reliance on your kindness, and a natural wish on my part to enlarge the field of my exertions as an excuse of making it.

I am always entirely unemployed during the recess. I need hardly say that I have many strong inducements for wishing to be so as little as possible; and thinking that perhaps in the course of the business with which you are connected, you are frequently to a certain extent engaged in the formation of commissions, or other public Boards on which the services of a Short Hand Writer are required, I have made up my mind to take the liberty of asking you, should you ever have an opportunity of recommendation if you would object to mentioning my name.—Of course the value of a recommendation from such a quarter would be incalculable, and I trust the recommendation itself would not be misplaced.

I will not detain you further than by again apologising for writing to you, and venturing to express a hope that you will not consider my application impertinent, and consequently unworthy of notice.

I am Sir | Your most obliged Servant
CHARLES DICKENS

1 Richard Earle (1796–1848), private secretary to the Hon. Edward Stanley (later 14th Earl of Derby), at this time Secretary of State for Ireland.

To Henry Kolle, [3 DECEMBER 1833]

Bentinck Street | Tuesday Morning

My dear Kolle

I intend with the gracious permission of yourself and Spouse to look in upon you some Evening this week. I do not write to you however for the purpose of ceremoniously making this important announcement but to beg Mrs. K's criticism of a little paper of mine (the first of a Series) in *the Monthly* (not the New Monthly) Magazine of this month. I haven't a Copy to send but if the Number falls in your way, look for the Article. It is the same that you saw lying on my table but the name is transmogrified from "A Sunday out of town" to "A dinner at Poplar Walk".[1]

Knowing the interest (or thinking I know the interest) you are kind enough to take in my movements I have the vanity to make this communication. Best Remembrances to Mrs. K "So no more at present" from

My dear Kolle | Yours Sincerely
CHARLES DICKENS

I am so dreadfully nervous, that my hand shakes to such an extent as to prevent my writing a word legibly.

1 CD's first published sketch.

To The Editor of The Monthly Magazine, [OCTOBER 1834]

My Dear Editor,

I celebrated a christening a few months ago in the *Monthly*,[1] and I find that Mr. Buckstone has officiated as self-elected godfather, and carried off my child to the Adelphi, for the purpose, probably, of fulfilling one of his sponsorial duties, viz., of teaching it the vulgar tongue.[2]

Now, as I claim an entire right to do 'what I like with my own', and as I contemplated a dramatic destination for my offspring, I must enter my protest against the kidnapping process.

It is very little consolation to me to know, when my handkerchief is gone, that I may see it flaunting with renovated beauty in Field-lane;[3] and if Mr. Buckstone has too many irons in the fire to permit him to get up his own 'things', I don't think he ought to be permitted to apply to my chest of drawers.

Just give him a good 'blow up' in your 'magazine',—will you?

I remain, your's,

BOZ.

1 'The Bloomsbury Christening' (Apr. 1834).
2 The first instance of CD's work being pirated. John Buckstone (1802–79†), actor, playwright, and theatre manager, had a long run with *The Christening*.
3 An alley leading to Saffron Hill, the thieves' haunt off Holborn, described in *OT*.

To Thomas Mitton,[1] [?21 NOVEMBER 1834]

Bentinck Street | Friday Morning

Dear Tom.

On waking this morning, I was informed that my father[2] (whom I have not seen, for he had gone out) had just been arrested by Shaw and Maxwell the quondam Wine People. Will you have the goodness the moment you receive this, to go over to Sloman's in Cursitor Street[3] and see him for me, and ascertain whether anything can be done?

I must work this morning, but tell him please I shall be with him about Six.—I dine at 5 if you can come up.

I fear it is an awkward business, and really I have no idea of *the extent* of his other embarrassments.

Believe me | Sincerely Yours
CHARLES DICKENS

I have not yet been taken,[4] but no doubt that will be the next act in this "domestic tragedy".

1 Thomas Mitton (1812–78), solicitor, one of CD's earliest close friends. They were clerks together for a short time during 1828–9 in New Square, Lincoln's Inn. He acted as CD's solicitor for many years.
2 John Dickens (1785–1851), assistant clerk in the Navy Pay Office; after 1826 journalist and parliamentary reporter. His financial irresponsibility and geniality can be seen in Mr Micawber in *DC*.
3 A detention house for debtors.
4 Perhaps CD had backed bills for his father, and might therefore be liable to arrest too.

To Henry Austin, [20 DECEMBER 1834]

Furnivals Inn | Saturday Morning

Dear Henry.

I am obliged to give you the very ridiculous notice that if you come and see me tomorrow we must *go out and get our dinner.* I think the best way will be to walk somewhere; the fact is that I have had an explosion with nineteen out of the twenty Laundresses[1] in the Inn already, and can't get "done for". Some Methodistical ruffian has been among 'em, and they have all got the cant about "profaning the Sabbath"— and wiolating that commandment which embraces within its scope not only the stranger within the gates, but cattle of every description, including Laundresses.

Tomorrow is my Mother's birth day, so I have promised on behalf of yourself and Beard that we will go from here, and spend the Evening there. If you will be down here as early as you can tomorrow morning—shall we say to breakfast; for I dont take that meal until half past ten?—we can walk to Norwood, or some pretty place where we can get a chop, and return here to our grog.

Believe me | Very Sincerely Yours
CHARLES DICKENS

1 Women servants in the Inns of Court.

To Thomas Beard, [11 JANUARY 1835]

Black Boy Hotel—Chelmsford | Sunday Morning

Dear Tom.

I am more anxious than I can well express to know the result of your Interview with Hodgkin,[1] having set my heart on its being favourable. If you are not engaged tomorrow, will you write me a line by Return of Post, and resolve my doubts. I go into Suffolk on Tuesday Morning early but my Head Quarters will be here, and I have no doubt I shall receive at once any letter that arrives, directed as above.

I wish of all things that you were with me—Barring the grime of Solitude I have been very comfortable since I left town and trust I shall remain so until I return, which I shall do about the latter end of the week, unless I receive orders from the Office to the contrary.

Owing to the slippery state of the roads on the morning I started, I magnanimously declined the honor of driving myself, and hid my dignity in the Inside of a Stage Coach. As the Election here had not commenced, I went on to Colchester (which is a very nice town) and returned here on the following morning. Yesterday I had to start at 8 OClock for Braintree—a place 12 miles off; and being unable to get a Saddle Horse, I actually ventured on a gig,—and what is more, I actually did the four and twenty miles without upsetting it. I wish to God you could have seen me tooling in and out of the banners, drums, conservative Emblems, horsemen, and go-carts with which every little Green was filled as the processions were waiting for Sir John Tyrell and Baring.[2] Every time the horse heard a drum he bounded into the hedge, on the left side of the road; and every time I got him out of that, he bounded into the hedge on the right side. When he *did* go however, he went along admirably. The road was clear when I returned, and with the trifling exception of breaking my Whip, I flatter myself I did the whole thing in something like style.

If any one were to ask me what in my opinion was the dullest and most stupid spot on the face of the Earth, I should decidedly say Chelmsford. Though only 29 miles from town, there is not a single shop where they sell Sunday Papers. I can't get an Athenæum, a Literary Gazette—no not even a penny Magazine. And here I am on a wet Sunday looking out of a damned large bow window at the rain as it falls into the puddles opposite, wondering when it will be dinner time, and cursing my folly in having put no books into my Portmanteau. The only book I have seen here, is one which lies upon the sofa. It is entitled "Field Exercises and Evolutions of the Army by Sir Henry Torrens". I have read it through so often, that I am sure I could drill a hundred Recruits from memory. There is not even anything to look at in the place, except two immense prisons, large enough to hold all the Inhabitants of the county—whom they can have been built for I can't imagine.

I fear among the gloomy reflections which will present themselves to my mind this day that of having entailed upon you the misery of decyphering such an unconnected mass as this, will not be the least. As I thought it very likely however, that you would never get beyond the first three sentences I have comprised in them, the whole object of my letter; knowing that whether you came to the end of it or not, you would believe without a written assurance that I am

Most Sincerely Yours
CHARLES DICKENS

My best remembrances to all.

1 Thomas Hodgskin (1787–1869†), economist, political theorist, and journalist. Edited *Hansard* 1834–7, where Beard was presumably hoping for a post.
2 Sir John Tysson Tyrell, Bt (1795–1877), and Alexander Baring (1773–1848†), the Tory candidates, were both nominated.

To *Thomas Beard,* [2 MAY 1835]

Wincanton Saturday Morng

Dear Tom. I arrived here (57 miles from Exeter) at 8 yesterday Evening having finished my whack[1] at the previous stage. I arranged with Neilson,[2] whom I occasionally saw in the course of my journey, that I would stop where he did; & finding him housed here, I ordered dinner, beds, & breakfasts for two. I am happy to say that our friend Unwin, when on duty, is the most zealous, active, and indefatigable little fellow I ever saw: I have now, not the slightest doubt (God willing) of the success of our Express. On our first stage we had very poor horses. At the termination of the second, The Times and I changed Horses together; they had the start two or three minutes: I bribed the post boys tremendously & we came in literally neck and neck—the most beautiful sight I ever saw. The next stage, your humble, caught them before they had changed; & the next Denison preceded Unwin about two minutes, leaving Neilson here to return to Exeter tomorrow Evening & I to get up by the Telegraph at 11. The roads were *extremely heavy,* & as *they* had 4, I ordered the same at every stage & empowered Unwin to do the same until he met his horses; indorsing on the parcel that the rain rendered it a matter of *absolute necessity.*

I have sketched, my dear fellow in a dozen most hasty words, our progress yester-night wh I hope, but can scarcely believe, you will be able to understand. I have only time to add that I trust you will not forget my packages & cream: that I received the bag, your kindness remembered: that I shall hope to hear from you the day of your return: that I shall impress on Powell the necessity of expressing the declaration:[3] that I think Lyons & Roney will fail; and that I am (it's an old story, but a true one)

Sincerely Yours
CHARLES DICKENS

1 His part of the report for the *Morning Chronicle* of Lord John Russell's speech at the nomination meeting for South Devon, where Russell had offered himself for re-election.

2 John Finlay Neilson (1809–81), *The Times* reporter. He later claimed that, in this race by horse-express from Exeter, he beat CD by an hour. This letter suggests otherwise, and CD regarded it as a triumph. Denison was the other *Times* reporter; Unwin was a *Morning Chronicle* reporter.

3 i.e. printing the result of the poll immediately. John Hill Powell, Lyons, and James Edward Roney all worked at the *Morning Chronicle* with CD; Roney shared lodgings with CD in Buckingham Street, Adelphi (according to a Dickens family tradition, in David Copperfield's rooms), probably in 1831.

To Catherine Hogarth,[1] [MAY 1835]

My dearest Kate.

Need I say that my unavoidable detention in town last night, distressed me exceedingly; or that it has rendered me doubly anxious to see you this morning as early as I can? I have written a note to your Mama begging her to inform me immediately how you are, and I hope to hear that I shall be able to ask the question of you myself at an early hour.

If I were to say on paper how interested I am in the slightest word that concerns you, much more on so important a point as your health, it would look like egotism: were I to express half my solicitude in your behalf it would appear like profession without sincerity, and were I to endeavour to embody the least of the feelings I entertain for you in words, it would be a useless, and hopeless attempt. For each and all my dear Girl you must give me credit, until time has enabled me to prove the sincerity and devotion of the affection I bear you.

Keep up your spirits above all things—if the consciousness of awakening sympathy and interest in the breast of any human being be a consolation in sickness, you may take my assurance that you possess both to an extent which you can hardly imagine—nor I describe.

Believe me | My Dearest Catherine | Ever Yours Affecy.
CHARLES DICKENS

1 Catherine Hogarth (1815–79), later CD's wife, eldest child of George and Georgina Hogarth. Met CD through her father, who was on the staff of the *Morning Chronicle* and actively promoted CD's career. This is the first letter from CD that Catherine kept.

To Catherine Hogarth, [?LATE MAY 1835]

Wednesday Morning

My dear Catherine.

It is with the greatest pain that I sit down, before I go to bed to-night, to say one word which can bear the appearance of unkindness or reproach; but I owe a duty to myself as well as to you, and as I was wild enough to think that an engagement of even three weeks might pass without any such display as you have favored me with twice already, I am the more strongly induced to discharge it.

The sudden and uncalled-for coldness with which you treated me just before I left last night, both surprised and deeply hurt me—surprised, because I could not have believed that such sullen and inflexible obstinacy could exist in the breast of any girl in whose heart love had found a place; and hurt me, because I feel for you far more than I have ever professed, and feel a slight from you more than I care to tell. My object in writing to you is this. If a *hasty* temper produce this strange behaviour, acknowledge it when I give you the opportunity—not once or twice, but again and again. If a feeling of you know not what—a capricious restlessness of you can't tell what, and a desire to teaze, you don't know why, give rise to it— overcome it; it will never make you more amiable, I more fond, or either of us, more happy. If three weeks or three months of my society has wearied you, do not trifle with me, using me like any other toy as suits your humour for the moment; but make the acknowledgment to me frankly at once—I shall not forget you lightly, but you will need no second warning. Depend upon it, whatever be the cause of your unkindness—whatever give rise to these wayward fancies—that what you do not take the trouble to conceal from a Lover's eyes, will be frequently acted before those of a husband.

I know as well, as if I were by your side at this moment, that your present impulse on reading this note is one of anger—pride perhaps, or to use a word more current with your sex—"spirit". My dear girl, I have not the most remote intention of awakening any such feeling, and I implore you, not to entertain it for an instant. I am very little your superior in years: in no other respect can I lay claim to the title, but I venture nevertheless to give you this advice first, because I cannot turn coolly away and forget a slight from you as I might from any other girl to whom I was not warmly and deeply attached; and secondly, because if you really love me I would have you do justice to yourself, and shew me that your love for me, like mine for you, is above the ordinary trickery, and frivolous absurdity which debases the name, and renders it ludicrous.

I have written these few lines in haste, but not in anger. I am *not* angry, but I *am hurt*, for the second time. Possibly you may not understand the sense in which I use the word; if so, I hope you never may. If you knew the intensity of the feeling which has led me to forget all my friends and pursuits to spend my days at your side; if you knew but half the anxiety with which I watched your recent illness, the joy with which I hailed your recovery, and the eagerness with which I would promote your happiness, you could more readily understand the extent of the pain so easily inflicted, but so difficult to be forgotten.

Ever yours most affectionately
CHARLES DICKENS

To Catherine Hogarth, [?JUNE 1835]

Saturday Morning | 6 O'Clock.

My Dearest Kate.

I am so completely worn out, that I can only say I shall expect you at 12. It's a childish wish my dear love; but I am anxious to hear and see you the moment I wake—Will you indulge me by making breakfast for me this Morning? It will give me pleasure; I hope will give you no trouble; and I am sure will be excellent practice for you against Christmas next. I shall expect you my dearest, and feel quite sure you will not disappoint me.

Believe me | My dearest Girl | Ever Yours most devoted
CHARLES DICKENS

Excuse my haste and drowsiness.

To Catherine Hogarth, [?OCTOBER 1835]

Furnivals Inn | Monday Morning

My Dearest Love.

"Barring" my cold, I am quite well this morning, as I am happy—most happy— to hear you are also. I have received the Adelphi order, and shall be with you, at a quarter before three o'clock.

—Not low this morning I hope?—You ought not to be, dear Mouse, and are very ungrateful if you are.

Love to Mary and your Mama | Believe me | Darling Tatie |
Ever yours truly and Affecy.
CHARLES DICKENS

To John Macrone,[1] [?27 OCTOBER 1835]

13 Furnivals Inn | Tuesday Morning October 26th.

My Dear Sir.

Precisely the idea you suggest about the metallic bubbles, entered my brain after I left you the other day—bubbles from a spring impregnated with steel, I *have* heard of:

but bubbles coming direct from a steel instrument would, I am inclined to think, be a natural curiosity. Are you particularly attached to the retention of the word "Bwain"— when we can't preserve the Parody on Head's title[2]—What do you think of

Sketches by Boz[3]
and
Cuts by Cruikshank[4]

or

————

Etchings by Boz
and
Wood Cuts by Cruikshank.

————

I think perhaps some such title would look more modest—whether modesty *ought* to have anything to do with such an affair, I must leave to your experience as a Publisher to decide.

I will go to the Chronicle Office this morning; and if I cannot get slips, procure copies, of the missing sketches. If you will have the kindness to send to Cochrane's[5] (you are more likely to get what we want than I am) for the October and November numbers of The Monthly for last year, you will find "The Steam Excursion" in one of them—I think the former. "The Great Winglebury Duel" (which is the title of the paper which will appear in The Monthly for December) I will get a proof of, in the course of a few days.

Now if the whole collection fall something short of the two volumes, which we shall ascertain I suppose by the printing, I will be ready with two or three new Sketches to make weight; and with this view I have begged Black[6] to get old Alderman Wood to take me to Newgate[7]—as an Amateur of course. I have long projected sketching its Interior, and I think it would tell extremely well. It would not keep you waiting, because the printer has plenty to go on with; and a day's time is a handsome allowance for me—much less[8] than I frequently had when I was writing for The Chronicle. In addition to "A Visit to Newgate", I find in some memoranda I have by me, the following Headings. "The Cook's Shop"—"Bedlam"—"The Prisoner's Van"—"The Streets—Noon and Night"—"Banking-Houses"—"Fancy Lounges"—"Covent Garden"—"Hospitals"—and "Lodging-Houses"—So we shall not want subjects at all events.

I am much gratified by the kind expression of your good opinion of my Sketches contained in your note, and hope—and believe into the bargain—that your favourable augury of the success of the book may be realized, even to *our* joint satisfaction.

I will call on you on Thursday Morning, unless I should previously hear you are otherwise engaged.

Believe me | Dear Sir | Very truly Yours
CHARLES DICKENS

1 John Macrone (1809–37†), publisher of *SB*. He and CD were on very good terms until their dispute over the Agreement for "Gabriel Vardon" (Nov.–Dec. 1836).

2 The original title suggested (perhaps "Bubbles from the Bwain of Boz and the Graver of Cruikshank") parodied *Bubbles from the Brunnens of Nassau, by an Old Man*, 1834—sketches of a visit to drink the mineral waters, by Sir Francis Bond Head.

3 Boz was the nickname of CD's younger brother Augustus, called Moses after Moses Primrose in *The Vicar of Wakefield*; "which being facetiously pronounced through the nose, became Boses, and being shortened, became Boz" (CD's preface to *PP*, 1847).

4 George Cruikshank (1792–1878†), graphic artist, and by 1835 the most popular illustrator of his day. He illustrated *SB*, and *OT*, the plot of which he later claimed to have virtually created.

5 James Cochrane (b. 1794), who had published the *Monthly Magazine* alone since Macrone withdrew from their partnership in Sept. 1834.

6 John Black (1783–1855†), editor of the *Morning Chronicle*, which he made the leading anti-Tory newspaper, strongly reformist and Benthamite. CD later referred to him as "Dear old Black! My first hearty out-and-out appreciator" (late May 1870).

7 London's main prison at this time, and site for public executions.

8 He clearly meant "more".

To *Catherine Hogarth*, [?19 NOVEMBER 1835]

Furnivals Inn | Thursday Evening

My dearest Girl,

I had two or three interruptions this morning, and have not yet (7 o'Clock) finished my Sketch,[1] although I am rapidly approaching that very desirable consummation. I fear I shall not be able to see you to-night, and therefore send out Fred.[2] I have some business to transact to morrow, and fear I should only make you late if you were to wait for my escort into town—I have therefore arranged that Fred shall be with you *at half past four precisely* (rather before than after) if that hour will suit you.

I received a note from Fraser[3] this morning in which he says that Black is out of town and has left no tickets, but that if he return by Saturday, as in all human probability he will, they are mine—the Adelphi I shall be sent to on Monday; but I hardly know how to arrange about it, as I fear I shall be late, and I do not like your traversing the West End of London, of all other parts, accompanied only by Fred.

If you knew now eagerly I long for your society this evening, or how much delight it would afford me to be able to turn round to you at our own fireside when my work is done, and seek in your kind looks and gentle manner the recreation and happiness which the moping solitude of chambers can never afford, you would believe me sincere in saying that necessity and necessity alone, induces me to forego the pleasure of your companionship for one evening in the week even. You will never do me the justice of believing it however, and all I can do until my book[4] is finished will be to reflect that I shall have (God willing) many opportunities of shewing you for years to come how unjust you used to be, and of convincing you then of what I would fain convince you now—that my pursuits and labours such as they are are not more selfish than my pleasures, and that your future advancement and happiness is the main-spring of them all.

Believe me | My dear Girl | Ever Yours most affecy.
CHARLES DICKENS

1 Presumably 'The Vocal Dressmaker' (*Bell's Life in London*, 22 Nov. 1835); it became 'The Mistaken Milliner', *SB*, second series.
2 One of CD's younger brothers, b. 1820.
3 Thomas Fraser (?1804–69), assistant editor on the *Morning Chronicle* 1835–6.
4 *Sketches*, First Series.

To Catherine Hogarth, [25 NOVEMBER 1835]

Furnivals Inn | Wednesday Evening

My dearest Kate

Macrone has urged me most imperatively and pressingly to "get on". I have made considerable progress in my "Newgate" sketch, but the subject is such a very difficult one to do justice to, and I have so much difficulty in remembering the place,[1] and arranging my materials, that I really have no alternative but to remain at home to-night, and "get on" in good earnest. You know I have frequently told you that my composition is peculiar; I never can write with effect—especially in the serious way—until I have got my steam up, or in other words until I have become so excited with my subject that I cannot leave off; and hoping to arrive at this state to-night, I have, after a great deal of combating with my wish to see you, arrived at the determination I have just announced—I hope to do a good deal.

I will not do you the injustice to suppose that knowing my reason and my *motive* for exertion, *you* of all people will blame me one instant for my self-denial. You may be disappointed:—I would rather you would—at not seeing me; but you cannot feel vexed at my doing my best with the stake I have to play for—you and a home for both of us.

Write me by Fred and Believe me, my own love

Ever Yours most sincerely & affy.
CHARLES DICKENS

1 Since his visit three weeks before, he had done a week's reporting at Bristol and Bath.

To Catherine Hogarth, [16 DECEMBER 1835]

White Hart Kettering | Wednesday Morning

My dear Girl.

As I received your very welcome letter just now, and am alone for a few minutes, I think I cannot do better than sit down and write another without delay, though what on earth I am to write about I know not. This place is fearfully dull, and I have seen neither a newspaper or a book since I came down here.

You will see or hear by the Chronicle of yesterday, that we had a slight flare[1] here yesterday morning, just stopping short of murder and a riot. Party feeling runs so high, and the contest is likely to be so sharp a one that I look forward to the probability of a scuffle before it is over. As the Tories are the principal party here, I am in no very good odour in the town, but I shall not spare them the more on that account in the descriptions of their behaviour I may forward to head quarters. Such a ruthless set of bloody-minded villains, I never set eyes on, in my life. In their convivial moments yesterday after the business of the day was over, they were perfect savages. If a foreigner were brought here on his first visit to an English town, to form his estimate of the national character, I am quite satisfied he would return forthwith to France, and never set foot in England again. The remark will apply in a greater or less degree to all Agricultural places during the pendency of an Election, but beastly as the electors usually are, these men are superlative blackguards. Would you believe that a large body of horsemen, mounted and armed, who galloped on a defenceless crowd yesterday, striking about them in all directions, and protecting a man who cocked a loaded pistol, were *led* by Clergymen, and Magistrates? Or that I saw one of these fellows with my own eyes, unbuckle one of his stirrup-leathers, and cut about him in the crowd, with the iron part of it—communicating to the blows all the additional force that swinging it at the end of the leather could give them? Anything more sickening and disgusting, or anything that roused my indignation so much, I never beheld.

I think I shall have to go over to Northampton to-day with the Times man, whose return from a gentleman's seat in the neighbourhood, whither he went on business before I was up, I am in momentary expectation of. If so, I shall sleep at Northampton to-night, and return here in the course of tomorrow morning. The polling begins on Friday and then we shall have an incessant repetition of the sounds and sights of yesterday 'till the Election is over—bells ringing, candidates speaking, drums sounding, a band of *eight trombones* (would you believe it?) blowing—men fighting, swearing drinking, and squabbling—all riotously excited, and all disgracing themselves. You will probably have heard from Fred that I shall have finished here by Monday. You shall hear from me again before then, and I will tell you the hour at which I shall expect to see you in Furnivals Inn. I expect a parcel from Fred to-night.

God bless you my dearest Katie.

Love to all, and Believe me | Ever affectionately Yours
CHARLES DICKENS

You won't forget the direction, if you feel disposed to write again.

1 i.e. a flare-up of violence.

To Catherine Hogarth, [18 DECEMBER 1835]

White Hart. Kettering. | Friday Noon

My dear Kate.

I am overjoyed to say that I have received a communication from the Office to the effect that it will be unnecessary for me to remain here for the Declaration of the Poll on Monday. I shall therefore leave by the "Peveril" tomorrow night at a quarter past one, and shall be in town about nine o'Clock on the following Morning.—I shall lie down for an hour or two, and be out at Brompton to dinner on Sunday.

I am very sorry my dear Girl that you should have thought my letter of the other day stiff and formal—I don't know how it is, but I am quite certain I had no notion of its being so, and if it really were (which I can hardly believe) it was quite unintentional. The noise and confusion here this morning—which is the first day of polling is so great that my head is actually splitting. There are about forty flags on either side, two tremendous bands, one hundred and fifty constables, and vehicles of every kind, sort, and description. These last mentioned nuisances are constantly driving about and in and out and up [and] down the town, conveying voters to the Poll; and the voters themselves are drinking and guzzling and howling and roaring in every house of Entertainment there is. Our house is so full, and the blue swine, or in other words the conservative electors are such beasts that we have retired into my bed room—a large apartment at the extreme end of a long gallery, with a couple of windows commanding an interesting view of the stable yard. There is a little passage leading to the room at the entrance of which is a door which we have fastened, and on the outside of which we have affixed a poker as a temporary knocker. Here we have removed the Bagatelle Board, and here we sit secure from interruption, with the bedstead wheeled into a corner. I have just ordered dinner in this curious den for five people—cod and oyster sauce, Roast beef, and a pair of ducks, plum pudding, and Mince Pies. Bearing in mind your objection to my doing anything in the Ducrow[1] way, I persuaded on the Times, Post, and Advertizer, to alter their original plan of making a day of it yesterday on saddle-horses, to hiring a four wheeled chaise. A driver was chosen by ballot, and your humble servant was unanimously appointed Guard. We started at about 11 oClock for the Duke of Buccleugh's seat[2] which is about 4 or 5 miles from hence: went over the House, dined at a country public house, and returned after dark, when our driver being very near-sighted and slightly overcome with potations of ale, and egg flip, ingeniously drove the party into a "water-splash". The Guard dismounted—the water being up to the calves of his legs—and after a great deal of dragging, splashing, and shouting, succeeded in leading the Horse back to the road, and we all arrived here in time for coffee. On the preceding day I was at Northampton, and "flore"³ slightly.

And now my dear Girl I have only time to add that business and want of space combined, compel me to close my letter abruptly. Its stiffness and formality I must leave you to judge of. The assurance that the prospect of seeing you two days earlier than I expected, gives me the utmost joy, I must judge of myself: only assuring you that it is most sincere and heartfelt. I am most happy to hear you have not been "coss"—though I perceive you have not yet subdued one part of your disposition— your distrustful feelings and want of confidence. However this may be, you may rest satisfied that I love you dearly—far too well to feel hurt by what in any one else would have annoyed me greatly. Tell Fred I had no time to write to him; and *not* to take any proofs to Brompton on Saturday Night, as I should like to see them when I return on Sunday Morning. Love to all. God bless you Pig, and Believe me (if you have any faith in your nature) Ever Yours most Sincerely & Affecy.

CHARLES DICKENS

Damn the Tories—They'll win here I am afraid.⁴

1 Andrew Ducrow (1793–1842†), popular equestrian performer.
2 Boughton House, about 2½ miles from Kettering.
3 Probably an allusion to a convivial party.
4 They did, by a majority of 597 (poll 3107).

To John Macrone, [21 DECEMBER 1835]

St. James's Square | Monday

My Dear Sir
    I called on you this morning although with very little hope of finding you returned so soon. When you come back, will you be kind enough to write to Cruikshank impressing the necessity of dispatch upon him?—I think he requires the spur.
    I will call on Thursday Morning and shall perhaps succeed in finding you at home.

Believe me | Very truly Yours
CHARLES DICKENS

To Catherine Hogarth, [21 FEBRUARY 1836]

Furnivals Inn | Sunday Evening

My Dearest Life

You must not be "coss" with what I cannot help. I like the *matter* of what I have done to-day, very much, but the *quantity* is not sufficient to justify my coming out to-night. If the representations I have so often made to you, about my working as a duty, and not as a pleasure, be not sufficient to keep you in the good humour, which you, of all people in the World should preserve—why then, my dear, you must be out of temper, and there is no help for it.

I can fancy, if you began to read this note with a frown, that a smile has taken its place by this time: and so I shall speak rationally about what I have been doing, as I hope I shall always be able to do, to my own Wife.—I have at this moment, got Pickwick, and his friends, on the Rochester Coach, and they are going on swimmingly, in company with a very different character from any I have yet described, who I flatter myself will make a decided hit.[1] I want to get them from the Ball, to their Inn, before I go to bed—and I think that will take me until one or two o'Clock, *at the earliest.* The Publishers will be here in the Morning, so you will readily suppose I have no alternative but to stick at my Desk.

Write me a long note by Fred, but if you *can* avoid crossing[2] it, do: for my eyes are none of the best at night, and I feel some difficulty in reading it by candle-light. I hope and believe I shall be able to get out between my turns, tomorrow night— about half past 9. But should I be prevented, I hereby solemnly pledge myself to be out, God willing, on Tuesday. Tell me all the news about Braham[3]—

Believe me | My dearest Love | Ever Yours most affecy.
CHARLES DICKENS

I wish you were a fixture here—I should like to have you by me—*so* much.

1 Jingle.
2 i.e. using the same sheet of paper twice, the second page written on top of the first at right angles.
3 John Braham (1777?–1856†), popular English tenor; in Dec. 1835 opened St. James's Theatre, known as 'Braham's Folly'.

To Thomas Barrow,[1] 31 MARCH 1836

15 Furnivals Inn. | Thursday March 31st. 1836

My Dear Uncle.

The great success of my book,[2] and the name it has established for me among the Publishers, enables me to settle at an earlier period than I at first supposed possible;

I have therefore fixed Saturday next, for my marriage with Miss Hogarth—the daughter of a gentleman who has recently distinguished himself by a celebrated work on Music, who was the most intimate friend and companion of Sir Walter Scott,[3] and one of the most eminent among the Literati of Edinburgh.

There is no Member of my family to whom I should be prouder to introduce my wife, than yourself, but I am compelled to say—and I am sure that you cannot blame me for doing so—that the same cause which has led me for a long time past, to deny myself the pleasure and advantage of your society, prevents my doing so. If I could not as a single man, I cannot as a married one, visit at a relation's house from which my father is excluded:[4] nor can I see any relatives here, who would not treat him, as they would myself.

This is a very painful subject, and I have many associations connected with you, which render it much more painful in this case, than in any other. I cannot forget that I was once your little companion and nurse, through a weary illness, nor shall I ever cease to remember the many proofs you have given me, in later days, of your interest, and affection.

When I say, Uncle, that I should be more happy than I can possibly express, if you would place it in my power, to know you once again on those terms of intimacy and friendship, I so sincerely desire, I hope you will not misunderstand my meaning. I do not ask you—I should conceive that I lowered and disgraced myself, if I did—to alter your determination. I may think that time might have softened the determined ani[mosity[5] y]ears ; I may [ ] do an injustice ([ ] I have no doubt) to my father's real character. I cannot, however, be an impartial judge, because I cannot be an unprejudiced one; and I do not presume therefore to arraign your decision.

Nothing that has occurred to me in my life, has given me greater pain, than thus denying myself the society of yourself and Aunt. I have only to add that the contents of this letter are unknown to everybody but Aunt Charlton,[6] to whom I have written on the same subject: and that come what may, I shall ever be, at heart,

Dear Uncle | Your most affectionate Nephew
[CHARLES DICKENS]

---

1 Thomas Culliford Barrow (?1793–1857), Mrs John Dickens's eldest brother.

2 *SB*, First Series.

3 Walter Scott (1771–1832†), poet and novelist; major influence on CD.

4 In 1819 Barrow had guaranteed an annuity of £26 to a third party in return for £200 paid to CD's father, who was unable to pay the annuity; in 1821 Barrow was called upon to repay the £200 himself. Hence the exclusion of John Dickens from Barrow's house.

5 Signature at end of letter has been cut away, affecting three lines on other side.

6 CD's maternal great-aunt (b. 1786).

To Robert Seymour,[1] [14 APRIL 1836]

15 Furnivals Inn | Thursday Evening

My Dear Sir—

I had intended to write you, to say how much gratified I feel by the pains you have bestowed on our mutual friend Mr. Pickwick, and how much the result of your labours, has surpassed my expectations. I am happy to be able to congratulate you, the publishers, and myself, on the success of the undertaking, which appears to have been most complete.

I have now, another reason for troubling you. It is this. I am extremely anxious about "The Stroller's Tale"[2]—the more especially as many literary friends, on whose judgment I place great reliance, think it will create considerable sensation. I have seen your design for an Etching to accompany it. I think it extremely good, but still, it is not quite my idea; and as I feel so very solicitous to have it as complete as possible, I shall feel personally obliged, if you will make another drawing. It will give me great pleasure to see you, as well as the drawing, when it is completed. With this view, I have asked Chapman and Hall, to take a glass of grog with me on Sunday Evening (the only night I am disengaged), when I hope you will be able to look in.[3]

The alteration I want, I will endeavour to explain. I think the woman should be younger—the "dismal man" decidedly should, and he should be less miserable in appearance. To communicate an interest to the plate, his whole appearance should express more sympathy and solicitude: and while I represented the sick man as emaciated and dying, I would not make him too repulsive. The furniture of the room, you have depicted, *admirably*.

I have ventured to make these suggestions, feeling assured that you will consider them in the spirit in which I submit them to your judgment. I shall be happy to hear from you, that I may expect to see you on Sunday Evening—[4]

Dear Sir | Very truly Yours
CHARLES DICKENS

1 Robert Seymour (1796–1836†), illustrator and caricaturist.
2 The first of the nine stories interpolated into *PP*.
3 This was their only meeting.
4 Seymour provided illustrations for the first two numbers of *PP*, but committed suicide on 20 Apr.

To Messrs Chapman & Hall,[1] 1 NOVEMBER 1836

Furnivals Inn. | Tuesday Evening | November 1st 1836.

My Dear Sirs,

I have been exceedingly gratified by your very kind letter; not so much by the intelligence you communicate to me of Pickwick's success, and the consequent advantage it holds out to me (though they are something) as by the very kind tone in which it is couched, and the very handsome terms in which your intelligence is communicated.

I am well aware of the lingering disease under which Mr. Pickwick has recently laboured, and of the great aggravation of the symptoms which has gradually taken place.[2] You may rest assured that the disease has reached its height, and that it will now take a favourable turn. Avoiding all showy promises, I will endeavour to prove to you, before this day week, that I am serious and in earnest. I only entreat you to recollect two things—first that I have many other occupations; and secondly that spirits are not to be forced up to Pickwick point, every day. Although thank God I have as few worldly cares as most people, you would scarcely believe how often I sit down to begin a number, and feeling unequal to the task, do what is far better than writing, under such circumstances—get up, and wait till I am. It is needless for me to say how cordially I am interested in its success, or how proud I am of it. If I were to live a hundred years, and write three novels in each, I should never be so proud of any of them, as I am of Pickwick, feeling as I do, that it has made its own way, and hoping, as I must own I do hope, that long after my hand is withered as the pens it held, Pickwick will be found on many a dusty shelf with many a better work.

There—enough of Pickwick, and now for future periodicals. I should be the most insensible, and at the same time the most jolter-headed scribe alive, if I had ever entertained the most remote idea of dissolving our most pleasant and friendly connection. So I hereby nominate and appoint William Hall and Edward Chapman of No. 186 Strand, their heirs, executors, administrators, and assigns, my periodical publishers, until I am advertised in the daily papers, as having been compressed into my last edition—one volume, boards, with brass plates; and in common with my very kind friend of the Advertiser, I hope it may be long before I come out in so unique a form.[3]

I had intended when I began this Letter, to close it by saying how much—how very much—I feel your honorable conduct. But as I know I should grow very sentimental if I said anything more about it, I will not trust myself to add more than that I am My dear Sirs,

Most faithfully yours
CHARLES DICKENS

1 William Hall (1800/1–47†) and Edward Chapman (1804–80†); booksellers and publishers. CD broke with them in 1844 but returned in 1859.

2 i.e. CD's increasing failure to produce his monthly instalments on time.

3 The *Morning Advertiser* reviewed all *PP* to date on 25 Oct. 1836, concluding: 'We sincerely hope that our youthful author may long be spared to contribute to the entertainment of the public, and that peace and health may attend his fireside.'

To Richard Bentley,[1] 2 NOVEMBER [1836]

Furnivals Inn | Wednesday Evening Novr. 2nd.

My dear Sir.

I have well weighed the subject on which we conversed this morning; and feeling perfectly satisfied that it will not interfere with Pickwick, shall be happy to undertake the editorship of the new Magazine,[2] on the following conditions being settled between us.

I should like in my agreement to have my duties specifically set forth, together with the emoluments you propose, and a stipulation relative to the quantity of matter I am to furnish monthly, which I understand is never to exceed a sheet. As I should immediately throw up my connection with the Chronicle in the event of my closing with you, I make it a sine quā non that my engagement is for a year certain. I have little doubt that it would last for many years, but as I must resign a certain income elsewhere, this condition is indispensable.

The terms I leave to you to propose. I need not enlarge on the rapidly increasing value of my time and writings to myself, or on the assistance "Boz's" name just now, would prove to the circulation, because I am persuaded that no one is better able to form a correct estimate on both points, than you are.

I thought it might facilitate our dispatch of business on Friday, if I stated these points at once. Within four and twenty hours after you make me a definite proposal, I will return a final answer. Of course I understand that until we agree to make it public, the project remains a secret.

I am | Dear Sir | Very faithfully Yours
CHARLES DICKENS

1 Richard Bentley (1794–1871†), prominent publisher. CD later quarrelled with him, and finally broke with the 'Burlington Street Brigand' in 1839.
2 *Bentley's Miscellany.*

To John Easthope,[1] [18 NOVEMBER 1836]

15 Furnivals Inn. | Friday Morning

Dear Sir.

If you imagine that I was guilty of the least intentional disrespect in not returning to the office the other day, you do me the greatest injustice. Having left Mrs. Dickens in a shop hard by; and having consumed in waiting at the office and going to Cecil Street, a much longer time than I supposed I should have been absent, I did not choose to leave her any longer in a strange place; knowing as I did how very easily I could account for my not returning (if you had thought anything of it at all, which

I considered highly improbable) when I did see you. I have not called since, because I have been very ill, and have not left the house for several days, and have since been obliged to devote my whole time, morning and night, to recovering the ground I had lost by indisposition.

You will permit me to assure you, very respectfully that you are greatly mistaken in imagining that I had *forgotten* that I was to supply a Sketch *weekly*. I merely pursued the same course as I adopted when I wrote the Sketches before. We had the same agreement then, but I wrote sometimes two in one week, sometimes none, as suited my convenience, and that of the paper. The very circumstance of the revising Barristers' Courts being open at the time, assured me that the Chronicle would sustain no injury by my doing so. Its columns must have been pretty full, for on one occasion, a Sketch was lying at the Office, I think three days, before it was inserted. I have only to add that I shall return the six guineas with the utmost pleasure, and that I wish I could return at the same time every additional six pence beyond my regular salary as a reporter that I have received from the Establishment, although I have rendered in return for it, the money's worth.

I should have been well content to have left; and to have considered the constrained and abrupt terms of your former letter, as one of those matters of course which so often pass between master and servant, when the servant gives his month's warning, and takes his services elsewhere. But I will say now, in the same frankness and honesty with which you express your feelings to me, that I *did* expect on leaving, to receive some slight written acknowledgment from the Proprietors of the Morning Chronicle of the sense they entertained of the services I had performed. I may say now, that on many occasions at a sacrifice of health, rest, and personal comfort, I have again and again, on important expresses in my zeal for the interests of the paper, done what was always before considered impossible, and what in all probability will never be accomplished again. During the whole period of my engagement wherever there was difficult and harassing duty to be performed—travelling at a few hours' notice hundreds of miles in the depth of winter—leaving hot and crowded rooms to write, the night through, in a close damp chaise—tearing along, and writing the most important speeches, under every possible circumstance of disadvantage and difficulty—for that duty have I been selected. And I did not think when I made great efforts to perform it, and to eclipse (as I have done, again and again) other papers with double the means, that my reward at last would be a regret that I had ever enjoyed a few week's rest, and a fear lest at the close of two years, I should have received six pounds six, too much! I have, however, the satisfaction of knowing that there is not another Newspaper Office in London where these services have not been watched and appreciated—that there is not one of my colleagues who will not cheerfully bear testimony to them—and with the respect and esteem of both Editors and reporters, I am happy to say that I can afford to part with the thanks of the Proprietors, although I feel much hurt, and much surprised at the conduct they think proper to pursue towards me.

Depend upon it, Sir, that if you would stimulate those about you to any exertions beyond their ordinary routine of duty, and gather round you competent successors to the young men whom you will constantly find quitting a most arduous and thankless profession, as other prospects dawn upon them, this is not the way to do it.

> I am | Dear Sir | Faithfully Yours
> CHARLES DICKENS

1 Sir John Easthope (1784–1865†), Liberal politician and chief proprietor of the *Morning Chronicle*.

To Hablot K. Browne,[1] [JANUARY 1837]

I think the Sergeant should look younger, and a great deal more sly, and knowing— he should be looking at Pickwick too, smiling compassionately at his innocence. The other fellows are noble—CD

1 Hablot Knight Browne, 'Phiz' (1815–82†), artist and illustrator. Succeeded Robert Buss (who had replaced Seymour) as illustrator of *PP*. Illustrated all CD's novels (except *OT*) up to and including *TTC*, 1859.

To Edward Chapman, [7 MAY 1837]

Doughty St. | Sunday Night

My Dear Sir
    We are in deep and severe distress. Miss Hogarth[1] after accompanying Mrs. Dickens & myself to the Theatre last night, was suddenly taken severely ill, and despite our best endeavours to save her, expired in my arms at two O'Clock this afternoon.

> Faithfully Yours
> CHARLES DICKENS[2]

1 Catherine's 17-year-old sister Mary, described by CD as 'the grace and life of our home'.
2 Signature very shaky, and the flourish omitted.

To Thomas Beard, [17 MAY 1837]

Collins's Farm. North End | Hampstead | Wednesday Evening

My Dear Beard.
    I received your kind letter in due course. I should have written to you myself, to communicate the dreadful occurrence, but I had so many distressing appeals to my attention and exertions, that I was compelled to postpone doing so for a time.

I presume you heard from my father, that on the Saturday Night we had been to the Theatre—that we returned home as usual—that poor Mary was in the same health and spirits in which you have so often seen her—that almost immediately after she went up stairs to bed she was taken ill—and that next day she died. Thank God she died in my arms, and the very last words she whispered were of me.

Of our sufferings at the time, and all through the dreary week that ensued, I will say nothing—no one can imagine what they were. You have seen a good deal of her, and can feel for us, and imagine what a blank she has left behind. The first burst of my grief has passed, and I can think and speak of her, calmly and dispassionately. I solemnly believe that so perfect a creature never breathed. I knew her inmost heart, and her real worth and value. She had not a fault.

Mrs. Hogarth has suffered and still continues to suffer most deep and bitter anguish. Kate, I am glad to say, made such strong efforts to console her, that she unconsciously summoned up all her fortitude at the same time, and brought it to her own assistance. She knows that if ever a mortal went to Heaven, her sister is there; she has nothing to remember but a long course of affection and attachment, perhaps never exceeded. Not one cross word or angry look on either side, even as children, rises in judgment against her; and she is now so calm and cheerful that I wonder to see her.

I have been so shaken and unnerved by the loss of one whom I so dearly loved that I have been compelled to lay aside all thoughts of my usual monthly work, for once;[1] and we have come here for quiet and change. We have a cottage of our own, with large gardens, and everything else on a small but comfortable scale. Kate is very anxious indeed to see you and as I can assure you that you will derive any thing but pain from seeing her, I hope you will join us in the old way. Name your own time, and believe me that there is no one whom it would give us so much pleasure to welcome as yourself.

> Believe me My Dear Beard | Ever Faithfully Yours
> CHARLES DICKENS

1 There was no June number of either *PP* or *OT*.

To John Forster,[1] [?26 MAY 1837]

48 Doughty Street. | Friday Morning

My Dear Forster.

Let me beg your acceptance of the accompanying Nos. of the Miscellany,—not as a matter of business, or with any view to notices thereof, past present or to come, but because I should really be greatly disappointed if I wrote anything which you had not an early opportunity of reading. This looks very like vanity I dare say, but

I do not mean it so. Believe me that it affords me great pleasure to hear that you continue to read my writings, and far greater gratification than I can well describe to *you* to hear from your own lips that poor Oliver "affects" you—which I take to be the highest of all praise.

> Believe me with great sincerity | Faithfully Yours
> CHARLES DICKENS

I shall expect you on Tuesday, remember.

1 John Forster (1812–76†), writer, editor, and critic. A friend, supporter, and adviser to many writers, including Leigh Hunt, Bulwer Lytton, Charles Lamb, and Robert Browning. From Oct. 1837 onwards he read, in MS or proof, everything that CD wrote. A close and affectionate friendship developed between them, and CD must soon have become aware of his notorious rudeness. Forster wrote the first biography of CD, having been authorized to do so. CD ended a long letter of praise for Forster's *Life and Adventures of Oliver Goldsmith*: 'I desire no better for my fame when my personal dustyness shall be past the controul of my love of order, than such a biographer and such a Critic' (22 Apr. 1848). Forster left his collection of CD's manuscripts to what is now the National Art Library at the V&A.

To Thomas Haines,[1] 3 JUNE 1837

48 Doughty St.—Mecklenburgh Square | Saturday June 3rd. 1837.

My Dear Sir.

Beard, our mutual friend, was to have been the medium of an introduction between us, but as he has not seen you for some time, I venture to introduce myself as "Boz", and when I tell you why I have not had patience to wait for his intervention, I dare say you will feel highly gratified.

In my next number of Oliver Twist, I must have a magistrate; and casting about for a magistrate whose harshness and insolence would render him a fit subject to be "shewn up" I have, as a necessary consequence, stumbled upon Mr. Laing[2] of Hatton Garden celebrity. I know the man's character perfectly well, but as it would be necessary to describe his appearance also, I ought to have seen him, which (fortunately or unfortunately as the case may be) I have never done.

In this dilemma it occurred to me that perhaps I might under your auspices be smuggled into the Hatton Garden office for a few moments some morning. If you can further my object, I shall be really very greatly obliged to you.

I am staying at Hampstead at present; but if you will direct a line to my house in town, stating when I shall call on you, or you on me, I will be punctual. Whether you can render me the assistance I require, or not, I shall be happy to avail myself of that opportunity of becoming known to you.

> Believe me | My Dear Sir | Faithfully Yours
> CHARLES DICKENS

1 Thomas Haines, for many years a respected reporter at the Mansion House police office.
2 Allan Laing (1788–1862), notoriously severe Hatton Garden police magistrate. CD pilloried him as Mr Fang in the July instalment of *OT* ch. II.

To John Forster, 2 JULY 1837

Hôtel Rignolle. | Calais, le 2nd. July 1837

My Dear Forster.

We[1] arrived here in great state this morning—I very sick, and Missis very well. Just as the boat was leaving Dovor, a breathless Boots put a letter from town, and "The Examiner" into my hands, the latter of which, I verily believe preserved me from that dismal extremity of qualmishness into which I am accustomed to sink when I have "the blue above and the blue below". I have always thought that the "silence wheresoe'er I go"[2] is a beautiful touch of Barry Cornwall's (otherwise Procter) descriptive of the depression produced by sea-voyaging. I know it's remarkably silent wherever *I* go, when I'm on the briny.

But seriously—how can I thank you for your beautiful notice?[3]— Can I do so better than by saying that I feel your rich, deep appreciation of my intent and meaning more than the most glowing abstract praise that could possibly be lavished upon me? You know I have ever done so, for it was your feeling for me and mine for you that first brought us together, and I hope will keep us so, till death do us part. Your notices make me grateful but very proud; so have a care of them, or you will turn my head.

We have arranged for a post coach to take us to Ghent, Brussels, Antwerp, and a hundred other places that I cannot recollect now and couldn't spell if I did. We went this afternoon in a barouche to some gardens where the people dance, and where they were footing it most heartily—especially the women who in their short petticoats and light caps look uncommonly agreeable. A gentleman in a blue surtout and silken Berlins[4] accompanied us from the Hotel, and acted as Curator.[5] He even waltzed with a very smart lady (just to show us, condescendingly, how it ought to be done) and waltzed elegantly too. We rang for slippers after we came back, and it turned out that this gentleman was the "Boots". Isn't this French?

I think we shall be home on Sunday Night or Monday Morning—I shall see you, please God, directly we return—at least, so soon as my sea-sickness shall have disappeared. Meanwhile curse my negligence for having forgotten Bentley's letter, and mislaid the draught. I sent another to him by the same Post which brings this,— very nearly the same I think. Mrs. D and Browne beg their best remembrances; and I beg you (no hard task I hope) to believe me ever

Faithfully and sincerely Yours
CHARLES DICKENS

1 CD, Catherine, and Hablot K. Browne; CD's first trip abroad.
2 From 'The Sea', B. W. Procter's *English Songs*, 1832.
3 Forster's highly complimentary review of *PP* No. 15 in *The Examiner* of 2 July.
4 Knitted gloves of Berlin wool.
5 i.e. guide.

To George Beadnell, [?LATE JULY 1837]

Doughty Street. | Monday Evening

My Dear Sir

I have purposely abstained from replying to your note before, in order that if our friend Mr. Clarke communicated with you again, you might be enabled to tell him with perfect truth that you had heard nothing from me.

My reason is this—if I were in the slightest instance whatever, to adopt any information so communicated, however much I invented upon it, the World would be informed one of these days—after my death perhaps—that I was not the sole author of the Pickwick Papers—that there were a great many other parties concerned— that a gentleman in the Fleet Prison perfectly well remembered stating in nearly the same words—&c &c &c. In short I prefer drawing upon my own imagination in such cases. Mr. Clarke's own story I have put into a Cobbler's mouth who tells it in the next number; and this is the only reality in the whole business of and concerning the Fleet. Fictitious narratives place the enormities of the system in a much stronger point of view, and they enable one to escape the personalities and endless absurdities into which there is a certainty of rushing if you take any man's account of his own grievances.

If you should receive any other application from the same quarter, perhaps you will have the goodness to say that you communicated the first to me, and there an end of it.

Believe me ever My Dear Sir | Faithfully and sincerely Yours
CHARLES DICKENS

Pray present my best Compts. to Mrs. & Miss Beadnell.

To Richard Bentley, 16 SEPTEMBER 1837

48 Doughty Street. | Saturday September 16th. 1837.

Sir.

When I left town, I placed a number of accepted articles in the Printer's hands, with directions to set them up in sheets, beginning at the commencement of the number, and to send proofs to me. The whole of this arrangement has been altered by you; proofs of articles which I never saw in Manuscript have been forwarded to me; and notwithstanding my written notice to the Printer that I would revise no such papers, this course has been persisted in, and a second sheet sent.

By these proceedings I have been actually superseded in my office as Editor of the Miscellany; they are in direct violation of my agreement with you, and a gross insult to me. I therefore beg to inform you that henceforth I decline conducting the Miscellany or contributing to it in any way; but in order that you may suffer no inconvenience or embarrassment from the shortness of this notice, I will write a paper this month, and edit the Magazine this month—no longer.

As I feel this course of treatment most strongly, I beg you to understand that it is my firm intention to abide by this determination, regarding the propriety of which, my feeling of what is due to myself, is strengthened by the best advice from others.

I am | Sir, | Yours
CHARLES DICKENS[1]

1 CD continued to edit *Bentley's Miscellany* until Jan. 1839.

To Mrs Georgina Hogarth,[1] [26 OCTOBER 1837]

Doughty Street. | Thursday Night

My Dear Mrs. Hogarth.

I need not thank you for your present of yesterday;[2] for you know the mournful pleasure I shall take in wearing it and the care with which I shall prize it, until—so far as relates to this life—I am like her.

I have never had her ring off my finger by day or night, except for an instant at a time to wash my hands, since she died. I have never had her sweetness and excellence absent from my mind so long. I can solemnly say that waking or sleeping I have never once lost the recollection of our hard trial and sorrow, and I feel that I never shall.

It will be a great relief to my heart when I find you sufficiently calm upon this sad subject to claim the promise I made you when she lay dead in this house, never to shrink from speaking of her as if her memory were to be avoided, but rather to take a melancholy pleasure in recalling the times when we were all so happy—so happy that increase of fame and prosperity has only widened the gap in my affections by causing me to think how she would have shared and enhanced all our joys, and how proud I should have been (as God knows I always was) to possess the affection of the gentlest and purest creature that ever shed a light on earth. I wish you could know how I weary now for the three rooms in Furnival's Inn, and how I miss that pleasant smile and those sweet words which, bestowed upon an evening's work in our merry banterings round the fire, were more precious to me than the applause of a whole world would be. I can recal everything we said and did in those happy days, and could shew you every passage and line we read together.

You and I will probably be oftener alone together in Kate's coming confinement, which will be a truly heavy time to me, reminding me how we spent the last. I see *now* that you are capable of making great efforts even against the affliction you have to deplore, and I hope that then our words may be where our thoughts are, and that we may call up these old memories,—not as shadows of the bitter past, but as lights upon a happier future.

Believe me My Dear Mrs. Hogarth, | Ever truly and affectionately Yours
CHARLES DICKENS

1 Catherine's mother.
2 A chain of Mary Hogarth's hair.

To *William Howison*, 21 DECEMBER 1837

48 Doughty Street London. | Thursday December 21st. 1837.

Sir.

I have to acknowledge the receipt of your letter informing me of the institution of an "Edinburgh Pickwick Club"—and conveying to me from its Members a most gratifying and welcome assurance of their good-will and regard.

I believe with you that this is the first society of the kind, established North of the Tweed, and I cannot tell you how much delight it has afforded me to hear of its existence. All my relations by marriage are of Scotland. Many of my dearest living friends are natives of your fine city, and my most cherished recollections are of a dearly loved friend and companion who drew her first breath in Edinburgh and died beside me.

I need not, I am sure, tell you that these are all reasons for endearing to me the place and everything savouring of it. If I wanted any additional sources of gratification beyond those which you acquaint me with, I should find them in the tone of your intelligence and the terms of your letter.

If a word of encouragement from me, can as you say endow you with double life, you will be the most lively club in all the Empire, from this time; for every hearty wish that I can muster for your long-continued welfare and prosperity, is freely yours. Mr. Pickwick's heart is among you always.

Nothing in the course of my brief career—numerous as my causes for gratification have been—has afforded me so much delight as the being so pleasantly and cheerily remembered by the rising spirits of distant places in their moments of relaxation and enjoyment. Trusting that I may long hold a place in your remembrances and that whenever I visit Scotland again I may find you flourishing with greater vigour than ever,

> I am | Sir | Very faithfully Yours
> CHARLES DICKENS

To John Forster, [? JANUARY 1838]

Dr. Forster

I shall expect you—chops await you.

> CD.

To Catherine Dickens, 1 FEBRUARY 1838

Greta Bridge. | Thursday February 1st. 1838.

My Dearest Kate.

I am afraid you will receive this, later than I could wish, as the Mail does not come through this place until 2 o'Clock tomorrow Morning. However, I have availed myself of the very first opportunity of writing, so the fault is *that* mail's, and not *this*.

We reached Grantham between 9 and 10 on Tuesday night, and found everything prepared for our reception in the very best Inn I have ever put up at. It is odd enough that an old lady who had been outside all day and came in towards dinner time turned out to be the Mistress of a Yorkshire School returning from the holiday-stay in London. She was a very queer old body, and shewed us a long letter she was carrying to one of the boys from his father, containing a severe lecture (enforced and aided by many texts from Scripture) *on his refusing to eat boiled meat*. She was very communicative, drank a great deal of brandy and water, and towards evening became insensible, in which state we left her.

Yesterday we were up again shortly after 7 and came on upon our journey by the Glasgow Mail which charged us the remarkably low sum of *six pounds, four* for two places inside. We had a very droll male companion until seven oClock in the evening, and a most delicious lady's maid for twenty miles who implored us to keep a sharp look-out at the coach windows as she expected her carriage was coming to meet her and she was afraid of missing it. We had many delightful vauntings of the same kind; and in the end it is scarcely necessary to say that the Coach did not come, and a very dirty girl did.

As we came further North, the snow grew deeper. About eight o'Clock it began to fall heavily, and as we crossed the wild heaths hereabout, there was no vestige of a track. The Mail kept on well, however, and at eleven we reached a bare place with a house standing alone in the midst of a dreary moor, which the Guard informed us was Greta Bridge. I was in a perfect agony of apprehension, for it was fearfully cold and there were no outward signs of anybody being up in the house. But to our great joy we discovered a comfortable room with drawn curtains and a most blazing fire. In half an hour they gave us a smoking supper and a bottle of mulled port (in which we drank your health) and then we retired to a couple of capital bedrooms in each of which was a rousing fire half way up the chimney.

We have had for breakfast, toasts, cakes, a yorkshire pie, a piece of beef about the size and much the shape of my portmanteau, tea, coffee, ham and eggs—and are now going to look about us. Having finished our discoveries, we start in a postchaise for Barnard Castle which is only four miles off, and there I deliver the letter given me by Mitton's friend. All the schools are round about that place, and a dozen old abbies besides, which we shall visit by some means or other tomorrow. We shall reach York on Saturday I hope, and (God willing) I trust I shall be at home on Wednesday Morning. If anything should occur to prevent me, I will write to you from York, but I think that is not likely.

I wish you would call on Mrs. Bartley and thank her for her letter; you can tell her when I expected to be in York.

A thousand loves and kisses to the darling boy whom I see in my mind's eye crawling about the floor of this Yorkshire Inn. Don't leave him alone too much. Bless his heart I would give two sovereigns for a kiss. Remember me too, to Frederick who I hope is attentive to you. Take care of yourself my dearest, and let me find by your letter at the York Post Office that you are in both good health and good spirits.

Is it not extraordinary that the same dreams which have constantly visited me since poor Mary died, follow me everywhere? After all the change of scene and fatigue, I have dreamt of her ever since I left home, and no doubt shall 'till I return. I should be sorry to lose such visions for they are very happy ones—if it be only the seeing her in one's sleep—I would fain believe too, sometimes, that her spirit may have some influence over them, but their perpetual repetition is extraordinary.[1]

Love to all friends. | Ever my dear Kate your affectionated husband
CHARLES DICKENS

1 The result of his telling Catherine about the dreams was that they stopped completely.

To Frederick Yates,[1] [?MID-MARCH 1838]

48 Doughty Street. | Friday Morning

My Dear Sir.

Supposing we arrange preliminaries to our mutual satisfaction, I propose to dramatize Oliver for the first night of next Season.[2]

I have never seen Mrs. Honnor to the best of my recollection, but from the mere circumstance of her being a Mrs, I should say at once that she was "a many sizes too large" for Oliver Twist. If it be played by a female, it should be a very sharp girl of thirteen or fourteen—not more, or the character would be an absurdity.

I don't see the possibility of any other house doing it before your next opening night.[3] If they do, it must be done in a very extraordinary manner, as the story (unlike that of Pickwick) is an involved and complicated one. I am quite satisfied that nobody can have heard what I mean to do with the different characters in the end, inasmuch as at present I don't quite know, myself; so we are tolerably safe on that head.

Any way, I am quite sure that your name as the Jew and mine as the author would knock any other attempts quite out of the field. I do not however see the least possibility of any other Theatre being able to steal a march upon you.

> Believe me always | Truly Yours
> CHARLES DICKENS

1 Frederick Yates (1797–1842†), actor and theatre manager.
2 Nothing came of this project.
3 Five different versions of *OT* were performed before Yates's production at the Adelphi in Feb. 1839. Gilbert À Beckett's version appeared in Mar. 1838, half-way through publication of the novel.

To George Lewes,[1] [?9 JUNE 1838]

Doughty Street | Saturday Morning

My Dear Sir

I write—fortunately for you—short notes, having no time (if I had the inclination) to make them longer.

I will take soundings in Counting-House Quarters and report about that very deep mine to which you devote yourself, in due course.[2]

I don't think I shall be in town again until next Saturday, but between twelve and two on that day I shall be here. I have I am sorry to say several unfixed dinner engagements afoot, but I have at present no reason to fear that any one of them will clash with whatever day may suit Leigh Hunt[3] best. I merely stipulate that you discharge me at an early hour, as I shall go back to Twickenham that night.

With reference to that question of yours concerning Oliver Twist I scarcely know what answer I can give you. I suppose like most authors I look over what I write with exceeding pleasure and think (to use the words of the elder Mr. Weller) "in my innocence that it's all wery capital". I thought that passage a good one *when* I wrote it, certainly, and I felt it strongly (as I do almost every word I put on paper) *while* I wrote it, but how it came I can't tell. It came like all my other ideas, such as they are, ready made to the point of the pen—and down it went. Draw your own conclusion and hug the theory closely.[4]

I strongly object to printing anything in italics but a word here and there which requires particular emphasis, and that not often. It is framing and glazing an idea and desiring the ladies and gentleman to walk up and admire it. The truth is, that I am a very modest man, and furthermore that if readers cannot detect the point of a passage without having their attention called to it by the writer, I would much rather they lost it and looked out for something else.

Faithfully Yours
CHARLES DICKENS

1 George Henry Lewes (1817–78†), writer and critic, and appreciative early reviewer of CD. They became friends; Lewes acted in CD's amateur company. He was later the partner of Marian Evans (George Eliot).
2 Lewes had presumably offered to write for *Bentley's Miscellany.*
3 Leigh Hunt (1784–1859†), poet, journalist, and literary critic. With his brother John, founder of the reformist weekly *The Examiner*; imprisoned 1813–15 for libelling the Prince of Wales. CD drew on him for Skimpole in *BH.*
4 The passage in the summer Nos. of *OT* which probably attracted Lewes, with his interest in mental phenomena, is the description in ch. 34 of Oliver's state suspended between sleeping and waking.

To John Forster, 23 JUNE 1838

Gammon Lodge | Saturday Evening | June 23rd. 1838

Sir.

I am requested to inform you that at a numerous meeting of the Gammon Aeronautical Balloon association[1] for the encouragement of Science and the Consumption of Spirits of Wine—Thomas Beard Esquire, Mrs. Charles Dickens, Charles Dickens Esquire, the Snodgering Blee, Popem Jee[2] and other distinguished characters being present and assenting—the vote of censure of which I inclose a copy was unanimously passed upon you for gross negligence in the discharge of your duty, and most unjustifiable disregard of the best interests of the Society.

I am Sir | Your most obedt. Servant
CHARLES DICKENS

Honorary Secretary

1 A balloon club for the children at Twickenham: Forster was president and had to supply the balloons. Serious balloon ascents were in the news.
2 Charley and Mamie. These are the first known of CD's many nicknames for his children.

To John Forster, 27 JULY 1838[1]

July 27th. 1838.

Dr. Sir.

Poets tell us that love is blind;— I fear indifference is more so. It is many months since I sent you a slight gage d'amour; it is many years (do not be alarmed, I am still very young) since I first became acquainted with your worth and excellence. I have seen you—met you—read your works—heard you speak—listened, in a breathless state, to your eloquent and manly expression of the sentiments which do you honor; and still by no word or sign have I discovered that you recognized in me the giver of the simple worthless riding whip which I have often seen in your hand, and once (when you [ ] it) nearly touched.

Mr. Forster—dear Mr. Forster let me say, as it is but on paper, and through the distant medium of an anonymous communication—I have loved you, and I could have wished, and have wished with all a woman's ardour that you were mine. You are no ordinary man. When I tell you this, believe that love—a love of which I am not ashamed, but proud, since its object exalts even that great passion—has rendered me superior to the common foibles of my sex. I love you still, but I know neither jealousy, envy, nor hatred. You love another. Heaven send you may be happy—as happy, Mr. Forster, as you deserve. As happy as in the wildest dreams of your youth you can ever have hoped to become.

I have but one object in writing, and that is soon stated. I might say two, since it will be a consolation to know that your eye traces these lines—but I will not. Think me capricious—strange—romantic—what you will—but when this engagement arising out of the acquaintance you have recently formed, *is* ratified (it may be already, I have no reason to doubt it) return that whip to the booking office of the Golden Cross Charing Cross,[2] directed "To T.B.K. To be called for." I shall receive it within four and twenty hours. The Reflection that you have used it, kept it, had it by you, looked upon it, wondered whence it came, and perhaps felt proud of it at times, will support me under the heavy infliction of knowing that you are another's.

Dear Mr. Forster, bless you. In the society of your future wife, and your excellent friends Mr. Dickens, Mr. Serjeant Talfourd[3] and Mr. Macready[4] who respect and admire you as a kindred spirit and find their genius mirrored in your own, may you be happy;—happier Dear Mr. Forster than

Louisa.

---

1 A joke letter, untidily written, with numerous cancellations, alterations, and blots.
2 The famous coaching inn, features in *SB*, *PP*, and *DC*.
3 Thomas Talfourd (1795–1854†), writer, judge, and politician. A man of charm and conviviality, at the heart of CD's social circle and model for Tommy Traddles in *DC*.
4 William Macready (1793–1873†), leading actor of his generation and theatre manager at Covent Garden and Drury Lane. He sought to raise the artistic and moral reputation of the stage, promoting Shakespeare and new dramatists, while driving prostitutes from public areas of the theatre. His friendship with CD was unbroken from 1837.

To *Johann Kuenzel*,[1] [?JULY 1838]

Doughty Street | Monday Evening.

My Dear Sir.

Pray keep the English Authors as long as you please. I only wish the collection were a more comprehensive and interesting one.

I am ashamed to confess that—in the hurry of many engagements—I have quite forgotten your request.[2] That I may forget it no longer, I will tell you "all I know" at once.

I was born at Portsmouth, an English Seaport town principally remarkable for mud, Jews, and Sailors, on the 7th. of February 1812. My father holding in those days a situation under Government in the Navy Pay Office, which called him in the discharge of his duty to different places, I came to London, a child of two years old, left it again at six, and then left it again for another Sea Port town—Chatham—where I remained some six or seven years, and then came back to London with my parents and half a dozen brothers and sisters, whereof I was second in seniority.

I had begun an irregular rambling education under a clergyman at Chatham, and I finished it at a good school in London—tolerably early, for my father was not a rich man, and I had to begin the world. So I began in a Lawyer's office—which is a very little world, and a very dull one—and leaving it at the expiration of two years, devoted myself for some time to the acquirement of such general literature as I could pick up in the Library of the British Museum,—and to the study of Short Hand, with a view to trying what I could do as a reporter—not for the Newspapers, but legal authorities—in our Ecclesiastical Courts. I was very successful in this pursuit—was induced to join the Mirror of Parliament—a publication, which was at that time devoted solely to the Debates—and afterwards to attach myself to the Morning Chronicle, where I remained until the four or five first numbers of the Pickwick Papers had appeared, and in the columns of which Journal most of my shorter sketches were originally published. Some few appeared in the old Monthly Magazine. I may tell you that I was considered very remarkable at the Chronicle for an extraordinary facility in writing and so forth—that I was very liberally paid during my whole connection with the paper—and that, when I quitted it, Pickwick was rapidly approaching the zenith of its fame and popularity.*

The rest of my career up to this time, you know. I may add for your guidance in any little notes you may throw together of my "Life and adventures" that I was a great reader as a child, being well versed in most of our English Novelists before I was ten[3] years old—that I wrote tragedies and got other children to act them—that I won prizes at school, and great fame—that I am positively assured I was a very clever boy—that I am now married to the eldest daughter of Mr. Hogarth of Edinburgh, a gentleman who has published two well-known Works on Music and was a great friend and companion of Sir Walter Scott's—and that, being now in my twenty-seventh year, I hope with God's blessing to retain my health, spirits, fancy, and perseverance (such as they are) for many years to come.

As to my means of observation, they have been pretty extensive. I have been abroad in the world from a mere child, and have lived in London and travelled by fits and starts through a great part of England, a little of Scotland, and less of France, with my eyes open. Heaven send that some kind wind may ere long blow me to Germany!

There—I have said more about myself in this one note than I should venture to say elsewhere in twenty years. If you can make anything of such a jumble of matter, and—more than all—interest anybody in it, your ability, my dear Sir, will have exalted your subject.

Believe me | Very truly Yours
CHARLES DICKENS

If it be any consolation to the German Ladies to know that I have two children, pray tell them so.

*The Sketches, I should have told you, had been previously collected and published with amazing success, and have since gone through many editions.

1 Johann Kuenzel (1810–73), German scholar and author. In England 1838–41 as tutor in the Duke of Sutherland's household.
2 For particulars about himself, to be published in the *Konversationslexikon*, Leipzig. CD's first autobiographical account of himself.
3 CD began to write 'twelve', crossed it out, and wrote 'ten' instead.

To John Forster, [2 OCTOBER 1838]

Doughty Street | Tuesday night

My Dear Forster

I need not tell you how delighted I have been with the notice in the Edinburgh.[1] It is all even *I* could wish, and what more can I say!

Hard at work still.—Nancy is no more. I shewed what I have done to Kate last night who was in an unspeakable *"state"*, from which and my own impression I augur well. When I have sent Sikes to the Devil, I must have yours.

Ever Faithfully
CHARLES DICKENS

1 Thomas Lister's article acclaimed CD as the 'truest and most spirited delineator of English life, amongst the middle and lower classes, since the days of Smollett and Fielding. . . . What Hogarth was in painting, such very nearly is Mr. Dickens in prose fiction,' *Edinburgh Review*, 1838.

To George Cruikshank, [?6 OCTOBER 1838]

Doughty Street | Saturday Morning

My dear Cruikshank

I find on writing it, that the scene of Sikes's escape will not do for illustration. It is so very complicated, with such a multitude of figures, such violent action, and torch-light to boot, that a small plate could not take in the slightest idea of it.

I am expecting to see you with some designs. When I do, we will settle upon the substitute for this.[1] I shall finish (please God) next week.

Always Believe me | Faithfully Yours
CHARLES DICKENS

1 Cruikshank illustrated part of the scene as 'The Last Chance', showing Sikes and his dog on the roof.

To Frederick Yates, [?29 NOVEMBER 1838]

48 Doughty Street | Thursday Morning

My Dear Sir.

I am very glad indeed that Nickleby[1] is doing so well. You are right about the popularity of the work, for its sale has left even that of Pickwick far behind.

My general objection to the adaptation of any unfinished work of mine simply is, that being badly done and worse acted it tends to vulgarize the characters, to destroy or weaken in the minds of those who see them the impressions I have endeavoured to create, and consequently to lessen the after-interest in their progress. No such objection can exist for a moment where the thing is so admirably done in every respect as you have done it in this instance. I felt it an act of common justice after seeing the piece, to withdraw all objection to its publication, and to say thus much to the parties interested in it, without reserve.[2]

Would you think me very unreasonable if I asked you not to compare Nicholas with Tom and Jerry?[3]

If you can spare us a private box for *next Tuesday,* I shall be much obliged to you. If it be on the stage so much the better, as I shall really be glad of an opportunity to tell Mrs Keeley[4] and O Smith[5] how very highly I appreciate their Smike and Newman Noggs. I put you out of the question altogether, for that glorious Mantalini is beyond all praise.

Faithfully Yours
CHARLES DICKENS

1 Yates's production at the Adelphi.
2 *PP, OT,* and *NN* had all been dramatized long before completion.

3 The heroes of Pierce Egan's popular *Life in London, or the Day and Night Scenes of Jerry Hawthorn, Esq. and Corinthian Tom*, 1821. The comparison was presumably made on the playbills. CD would have disliked Egan's coarse language and glorification of fast Regency life.

4 Mary Ann Keeley (1805–99†), successful actress, played in many adaptations of CD's novels. Wife of actor Robert Keeley; CD greatly admired them both.

5 Richard John Smith (1786–1855†), actor, known as O Smith for his success as Obi in the melodrama *Three Fingered Jack*. Played Hugh in *BR*, and Scrooge.

To *William Hughes*,[1] 12 DECEMBER 1838

Doughty Street. London. | December the twelfth | 1838.

Respected Sir.

I have given Squeers one cut on the neck and two on the head, at which he appeared much surprised and began to cry, which being a cowardly thing is just what I should have expected from him—wouldn't you?

I have carefully done what you told me in your letter, about the lamb and the two sheeps for the little boys. They have also had some good ale and porter, and some wine. I am sorry you didn't say *what* wine you would like them to have. I gave them some sherry which they liked very much, except one boy who was a little sick and choaked a good deal. He was rather greedy, and that's the truth, and I believe it went the wrong way, which I say served him right, and I hope you will say so, too.

Nicholas had his roast lamb as you said he was to, but he could not eat it all, and says if you do not mind his doing so, he should like to have the rest hashed tomorrow, with some greens which he is very fond of and so am I. I said I was sure you would give him leave. He said he did not like to have his porter hot, for he thought it spoilt the flavour, so I let him have it cold. You should have seen him drink it. I thought he never would have left off. I also gave him three pounds of money—all in six pences to make it seem more—and he said directly that he should give more than half of it to his mama and sister and divide the rest with poor Smike. And I say he is a good fellow for saying so, and if anybody says he isn't, I am ready to fight him whenever they like.—There.

Fanny Squeers shall be attended to, depend upon it. Your drawing of her is very like, except that I don't think the hair is quite curly enough. The nose is particularly like hers, and so are the legs. She is a nasty disagreeable thing and I know it will make her very cross when she sees it, and what I say is that I hope it may. You will say the same, I know—at least I think you will.

I meant to have written you a longer letter but I cannot write very fast when I like the person I am writing to, because that makes me think about them, and I like you and so I tell you. Besides it is just eight o'clock at night, and I always go to bed at eight o'Clock except when it is my birthday, and then I sit up to supper. So I will not say anything more besides this—and that is my love to you and

Neptune, and if you will drink my health every Christmas Day, I will drink yours—
Come.

> I am | Respected Sir | Your affectionate friend
> CHARLES DICKENS

I don't write my name very plain, but you know what it is, you know, so never
mind.

1 William Hughes (1833–1907), aged 5, younger brother of the author of *Tom Brown's Schooldays*.

To *Anna Maria Hall*,[1] 29 DECEMBER 1838

Doughty Street | December 29th. 1838.

My Dear Mrs. Hall.

I am exceedingly obliged to you for your kind note, and the interesting anecdote
which you tell so well. I have laid it by in the MS of the first number of Nickleby, and
shall keep it there in confirmation of the truth of my little picture.

Depend upon it that the rascalities of those Yorkshire schoolmasters *cannot* easily
be exaggerated, and that I have kept down the strong truth and thrown as much
comicality over it as I could, rather than disgust and weary the reader with its fouler
aspects. The identical scoundrel you speak of, I saw—curiously enough. His name is
Shaw;[2] the action was tried (I believe) eight or ten years since, and if I am not much
mistaken another action was brought against him by the parents of a miserable child,
a cancer in whose head *he* opened with an inky penknife, and so caused his death.[3]
The country for miles round was covered, when I was there, with deep snow. There
is an old Church near the school, and the first grave-stone I stumbled on that dreary
winter afternoon was placed above the grave of a boy, eighteen long years old, who
had died—suddenly, the inscription said; I suppose his heart broke—the Camel falls
down "suddenly" when they heap the last load upon his back—died at that wretched
place. I think his ghost put Smike into my head, upon the spot.

I went down in an assumed name, taking a plausible letter to an old Yorkshire
attorney from another attorney in town, telling him how a friend had been left a
widow, and wanted to place her boys at a Yorkshire school in hopes of thawing the
frozen compassion of her relations. The man of business gave an introduction to
one or two schools, but at night he came down to the Inn where I was stopping, and
after much hesitation and confusion—he was a large-headed flat-nosed red-faced old
fellow—said with a degree of feeling one would not have given him credit for, that
the matter had been upon his mind all day—that they were sad places for mothers to
send their orphan boys too—that he hoped I would not give up him as my adviser—
but that she had better do anything with them—let them hold horses, run errands—

fling them in any way upon the mercy of the World—rather than trust them there. This was an attorney, a well-fed man of business, and a rough Yorkshireman!

Mrs. Dickens and myself will be delighted to see the friend you speak of—we unite in regards to yourself and Mr. Hall[4]—and I throw myself single-handed upon your good nature, and beseech you to forgive me this long story—which you ought to do, as you have been the means of drawing it from me. Believe me, Dear Mrs. Hall

Very faithfully Yours
CHARLES DICKENS

1 Anna Maria Hall (1800–81†). Prolific writer and editor, and active philanthropist. Married to Samuel Carter Hall.
2 William Shaw, owner of Bowes Academy, Yorkshire; widely recognized as the original of Squeers. CD and Browne visited him on 2 Feb. 1838.
3 CD confuses Shaw with the Yorkshire schoolmaster whom he was told about as a boy. See his preface to *NN*, 1848.
4 Samuel Carter Hall (1800–89†), prolific journal editor and writer. Champion of modern British artists, and active in temperance and other philanthropic movements. Claimed to have known almost every distinguished artist and writer of his day, and thought to be a model for Pecksniff in *MC*.

To John Forster, [21 JANUARY 1839]

Doughty Street | Monday Morning

My Dear Forster

With this you will receive a copy of a letter, which I am going to send to Bentley tomorrow morning.[1] Keep it for I have no other.

From what I have already said to you, you will have been led to expect that I entertained some such intention. I know you will not endeavour to dissuade me from sending it for such an attempt would be utterly useless. Go it MUST.

It is no fiction to say that at present I *cannot* write this tale. The immense profits which Oliver has realised to its publisher, and is still realising; the paltry, wretched, miserable sum it brought to me (not equal to what is every day paid for a novel that sells fifteen hundred copies at most); the recollection of this, and the consciousness that I have still the slavery and drudgery of another work on the same journeyman-terms; the consciousness that my books are enriching everybody connected with them but myself, and that I, with such a popularity as I have acquired, am struggling in old toils, and wasting my energies in the very height and freshness of my fame, and the best part of my life, to fill the pockets of others, while for those who are nearest and dearest to me I can realise little more than a genteel subsistence: all this puts me out of heart and spirits: and I cannot—cannot and will not—under such circumstances that keep me down with an iron hand, distress myself by beginning this tale until I have had time to breathe; and until the intervention of the summer, and some cheerful days in the country, shall have restored me to a more genial and composed state of feeling.

There—for six months Barnaby Rudge stands over. And but for you, it should stand over altogether. For I do most solemnly declare that morally, before God and man, I hold myself released from such hard bargains as these,[2] after I have done so much for those who drove them. This net that has been wound about me so chafes me, so exasperates and irritates my mind, that to break it at whatever cost— *that* I should care nothing for—is my constant impulse. But I have not yielded to it. I merely declare that I must have a postponement very common in all literary agreements; and for the time I have mentioned—six months from the conclusion of Oliver in the Miscellany—I wash my hands of any fresh accumulation of labour, and resolve to proceed as cheerfully as I can with that which already presses upon me.

Always faithfully Yours
CHARLES DICKENS

1 Requiring a postponement of six months before beginning *BR* in *Bentley's Miscellany*. It was finally published in *MHC* in 1841.
2 The terms for *BR* would have given CD £800, £40 less than he had had for *OT*.

To *William Bradbury*,[1] 3 MARCH [1839]

48 Doughty Street | Sunday Morning March 3rd.

My Dear Sir.

I read your note last night with heartfelt pain and sorrow. But I hope and believe that from the very depth and strength of your affection for your dead child, will arise your best and truest consolation.

The certainty of a bright and happy world beyond the Grave, which such young and untried creatures (half Angels here) *must* be called away by God to people—the thought that in that blessed region of peace and rest there is one spirit who may well be supposed to love and watch over those whom she loved so dearly when on earth— the happiness of being always able to think of her as a young and promising girl, and not as one whom years and long sorrow and suffering had changed—above all, the thought of one day joining her again where sorrow and separation are unknown— these are all sources of consolation which none but those who have suffered deep affliction can know in all their force, and which will whisper comfort and resignation to you and your poor wife.

To many, these would sound as very very slight considerations to fortify the mind against such a loss. It is nearly two years ago since I lost in one short night a young and lovely creature whom—I can say even to *you* now—I loved with the warmest affection that our nature is capable of, and in whom I had the fondest father's pride. The first burst of anguish over, I have never thought of her with pain—never. I have never connected her idea with the grave in which she lies. I look upon it as I sometimes do upon the clothes she used to wear. They will moulder away in their secret places, as her earthly form will in the ground, but I have long since learnt to separate her from all this litter of dust and ashes, and to picture her to myself with every well-remembered grace and beauty heightened by the light of Heaven and the power of that Merciful Being who would never try our earthly affections so severely but to make their objects happy, and lead our thoughts to follow them.

I venture to hope my dear Sir, that the day is not far distant when you will be able to think of this dear child with a softened regret which will have nothing of bitterness in its composition—when it will be a melancholy but not a painful satisfaction to call up old looks and thoughts and turns of speech—and when you will be able to reflect with a grateful heart that those who yield most promise and are most richly endowed, commonly die young, as though from the first they were the objects of the Almighty's peculiar love and care. It is, no doubt, a heavy blow to lose so sweet a child; but who that loved her would call her back, if any soul could return to tell the bliss of that distant land to which she has winged her early flight?

Receive my Dear Sir the assurance I cannot refrain from conveying to you at such a time as this, of my earnest and sincere sympathy and warm regard. And may the influence which the blessed spirits of those who have toiled on earth, have been supposed by many good and wise men to exercise over sorrowing mortals, bring comfort to you and yours in this sad bereavement.

> My Dear Sir, I am always, | Faithfully Yours
> CHARLES DICKENS

1 William Bradbury (1800–69†), in partnership with Frederick Evans (1803–70†), as printers and publishers. Until CD quarrelled with Chapman & Hall in 1844, they were his printers; thereafter they were his publishers until 1858. Proprietors of *Punch* from Dec. 1841. For many years CD had the highest opinion of them both as printers and publishers, and relations were very cordial.

To John Forster, [5 MARCH 1839]

New London Inn. Exeter. | Tuesday Night.

My Dear Forster.

I took a cottage for them[1] this morning. If they are not pleased with it—I shall be grievously disappointed; that's all. It is at a place called Alphington, exactly one mile beyond Exeter on the Dawlish, I think, but I know on the Plymouth-Road. There are two white cottages together, built of brick with thatched roofs. One is theirs and the other belongs to their landlady one Mrs. Pannell. I almost forget the number of rooms and cannot say positively until I have been there again, but I can report on solemn affirmation that on the ground floor there are an excellent parlor, a nice kitchen, and a little third room of comfortable proportions; and that in the yard behind there are meat-safes cellars coal holes wood houses and such like accomodations in rural abundance. Upstairs there is really a beautiful little room over the parlor which I am furnishing as a drawingroom, and I am not sure whether there are two or three bedrooms besides. There is a splendid garden and the rent of the whole (the landlady paying all taxes) is twenty pounds a year! The paint and paper throughout is new and fresh and cheerful-looking: the place is clean beyond all description; and the neighbourhood I suppose the most beautiful in this most beautiful of English counties.

Mrs. Pannell of whom I must make most especial mention is a Devonshire widow with whom I had the honor of taking lunch to-day. She is a fat, infirm, splendidly-fresh-faced country dame, rising sixty and recovering from an attack "on the Nerves"—I thought they never went off the stones,[2] but I find they try country air with the best of us. In the event of my mother's being ill at any time, I really think the vicinity of this good dame (the very picture of respectability and good humour) will be the greatest possible comfort. *Her* furniture and domestic arrangements are a capital picture, but that, with sundry imitations of herself and some "ladies" who called while I was there (evidently with a view to the property) I must reserve 'till I see you, when I anticipate a hearty laugh. The cottages communicate at the back—that is, our people pass close behind hers to get to their garden—she bears the highest character with the bankers and the clergyman—who formerly lived in *my* cottage himself—and is a kind-hearted worthy capital specimen of the sort of life, if she is properly managed, or I have no eye for the real and no idea of finding it out.

The good lady's brother and his wife live in the next nearest cottage, and the brother transacts the good lady's business, the nerves not admitting of her transacting it herself, although they leave her in her debilitated state something sharper than the finest lancet. Now the brother having coughed all night 'till he coughed himself into such a perspiration that you might have "wringed his hair", according to the asseverations of eye witnesses, his wife was sent for to negociate with me, and if you could have seen me sitting in the kitchen with the two old women, endeavouring to make them comprehend that I had no evil intentions or covert designs and that I had come down all that way to take some cottage and had *happened* to walk down that road and see that particular one, you would never have forgotten it. Then to see the servant-girl run backwards and forwards to the sick man, and when the sick man had signed one agreement which I drew up and the old woman instantly put away in a disused tea-caddy, to see the trouble and the number of messages it took before the sick man could be brought to sign another (a duplicate) that we might have one apiece, was one of the richest scraps of genuine drollery I ever saw in all my days. How, when the business was over, we became conversational—how I was facetious and at the same time virtuous and domestic—how I drank toasts in the beer, and stated on interrogatory that I was a married man and the father of two blessed infants—how the ladies marvelled thereat—how one of the ladies, having been in London, enquired where I lived and being told, remembered that Doughty Street and the Foundling Hospital were in the Old Kent Road, which I didn't contradict,—all this and a great deal more must come with Stebbing when I return, and will make us laugh then I hope, and makes me laugh now to think of. Of my subsequent visit to the Upholsterer recommended by Mrs. Pannell—of the absence of the upholsterer's wife and the timidity of the upholster, fearful of acting in her absence—of my sitting behind a high desk in a little dark shop calling over the articles in requisition and checking off the prices as the upholsterer exhibited the goods and called them out—of my coming over the upholsterer's daughter with many virtuous endearments to propitiate the establishment and reduce the bill—of these matters I say nothing, either, for the same reason as that just mentioned. The discovery of the cottage I seriously look upon as a blessing (not to speak it profanely) upon our efforts in this, I hope no longer sad, cause. I had heard nothing from the Bank and walked straight there, by some strange impulse, directly after breakfast. I am sure they may be happy there, if they will. If I were older and my course of activity were run, I am sure *I* could, with God's blessing, for many and many a year.

The Theatre is open here, and Charles Kean[3] is playing for his last night to-night. If it had been the "rig'lar" drama I should have gone, but I was afraid Sir Giles Overreach (are there two r's?) might upset me so I stayed away. My quarters are excellent and the head-waiter is *such* a Waiter! Knowles—not Sheridan Knowles,[4] but Knowles of the Cheatham Hill Road—is an ass to him. This sounds bold but truth is stranger than fiction. By the bye, not the least comical thing that has occurred was the visit of the upholsterer (with some further calculations) since I began this letter. I think they took me here for the wonderful Being I am; they were amazingly sedulous, and no doubt looked for my being visited by the nobility and gentry of the neighbourhood. My first and only visitor came to-night.—A ruddy-faced man in faded black with extracts from a feather bed all over him—an extraordinary and quite miraculously dirty face—a thick stick—and the personal appearance altogether of an amiable bailiff in a green old age. I have not seen the proper waiter since, and more than suspect I shall not recover this blow. He was announced (by *the* waiter) as "a person". I expect my bill every minute.

I have left so little room for business that I must be brief. I wrote to-day for my mother to come down on *Thursday,* and inclosed her—for herself—the wherewithal. Please to advance to father for himself and Augustus to follow on Saturday five pounds. Don't forget your letter by Friday's post, and let it be a long one. If you *should* have time to see little Evans or Hicks you will relieve my mind by telling them how it is that they will not get the copy for the next No. as soon as I promised. I want my mother for some matters of curtains, blinds, and so forth in which—with her—I can save greatly. Forgive this jumble of incoherence (penned under the pressure of two other letters and some sleepiness) and believe me my dear Forster if I need ask it

Always Your attached friend
CHARLES DICKENS

I hope to be home on Monday Evening at half past eight.

The waiter is laughing outside the door with another waiter—This is the latest intelligence of my condition.

I open this on Wednesday Morning to say that Charles Kean is gone, and I have moved into his sitting room. I am sitting at this instant in his wery chair!!! I was bursting into the water-closet this morning, when a man's voice (of tragic quality) cried out—"There is somebody here." It was his. I shall reserve this for his Biographer.

1 CD's parents and youngest brother Augustus (b. 1827). CD wanted his father out of London.
2 Paving-stones, i.e. the town.
3 Charles Kean (1811–68†), actor and theatre manager. Much acclaimed for his Hamlet in 1838, he and Macready were rivals. Sir Giles Overreach is in Philip Massinger's *A New Way to Pay Old Debts* (1633).
4 James Sheridan Knowles, the playwright.

To Daniel Maclise,[1] 28 JUNE 1839

Elm Cottage Petersham | Friday June 28th. 1839.

My Dear Maclise.

When I had read your note, I fell into a stupefaction from which I have not yet recovered, and under which I am still labouring so heavily that I have only sense and energy sufficient to say "Come down—Come down—Revive yourself by country air—Come down—and that without loss of time—and leave the rest to me, and I'll warrant you good health for 12 months at least. Come to the Shakspeare on Saturday, bring your bag with you, and return with me and the trusty Topping."[2]

Beard is hearty, new and thicker ropes have been put up at the tree, the little birds have flown, their very nests have disappeared, the roads about are jewelled after dusk by glow-worms, the leaves are all out and the flowers too, swimming feats from Petersham to Richmond Bridge have been achieved before breakfast, I myself have risen at 6 and plunged head foremost into the water to the astonishment and admiration of all beholders, a series of performances have been invented for the swing which out-Blackmore Mr. Blackmore.[3] You haven't a notion of the glories we have been working, which to be appreciated must be seen.

Your intelligence has so exhausted me, that I have but strength enough for one more word COME; and in that one strong gasp, I sink backward on the large sofa, and can add no more.

Ill! *He* ill![4]
Any time while the—
Sick a gettin' up—[5]
    My strength is gone

1 Daniel Maclise (1806–70†), one of the most admired painters of his day; met CD in 1836. They became close friends, although they drifted apart in later years as Maclise suffered from depression and became reclusive. His celebrated portrait of CD was painted in 1839.
2 William Topping, CD's manservant.
3 The 'undaunted Mr. Blackmore' is described in 'Vauxhall-Gardens by Day', *SB*. A contemporary advertisement acclaims his 'peculiar and surprising exercises on the Slack Rope'.

4 CD has drawn quavery lines under this and the next line; the writing of the last three lines is increasingly shaky.
5 'Sich a Getting Up Stairs' was a popular comic American song.

To *Hablot K. Browne*, [EARLY JULY 1839]

— A hairdresser's shop at night[1]—not a dashing one, but a barber's. Morleena Kenwig[s] on a tall chair having her hair dressed by an underbred attendant with his hair parted down the middle, and frizzed up into curls at the sides. Another customer, who is being shaved, has just turned his head in the direction of Miss Kenwigs, and she and Newman Noggs (who has brought her there, and has been whiling away the time with an old newspaper), recognise, with manifestations of surprise, and Morleena with emotion, Mr. Lillyvick, the collector. Mr. Lillyvick's bristly beard expresses great neglect of his person, and he looks very grim and in the utmost despondency.—

1 The subject for the first illustration for the Aug. *NN*, 'Great excitement of Miss Kenwigs at the hairdresser's Shop', ch. 52.

To [?*Mrs Godfrey*], 25 JULY 1839

Elm Cottage Petersham | Thursday July 25th. 1839.

My Dear Madam

The tales you have sent me will be quite sufficient in point of quantity to make the little book for your own distribution, in which I will immediately have them printed for you—indeed, I would suggest the omission of the tale about the pin cushion, as it does not seem to me very likely to please and you will have quite enough for your purpose without it.

There is some want of explanation concerning Brownwing himself and the little girls to whom he addresses his tales. That, if you please, I will supply. A very few words will render this quite intelligible to children, and as I have marked the passages where they appear to be wanted, I can perhaps set this right more readily than you could.

In acknowledging the receipt of your parcel, and requesting you to let me know whether you will like your name in the little title page and the addition (as I suppose you will) of the name of your school, I feel it necessary to suggest to you whether you do not think there are some passages in the story "The loss of beauty" which are calculated (and very naturally so) to give offence to the very class of persons with whom you desire to stand well—whether it does not appear to be designed more for the correction of parents than the instruction of children—whether the points about the grandmama do not touch upon very delicate ground and one upon which there is always more or less of sore feeling in families where there is a grandmama and whether, the teaching children (who always apply stories to their own cases) to decide so positively in her favour against their own parent is exactly judicious and very likely to create a prepossession in your own favour? You should be a better judge of this than I, but I know you will rather thank me than be displeased for mentioning these doubts as they have occurred to me on reading your tales.

There is one other point upon which I have at all times and in all cases so strong and violent a feeling, that (although I do not ask you to make any alteration, for my opinions are peculiar, I daresay, and quite as likely to be wrong as yours) I cannot forbear expressing my opinion upon it. I do most decidedly object, and have a most invincible and powerful repugnance to that frequent reference to the Almighty in small matters, which so many excellent persons consider necessary in the education of children. I think it monstrous to hold the source of inconceivable mercy and goodness perpetually up to them as an avenging and wrathful God who—making them in His wisdom children before they are men and women—is to punish them awfully for every little venial offence which is almost a necessary part of that stage of life. I object decidedly to endeavouring to impress them with a fear of death, before they can be rationally supposed to become accountable creatures, and so great a horror do I feel at the thought of imbuing with strict doctrines those who have just reflection enough to know that if God be as rigid and just as they are told He is, their fathers and mothers and three fourths of their relations and friends must be doomed to Eternal Perdition, and if I were left to choose between the two evils I would far rather that my children acquired their first principles of religion from a contemplation of nature and all the goodness and beneficence of the Great Being Who created it, than I would suffer them with such strict construction ever to open a Bible or a Prayer Book, or enter a place of Worship. I do declare to you my dear Madam, that I daily see such evil and misery springing up from this fatal mistake, that whenever I see the slightest approach to it, I cannot in my conscience let it go by without my most solemn protest.

> I am always Dear Madam | Faithfully Yours
> CHARLES DICKENS

To John Forster, [18 SEPTEMBER 1839]

Broadstairs. | Wednesday Afternoon.

My Dear Forster.

I plainly see that I must come to town on Saturday, or I shall delay the proofs terribly, and perhaps endanger the appearance of the No. This necessity will bring one pleasure with it, for it will enable us to come back together on Sunday, and further to dine together on Saturday if you will give me a chop. I am very anxious that you should see the conclusion of Nickleby, the preface &c before it finally leaves my hands. I have therefore written to Hicks telling him to send proofs to your chambers on Saturday evening, and a note beforehand, saying when they may be expected. If you don't object, we will devote the evening to a careful reading. Will you send for me to Doughty Street telling them to have a bed ready for me, and ordering Topping to be at your place to take my bag? I shall be with you (I hope) between 4 and 5.

I have not written to Macready, for they have not yet sent me the little page of Dedication, which is merely "To W. C. Macready Esquire the following pages are inscribed, as a slight token of admiration and regard, by his friend the Author"— duly set out in lines and various types of course. I will write to him when I get it. Meanwhile will you let him know that I have fixed the Nickleby dinner for *Saturday the 5th. of October*—place, the Albion in Aldersgate Street. Time, six for half past exactly.

I shall not finish entirely, before Friday—sending Hicks the last 20 pages of MS by the Night coach. I have had pretty stiff work as you may suppose, and I have taken great pains. I shall be more glad than I can tell you to see you again, and look forward to Saturday and the evenings that are to follow it, with most joyful anticipation.

The discovery is made,[1] Ralph is dead, the loves have come all right, Tim Linkinwater has proposed, and I have now only to break up Dotheboys and the book together. I have had a good notion for Barnaby, of which more anon.

It has been blowing great guns here for the last three days, and last night—I wish you could have seen it—there was *such* a sea! Fred (who is here) and I, staggered down to the Pier and creeping under the lee of a large boat which was high and dry, watched it breaking for nearly an hour. Of course we came back wet through, but it was most superb. One steamboat after getting to Ramsgate could not make her way into the harbour and was obliged to go back to Margate and put in there, and the boat from London didn't come at all. Heaven knows what became of it—nobody here does.

What a strange thing it is that all sorts of fine things happen in London when I'm away! I almost blame myself for the death of that poor girl who leaped off the Monument—she would never have done it if I had been in town; neither would the two men have found the skeleton in the Sewers. If it had been a female skeleton, I should have written to the coroner and stated my conviction that it *must* be Mrs. Sheppard. A famous subject for an illustration by George—Jonathan Wild forcing Mrs. Sheppard down the grown-up seat of a gloomy privy, and Blueskin or any such second robber cramming a child (anybody's child) down the little hole— Mr. Wood looking on in horror—and two other spectators, one with a fiendish smile and the other with a torch, aiding and abetting![2]

My love to Macready, and to you—and no more at present from yours ever faithfully CD—except best regards from all here.

1 That Ralph Nickleby was Smike's father.
2 A parody of Cruikshank's illustration to *Jack Sheppard* in the current No. of *Bentley's Miscellany*, 'Jonathan Wild throwing Sir Rowland Trenchard down the well-hole'. Blueskin was Sheppard's partner; Mr Wood a respectable carpenter.

To John Overs,[1] 27 SEPTEMBER 1839

Broadstairs. | September 27th. 1839.

Dr. Sir.

I can have no objection to your stating either to the Editor of Tait's Magazine, or of Blackwood's, the substance of what I wrote to you concerning your Songs, or (if you have the note by you) the exact terms in which I expressed myself.

I should have answered your letter before, but I have been out of town, in different places, for some months and did not receive it in due course. This is the reason why I have not returned your play long ago. I shall be in town towards the end of next week, and will send it to you.

I am sorry to say—and would not say, but that I know you wish me to speak plainly, and that I ought to do so—that of the play itself, I cannot speak favorably. The production is most honorable and creditable to you, but it would not benefit you, either in pocket or reputation, if it were printed;—and acted, I do not think it ever could be. Not to mention that the verse contains most singular instances of inverted expressions (which I may describe more familiarly as putting the cart before the horse) and many words not to be found in the language— not to mention these faults which are easily susceptible of correction, there are some in the plot and characters, which seem to me incurable. The father is such a dolt, and the villain *such* a villain, the girl so especially credulous and the means used to deceive them so very slight and transparent, that the reader *cannot* sympathize with their distresses. Action too is terribly wanting, and the characters not being strongly marked (except in improbabilities) the dialogues grow tedious and wearisome. I read it with great care, and not long ago either, but I don't remember at this moment any difference in the mode or matter of their speech which enables me to distinguish, in recollection, one character from the other— except the maiden lady and the villain, of whom the former is very good, and the latter but an average villain who speaks in dashes and interjections and constantly interrupts himself.

I think so highly of the exertions you have made and the difficulties against which you have struggled, that I am unwilling you should suppose you had no mart for worthy labour, and were *kept down* by obstacles against which you could not contend. I firmly believe that if this play had been written by Sheridan Knowles or Sir Edward Bulwer,[2] it would not have been acted. I am *sure* it would not, from what I know of the proceedings of both those gentlemen, and the friendly criticism and judgment to which they have several times submitted. Remember how very difficult it is to produce a good play, how very few men can do it, and how many fail and how few try—or if they do try, ever permit their trials to see the light.

Calling these things to mind, you will not (I am sure) be discouraged or hurt by what I tell you—remembering too, that I communicate but my individual opinion, and that I am as likely to commit an error in judgment as anybody else.

Yours truly
CHARLES DICKENS

1 John Overs (1808–44†), author and cabinet-maker. CD helped him with his writing; advised him on its publication; wrote to several periodical editors on his behalf, and corrected the proofs of his *Evenings of a Working Man*, 1844, for which he wrote a commendatory preface. He also gave him financial help, and got him a job at Macready's theatre. Forty-two letters from CD to Overs survive.
2 Edward George Earle Lytton Bulwer (1803–73†), politician and popular writer, who published under the name Edward Bulwer Lytton. He and CD had long admired each other's work; their joint founding of the Guild of Literature and Art drew them together in 1850.

To John Forster, [?10 JANUARY 1840]

I will dine with you. I intended to spend the evening in strict meditation (as I did last night); but perhaps I had better go out, lest all work and no play should make me a dull boy. *I* have a list of titles too, but the final title I have determined on—or something very near it. I have a notion of this old file in the queer house, opening the book by an account of himself, and, among other peculiarities, of his affection for an old quaint queer-cased clock; showing how that when they have sat alone together in the long evenings, he has got accustomed to its voice, and come to consider it as the voice of a friend; how its striking, in the night, has seemed like an assurance to him that it was still a cheerful watcher at his chamber-door; and how its very face has seemed to have something of welcome in its dusty features, and to relax from its grimness when he has looked at it from his chimney-corner. Then I mean to tell how that he has kept odd manuscripts in the old, deep, dark, silent closet where the weights are; and taken them from thence to read (mixing up his enjoyments with some notion of his clock); and how, when the club came to be formed, they, by reason of their punctuality and his regard for this dumb servant, took their name from it. And thus I shall call the book either Old Humphrey's Clock, or Master Humphrey's Clock; beginning with a woodcut of old Humphrey and his clock, and explaining the why and wherefore. All Humphrey's own papers will be dated then From my clock-side, and I have divers thoughts about the best means of introducing the others. I thought about this all day yesterday and all last night till I went to bed. I am sure I can make a good thing of this opening, which I have thoroughly warmed up to in consequence.

To George Cattermole,[1] 13 JANUARY 1840

1 Devonshire Terrace | Monday January 13th. 1840

My Dear Cattermole.

I am going to propound a mightily grave matter to you. My new periodical work appears—or I should rather say the first No. does—on Saturday the 28th. of March; and as it has to be sent to America and Germany and must therefore be considerably in advance, it is now in hand—I having in fact begun it on Saturday last. Instead of being published in *monthly* parts at a *shilling* each, only, it will be published in *weekly* parts at three pence *and* monthly parts at a shilling—my object being to baffle the imitators and make it as novel as possible. The plan is a new one—I mean the plan of the fiction—and it will comprehend a great variety of tales. The title is, *"Master Humphrey's Clock"*.

Now, among other improvements, I have turned my attention to the illustrations, meaning to have wood-cuts dropped into the text, and no separate plates. I want to know whether you would object to make me a little sketch *for* a wood-cut— in indian ink would be quite sufficient—about the size of the inclosed scrap: the subject an old quaint room with antique Elizabethian furniture, and in the chimney-corner an extraordinary old clock—*the* clock belonging to Master Humphrey in fact—and no figures. This I should drop into the text at the head of my opening page.

I want to know besides—as Chapman and Hall are my partners in the matter there need be no delicacy about my asking or your answering the question—what would be your charge for such a thing, and whether (if the work answers our expectations) you would like to repeat the joke at regular intervals, and if so, on what terms. I should tell you that I intend asking Maclise to join me likewise,[2] and that the copying the drawing on wood, and the cutting, will be done in first-rate style. We are justified by past experience in supposing that the sale would be enormous, and the popularity very great; and when I explain to you the notion I have in my head, I think you will see that it opens a vast number of very good subjects.

I want to talk the matter over with you, and wish you would fix your own time and place—either here, or at your house, or at the Athenæum,[3] though this would be the best place, because I have my papers about me. If you could take a chop with me, for instance, on Tuesday or Wednesday, I could tell you more in two minutes than in twenty letters, albeit I have endeavoured to make this as business-like and stupid as need be.

Of course all these tremendous arrangements are as yet a profound secret, or there would be fifty Humphreys in the field.[4] So write me a line like a worthy gentleman, and convey my best remembrances to your worthy lady.

Believe me always, My Dear Cattermole | Faithfully Yours
CHARLES DICKENS

1 George Cattermole (1800–68†), watercolour painter and illustrator, skilled in antiquarian and architectural subjects. Co-illustrator of *BR* and *OCS*. Friendly with CD (who affectionately nicknamed him Kittenmoles), and acted in his amateur company.
2 Maclise provided one illustration, Cattermole *c.*40, and Browne 132.
3 The London club.
4 Cf. *Richard III*, v. vii. 11: 'I think there be six Richmonds in the field.'

To Daniel Maclise, [13 FEBRUARY 1840]

V. R.[1]

Devonshire Terrace | Thursday Afternoon

My Dear Maclise

I send you a copy of Pickwick and the two little books.[2] Let the authorship of the last-named trifles remain in the bosom of your family.

The last aggravating word has touched that tender chord in my heart which you understand so well. Have you heard from Forster this morning? I have, but oh what a mockery it is. *He does not love her.*

I have seen my wife—spoken to her—been in her society. I burst into tears on hearing the voices of my infant children. I loathe my parents. I hate my house. I love nobody here but the Raven,[3] and I only love him because he seems to have no feeling in common with anybody. What is to be done. Heavens my friend, what is to be done!

What if I murder Chapman and Hall. This thought has occurred to me several times. If I did this she would hear of me; perhaps sign the warrant for my execution with her own dear hand. What if I murder myself. Mr. Wakley is a beast—a coarse unsympathizing coroner—and would not understand such feelings as mine. I feel that, and lay down my razor as the thought occurs to me. Is there no sentimental coroner? I have heard of Mr. Baker but I don't know how his mind is constituted. I have also heard of Mr. Higgs, but the name is not promising. I think there is one named Grubb. Perhaps *he* has high feeling and could comprehend me. The Serpentine is in his district, but then the Humane Society[4] steps in. They might disfigure me with drags—perhaps save me and expect me at the next Anniversary Dinner to walk round Free-Mason's Hall with a bible under my arm. She would never love me after *that.*—All is difficulty and darkness.

What is to be done? Would any alliance with the Chartists serve us? They have no doubt in contemplation attacks upon the palace, and being plain men would very likely resign *her* to us with great cheerfulness. Let us then toss—the best out of three—and the loser to poison himself. Is this feasible?

I dreamt of Lady Fanny Cowper[5] all night, but I didn't love her, sleeping, nor do I now that I am awake although I did but a few days back. I feel tenderly towards your sister because she knows our secret. With the great exception that I need not name, she is now the only woman on Earth that I do not shrink from in horror. Here is a state of mind!

How are you to-day. It will be some consolation to me to receive a detail of your sufferings. On Saturday Morning I shall call upon you. Conceive my misery until then! Tonight—tomorrow—all tories— nothing but slight and insult upon her generous head—Gracious Powers where will this end!

I am utterly miserable and unfitted for my calling. What the upshot will be, I don't know, but something tremendous I am sure.—I feel that I am wandering.

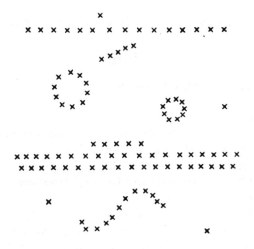

Your distracted friend
CHARLES DICKENS

1 Written large and bold. Following Queen Victoria's marriage in 1840, CD pretended he had 'fallen hopelessly in love' with her. The joke may have been based on attempts by various madmen to enter Buckingham Palace and Windsor Castle.
2 CD's *Sketches of Young Couples* and *Sketches of Young Gentlemen* had recently been published anonymously.
3 CD had two pet ravens in succession; see his preface to *BR*.
4 Its principal depot was on the Serpentine, a spot associated with suicides.
5 The Queen's favourite Maid of Honour.

To Leigh Hunt, 12 MAY 1840

1 Devonshire Terrace | Tuesday May 12th. 1840.

My Dear Hunt.

A crowd of thanks, treading on each others' heels and tripping one another up most pleasantly—a crowd of thanks, I say, for that Rustic Walk which I have just taken with you, and for the dinner,¹ and for the no-mention of the bill, or of the little squat doll-looking tumbler which you knocked over with your elbow when you were talking so merrily, and broke. As to the apostrophe I wouldn't lay a hand upon it for the world; and shew me the printer who dares to mar it!

I should have been exceedingly glad to shake hands with your son;[2] but when he called, I was on a rustic walk with Maclise, and was doing all that you did—only not so well—and eating lamb chops, and drinking beer, and laughing like a coal-heaver,—and all this at the Eel Pie House on Twickenham Island, which teaches one geography on the practical method, and illustrates that problem about the tract of country "entirely surrounded by water", rendering it intelligible and pleasant to the meanest capacity.

Good God how well I know that room! Don't you remember a queer, cool, odd kind of smell it has, suggestive of porter and even pipes at an enormous distance? Don't you remember the tea-board, and the sand, and the press on the landing outside full of clean linen intensely white? Don't you recollect the little pile of clean spittoons in one nook near the fireplace, looking like a collection of petrified three-cornered hats once worn by the dead-and-gone old codgers who used to sit and smoke there? The very sound of the bell—flat like a sheep-bell as if it had caught its tones from listening to it in its idle, shady, drowsy time of rest—the jingling wire more noisy than the bell—I have it in my ears. And closing my eyes, I'm down stairs in the bar where the soda water comes out of the window seat on which the landlady sits o' fine evenings, where the lemons hang in a grove each in its own particular net, where "the cheese" is kept, with great store of biscuits hard by in a wicker basket—where those wonderful bottles are, that hold cordials. You know 'em? great masses of grapes painted on 'em in green, blue, and yellow, and the semblance of an extraordinary knot of ribbon supporting the emblem of a label, whereon is the name of the compound? On one of these is "Lovitch". Great Heaven what is Lovitch? Has it any connection with peppermint, or is it another name for nectar? Tell me my heart, can *this* be Love-itch.

Oh Hunt I'm *so* lazy, and all along o' you! The sun is in my eyes, the hum of the fields in my ears, the dust upon my feet—and a boy, redolent of the steam engine and sweltering in warm ink is slumbering in the passage, waiting for "Copy".

Tell your son I can shake hands with him though he comes without a letter in his palm. And believe me always

Heartily Yours, in *the* faith,
CHARLES DICKENS

---

1 Hunt had clearly sent CD a MS copy of his poem extolling the pleasures of a country walk and dinner in an old inn. The 'apostrophe' probably refers to the opening lines of 'The Dinner': 'Blessings be thine, and a less hard old sofa, | Thou poor apartment.'

2 Thornton Leigh Hunt (1810–73†), journalist, and later collaborator on the *Leader* with Lewes; fathered four children with Lewes's wife.

To *Thomas Beard,* 1 JUNE 1840

37 Albion Street Broadstairs. | Monday Night June 1st. 1840

My Dear Beard.

With that tremendous energy which characterizes the proceedings of this establishment, we thought of coming here one day last week, and accordingly came this very morning. We have been in the house two hours, and the dining-parlor closet already displays a good array of bottles, duly arranged by the writer hereof—the Spirits labelled "Gin", "Brandy", "Hollands" in autograph character—and the wine tasted and approved. The castors already boast mushroom ketchup, harvey, cayenne, and such like condiments; the writing table is set forth with a neatness peculiar to your estimable friend; and the furniture in all the rooms has been entirely re-arranged by the same extraordinary character. The sea is rolling away, like nothing but the sea, in front of the house, and there are two pretty little spare bedrooms waiting to be occupied.

We mean to stay here a Month, and to return, please God, for another Month in the beginning of September. For occasional manly sports in July and August, I shall endeavour to find some queer cabin at Cobham in Kent.

Meantime verbum sap. Every Saturday Morning at 9 o'Clock there is a Ramsgate steamer leaving London Bridge Wharf, which, being boarded off this place by a boat belonging to it, will deposit you in the family's arms. On Monday Mornings you can leave here either at 8 or 9, and be in town, as you please, at about ½ past 3 or ½ past 4.

Therefore, as I am very tired and just now going to bed preparatory to close work tomorrow, I merely forward you these instructions, expecting by return of post a becoming assurance of your duty and submission.

> My Dear Beard | Heartily Yours
> CHARLES DICKENS

To *John Forster,* [17 JUNE 1840]

It's now four o'clock and I have been at work since half-past eight. I have really dried myself up into a condition which would almost justify me in pitching off the cliff, head first—but I must get richer before I indulge in a crowning luxury. Number 15,[1] which I began to-day, I anticipate great things from. There is a description of getting gradually out of town, and passing through neighbourhoods of distinct and various characters, with which, if I had read it as anybody else's writing, I think I should have been very much struck. The child and the old man are on their journey of course, and the subject is a very pretty one.

Pondering on what might be done to help off the unsold stock of OT *when he had regained the copyright from Bentley, CD suggests:*

Would it not be best to print new title-pages to the copies in sheets and publish them as a new edition, with an interesting Preface? I am talking about all this as though the treaty were concluded, but I hope and trust that in effect it is, for negotiation and delay are worse to me than drawn daggers.

1 *OCS* chs. 15 and 16 (published 11 July).

To the Marquis of Normanby,[1] 3 JULY 1840

1 Devonshire Terrace | York Gate Regents park | Friday 3rd July 1840

My Lord.

I make no apology for addressing a few words to you, as I trust you will feel that none is needed. The subject to which I take the liberty of calling your attention is one of great importance, and one to which the Government of which you are so distinguished and worthy a Member, has long directed its enlightened and merciful attention.[2]

I believe there are few persons more strongly impressed with the excellence and wisdom of the alterations that have been silently working for some years in our treatment and punishment of criminals, than I am. But I fear that their value is not sufficiently appreciated or felt—and that their effect in deterring offenders from the commission of guilty deeds, is very materially impaired—in consequence of their nature and extent not being sufficiently known. The terrors of transportation and confinement under the present system, are known to few but those who have penetrated to the heart of parliamentary reports and commissioners' enquiries; by that class for whose especial benefit and correction they are intended, they are known least of all.

I have felt this for a long time, and have had my old thoughts upon the subject wakened up afresh by the sentence passed upon the convict Gould[3] the other day, which is shorn of its impressiveness and example by the one unfortunate circumstance that the people do not know, and do not suspect, what his real punishment is. They remember to have read in the newspapers how some men who were transported to New South Wales thirty years ago, died worth their ten and twenty thousand pounds apiece; and they have a dim idea that the transport-ships are rather close, and the climates to which they go, very bright and hot; beyond this, they know and think nothing about it.

It has occurred to me that a strong and vivid description of the terrors of Norfolk Island[4] and such-like places, told in a homely Narrative with a great appearance of truth and reality and circulated in some very cheap and easy form (if with the direct authority of the Government, so much the better) would have a very powerful impression on the minds of the badly-disposed, and would do a great deal to promote the object that your Lordship and all good Governors have at heart. I think, even, that if it were read in prisons, jails for untried criminals, and houses of correction whither they are sent for short terms, it would have a deep and salutary effect in inspiring all *rising* convicts with a tremendous fear of the higher penalties of the law. Am I am sure that the more these penalties are known and surrounded with terrors, the more they will be avoided by the young and wavering.

If this very hasty and meagre hint of the idea I have, is intelligible to you My Lord, I have merely to add that I am ready, and should be very glad, to undertake this task and to place the best description I could produce in your hands, to be used as you think best, *but I would have it on the pillow of every prisoner in England.*[5] You will permit me to add, further, that I make this offer as a humble tribute of my respect for the liberal and wise Government under which the people live at present,[6] and that so far from seeking any fee or reward, I would beg, if I did this at all, to be understood as doing it quite disinterestedly and gratuitously, otherwise I should lose my chief pride and pleasure in the theme.

I am My Lord | Your faithful Servant
CHARLES DICKENS

1 Constantine Henry Phipps, 1st Marquess of Normanby (1797–1863†), politician and diplomatist. MP with liberal views, held office in Melbourne's government. CD later met his son, Lord Mulgrave, on the trip to America, 1842, and visited the Normanbys in 1844. *D&S* is dedicated 'with great esteem to the Marchioness of Normanby'.

2 i.e. the appointment, in 1833, of the Commissioners on Criminal Law, enjoined to rationalize the structure of non-capital crimes and punishments. In their *Fourth Report*, 1839, after legislation had removed the death penalty for the majority of offences, they set out to control judicial discretion in sentences of transportation and imprisonment.

3 Richard Gould, acquitted for the murder of John Templeman on 14 Apr. He confessed to being an accomplice in the murder, hoping to receive the reward of £200 authorized by Lord Normanby for the apprehension of the murderer and knowing he could not be retried for the crime. He was tried for burglary on 22 June and sentenced to transportation for life. Reported in *The Times*.

4 The penal station situated between Australia and New Zealand, the most severe of the convict settlements.

5 CD's offer was not accepted.

6 Lord Melbourne's Whig government, 1835–41.

To Edward Marjoribanks,[1] 6 JULY 1840

1 Devonshire Terrace, York Gate | 6th. July 1840.

My Dear Sir.

A kind of impossible possibility occurred to me this morning, and filled me with a shadowy dread. I have determined to apply to you to solve my doubts. Miss Coutts's[2] card for the fifteenth has solemn mention of a Royal Duke and Duchess—*are* gentlemen expected to wear court-dresses in consequence?

Forgiving my troubling you. I have already appeared in that very extraordinary costume and am prepared for the worst; but I have no confidence in my legs, and should be glad to hear that the etiquette went in favor of trowsers.

My Dear Sir Believe me | Faithfully Yours
CHARLES DICKENS

1 Edward Marjoribanks (1776–1868), partner in Coutts's Bank, where CD banked from 1837.
2 Angela Burdett Coutts (1814–1906†), heiress and philanthropist. Probably first met CD in 1838 through Edward Marjoribanks. In 1837 she inherited a fortune from her grandfather's second wife; CD helped guide her many charitable enterprises and they also became good friends. *MC* is dedicated to her.

To *Charles Edwards Lester*,[1] 19 JULY 1840

Devonshire Terrace. | Sunday July 19th. 1840.

Dear Sir.

As I have not the complete MS of Oliver (I wish I had, as it would one day have an interest for my children) I am enabled to send you a scrap, in compliance with your request; and have much pleasure in doing so.

Pray make my regards to your lady, and give her from me the other little packet inclosed. It is the first specimen of the kind I have parted with—except to a hairdresser—and will most likely be the last, for if I were to be liberal in this respect, my next portrait would certainly be that of a perfectly bald gentleman.

Believe me Dear Sir | Faithfully Yours
CHARLES DICKENS

P.S. I should tell you perhaps as a kind of certificate of the Oliver scrap, that it is a portion of the original and only draught.—I never copy.

1 Charles Edwards Lester (1815–90) of New York, journalist and writer of history and biography.

To *William Macready*, 17 AUGUST [1840]

Devonshire Terrace | Monday August 17th.

My Dear Macready.

Many thanks for the book. I think so well of it *as to have it bound,* and when that's done, you must put your name in it for me.

Tuesday the Twenty Fifth shall (God willing) be the day.[1] We have arranged accordingly. Time and so forth we will settle next Sunday.

What can I say to you, about last night?[2] Frankly, nothing. Nothing can enhance the estimation in which I hold you, or the affectionate and sincere attachment I bear towards you, my dear friend,—and not even your manly and generous interposition can make me eloquent upon a subject on which I feel so deeply and singly.

I am very much grieved, and yet I am not penitent and cannot be, reason with myself as I will. With all the regard I have for Forster, and with all the close friendship between us, I cannot close my eyes to the fact that we do not quarrel with other men; and the more I think of it, the more I feel confident in the belief that there is no man, alive or dead, who tries his friends as he does. I declare to you solemnly, that when I think of his manner (far worse than his matter) I turn burning hot, and am ashamed and in a manner degraded to have been the subject of it.

I have found the soul of goodness in this evil[3] thing at all events, and when I think of all you said and did, I would not recal (if I had the power) one atom of my passion and intemperance, which carried with it a breath of yours.

Ever believe me | My Dear Macready | Yours affectionately and heartily
CHARLES DICKENS

1 For Katey's christening: Macready was godfather.
2 In his diary Macready recorded the 'painful scene' after dinner, with Forster displaying his 'usual want of tact' and CD flying into a 'violent . . . passion'.
3 Cf. *Henry V*, IV. i. 4.

To John Forster, [4 OCTOBER 1840]

You will receive the proof herewith. I have altered it. You must let it stand now. I really think the dead mankind a million fathoms deep, the best thing in the sentence.[1] I have a notion of the dreadful silence down there, and of the stars shining down upon their drowned eyes—the fruit, let me tell you, of a solitary walk by starlight on the cliffs. As to the child-image I have made a note of it for alteration. In number thirty there will be some cutting needed, I think. I have, however, something in my eye near the beginning which I can easily take out. You will recognize a description of the road we travelled between Birmingham and Wolverhampton: but I had conceived it so well in my mind that the execution doesn't please me quite as well as I expected. I shall be curious to know whether you think there's anything in the notion of the man and his furnace-fire.[2] It would have been a good thing to have opened a new story with, I have been thinking since.

1 *OCS* ch. 42.
2 *OCS* ch. 44.

To **Thomas Hill**,[1] 14 OCTOBER [1840]

Devonshire Terrace. | Wednesday 14th. October

My Dear Sir.

Designers, printers, publishers, wood-cutters—in short, the whole of the works of Master Humphrey's Clock dine here next Tuesday at Six for half past exactly, to celebrate the completion of the first Volume. I look upon you as an essential part of the publication; and count surely on your joining us.

I regretted to hear from my brother Fred, that you had not been very well—though I look upon your being anything but well and cheerful, as a sort of practical joke; not an agreeable thing, but still a thing too preposterous to be considered seriously.

Always Heartily Yours
CHARLES DICKENS

1 Thomas Hill (1790–1840†), book-collector and part proprietor of the *Monthly Mirror*; kind-hearted and hospitable.

To **Daniel Maclise**, 20 NOVEMBER 1840

Friday November twentieth Eighteen forty

My Dear Mac

I have been writing all day, and mean to take a great, London, backslums kind of walk tonight, seeking adventures in knight errant style. Will you come with me? And (as a preparation, will you dine with us at *a quarter before 5*?—Leg of mutton stuffed with oysters.

Reply "Yes".

Always & Ever
CD

To [**Robert Horrell**],[1] 25 NOVEMBER 1840

1 Devonshire Terrace | York Gate Regents Park.
Twenty fifth November 1840.

Sir.

I have read the little poems you sent me (and which I now return), and in compliance with your request, have to give you my opinion of them. I am by no means satisfied, nor do I wish you to be, that my conclusions are infallible; and I scarcely expect, and certainly do not desire, that you should attach any weight to them, whatever.

First, as the more grateful task, let me say what I have to say of praise. You are a very young man you tell me, with other occupations to employ your time; and you can only cultivate these thoughts and aspirations by stealth. A love of the good and beautiful, and a desire to illustrate it in one so circumstanced is always a thing to be commended—to be very highly commended. It should increase your own happiness whether it adds to the happiness and entertainment of mankind or no, and from pursuits so worthy and humanizing, I would not turn you aside by one discouraging word. The pursuit of excellence in any path which has the light of Truth upon it, is, in the abstract, a noble employment, and like the search for the Philosopher's Stone will reward you with a hundred incidental discoveries though you fall short of the one great object of your desire.

Beyond this, I think that you have many good thoughts—occasionally a power of expressing them, very simply and well—a love of nature and all creation—and, of course, (for these are its necessary companions) deep feeling and strong sympathy.

On the other hand, you have very much to learn. Your versification is often harsh and irregular, your conceits strained and unnatural, your images fraught with more sound than sense. The first fault is one which only time and reading can remove; a few instances of the other two, I have marked as they have struck me in the perusal. To spell a tiger from all thoughts of harm—to clasp blood springs with tendril fingers (which appears difficult, to say the least)—to make the sun unfurl his bannered robe—to engrave words *with* fire—to describe the birds as couching with gasping pants of bliss—to tear a man to pieces with links—to fold love's banner o'er a lady's brow—are so near being absurdities that I hardly know what else to call them. You may find, I know, startling and monstrous conceits in the writings of our greatest Poets; but you must remember that *they* were great, not because of these blots, but in despite of them, having for every one a crowd of beautiful and grand thoughts which bore down all before them. Never imitate the eccentricities of genius, but toil after it in its truer flights. They are not so easy to follow, but they lead to higher regions.

You have too much about faëry land, and faëry things—by far too much mention of nerves and heart strings—more agonies of despondency than suit my taste— mysterious promptings too in your own breast which are much better there, than anywhere else. It is not the province of a Poet to harp upon his own discontents, or to teach other people that they ought to be discontented. Leave Byron to his gloomy greatness, and do you

> Find tongues in trees, books in the running brooks,
> Sermons in stones, and good in everything.[2]

The young painter's last dream pleased me very much in its opening; the change of time and coming on of morning are very beautifully described, and the aspect of his room and the familiar things about it I really think *highly* of. But surely in the close of this piece you have quite perverted its proper object and intention. To make that face his comfort and trust—to fill him with the assurance of meeting it one day in Heaven—to make him dying, attended, as it were, by an angel of his own creation—to inspire him with gentle visions of the reality sitting by his bedside and shedding a light even on the dark path of Death—and so to let him gently pass away, whispering of it and seeking the hand to clasp in his—would be to complete a very affecting and moving picture. But, to have him struggling with Death in all its horrors, yelling about foul fiends and bats' wings, with starting eyes and rattles in his throat, is a ghastly, sickening, hideous end, with no beauty, no moral, nothing in it but a repulsive and most painful idea. If he had been the hero of an epic in seventy books, and had out-Lucifered Lucifer in every line of them, you could scarcely have punished him at last in a more revolting manner. I do hope that you will write this piece again with some such alteration. If you ever do so, I shall be glad to see it.

"Withered Leaves" opens, I think, very prettily. But it is not so well sustained, and treads rather closely at last (in the idea; not in the manner of expressing it) upon a song of Mr. Lover's, founded on an Irish Superstition. It is called, if I remember right, the Four Leaved Shamrock.[3] The Ode to the Moon, very good. These are the only *data* I have, by which to form an opinion of your powers.

The advice I have to give you, is given in a very few words. I don't think you would ever find a publisher for a volume of such compositions unless at your own expence; and if you could, and have anything in you, the time would very soon come, when you would most heartily regret the having rushed into print. There are a great many people who write as well—many who write better. If you are to pass them, or are to take any place in the procession of Fame, you will do so none the later for keeping these effusions in your desk. At the same time, I see no objection to your sending some piece of moderate length—the painter for instance, but not in its present form—to such a Magazine as Blackwood's; and no improbability—no unusual improbability I mean—in the way of its acceptance and insertion. If you do this, give yourself the advantage of plain penmanship and a sheet of paper large enough to hold the lines, or it will never be read. And don't write to the Editor to tell him who you are or what you are, for he will care very little about that, and the public will care less.

It is impossible for me to say on such means as you have given me, whether I think you ever will be a great man, or whether you have God's gifts to become one. Some men would consider it their bounden duty to warn you off the dangerous ground of Poetry, but that I will not do,—firstly because I know you would still trespass there as boldly as ever, and secondly because for aught I know the land may be yours by right. Therefore, I make such remarks upon your writings as occur to me in reading them, and point out to you the course you would do best to take—the course I took myself when I was about one and twenty—and the course most writers have adopted when unknown and untried.

It is impossible that being unknown and untried, I could introduce you to a publisher with any beneficial result. I could not say that I thought your book would *pay* (that would be his first question); I could not even tell him that it was likely to attract public attention. I know but a dozen leaves of it, and if I said of those leaves to him, what I have said to you, he would be perfectly satisfied; and with the utmost deference and respect, and with the sincerest possible thanks, would decline the honor I proposed to confer upon him, and express the deepest gratitude for the preference.

You wish to know whether you do right in sacrificing so much time to what may fail at last. If you do so at the cost of any bitterness of heart, or any disgust with the employment in which you are engaged, you certainly do *wrong*. If you have strength of mind to do your duty cheerfully, and to make these toils a relaxation and solace of which nobody can deprive you, you do *right*. This is a question which none but yourself can determine. It is settled easily. When you have finished something carefully and to please yourself, make the trial I have suggested. If it fail in one quarter, try it again in another. If it fail in half a dozen, and each failure bring with it vexation and disappointment, lock up your papers, burn your pen, and thank Heaven you are not obliged to live by it.

Faithfully Yours
CHARLES DICKENS

1 Robert Horrell wrote to CD under the assumed name of S. Harford. He was a young solicitor's clerk in Exeter who later went to Australia for his health but died in his twenties. CD wrote seven letters to him: this is the second.
2 *As You Like It*, II. i. 16–17.
3 One of Samuel Lover's 'Songs of the Superstitions of Ireland' (*Songs and Ballads*, 1839).

To George Cattermole, [?22 DECEMBER 1840]

Dr. George

The child lying dead in the little sleeping room which is behind the oaken screen. It is winter time, so there are no flowers; but upon her breast, and pillow, and about her bed, there may be slips of holly, and berries, and such free green things.—Window overgrown with ivy—. The little boy who had that talk with her about angels, *may* be by the bedside, if you like it so, but I think it will be quieter and more peaceful if she is quite alone. I want it to express the most beautiful repose and tranquillity, and to have something of a happy look, if death can.[1]

2nd.

The child has been buried *inside* the church, and the old man who cannot be made to understand that she is dead, repairs to the grave every day, and sits there all day long, waiting for her arrival, to begin another journey. His staff and knapsack, her little bonnet and basket, &c lie beside him. "She'll come tomorrow" he says when it gets dark, and goes sorrowfully home. I think an hour-glass running out, would help the notion.—Perhaps *her* little things upon his knee, or in his hands—[2]

I am breaking my heart over this story, and cannot bear to finish it.

Love to Missis | Ever & always heartily

CD

1 Cattermole drew Nell alone in the 'little sleeping room', *OCS* ch. 71.
2 Cattermole's drawing is in *OCS* ch. 72.

To John Forster, 5 JANUARY [1841]

Devonshire Terrace. | Tuesday Morning | Fifth January.

My Dear Forster.

On the whole we were tremendous last night, though rather slack at first. We had two very long Sir Roger de Coverleys,[1] and after supper about eight very good Charades. Among them was conspicuous "Morning Herald" invented by your humble.

I shall certainly not stir out today, for we were not home until half-past five, and not up until half-past twelve. Unless I look very sharp, I shall not have done the No. by tomorrow night[2]—for I drank punch last evening in considerable quantities.

Always Faithfully

CD.

As you don't say how the face is, I suppose it was a false alarm.

1 An English country dance.
2 *OCS* chs. 69 and 70.

To John Forster, [?8 JANUARY 1841]

Done! Done!!![1] Why bless you, I shall not be done till Wednesday night. I only began yesterday, and this part of the story is not to be galloped over, I can tell you. I think it will come famously—but I am the wretchedest of the wretched. It casts the most horrible shadow upon me, and it is as much as I can do to keep moving at all. I tremble to approach the place a great deal more than Kit; a great deal more than Mr. Garland; a great deal more than the Single Gentleman. I shan't recover it for a long time. Nobody will miss her like I shall. It is such a very painful thing to me, that I really cannot express my sorrow. Old wounds bleed afresh when I only think of the way of doing it: what the actual doing it will be, God knows. I can't preach to myself the schoolmaster's consolation, though I try. Dear Mary died yesterday, when I think of this sad story. I don't know what to say about dining to-morrow—perhaps you'll send up to-morrow morning for news? That'll be the best way. I have refused several invitations for this week and next, determining to go nowhere till I had done. I am afraid of disturbing the state I have been trying to get into, and having to fetch it all back again.

1 i.e the closing chapters of *OCS*.

To John Forster, 17 JANUARY 1841

Devonshire Terrace | Monday Seventeenth January | 1841.

My Dear Forster.

I can't help letting you know how much your yesterday's letter pleased me.[1] I felt sure you liked the Chapters when we read them on Thursday night, but it was a great delight to have my impression so strongly and heartily confirmed.

You know how little value I should set on what I had done, if all the world cried out that it was good, and those whose good opinion and approval I value most, were silent. The assurance that this little closing of the scene, touches and is felt by you so strongly, is better to me than a thousand most sweet voices out of doors.[2]

When I first began (on your valued suggestion) to keep my thoughts upon this ending of the tale, I resolved to try and do something which might be read by people about whom Death had been,—with a softened feeling, and with consolation. I was moved, therefore, to have poor Bradbury's note yesterday,[3] and was glad to think he felt as I would have had him.

After you left last night I took my desk up stairs, and writing until four o'Clock this morning, finished the old story. It makes me very melancholy to think that all these people are lost to me for ever, and I feel as if I never could become attached to any new set of characters.

I wish you would give my love to Macready (I suppose you dine there today) and tell him that on Friday night, I will send him the next week's number, in order that he may read the two together, which I should like him very much to do. Tomorrow morning, please God, I shall be with you—about twelve.

Always My Dear Forster | Your affectionate friend
CHARLES DICKENS

1 Forster had described the death of 'dear little Nell' as 'your literary masterpiece'.
2 Cf. *Coriolanus*, ii. iii. 169.
3 William Bradbury, who as printer would have read the chapters in MS, had lost his young daughter in 1839.

To George Cattermole, 30 JANUARY 1841

Devonshire Terrace | Saturday Evening | January Thirtieth | 1841.

My Dear George.

I send you the first four Slips of No. 48,[1] containing the description of the Locksmith's house, which I think will make a good subject, and one you will like. If you put the 'Prentice in it, shew nothing more than his paper cap, because he will be an important character in the story, and you will need to know more about him as he is minutely described. I may as well say that he is *very short*. Should you wish to put the locksmith in, you will find him described in No. 2 of Barnaby (which I told C and H to send you)—Browne has done him in one little thing, but so very slightly that you will not require to see his sketch, I think.

Now, I must know what you think about the Raven,[2] my buck, otherwise I am in this fix.—I have given Browne *no* subject for this No., and time is flying. If you would like to have the Raven's first appearance, and don't object to having both subjects, so be it. I shall be delighted. If otherwise, I must feed that hero forthwith.

I cannot close this hasty note, my dear fellow, without saying that I have deeply felt your hearty and most invaluable co-operation in the beautiful illustrations you have made for the last story—that I look at them with a pleasure I cannot describe to you in words—and that it is impossible for me to say how sensible I am of your earnest and friendly aid. Believe me that this is *the very first time* any designs for what I have written have touched and moved me, and caused me to feel that they expressed the idea I had in my mind. I am most sincerely and affectionately grateful to you, and am full of pleasure and delight.

Believe me,

My Dear Cattermole | Always Heartily Yours
C.D

Over

We are just the same at home. But next week, I should say, *must* put us all to rights.[3]

---

1 Of *MHC*, chs. 3 and 4 of *BR*.

2 On 28 Jan. CD had asked Cattermole 'whether you *feel* Ravens in general, and would fancy Barnaby's raven in particular. . . . I have been studying my bird, and think I could make a very queer character of him.' Cattermole declined, and Browne did all the illustrations containing Grip the raven.

3 CD's fourth child, Walter, was born on 8 Feb.

To *Thomas Mitton*, 6 MARCH 1841

Devonshire Terrace. | Saturday Sixth March 1841.

My Dear Mitton.

I return you the form of advertisement, corrected;[1] and have marked upon the back the papers in which it must be inserted, which, indeed, are all the morning and evening ones. The Sundays we may leave alone.

Let there be no misunderstanding, for this is a very serious matter, relative to what I said to you this morning. Mind. If he communicate with you, the following are the only conditions to which I will assent.

First. That he goes abroad—to Calais, Boulogne, or Antwerp. The last, I think, is the best place, but let him please himself.

Secondly. That he takes Augustus with him, whom, immediately on their arrival, I will send as a weekly boarder to the best school I can find in the place, and clothe, and find in pocket money. I say weekly boarder, because I should wish the boy, for more reasons than one, to be at home from Saturday night to Monday Morning.

Thirdly. That if my mother should object to go—I think it very likely she may, but I have had no communication whatever with her upon the subject—he allows her out of his pension, for her support, forty pounds a year.

On these conditions, I will allow him £20 a year, which will make his income a hundred—a very good one mind, abroad—put the amount of the last quarter's allowance to whatever the furniture at Alphington will fetch, and apply the amount to paying or compounding for the Devonshire debts—and I will give him besides £10 to leave England with.

If these concessions are accepted, you have full power from me to carry them out immediately. *But I will consent to nothing short of, or beyond them*; and I know after the solemn injunctions I have laid upon you to the contrary, that you will not hold yourself justified in entertaining any other proposition for a moment.[2]

Always | Dear Mitton | Faithfully Yours
CHARLES DICKENS

---

1 CD's father had borrowed money from CD's acquaintance Thomas Latimer in Exeter, promising that CD's publishers would pay. CD apologized to Latimer for this 'moral outrage which words can scarcely censure enough', and placed an advertisement in all the main London newspapers, announcing that 'Charles Dickens will not discharge or liquidate any debt or debts, save those of his own or his wife's contracting'.

2 John Dickens did not accept this plan and continued to live at Alphington.

To Daniel Maclise, 12 MARCH 1841

Devonshire Terrace. | Friday Evening | March The Twelfth 1841.

My Dear Maclise.

You will be greatly shocked and grieved to hear that the Raven[1] is no more.

He expired to-day at a few minutes after Twelve o'Clock at noon. He had been ailing (as I told you t'other night) for a few days, but we anticipated no serious result, conjecturing that a portion of the white paint he swallowed last summer might be lingering about his vitals without having any serious effect upon his constitution. Yesterday afternoon he was taken so much worse that I sent an express for the medical gentleman (Mr. Herring)[2] who promptly attended, and administered a powerful dose of castor oil. Under the influence of this medicine, he recovered so far as to be able at 8 o'Clock p.m. to bite Topping. His night was peaceful. This morning at daybreak he appeared better; received (agreeably to the doctor's directions) another dose of castor oil; and partook plentifully of some warm gruel, the flavor of which he appeared to relish. Towards eleven o'Clock he was so much worse that it was found necessary to muffle the stable knocker. At half past, or thereabouts, he was heard talking to himself about the horse and Topping's family, and to add some incoherent expressions which are supposed to have been either a foreboding of his approaching dissolution, or some wishes relative to the disposal of his little property—consisting chiefly of halfpence which he had buried in different parts of the garden. On the clock striking twelve he appeared slightly agitated, but he soon recovered, walked twice or thrice along the coach-house, stopped to bark, staggered, exclaimed "Halloa old girl!" (his favorite expression) and died.

He behaved throughout with a decent fortitude, equanimity, and selfpossession, which cannot be too much admired. I deeply regret that being in ignorance of his danger I did not attend to receive his last instructions. Something remarkable about his eyes occasioned Topping to run for the doctor at Twelve. When they returned together our friend was gone. It was the medical gentleman who informed me of his decease. He did it with great caution and delicacy, preparing me by the remark that "a jolly queer start had taken place", but the shock was very great notwithstanding.

I am not wholly free from suspicions of poison—a malicious butcher has been heard to say that he would "do" for him—his plea was, that he would not be molested in taking orders down the Mews, by any bird that wore a tail—other persons have also been heard to threaten—among others, Charles Knight[3] who has just started a weekly publication, price fourpence; Barnaby being, as you know, Threepence. I have directed a post mortem examination, and the body has been removed to Mr. Herring's school of Anatomy for that purpose.

I could wish, if you can take the trouble, that you would inclose this to Forster when you have read it. I cannot discharge the painful task of communication more than once. Were they Ravens who took Manna to somebody in the wilderness? At times I hope they were, and at others I fear they were not, or they would certainly have stolen it by the way. In profound sorrow, I am ever Your bereaved friend. CD.

Kate is as well as can be expected, but terribly low as you may suppose. The children seem rather glad of it. He bit their ancles. But that was play——

1 One of the two ravens who were the originals of Grip in *BR*. Stuffed, in a glass case, he fetched £126 in Christie's sale of 9 July 1870. At some time CD wrote a letter to the raven who was being looked after by Edwin Landseer while CD was out of London.
2 William Herring, dealer in birds and live animals, 21 Quickset Row, London W.
3 Charles Knight (1791–1873†), writer, and publisher for the Society for the Diffusion of Useful Knowledge. *London*, edited by him, issued in weekly parts 1841–4, at 4*d*. Later wrote for *HW*.

To John Scott,[1] 22 MARCH 1841

1 Devonshire Terrace. | York Gate Regents Park.
March The Twenty Second 1841.

My Dear Sir.

I really cannot tell you how much pleasure I have derived from the receipt of your warm-hearted and welcome note; nor can I thank you for it sufficiently.

Although I know in my heart and conscience that every action of my life and every impulse by which I am guided give the lie to the assertion, I am still greatly pained to learn that you have ever heard me charged with forgetting old friends or associates. Those who know me best, best know how such a charge would wound me, and how very undeserved it is. There is no character I so detest and abhor as a man who presumes on his prosperity. I feel its baseness so strongly that if I supposed my children could at any future time believe me to have been a creature of that kind, I should be wretched.

Happily, although I have made many friends, I have never since my schooltime lost *one*. The pleasantest and proudest part of my correspondence is that in which I have stored the congratulations of some from whom I had been separated by distance or accident for several years; and believe me that from a little pale schoolmaster who taught me my letters (and who turned up miraculously the other day in a high state of preservation) to those who have more recent and more fleeting claims on my regard, I have never in my life—and especially in my later life—no, not once, treated any single human being with coldness or hauteur. I have a capacity, and a strong inclination, for feeling warmly towards all those whom I have known in less successful times; and any man who reports me unjustly in this respect, either does me wilfully an envious and grudging wrong, or acquiesces too easily in a falsehood, of which he may convince himself at the smallest possible expence of trouble and justice.

Let me thank you again, very faintly and imperfectly, for your honest letter. I shall put it among the grateful records to which I have referred; and I do not despair of increasing their bulk before I die, by communications not very dissimilar, even from those who now mistake me most.

Pray, if you should have reason to think when you read the Clock that I have written anything about this time in extremely good spirits, believe that you have had a large share in awakening them—and believe besides that I am with sincerity

My Dear Sir | Faithfully Yours
CHARLES DICKENS

1 Probably a friend of CD's in his reporting days.

To *Washington Irving,*[1] 21 APRIL 1841

1 Devonshire Terrace York Gate | Regents Park London
April The Twenty First 1841.

My Dear Sir.
There is no man in the World who could have given me the heartfelt pleasure you have, by your kind note of the Thirteenth of last Month.[2] There is no living writer, and there are very few among the dead, whose approbation I should feel so proud to earn. And with everything you have written, upon my shelves, and in my thoughts, and in my heart of hearts, I may honestly and truly say so. If you could know how earnestly I write this, you would be glad to read it—as I hope you will be, faintly guessing at the warmth of the hand I autographically hold out to you, over the broad Atlantic.

I wish I could find in your welcome letter, some hint of an intention to visit England. I can't. I have held it at arm's length, and taken a bird's-eye view of it after reading it a great many times, but there is no greater encouragement in it this way than on a microscopic inspection. I should love to go with you—as I have gone, God knows how often—into Little Britain, and Eastcheap, and Green Arbour Court, and Westminster Abbey.[3] I should like to travel with you, outside the last of the coaches, down to Bracebridge Hall. It would make my heart glad to compare notes with you about that shabby gentleman in the oilcloth hat and red-nose who sat in the nine-cornered back parlor at the Masons' Arms—and about Robert Preston— and the tallow chandler's widow whose sitting room is second nature to me—and about all those delightful places and people that I used to walk about and dream of in the daytime when a very small and not over-particularly-taken-care-of boy. I have a good deal to say too about that dashing Alonzo De Ojeda that you can't help being fonder of than you ought to be—and much to hear concerning Moorish Legend, and poor unhappy Boabdil. Diedrich Knickerbocker I have worn to death in my pocket—and yet I should shew you his mutilated carcass—with a joy past all expression.

I have been so accustomed to associate you with my pleasantest and happiest thoughts, and with my leisure hours, that I rush at once into full confidence with you, and fall—as it were naturally, and by the very laws of gravity—into your open arms. Questions come thronging to my pen as to the lips of people who meet after long hoping to do so. I don't know what to say first, or what to leave unsaid, and am constantly disposed to break off and tell you again how glad I am this moment has arrived.

My Dear Washington Irving I cannot thank you enough for your cordial and generous praise, or tell you what deep and lasting gratification it has given me. I hope to have many letters from you, and to exchange a frequent correspondence. I send this to say so. After the first two or three, I shall settle down into a connected style, and become gradually rational.

You know what the feeling is after having written a letter, sealed it, and sent it off. I shall picture you reading this and answering it, before it has lain one night in the Post Office. Ten to one that before the fastest packet could reach New York, I shall be writing again.

Do you suppose the Post office clerks care to receive letters? I have my doubts. They get into a dreadful habit of indifference. A Postman, I imagine, is quite callous. Conceive his delivering one to himself, without being startled by a preliminary double knock—!

Always your faithful friend
CHARLES DICKENS

1 Washington Irving (1783–1859; *ANB*); hailed by English critics as America's first major author.
2 About little Nell and *OCS*; it 'very strongly revived' CD's idea of going to America, see Forster, 196.
3 All described in Irving's *The Sketch-Book of Geoffrey Crayon, Gent.*, 1820. The references to many of Irving's books throughout this paragraph show CD's familiarity with them.

To Augustus Tracey,[1] 26 APRIL [1841]

1 Devonshire Terrace | York Gate Regents Park.
Monday Evg. April The Twenty Sixth.

My Dear Sir.

Since I left you to-day, I have been greatly distressed in my mind, concerning our wretched friend the (supposed) tailor. May I ask you to apply the inclosed trifle in any way that you think will do him the most good, and to exercise your own discretion— for none can have so good a one as you in such a case—either to pay his fine and give him the rest, or keep him his five days, and then let him have the whole to start with. In either case, I would like to send him, besides, a suit of cast-off clothes, which (if you give me your permission to forward them to the jail; I don't like to venture on sending them without it) my man shall bring directly.

I cannot express to you how much moved I have been by witnessing the results of your humanity and goodness. Men who have so much in their power and acquit themselves so well, deserve the gratitude of mankind. Accept the thanks and assurances of esteem of one among them who loves, and truly loves the rest. It is the only qualification I have for offering them to you.

Very faithfully Yours
CHARLES DICKENS

1 Lieutenant Augustus Tracey, RN (1798–1878). In the navy 1811–34, then governor of the Westminster House of Correction, Tothill Fields. Became a friend of CD's, taking a keen interest in Urania Cottage (see below, from 1846 onwards), many of whose inmates came from his prison.

To Basil Hall,[1] 27 APRIL 1841

Devonshire Terrace | April The Twenty Seventh 1841.

My Dear Hall.

Post just going—compression of sentiments required—Bust received[2]—likeness *amazing*—recognizable instantly if encountered on the summit of the Great Pyramid—Scotch anecdote most striking and most distressing[3]—dreamed of it—babbies well—wife ditto—yours the same, I hope?—Seaport sketches one of those ideas that improves in promise as they are pondered on—*Good,* I am certain—Ever faithfully, and at present hastily—

BOZ.

1 Basil Hall (1788–1844†), naval officer, author, and travel writer. An admirer of CD's work, he sent him long descriptions of potential material.
2 Hall had asked CD for a bust to be done of him by the sculptor Samuel Joseph. The whole letter is written in the style of Alfred Jingle, in *PP*.
3 One of Hall's suggestions for CD's pen. The Seaport sketches refer to Hall's proposed book about Portsmouth.

To John Blackburn,[1] 3 MAY 1841

Devonshire Terrace | Monday May The Third 1841

My Dear Sir.

Many thanks to you for the Magazine, which is a great curiosity. As you may suppose that I haven't read my second self "right through", you will not give me any credit for returning them within the specified time.[2]

Good God how hot these Oriental Magazines look! You're so used to them, that I dare say you don't see it, but the pages are parched—burnt up—suggestive of drought and scorching heat. Some Indian birds we have, began to sing directly the parcel was brought in. *I* began to drink claret out of a tumbler before I had turned over the leaves of the Second Number. And all last night, I dreamed about Vishnu, and Hindoo Temples, and Indian Jugglers sitting upon nothing, and Tigers coming unexpectedly to dinner parties and bounding away into remote Jungles with English Butlers—Elephants too were so common as to be quite ridiculous; and I ate rice by hundred weights.

Faithfully Yours
CHARLES DICKENS

1 John Blackburn, sub-editor of the *Englishman*, Calcutta, and author of *The Overland Traveller, or Guide to Persons Proceeding to Europe via the Red Sea, from India*, Calcutta, 1838.
2 Blackburn had probably sent him the numbers of the *Lighthouse*, Madras, containing 'Pickwick in India', in seven chapters, by the Editor.

To John Forster, [3 JUNE 1841]

Say what you please of Gordon,[1] he must have been at heart a kind man, and a lover of the despised and rejected, after his own fashion. He lived upon a small income, and always within it; was known to relieve the necessities of many people; exposed in his place the corrupt attempt of a minister to buy him out of Parliament; and did great charities in Newgate. He always spoke on the people's side, and tried against his muddled brains to expose the profligacy of both parties. He never got anything by his madness, and never sought it. The wildest and most raging attacks of the time, allow him these merits: and not to let him have 'em in their full extent, remembering in what a (politically) wicked time he lived, would lie upon my conscience heavily. The libel he was imprisoned for when he died, was on the queen of France; and the French government interested themselves warmly to procure his release—which I think they might have done, but for Lord Grenville.

1 Lord George Gordon (1751–93†), political and religious agitator; the anti-Catholic march he led to Parliament caused the Gordon Riots which feature in *BR* chs. 35 and 36.

To John Forster, [26 JUNE 1841, Edinburgh]

The great event[1] is over; and being gone, I am a man again.[2] It was the most brilliant affair you can conceive; the completest success possible, from first to last. The room was crammed, and more than seventy applicants for tickets were of necessity refused yesterday. Wilson[3] was ill, but plucked up like a lion, and spoke famously. I send you a paper herewith but the report is dismal in the extreme. They say there will be a better one—I don't know where or when. Should there be, I will send it to you. I *think* (ahem!) that I spoke rather well.[4] It was an excellent room, and both the subjects (Wilson and Scottish Literature, and the Memory of Wilkie)[5] were good to go upon. There were nearly two hundred ladies present. The place is so contrived that the cross table is raised enormously: much above the heads of people sitting below: and the effect on first coming in (on me, I mean) was rather tremendous. I was quite self-possessed however, and, notwithstanding the enthoosemoosy, which was very startling, as cool as a cucumber. I wish to God you had been there, as it is impossible for the "distinguished guest" to describe the scene. It beat all natur'.

1 The dinner in CD's honour held at the Waterloo Rooms, Edinburgh, on 25 June.
2 *Macbeth*, III. iv. 108.
3 John Wilson (1785–1854†), 'Christopher North' of *Blackwood's Edinburgh Magazine* and foremost critic of his time.
4 For the texts of CD's speeches, see *Speeches*, 9–14.
5 David Wilkie (1785–1841†), painter of genre, historical subjects, and portraits.

To John Forster, 11 JULY 1841 [Dalmally]

I was not at all ill pleased to have to come again through that awful Glencoe. If it had been tremendous on the previous day, yesterday it was perfectly horrific. It had rained all night, and was raining then, as it only does in these parts. Through the whole glen, which is ten miles long, torrents were boiling and foaming, and sending up in every direction spray like the smoke of great fires. They were rushing down every hill and mountain side, and tearing like devils across the path, and down into the depths of the rocks. Some of the hills looked as if they were full of silver, and had cracked in a hundred places. Others as if they were frightened, and had broken out into a deadly sweat. In others there was no compromise or division of streams, but one great torrent came roaring down with a deafening noise, and a rushing of water that was quite appalling. Such a *spaet*, in short (that's the country word), has not been known for many years, and the sights and sounds were beyond description. The post-boy was not at all at his ease, and the horses were very much frightened (as well they might be) by the perpetual raging and roaring; one of them started as we came down a steep place, and we were within that much (——) of tumbling over a precipice; just then, too, the drag broke, and we were obliged to go on as we best could, without it: getting out every now and then, and hanging on at the back of the carriage to prevent its rolling down too fast, and going Heaven knows where.

Well, in this pleasant state of things we came to King's-house again, having been four hours doing the sixteen miles. The rumble[1] where Tom sat was by this time so full of water, that he was obliged to borrow a gimlet, and bore holes in the bottom to let it run out. The horses that were to take us on, were out upon the hills, somewhere within ten miles round; and three or four bare-legged fellows went out to look for 'em, while we sat by the fire and tried to dry ourselves. At last we got off again (without the drag and with a broken spring, no smith living within ten miles), and went limping on to Inverouran. In the first three miles we were in a ditch and out again, and lost a horse's shoe. All this time it never once left off raining; and was very windy, very cold, very misty, and most intensely dismal. So we crossed the Black-mount, and came to a place we had passed the day before, where a rapid river runs over a bed of broken rock. Now, this river, sir, had a bridge last winter, but the bridge broke down when the thaw came, and has never since been mended; so travellers cross upon a little platform, made of rough deal planks stretching from rock to rock; and carriages and horses ford the water, at a certain point. As the platform is the reverse of steady (we had proved this the day before), is very slippery, and affords anything but a pleasant footing, having only a trembling little rail on one side, and on the other nothing between it and the foaming stream, Kate decided to remain in the carriage, and trust herself to the wheels rather than to her feet. Fletcher[2] and I had got out, and it was going away, when I advised her, as I had done several times before, to come with us; for I saw that the water was very high, the current being greatly swollen by the rain, and that the post-boy had been eyeing it in a very disconcerted manner for the last half hour. This decided her to come out; and Fletcher, she, Tom, and I, began to cross, while the carriage went about a quarter of a mile down the bank, in search of a shallow place. The platform shook so much that we could only come across two at a time, and then it felt as if it were hung on springs. As to the wind and rain! . . . well, put into one gust all the wind and rain you ever saw and heard, and you'll have some faint notion of it!

When we got safely to the opposite bank, there came riding up a wild highlander, in a great plaid, whom we recognized as the landlord of the inn, and who without taking the least notice of us, went dashing on,—with the plaid he was wrapped in, streaming in the wind,—screeching in Gaelic to the post-boy on the opposite bank, and making the most frantic gestures you ever saw, in which he was joined by some other wild man on foot, who had come across by a short cut, knee-deep in mire and water. As we began to see what this meant, we (that is, Fletcher and I) scrambled on after them, while the boy, horses, and carriage were plunging in the water, which left only the horses' heads and the boy's body visible. By the time we got up to them, the man on horseback and the man on foot were perfectly mad with pantomime; for as to any of their shouts being heard by the boy, the water made such a great noise that they might as well have been dumb. It made me quite sick to think how I should have felt if Kate had been inside. The carriage went round and round like a great stone, the boy was as pale as death, the horses were struggling and plashing and snorting like sea-animals, and we were all roaring to the driver to throw himself off and let them and the coach go to the devil, when suddenly it came all right (having got into shallow water), and, all tumbling and dripping and jogging from side to side, climbed up to the dry land. I assure you we looked rather queer, as we wiped our faces and stared at each other in a little cluster round about it. It seemed that the man on horseback had been looking at us through a telescope as we came to the track, and knowing that the place was very dangerous, and seeing that we meant to bring the carriage, had come on at a great gallop to show the driver the only place where he could cross. By the time he came up, the man had taken the water at a wrong place, and in a word was as nearly drowned (with carriage, horses, luggage, and all) as ever man was. Was *this* a good adventure?

We all went on to the inn—the wild man galloping on first, to get a fire lighted—and there we dined on eggs and bacon, oat-cake, and whiskey; and changed and dried ourselves. The place was a mere knot of little outhouses, and in one of these there were fifty highlanders *all drunk.* . . . Some were drovers, some pipers, and some workmen engaged to build a hunting-lodge for Lord Breadalbane hard by, who had been driven in by stress of weather. One was a paper-hanger. He had come out three days before to paper the inn's best room, a chamber almost large enough to keep a Newfoundland dog in; and, from the first half hour after his arrival to that moment, had been hopelessly and irreclaimably drunk. They were lying about in all directions: on forms, on the ground, about a loft overhead, round the turf-fire wrapped in plaids, on the tables, and under them. We paid our bill, thanked our host very heartily, gave some money to his children, and after an hour's rest came on again. At ten o'clock at night, we reached this place, and were overjoyed to find quite an English inn, with good beds (those we have slept on, yet, have always been of straw), and every possible comfort. We breakfasted this morning at half past ten, and at three go on to Inverary to dinner. I believe the very rough part of the journey is over, and I am really glad of it. Kate sends all kind of regards. I shall hope to find a letter from you at Inverary when the post reaches there, to-morrow. I wrote to Oban yesterday, desiring the post-office keeper to send any he might have for us, over to that place. Love to Mac.

1 Back portion of a carriage adapted for servants' seats or luggage. Tom was CD's servant.
2 Angus Fletcher (1799–1862), sculptor, studied in London and Italy; his bust of CD was shown at the Royal Academy 1839.

To Mary Hurnall, 21 JULY 1841

1 Devonshire Terrace | York Gate Regents Park. | July The Twenty First 1841.

Dear Madam.

I have been in Scotland for some weeks past, and find so many letters to answer on my return,[1] that I am obliged to send a more brief reply to yours than I desire.

Accept my sincere thanks, both for your note, and the Invitation it contains. I fear it is not likely that it will ever be in my power to accept it in deed, but in spirit I do, and so do Mrs. Dickens and my children—you are right; I have four.

Be assured that I am not unmindful of my promise, and that if you should come back to London at any time, I shall, please God, make a point of seeing you.

Your remark—a very natural and proper one—on the blind man in Barnaby, is only another proof to me, among many others which present themselves in various forms every day, of the great disadvantages which attend a detached and desultory form of publication. My intention in the management of this inferior and subordinate character, was to remind the World who have eyes, that they have no *right* to expect in sightless men a degree of virtue and goodness to which they, in full possession of all their senses, can lay no claim—that it is a very easy thing for those who misuse every gift of Heaven to consider resignation and cheerfulness the duty of those whom it has deprived of some great blessing—that whereas we look upon a blind man who does wrong, as a kind of monster, we ought in Truth and Justice to remember that a man who has eyes and is a vicious wretch, is by his very abuse of the glorious faculty of sight, an immeasurably greater offender than his afflicted fellow. In a word, I wished to show that the hand of God is at least as manifest in making eyes as in unmaking them, and that we do not sufficiently consider the sorrows of those who walk in darkness on this earth, when we set it up as a rule that they *ought* to be better than ourselves, and that they are required to be by their calamity. Calamity with us, is made an excuse for doing wrong. With them, it is erected into a reason for their doing right. This is really the justice of rich to poor, and I protest against it because it is so.[2]

All this you would have seen if you could have had the whole book before your mental vision. As it is, I can only hope to bring my meaning before you by very slow and gradual degrees, and after you have formed a first impression on the subject.

That it is a real pleasure and delight to me to know that I afford you any consolation or amusement, you may believe with your whole heart. And believe also that I am, Dear Madam with an unaffected interest in your happiness

Faithfully Yours
CHARLES DICKENS

1 Twelve letters which CD wrote on this day survive.
2 The coincidence of Mrs Hurnall's protest at CD's treatment of Stagg, and the change in CD's treatment of him, suggests that CD received her letter in Scotland, between writing chs. 45 and 46.

To Chauncy Hare Townshend,[1] 23 JULY [1841]

Devonshire Terrace. | Twenty Third July.

My Dear Townshend.

On Wednesday I will dine with you please God. At what hour?

I am horribly hard at work, after my Scotch honors, and dare not be mesmerized, lest it should damage me at all. Even a day's head ache would be a serious thing just now.

—But a time *will* come—as they say in melo dramas—no more—

Except that I am always | Faithfully Yours
CHARLES DICKENS

1 Revd Chauncy Hare Townshend (1798–1868†), poet and collector. First met CD in 1840. An important and lifelong relationship to CD, but very few letters to him survive.

To George Cattermole, 28 JULY 1841

Devonshire Terrace. | Wednesday Evening | July The Twenty Eighth 1841.

My Dear George.
   Can you do for me by *Saturday Evening*—I know the time is short, but I think the subject will suit you, and I am greatly pressed—a party of rioters (with Hugh and Simon Tappertit conspicuous among them) in old John Willet's bar—turning the liquor taps to their own advantage—smashing bottles—cutting down the grove of lemons—sitting astride on casks—drinking out of the best punchbowls—eating the great cheese—smoking sacred pipes &c &c—John Willet, fallen backward in his chair, regarding them with a stupid horror, and quite alone among them, with none of the Maypole customers at his back.
   It's in your way, and you'll do it a hundred times better than I can suggest it to you, I know.[1]

Faithfully Always
CHARLES DICKENS

1 Cattermole's illustration, 'The mob at the Maypole', appeared in *BR* ch. 54, published 21 Aug.

To John Forster, [?MID-AUGUST 1841]

   Thank God there is a Van Diemen's-land.[1] That's my comfort. Now, I wonder if I should make a good settler! I wonder, if I went to a new colony with my head, hands, legs, and health, I should force myself to the top of the social milk-pot and live upon the cream! What do you think? Upon my word I believe I should.

1 Annexed by the British government 1803; given colonial status and name changed to Tasmania 1856.

To [Edward Chapman], 16 SEPTEMBER 1841

Broadstairs. | Thursday Sixteenth September 1841.

My Dear Sir.
   Know for your utter confusion, and to your lasting shame and ignominy, that the initial letter *has been* purwided—that it was furnished to the artist at the same time as the subject—and that it is a

D[1]

—which   stands   for   Double—Demnible—Doubtful—Dangerous—Doleful—Disastrous—Dreadful—Deuced—Dark—Divorce—and Drop—all applicable to the Precipice on which you stand.[2]

Farewell! If you did but know—and would pause, even at this late period—better an action for breach than—but we buy experience. Excuse my agitation. I scarcely know what I write.—To see a fellow creature—and one who has so long withstood— still if—Will *nothing* warn you—

In extreme excitement
CD
My hand fails me
P.S. | Pause. | Put it off
P.P.S. | Emigrate
P.P.P.S—| And leave me | the business ——
I mean the Strand | one.

1 Within Browne's 'D'—the initial letter of ch. 65—Barnaby and his father await liberation.
2 Chapman was about to get married; he was 37.

To John Forster, [18 SEPTEMBER 1841]

I have let all the prisoners out of Newgate, burnt down Lord Mansfield's, and played the very devil.[1] Another number will finish the fires, and help us on towards the end. I feel quite smoky when I am at work. I want elbow-room terribly.

1 i.e he had finished chs. 65 and 66, published 2 Oct.

To John Forster, [25 OCTOBER 1841]

As no steps had been taken towards the funeral,[1] I thought it best at once to bestir myself; and not even you could have saved my going to the cemetery. It is a great trial to me to give up Mary's grave;[2] greater than I can possibly express. I thought of moving her to the catacombs, and saying nothing about it; but then I remembered that the poor old lady[3] is buried next her at her own desire, and could not find it in my heart, directly she is laid in the earth, to take her grandchild away. The desire to be buried next her is as strong upon me now, as it was five years ago; and I *know* (for I don't think there ever was love like that I bear her) that it will never diminish. I fear I can do nothing. Do you think I can? They would move her on Wednesday, if I resolved to have it done. I cannot bear the thought of being excluded from her dust; and yet I feel that her brothers and sisters, and her mother, have a better right than I to be placed beside her. It is but an idea. I neither think nor hope (God forbid) that our spirits would ever mingle *there.* I ought to get the better of it, but it is very hard. I never contemplated this—and coming so suddenly, and after being ill, it disturbs me more than it ought. It seems like losing her a second time.

1 Catherine's brother George had died suddenly on 24 Oct.
2 CD wrote to Catherine's mother, 'I had always intended to keep poor Mary's grave for us and our dear children, and for you,' 24 Oct., but agreed that George should be buried there instead.
3 Catherine's grandmother, Mrs George Thomson.

To John Forster, [?OCTOBER 1841]

Of my distress I will say no more than that it has borne a terrible, frightful, horrible proportion to the quickness of the gifts you remind me of. But may I not be forgiven for thinking it a wonderful testimony to my being made for my art, that when, in the midst of this trouble and pain, I sit down to my book, some beneficent power shows it all to me, and tempts me to be interested, and I don't invent it—really do not—*but see it,* and write it down. . . . It is only when it all fades away and is gone, that I begin to suspect that its momentary relief has cost me something.

To Angela Burdett Coutts, 27 OCTOBER 1841

Devonshire Terrace. | Twenty Seventh October 1841.

Dear Miss Coutts.

Let me thank you for your kind recollection of me, yesterday. I was greatly pleased to hear from you once more, I assure you.

I should have called in Stratton Street immediately on my return to town, but I have been exceedingly unwell. It is scarcely three weeks, since I was obliged to submit to a painful surgical operation[1] (for which agreeable change I left the seaside) and although I have recovered with a rapidity whereat the Doctors are astounded, I have only just begun to feel my legs at all steady under my diminished weight. I almost thought, at first, that I was about to go through life on Two pillars of jelly, or tremulous Italian cream,—but I am happy to say that I am again conscious of floors and pavements.

They tell me that in two or three days I may go to Windsor, and set up for myself as one who has no need of the Faculty. I shall not be there, I hope, more than a fortnight at the utmost, and on my return I shall be only too well pleased to present myself at Roehampton,[2] or, if you should have left there, at your house in town. I defer all particulars about America, until then.

Some friends in Yorkshire have sent me a raven, before whom *the* Raven (the dead one) sinks into insignificance. He can say anything—and he has a power of swallowing door-keys and reproducing them at pleasure, which fills all beholders with mingled sensations of horror and satisfaction—if I may [say] so; with a kind of awful delight. His infancy and youth have been passed at a country public house, and I am told that the sight of a drunken man calls forth his utmost powers. My groom is unfortunately sober, and I have had no opportunity of testing this effect,—but I have told him to "provide himself" elsewhere, and am looking out for another who can have a dissolute character from his last master.

With best regards to Miss Meredith,[3] I am always Dear Miss Coutts

Most Faithfully Yours
CHARLES DICKENS

1 For fistula.
2 Where Miss Coutts had a house for a short time.
3 Hannah Meredith (d. 1878), later Brown, Miss Coutts's former governess and now companion.

To George Fletcher, 2 NOVEMBER 1841

1 Devonshire Terrace | York Gate Regents Park
Second November, 1841.

Sir.

It is no less painful to me to refuse, than it is to you to ask. Let me do so, briefly.

Nearly every day of my life, I receive letters akin to that which you have sent me. My inclination is, God knows, never to send an applicant away, empty-handed. But if I were the richest man in England, I should have to disappoint, almost as often as I helped. Judge then, being what I am, how frequently I am forced to hold my hand.

Fame's Trumpet should blow a little more of the wealth arising from the circulation of my works, into the Booksellers' pockets, and less into my own.[1] With a hundred claims upon my superfluity, I cannot render more than sympathy to such a case as yours. *If I could, I would.*

CHARLES DICKENS

1 i.e. it should be more widely known how much went into his publishers' (his 'Booksellers' ') pockets, how little into his own.

To John Landseer,[1] 5 NOVEMBER 1841

1 Devonshire Terrace | York Gate Regents Park
Fifth November 1841.

My Dear Sir.

Let me thank you, both for your call and your note—and let me add that it affords me real pleasure to communicate with you in any way.

You are quite right in considering it very remarkable and worthy of notice, that Wilkes should have been the active magistrate in the suppression of the Gordon Riots.[2] I determined however, after some consideration, not to notice it in Barnaby, for this reason.—It is almost indispensable in a work of fiction that the characters who bring the catastrophes about, and play important parts, should belong to the Machinery of the Tale,—and the introduction towards the end of a story where there is always a great deal to do, of new actors until then unheard of, is a thing to be avoided, if possible, in every case. Now, if I had talked about Wilkes, it would have been necessary for me to glance at his career and previous position (for in that lies the singularity you speak of)—and if I had stopped to do that, I should have stopped the riots which must go on to the end headlong, pell mell, or they lose their effect. I therefore resolved to defer that point, with some others of equal curiosity and interest, until the appearance of another Edition would afford me an opportunity of relating them in *Notes,* where they would not stem the current of the Tale, or embarrass the action.

I need not tell you who are so well acquainted with "Art" in all its forms, that in the description of such scenes, a broad, bold, hurried effect must be produced, or the reader instead of being forced and driven along by imaginary crowds will find himself dawdling very uncomfortably through the town, and greatly wondering what may be the matter. In this kind of work the object is,—not to tell everything, but to select the striking points and beat them into the page with a sledge-hammer. And herein lies the difficulty. No man in the crowd who was pressed and trodden here and there, saw Wilkes. No looker-on from a window at the struggle in the street, beheld an Individual, or anything but a great mass of magistrates, rioters, and soldiery, all mixed up together. Being always in one or other of these positions, my object has been to convey an idea of multitudes, violence, and fury; and even to lose my own dramatis personae in the throng, or only see them dimly, through the fire and smoke.

Until I received your second note last evening, I did not observe the slip of the pen to which it alluded. Even if I had done so, I should have understood, of course, what you had intended to write.

Believe me | My Dear Sir
Faithfully Yours
CHARLES DICKENS

---

1 John Landseer (1763/9–1852†), engraver and antiquary. Father of the celebrated painter Edwin Landseer, whom he rebuked for reading *OT* ('some of Dickens's nonsense') in front of his pupils at the Royal Academy.

2 John Wilkes was city chamberlain and magistrate at the time of the riots, and energetic in suppressing them. He had previously been briefly imprisoned for seditious libel of George III and the government.

To Charles Smithson,[1] 20 DECEMBER 1841

Devonshire Terrace. | Twentieth December 1841.

My Dear Smithson.

The Pie was no sooner brought into my room yesterday evening, than I fainted away.

Topping put his shoulder out, in carrying it from the waggon to the hall-door; and John[2] is in the hospital with a damaged spine—having rashly attempted to lift it.

There never *was* such a Pie! We are mad to know what it's made of, but haven't the courage to cut it. Indeed we haven't a knife large enough for the purpose. We think of hiring Fletcher to eat it. We sit and stare at it in a dull astonishment, and grow dizzy in the contemplation of its enormous magnitude.

It prevents my writing at any length, as my faculties are absorbed in crust. I have a shadowy recollection that I owe Mrs. Smithson a large sum of money and that it preys upon my mind. Fred was to have told me the amount, but he forgot it on his way home. I seem to remember, too, that you paid for THE Raven—Good God!—if you could only hear him talk, and see him break the windows!

You will be glad to hear—I can only hint at his perfections—that he disturbs the church service, and that his life is threatened by the Beadle. Maclise says he *knows* he can read and write. I quite believe it; and I go so far as to place implicit reliance on his powers of cyphering.

Ease my mind, or ask Mrs. Smithson to ease it, on the subject of my liabilities. I am going to send her two books, and will remit (if you or she will put me in a condition to do so) at the same time.

Kate joins me in hearty wishes that you and yours (including "beauteous Bill") may enjoy very many happy Christmases, and New Years.

Since writing the above, I have looked at the Pie, and—I am very weak[3]

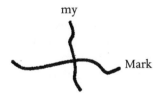

my

Mark

---

1 Charles Smithson (?1804–44), solicitor with Thomas Mitton. The raven was a gift from him.
2 John Thompson, CD's manservant until 1867, when he was dismissed for theft from the *AYR* office.
3 This last sentence in very quavery writing.

To John Forster, [29 JANUARY 1842, Tremont House, Boston, USA]

As the Cunard boats have a wharf of their own at the custom-house, and that a narrow one, we were a long time (an hour at least) working in. I was standing in full fig on the paddle-box beside the captain, staring about me, when suddenly, long before we were moored to the wharf, a dozen men came leaping on board at the peril of their lives, with great bundles of newspapers under their arms; worsted comforters (very much the worse for wear) round their necks; and so forth. "Aha!" says I, "this is like our London-bridge": believing of course that these visitors were news-boys. But what do you think of their being EDITORS? And what do you think of their tearing violently up to me and beginning to shake hands like madmen? Oh! If you could have seen how I wrung their wrists! And if you could but know how I hated one man in very dirty gaiters, and with very protruding upper teeth, who said to all comers after him, "So you've been introduced to our friend Dickens—eh?" There was one among them, though, who really was of use; a Doctor S, editor of the—¹ He ran off here (two miles at least), and ordered rooms and dinner. And in course of time Kate, and I, and Lord Mulgrave² (who was going back to his regiment at Montreal on Monday, and had agreed to live with us in the meanwhile) sat down in a spacious and handsome room to a very handsome dinner, 'bating peculiarities of putting on table, and had forgotten the ship entirely. A Mr. Alexander, to whom I had written from England promising to sit for a portrait, was on board directly we touched the land, and brought us here in his carriage. Then, after sending a present of most beautiful flowers, he left us to ourselves, and we thanked him for it.

How can I tell you what has happened since that first day? How can I give you the faintest notion of my reception here; of the crowds that pour in and out the whole day; of the people that line the streets when I go out; of the cheering when I went to the theatre; of the copies of verses, letters of congratulation, welcomes of all kinds, balls, dinners, assemblies without end? There is to be a public dinner to me here in Boston, next Tuesday, and great dissatisfaction has been given to the many by the high price (three pounds sterling each) of the tickets. There is to be a ball next Monday week at New York, and 150 names appear on the list of the committee. There is to be a dinner in the same place, in the same week, to which I have had an invitation with every known name in America appended to it. But what can I tell you about any of these things which will give you the slightest notion of the enthusiastic greeting they give me, or the cry that runs through the whole country! I have had deputations from the Far West, who have come from more than two thousand miles distance: from the lakes, the rivers, the back-woods, the log-houses, the cities, factories, villages, and towns. Authorities from nearly all the States have written to me. I have heard from the universities, congress, senate, and bodies, public and private, of every sort and kind. "It is no nonsense, and no common feeling," wrote Dr. Channing³ to me yesterday. "It is all heart. There never was, and never will be, such a triumph." And it is a good thing, is it not, . . . to find those fancies it has given me and you the greatest satisfaction to think of, at the core of it all? It makes my heart quieter, and me a more retiring, sober, tranquil man to watch the effect of those thoughts in all this noise and hurry, even than if I sat, pen in hand, to put them down for the first time. I feel, in the best aspects of this welcome, something of the presence and influence of that spirit which directs my life, and through a heavy sorrow has pointed upwards with unchanging finger for more than four years past. And if I know my heart, not twenty times this praise would move me to an act of folly.

1 Joseph Palmer, MD (1796–1871), reporter for the *Boston Transcript*. Forster customarily changed the initials of people referred to by CD to conceal identities.
2 George Constantine Phipps, 2nd Marquess of Normanby (1819–90†), later colonial governor; passenger on the Atlantic crossing to America with the Dickenses.
3 William Channing, DD (1782–1842; *ANB*), Unitarian clergyman and author. A social reformer, he influenced contemporary American writers. CD and Catherine breakfasted with him on 2 Feb.

To Unknown Ladies of Plymouth, Massachusetts,[1] 2 FEBRUARY [1842]

Tremont House, February 2d.

My Dear Ladies,

I wish I could bring my whole head among you, but being prevented, (by reason of the arrangements I have made for going elsewhere) I confess that I am afraid to send you a lock of my hair, as the precedent would be one of a most dangerous and alarming kind, and likely to terminate before long in my total baldness.

You see how very candidly I deal with you. If I had been of a deceitful nature, nothing would have been easier for me to do, than to have got a lock of hair from one of the waiters, and forwarded it to you by post.

But, as I have had much pleasure in the receipt of your letter, and feel that I may treat you with perfect confidence, I prefer even to refuse your request, and to throw myself upon your merciful consideration.

> Dear Ladies, I am ever | Faithfully yours,
> CHARLES DICKENS

1 Published in the *New York Herald*, 27 Feb.

To Jonathan Chapman,[1] 22 FEBRUARY 1842

Carlton House, New York. | Twenty Second February 1842.

My Dear Friend.

Here's my hand.—Our alliance is complete. Let the Sea rise never so high between us, we will rise higher. And when you come to England, we will have such walks and talks together, as shall indemnify us for years of separation.

I am sick to death of the life I have been leading here—worn out in mind and body—and quite weary and distressed. I have declined all future Invitations of a public nature; and mean to be resolute from this time forth. I am a splendid illustration of the wisdom of the fable concerning the old man and his ass. Half the population take it ill if I *do* go where I am asked; and the other half take it ill if I *don't*. So I mean, in future, to consult my own wishes,—and those of no other person in this Hemisphere.

I have never in my life been so shocked and disgusted, or made so sick and sore at heart, as I have been by the treatment I have received here (in America I mean), in reference to the International Copyright question. I,—the greatest loser by the existing Law, alive,—say in perfect good humour and disinterestedness (for God knows that I have little hope of its ever being changed in my time) that I hope the day will come when Writers will be justly treated; and straightway there fall upon me scores of your newspapers; imputing motives to me, the very suggestion of which turns my blood to gall; and attacking me in such terms of vagabond scurrility as they would denounce no murderer with. I vow to Heaven that the scorn and indignation I have felt under this unmanly and ungenerous treatment has been to me an amount of agony such as I never experienced since my birth. But it has had the one good effect of making me iron upon this theme; and iron I will be, here and at home, by word of mouth and in writing, as long as I can articulate a syllable, or hold a pen.

I open my whole heart to you, you see! I write in such a spirit of confidence that I pour out all I have felt upon this subject,—though I have said nothing in reference to it, even to my wife. This is a foretaste of what you have brought upon yourself.

I shall be in Washington, about the sixth or seventh of March. While I am there, I will write to you again; and I shall hope to see your handwriting before I go further South. How I wish that you were not Mayor of Boston, and would join us there, and travel with us until the end of May!

Always Your faithful | And affectionate friend
CHARLES DICKENS

1 Jonathan Chapman (1807–48), Whig mayor of Boston 1840–42; he escorted CD round Boston.

To *William Macready*, 22 MARCH 1842

Baltimore. Twenty Second March 1842.

My Dear Friend.

I beg your pardon—but you were speaking of rash leaps at hasty conclusions. Are you quite sure you designed that remark for me? Have you not, in the hurry of correspondence, slipped a paragraph into my letter, which belongs of right to somebody else? When did you ever know me leap at a *wrong* conclusion? I pause for a reply.[1] Pray Sir did you ever find me admiring Mr. Bryden?[2] On the contrary, did you never hear of my protesting through good, better, and best report, that he was not an open or a candid man and would one day *beyond all doubt* displease you by not being so. I pause again for a reply.

Are you quite sure, Mr. Macready,—and I address myself to you with the sternness of a man in the pit—are you quite sure Sir, that you do not view America through the pleasant mirage which often surrounds a thing that has been, but not a thing that is. Are you quite sure that when you were here,[3] you relished it as well as you do now, when you look back upon it. The early spring birds, Mr. Macready, *do* sing in the groves, that you were very often not over well pleased with many of the new Country's social aspects. Are the birds to be trusted?[4] Again I pause for a reply.

My dear Macready, I desire to be so honest and just to those who have so enthusiastically and earnestly welcomed me, that I burned the last letter I wrote to you—even to *you* to whom I would speak as to myself—rather than let it come with anything that might seem like an ill-considered word of disappointment. I preferred that you should think me neglectful (if you could imagine anything so wild) rather than I should do wrong in this respect.—Still it is of no use. I *am* disappointed. This is not the Republic I came to see. This is not the Republic of my imagination. I infinitely prefer a liberal Monarchy—even with its sickening accompaniments of Court Circulars, and Kings of Prussia—to such a Government as this. In every respect but that of National Education, the Country disappoints me. The more I think of its youth and strength, the poorer and more trifling in a thousand respects, it appears in my eyes. In everything of which it has made a boast—excepting its education of the people, and its care for poor children—it sinks immeasurably below the level I had placed it upon. And England, even England, bad and faulty as the old land is, and miserable as millions of her people are, rises in the comparison. Strike down the established church, and I would take her to my heart for better or worse, and reject this new love without a pang or moment's hesitation.

You live here, Macready, as I have sometimes heard you imagining! *You!* Loving you with all my heart and soul, and knowing what your disposition really is, I would not condemn you to a year's residence on this side of the Atlantic, for any money. Freedom of opinion! Where is it? I see a press more mean and paltry and silly and disgraceful than any country ever knew,—if that be its standard, here it is. But I speak of Bancroft, and am advised to be silent on that subject, for he is "a black sheep—a democrat". I speak of Bryant, and am entreated to be more careful—for the same reason. I speak of International copyright, and am implored not to ruin myself outright. I speak of Miss Martineau,[5] and all parties—slave upholders and abolitionists; Whigs, Tyler Whigs, and Democrats, shower down upon her a perfect cataract of abuse. "But what has she done? Surely she praised America enough!"— "Yes, but she told us of some of our faults, and Americans can't bear to be told of their faults. Don't split on that rock, Mr. Dickens, don't write about America—we are so very suspicious."—Freedom of opinion! Macready, if I had been born here, and had written my books in this country,—producing them with no stamp of approval from any other land—it is my solemn belief that I should have lived and died, poor, unnoticed, and "a black sheep"—to boot. I never was more convinced of anything than I am of that.

The people are affectionate, generous, open-hearted, hospitable, enthusiastic, good humoured, polite to women, frank and cordial to all strangers; anxious to oblige; far less prejudiced than they have been described to be; frequently polished and refined, very seldom rude or disagreeable. I have made a great many friends here, even in public conveyances, whom I have been truly sorry to part from. In the towns, I have formed perfect attachments. I have seen none of that greediness and indecorum on which travellers have laid so much emphasis. I have returned frankness with frankness—met questions not intended to be rude, with answers meant to be satisfactory—and have not spoken to one man, woman, or child of any degree, who has not grown positively affectionate before we parted. In the respects of not being left alone, and of being horribly disgusted by tobacco chewing and tobacco spittle, I have suffered considerably. The sight of Slavery in Virginia; the hatred of British feeling upon that subject; and the miserable hints of the impotent indignation of the South, have pained me very much—on the last head, of course, I have felt nothing but a mingled pity and amusement; on the others, sheer distress. But however much I like the ingredients of this great dish, I cannot but come back to the point from which I started, and say that the dish itself goes against the grain with me, and that I don't like it.

You know that I am, *truly,* a Liberal. I believe I have as little Pride as most men; and I am conscious of not the smallest annoyance from being hail fellow well met, with everybody. I have not had greater pleasure in the company of any set of men among the thousands whom I have received (I hold a regular Levee every day, you know, which is duly heralded and proclaimed in the Newspapers) than in that of the Carmen of Hertford, who presented themselves in a body in their blue frocks, among a crowd of well-dressed ladies and gentlemen, and bad me welcome through their spokesmen. They had all read my books, and all perfectly understood them. It is not these things I have in my mind when I say that the man who comes to this Country a Radical and goes home again with his old opinions unchanged, must be a Radical on reason, sympathy, and reflection, and one who has so well considered the subject, that he has no chance of wavering.

We have been to Boston, Worcester, Hertford, New Haven, New York, Philadelphia, Baltimore, Washington, Fredericksburgh, Richmond, and back to Washington again. The premature heat of the weather (it was 80 yesterday in the shade) and Clay's advice—how you would like Clay!⁶—made me determine not to go to Charleston; but having got to Richmond, I think I should have turned back, under any circumstances. We remain at Baltimore for two days, of which this is one. Then we go to Harrisburgh. Then by the Canal boat and the Railroad over the Alleghany Mountains, to Pittsburgh. Then down the Ohio to Cincinnati; then to Louisville, and then to St. Louis. I have been invited to a public entertainment in every town I have entered, and have refused them; but I have excepted St. Louis, as the farthest point of my travels. My friends there have passed some resolutions which Forster has, and will shew you. From St. Louis we cross to Chicago, traversing immense prairies. Thence by the lakes and Detroit to Buffalo, and so to Niagara. A run into Canada follows of course, and then—let me write the blessed word in capitals—we turn towards H O M E.[7]

Kate has written to Mrs. Macready, and it is useless for me to thank you my dearest friend, or her, for your care of our dear children, which is our constant theme of discourse. Forster has gladdened our hearts with his account of the triumph of Acis and Galatea,—and I am anxiously looking for news of the Tragedy.—Forrest[8] breakfasted with us at Richmond last Saturday—he was acting there, and I invited him—and he spoke very gratefully and very like a man, of your kindness to him when he was in London.

David Colden is as good a fellow as ever lived; and I am deeply in love with his wife. Indeed we have received the greatest and most earnest and zealous kindness from the whole family, and quite love them all. Do you remember one Greenhow, whom you invited to pass some days with you at the hotel on the Kaatskill Mountains? He is translator to the State Office at Washington— has a very pretty wife—and a little girl of five years old. We dined with them, and had a very pleasant day. The President invited me to dinner, but I couldn't stay for it. I had a private audience, however, and we attended the Public drawing room besides.

Now don't you rush at the quick conclusion, that *I* have rushed at a quick conclusion. Pray be upon your guard. If you can by any process estimate the extent of my affectionate regard for you, and the rush I shall make when I reach London to take you by your true right hand, I don't object. But let me entreat you to be very careful how you come down upon the sharp-sighted Individual who pens these words, which you seem to me to have done in what Willmott[9] wod. call "one of Mr. Macready's rushes"—As my pen is getting past its work I have taken a new one to say, that I am ever, My Dear Macready your faithful friend. CD.

1 Brutus to Plebeians, *Julius Caesar*, III. ii. 34.

2 Brydone, Macready's inefficient business manager.

3 On an eight-months' tour, 1826–7.

4 No doubt a reference to the lawyer and philanthropist David Colden (1797–1850) and his wife, who were friends of Macready's and attentive hosts to CD while he was in New York.

5 Harriet Martineau (1802–76†), English writer and journalist. Had met CD by 1836; he read her books, *Society in America* and *Retrospect of Western Travel*, before his visit.

6 Henry Clay (1777–1852), senator for Kentucky, Whig leader, and a strong advocate for international copyright.

7 Written in large Gothic capitals.

8 Edwin Forrest (1806–72; *ANB*), acclaimed American actor; acted in London 1836, and later in 1845, when he and Macready became bitter rivals.

9 Willmott was the head prompter at Drury Lane.

To *Rebecca Nichols,*[1] 19 APRIL 1842

Cincinnati. | Nineteenth April 1842.

My Dear Madam

I am very much obliged to you for your beautiful lines upon the death of Nell; which I have read with great interest and pleasure.

> Believe me | Faithfully Yours
> CHARLES DICKENS

1 Rebecca Nichols (1819–1903), poet and newspaper editor, then living in Cincinnati. Her poem, commemorating Nell in spring, summer, and autumn, began: 'Spring, with breezes cool and airy, | Opened on a little fairy.'

To *John Forster,* 24 and 26 APRIL 1842

Sandusky | Sunday, Twenty-fourth April, 1842.

I say nothing of Kate's troubles—but you recollect her propensity? She falls into, or out of, every coach or boat we enter; scrapes the skin off her legs; brings great sores and swellings on her feet; chips large fragments out of her ankle-bones; and makes herself blue with bruises. She really has, however, since we got over the first trial of being among circumstances so new and so fatiguing, made a *most admirable* traveller in every respect. She has never screamed or expressed alarm under circumstances that would have fully justified her in doing so, even in my eyes; has never given way to despondency or fatigue, though we have now been travelling incessantly, through a very rough country, for more than a month, and have been at times, as you may readily suppose, most thoroughly tired; has always accommodated herself, well and cheerfully, to everything; and has pleased me very much, and proved herself perfectly game.

We remained at Cincinnati, all Tuesday the nineteenth, and all that night. At eight o'clock on Wednesday morning the twentieth, we left in the mail stage for Columbus: Anne, Kate, and Mr. Q inside; I on the box.[1] The distance is a hundred and twenty miles; the road macadamized; and for an American road, very good. We were three and twenty hours performing the journey. We travelled all night; reached Columbus at seven in the morning; breakfasted; and went to bed until dinner time. At night we held a levee for half an hour, and the people poured in as they always do: each gentleman with a lady on each arm, exactly like the Chorus to God Save the Queen. I wish you could see them, that you might know what a splendid comparison this is. They wear their clothes, precisely as the chorus people do; and stand—supposing Kate and me to be in the centre of the stage, with our backs to the footlights—just as the company would, on the first night of the season. They shake hands exactly after the manner of the guests at a ball at the Adelphi or the Haymarket; receive any facetiousness on my part, as if there were a stage direction "all laugh"; and have rather more difficulty in "getting off" than the last gentlemen, in white pantaloons, polished boots, and berlins, usually display, under the most trying circumstances. . . .

We are in a small house here, but a very comfortable one, and the people are exceedingly obliging. Their demeanour in these country parts is invariably morose, sullen, clownish, and repulsive. I should think there is not, on the face of the earth, a people so entirely destitute of humour, vivacity, or the capacity of enjoyment. It is most remarkable. I am quite serious when I say that I have not heard a hearty laugh these six weeks, except my own; nor have I seen a merry face on any shoulders but a black man's. Lounging listlessly about; idling in bar-rooms; smoking; spitting; and lolling on the pavement in rocking-chairs, outside the shop doors; are the only recreations. I don't think the national shrewdness extends beyond the Yankees; that is, the Eastern men. The rest are heavy, dull, and ignorant. . . .

Tuesday, April Twenty-sixth, 1842.
NIAGARA FALLS!!! (upon the *English Side*).

We purpose remaining here a week. In my next I will try to give you some idea of my impressions, and to tell you how they change with every day. At present it is impossible. I can only say that the first effect of this tremendous spectacle on me, was peace of mind—tranquillity—great thoughts of eternal rest and happiness— nothing of terror. I can shudder at the recollection of Glencoe (dear friend, with Heaven's leave we must see Glencoe together), but whenever I think of Niagara, I shall think of its beauty.

If you could hear the roar that is in my ears as I write this. Both Falls are under our windows. From our sitting-room and bed-room we look down straight upon them. There is not a soul in the house but ourselves. What would I give if you and Mac were here, to share the sensations of this time! I was going to add, what would I give if the dear girl whose ashes lie in Kensal-green, had lived to come so far along with us—but she has been here many times, I doubt not, since her sweet face faded from my earthly sight. . . .

I do perceive a perplexingly divided and subdivided duty, in the matter of the book of travels. Oh! the sublimated essence of comicality that I *could* distil, from the materials I have! . . . You are a part, and an essential part, of our home, dear friend, and I exhaust my imagination in picturing the circumstances under which I shall surprise you by walking into 58, Lincoln's-inn fields. We are truly grateful to God for the health and happiness of our inexpressibly dear children and all our friends. But one letter more—only one. . . . I don't seem to have been half affectionate enough, but there *are* thoughts, you know, that lie too deep for words.

---

1 Outside the coach, his favourite seat. Anne was Catherine's maid, Anne Brown, later Cornelius. She left on her marriage in 1853 but returned to Tavistock House after CD and Catherine separated. Mr Q. was George Putnam, engaged as secretary to CD while in America.

To *Cornelius Felton*,[1] 21 MAY 1842

Montreal. | Saturday Twenty First May 1842.

My Dear Felton.

I was delighted to receive your letter, yesterday; and was well pleased with its contents. I anticipated objection to Carlyle's Letter.[2] I called particular attention to it for three reasons. Firstly, because he boldly *said* what all the others *think*; and therefore deserved to be manfully supported. Secondly, because it is my deliberate opinion that I have been assailed on this subject in a manner in which no man with any pretensions to public respect, or with the remotest right to express an opinion on a subject of universal literary interest, would be assailed in any other country on the face of the Earth. Thirdly, because I have seen enough to be assured that it is of no use to clutch these robbers in any other part of their ungodly persons but the throat. And Fourthly (I will add a fourth reason) because, meaning to let my indignation loose when I get home, I do not choose to curb it here, when I have an opportunity of giving it vent.

I really cannot sufficiently thank you, dear Felton, for your warm and hearty interest in these proceedings. But it would be idle to pursue that theme, so let it pass.

The wig and whiskers are in a state of the highest preservation. The play comes off, next Wednesday night, the Twenty Fifth.[3] What would I give to see you in the front row of the centre box—your spectacles gleaming not unlike those of my dear friend Pickwick—your face radiant with as broad a grin as a staid Professor may indulge in—and your very coat, waistcoat, and shoulders, expressive of the rum and water we should drink together, when the performance was over! I would give something (not so much, but still a good round sum) if you could only stumble into that very dark and dusty Theatre in the day time (at any minute between 12 and 3) and see me, with my coat off, the Stage Manager and Universal Director, urging impracticable ladies and impossible gentlemen on to the very confines of insanity—shouting and driving about, in my own person, to an extent which would justify any philanthropic stranger in clapping me into a strait waistcoat without further enquiry—endeavouring to goad Hamlet into some dim and faint understanding of a prompter's duties—and struggling in such a vortex of noise, dirt, bustle, confusion, and inextricable entanglement of speech and action, as you would grow giddy in contemplating. We perform a Roland for an Oliver—A Good Night's Rest—and Deaf as a Post.[4] This kind of voluntary hard labour used to be my great delight. The furor has come strong upon me again; and I begin to be once more of opinion that nature intended me for the Lessee of a National Theatre—and that pen ink and paper have spoiled a Manager.

Oh! How I look forward across that rolling water to Home, and its small tenantry! How I busy myself in thinking how my books look; and where the tables are; and in what positions the chairs stand, relatively to the other furniture; and whether we shall get there in the night, or in the morning, or in the afternoon—and whether we shall be able to surprise them—or whether they will be too sharply looking out for us—and what our pets will say—and how they'll look—and who will be the first to come and shake hands—and so forth! If I could but tell you how I have set my heart on rushing into Forster's study (Forster is my great friend, and writes at the bottom of all his letters—"My Love to Felton") and into Maclise's painting room, and into Macready's managerial ditto, without a moment's warning—and how I picture every little trait and circumstance of our arrival to myself, down to the very colour of the bow on the cook's cap—you would almost think I had changed places with my eldest son, and was still in pantaloons of the thinnest texture. I left all these things—God only knows what a love I have for them—as coolly and calmly as any animated cucumber; but when I come upon them again I shall have lost all power of self-restraint, and shall as certainly make a fool of myself (in the popular meaning of that expression) as ever Grimaldi[5] did in his way, or George The Third in his.

And not the less so, dear Felton, for having found some warm hearts, and left some instalments of earnest and sincere affection, behind me on this continent. And whenever I turn my mental telescope hitherward, trust me that one of the first figures it will descry will wear spectacles so like yours that the maker couldn't tell the difference, and shall address a Greek class in such an exact imitation of your voice, that the very students, hearing it, should cry "That's he! Three cheers for Felton Hoo—ray—ay—ay—ay—ay!"

—About those joints of yours—I think you are mistaken. They *can't* be stiff. At the worst, they merely want the air of New York, which, being impregnated with the flavor of last year's oysters, has a surprising effect in rendering the human frame supple and flexible, in all cases of rust.

A terrible idea occurred to me, as I wrote those words—The oyster cellars—what do they do, when oysters are not in season? Is pickled salmon vended there—do they sell crabs, shrimps, winkles, herrings?—The oyster openers, what do *they* do? Do they commit suicide in despair, or wrench open tight drawers and cupboards and hermetically-sealed bottles—for practice? Perhaps they are dentists out of the oyster season. Who knows!

Kate sends her love to you, and Mrs. Felton, and your little girl—in which I join with all my heart. Being ever my dear Felton

[CHARLES DICKENS]

1 Cornelius Felton (1807–62; *ANB*), professor of Greek and later president of Harvard. He became CD's closest American friend, and wrote a spirited defence of *AN* for the *North American Review* (Jan. 1843).

2 Thomas Carlyle (1795–1881†), author, biographer, and historian. Greatly admired by CD, especially for *The French Revolution* (1837) and *Past and Present* (1843). They first met in 1840. Carlyle's letter accompanied an open letter on copyright to American newspapers signed by twelve British authors, as requested by CD. His comparison of American pirates of English books with Rob Roy and his cattle-thieves provoked furious resentment.

3 CD and Catherine were invited to act in private theatricals at the Montreal Theatre, with the officers garrisoned there.

4 CD played Alfred Highflier in Thomas Morton's comedy *A Roland for an Oliver*, Mr Snobbington in Charles Mathews's interlude *A Good Night's Rest; or, Past Two O'clock in the Morning*, and Gallop in John Poole's farce *Deaf as a Post*.

5 Joseph Grimaldi (1778–1837†), actor, clown, and pantomimist, whose memoirs CD edited in 1838.

To John Forster, 26 MAY [1842]

[Rasco's] Hotel, Montreal, Canada, twenty-sixth of May

This, like my last, will be a stupid letter, because both Kate and I are thrown into such a state of excitement by the near approach of the seventh of June, that we can do nothing, and think of nothing.

The play came off last night. The audience, between five and six hundred strong, were invited as to a party; a regular table with refreshments being spread in the lobby and saloon. We had the band of the twenty-third[1] (one of the finest in the service) in the orchestra, the theatre was lighted with gas, the scenery was excellent, and the properties were all brought from private houses. Sir Charles Bagot, Sir Richard Jackson, and their staffs were present; and as the military portion of the audience were all in full uniform, it was really a splendid scene.

We "went" also splendidly; though with nothing very remarkable in the acting way. We had for Sir Mark Chase a genuine odd fish, with plenty of humour; but our Tristram Sappy was not up to the marvellous reputation he has somehow or other acquired here. I am not however, let me tell you, placarded as stage-manager for nothing. Everybody was told they would have to submit to the most iron despotism; and didn't I come Macready over them? Oh no. By no means. Certainly not. The pains I have taken with them, and the perspiration I have expended, during the last ten days, exceed in amount anything you can imagine. I had regular plots of the scenery made out, and lists of the properties wanted; and had them nailed up by the prompter's chair. Every letter that was to be delivered, was written; every piece of money that had to be given, provided; and not a single thing lost sight of. I prompted, myself, when I was not on; when I was, I made the regular prompter of the theatre my deputy; and I never saw anything so perfectly touch and go, as the first two pieces. The bedroom scene in the interlude was as well furnished as Vestris[2] had it; with a "practicable" fireplace blazing away like mad, and everything in a concatenation accordingly. I really do believe that I was very funny: at least I know that I laughed heartily at myself, and made the part a character, such as you and I know very well: a mixture of T——, Harley, Yates, Keeley and Jerry Sneak.[3] It went with a roar, all through; and, as I am closing this, they have told me I was so well made up that Sir Charles Bagot, who sat in the stage box, had no idea who played Mr. Snobbington, until the piece was over.

But only think of Kate playing! and playing devilish well, I assure you! All the ladies were capital, and we had no wait or hitch for an instant. You may suppose this, when I tell you that we began at eight, and had the curtain down at eleven. It is their custom here, to prevent heartburnings in a very heartburning town, whenever they have played in private, to repeat the performance in public. So, on Saturday (substituting, of course, real actresses for the ladies), we repeat the two first pieces to a paying audience, for the manager's benefit. . . .

I send you a bill,[4] to which I have appended a key.

I have not told you half enough. But I promise you I shall make you shake your sides about this play. Wasn't it worthy of Crummles that when Lord Mulgrave and I went out to the door to receive the Governor-general, the regular prompter followed us in agony with four tall candlesticks with wax candles in them, and besought us with a bleeding heart to carry two apiece, in accordance with all the precedents? . . .

I have hardly spoken of our letters, which reached us yesterday, shortly before the play began. A hundred thousand thanks for your delightful mainsail[5] of that gallant little packet. I read it again and again; and had it all over again at breakfast time this morning. I heard also, by the same ship, from Talfourd, Miss Coutts, Brougham, Rogers,[6] and others. A delicious letter from Mac too, as good as his painting I swear. Give my hearty love to him. . . . God bless you, my dear friend. As the time draws nearer, we get FEVERED with anxiety for home. . . . Kiss our darlings for us. We shall soon meet, please God, and be happier and merrier than ever we were, in all our lives. . . . Oh home—home—home—home—home—home—HOME !!!!!!!!!!

1 The 23rd Royal Welch Fusiliers.
2 Lucia Elizabeth Vestris (1797–1856†), actress and theatre manager, married to Charles Mathews; she produced *Two in the Morning* at Covent Garden in 1840.
3 T— is possibly Talfourd; Harley, Yates, and Keeley were actors, and Jerry Sneak a hen-pecked husband in Samuel Foote's *The Mayor of Garratt* (1764).
4 The playbill for the performance of 25 May.
5 i.e. Forster's covering letter.
6 Samuel Rogers (1763–1855†), poet. CD met him in 1839. *OCS* is dedicated to him.

To Thomas Longman,[1] [1 JULY 1842]

Athenaeum, Friday Afternoon.

My dear Sir,

If I could possibly have attended the meeting yesterday[2] I would most gladly have done so. But I [had] been up the whole night, and was too much exhausted even to write and say so before the proceedings came on.

I have fought the fight across the Atlantic with the utmost energy I could command; have never been turned aside by any consideration for an instant; am fresher for the fray than ever; will battle it to the death, and die game to the last.

I am happy to say that my boy is quite well again. From being in perfect health he fell into alarming convulsions with the surprise and joy of our return.

I beg my regards to Mrs. Longman,

And am always, | Faithfully yours
[CHARLES DICKENS]

1 Thomas Longman (1804–79†), publisher, head of Longmans from 1842. He and his wife were friendly with CD.
2 Held at the Freemasons' Tavern, to combat the foreign piracy of British literary works.

To The Editor of **The Morning Chronicle,** 25 JULY 1842

Monday morning, July 25, 1842

Sir,

As the Mines and Collieries Bill[1] will be committed in the House of Lords to-night; or, in other words, as it will arrive to-night at that stage in which the tender mercies of the Colliery Lords will so distort and maim it, that its relations and friends elsewhere will be sorely puzzled to know it again when it is returned to them, I venture to trouble you with a few remarks upon the subject. From its first public exposition it has had such ready sympathy from you, and has received such able and manly support in your journal, that I offer no apology for this intrusion on your time and space.

That for very many years these mines and all belonging to them, as they have been out of sight in the dark earth, have been utterly out of legislative mind; that for so many years all considerations of humanity, policy, social virtue, and common decency, have been left rotting at the pit's mouth, with other disregarded dunghill matter from which lordly colliers could extract no money; that for very many years, a state of things has existed in these places, in the heart and core of a Christian country, which, if it had been discovered by mariners or missionaries in the Sandwich Islands, would have made the fortune of two quarto volumes, filled the whole bench of bishops with emotion, and nerved to new and mighty projects the Society for the Propagation of the Gospel in Foreign Parts, is well known to every one. That the evidence taken by the commissioners wrought (as well it might) an extraordinary impression on the public mind, from the first moment of its diffusion; that the bill founded upon it, passed the House of Commons with the hearty consent of all parties, and the ready union of all interests; that the people of every class, and their representatives of every class, were no sooner made acquainted with the evil, than they hastened to apply the remedy, are recent and notorious facts. It was reserved for the House of Lords alone to discover that this kind of legislation was very bad and odious, and would never do.[2] Let us see on what grounds.

It is an interference with the rights of labour, because it proposes to banish women from the mines. It proceeds on insufficient evidence, because the witnesses were not upon oath. The sub-commissioners who examined the witnesses did so improperly. Nobody knows how or why—but somebody says so. To these formidable heads of objection Lord Londonderry adds (with true Lord Londonderry *naïveté*) that the prints upon their lordships' table are excessively disgusting.[3] Wherefore, he argues, (with true Lord Londonderry logic) that the parties who originated them are excessively hypocritical.

In addition to these grounds of opposition, it was stoutly contended by their collier lordships that there are no grievances, no discomforts, no miseries whatever, in the mines; that all labourers in mines are perpetually singing and dancing, and festively enjoying themselves; in a word, that they lead such rollicking and roystering lives that it is well they work below the surface of the earth, or society would be deafened by their shouts of merriment. This is humorous, but not new. Exactly the same things have been said of slavery, factory-work, Irish destitution, and every other grade of poverty, neglect, oppression, and distress. There is a kind of opposition to truth, which may be called the out-and-out, or whole-hog opposition. It stops at nothing, and recognises no middle course. Show beyond all dispute, and the remotest possibility of doubt, that any class of persons are in especial need of legislative protection and assistance, and opponents of this stamp will instantly arise, and meet you with the assertion, not that that class are moderately well off, or have an average amount of comfort; but that of all earthly ranks and conditions, theirs is the most surpassingly and exquisitely desirable. Now, happiness capers and sings on a slave plantation, making it an Eden of ebony. Now, she dwelleth in a roofless cabin, with potatoes thrice a week, buttermilk o' Sundays, a pig in the parlour, a fever in the dungheap, seven naked children on the damp earth-floor, and a wife newly delivered of an eighth, upon a door, brought from the nearest hut that boasts one—five miles off. Now, she rambles through a refreshing grove of steam engines, at midnight, with a Manchester child, patting him occasionally on the head with a billy-roller. And now she sits down in the dark, a thousand feet below the level of the sea, passing the livelong day beside a little trapper six years old.[4] If I were not this great peer, quoth Lord Londonderry, I would be that small trapper. If I were not a lord, doomed unhappily in my high place to preserve a solemn bearing, for the wonder and admiration of mankind, and hold myself aloof from innocent sports, I would be a jolly little trapper. Oh, for the cindery days of trapper infancy! The babes in the wood had a rich and cruel uncle. When were the children in the coals ever murdered for their inheritance? Jolly, jolly trappers![5]

It is an interference with the rights of labour to exclude women from the mines—women who work by the side of naked men—(daughters often do this beside their own fathers)—and harnessed to carts in a most revolting and disgusting fashion, by iron chains. Is it among the rights of labour to blot out from that sex all form and stamp, and character of womanhood—to predestine their neglected offspring, from the hour of their conception in the womb, to lives of certain sin and suffering, misery and crime—to divest them of all knowledge of home, and all chance of womanly influence in the humble sphere of a poor peasant's hearth—to make them but so many weaker men, saving in respect of their more rapid and irresistible opportunities of being brutalised themselves, and of brutalizing others; and their capacity of breeding for the scaffold and the gaol? When we talk of "rights of labour," do we picture to ourselves a hideous phantom whispering discontent in the depths of pits and mines, sharpening the Chartist's pike by stealth,[6] and skulking from the farmer's rickyard? Or are we men, possessing the common average of reason bestowed by God upon the descendants of Adam, who well know that what these lords proclaim to be the rights of labour are its wrongs? Who well know that the opposition to this vital clause originates with men who stand, it may be almost said, upon their trial—who in any other tribunal would be heard with caution and distrust; and could not sit upon the jury, far less carry in their pockets friendly verdicts from absent jurymen, by the score! To speak more plainly yet, do we not know, right well, that the real leader of the opposition to this very clause is himself the owner of the worst-conducted mine in that worst district of Scotland; who has at this moment 400 women in his weekly pay and service? And is there a man alive (out of the House of Lords) who does not read in this phrase "rights of labour," fears of possible claims for higher wages from the men, when the women no longer prostitute all the faculties of their minds and bodies to the degrading work they have pursued too long? Who does not see upon its face distinctly pictured apprehensions of a louder cry for bread? The mining labourers, with no complaint or hope of change, are bound to work, from year to year, and from age to age, their fingers to the bone; to turn their women into men, and children into devils; and do all this to live. These are the "rights of labour" with your collier lords!

The evidence is insufficient, because not taken upon oath. It was well observed in your journal some days since, that this was made no ground of objection to the Poor Law Bill upon its introduction; and that it arises for the first time. But why this extraordinary distinction between the Poor Law Act, and that for the better regulation of mines and collieries? Simply, because in the one case property sought protection against poverty; and in the other, poverty seeks protection against property. "A man may see how this world goes, with no eyes. Look with thine ears; see how yon justice rails upon yon simple thief. Hark in thine ear: change places: and handy-dandy, which is the justice, which is the thief."[7]

Abuse of the sub-commissioners is a very fruitful theme, and it daily grows in favour with these lords. Now, the sub-commissioners were chosen from among barristers, medical gentlemen, and civil engineers. I have examined the result of their labours, very attentively; and I honestly believe that a more impartial, able, and carefully-conducted investigation never was pursued. I believe that is the almost universal opinion; and I only concur with every friend of humanity, when I express my gratitude to these gentlemen, for the extraordinary pains they have taken to arrive at the truth; and the luminous manner in which they have stated it. But they by no means please the collier lords. I should be greatly surprised if they did. Barristers are not so liable as other men to be easily imposed on by false statements; surgeons cannot be blinded to the present and probable effects of a pernicious atmosphere, and the work of beasts of burden, on tender years and frames. Civil engineers are well acquainted with the dangers that lurk in ill-conducted pits, where no provision is made for the safety of the labourers. Lord Littleton's valet, Lord Londonderry's butler, and any steward or overseer of the Duke of Hamilton would have known better. They would have made an excellent commission. With three such sub-commissioners (one to form a quorum) the collier lords would have got on briskly. Jolly little trappers would have been quoted against us by the dozen, and not a whisper would have been heard about their jolly little affidavits.

It is something so new for a rational being to agree with Lord Londonderry on any subject, that I am happy to be enabled to lay claim to that distinction. The pictures on the table of the House of Lords are unquestionably disgusting. They exhibit human beings in a condition which it is horrible to contemplate—which is disgraceful to the country, dangerous to the community, repulsive and offensive to all right-thinking persons, in the highest degree. But Lord Londonderry's objection is not to the existence of this deplorable state of society; it is confined to the naughty pictures that set it forth and illustrate it; "Keep it in the mines," says he, "but don't lay it on the table. Preserve it, but don't paint it. I equally protest against legislation and lithograph." In like manner the delicacy of the distillers of Hogarth's time was grievously outraged by the print of "Gin Lane," and nearly all the stout landladies dwelling about Covent-garden voted "The Harlot's Progress" indecent and immoral.

Without taking up your time by following Lord Londonderry into his acute deduction before mentioned, that because these prints disgust him, therefore the gentlemen with whom they originated are of necessity hypocrites, I would beg, in conclusion, earnestly to impress on your readers that these are the only objections which have been urged against the Mines and Collieries Bill; and that these are the men who will to-night, by motions for delay, and other means, so pare, and cut, and fritter it away, as to reduce it to the very ghost and shadow of its former self, and to a mere absurd nonentity. Of the few petitions which have been presented against it by these same hands, purporting to come from the labourers in mines, I say nothing, as it is not very difficult to understand how signatures are procured to them, and as Lord Londonderry himself admitted a few nights ago, in his usually happy manner, on presenting one of these very documents, that the prospect of this relief "had thrown them into a fever."

In these times, when so wide a gulf has opened between the rich and poor, which, instead of narrowing, as all good men would have it, grows broader daily; it is most important that all ranks and degrees of people should understand whose hands are stretched out to separate these two great divisions of society each of whom, for its strength and happiness, and the future existence of this country, as a great and powerful nation, is dependent on the other. Therefore it is that I implore your readers closely to watch the fate of this measure, which has for its sole object the improvement of the condition and character of one great class of hewers of wood and drawers of water, whose lives, at the very best, must be fraught with danger, toil, and hardship; to compare the fate of this bill in the House of Lords, with its reception by the country, and its progress through the House of Commons, and to bestow their best attention on the debate of this night.[8]

B.[9]

1 'An Act to prohibit the Employment of Women and Girls in Mines and Collieries, to regulate the Employment of Boys, and make Provisions for the Safety of Persons working therein', moved by Lord Ashley on 7 June. CD supported the Children's Employment Commission, whose report led to the Bill.

2 The Lords, with a powerful section of mine-owning peers, were predictably hostile to the Bill; the main opponent was Lord Londonderry, who owned vast coalfields.

3 Prints (often reproduced) from drawings of women and children at work in the mines, done on the spot.

4 The youngest children worked as 'trappers', to open and shut the doors for the coal-carts. They sat alone in the dark for twelve hours or more a day.

5 Lord Londonderry had presented a petition against the Bill from colliery owners of Northumberland and Durham, which, according to the *Morning Chronicle*, claimed that 'the boys engaged in the collieries were as happy as the day was long, and they sat at their little trap doors amusing themselves cutting out figures'.

6 Chartism was the working-class movement for social and political reform.
7 *King Lear*, IV. vi. 150–4.
8 After amendments, the Bill received the Royal Assent on 10 Aug.
9 This letter was not published under CD's name, but the signature 'B' would have suggested Boz.

To Jonathan Chapman, 15 OCTOBER 1842

1 Devonshire Terrace | York Gate Regents Park.
Fifteenth October 1842.

My Dear Friend.

I was heartily glad to see your hand-writing when the Cunard Boat which brought your letter, came in. And I was heartily glad to read it—not the less so, because it led me to the belief that your tenderness for me was keener and less bold than any anxiety you would ever entertain for yourself.[1]

In lieu of the American people (or the worst among them) as a mass, consider them, for a moment, as a man. If you could only retain the friendship of an Individual by the sacrifice of everything which elevates you in your own respect—by fearing to speak the Truth—by keeping a timid silence—by debating within yourself at every turn, as though he were a rich relation, "will he like this; will he be angry if I say that; will he find out that I am but a toy for his amusement, if I do the other"—would you seek to hold it, for a day? If I know you, No. Neither would I. And because I claim to have been kindly received in America, by reason of something I had done to amuse its people and prepossess them in my favor; and not with reference to something I was not to do; therefore I write about its people, and write freely. And as I have never been deterred by hopes of promotion or visions of greatness, from pointing out abuses at home, so no amount of popular breath shall blow me from my purpose, if I see fit to point out what in my judgment are abuses abroad. And if my being an honest man, bring down caprice, and weathercock fickleness, and the falsest kind of insult on my head, what matters it to me—or to you—or to any man who is worth the name, and, being right, can look down on the crowd, and whistle while they hiss?

What is to prevent my writing? The certainty of not pleasing them. How does the certainty appear? By every claim I have upon them being disregarded and cast ruthlessly aside, at the printed bidding of some abandoned fellow; and aspersions being greedily believed which make me out a lying adventurer. My dear Chapman, if we yielded to such reasons or such men as these; in five year's time there would be no such thing as Truth in the world; and from that hour downward, her cause would be a hopeless, desperate venture.

I am well convinced that in your heart of hearts, you think and feel with me. I am well convinced that there is not, in my book, one solitary line in which you, and such as you, will not most thoroughly concur. I dispassionately believe that in the slow fulness of time, what I have written, will have some effect in purging your community of evils which threaten its very existence. And I know that it is written kindly and good-humouredly; and that I have never, for an instant, suffered myself to be betrayed into a hasty or unfair expression, or one I shall, at any time, regret. Believe me, my dear friend, the fact is literally so; and that you will find it so, to your entire contentment. And when you meet with evidences of a change in the popular opinion towards me, is it not enough to say within yourself, "if he had not brought about that change himself, he would not be the man who is my friend, but would be some other fellow whom I could hear dispraised with supreme indifference"?

Longfellow[2] from Cambridge is staying with us just now, and will return, I believe, by the Great Western[3] next Saturday. I shall charge him with a copy of my book for you. I have caused my publishers to take such precautions as will prevent (I hope) its reaching America by the Steamer which will bring you this letter.

Our darlings are all well, and send all manner of messages in broken English, to yours. Mrs. Dickens joins me in cordial and sincere remembrances to yourself, and to Mrs. Chapman. And I am always—stay; not always—conditionally—conditionally on your not, at any future time, talking about the length of your letters, or committing any such monstrous absurdity—Your faithful friend

CHARLES DICKENS

1 Chapman had written to CD about the 'journalistic mud' being 'flung at him since his departure'.
2 Henry Wadsworth Longfellow (1807–82; *ANB*), American poet, and professor of modern languages at Harvard. He called on CD, whom he admired greatly, in Boston.
3 Isambard Kingdom Brunel's wooden paddle steamer, the first steamship to make regular crossings of the Atlantic.

To Daniel Maclise, 9 NOVEMBER 1842

Ninth November 1842. Wednesday

My Dear Mac
    It's a holiday—Lord Mayor's Day. We pledged ourselves to keep it. Do you remember? Shave. I'll come down, directly.

Faithfully Always
CD.

To Angela Burdett Coutts, 12 NOVEMBER 1842

Devonshire Terrace | Twelfth November 1842.

My Dear Miss Coutts.
    Your most kind note found me in the agonies of plotting and contriving a new book;[1] in which stage of the tremendous process, I am accustomed to walk up and

down the house, smiting my forehead dejectedly; and to be so horribly cross and surly, that the boldest fly at my approach. At such times, even the Postman knocks at the door with a mild feebleness, and my publishers always come two together, lest I should fall upon a single invader and do murder on his intrusive body.

I am afraid if I came to see you under such circumstances, you would be very glad to be rid of me in two hours at the most; but I would risk even that disgrace, in my desire to accept your kind Invitation, if it were not indispensable just now, that I should be always in the way.[2] In starting a work which is to last for twenty months, there are so many little things to attend to, which require my personal superintendence, that I am obliged to be constantly on the watch; and I may add, seriously, that unless I were to shut myself up, obstinately and sullenly in my own room for a great many days without writing a word, I don't think I ever should make a beginning.

For these reasons, I am fain to be resolute and virtuous, and to deny myself and Mrs. Dickens the great pleasure you offer us. I have not answered your letter until now, because I have really been tempted and hesitating. But the lapse of every new day, only gives me a stronger reason for being perseveringly uncomfortable, that out of my gloom and solitude, something comical (or meant to be) may straightway grow up.

If you should still be in your present retreat when I have got my first number written (after which, I go on with great nonchalance) we shall be more than glad to come to you for one or two days. In the meantime Mrs. Dickens begs me to add her best remembrances to my own; and to say that if you can oblige her with your box at Covent Garden on any of Miss Kemble's nights, she will be very thankful.

> I am always Dear Miss Coutts | Yours faithfully and obliged
> CHARLES DICKENS

It is impossible for me to say how I should argue with Miss Meredith, under existing circumstances.[3]

1 He had allowed himself a break of nearly a month since finishing *AN*, before settling to *MC*.
2 i.e. within reach or call.
3 CD's arguments with her became a standing joke. She is thought to be the model for Miss Dartle in *DC*.

To *William Macready*, 12 NOVEMBER 1842

Devonshire Terrace | Saturday Twelfth Novr. 1842.

My Dear Macready

You pass this house every day, on your way to, or from, the Theatre. I wish you would call once as you go by—and soon, that you may have plenty of time to deliberate on what I wish to suggest to you. The more I think of Marston's Play[1] the more sure I feel that a Prologue, to the purpose, would help it materially, and almost decide the fate of any ticklish point on the first night. Now I have an idea (not easily explainable in writing, but told in five words) which would take the prologue out of the conventional dress of prologues—quite—get the curtain up with a dash—and begin the play with a sledge hammer blow. If, on consideration, you should think with me, I will write the Prologue, heartily.[2]

Faithfully Yours ever
CHARLES DICKENS

1 *The Patrician's Daughter*, a verse tragedy set in 1842 by John Westland Marston (1815–90), and dedicated to Macready.
2 A remarkable offer in the light of the preceding letter to Miss Coutts about the demands made by his new book. CD's prologue consists of forty-eight lines in heroic couplets, and was designed to prepare the audience for the play's contemporary setting.

To Thomas Beard, 18 DECEMBER [1842]

Eighteenth December | Sunday

My Dear Beard

I want your help in a pious fraud—such a pious one, that I have no doubt you will give it me.

I am very anxious for many reasons, to possess a little picture which Maclise is at this minute painting;[1] and I know very well, that if I were to say so, he would either insist upon giving it to me, or would set some preposterous price upon it, which he can by no means afford to take. Now, I think I may purchase it without his knowing I am the purchaser; and if I can, he is a cleverer fellow than I take him to be (highly as I estimate his abilities), if he can ever return the money to me afterwards.

Behold my project.

I want you to write him a note, and say that Mr. So and So of such and such a place in Sussex—one of your country friends—is enthusiastic in his admiration of him, and is very anxious to possess a small picture (he can't afford a large one) of his painting. That he has commissioned you to ask him what he has now by him, and has empowered you to purchase any subject, with *one* figure in it. That you have spoken to me on the subject, and I have mentioned privately to you, his having a most charming picture of a girl at a Waterfall. That you wish to buy the girl at the Waterfall, forthwith. That you will take it as a personal favor, if he will sell you the girl at the Waterfall. And that you are prepared to give him the money *down,* for the girl at the Waterfall, if he will let you know what sum you shall forward to him as her ransom from his damned uncomfortable studio.

A hundred, or a hundred and fifty Guineas, will most likely be the mark. If you can only buy it, I will give you the needful instantly wherewith to close the bargain; and a hundred and fifty thousand thanks, *in.*

All minor points I leave to your discretion.—I suppose you *an't* at home, and *couldn't* dine here today at half past five—could you?

Always Faithfully
CD.

1 *Waterfall at St Nighton's Kieve, near Tintagel*, for which the model was Georgina Hogarth. The pious fraud succeeded; CD paid 100 guineas for the picture, which is now in the V&A.

To Cornelius Felton, 31 DECEMBER 1842

London. 1 Devonshire Terrace, York Gate, Regents Park
Thirty First December 1842

My dear Felton. Many and many happy New Years to you and yours! As many happy children as may be quite convenient, (no more); and as many happy meetings between them and our children and between you and us, as the kind Fates in their utmost kindness shall favorably decree!

The American book (to begin with that), has been a most complete and thorough-going success—Four large Editions have now been sold *and paid for*; and it has won golden opinions from all sorts of men—except our friend in Fraser, who is a miserable creature;[1] a disappointed man in great poverty, to whom I have ever been most kind and considerate (I need scarcely say that); and another friend in Blackwood—no less a person than an illustrious gentleman named Warren, who wrote a story called Ten Thousand a Year.[2] They have done no harm, and have fallen short of their mark, which, of course, was to annoy me. Now I am perfectly free from any diseased curiosity in such respects, and whenever I hear of a notice of this kind, I never read it. Whereby I always conceive (don't you?) that I get the Victory. With regard to your Slave owners, they may cry, 'till they are as black in the face as their own Slaves, that Dickens lies. Dickens does not write for their satisfaction, and Dickens will not explain for their comfort. Dickens has the name and date of every newspaper in which every one of those advertisements[3] appeared;—as they know perfectly well; but Dickens does not choose to give them, and will not, at any time between this and the Day of Judgment. Neither will Dickens correct, to the joy of the Republican Free (and Easy) Newspapers, any little local errors into which he has fallen—not even that of Brock's Monument, which is a misprint[4]—but he will leave the book with all its imperfections on its head, just as it first came out, and alter nothing.

I have been hard at work on my new book, of which the first Number has just appeared.[5] The Paul Jones's's[6] who pursue Happiness—and Profit—at other mens' cost, will no doubt enable you to read it, almost as soon as you receive this. I hope you will like it. And I particularly commend, my dear Felton, one Mr. Pecksniff and his daughters, to your tender regard. I have a kind of liking for them, myself.

Blessed star of morning, such a trip as we had into Cornwall, just after Longfellow went away! The "we", means Forster, Maclise, Stanfield (the renowned Marine

Painter)[7] and the Inimitable Boz. We went down into Devonshire by the Railroad, and there we hired an open carriage from an Innkeeper, patriotic in all Pickwick matters; and went on with Post Horses. Sometimes we travelled all night; sometimes all day; sometimes both. I kept the joint stock purse; ordered all the dinners and drinks; paid all the turnpikes; conducted facetious conversations with the postboys; and regulated the pace at which we travelled. Stanfield (an old sailor) consulted an enormous map on all disputed points of wayfaring: and referred moreover to a pocket compass and other scientific Instruments. The luggage was in Forster's department; and Maclise, having nothing particular to do, sang songs. Heavens! If you could have seen the necks of bottles—distracting in their immense varieties of shape—peering out of the carriage pockets! If you could have witnessed the deep devotion of the post boys—the wild attachment of the Hostlers—the maniac glee of the waiters. If you could have followed us into the earthy old Churches we visited, and into the strange caverns on the gloomy seashore, and down into the depths of Mines, and up to the tops of giddy heights where the unspeakably green water was roaring I dont know how many hundred feet below! If you could have seen but one gleam of the bright fires by which we sat in the big rooms of ancient Inns at night, until long after the small hours had come and gone—or smelt but one steam of the *hot* Punch (not white, dear Felton, like that amazing compound I sent you a taste of, but a rich, genial, glowing brown) which came in every evening in a huge broad china Bowl! I never laughed in my life as I did on this journey. It would have done you good to hear me. I was choaking and gasping and bursting the buckle off the back of my stock, all the way. And Stanfield (who is very much of your figure and temperament, but fifteen years older) got into such apoplectic entanglements that we were often obliged to beat him on the back with Portmanteaus before we could recover him. Seriously, I do believe there never was such a trip. And they made such sketches, those two men, in the most romantic of our halting places, that you would have sworn we had the Spirit of Beauty with us, as well as the Spirit of Fun.—But stop 'till you come to England—I say no more—.

The actuary of the National Debt couldn't calculate the number of children who are coming here on Twelfth Night, in honor of Charley's birthday, for which occasion I have provided a Magic Lantern and divers other tremendous engines of that nature. But the best of it, is, that Forster and I have purchased between us the entire stock in trade of a conjurer,[8] the practice and display whereof is entrusted to me. And oh my dear eyes, Felton, if you could see me conjuring the company's watches into impossible tea caddies, and causing pieces of money to fly, and burning pocket handkerchiefs without hurting 'em,— and practising in my own room, without anybody to admire—you would never forget it as long as you live. In those tricks which require a confederate I am assisted (by reason of his imperturbable good humour) by Stanfield, who always does his part exactly the wrong way: to the unspeakable delight of all beholders. We come out on a small scale tonight, at Forster's, where we see the Old Year out and the New One in. Particulars of Success shall be forwarded in my next.

I have quite made up my mind that Forster really believes he *does* know you personally, and has, all his life. He talks to me about you with such gravity that I am afraid to grin; and feel it necessary to look quite serious. Sometimes he *tells* me things about you—doesn't ask me, you know—so that I am, occasionally perplexed beyond all telling, and begin to think it was he, and not I, who went to America. It's the queerest thing in the World.

The book I was to have given Longfellow for you, is not worth sending by itself: being only a Barnaby. But I will look up some Manuscript for you (I think I have that of the American Notes complete) and will try to make the parcel better worth its long conveyance. With regard to Maclise's pictures, you certainly are quite right in your impression of them; but he is "such a discursive devil", (as he says of himself) and flies off at such odd tangents that I feel it difficult to convey to you any general notion of his purpose. I will try to do so, when I write again.

I want very much to know about Howe and that charming girl;[9] and to hear whether he has got as far as the finger (or squeezing) language yet. Give me full particulars. Will you remember me cordially to Sumner, and say I thank him for his welcome letter? The like to Hillard, with many regards to himself and his most sensible wife, with whom I had one night a little conversation which I shall not readily forget. The like to Washington Allston, and all friends who care for me, and have outlived my book. Kate joins me in earnest and affectionate remembrances to yourself and Mrs. Felton and your little daughters. So does Charley. So does Mary. So does Kate. So does Walter. Always My Dear Felton

With true regard and affection Yours
CHARLES DICKENS

1 Most reviews of *AN* were favourable, especially of CD's accounts of prisons and comments on slavery. The anonymous reviewer in *Fraser's Magazine* objected: 'Everything is made to wear Boz's peculiar colours.'

2 Samuel Warren (1807–77†), lawyer and writer. His novel *Ten Thousand a Year* (1839–41) was a best-seller.

3 The advertisements for runaway slaves quoted in *AN* ch. 17.

4 A monument to a British commander at the site of the battle of Queenston Heights Ontario, 1812. It was blown up in 1840. CD's 'misprint' was a minor mistake concerning the course of the battle.

5 The first No. of *MC* was published that day.

6 John Paul Jones (1747–92†), American naval officer, hero of the Revolutionary War; known in England as an adventurer and privateer.

7 Clarkson Stanfield (1793–1867†), painter. Ran away to sea in 1808, and in 1812 was pressed into the navy. Following his discharge for ill-health he took up scene-painting to great acclaim, especially for his dioramas. After 1834 he concentrated on paintings of marine subjects and landscapes. Met CD through Macready in 1837 and they formed a warm friendship. *LD* is dedicated to Stanfield 'by his attached friend'.

8 From Hamley's toy shop in High Holborn, then called 'Noah's Ark'.

9 Samuel Howe, director of the Perkins Institution and Massachusetts Asylum for the Blind, near Boston. The girl was Julia Ward, who married Howe in 1843. The other references in this paragraph are to people CD met during his American trip.

To John Forster, [?MID-FEBRUARY 1843]

As to the way in which these characters have opened out,[1] that is, to me, one of the most surprising processes of the mind in this sort of invention. Given what one knows, what one does not know springs up; and I am as absolutely certain of its being true, as I am of the law of gravitation—if such a thing be possible, more so.

1 CD was probably writing the March No. of *MC* chs. 6–8, in which the most prominent characters are Pecksniff and Tom Pinch.

To Alfred Tennyson,[1] 9 MARCH 1843

Devonshire Terrace | Ninth March 1843.

My Dear Tennyson.

For the love I bear you, as a man whose writings enlist my whole heart and nature in admiration of their Truth and Beauty, set these books upon your shelves, believing that you have no more earnest and sincere homage than mine.

Faithfully | and Gratefully | Your friend
CHARLES DICKENS

1 Alfred Tennyson (1809–92†), poet, later poet laureate. CD invited him to dinner at Devonshire Terrace in Apr. 1843.

To Douglas Jerrold,[1] 3 MAY 1843

Devonshire Terrace | Third May 1843

My Dear Jerrold.

Let me thank you, most cordially, for your books—not only for their own sakes (and I have read them with perfect delight) but also for this hearty and most welcome mark of your recollection of the friendship we have established; in which light I know I may regard and prize them.

I am greatly pleased with your opening paper in the Illuminated.[2] It is very wise, and capital; written with the finest end of that iron pen of yours; witty, much needed, and full of Truth. I vow to God that I think the Parrots of Society are more intolerable and mischievous than its Birds of Prey. If ever I destroy myself, it will be in the bitterness of hearing those infernal and damnably good old times, extolled. Once in a fit of madness, after having been to a Public Dinner which took place just as this Ministry came in, I wrote the Parody[3] I send you enclosed, for Fonblanque. There is nothing in it but wrath; but that's wholesome—so I send it to you.

I am writing a little history of England[4] for my boy, which I will send you when it is printed for him, though your boys are too old to profit by it. It is curious that I have tried to impress upon him (writing, I dare say, at the same moment with you) the exact spirit of your paper. For I don't know what I should do, if he were to get hold of any conservative or High church notions; and the best way of guarding against any such horrible result, is, I take it, to wring the parrots' necks in his very cradle.

Oh Heaven, if you could have been with me at a Hospital Dinner[5] last Monday! There were men there—your City aristocracy—who made such speeches, and expressed such sentiments, as any moderately intelligent dustman would have blushed through his cindery bloom to have thought of. Sleek, slobbering, bow-paunched, overfed, apoplectic, snorting cattle—and the auditory leaping up in their delight! I never saw such an illustration of the Power of Purse, or felt so degraded and debased by its contemplation, since I have had eyes and ears. The absurdity of the thing was too horrible to laugh at. It was perfectly overwhelming. But if I could have partaken it with anybody who would have felt it as you would have done, it would have had quite another aspect—or would at least, like a "classical" mask (oh damn that word!) have had one funny side to relieve its dismal features.

Supposing fifty families were to emigrate into the wilds of North America—yours, mine, and forty eight others: picked for their concurrence of opinion on all important subjects, and for their resolution to found a Colony of Common Sense. How soon would that Devil, Cant, present itself among them in one shape or other—the day they landed, do you say—or the day after?

That is a great mistake (almost the only one I know) in the Arabian Nights, where the Princess restores people to their original beauty by sprinkling them with the Golden Water. It is quite clear that she must have made monsters of them by such a christening as that.

My wife is very sorry to hear of your daughter's illness, and sends many kind messages to her and Mrs. Jerrold—whereof the best, is, that she hopes the latter will never stand upon ceremony, but always on something better.

My Dear Jerrold | Faithfully your friend
CHARLES DICKENS

---

1 Douglas Jerrold (1803–57†), playwright and journalist. CD invited him to contribute to the first number of *Bentley's Miscellany* in 1836. They became good friends; Jerrold acted in CD's amateur theatricals. A regular contributor to *Punch* from its launch in 1841.

2 A monthly illustrated magazine which Jerrold edited until 1844.

3 'The Fine Old English Gentleman', a satirical ballad mocking 'fine old English Tory times', published anonymously in *The Examiner*, 7 Aug. 1841. Sir Robert Peel's Conservative government came to power in Aug. 1841.

4 *A Child's History of England* appeared in *HW*, 1851–3.

5 The seventh anniversary dinner of the Charterhouse Square Infirmary on 1 May.

To Mrs Georgina Hogarth, 8 MAY 1843

Devonshire Terrace, 8th May, 1843.

My Dear Mrs. Hogarth,

I was dressing to go to church yesterday morning—thinking, very sadly, of that time six years[1]—when your kind note and its accompanying packet were brought to me. The best portrait that was ever painted would be of little value to you and me, in comparison with that unfading picture we have within us; and of the worst (which ——'s really is) I can only say, that it has no interest in my eyes, beyond being something which she sat near in its progress, full of life and beauty. In that light, I set some store by the copy you have sent me; and as a mark of your affection, I need not say I value it very much. As any record of that dear face, it is utterly worthless.

I trace in many respects a strong resemblance between her mental features and Georgina's[2]—so strange a one, at times, that when she and Kate and I are sitting together, I seem to think that what has happened is a melancholy dream from which I am just awakening. The perfect like of what she was, will never be again, but so much of her spirit shines out in this sister, that the old time comes back again at some seasons, and I can hardly separate it from the present.

After she died, I dreamed of her every night for many months—I think for the better part of a year—sometimes as a spirit, sometimes as a living creature, never with any of the bitterness of my real sorrow, but always with a kind of quiet happiness, which became so pleasant to me that I never lay down at night without a hope of the vision coming back in one shape or other. And so it did. I went down into Yorkshire, and finding it still present to me, in a strange scene and a strange bed, I could not help mentioning the circumstance in a note I wrote home to Kate. From that moment I have never dreamed of her once, though she is so much in my thoughts at all times (especially when I am successful, and have prospered in anything) that the recollection of her is an essential part of my being, and is as inseparable from my existence as the beating of my heart is.

Always affectionately
[CHARLES DICKENS]

---

1 The death of Mary Hogarth. The only known painting of her was done after her death, perhaps from an earlier sketch, by Hablot K. Browne.
2 Georgina Hogarth (1827–1917), Catherine's sister; she came to live with the family in 1842, and helped care for the children. CD referred to her as 'my little housekeeper' (29 Aug. 1850); he appointed her and Forster as executors of his will.

To [*Augustus Tracey*], 7 JUNE 1843

1 Devonshire Terrace | York Gate Regents Park | Seventh June 1843.

Governor.

Now, we don't want none of your sarse—and if you bung any of them tokes[1] of yours in this direction, you'll find your shuttlecock sent back as heavy as it came. Who wants your Bridewell umberellers? Do you suppose people can't perwide theirselves with crooked handles, without axing *you*? Who ever see your umbereller? *I* didn't. Go and look for it in the Gruel; and if it an't there, search the Soup. It an't so thick, but wot you'll find three and sixpence worth of ginghum[2] among the ox heads as you pave your garden with. Ah. Oh. Yes. No. Yor'ne too cheekish by half Governor. That's where it is. You'd better take it out of yourself by a month and labour, on the Mill. If that don't answer, let off one of them blunderbusses in the office agin your weskut. *That's* what your complaint wants.

his

Villium   Gibbuns

Mark.

Memorandum added by the Chaplain
P.S. The unfortunate man forgot to state that the umbrella was Found in his possession while he penned the above—that his wretched wife was as well as could be expected; also her sister—that he had determined not to ask the Governor in Dr Howe's behalf, for a ticket to the St. Giles's Lions[3] (thinking the said Doctor troublesome in that respect) but had conferred with Mr. Crea[4] according to the Governor's kind suggestion; and would write the Governor when the Night was fixed.

1 Pieces of dry bread, prison slang.
2 An umbrella.
3 Samuel Howe was visiting, and presumably proposed a visit to the 'thieves' quarter'.
4 The head turnkey at Tracey's prison, Tothill Fields.

To *Hablot K. Browne*, [?15–18 AUGUST 1843]

2nd Subject

The First Subject having shewn the settlement of Eden on paper, the second shews it in reality.[1] Martin and Mark are displayed as the tenants of a wretched log hut (*for a pattern whereof, see a Vignette brought by Chapman and Hall*) in a perfectly flat swampy, wretched forest of stunted timber in every stage of decay, with a filthy river running before the door, and some other miserable loghouses indicated among the trees, whereof the most ruinous and tumbledown of all, is labelled BANK. And National Credit Office. Outside their door, as the custom is, is a rough sort of form or dresser, on which are set forth their pot and kettle and so forth: all of the commonest kind. On the outside of the house at one side of the door, is a written placard CHUZZLEWIT AND CO. ARCHITECTS AND SURVEYORS; and upon a stump of tree, like a butcher's block, before the cabin, are Martin's instruments—a pair of rusty compasses &c On a three legged stool beside this block, sits Martin in his shirt sleeves, with long dishevelled hair, resting his head upon his hands: the picture of hopeless misery—watching the river, as sadly remembering that it flows towards home. But Mr. Tapley, up to his knees in filth and brushwood, and in the act of endeavouring to perform some impossibilities with a hatchet, looks towards him with a face of unimpaired good humour, and declares himself perfectly jolly. Mark the only redeeming feature. Everything else dull, miserable, squalid, unhealthy, and utterly devoid of hope: diseased, starved, and abject.

The weather is intensely hot, and they are but partially clothed.

1 'The thriving City of Eden as it appeared in Fact' is the title of this illustration for *MC* ch. 23.

To John Forster, [?29 AUGUST 1843, Broadstairs]

I performed an insane match against time of eighteen miles by the milestones in four hours and a half, under a burning sun the whole way. I could get no sleep at night, and really began to be afraid I was going to have a fever. You may judge in what kind of authorship-training I am to-day. I could as soon eat the cliff as write about anything.

To Angela Burdett Coutts, 16 SEPTEMBER 1843

Broadstairs | Sixteenth September 1843

Dear Miss Coutts.

I wished very much to have had the pleasure of coming to Putney on Friday, and to have remained there that night, in compliance with your kind Invitation. But when I got to town on Thursday, I had still an unfinished number on my hands and mind. So I came back here again yesterday—too late for the post, or I would have saved it, and written to you. Pray tell Miss Meredith, with my best regards, that I have written the second chapter in the next number, with an eye to her experiences.[1] It is especially addressed to them, indeed.

On Thursday night, I went to the Ragged School; and an awful sight it is.[2] I blush to quote Oliver Twist for an authority, but it stands on that ground, and is precisely such a place as the Jew lived in. The school is held in three most wretched rooms on the first floor of a rotten house; every plank, and timber, and brick, and lath, and piece of plaster in which, shakes as you walk. One room is devoted to the girls: two to the boys. The former are much the better-looking—I cannot say better dressed, for there is no such thing as dress among the seventy pupils; certainly not the elements of a whole suit of clothes, among them all. I have very seldom seen, in all the strange and dreadful things I have seen in London and elsewhere, anything so shocking as the dire neglect of soul and body exhibited in these children. And although I know; and am as sure as it is possible for one to be of anything which has not happened; that in the prodigious misery and ignorance of the swarming masses of mankind in England, the seeds of its certain ruin are sown, I never saw that Truth so staring out in hopeless characters, as it does from the walls of this place. The children in the Jails are almost as common sights to me as my own; but these are worse, for they have not arrived there yet, but are as plainly and certainly travelling there, as they are to their Graves.

The Masters are extremely quiet, honest, good men. You may suppose they are, to be there at all. It is enough to break one's heart to get at the place: to say nothing of getting at the children's minds afterwards. They are well-grounded in the Scotch—the Glasgow—system of elementary instruction, which is an excellent one;[3] and they try to reach the boys by kindness. To gain their attention in any way, is a difficulty, quite gigantic. To impress them, even with the idea of a God, when their own condition is so desolate, becomes a monstrous task. To find anything within them—who know nothing of affection, care, love, or kindness of any sort— to which it is possible to appeal, is, at first, like a search for the philosopher's stone. And here it is that the viciousness of insisting on creeds and forms in educating such miserable beings, is most apparent. To talk of Catechisms, outward and visible signs, and inward and spiritual graces, to these children, is a thing no Bedlamite would do, who saw them. To get them, whose whole lives from the moment of their birth, are one continued punishment, to believe even in the judgment of the Dead and a future state of punishment for their sins, requires a System in itself.

The Masters examined them, however, on these points, and they answered very well—sometimes in a shout all at once, sometimes only one boy, sometimes half a dozen. I put a great many questions to them upon their answers, which they also answered very well. There was one boy, who had been selling Lucifer Matches all day in the streets—not much older than Charley—clad in a bit of a sack—really a clever child, and handsome too, who gave some excellent replies, though, of course, in language that would be very strange in your ears. Hardly any of them can read yet. For the masters think it most important to impress them at first with some distinction (communicated in dialogue) between right and wrong. And I quite agree with them. They sell trifles in the streets, or beg (or some, I dare say, steal) all day; and coming tired to this place at night, are very slow to pick up any knowledge. That they *do* come at all, is, *I* think, a Victory.

They knew about the Saviour, & the Day of Judgment. The little match boy told me that God was no respecter of persons, and that if he (the match boy) prayed "as if he meant it", and didn't keep company with bad boys, and didn't swear, and didn't drink, he would be as readily forgiven in Heaven, as the Queen would. They understood that the Deity was everywhere, and had knowledge of everything; and that there was something in them which they couldn't see or lay their hands on, which would have to account to him after they were dead. They were very quiet and orderly, while the Master said a little prayer; and sang a short hymn before they broke up. The singing was evidently a great treat, and the match boy came out very strong, with a Shake, and a Second.

I am happy to say I afforded great amusement at first—in particular by having a pair of white trousers on, and very bright boots. The latter articles of dress, gave immense satisfaction, and were loudly laughed at. Mr. Stanfield, who was with me,—in consequence of looking rather burly and fat in the small room— was received with a perfect cheer; and his sudden retirement, in consequence of being overcome by the closeness of the atmosphere, and the dread of Typhus Fever, was much regretted. When they saw that I was quite serious, and had an interest in their answers, they became quiet, and took pains. They were still better-behaved on seeing that I stood with my hat off, before the master (though I heard one boy express his opinion that I certainly wasn't a barber, or I should have cut my hair); and so far as their behaviour is concerned, I should not have the least doubt of my ability—or that of anybody else who went the right way to work—to reduce them to order in five minutes, at any time.

The school is miserably poor, you may believe, and is almost entirely supported by the teachers themselves. If they could get a better room (the house they are in, is like an ugly dream); above all, if they could provide some convenience for washing; it would be an immense advantage. The moral courage of the teachers is beyond all praise. They are surrounded by every possible adversity, and every disheartening circumstance that can be imagined. Their office is worthy of the apostles.

My heart so sinks within me when I go into these scenes, that I almost lose the hope of ever seeing them changed. Whether this effort will succeed, it is quite impossible to say. But that it is a great one, beginning at the right end, among thousands of immortal creatures, who cannot, in their present state, be held accountable for what they do, it is *as* impossible to doubt. That it is much too squalid and terrible to meet with any wide encouragement, I greatly fear. There is a kind of delicacy which is not at all shocked by the existence of such things, but is excessively shocked to know of them; and I am afraid it will shut its eye on Ragged Schools until the Ragged Scholars are perfect in their learning out of doors, when Woe to whole garments.

I need not say, I am sure, that I deem it an experiment most worthy of your charitable hand. The reasons I have, for doubting its being generally assisted, all assure me that it will have an interest for you. For I know you to be very, very far-removed, from all the Givers in all the Court Guides between this, and China.

If you will let me know whether there is anything you would like me to do in the matter, I shall be truly rejoiced to do it—I shall certainly visit the school again; for some important topics have occurred to me, in reference to which, I want to offer strong suggestions to the Masters.

We return to town on the second of next month. I am going down to Manchester for a couple of days, on the fifth, to preside at the re-opening of their Athenæum, whereat some couple of thousand people are to be assembled. If you are at Putney on the Third or Fourth, perhaps you will let me come to see you.

With best regards to Miss Meredith—and Mr. Young if the bird of passage known by that name be still with you—I am always Dear Miss Coutts

> Yours faithfully and obliged
> CHARLES DICKENS

1 *MC* ch. 25; Mrs Gamp was based on a nurse hired by Miss Coutts to take care of Miss Meredith.
2 The Ragged School movement provided free education for the poorest children. CD visited the Field Lane Ragged School, near Saffron Hill, London EC, which opened in 1841. Fagin's den in *OT* is in Saffron Hill. See also above, Oct. 1834.
3 i.e. the methods introduced by David Stow, including group teaching and learning by doing.

To John Forster, [24 SEPTEMBER 1843]

I sent Miss Coutts a sledge-hammer account of the Ragged schools; and as I saw her name for two hundred pounds in the clergy education subscription-list, took pains to show her that religious mysteries and difficult creeds wouldn't do for such pupils. I told her, too, that it was of immense importance they should be washed. She writes back to know what the rent of some large airy premises would be, and what the expense of erecting a regular bathing or purifying place; touching which points I am in correspondence with the authorities. I have no doubt she will do whatever I ask her in the matter. She is a most excellent creature, I protest to God, and I have a most perfect affection and respect for her.

To Samuel Starey,[1] 24 SEPTEMBER 1843

Broadstairs, Kent. | Twenty Fourth September 1843.

Dear Sir.

Allow me to ask you a few questions in reference to that most noble undertaking in which you are engaged—with a view, I need scarcely say, to its advancement and extended usefulness. For the present, I could wish them, if you please to be considered as put in confidence, but not to the exclusion of the gentlemen associated with you in the management of the Ragged School on Saffron Hill.

It occurred to me when I was there as being of the most immense importance that if practicable the boys should have an opportunity of Washing themselves, before beginning their tasks.

Do you agree with me? If so, will you ascertain at about what cost, a washing-place—a large trough or sink, for instance, with a good supply of running water, soap, and towels,—could be put up? In case you consider it necessary that some person should be engaged to mind it, and to see that the boys availed themselves of it in an orderly manner, please to add the payment of such a person to the expence.

Have you seen any place, or do you know of any place, in that neighbourhood— any one or two good spacious lofts or rooms—which you would like to engage (if you could afford it) as being well suited for the school? If so, at what charge could it be hired, and how soon?

In the event of my being able to procure you the funds for making these great improvements, would you see any objection to expressly limiting Visitors (I mean visiting teachers—volunteers, whoever they may be—) to confining their questions and instructions, as a point of honor, to the broad truths taught in the School by yourself and the gentlemen associated with you? I set great store by this question, because it seems to me of vital importance that no persons, however well intentioned, should perplex the minds of these unfortunate creatures with religious Mysteries that young people with the best advantages, can but imperfectly understand. I heard a lady visitor, the night I was among you, propounding questions in reference to "the Lamb of God" which I most unquestionably would not suffer any one to put to my children: recollecting the immense absurdities that were suggested to my own childhood by the like injudicious catechizing.

I return to town on Monday the second of next Month. If you write to me before then, please to address your letter here. If after that date, to my house in town.

With a cordial sympathy in your Great and Christian Labour, I am Dear Sir

> Faithfully Yours
> CHARLES DICKENS

1 Samuel Starey (d. 1904), lawyer's clerk, treasurer of Field Lane Ragged School.

To *Thomas Mitton*, 28 SEPTEMBER 1843

Broadstairs | Twenty Eighth September 1843

My Dear Mitton

He is certain to do it again.[1] There was no help but to pay it, as you so kindly did. But he is sure to do it again.

Even now, with the knowledge of him which I have so dearly purchased, I am amazed and confounded by the audacity of his ingratitude. He, and all of them, look upon me as a something to be plucked and torn to pieces for their advantage. They have no idea of, and no care for, my existence in any other light. My soul sickens at the thought of them.

There seems to be no hope of anything—or next to no hope—for Alfred,[2] yet. I had been debating in my own mind what to do for the present, and had resolved to give him a pound a week and his boathire to and fro, and to make use of him as a Secretary. I have tried him in that capacity here, and he does exceedingly well: being very quick, and very neat. I think I should have proposed it to him this very day. But his father's letter—a threatening letter, before God!—to me!—chokes the words in my throat.

What do you think of this? If you think it the best thing I can do, and should see my disinterested and most affectionate parent, will you undertake to tell him that his letter has disgusted me beyond expression; and that I have no more reference to anything he wants or wishes or threatens or would do or wouldn't do, in taking on myself this new Burden, than I have reference to the Bell of Saint Paul's Cathedral or the Statue at Charing Cross?

Nothing makes me so wretched, or so unfit for what I have to do, as these things. They are so entirely beyond my own controul, so far out of my reach, such a drag-chain on my life, that for the time they utterly dispirit me, and weigh me down.

I shall be punctual on Tuesday. In the meantime, perhaps I shall receive a line from you.

Faithfully Ever
CHARLES DICKENS

I received Smithson's communication, and answered it by Return.

---

1 John Dickens was in debt again. CD's account-book shows a payment to Mitton of £15. 9s. 6d. on 16 Oct.
2 One of CD's younger brothers, b. 1822.

To John Forster, [2 NOVEMBER 1843]

I expected you to be startled. If I was startled myself, when I first got this project of foreign travel into my head, MONTHS AGO, how much more must you be, on whom it comes fresh: numbering only hours! Still, I am very resolute upon it—very. I am convinced that my expenses abroad would not be more than half of my expenses here; the influence of change and nature upon me, enormous. You know, as well as I, that I think Chuzzlewit in a hundred points immeasurably the best of my stories. That I feel my power now, more than I ever did. That I have a greater confidence in myself than I ever had. That I *know,* if I have health, I could sustain my place in the minds of thinking men, though fifty writers started up to-morrow. But how many readers do *not* think! How many take it upon trust from knaves and idiots, that one writes too fast, or runs a thing to death! How coldly did this very book go on for months, until it forced itself up in people's opinion, without forcing itself up in sale! If I wrote for forty thousand Forsters, or for forty thousand people who know I write because I can't help it, I should have no need to leave the scene. But this very book warns me that if I *can* leave it for a time, I had better do so, and must do so. Apart from that again, I feel that longer rest after this story would do me good. You say two or three months, because you have been used to see me for eight years never leaving off. But it is not rest enough. It is impossible to go on working the brain to that extent for ever. The very spirit of the thing, in doing it, leaves a horrible despondency behind, when it is done; which must be prejudicial to the mind, so soon renewed, and so seldom let alone. What would poor Scott have given to have gone abroad, of his own free will, a young man, instead of creeping there, a driveller, in his miserable decay![2] I said myself in my note to you—anticipating what you put to me—that it was a question *what* I should come out with, first. The travel-book, if to be done at all, would cost me very little trouble; and surely would go very far to pay charges, whenever published. We have spoken of the baby,[3] and of leaving it here with Catherine's mother. Moving the children into France could not, in any ordinary course of things, do them anything but good. And the question is, what it would do to that by which they live: not what it would do to them.—I had forgotten that point in the B. and E. negociation; but they certainly suggested instant publication of the reprints, or at all events of some of them; by which of course I know, and as you point out, I could provide of myself what is wanted. I take that as putting the thing distinctly as a matter of trade, and feeling it so. And, as a matter of trade with them or anybody else, as a matter of trade between me and the public, should I not be better off a year hence, with the reputation of having seen so much in the meantime? The reason which induces you to look upon this scheme with dislike—separation for so long a time—surely has equal weight with me. I see very little pleasure in it, beyond the natural desire to have been in those great scenes; I anticipate no enjoyment at the time. I have come to look upon it as a matter of policy and duty. I have a thousand other reasons, but shall very soon myself be with you.

1 Sales of *MC* were initially poor, but increased with Martin's visit to America.
2 The novelist Walter Scott went abroad during his last illness in October 1831.
3 The child expected in Jan. 1844.

To *William Macready*, 3 JANUARY 1844

Devonshire Terrace | Third January 1844.

My very dear Macready.

You know all the news, and you know I love you; so I no more know why I write, than I do why I "come round" after the play to shake hands with you in your dressing-room.[1] I say, *Come*, as if you were at this present moment the lessee of Drury Lane, and had Jones with a long face on one hand—Smith, elaborately explaining that everything in creation is a joint stock Company, on the other—the Inimitable B by the fire, in conversation with Serle—and Forster confidential with everybody about nothing particular.[2] Well a day!—I see it all, and smell that extraordinary compound of odd scents peculiar to a theatre, which bursts upon me when I swing open the little door in the hall; accompanies me, as I meet perspiring supers in the narrow passage; goes with me, up the two steps; crosses the stage; winds round the third entrance P.S.[3] as I wind; and escorts me safely into your presence, where I find you *un*winding something slowly round and round your chest, which is so long that no man ever saw the end of it.

Oh that you had been in Clarence Terrace on Nina's[4] birthday! Good God how we missed you, talked of you, drank your health, and wondered what you were doing! Perhaps you are Falkland[5] enough (I swear I suspect you of it) to feel rather sore—just a little bit you know; the merest trifle in the world—on hearing that Mrs. Macready looked brilliant—blooming, young, and handsome; and that she danced a country dance with the writer hereof (Acres to your Falkland) in a thorough spirit of beaming good humour and enjoyment. Now you don't like to be told that? Nor do you quite like to hear that Forster and I conjured bravely—that a hot plum pudding was produced from an empty saucepan, held over a blazing fire, kindled in Stanfield's hat, without damage to the lining—that a box of bran was changed into a live Guinea Pig, which ran between my God child's[6] feet, and was the cause of such a shrill uproar and clapping of hands that you might have heard it (and I daresay did) in America—that three half crowns being taken from Major Burns and put into a tumbler-glass before his eyes did then and there give jingling answers unto questions asked of them by me, and knew where you were, and what you were doing; to the unspeakable admiration of the whole assembly. Neither do you quite like to be told that we are going to do it again, next Saturday, with the addition of Demoniacal dresses from a Masquerade Shop. Nor, that Mrs. Macready, for her gallant bearing always, and her best sort of best affection, is the best creature I know. Never mind. No man shall gag me; and those are my opinions.

My dear Macready, the lecturing proposition is not to be thought of. I have not the slightest doubt or hesitation in giving you my most strenuous and decided advice, against it.[7] I am not at all clear, even of its success in America, for as it is invariably the characteristic of low, coarse, and mean minds in the circle of one's own acquaintance to delight in new faces and change of friends, so it is one of the most striking features in that low, coarse, and mean Nation to be perpetually playing skittles with different sets of Idols. And I am by no means sure, that *any* second visit of yours to any place for any purpose will be the success it ought to be, and would, with people of a higher standard, most indubitably prove. But setting aside this, *and looking only to its effect at home*, I am immoveable in my conviction that the impression it would produce would be one of failure, and a reduction of yourself to the level of those who do the like here. To us who know the Boston names and honor them, and who know Boston and like it (Boston is what I would have the whole United States to be) the Boston requisition would be a valuable document of which you and your friends might well be proud. But these names are perfectly unknown to the public here, and would produce not the least effect. The only thing known to the public here, is, that they ask (when I say "they", I mean the people) everybody to lecture. It is one of the things I have ridiculed in Chuzzlewit. Lecture, you, and you fall into the roll of Lardners, Vandenhoffs, Eltons, Knowleses, Buckinghams.[8]—You are off your pedestal, have flung away your glass slipper, and changed your triumphal coach into a seedy old pumpkin. I am quite sure of it, and cannot express my strong conviction, in language of sufficient force.

"Puff-ridden"! Why to be sure they are. The Nation is a miserable Sindbad, and its boasted press (the braggarts!) the loathsome, foul old man upon his back. And yet with that extraordinary disregard of Truth, that monstrous audacity of assertion, which makes a Gentleman in heart so rare a man among the people, they will tell you, and proclaim to the four winds, for repetition here, that they don't heed their ignorant and brutal papers. As if the papers could exist if they didn't heed them! As if a man could live in the United States a month, and not see the whole country is led and driven by a herd of rascals, who are the human lice of God's creation! Let any two of these vagabonds in any town you go to, take it into their heads to make you an object of attack, or to direct the general attention elsewhere, and what avail those wonderful images of passion which you have been all your life perfecting, and which I no more believe the rotten heart of that false land is capable of feeling, otherwise than as a fashion, a fancy, than I believe, or ever did believe, it made a distinction between me and Fanny Elssler,[9] or between her and La Fayette. Pah! I never knew what it was to feel disgust and contempt, 'till I travelled in America.

I have sent you, to the charge of our trusty and well-beloved Colden, a little book I published on the 17th of December,[10] and which has been a most prodigious success—the greatest, I think, I have ever achieved. It pleases me to think that it will bring you Home for an hour or two. And I long to hear you have read it, on some quiet morning. Do they allow you to be quiet, by the way? "Some of our most fash'nable people Sir", denounced me awfully, for liking to be alone sometimes.

Now that we have turned Christmas, I feel as if your face were directed homewards, Macready. The downhill part of the road is before us now, and we shall travel on to midsummer at a dashing pace. Damn them, I can't damage you by coming with open arms to Liverpool (for you won't be going back again in a hurry, much as you relish them); and please Heaven I will be there, when you come steaming up the Mersey, with that red funnel smoking out unutterable things, and your heart much fuller than your trunks, though something lighter! If I be not the first Englishman to shake hands with you on English Ground, the man who gets before me will be a brisk and active fellow, and even then need put his best leg foremost. So I warn Forster to keep in the rear, or he'll be blown.

If you should have any leisure to project, and put on paper, the outline of a scheme for opening any Theatre on your return, upon a certain List Subscribed, and on certain understandings with the actors, it strikes me that it would be well to break ground, while you are still away. Of course I need not say that I will see anybody or do anything—even to the calling together of the actors—if you should ever deem it desirable. My opinion is, that our respected and valued friend Mr. Bunn,[11] will stagger through another season, if he don't rot first. I understand he is in a partial state of decomposition at this minute. He was very ill, but got better. How is it that Bunns always *do* get better, and strong hearts are so easy to die!

Burn this letter, lest it should be abstracted from your desk (as Jeffrey's pocket book was[12]) and published in a newspaper. Being confidentially addressed to yourself, it would be very extensively read. I hope you saw Mr. Park Benjamin in New York—a literary gentleman, and "smart", oh very smart. Also Mr. James Gordon Bennet (think of his proposing to Chapman and Hall to publish his travels in England!) and Colonel Webb, and all that holy brotherhood.[13] Kate sends her tender love. So does Georgy. So does Charley, so does Mamy, so does Katey, so does Walter, so does the other one who is to be born next week. Look homeward always, as we look abroad to you. God bless you my dear Macready.

Ever your affectionate friend

C.D.

1 Macready was touring America.
2 Friends and acquaintances in the theatre. Jones was Macready's treasurer at Drury Lane, Smith an actuary, and Serle an actor and dramatist.
3 Prompt Side.
4 Macready's eldest child.
5 An allusion to the jealous disposition of Falkland, in Sheridan's *The Rivals*.
6 Henry Macready, b. 21 Dec. 1838.
7 Macready was invited to give readings from Shakespeare, but did not do so.
8 Dionysius Lardner was a popular scientific writer; John Vandenhoff and Edward Elton were actors, and James Buckingham an author and traveller.
9 The Austrian dancer Fanny Elssler was so successful when she toured America in 1840–2 that Congress avoided sitting on the days of her performances in Washington. The French aristocrat La Fayette served with distinction as a general under George Washington in the American Revolutionary War.
10 CC.
11 Alfred Bunn (1796–1860†), theatre manager and librettist; lessee of Drury Lane.
12 Francis Jeffrey, Lord Jeffrey (1773–1850†), judge, writer, and influential critic. An admirer of CD, whom he befriended. In 1815 his private journal was published in a Philadelphia paper.
13 Park Benjamin (1809–64) was founder and editor of the weekly *New World*; James Gordon Bennet (1795–1872) was editor of the *New York Herald*; Colonel James Watson Webb (1802–84) editor of the *Morning Courier and New-York Enquirer*, and perhaps the original of Colonel Diver, *MC* ch.16.

To Clarkson Stanfield & Family, 7 FEBRUARY 1844

How are you getting on? Say that you are well enough to come and dine here today at half past five—*do* say that much—for on this day two and thirty years ago, the planet Dick appeared on the horizon. To the great admiration, wonder and delight of all who live, and the unspeakable happiness of mankind in general. Best regards at home from all here.

To Mr. Parkin, 9 MARCH 1844

1 Devonshire Terrace | York Gate Regents Park | Ninth March 1844.

Mr. Charles Dickens presents his compliments to Mr. Parkin, and begs to thank him for his note. The dreadful thought that there was no Suet in the pudding, had already suggested itself to Miss Pinch's mind. Mr. Dickens will be careful that the

Public shall not be deluded on the subject, and that the indispensability of Suet shall be distinctly recognized.[1]

1 Suet is not mentioned in the Mar. No. of *MC*, but in the May No. is recognized as indispensable.

To *Thomas Thompson*,[1] 11 MARCH 1844

Devonshire Terrace. Monday, Eleventh March, 1844

My dear Thompson,

I swear to you that when I opened and read your letter this morning (I laid down my pen to break the seal, being just shut up in my room) I felt the blood go from my face to I don't know where, and my very lips turn white. I never in my life was so surprised, or had the whole current of my life so stopped, for the instant, as when I felt, at a glance, what your letter said. Which I did, correctly. For when I came to read it attentively, and several times over, I found nothing new in it.

This was not because it contained a word to astonish *me,* but because I never had imagined you remaining in Liverpool, or seriously admiring her.[2] Forgive me when I say that I did not think it lay in your temper or habit to do so unless it had become a thing of pretty long custom. I supposed you had returned to Yorkshire—I expected you in town any day—and have often wondered within myself whether you would still have an interest in recalling with me her uncommon character and wonderful endowments. I know that in many points I am an excitable and headstrong man, and ride O God what prancing hobbies!—and although I knew that the impression she had made on me was a true, deep, honest, pure-spirited thing, I thought my nature might have been prepared to receive it, and to exaggerate it unconsciously, and to keep it green long after such a fancy as I deemed it probable you might have conceived had withered. So much for my injustice, which I *must* release myself of in the first instance.

You asked me to write, and I think you want me to write freely. I will tell you what I would do myself, if I were in your case and I will tell you without the least reserve.

If I had all your independent means, and twenty times my own reputation and fame, and felt as irresistibly impelled towards her as I should if I were in your place and as you do, I would not hesitate, or do that slight to the resolution of my own heart which hesitation would imply. But would win her if I could, by God. I would answer it to myself, if my world's breath whispered me that I had known her but a few days, that hours of hers are years in the lives of common women. That it is in such a face and such a spirit, as part of its high nature, to do at once what less etherial creatures must be long in doing. That as no man ever saw a soul or caught it in its flight, no man can measure it by rule and rod. And that it has a right in such lofty development to pitch all forms laid down by bodies to the devil—the only thing, as far as I know, who was never in love himself, or inspired it in others.

And to the father I *would* point out, in very tenderness and sorrow for this gentle creature, who otherwise is lost to this sad world which needs another, Heaven knows, to set it right—lost in her youth as surely as she lives—that the course to which he is devoting her, should not be called her life but Death; for its speedy end is certain. I saw an angel's message in her face that day that smote me to the heart. He may not know this, being always with her; it is very likely he does not; and I would tell it him. Repose, change, a mind at rest, a foreign climate would be, in a springtime like hers, the dawning of a new existence. I believe, I do believe and hope, that this would save her; and that many happy years hence, she would be strong and hardy. But at the worst, contemplating the chance, the distant chance in such a case, of what is so dreadful, I could say in solemn and religious earnestness that I could bear better her passing from my arms to Heaven than I could endure the thought of coldly turning off into the World again to see her no more; to have my very name forgotten in her ears; to lose the recollection of her myself but at odd times and in remorseful glances backwards; and only to have the old thoughts stirred up at last by some indifferent person saying "You recollect her? Ah! She's dead."

As I live, I write the Truth and feel it.

So many ideas spring up within me, of the quiet happiness we might enjoy abroad, all of us together, in some delicious nook, where we should make merry over all this, that I don't know whether to be glad or sorry at my own hopefulness—Such Italian Castles, bright in sunny days, and pale in moonlight nights, as I am building in the air!—

But time is precious, and Dick is (to a certain extent) a prosing Donkey, if you give him the rein. So as it is pouring very hard, and John will probably contract an asthma in running at the rate of seven miles an hour to the post-office to save the post, I will go on with my building after I have dispatched this.

I never was more in earnest, my dear Thompson, in my life.

> Always faithfully your friend
> CHARLES DICKENS

P.S. I am truly sorry to hear about Smithson[3] but I have been afraid of it for a long time. Write, if you remain.

P.P.S. I don't seem to have said half enough.

---

1 Thomas James Thompson (1812–81), a widower, and friend of CD's since 1838.
2 Christiana Weller (1825–1910), a young concert pianist, whom CD and Thompson had just met and seen perform. In April CD wrote to Christiana on Thompson's behalf.
3 Thompson's brother-in-law; died 30 Mar.

To The Committee of The Metropolitan Drapers' Association,[1] 28 MARCH 1844

Devonshire Terrace, 28th March, 1844

Gentlemen,

I beg to assure you, that it gives me great satisfaction to have the honour of enrolling my name among the Vice-Presidents of your Association.

My engagements will not permit, I regret to say, of my attending your Meeting at the Hanover Square Rooms on Monday Evening. But though absent in the body, I am with you in the spirit there and always. I believe that the objects you have in view, are not of greater importance to yourselves than to the welfare and happiness of society in general; to whom the comfort, happiness, and intelligence of that large class of industrious persons whose claims you advocate, is, if rightly understood, a matter of the highest moment and loftiest concern.

I understand the late-hour system to be a means of depriving very many young men of all reasonable opportunities of self-culture and improvement, and of making their labour irksome, weary, and oppressive. I understand the early-hour system to be a means of lightening their labour without disadvantage to any body or any thing, and of enabling them to improve themselves, as all rational creatures are intended to do, and have a right to do; and, therefore I hold that there is no more room for choice or doubt between the two, than there is between good and bad, or right and wrong.

I am, Gentlemen, | Your faithful Servant,
CHARLES DICKENS

1 Established 1842. Its president was James Emerson Tennent (1804–69†), traveller, politician, and MP. Fellow law student of Forster, and long known to CD. *OMF* is dedicated to him 'as a memorial of friendship'.

To Thomas Powell,[1] 16 APRIL 1844

Devonshire Terrace. | Sixteenth April 1844.

My Dear Powell.

Lord bless you! Thursday or Friday!!! Why, I composed (though I say it, as shouldn't) the best little party you can imagine; comprehending everybody I had room for, whom I thought Mr. Chapman would like to know.[2] Let me see. Rogers for Poetry, Sydney Smith for Orthodoxy, Charles Kemble and Young for Theatricality, Lord Denman for Benchity, Lord Dudley Stuart for Polarity, Mr. and Mrs. Milner Gibson for Anti Corn Law Leaguality, Mrs. Norton for beauty, and divers others for variety. Lord love you! Why, at this time of the year it couldn't be done again under three weeks. Not to mention the Dwarf—General Tom Thumb—whom on the word of a Spiritiwal creetur, I had summoned, and have summoned, for the Evening in question. No. We won't come down with the run. We'll have a long notice, and see what can be done with the second wentur. When we doos go in, we plays to win Sir.

Says Shrimp to me (I allude to the humble individual who has the honor to be my brother) "Mr. Powell is coming up one evening".—"Shrimp", said I. "Why evening? We dine at half past 5. Cannot said Powell, with a day's notice (to ensure my not being out) come up to dinner?" I saw that I had touched him; and had a modest confidence in my Message reaching you safely. Whether Shrimp broke down, or Prawn (otherwise Powell) I don't know. But until this point is cleared up, I decline to acknowledge the receipt of potted chair.[3] If indeed that *be* chair in a black bag; which I don't believe.

Faithfully Ever

CD.

1 Thomas Powell (1809–87), miscellaneous writer, embezzler, and forger; ingratiated himself in literary circles until his fraudulent activities at Thomas Chapman's were discovered in 1846.
2 A message to Powell through 'Shrimp' (Augustus, CD's youngest brother) seems to have been misunderstood; CD pretends that this throws out all his plans for a splendid dinner-party of assorted notables to meet Thomas Chapman.
3 Potted char, the fish. Powell sent edible presents to those with whom he wanted to ingratiate himself.

To Charles Watson, 25 APRIL 1844

1 Devonshire Terrace | York Gate Regents Park | Twenty Fifth April 1844.

Sir.

I beg to acknowledge the receipt of your obliging letter of the Twenty Third Instant.

I am perfectly aware that there are several passages in my books which, with very little alteration—sometimes with none at all—will fall into blank verse, if divided off into Lines. It is not an affectation in me, nor have I the least desire to write them in that metre; but I run into it, involuntarily and unconsciously, when I am very much in earnest. I even do so, in speaking.

I am not prepared to say that this may not be a defect in prose composition; but I attach less importance to it than I do to earnestness. And considering that it is a very melodious and agreeable march of words, usually; and may be perfectly plain and free; I cannot agree with you that it is likely to be considered by discreet readers as turgid or bombastic, unless the sentiments expressed in it, be of that character. Then indeed it matters very little how they are attired, as they cannot fail to be disagreeable in any garb.

Upon the whole I am inclined to think that if I had altered the passages which give you offence, you would not have liked my books so well as you are kind enough to say you do; and would not have given me that credit for being in earnest which has procured for me the pleasure of receiving your good-humoured and agreeable letter.[1]

Faithfully Yours
CHARLES DICKENS

1 CD later wrote to Forster about *The Battle of Life*: 'If in going over the proofs you find the tendency to blank verse (I *cannot* help it, when I am very much in earnest) too strong, knock out a word's brains here and there' (13 Nov. 1846).

To Hablot K. Browne, [?JUNE 1844]

FRONTISPIECE

I have a notion of finishing the book, with an apostrophe to Tom Pinch, playing the organ. I shall break off the last Chapter suddenly, and find Tom at his organ, a few years afterwards. And instead of saying what became of the people, as usual, I shall suppose it to be all expressed in the sounds; making the last swell of the Instrument a kind of expression of Tom's heart. Tom has remained a single man, and lives with his sister and John Westlock who are married—Martin and Mary are married—Tom is a godfather of course—Old Martin is dead, and has left him some money—Tom has had an organ fitted in his chamber, and often sits alone, playing it; when of course the old times rise up before him. So the Frontispiece is Tom at his organ with a pensive face; and any little indications of his history rising out of it, and floating about it, that you please; Tom as interesting and amiable as possible.

VIGNETTE FOR TITLE PAGE.

The finger post at the end of the lane, which has been so often mentioned. You can either have Tom Pinch waiting with John Westlock and his boxes, as at the opening of the book; or Mr. Pecksniff blandly receiving a new pupil from the coach (perhaps this will be better);[1] and by no means forgetting the premium in his welcome of the Young Gentleman.
Will you let me see the Designs for these two?
(Over)

1st. Subject.

The Room in the Temple. Mrs. Lupin, with Mary in her charge, stands a little way behind old Martin's chair. Young Martin is on the other side. Tom Pinch and his sister are there too. Mr. Pecksniff hastens in to rescue his venerable friend from this horde of plunderers and deceivers. The old man in a transport of burning indignation, rises from his chair, and uplifting his stick, knocks the good Pecksniff down; before John Westlock and Mark who gently interpose (though they are very much delighted) can possibly prevent him. Mr. Pecksniff on the ground. The old man full of fire, energy and resolution.

Lettering.
Warm Reception of Mr. Pecksniff by his Venerable friend.

2nd. SUBJECT.

Represents Miss Charity Pecksniff on the bridal morning. The bridal breakfast is set out in Todgers's drawing-room. Miss Pecksniff has invited the strong-minded woman, and all that party who were present in Mr. Pecksniff's parlor, in the second number, to behold her triumph. She is not proud, but forgiving. Jinkins is also present and wears a white favor in his button hole. Merry is *not* there. Mrs. Todgers is decorated for the occasion. So are the rest of the company. The bride wears a bonnet with an orange flower. They have waited a long time for Moddle. Moddle has not appeared. The strong-minded woman has expressed a hope that nothing has happened to him; the daughters of the strong-minded woman (who are bridesmaids) have offered consolation of an aggravating nature. A knock is heard at the door. It is not Moddle but a letter from him. The bride opens it, reads it, shrieks, and swoons. Some of the company catch it up crowd about each other, and read it over one another's shoulders. Moddle writes that he can't help it—that he loves another—that he is wretched for life—and has that morning sailed from Gravesend for Van Diemen's Land.

Lettering. *The Nuptials of Miss Pecksniff receive a temporary check.*

1 This second alternative was chosen.

To Count D'Orsay,[1] 7 AUGUST 1844

Albaro, Near Genoa. Wednesday August Seventh 1844

My Dear Count D'Orsay.

I hope you will not think me tardy in commencing that correspondence—with yourself and Lady Blessington[2] alternately—from which I am to derive so much interest and happiness during my stay in these latitudes. I should have flung my loving glove into Gore House before now; but that the restlessness of a perfectly new life, and the illness of my pet little daughter (the smaller of the two Kensington lunchers) have sadly interfered with my good resolutions. Once off, however, I think I can back myself to keep going. I am a bad starter—nothing more.

We had a charming journey here. I cannot tell you what an immense impression Paris made upon me. It is the most extraordinary place in the World. I was not prepared for, and really could not have believed in, its perfectly distinct and separate character. My eyes ached and my head grew giddy, as novelty, novelty, novelty; nothing but strange and striking things; came swarming before me. I cannot conceive any place so perfectly and wonderfully expressive of its own character; its secret character no less than that which is on its surface; as Paris is. I walked about the streets—in and out, up and down, backwards and forwards—during the two days we were there; and almost every house, and every person I passed, seemed to be another leaf in the enormous book that stands wide open there. I was perpetually turning over, and never coming any nearer the end. There never was such a place for a description. If I had only a larger sheet of paper (I have ordered some for next time) I am afraid I should plunge, wildly, into such a lengthened account of those two days as would startle you. This is the sole and solitary sheet in the house this morning (except those on the beds)—which looks providential, and seems to be an interposition in your favor.

Let me explain to you where I am. Do you recollect Byron's old house? Yes? Well. It isn't that—as they always say on the stage, when the two comic men are sitting in chairs before the lamps—but keeping on, up the hill past Byron's house, you come to another large house at the corner of a lane, with a little tumble-down blackguard old green-grocer's shop at the other corner, on which is painted, if I recollect right, Croce di San Lorenzo. The Governor lives in the large house opposite the Green Grocer's now; and turning down between the Governor's *and* the Green Grocer's, you go down a long, straggling, very narrow lane until you come to mine: which is on the left hand, with the open Sea before it—a fort close by, on the left—a vineyard sloping down towards the shore—and an old ruined church dedicated to St. John the Baptist (which I dare say Lady Blessington will remember) blotting out just so much of the sea as its walls and tower can hide. It is properly called The Villa di Bella Vista; but *I* call it the Villa di Bagnerello—that being the name of an amiable but drunken butcher into whose hands it has fallen, and who, being universally known (in consequence of being carried home from some wine shop or other every night), is a famous address: which the dullest errandboy recognizes immediately.

There is a delicious air here—almost always a sea breeze—and very good bathing. The house is bare of furniture, but especially clean. The Sala is very large, and the bedrooms excellent. As it would never do for a winter residence, however, I have been looking about me, and have concluded an arrangement, I hope, for the Peschiere:[3] entering on the possession of that Palazzo, on the first of October. I have the whole Palace except the Ground Piano. I don't know whether you ever saw the rooms. They are very splendid indeed; and every inch of the walls is painted in fresco. The Gardens also, are beautiful. The last English resident paid Eight hundred francs a month; but I take the unexpired term of the present occupier (an English Colonel) who has had it for a year and a half, and got it much cheaper in consequence. My rent will be five hundred, which, as rent goes in Genoa, will be very cheap. I had thought of a Piano in the Solicetti on the Acqua Sola; but I am doubtful whether it might not be a thought too breezy in the windy weather; to say nothing of an intolerable bell which is always clashing and clanging hard by; or of the hospital, which is close to the windows.

I have been turning my plans over in my mind; and I think I shall remain quiet until I have done my little Christmas Book—that will be, perhaps, about the middle of October. In November, I think I shall start, with my servant (I have a most admirable and useful fellow—a frenchman) for Verona, Mantua, Milan, Turin,

Venice, Florence, Pisa, Leghorn[4] &c. I shall come back here for Christmas, and remain here through January. In February, I think I shall start off again (attended as before) and taking the Steamboat to Civita Vecchia, go to Rome—from Rome to Naples—and from Naples to Mount Ætna, which I very much desire to see. Then I purpose returning to Naples, and coming back here, direct, by Steamer. For Easter Week, I design returning to Rome again; taking Mrs. Dickens and her sister with me, that time; then coming back here, picking up my caravan, starting off to Paris, and remaining there a month or so, before I return to England. What do you think of that?

Now is it not a pity that Maclise don't come here straightway, and see all this along with me? I feel that it would be of immense service to him; and the delight to me would be, of course, unspeakable. I believe that in his heart he thinks so too; but there never lived a man who had such extraordinary difficulty in making up his mind *to anything,* as he has. I have observed indecision in many and divers men; but never in any one to one hundredth part of the extent to which it exists in him. Do pour a broadside into him, dear Count D'Orsay. You have great influence with him. Stir him up with a pole as long as that dress cane you once gave me; and let us see if one of the eighteen spare beds in the Peschiere cannot be tenanted by an R.A.

I am disgusted with the Fine Arts Commission—by the way, the frescoes in the Peschiere were reported to them as among the finest in Italy. I think their putting Maclise anywhere but at the very head and front of the Competitors, abominable.[5] And I think the terms on which their designs are to be sent in, are disgraceful to the Commissioners as gentlemen—disgraceful to the selected artists, as men of talent—and disgraceful to the country in which the paltry, huckstering piece of power is exercised. If I were one of the exhibitors, I would see the New Houses of Parliament blown up higher than ever the old ones were like to have been, before I would coin the smallest corner of my brain for their service. A word in your ear, my dear Count D'Orsay. Do you think that when they were placing the artists, Rogers had any recollection of—the faintest and dimmest pleasure of memory in—a certain little pen and ink likeness of himself, once published in Frazer's Magazine?[6] God forgive me. But I shrewdly suspect that too smooth head of his, I swear!

What a sad place Italy is! a country gone to sleep, and without a prospect of waking again! I never shall forget, as long as I live, my first impressions of it, as I drove through the streets of Genoa, after contemplating the splendid View of the town, for a full hour, through a telescope, from the deck of the steamboat. I thought that of all the mouldy, dreary, sleepy, dirty, lagging, halting, God-forgotten towns in the wide world, it surely must be the very uttermost superlative. It seemed as if one had reached the end of all things—as if there were no more progress, motion, advancement, or improvement of any kind beyond; but here the whole scheme had stopped centuries ago, never to move on any more, but just lying down in the sun to bask there, 'till the Day of Judgment.

I have a great interest in it now; and walk about, or ride about, the town when I go there, in a dreamy sort of way, which is very comfortable. I seem to be thinking, but

I don't know what about—I haven't the least idea. I can sit down in a church, or stand at the end of a narrow Vico, zig-zagging uphill like a dirty snake: and not feel the least desire for any further entertainment. Just in the same way, I lie down on the rocks in the evening, staring the blue water out of countenance; or stroll up the narrow lanes, and watch the lizards running up and down the walls (so slight and fast, that they always look like the shadows of something else, passing over the stones) and diving into their holes so suddenly that they leave bits of their tails hanging out, and don't know it. I never knew what it was to be lazy, before.—I should think a dormouse was in very much the same condition before he goes under the wool in his cage—or a tortoise before he buries himself. I feel that I am getting rusty.—I should creak when I tried to think, if it were not for some feeble efforts I am making to acquire the language: each one a tiny drop of oil upon my hinges: and the only oil they ever get.

Were you ever at Lyons? *That's* the place. It's a great Nightmare—a bad conscience—a fit of indigestion—the recollection of having done a murder. An awful place! I made a good mistake there, at which I used to laugh afterwards; before I had lost the strength of mind which laughing requires. There is a curious clock in the cathedral—I dare say you have seen it. At all events, it is covered at the top with little doors, and when the Sacristan gets inside and sets the works a going, the doors fly open, one after another, and little scriptural images bolt out suddenly, and retire again; while some shrill little bells exert themselves to the utmost. One of these doors flying open, disclosed the Virgin Mary—with a very blunt nose, like the hangman in Punch's Show. She hadn't sat there long when another little door, after trying to open itself a great many times (you know the queer, jerking manner of clockwork) flew wide open all at once, and disclosed a little doll with Wings, who dived out with surpassing suddenness, and at sight of the Virgin instantly dived in again, while its little street-door shut up of itself, with a bang. "Aha!" said I. "Yes, Yes—The Devil, of course. We have very soon settled *his* business".—"The Devil!" said the Sacristan, looking out of the clock, pale with horror. "The Angel Gabriel Monsieur! The Annunciation Monsieur!" Which it seemed (to my great confusion) had actually been represented.

My dear Count D'Orsay, I am afraid this is the rustiest of letters, but blame Italy for it. Not me. I shall look to hear from you, or Lady Blessington, most eagerly. My most cordial and sincere regards to her. She cannot think how sorry she made me, by her heartiness and interest at parting—and yet how very glad, at the same time. Remember me, very cordially, to Miss Power and her sister. And believe me with the sincerest regard

Always Faithfully Your friend
CHARLES DICKENS

What Portraits are you painting? What figures are you modelling? Has that libellous artist—I am still strong on that point: feeble as I have become—finished his slander on Miss Power?

P.S. Address to the Poste Restante. The Albaro postman gets drunk—loses letters—and goes down on his knees in sober repentance. Poste Restante, Genoa.

1 Alfred, Count D'Orsay (1801–52†), artist and dandy, acted as host of Lady Blessington's fashionable though bohemian salon at Gore House, Piccadilly. The couple's affair was common knowledge.
2 Marguerite, Countess of Blessington (1789–1849†), hostess and author. Her niece Marguerite Power lived at Gore House with her.
3 The Palace of the Marchese Pallavicini, within the walls of Genoa; known as the Peschiere from the fishponds which were a feature of its gardens.
4 Livorno.
5 The Fine Arts Commissioners had prescribed subjects for frescoes in the new House of Lords. Six artists (including Maclise) were chosen to submit sketches, but the subjects were also open to general competition.
6 Rogers was the subject of one of Maclise's caricatures, 'The Gallery of Illustrious Literary Characters', *Fraser's*, Sept. 1830.

To Clarkson Stanfield, 24 AUGUST 1844

Albaro Saturday Night Twenty Fourth August 1844

My Dear Stanfield. I love you so truly, and have such pride and joy of heart in your friendship, that I don't know how to begin writing to you. When I think how you are walking up and down London in that portly surtout, and can't receive proposals from Dick to go to the theatre, I fall into a state between laughing and crying, and want some friendly back to smite.—"Je-im! Aye aye your honor",—is in my ears every time I walk upon the seashore here; and the number of expeditions I make into Cornwall,[1] in my sleep—the springs of flys I break, the songs I sing, and the bowls of punch I drink—would soften a heart of stone.

We have had weather here since five o'Clock this morning, after your own heart. Suppose yourself the admiral in Black Eyed Susan[2]—after the acquittal of William, and when it was feasible to be on friendly terms with him.—I am T.P.[3] My trousers are very full at the ankles—my black neck kerchief is tied in the regular style—the name of my ship is painted round my glazed hat.—I have a red waistcoat on—and the seams of my blue jacket are "paid"[4]—permit me to dig you in the ribs, when I make use of this nautical expression—with white. In my left hand I hold the baccy box, connected with the Story of Sandomingerbilly.[5] I lift up my eyebrows as far as I can (on the T.P. model) take a quid from the box—screw the lid on again (chewing at the same time, and looking pleasantly at the pit)—brush it with my right elbow—cock up my right leg—scrape my right foot on the ground—hitch up my trousers—and in reply to a question of yours: namely "Indeed! What weather, William?" deliver myself as follows:

Lord love your honor! Weather!! Such weather as would set all hands to the pumps aboard one of your fresh water cockboats, and set the purser to his wits' ends to stow away for the use of the Ship's company, the casks and casks full of blue water as would come powering in over the gunnel! The dirtiest night, your honor, as ever you see 'atween Spithead at Gunfire and the Bay of Biscay! The wind Sou West, and your Honor dead in the wind's eye; the breakers running high upon the rocky beach—the light 'us no more looming through the fog, than Davey Jones's sarser eye through the blue sky of Heaven in a calm, or the blue toplights of your Honor's lady, cast down in a modest overhauling of her catheads,—avast!" (whistling) "my dear eyes here am I a goin, head-on, to the breakers!" (bowing)

Admiral (smiling)—"No William! I admire plain-speaking as you know. And so does old England William, and old England's Queen. But you were saying—"

William. "Aye aye your Honor—I", (scratching his head) "I've lost my reckoning. Damme!—I ast pardon—but won't your honor throw a hencoop, or any ould end of towline to a man as is overboard?"

Admiral. (smiling still) "You were saying, William, that the wind—"

William. (again cocking up his leg and slapping the thigh very hard) "Avast heaving your honor! I see your honor's signal fluttering in the breeze, without a glass! As I was a saying, your honor, the wind a blowin from the Sou West—due Sou West your honor: not a pint to Larboard nor a pint to Starboard—the clouds a gatherin in the distance, for all the world like Beachey Head in a fog—the sea a rowling in, in heaps of foam, and running higher than the mainyard arm—the craft a scuddin by, all taught and under storms'els, for the harbor—not a blessed star a twinklin out aloft— aloft, your honor, in the little Cherub's Native Country—and the spray a flying like the white foam from Jolly's lips, when Poll of Portsea took him for a tailor!" (laughs)

Admiral (laughing also) "You have described it well, William, and I thank you. But who are these!"

(Enter Supers—in calico jackets to look like cloth—some in brown holland petticoat trousers and big boots, all in belts with very large buckles. Last Super rolls on a cask and pretends to tap it. Other supers apply tin mugs to the bunghole, and drink—previously holding them upside down.)

William (after shaking hands with everybody) "Who are these your Honor! Mess mates as staunch and true as ever broke biscuit. An't you my lads!"

All. "Aye aye William. That we are. That we are!"

Admiral. (much affected) "Oh England! What wonder that—! But I will no longer detain you from your sports my humble friends" (Admiral speaks very loud, and looks hard at the orchestra this being the cue for the dance)—"from your sports my humble friends. Farewell!"

All. Hurrah! Hurrah! (Exit Admiral)

(*Voice behind*) Suppose the dance, Mr. Stanfield. Are you all ready? Go—then!

My dear Stanfield, how I wish you would come this way, and see me in the Palazzo Peschiere! Was ever man so welcome as I would make you! What a truly gentlemanly action it would be, to bring Mrs. Stanfield—and the baby! and how Kate and her sister would wave pocket handkerchiefs from the Wharf, in joyful welcome! Ah, what a glorious proceeding!

Do you know this place? Of course you do. I won't bore you with anything about it, for I know Forster reads my letters to you; but *what* a place it is! The views from the hills here, and the immense variety of prospects of the sea, are as striking, I think, as such Scenery can be. Above all, the approach to Genoa, by sea from Marseilles, constitutes a Picture which you ought to paint; for nobody else can ever do it! Villain! You made that bridge at Avignon, better than it is.[6] Beautiful as it undoubtedly is, you made it fifty times better. And if I were Morrison,[7] or one of that school (bless the dear fellows one and all!) I wouldn't stand it, but would insist on having another picture gratis, to atone for the imposition.

The night is like a seaside night in England, towards the end of September. They say it is the prelude to clear weather. But the wind is roaring now, and the sea is raving, and the rain is driving down, as if they had all set in for a real hearty pic nic, and each had brought its own contribution to the general festivity. I don't know whether you are acquainted with the Coast Guard men in these parts? They are extremely civil fellows, of a very amiable manner and appearance, but the most innocent men, in matters you would suppose them to be well acquainted with, in virtue of their office: that I ever encountered. One of them asked me, only yesterday, if it would take a Year to get to England in a ship. Which I thought for a Coast Guard man was rather a tidy question.—It would take a long time to catch a ship going there, if he were on board a pursuing cutter though. I think he would scarcely do it in twelve months, indeed.

Forster told me, in a letter I received from him yesterday, of your mistake at the Parthenon, in respect of that marvellous likeness of Liston.[8] I laughed immoderately. He gave me an admirable description of the scene; and when I recollected the laborious manner in which I had impressed the fact of the strong resemblance upon you, in that very room—and the courteous, Academical sympathy for my uneducated eye, with which you had conceded—"Well! he *is* like him Dick"—I grinned from ear to ear. So you were at Astley's[9] t'other night! "Now Mr. Stickney Sir! what can I come for to go for to do, for to bring, for to fetch, for to carry for you Sir?"—"He he he! Oh! I say Sir!"—"Well Sir?"—"Miss Woolford knows me Sir. She laughed at me!"—I see him run away after this;—not on his feet, but on his knees and the calves of his legs alternately —and that smell of sawdusty horses, which was never in any other place in the world, salutes my nose with painful distinctness.

What do you think of my suddenly finding myself a Swimmer? But I have really made the discovery; and skim about a little blue bay just below the house here, like a fish in high spirits. I hope to preserve my bathing dress for your inspection and approval—or possibly to enrich your collection of Italian Costumes—on my return. Do you recollect Yarnold in Massaniello?[10] I find that I unintentionally "dress at him", before plunging into the sea. I enhanced the likeness very much last Friday Morning, by singing a barcarole on the rocks. I was a trifle too flesh-coloured (the stage knowing no medium between bright salmon, and dirty yellow); but apart from that defect, not badly made up, by any means.

I see in Galignani,[11] that a Public dinner is to be given to Mr. Bunn. It is a great mortification to me, not to be in England; that I might have the honor and gratification of enrolling my name in the list of stewards, and humbly testifying by that action and by my poor presence at the Festival, my sympathy with, and admiration for, a public servant, who, as a gentleman, a manager, a man: and considered either as a public or a private Individual; has no parallel in the country which claims him for her son. When I see such honors paid to this distinguished gentleman, whose speech, whose life, and whose every proceeding in every capacity, so justly entitle him to that meed of public approbation which he has so well earned, I feel, indeed that the regeneration of the Drama is at hand; and that its golden age (or it may be, brazen; at this distance the metals resemble each other, very nearly) has not departed from our happy shores. If you think Lord Glengall likely to buy this, for his speech, I will take five guineas for it, and subscribe the Sum to the Society for the Propagation of the Gospel in Foreign Parts.

When you write to me, my dear Stanny; as I hope you will soon; address, Poste Restante Genoa. I remain out here until the end of September, and send in for my letters daily. There *is* a Postman for this place, but he gets drunk and loses the letters; after which he calls to say so, and to fall upon his knees—which is affecting, but not satisfactory. About three weeks ago, I caught him at a Wine shop near here; playing bowls in the garden. It was then about five o'Clock in the afternoon; and he had been airing a newspaper addressed to me, since 9 o'Clock in the Morning.

Kate and Georgina unite with me in most cordial remembrances to Mrs. and Miss Stanfield, and to all the children; who I hope are well and thriving. They particularize all sorts of messages, but I tell them they had better write themselves if they want to send any. Though I don't know that their writing would end in the safe deliverance of those commodities after all; for when I began this letter, I meant to give utterance to all kinds of heartiness, my dear Stanfield; and I come to the end of it without having said anything more than that I am—which is new to you—under every circumstance and everywhere

Your most affectionate friend
CHARLES DICKENS

1 See above, 31 Dec. 1842.
2 Douglas Jerrold's highly successful play.
3 Thomas Potter ('Tippy') Cooke (1786–1864†), actor. Had been in the navy and excelled in sailor roles, notably Sweet William in *Black-Eyed Susan*.
4 Smeared with pitch or tar to make waterproof.
5 St Domingo Billy, the shark who swallowed tobacco-boxes in *Black-Eyed Susan*. Many phrases in the following dialogue recall the play.
6 Stanfield exhibited *Avignon on the Rhone* in 1840 and *The Bridge at Avignon* in 1848.
7 James Morrison (1789–1857†), wealthy merchant, politician, and art collector.
8 Lord Morpeth humorously acknowledged his remarkable likeness to the actor John Liston in CD's presence.
9 Astley's Amphitheatre, the circus visited by the Nubbles family, *OCS* ch. 39. Stickney was the ringmaster and Miss Woolford the chief equestrienne.
10 Yarnold was an actor in Macready's company at Covent Garden and the Lyceum. He played the hero's friend Moreno in Auber's opera *Masianello*, with bare arms and a striped shirt.
11 *Galignani's Messenger*, a daily English newspaper with extracts from the London press, published in Paris.

To John Forster, [?30 SEPTEMBER 1844]

Let me tell you of a curious dream I had, last Monday night; and of the fragments of reality I can collect, which helped to make it up. I have had a return of rheumatism in my back, and knotted round my waist like a girdle of pain; and had laid awake nearly all that night under the infliction, when I fell asleep and dreamed this dream. Observe that throughout I was as real, animated, and full of passion as Macready (God bless him!) in the last scene of Macbeth. In an indistinct place, which was quite sublime in its indistinctness, I was visited by a Spirit. I could not make out the face, nor do I recollect that I desired to do so. It wore a blue drapery, as the Madonna might in a picture by Raphael; and bore no resemblance to any one I have known except in stature. I think (but I am not sure) that I recognized the voice. Anyway, I knew it was poor Mary's spirit. I was not at all afraid, but in a great delight, so that I wept very much, and stretching out my arms to it called it "Dear." At this, I thought it recoiled; and I felt immediately, that not being of my gross nature, I ought not to have addressed it so familiarly. "Forgive me!" I said. "We poor living creatures are only able to express ourselves by looks and words. I have used the word most natural to *our* affections; and you know my heart." It was so full of compassion and sorrow for me—which I knew spiritually, for, as I have said, I didn't perceive its emotions by its face—that it cut me to the heart; and I said, sobbing, "Oh! give me some token that you have really visited me!" "Form a wish," it said. I thought, reasoning with myself: "If I form a selfish wish, it will vanish." So I hastily discarded such hopes and anxieties of my own as came into my mind, and said, "Mrs. Hogarth is surrounded with great distresses"—observe, I never thought of saying "your mother" as to a mortal creature—"will you extricate her?" "Yes." "And her extrication is to be a certainty to me, that this has really happened?" "Yes." "But answer me one other question!" I said, in an agony of entreaty lest it should leave me. "What is the True religion?" As it paused a moment without replying, I said—Good God, in such an agony of haste, lest it should go away!—"You think, as I do, that the Form of religion does not so greatly matter, if we try to do good?—or," I said, observing that it still hesitated, and was moved with the greatest compassion for me, "perhaps the Roman Catholic is the best? perhaps it makes one think of God oftener, and believe in him more steadily?" "For *you*," said the Spirit, full of such heavenly tenderness for me, that I felt as if my heart would break; "for *you*, it is the best!" Then I awoke, with the tears running down my face, and myself in exactly the condition of the dream. It was just dawn. I called up Kate, and repeated it three or four times over, that I might not unconsciously make it plainer or stronger afterwards. It was exactly this. Free from all hurry, nonsense, or confusion, whatever. Now, the strings I can gather up, leading to this, were three. The first you know, from the main subject of my last letter. The second was, that there is a great altar in our bedroom, at which some family who once inhabited this palace had mass performed in old time: and I had observed within myself, before going to bed, that there was a mark in the wall, above the sanctuary, where a religious picture used to be; and I had wondered within myself what the subject might have been, *and what the face was like*. Thirdly, I had been listening to the convent bells (which ring at intervals in the night), and so had thought, no doubt, of Roman Catholic services. And yet, for all this, put the case of that wish being fulfilled by any agency in which I had no hand; and I wonder whether I should regard it as a dream, or an actual Vision!

1 CD wrote to Forster on 23 Sept. with commissions in regards to his wife's family. This was the first time CD dreamed of Mary since Feb. 1838 and he refers to it in his letter to Thomas Stone, 2 Feb. 1851; see below.

To John Forster, [8 OCTOBER 1844]

He so missed his long night-walks that he seemed dumbfounded without them. I can't help thinking of the boy in the school-class whose button was cut off by Walter Scott and his friends.[1] Put me down on Waterloo-bridge at eight o'clock in the evening, with leave to roam about as long as I like, and I would come home, as you know, panting to go on. I am sadly strange as it is, and can't settle. You will have lots of hasty notes from me while I am at work: but you know your man; and whatever strikes me, I shall let off upon you as if I were in Devonshire-terrace. It's a great thing to have my title, and see my way how to work the bells. Let them clash upon me now from all the churches and convents in Genoa, I see nothing but the old London belfry I have set them in.[2] In my mind's eye, Horatio. I like more and more my notion of making, in this little book, a great blow for the poor. Something powerful, I think I can do, but I want to be tender too, and cheerful; as like the Carol in that respect as may be, and as unlike it as such a thing can be. The duration of the action will resemble it a little, but I trust to the novelty of the machinery to carry that off; and if my design be anything at all, it has a grip upon the very throat of the time.

1 Scott recounts supplanting the boy who always came top by, 'in an evil moment', cutting off the waistcoat button with which the boy 'always fumbled with his fingers' when asked a question. Without the button, the boy 'stood confounded', and never did well thereafter. 'Poor fellow! I believe he is dead; he took early to drinking.' J. G. Lockhart, *Memoirs of the Life of Sir Walter Scott* (Edinburgh: Robert Cadell, 1837), 1, 94.
2 Described at the opening of *TC*.

To Catherine Dickens, 8 NOVEMBER 1844

Parma. Albergo Della Posta. Friday November Eighth 1844.

My Dearest Kate. "If Missis could see us to-night, what would she say!"—That was the brave C's[1] remark last night at Midnight; and he had reason. We left Genoa, as you know, soon after 5 on the evening of my departure; and in company with the lady whom you saw, and the Dog whom I don't think you did see—travelled all night *at the rate of Four Miles an Hour*, over bad roads, without the least refreshment, until

Daybreak, when the Brave and myself escaped into a miserable Caffe while they were changing horses, and got a cup of that drink, hot. That same day a few hours afterwards—between 10 and 11, we came to (I hope) the damndest Inn in the world, where, in a vast chamber, rendered still more desolate by the presence of a most offensive specimen of what D'Israeli calls The Mosaic Arab (who had a beautiful girl with him) I regaled upon a breakfast, almost as cold and damp and cheerless as myself. Then, in another coach, much smaller than a small fly, I was packed up with an old Padre, a Young Jesuit, a provincial avvocato, a private gentleman with a very red nose and a very wet brown umbrella, and the Brave C; and so went on again, at the same pace through the same Mud and Rain, until Four in the afternoon, when there was a place in the coupee (two indeed) which I took: holding that select compartment in company with a very ugly, but very agreeable Tuscan "Gent", who said "Gia" instead of "Si" and rung some other changes on this changing language, but with whom I got on very well: being extremely conversational. We were bound, as you know,—perhaps,—for Piacenza, but it was discovered that we couldn't get to Piacenza; and about 10 o'Clock at night we halted at a place called Stradella, where the Inn was a series of queer Galleries open to the night, with a great courtyard full of Waggons, and horses, and Veloceferi and what not, in the center. It was bitter cold and very wet; and we all walked into a bare room (Mine!) with two immensely broad beds on two deal dining tables—a third great empty table—the usual washing-stand tripod with a slop basin on it—and two chairs. And here we walked up and down for three quarters of an hour or so, while dinner, or supper, or whatever it was, was getting ready. This was set forth (by way of variety) in the old Priest's bedroom, which had two more immensely broad beds on two more deal dining-tables in it. The first dish was a cabbage boiled in a great quantity of rice and hot water: the whole flavored with cheese. I was so cold that I thought it comfortable: and so hungry that a bit of cabbage, when I found such a thing floating my way, charmed me. After that, we had a dish of very little pieces of Pork, fried: with pigs kidneys. After that, a fowl. After that, something very red and stringy, which I think was veal; and after that two tiny little new-born-baby-looking turkeys. Very red and very swollen. Fruit, of course, to wind up. And Garlic in one shape or another with every course. I made three Jokes at supper (to the immense delight of the company) and retired early. The brave brought in a bush or two, and made a fire: and after that, a glass of screeching hot brandy and water; that bottle of his, being full of brandy. I drank it at my leisure—undressed before the fire—and went into one of the beds. The brave reappeared about an hour afterwards, and went into the other; previously tying a pocket-handkerchief round and round his head in a strange fashion: and giving utterance to the sentiment with which this letter begins. At 5 this morning, we resumed our journey—still through mud and rain—and at about 11, arrived at Piacenza; where we fellow passengers took leave of one another in the most affectionate manner. As there was no coach on, 'till six at night—and as it was a very grim, despondent sort of place—and as I had had enough of Diligences for one while—I posted forward here, in the strangest carriages ever beheld, which we changed, when we changed horses. We arrived here before 6. The hotel is quite French. I have dined, very well, in my own room on the second floor; and it has two beds in it, screened off from the room by drapery. I only use one tonight; and that is already made.

I purpose posting on to Bologna, if I can arrange it, at 12 tomorrow: seeing the sights here, first. If there be a Mail from Bologna to Venice, and it serves my time, I will write you again on my arrival at the latter place. You *may* not have that letter before you leave for Milan. But we will take our chance of it.

My dear Kate, be very careful if no opportunity occur for Susan's[2] leaving Genoa before you come to Milan, that you set aside every little consideration, and bring her with you. Remember how much we owe to Macready, and to Mrs. Macready too, for their constancy to us when we were in such great anxiety about the Darlings;[3] and do not let any natural dislike to her inanities, interfere in the slightest degree with an obligation so sacred. You are too easily run away with—and Georgy is too—by the irritation and displeasure of the moment, in such a case. Far too easily, for the lasting honorable and just remembrance of such a bond; and I was pained to see (as I should have told Georgy before I left if I had had an opportunity) that in such a case as the Messages to Forster (she will know what I mean) she does a glaringly foolish and unnecessary silliness, and places huge means of misrepresentation in very willing hands. I should never forgive myself or you, if the smallest drop of coldness or misunderstanding were created between me and Macready, by means so monstrously absurd. And mind what I say. It will be created—I see it very clearly—unless you are as careful with that girl as if you were treading on hot ploughshares; and unless you are something more tender too. I am sure her presence at the Peschiere during the past month, has worried nobody more than me. I am sure her presence at our short reunion at Milan would be a positive grievance to me. But I do hold hospitality, even when there is no other tie upon it, to be so high a thing, that I spare even Fletcher, when I am tempted to "put him down". And do, for God's sake, look beyond the hour into six or twelve months hence. Say I beg to be remembered kindly to her; and whether she leaves you, or not, have it understood that you intended to bring her to Milan. And observe. *I positively object, and say No, to her going to Rome under the protection of any entire stranger. I cannot allow it to be, until I have seen Macready.* I have thought of this, very much.

It is dull work, this travelling alone. My only comfort is, in Motion. I look forward with a sort of shudder to Sunday, when I shall have a day to myself in Bologna; and I think I must deliver my letters in Venice, in sheer desperation. Never did anybody want a companion after dinner (to say nothing of after supper) so much as I do.

There has been Music on the landing outside my door to night. Two violins and a violincello. One of the violins played a Solo; and the others, struck in, as an orchestra does now and then—very well. Then he came in, with a small tin platter. "Bella Musica!" said I. "Bellissima Musica Signore. Mi piace Multissimo." "Sono Felici Signore!" said he. I gave him a franc. "E multissimo generoso. Tanto generoso Signore!"

It was a joke to laugh at, when I was learning, but I swear that unless I could stagger on, Zoppa-wise,[4] with the people, I verily believe I should turn back, this morning.

In all other respects, I think the entire change has done me service—undoubted service, already. I am free of the Book: and am red-faced;[;] and feel marvellously disposed to sleep.

So for all the straggling qualities of this straggling letter, want [of sleep] must be responsible. Give my best love to Georgy, and my paternal blessing to

Mamey

Katey

Charley

Walley

and

Chickenstalker.

Ever My Dearest | Yours with true affection

CHARLES DICKENS

P.S. Keep things in their places. I can't bear to picture them otherwise.

P.P.S. I *think* I saw Roche sleeping with his head on the lady's shoulder—in the coach. I couldn't swear it, and the light was deceptive. But I think I did.

1 CD's courier, 'my right hand', Louis Roche.
2 Mrs Macready's sister.
3 Macready had reassured CD and Catherine by making himself responsible for their children during CD's American trip.
4 Haltingly, from the Italian for lame.

To John Forster, [12 NOVEMBER 1844, Venice]

I began this letter, my dear friend, with the intention of describing my travels as I went on. But I have seen so much, and travelled so hard (seldom dining, and being almost always up by candle light), that I must reserve my crayons for the greater leisure of the Peschiere after we have met, and I have again returned to it. As soon as I have fixed a place in my mind, I bolt—at such strange seasons and at such unexpected angles, that the brave C stares again. But in this way, and by insisting on having everything shewn to me whether or no, and against all precedents and orders of proceeding, I get on wonderfully.

I must not anticipate myself. But, my dear fellow, nothing in the world that ever you have heard of Venice, is equal to the magnificent and stupendous reality. The wildest visions of the Arabian Nights are nothing to the piazza of Saint Mark, and the first impression of the inside of the church. The gorgeous and wonderful reality of Venice is beyond the fancy of the wildest dreamer. Opium couldn't build such a place, and enchantment couldn't shadow it forth in a vision. All that I have heard of it, read of it in truth or fiction, fancied of it, is left thousands of miles behind. You know that I am liable to disappointment in such things from over-expectation, but Venice is above, beyond, out of all reach of coming near, the imagination of a man. It has never been rated high enough. It is a thing you would shed tears to see. When I came *on board* here last night (after a five miles' row in a gondola; which somehow or other, I wasn't at all prepared for); when, from seeing the city lying, one light, upon the distant water, like a ship, I came plashing through the silent and deserted streets; I felt as if the houses were reality—the water, fever-madness. But when, in the bright, cold, bracing day, I stood upon the piazza this morning, by Heaven the glory of the place was insupportable! And diving down from that into its wickedness and gloom—its awful prisons, deep below the water; its judgment chambers, secret doors, deadly nooks, where the torches you carry with you blink as if they couldn't bear the air in which the frightful scenes were acted; and coming out again into the radiant, unsubstantial Magic of the town; and diving in again, into vast churches, and old tombs—a new sensation, a new memory, a new mind came upon me. Venice is a bit of my brain from this time.[1] My dear Forster, if you could share my transports (as you would if you were here) what would I not give! I feel cruel not to have brought Kate and Georgy; positively cruel and base. Canaletti and Stanny,[2] miraculous in their truth. Turner, very noble. But the reality itself, beyond all pen or pencil. I never saw the thing before that I should be afraid to describe. But to tell what Venice is, I feel to be an impossibility. And here I sit alone, writing it: with nothing to urge me on, or goad me to that estimate, which, speaking of it to anyone I loved, and being spoken to in return, would lead me to form. In the sober solitude of a famous inn; with the great bell of Saint Mark ringing twelve at my elbow; with three arched windows in my room (two stories high) looking down upon the Grand Canal and away, beyond, to where the sun went down to-night in a blaze; and thinking over again those silent speaking faces of Titian and Tintoretto; I swear (uncooled by any humbug I have seen) that Venice is *the* wonder and the new sensation of the world! If you could be set down in it, never having heard of it, it would still be so. With your foot upon its stones, its pictures before you, and its history in your mind, it is something past all writing of or speaking of—almost past all thinking of. You couldn't talk to me in this room, nor I to you, without shaking hands and saying "Good God my dear fellow, have we lived to see this!"

1 Writing to Jerrold from Cremona about Venice four days later, CD emphasized the contradictions: 'Dreamy, beautiful, inconsistent, impossible, wicked, shadowy, damnable old place.' He criticized those 'who will declaim to you in speech and print by the hour together, on the degeneracy of the times in which a Railroad is building across the Water to Venice! Instead of going down upon their knees, the drivellers, and thanking Heaven that they live in a time when Iron makes Roads instead of Prison Bars, and engines for driving screws into the skulls of innocent men' (16 Nov. 1844).
2 Clarkson Stanfield painted many pictures of Venice.

To Catherine Dickens, 2 DECEMBER 1844

Piazza Coffee House, Covent Garden. | December Second 1844. Monday.

My Dearest Kate. I received, with great delight, your *excellent* letter of this morning. Do not regard this, as my answer to it. It is merely to say that I have been at Bradbury and Evans's all day, and have barely time to write more, than that I *will* write tomorrow. I arrived about 7 on Saturday Evening, and rushed into the arms of Mac and Forster—Both of whom, send their best loves to you and Georgy. With a heartiness, not to be described.

The little book, is now, so far as I am concerned, all ready. One cut of Doyle's,[1] and one of Leech's,[2] I found so unlike my idea, that I had them both to breakfast with me this morning, and with that winning manner which you know of, got them with the highest good humour, to do both afresh. They are now hard at it. Stanfield's readiness—delight—wonder at my being pleased—in what *he* has done is delicious. Mac's frontispiece is charming. The book is quite splendid,—the expences will be very great, I have no doubt.

Anybody who has heard it, has been moved in the most extraordinary manner. Forster read it (for dramatic purposes) to À Beckett[3]—not a man of very quiet feeling. He cried so much, and so painfully, that Forster didn't know whether to go on or stop; and he called next day to say that any expression of his feeling was beyond his power. But that he believed it, and felt it, to be—I won't say what.

As the reading comes off tomorrow night,[4] I had better not despatch my letter to you, until *Wednesday's* Post. I must close to save this (heartily tired I am; and I dine at Gore House today!) so with love to Georgy, Mamey, Katey, Charley, Walley, and Chickenstalker, Ever believe me Yours with true affection. CD.

P.S. If you had seen Macready last night—undisguisedly sobbing, and crying on the sofa, as I read—you would have felt (as I did) what a thing it is to have Power.

P.P.S. "In[".][5]

1　Richard Doyle (1824–83†), illustrator and watercolour painter, designed the opening of each quarter of *TC*.
2　John Leech (1817–64†), humorous artist and illustrator. Chief cartoonist for *Punch*; provided illustrations for CD's Christmas books and was sole illustrator of *CC*. Friendly with CD; their families often holidayed together.
3　CD apparently authorized the dramatization of *TC* by Gilbert À Beckett and Mark Lemon, which was put on at the Adelphi two days after the book's publication.
4　Forster describes CD's reading of *TC*, which was sketched by Maclise, see Forster, 363.
5　A tear has removed several letters; perhaps CD wrote 'Inimitable!'

To John Forster, [? AUGUST–DECEMBER 1844, Genoa]

We are very sorry to lose the benefit of his advice[1]—or, as my father would say, to be deprived, to a certain extent, of the concomitant advantages, whatever they may be, resulting from his medical skill, such as it is, and his professional attendance, in so far as it may be so considered.

1 The physician Sir James Murray. John Dickens's style of speech is a model for Mr Micawber in *DC*.

To John Forster, [?30–1 DECEMBER 1844, Genoa]

ARE we to have that play??? Have I spoken of it, ever since I came home from London, as a settled thing! I do not know if I have ever told you seriously, but I have often thought, that I should certainly have been as successful on the boards as I have been between them. I assure you, when I was on the stage at Montreal (not having played for years) I was as much astonished at the reality and ease, to myself, of what I did as if I had been another man. See how oddly things come about! When I was about twenty, and knew three or four successive years of Mathews's At Homes[1] from sitting in the pit to hear them, I wrote to Bartley who was stage manager at Covent-garden, and told him how young I was, and exactly what I thought I could do; and that I believed I had a strong perception of character and oddity, and a natural power of reproducing in my own person what I observed in others. There must have been something in the letter that struck the authorities, for Bartley wrote to me, almost immediately, to say that they were busy getting up the Hunchback (so they were!) but that they would communicate with me again, in a fortnight. Punctual to the time, another letter came: with an appointment to do anything of Mathews's I pleased, before him and Charles Kemble, on a certain day at the theatre. My sister Fanny was in the secret, and was to go with me to play the songs. I was laid up, when the day came, with a terrible bad cold and an inflammation of the face; the beginning, by the bye, of that annoyance in one ear to which I am subject at this day. I wrote to say so, and added that I would resume my application next season. I made a great splash in the gallery soon afterwards; the Chronicle opened to me; I had a distinction in the little world of the newspaper, which made me like it; began to write; didn't want money; had never thought of the stage, but as a means of getting it; gradually left off turning my thoughts that way; and never resumed the idea. I never told you this, did I? See how near I may have been, to another sort of life.

This was at the time when I was at Doctors' Commons as a shorthand writer for the proctors. And I recollect I wrote the letter from a little office I had there, where the answer came also. It wasn't a very good living (though not a *very* bad one), and was wearily uncertain; which made me think of the Theatre in quite a business-like way. I went to some theatre every night, with a very few exceptions, for at least three years: really studying the bills first, and going to where there was the best acting: and always to see Mathews whenever he played. I practised immensely (even such things as walking in and out, and sitting down in a chair): often four, five, six hours a day: shut up in my own room, or walking about in the fields. I prescribed to myself, too, a sort of Hamiltonian system for learning parts;[2] and learnt a great number. I haven't even lost the habit now, for I knew my Canadian parts immediately, though they were new to me. I must have done a good deal: for, just as Macready found me out, they used to challenge me at Braham's; and Yates, who was knowing enough in those things, wasn't to be parried at all. It was just the same, that day at Keeley's, when they were getting up the Chuzzlewit last June.

1 Charles Mathews (1776–1835†), actor, playwright, and comedian; his popular 'At Homes' were monologues laced with anecdotes, jokes, and songs.
2 James Hamilton (1769–1829†), teacher of languages, which he did 'by observation, not by rules'.

To [*Emile de la Rue*],[1] 15 JANUARY [1845, Genoa]

Wednesday January Fifteenth. Having been asleep some twenty minutes, I drew her into a conversation, as follows—occasionally with some little difficulty, and by dint of repeating the same question three or four times. "Well! where are you today? On the Hillside as usual?"—"Yes."—"Quite alone?"—"No."—"Are there many people there?"—"Yes. A good many." "Men, or women?"—"Both." "How they are dressed?"—"I can't see. I have too many things to look at."—"But you can tell me what they are doing. Can't you?"—"Yes. They are walking about, and talking."—"To you?"—"No. To each other."—"What are they saying?"—"I don't know."—"Try and find out"—"I am too busy."—"But not so busy that you can't listen to them, surely?"—"Yes I am. I have so many things to attend to."—"Are they a crowd?"— "Yes; quite a crowd."

Suddenly, she cried out, in great agitation. "Here's my brother! Here's my brother!"—and she breathed very quickly, and her figure became stiff. "Where? In the crowd?"—"No. In a room."—"Who is with him?"—"Nobody."—"What is he doing?"—"Leaning against a window: looking out. Oh he is so sad! He is so sad!"— shedding tears as she spoke, and shewing the greatest sympathy. "What Brother? The Brother I know?"—"No no. Not the Brother you know. Another."—"What is his name?"—"Charles. Oh how sad he is!"—"What makes him so?"—"I don't know, I don't know. I must try to find out."—"Watch the door, and perhaps somebody will come in"—"Yes yes, I will. I am very busy, looking. I am trying to see."

After a pause, I said:

"Well! Has anybody come in?"—"No. He is still alone."—"Leaning against the window?"—"No. Walking up and down the room."—"Still sad?"—"Oh! Very sad! What *can* make him so sad!"—"Tell me what you see through the window."—"No. I can't, I can't. I am looking at him."—"Yes. But look at the window too. I'm sure you will if I ask you. What do you see through the window? Fields?"—"No no. The sea."—"How is your brother dressed?"—"In his uniform."—"With a sword?"— "No."—"With a hat?"—"No."—"You will be sure to tell me, if anyone comes in?"— "Yes yes. But I am trying to find out what makes him so sad, poor fellow!"—still crying, and in great distress. After a time, she said, with increased agitation. "He is thinking of me!"—and after another interval, she cried that she had found out the reason of his despondency. That he thought himself forgotten. That the letters had miscarried, and he had not received them. Then she fell back in the chair, like one whose mind was relieved; and said it was gone and she saw him no more.

She said all this, with as much earnestness as if the scene had been actually present to her view; and spoke in the peculiar tone of voice which is natural to a person who watches intently, and is afraid of losing any glimpse of what is passing. She several times brushed her closed eyes with her hands, as if to wipe away her tears, and see him more distinctly.

I do not make any note of the other visions of today, on this paper; as they are incomplete. And I am very curious to see whether she resumes them tomorrow. It is sufficient to remark just now, that she always imagines herself lying on a hill-side with a very blue sky above, green grass about her, and a pleasant air stirring. That the sensation of pain, suggests to her the rolling of stones down this hill, by some unseen people: which she is much distressed in her endeavours to avoid: and which occasionally strike her. There is a man haunting this place—dimly seen, but heard talking sometimes—whom she is afraid of, and "dare not" look at. I connect it with the figure whom she calls her bad spirit; in consequence of her trembling very much, when I once asked her, lying on this imaginary hill, if that phantom were to be seen: when she implored me not to speak of him. She said today that this creature was talking of me; and at my request, she tried hard to overhear what he said. But "she couldn't make it all out", she complained, and suddenly added, "Don't go away upon a Monday. Be sure not to go away upon a Monday. It's not he who says that. *I* say it." Immediately afterwards, she complained of being tired, and begged me to awaken her.[2]

1 Emile de la Rue (d. 1870), Swiss banker resident in Genoa. These notes were made during one of the many sessions in which CD was mesmerizing de la Rue's English wife Augusta.
2 Followed by a flourish, such as CD uses to indicate 'finis' of a chapter.

To Emile de la Rue, 27 JANUARY 1845 [near Poderina]

La Scala, No 2 (for we were in another | place of the same name, the night | before last.)
Monday January 27th. 1845.

My Dear de la Rue.

Having disposed, in this very lone house, of a much better dinner than any reasonable person could have expected to find in such a place, I am going to bestow a little tediousness[1] on you. And I heartily wish you were "crackling" your very loudest in your own Palazzo, and I were writing it in my accustomed literary station in your drawing-room; instead of sitting (as I am) at the corner of an immense table, much larger than any table on which Billiards were ever played: with one very sharp corner forcing my centre waistcoat-button into my chest, and stamping a lively impression of it into my skin. Which is the only position in which I can find the least approach to warmth. In consequence of all the fire going up the chimney; and nothing of it coming into the room except the smoke.

I shall come to the subject which is nearest to my heart (and yours) last. As Hope stepped out of Pandora's box when all its stock of troubles was exhausted, so that topic shall shew itself from the depths of my letter, when other and less interesting matters are disposed of.

They are few enough. You know how gloomy it was, when we left Genoa, and you know how it rained next day. On reflection, I don't think anybody knows that, to the full extent, except myself, my wife, Roche and the Vetturino[2]—and the four horses: I had almost forgotten the horses. Perhaps because they were under water nearly all the way. Something wet and heavy—feeling, to the touch, like the toast out of a jug of toast and water—was put into the carriage by a postilion, after it was dark on that Monday night, and when we were within some four miles from Spezzia. It appeared, on examination, to be a letter from Fletcher, who had got wet through, in crossing the Magra[3] to meet us; and described himself as taking dinner in a blanket while his clothes were drying.

When we reached the Inn we found him in this state; very red and warm; and looking like a perfectly new-born baby, suddenly grown up. He had by that time taken two dinners; and on my ordering our own, he requested that a knife and fork might be placed for him—and so took a third. You recollect the dimensions (in round numbers) of his nose? Well! By the time he had finished this third dinner, his eyes protruded infinitely beyond the tip of that feature. You never saw such a human Prawn as he looked, in your life. When he retired to bed in a state of insensibility, I had the faintest expectation possible, of ever seeing him again, alive.

But he got through it, somehow or other, and turned up again at breakfast. He was soft and pulpy, all over: and much swollen. This last appearance subsided in course of time, and the Magra subsiding also, we got over it (not, as I thought, without some danger) on Tuesday afternoon. We remained with Mr. Walton until Thursday Morning—started for Pisa that day (taking him and Fletcher with us)—dined and slept at Pisa that night—climbed up the Leaning Tower next morning—took the Railroad to Leghorn that afternoon—and dined at Mr Gower's that Evening. Next day we started from Pisa, alone—slept at the other La Scala, that night—at Siena last night; where there is a very beautiful Cathedral, a picturesque Piazza, and a very quaint old town—and arrived here this evening, at Six. That is to say, Two Hours ago. It rained rather heavily in the night, last night. But since this day week, the weather has been fine and pleasant: though generally cool, and sometimes very cold.

Before I take up your Diary and read it over for the hundredth time; let me tell you what happened today. And if you think it will interest Madame De la Rue, pray read it to her: giving her, at the same time, something as near my love as you may feel disposed to deliver. I was on the Box of the Carriage; and, as usual, at Eleven by the Genoa time, composed myself for one hour's abstraction, in rigid pursuance of our agreement. Now, it happened that I was not alone, as it is my custom to be then; but that Mrs. Dickens had been hoisted up, to get the air. As I very often sit a long time without saying anything at all—when I am thinking, or when I am thinking

I am thinking—and as she is well used to it, I didn't mind her, but sat quite still and quiet. Observe.—I didn't move hand or foot. I engaged myself, in imagination, in mesmerizing our Patient; and my whole Being, for the time, was set upon it, certainly, with the greatest stedfastness. But it was impossible for anybody to know in what I was engaged, otherwise than that I was very intent on some subject. Will you believe me when I tell you that I had not remained thus, more than five or ten minutes, when I was disturbed by Mrs. Dickens' letting her muff fall. And *can* you believe me when I tell you that looking at her I found her, as I live! in the Mesmeric trance, with her eyelids quivering in a convulsive manner peculiar to some people in that state—her hands and feet suddenly cold—her senses numbed—and that on my rousing her, with some difficulty, and asking her what was the matter, she said she had been magnetized? She was so discomposed that it was necessary to put her into the carriage immediately; and she had a bad fit of trembling until the influence wore off.

No word had ever passed my lips in reference to my compact with Madame De La Rue. She was as utterly ignorant of it, as she is of any business-secret in your banking house. There is no possibility of any mistake or exaggeration in this. She is quite well, and has been ever since we left Genoa. Within five minutes of my shutting myself up within myself, I had been teaching her some Italian words; and I supposed her to be still engaged in conning them over, when this surprise occurred. It was really quite a fearful thing, and the strongest instance of the strange mysteries that are hidden within this power, that I have ever seen or heard of. Picture to yourself the stupendous difficulty of believing such a statement, if you read it in Print. Even imagine the difficulty of getting anybody to believe it, who knew the parties and could not doubt their veracity. Yet there can be nothing more true. For it is Truth itself. I have purposely stated it in the plainest manner, and have not presented it to you in anything like the remarkable aspect, in which it actually occurred.

Now, with reference to your Journal. Pray do not think you have put down too much, and pray do not depart from that system of writing it, as nothing could be more concise and intelligible. I cannot express to you the delight with which I read it, for with that strong trust in me on the part of Madame de la Rue—that most indubitable token of the strength of our position, and the power of the Magnetism— how can we despair of anything, or fail to hope for everything! Preserving that, and steadily increasing it (which is my desire and expectation) I do hope and believe that with God's leave the worst parts of her disorder will fall down prostrate, and be crushed the soonest, before it. If she were clairvoyant, or (to say the wildest thing I can think of) if she were omniscient, I should not value the wonder more than I do this gentle Trust of hers in my power to help her—I should not care for it, as a bright star of Hope, half so much. It is an assurance to me that the root of that Tree which shall peacefully shelter your Home for years to come, has struck deep into the Earth; and that the relief she has already experienced in her Mind is hardly to be estimated.

But this last assurance I have from herself. Set down in her own words, and not to be read with dry eyes. It is in that letter which you forwarded to me at Leghorn; and from it, I learn that her *mental* agony has been immensely beyond anything she has ever led you (on whom, she says, she could not bear to bring more sorrow than she could help: having already brought so much) to suppose. She speaks of that, as a thing past. She speaks, with confidence, of her nightly horrors as dreadful trials whose days were numbered—almost as trials already past. It is impossible to imagine the weight of the load she has begun to lay down in this respect, without the affecting knowledge of her grateful heart.

She has now no secret in connexion with the devilish figure; for that chain is utterly broken. That it bound her to the disease, and the disease to her, and that it must have linked her (she says so) in the course of time to Madness, I have no earthly doubt. I cannot yet quite make up my mind, whether the phantom originates in shattered nerves and a system broken by Pain; or whether it is the representative of some great nerve or set of nerves on which her disease has preyed —and begins to loose its hold now, because the disease of those nerves is itself attacked by the inexplicable agency of the Magnetism. I think upon the whole, I incline to this last opinion; but I could not make up my mind without more observation of, and more conversation with, herself. I should also like to discuss it, at full length, with you.

However this may be, what I want to impress upon you; and what your affection will, I know, readily see, is this. That figure is so closely connected with the secret distresses of her very soul—and the impression made upon it is so entwined with her confidence and trust in me, and her knowledge of the power of the Magnetism—*that it must not make head again.* From what I know from her, I know there is more danger and delay in one appearance of that figure than in a dozen fits of the severest bodily pain. Believe nothing she says of her capacity of endurance, if the reappearance of that figure should become frequent. Consult that, mainly, and before all other signs. I shudder at the very thought of the precipice on which she has stood, when that Fancy has persecuted her. If you find her beset by it, induce her to be got to me by one means or other; for there the danger lies so deep, that she herself can hardly probe it, even now.

My dear De la Rue, I have written, or have meant to write, very strongly on this point, for I hold her clue now, and am acquainted with its vast importance. This letter will cross your second, which is already, I hope, on its way to Rome. I will write to you, when I have heard from her and you at that place. I have come to the end of my paper, and to bed time, at the same moment. Very many thanks for your kindness to my pet little sister in law. Best remembrances from Mrs. Dickens. All cordial assurances of friendship and regard From Yours Heartily

CHARLES DICKENS

1 Cf. *Much Ado about Nothing*, III. v. 21–2.
2 One who drives a vettura, a four-wheeled carriage.
3 River in northern Italy.

To John Forster, [?EARLY JULY 1845]

I really think I have an idea, and not a bad one, for the periodical. I have turned it over, the last two days, very much in my mind: and think it positively good. I incline still to weekly; price three halfpence, if possible; partly original partly select; notices of books, notices of theatres, notices of all good things, notices of all bad ones; Carol philosophy, cheerful views, sharp anatomization of humbug, jolly good temper; papers always in season, pat to the time of year; and a vein of glowing, hearty, generous, mirthful, beaming reference in everything to Home, and Fireside. And I would call it, sir,—

THE CRICKET
A cheerful creature that chirrups on the Hearth.

Natural History.

Now, don't decide hastily till you've heard what I would do. I would come out, sir, with a prospectus on the subject of the Cricket that should put everybody in a good temper, and make such a dash at people's fenders and arm-chairs as hasn't been made for many a long day. I could approach them in a different mode under this name, and in a more winning and immediate way, than under any other. I would at once sit down upon their very hobs; and take a personal and confidential position with them which should separate me, instantly, from all other periodicals periodically published, and supply a distinct and sufficient reason for my coming into existence. And I would chirp, chirp, chirp away in every number until I chirped it up to —— well, you shall say how many hundred thousand! . . . Seriously, I feel a capacity in this name and notion which appears to give us a tangible starting-point, and a real, defined, strong, genial drift and purpose. I seem to feel that it is an aim and name which people would readily and pleasantly connect with *me*; and that, for a good course and a clear one, instead of making circles pigeon-like at starting, here we should be safe. I think the general recognition would be likely to leap at it; and of the helpful associations that could be clustered round the idea at starting, and the pleasant tone of which the working of it is susceptible, I have not the smallest doubt. . . . But you shall determine. What do you think? And what do you say? The chances are, that it will either strike you instantly, or not strike you at all. Which is it, my dear fellow? You know I am not bigoted to the first suggestions of my own fancy; but you know also exactly how I should use such a lever, and how much power I should find in it. Which is it? What do you say?—I have not myself said half enough. Indeed I have said next to nothing; but like the parrot in the negro-story, I "think a dam deal".

To Mr. Head,[1] 13 AUGUST 1845

Devonshire Terrace. | Wednesday Thirteenth August | 1845.

Mr. Head. I send you, on the other side, the names of the three other gentlemen who have decided to have their dresses made by you. And against their names, I have written their addresses, and the best time for measuring them. *Be very careful that the colors are bright; and that they will shew well by Lamplight.*

I enclose you three sketches, which express the figure of Bobadil,[2] as I wish to make up. The sword I have; and I do not want spurs. But I wish the tops of the boots, and the gauntlets, and the hat-brim, to be very large. And I want the boots, gauntlets, and hat, *first*—and as soon as convenient to you. Do not forget the sword-belt. I want that to come home at the same time as the boots and gauntlets.

I wish particularly to see the red, of which you propose to make Bobadil's breeches and hat. I want it to be a very gay, fierce, bright color.

You can send to me, either between 10 and 11 tomorrow morning, or between 6 and 8 tomorrow evening. But it must be tomorrow, as I am going out of town next day for four or five days. Send a pattern of the red, at the same time. I will give an old pair of gloves to the person whom you send, that you may know the size of my hands for the gauntlets.

If you do these dresses well, as I have no doubt you will, I think it will throw some good jobs into your way, another time. If you want your Messenger to see any of the other prints to refresh your memory, I will shew them to him.

Yours
CHARLES DICKENS

P.S. Take care of the sketches.

Over
Wellbred. Mr. Thompson, 35 Gloucester Road, Hyde Park Gardens. Best time for measuring this gentleman, I should think tomorrow before 12.

Cash. Mr. Augustus Dickens. This gentleman will call on you at the Theatre, between 4 and 5 on Friday afternoon, to be measured. His dress to be of cloth.

Young Knowell. Mr. Frederick Dickens. This gentleman will write you a note, on Monday, and tell you when he will call at the Theatre for the same purpose

---

Master Mathew. Mr. Leech, Brook Green Hammersmith. This gentleman can be measured at his house on Friday Morning

---

1 Theatrical costumier used by Macready.
2 CD took the part of Bobadil, a boastful but cowardly soldier, in Ben Jonson's *Every Man In His Humour*, performed by his amateur company at the St James's Theatre. C. R. Leslie's picture of him in this part is well known from a contemporary engraving.

To *Frederick Dickens*, 7 OCTOBER 1845

Devonshire Terrace. | Wednesday Evening | Seventh October 1845.

My Dear Fred.

I claim no right whatever to oppose your wishes.¹ You ask me for my counsel: and I give it you. I do not expect you to take it, nor shall I be in the least offended if you do not. But I would earnestly advise you not to be hasty in rejecting it.

So far as I know myself, I think I have some reason to suppose that I am not accustomed to take "stern" views of any subject. That it is not my nature in any case. And that if I had a tendency that way it would be very unlikely to beset me in reference to any matter nearly concerning *you*.

Marriage, with your income, is a very serious affair. Something on the lady's part, would certainly be desirable. But failing that, (on which I do not lay extraordinary stress, as the affections are not commonly regulated by the pocket) I do hold it very essential that the family with which you connect yourself should seem, in what one knows of them, to give you some sort of warrant for trusting in them as good, straight-forward, agreeable persons—pleasant to associate with, when their freshness has gone off—commonly discreet and rational in ordinary life—and such good governors of themselves in their sentiments, sympathies, antipathies, and what not, as to render them reasonably likely to stand the wear and tear of Home-test; which brings all metal to the proof in a very searching manner.

I do not think the Wellers are this kind of people. I want odd phrases to express my meaning when I think of them. Perhaps I cannot express myself better than by saying they are, in my opinion, an "impracticable family." They don't seem to me to have any ballast. They are very amiable, but especially uncomfortable. They are feverish, restless, flighty, excitable, uncontrollable, wrong-headed; under no sort of wholesome self-restraint; and bred to think the absence of it a very intellectual and brilliant thing. The presence of this flutter and fever in anybody's house—but especially in a poor man's, with the world before him—is not the presence that would make it comfortable, rich, or happy.

Anna is very young—surely *very* young. I grant her good looks. I grant her cleverness (I think very highly of it); but I doubt her quiet wisdom in the quiet life to which you must inevitably retreat. I doubt whether that "Soul" of which the family make such frequent mention, may not be something too expansive for a domestic parlor—a little too vague for the defined and marked-out tenor of your way. I doubt whether she be in a condition to know her own mind, or your mind, or anything else, with any sort of distinctness, or with any enduring perception. The world about her seems to be a Great Electrifying Machine, from which she gets all sorts of unaccountable shocks and knocks and starts; and it seems to me to be an open question whether she will ever be shocked and knocked and started into a reasonable woman.

You will say, very naturally and with good reason, that I may be wrong in this, and how do I know it? But I may say, at least as naturally and with no less reason, that *you* may be wrong in *your* estimate, and how do *you* know better. When I went away to Italy, she was a mere child. Consider. Have your opportunities been so very numerous or good, that you can pronounce with any sort of clearness, on the dawning character half developed in her, since. These things of which I speak, are on the surface: broadly open to all observers. Have you been able to see so far below it, as to find the quiet source of all these eddies and currents?

The change in Thompson's affairs has, very naturally, hurried you on, it seems to me. For it has disturbed you in your opportunities of intercourse with her, and driven you into the devising of some new occasions. But do you believe you are so much attached to her, that you cannot withdraw now, if you will? And do you believe that your Heart is already shut up against all other comers? I have nothing in my mind but your Happiness. If I thought your Happiness would be secured by this pursuit, I would encourage you at all hazards. But the little foibles of the Wellers seem to me as dangerous to domestic peace as many graver—infinitely graver— faults would be. And I should be wanting in that affection for which you give me credit (not, I can sincerely say, without as good reason as ever a Brother had; for my love for you has always been a strong and true and tender one) if I did not entreat you to be cautious—to avoid all rash conclusion—and to look steadily along the far perspective of weary years to which one hasty moment may conduct you: shutting out retreat.

I have assumed that Anna may reciprocate your attachment—that the father may approve of it—that the weakness of the mother may happen to stagger into your side of the balance—that the commercial arithmetic of Mr. Shaw may find no flaw in your proposals—that nobody's Soul may make your probation a wretched and uncertain one—but think of all these chances my dear Fred. And whatever you resolve on (for I see the resolution lies with you at last) come and tell me what it is. If I cannot dissuade you from your purpose, I may guide you in its execution.

Ever Yours affectionately
CHARLES DICKENS

---

1 Fred wished to marry Christiana Weller's 15-year-old sister Anna. On 4 Oct. CD wrote to Stanfield that he was 'engaged in some painful business' on behalf of Thomas Thompson, whose marriage plans with Christiana had been temporarily and inexplicably 'shattered'.

To *William Macready*, 17 OCTOBER 1845

Devonshire Terrace | Friday Evening | Seventeenth October 1845.

My Dear Macready.

You once (only once) gave the World assurance of a Waistcoat. You wore it Sir—I think in "Money".[1] It was a remarkable and precious Waistcoat wherein certain broad stripes of blue or purple, disported themselves as by a combination of extraordinary circumstances, too happy to occur again. I have seen it on your Manly chest in Private Life. I saw it, Sir, (I think) the other day, in the cold light of morning—with feelings easier to be imagined than described. Mr. Macready, Sir! Are you a father? If so, lend me that Waistcoat for five minutes. I am bidden to a wedding[2] (where fathers are made); and my artist cannot, I find (how should he?) imagine such a waistcoat. Let me shew it to him as a sample of my tastes and wishes; and—ha ha ha ha!—*Eclipse* the Bridegroom!

I will send a trusty Messenger at halfpast 9 precisely—in the Morning—He is sworn to secrecy—He durst not for his life betray us—or Swells in ambuscade would have the Waistcoat at the cost of his Heart's blood.

Thine
The Unwaistcoated One.

1 Macready played Evelyn in Bulwer Lytton's *Money* in 1840, with great success. Count D'Orsay designed the costumes.
2 Thomas Thompson and Christiana Weller were married at St Luke's Chelsea, 21 Oct.

To *Messrs Bradbury & Evans*, 30 JANUARY 1846

Devonshire Terrace | Friday Morning | Thirtieth January 1846.

My Dear Bradbury and Evans.

I cut the main subject of our conversation last night as short as possible, because I always desire to restrain myself from acting on impulse in any such case.

I quite agree with you in the necessity of the Paper[1] being made perfect, if possible, and in the expediency of finding out where it can be improved. On the other hand, I doubt your counsellors in general, very much indeed. I examine and test anyone who counsels me, very closely; and when it is such a man as Mr. Tooke[2] (of whom I spoke to you last night), I discard *his* advice altogether. But I have already told Mr. Paxton,[3] and I have already warned you, that very sensible and far-seeing gentlemen well accustomed to newspapers regard the Railway policy of the D.N. as being too one-sided, and as threatening to taint it. And I think if you could get beyond deposit men, and provisional directors, and committee men, and the like, you would find this out. I have very little doubt if you do not, that the Times will discover it for you.

This, however, is not the point of my letter.

You know that I recommended Mr. Powell to you, as the man, of all others in London, best qualified to act as one of the Sub Editors of an enterprising Paper. You know that I was very anxious to secure him, and considered it a very great point when he was engaged, and have always spoken of him with great confidence.

One week after the starting of the Paper, you come to me, and give me to understand, on certain nameless authority (which you call "gatherings") that he is quite unfit for the place he holds! I wish to know from whom you learn this: and I consider myself justified in putting you upon your honor to withhold from me the name of no person with whom you have taken counsel on this subject.

When I tell you, distinctly, that I shall leave the Paper immediately, if you do not give me this information, I think it but fair to add that it is extremely probable I shall leave it when you have done so. For it would be natural in any man, and is especially so in one in my position, to consider this, disrespectful, and quite unendurable. I am thoroughly disgusted, and shall act accordingly.

Faithfully Yours
CHARLES DICKENS

1 The *Daily News*, a new newspaper intended to be a Liberal rival of *The Times*. CD was briefly editor.
2 Thomas Tooke (1774–1858†), economist, free-trader, and writer on the currency, seems the more likely 'counsellor' for Bradbury & Evans. But CD's animus might suggest William Tooke (1777–1863†), solicitor and treasurer of the Royal Literary Fund.
3 Joseph Paxton (1803–65†), landscape gardener, architect, and designer of the 1851 Great Exhibition. Director of railway companies during the railway mania of 1845–6, he raised £25,000, half of the initial capital, to found the *Daily News* with Bradbury.

To Count D'Orsay, 24 APRIL 1846

Devonshire Terrace | Twenty Fourth April 1846.

My Dear Count D'Orsay.

I send you, for trial, half a dozen of the wine I spoke of. I have plenty more, if you like it. It is called the Zeller Wine,[1] and is perfectly pure and genuine. I bought it out of an enormous cask under the Town Hall at Offenburg; on the top of which Town Hall, there is an old, old Stork's nest, where the Storks, with their long legs, sit on a summer night, meditating or fly for a change to the neighbouring chimnies and sit there until it is too dark to see them. I have no doubt they improve the flavor of the wine, but I don't know how.

Ever Affectionately Yours
CHARLES DICKENS

1 i.e. Zeller-Baden: a red wine, kept in the wood and bottled as required.

To *Angela Burdett Coutts,* 26 MAY 1846

Devonshire Terrace | Twenty Sixth May 1846.

My Dear Miss Coutts.

I find those who are best acquainted with the subject and the class of persons to be addressed, decidedly in favor of the School and the Church[1] being *Free.* You may remember this to have been my impression at first, but I have not expressed any opinion of my own to those whom I have sounded on the subject.

In reference to the Asylum,[2] it seems to me very expedient that you should know, if possible, whether the Government would assist you to the extent of informing you from time to time into what distant parts of the World, women could be sent for marriage, with the greatest hope for their future families, and with the greatest service to the existing male population, whether expatriated from England or born there. If these poor women *could* be sent abroad with the distinct recognition and aid of the Government, it would be a service to the effort. But I have (with reason) a doubt of all Governments in England considering such a question in the light, in which men undertaking that immense responsibility, are bound, before God, to consider it. And therefore I would suggest this appeal to you, merely as something which you owe to yourself and to the experiment; the failure of which, does not at all affect the immeasurable goodness and hopefulness of the project itself.

I do not think it would be necessary, in the first instance at all events, to build a house for the Asylum. There are many houses, either in London or in the immediate neighbourhood, that could be altered for the purpose. It would be necessary to limit the number of inmates, but I would make the reception of them as easy as possible to themselves. I would put it in the power of any Governor of a London Prison to send an unhappy creature of this kind (by her own choice of course) straight from his prison, when her term expired, to the Asylum. I would put it in the power of any penitent creature to knock at the door, and say For God's sake, take me in. But I would divide the interior into two portions; and into the first portion I would put all new-comers without exception, as a place of probation, whence they should pass, by their own good-conduct and self-denial alone, into what I may call the Society of the house. I do not know of any plan so well conceived, or so firmly grounded in a knowledge of human nature, or so judiciously addressed to it, for observance in this place, as what is called Captain Maconnochie's Mark System,[3] which I will try, very roughly and generally, to describe to you.

A woman or girl coming to the Asylum, it is explained to her that she has come there for *useful* repentance and reform, and because her past way of life has been dreadful in its nature and consequences, and full of affliction, misery, and despair *to herself.* Never mind Society while she is at that pass. Society has used her ill and turned away from her, and she cannot be expected to take much heed of its rights or wrongs. It is destructive to *herself,* and there is no hope in it, or in her, as long as she pursues it. It is explained to her that she is degraded and fallen, but not lost, having this shelter; and that the means of Return to Happiness are now about to be put into her own hands, and trusted to her own keeping. That with this view, she is, instead of being placed in this probationary class for a month, or two months, or three months, or any specified *time* whatever, required to earn there, a certain number of *Marks* (they are mere scratches in a book) so that she may make her probation a very short one, or a very long one, according to her own conduct. For so much work, she has so many Marks; for a day's good conduct, so many more. For every instance of ill-temper, disrespect, bad language, any outbreak of any sort or kind, so many—a very large number in proportion to her receipts—are deducted. A perfect Debtor and Creditor account is kept between her and the Superintendent, for every day; and the state of that account, it is in her own power and nobody else's, to adjust to her advantage. It is expressly pointed out to her, that before she can be considered qualified to return to any kind of society—even to the Society of the Asylum—she must give proofs of her power of self-restraint and her sincerity, and her determination to try to shew that she deserves the confidence it is proposed to place in her. Her pride, her emulation, her sense of shame, her heart, her reason, and her interest, are all appealed to at once, and if she pass through this trial, she *must* (I believe it to be in the eternal nature of things) rise somewhat in her own self-respect, and give the managers a power of appeal to her, in future, which nothing else could invest them with. I would carry a modification of this Mark System through the whole establishment; for it is its great philosophy and its chief excellence that it is not a mere form or course of training adapted to the life within the house, but is a preparation—which is a much higher consideration—for the right performance of duty outside, and for the formation of habits of firmness and self-restraint. And the more these unfortunate persons were educated in their duty towards Heaven and Earth, and the more they were tried on this plan, the more they would feel that to dream of returning to Society, or of becoming Virtuous Wives, until they had earned a certain gross number of Marks required of everyone without the least exception, would be to prove that they were not worthy of restoration to the place they had lost. It is a part of this system, even to put at last, some temptation within their reach, as enabling them to go out, putting them in possession of some money, and the like; for it is clear that unless they are used to some temptation and used to resist it, within the walls, their capacity of resisting it without, cannot be considered as fairly tested.

What they would be taught in the house, would be grounded in religion, most unquestionably. It must be the basis of the whole system. But it is very essential in dealing with this class of persons to have a system of training established, which, while it is steady and firm, is cheerful and hopeful. Order, punctuality, cleanliness, the whole routine of household duties—as washing, mending, cooking—the establishment itself would supply the means of teaching practically, to every one. But then I would have it understood by all—I would have it written up in every room—that they were not going through a monotonous round of occupation and self-denial which began and ended there, but which began, or was resumed, under that roof, and would end, by God's blessing, in happy homes of their own.

I have said that I would put it in the power of Governors of Prisons to recommend Inmates. I think this most important, because such gentlemen as Mr. Chesterton[4] of the Middlesex House of Correction, and Lieutenant Tracey of Cold Bath Fields, Bridewell, (both of whom I know very well) are well acquainted with the good that is in the bottom of the hearts, of many of these poor creatures, and with the whole history of their past lives; and frequently have deplored to me the not having any such place as the proposed establishment, to which to send them—when they are set free from Prison. It is necessary to observe that very many of these unfortunate women are constantly in and out of the Prisons, for no other fault or crime than their original one of having fallen from virtue. Policemen can take them up, almost when they choose, for being of that class, and being in the streets; and the Magistrates commit them to Jail for short terms. When they come out, they can but return to their old occupation, and so come in again. It is well-known that many of them fee the Police to remain unmolested; and being too poor to pay the fee, or dissipating the money in some other way, are taken up again, forthwith. Very many of them are good, excellent, steady characters when under restraint—even without the advantage of systematic training, which they would have in this Institution—and are tender nurses to the sick, and are as kind and gentle as the best of women.

There is no doubt that many of them would go on well for some time, and would then be seized with a violent fit of the most extraordinary passion, apparently quite motiveless, and insist on going away. There seems to be something inherent in their course of life, which engenders and awakens a sudden restlessness and recklessness which may be long suppressed, but breaks out like Madness; and which all people who have had opportunities of observation in Penitentiaries and elsewhere, must have contemplated with astonishment and pity. I would have some rule to the effect that no request to be allowed to go away would be received for at least four and twenty hours, and that in the interval the person should be kindly reasoned with, if possible, and implored to consider well what she was doing. This sudden dashing down of all the building up of months upon months, is, to my thinking, so distinctly a Disease with the persons under consideration that I would pay particular attention to it, and treat it with particular gentleness and anxiety; *and I would not make one, or two, or three, or four, or six departures from the Establishment a binding reason against the readmission of that person, being again penitent,* but would leave it to the Managers to decide upon the merits of the case: giving very great weight to general good conduct within the house.

I would begin with some comparatively small number—say thirty—and I would have it impressed upon them, from day to day, that the success of the experiment rested with them, and that on their conduct depended the rescue and salvation, of hundreds and thousands of women yet unborn. In what proportion this experiment would be successful, it is very difficult to predict; but I think that if the Establishment were founded on a well-considered system, and were well managed, one half of the Inmates would be reclaimed from the very beginning, and that after a time the proportion would be very much larger. I believe this estimate to be within very reasonable bounds.

The main question that arises, is, if the co-operation of the Government—beginning at that point when they are supposed to be reclaimed—cannot be secured, how are they to be provided for, permanently? Supposing the mark system and the training to be very successful, and gradually to acquire a great share of public confidence and respect, I think it not too sanguine to suppose that many good people would be glad to take them into situations. But the power of beginning life anew, in a world perfectly untried by them, would be so important in many cases, as an effectual detaching of them from old associates, and from the chances of recognition and challenge, that it is most desirable to be, somehow or other, attained.

I do not know whether you would be disposed to entrust me with any share in the supervision and direction of the Institution. But I need not say that I should enter on such a task with my whole heart and soul; and that in this respect, as in all others, I have but one sincere and zealous wish to assist you, by any humble means in my power, in carrying out your benevolent intentions.

And at all events it would be necessary for you to have, in the first instance, on paper, all the results of previous experience in this way, as regards scheme, plan, management, and expence. These I think I could procure, and render plain, as quietly and satisfactorily as anyone. And I would suggest to you, this course of action.

That,—the School and Church proceeding—this Design remain in abeyance for the present. That when I go to Paris (whither I shall remove, please God, before Christmas) I examine every Institution of this sort existing there, and gather together all the information I possibly can. I believe more valuable knowledge is to be got there, on such a subject, than anywhere else; and this, combined with the results of our English experience, I would digest into the plainest and clearest form; so that you could see it, as if it were a Map. And in the meantime you would have these advantages.

1. That in the establishment of your school and Dispensary, you might find or make some Instruments that would be very important and useful in the working out of this scheme.

2. That there will then have been matured, and probably tried, certain partial schemes going a very little way on this same road, which are now on foot in the City of London, and the success or failure of which will be alike instructive.

3. That there is a very great probability of the whole Transportation system being shortly brought under the consideration of the Legislature; and it is particularly worthy of consideration that the various preliminary reports on the subject, (which I have lately been reading) recognize the question of sending out women to the different settlements, as one of very great importance.

I have that deep sense, dear Miss Coutts, of the value of your confidence in such a matter, and of the pure, exalted, and generous motives by which you are impelled, that I feel a most earnest anxiety that such an effort as you contemplate in behalf of your Sex, should have every advantage in the outset it can possibly receive, and should, if undertaken at all, be undertaken to the lasting honor of your name and Country. In this feeling, I make the suggestion I think best calculated to promote that end. Trust me, if you agree in it, I will not lose sight of the subject, or grow cold to it, or fail to bestow upon it my best exertions and reflection. But, if there be any other course you would prefer to take; and you will tell me so; I shall be as devoted to you in that as in this, and as much honored by being asked to render you the least assistance.

Ever Faithfully Yours
CD.

1 The church of St Stephen, Westminster, which Miss Coutts built 1847–50, and the associated school for poor children.
2 The beginning of the plan for Urania Cottage, established 1847, for the reclamation of young women from the prisons and streets. Almost all the principles and policies outlined in this letter were adopted.
3 Alexander Maconochie (1787–1860†), geographer and radical penal reformer; governor of Norfolk Island 1840–4. CD invited him to dinner Mar. 1846.
4 George Laval Chesterton (d. 1868), governor of Coldbath Fields Prison 1829–54. CD had been visiting his prison since 1835; the two men were friends.

To Lord Morpeth,[1] 20 JUNE 1846

Rosemont, Lausanne, Switzerland | Saturday June Twentieth 1846.

My Dear Lord Morpeth.

Let me premise in the very first line of this letter, that you are to read it at your convenience—and that if you be not at perfect leisure when you receive it, I beg you to fold it up again, until you have a few spare minutes to bestow on its perusal.

I wish to confide to you, a very earnest desire of mine, and to leave it entirely to your discretion and inclination, whether it shall remain a point in confidence between yourself and me, or whether you shall communicate it, at your own time, to anyone else.

I have an ambition for some public employment—some Commissionership, or Inspectorship, or the like, connected with any of those subjects in which I take a deep interest, and in respect of which the Public are generally disposed to treat me with confidence and regard. On any questions connected with the Education of the People, the elevation of their character, the improvement of their dwellings, their greater protection against disease and vice—or with the treatment of Criminals, or the administration of Prison Discipline, which I have long observed closely—I think I could do good service, and I am sure I should enter with my whole heart. I have hoped, for years, that I may become at last a Police Magistrate, and turn my social knowledge to good practical account from day to day; and I have the strongest hope that in any such position as I have glanced at, I could prove my fitness for improving the execution of that trust. It is not a very towering ambition perhaps; but never was a man's ambition so peculiarly associated with his constant sympathies—and, as I fancy, with his capabilities—as this of mine.[2]

Before I left London, political circumstances pointed so directly to a change in the Government, and the restoration, before long, of the Party with which you are proudly and honorably associated, that I more than once had the idea of speaking to some distinguished Member of it on this subject, and begging leave to mention the fact that I sought employment of this kind—and there an end. Had Lord Holland been living, I think I should have done so to him without hesitation. But, at one time thinking of you, and at another of Lord Lansdowne, and at another of Lord Normanby (from whom I have received great personal kindness) I grew undecided and uneasy, and came away, at last, without doing anything.

Reverting to the question in this retirement, I have, somehow, accustomed myself to look at it, as it were from a distant time as well as a distant place. Fancying this letter a hundred years old, I cannot discern any reason why a Descendant of mine should come to the knowledge of it, with the least misgiving or reluctance. Therefore I think I may banish those feelings from my own mind, and boldly (though with an unaffected diffidence) state my object.

I feel that in doing so, I am as little open to the suspicion of sordid motives as any man, with such an object, can be. I entertain the wish, common to most Literary Men, of having some permanent dependance besides Literature. But I have no thought of abandoning that pursuit, which is a great happiness to me: and only seek this new avocation as its not unnatural offspring and companion. My writings, such as they are, are my credentials; and they have never been in greater favor at home and abroad, nor has my pen ever been more profitable to me, than at this time.

You may laughingly ask why I select you, after all, as the recipient of this letter? I will tell you the plain truth, without the slightest ornament. Though I have had the pleasure of your personal acquaintance—I had almost written, friendship—for but a short time, I am sure you have, naturally, a strong and kind inclination towards one in my position, which may be most implicitly confided in. In that assurance, I put my trust in you without reserve, and leave the substance of this letter to be remembered or forgotten by you, with a perfect reliance on your generous consideration.

I am ever | Dear Lord Morpeth
Yours faithfully and obliged
CHARLES DICKENS

1 George Howard, Viscount Morpeth, later 7th Earl of Carlisle (1802–64†), Whig politician; had been in America at the same time as CD.

2 According to Forster, the reply did not encourage CD to think of it further (Forster, 388). Police magistrates had to be barristers of seven years' standing, so CD would not have been eligible.

To John Forster, [?28 JUNE 1846, Rosemont]

I have not been idle since I have been here, though at first I was "kept out" of the big box[1] as you know. I had a good deal to write for Lord John about the Ragged schools. I set to work and did that. A good deal for Miss Coutts, in reference to her charitable projects. I set to work and did *that*. Half of the children's New Testament[2] to write, or pretty nearly. I set to work and did *that*. Next I cleared off the greater part of such correspondence as I had rashly pledged myself to; and then . . .

BEGAN DOMBEY!

I performed this feat yesterday—only wrote the first slip—but there it is, and it is a plunge straight over head and ears into the story. . . . Besides all this, I have really gone with great vigour at the French, where I find myself greatly assisted by the Italian; and am subject to two descriptions of mental fits in reference to the Christmas book: one, of the suddenest and wildest enthusiasm; one, of solitary and anxious consideration. . . . By the way, as I was unpacking the big box I took hold of a book, and said to "Them",—"Now, whatever passage my thumb rests on, I shall take as having reference to my work." It was TRISTRAM SHANDY, and opened at these words, "What a work it is likely to turn out! Let us begin it!"[3]

1 This contained CD's writing materials and ornaments from his desk.
2 Now generally known as 'The Life of Our Lord'; finally published in 1934.
3 Bk. 8, ch. 1.

To John Forster, [18 JULY 1846, Rosemont]

I think the general idea of Dombey is interesting and new, and has great material in it. But I don't like to discuss it with you till you have read number one, for fear I should spoil its effect. When done—about Wednesday or Thursday, please God—I will send it in two days' posts, seven letters each day. If you have it set at once (I am afraid you couldn't read it, otherwise than in print) I know you will impress on B. & E. the necessity of the closest secrecy. The very name getting out, would be ruinous. The points for illustration, and the enormous care required, make me excessively anxious. The man for Dombey, if Browne could see him, the class man to a T, is Sir A—— E——, of D——'s.[1] Great pains will be necessary with Miss Tox. The Toodle family should not be too much caricatured, because of Polly. I should like Browne to think of Susan Nipper, who will not be wanted in the first number. After the second number, they will all be nine or ten years older,[2] but this will not involve much change in the characters, except in the children and Miss Nipper. What a brilliant thing to be telling you all these names so familiarly, when you know nothing about 'em! I quite enjoy it. By the bye, I hope you may like the introduction of Solomon Gills. I think he lives in a good sort of house. . . . One word more. What do you think, as a name for the Christmas book, of THE BATTLE OF LIFE? It is not a name I have conned at all, but has just occurred to me in connection with that foggy idea. If I can see my way, I think I will take it next, and clear it off. If you knew how it hangs about me, I am sure you would say so too. It would be an immense relief to have it done, and nothing standing in the way of Dombey.

1 Unidentified. Forster repudiates the notion of any original for Mr Dombey (Forster, 485).
2 CD changed his plan: Paul is 'nearly five' at the beginning of No. 3, during which a year passes.

To John Forster, [25–26 JULY 1846, Rosemont]

Sending the manuscript of the first four chapters: I will now go on to give you an outline of my immediate intentions in reference to Dombey. I design to show Mr. D with that one idea of the Son taking firmer and firmer possession of him, and swelling and bloating his pride to a prodigious extent. As the boy begins to grow up, I shall show him quite impatient for his getting on, and urging his masters to set him great tasks, and the like. But the natural affection of the boy will turn towards the despised sister; and I purpose showing her learning all sorts of things, of her own application and determination, to assist him in his lessons: and helping him always. When the boy is about ten years old (in the fourth number), he will be taken ill, and will die; and when he is ill, and when he is dying, I mean to make him turn always for refuge to the sister still, and keep the stern affection of the father at a distance. So Mr. Dombey—for all his greatness, and for all his devotion to the child—will find himself at arms' length from him even then; and will see that his love and confidence are all bestowed upon his sister, whom Mr. Dombey has used—and so has the boy himself too, for that matter—as a mere convenience and handle to him. The death of the boy is a death-blow, of course, to all the father's schemes and cherished hopes; and "Dombey and Son", as Miss Tox will say at the end of the number, "is a Daughter after all." . . . From that time, I purpose changing his feeling of indifference and uneasiness towards his daughter into a positive hatred. For he will always remember how the boy had his arm round her neck when he was dying, and whispered to her, and would take things only from her hand, and never thought of him. . . . At the same time I shall change *her* feeling towards *him* for one of a greater desire to love him, and to be loved by him; engendered in her compassion for his loss, and her love for the dead boy whom, in his way, he loved so well too. So I mean to carry the story on, through all the branches and off-shoots and meanderings that come up; and through the decay and downfall of the house, and the bankruptcy of Dombey, and all the rest of it; when his only staff and treasure, and his unknown Good Genius always, will be this rejected daughter, who will come out better than any son at last, and whose love for him, when discovered and understood, will be his bitterest reproach. For the struggle with himself, which goes on in all such obstinate natures, will have ended then; and the sense of his injustice, which you may be sure has never quitted him, will have at last a gentler office than that of only making him more harshly unjust. . . . I rely very much on Susan Nipper grown up, and acting partly as Florence's maid, and partly as a kind of companion to her, for a strong character throughout the book. I also rely on the Toodles, and on Polly, who, like everybody else, will be found by Mr. Dombey to have gone over to his daughter and become attached to her. This is what cooks call "the stock of the soup". All kinds of things will be added to it, of course. . . .

About the boy,[1] who appears in the last chapter of the first number, I think it would be a good thing to disappoint all the expectations that chapter seems to raise of his happy connection with the story and the heroine, and to show him gradually and naturally trailing away, from that love of adventure and boyish light-heartedness, into negligence, idleness, dissipation, dishonesty, and ruin. To show, in short, that common, every-day, miserable declension of which we know so much in our ordinary life; to exhibit something of the philosophy of it, in great temptations and an easy nature; and to show how the good turns into bad, by degrees. If I kept some little notion of Florence always at the bottom of it, I think it might be made very powerful and very useful. What do you think? Do you think it may be done, without making people angry? I could bring out Solomon Gills and Captain Cuttle well, through such a history; and I descry, anyway, an opportunity for good scenes between Captain Cuttle and Miss Tox.[2] This question of the boy is very important. . . . Let me hear all you think about it. Hear! I wish I could.

1 Walter Gay.
2 No such scenes were written.

To John Forster, [30 AUGUST 1846, Rosemont]

You can hardly imagine what infinite pains I take, or what extraordinary difficulty I find in getting on FAST. Invention, thank God, seems the easiest thing in the world; and I seem to have such a preposterous sense of the ridiculous, after this long rest, as to be constantly requiring to restrain myself from launching into extravagances in the height of my enjoyment. But the difficulty of going at what I call a rapid pace, is prodigious: it is almost an impossibility. I suppose this is partly the effect of two years' ease, and partly of the absence of streets and numbers of figures. I can't express how much I want these. It seems as if they supplied something to my brain, which it cannot bear, when busy, to lose. For a week or a fortnight I can write prodigiously in a retired place (as at Broadstairs), and a day in London sets me up again and starts me. But the toil and labour of writing, day after day, without that magic lantern, is IMMENSE!! I don't say this, at all in low spirits, for we are perfectly comfortable here, and I like the place very much indeed, and the people are even more friendly and fond of me than they were in Genoa. I only mention it as a curious fact, which I have never had an opportunity of finding out before. *My* figures seem disposed to stagnate without crowds about them. I wrote very little in Genoa (only the Chimes), and fancied myself conscious of some such influence there—but Lord! I had two miles of streets at least, lighted at night, to walk about in; and a great theatre to repair to, every night.

I shall gladly acquiesce in whatever more changes or omissions you propose. Browne seems to be getting on well. . . . He will have a good subject in Paul's christening. Mr. Chick is like D, if you'll mention that when you think of it. The little chapter of Miss Tox and the Major, which you alas! (but quite wisely) rejected from the first number, I have altered for the last of the second. I have not quite finished the middle chapter yet—having, I should say, three good days' work to do at it; but I hope it will be all a worthy successor to number one. I will send it as soon as finished.

To John Forster, [?6 SEPTEMBER 1846, Rosemont]

The weather obstinately clearing, we started off last Tuesday for the Great St. Bernard, returning here on Friday afternoon. The party consisted of eleven people and two servants—Haldimand, Mr. and Mrs. Cerjat and one daughter, Mr. and Mrs. Watson,[1] two Ladies Taylor, Kate, Georgy, and I. We were wonderfully unanimous and cheerful; went away from here by the steamer; found at its destination a whole omnibus provided by the Brave[2] (who went on in advance everywhere); rode therein to Bex; found two large carriages ready to take us to Martigny; slept there; and proceeded up the mountain on mules next day. Although the St. Bernard convent is, as I dare say you know, the highest inhabited spot but one in the world, the ascent is extremely gradual and uncommonly easy: really presenting no difficulties at all, until within the last league, when the ascent, lying through a place called the valley of desolation, is very awful and tremendous, and the road is rendered toilsome by scattered rocks and melting snow. The convent is a most extraordinary place, full of great vaulted passages, divided from each other with iron gratings; and presenting a series of the most astonishing little dormitories, where the windows are so small (on account of the cold and snow), that it is as much as one can do to get one's head out of them. Here we slept: supping, thirty strong, in a rambling room with a great wood-fire in it set apart for that purpose; with a grim monk, in a high black sugar-loaf hat with a great knob at the top of it, carving the dishes. At five o'clock in the morning the chapel bell rang in the dismallest way for matins: and I, lying in bed close to the chapel, and being awakened by the solemn organ and the chaunting, thought for a moment I had died in the night and passed into the unknown world.

I wish to God you could see that place. A great hollow on the top of a range of dreadful mountains, fenced in by riven rocks of every shape and colour: and in the midst, a black lake, with phantom clouds perpetually stalking over it. Peaks, and points, and plains of eternal ice and snow, bounding the view, and shutting out the world on every side: the lake reflecting nothing: and no human figure in the scene. The air so fine, that it is difficult to breathe without feeling out of breath; and the cold so exquisitely thin and sharp that it is not to be described. Nothing of life or living interest in the picture, but the grey dull walls of the convent. No vegetation of any sort or kind. Nothing growing, nothing stirring. Everything iron-bound, and frozen up. Beside the convent, in a little outhouse with a grated iron door which you may unbolt for yourself, are the bodies of people found in the snow who have never been claimed and are withering away—not laid down, or stretched out, but standing up, in corners and against walls; some erect and horribly human, with distinct expressions on the faces; some sunk down on their knees; some dropping over on one side; some tumbled down altogether, and presenting a heap of skulls and fibrous dust. There is no other decay in that atmosphere; and there they remain during the short days and the long nights, the only human company out of doors, withering away by grains, and holding ghastly possession of the mountain where they died.

It is the most distinct and individual place I have seen, even in this transcendent country. But, for the Saint Bernard holy fathers and convent in themselves, I am sorry to say that they are a piece of as sheer humbug as we ever learnt to believe in, in our young days. Trashy French sentiment and the dogs (of which, by the bye, there are only three remaining) have done it all. They are a lazy set of fellows; not over fond of going out themselves; employing servants to clear the road (which has not been important or much used as a pass these hundred years); rich; and driving a good trade in Innkeeping: the convent being a common tavern in everything but the sign. No charge is made for their hospitality to be sure; but you are shown to a box in the chapel, where everybody puts in more than could, with any show of face, be charged for the entertainment; and from this the establishment derives a right good income. As to the self-sacrifice of living up there, they are obliged to go there young, it is true, to be inured to the climate: but it is an infinitely more exciting and various life than any other convent can offer; with constant change and company through the whole summer; with a hospital for invalids down in the valley, which affords another change; and with an annual begging-journey to Geneva and this place and all the places round for one brother or other, which affords farther change. The brother who carved at our supper could speak some English, and had just had Pickwick given him!—what a humbug he will think me when he tries to understand it! If I had had any other book of mine with me, I would have given it him, that I might have had some chance of being intelligible.

I hope to finish the second number to-morrow, and to send it off bodily by Tuesday's post. On Wednesday I purpose, please God, beginning the Battle of Life. I shall peg away at that, without turning aside to Dombey again; and *if* I can only do it within the month!

1 This was the circle of English residents at Lausanne, who became CD's friends. *DC* is dedicated to 'The Hon. Mr and Mrs Richard Watson, of Rockingham, Northamptonshire'. CD adopted some features of Rockingham Castle for Chesney Wold in *BH*.
2 The courier, Louis Roche.

To John Forster, [?20 SEPTEMBER 1846, Rosemont]

The absence of any accessible streets continues to worry me, now that I have so much to do, in a most singular manner. It is quite a little mental phenomenon. I should not walk in them in the day time, if they were here, I dare say: but at night I want them beyond description. I don't seem able to get rid of my spectres unless I can lose them in crowds. However, as you say, there are streets in Paris, and good suggestive streets too: and trips to London will be nothing then. WHEN I have finished the Christmas book, I shall fly to Geneva for a day or two, before taking up with Dombey again. I like this place better and better; and never saw, I think, more agreeable people than our little circle is made up of. It is so little, that one is not "bothered" in the least; and their interest in the Inimitable seems to strengthen daily. I read them the first number last night "was a" week, with unrelateable success; and old Mrs. Marcet, who is devilish 'cute, guessed directly (but I didn't tell her she was right) that little Paul would die. They were all so apprehensive that it was a great pleasure to read it; and I shall leave here, if all goes well, in a brilliant shower of sparks struck out of them by the promised reading of the Christmas book.

You remember your objection about the two stories. I made over light of it. I ought to have considered that I have never before really tried the opening of two together—having always had one pretty far ahead when I have been driving a pair of them. I know it all now. The apparent impossibility of getting each into its place, coupled with that craving for streets, so thoroughly put me off the track, that, up to Wednesday or Thursday last, I really contemplated, at times, the total abandonment of the Christmas book this year, and the limitation of my labours to Dombey and Son! I cancelled the beginning of a first scene—which I have never done before— and, with a notion in my head, ran wildly about and about it, and could not get the idea into any natural socket. At length, thank Heaven, I nailed it all at once; and after going on comfortably up to yesterday, and working yesterday from half-past nine to six, I was last night in such a state of enthusiasm about it that I think I was an inch or two taller. I am a little cooler to-day, with a headache to boot; but I really begin to hope you will think it a pretty story, with some delicate notions in it agreeably presented, and with a good human Christmas groundwork.[2] I fancy I see a great domestic effect in the last part.

1 From the proofs.
2 The ball at the end of part 2 of *The Battle of Life* is in 'the Christmas season'.

To John Forster, [11 OCTOBER 1846, Rosemont]

The Dombey success is BRILLIANT! I had put before me thirty thousand as the limit of the most extreme success, saying that if we should reach that, I should be more than satisfied and more than happy; you will judge how happy I am! I read the second number here last night to the most prodigious and uproarious delight of the circle. I never saw or heard people laugh so. You will allow me to observe that my reading of the Major has merit.

I was thinking the other day that in these days of lecturings and readings, a great deal of money might possibly be made (if it were not infra dig) by one's having Readings of one's own books. It would be an *odd* thing. I think it would take immensely. What do you say? Will you step to Dean-street, and see how Miss Kelly's engagement-book (it must be an immense volume!) stands? Or shall I take the St. James's?

You will know, long before you get this, all about the revolution at Geneva. There were stories of plots against the Government when I was there, but I didn't believe them; for all sorts of lies are always afloat against the radicals, and wherever there is a consul from a Catholic Power the most monstrous fictions are in perpetual circulation against them: as in this very place, where the Sardinian consul was gravely whispering the other day that a society called the Homicides had been formed, whereof the president of the council of state, the O'Connell[1] of Switzerland

and a clever fellow, was a member; who were sworn on skulls and cross-bones to exterminate men of property, and so forth. There was a great stir here, on the day of the fight in Geneva. We heard the guns (they shook this house) all day; and seven hundred men marched out of this town of Lausanne to go and help the radical party—arriving at Geneva just after it was all over. There is no doubt they had received secret help from here; for a powder barrel, found by some of the Genevese populace with "Canton de Vaud" painted on it, was carried on a pole about the streets as a standard, to show that they were sympathized with by friends outside. It was a poor mean fight enough, I am told by Lord Vernon, who was present and who was with us last night. The Government was afraid; having no confidence whatever, I dare say, in its own soldiers; and the cannon were fired everywhere except at the opposite party, who (I mean the revolutionists) had barricaded a bridge with an omnibus only, and certainly in the beginning might have been turned with ease. The precision of the common men with the rifle was especially shown by a small party of *five,* who waited on the ramparts near one of the gates of the town, to turn a body of soldiery who were coming in to the Government assistance. They picked out every officer and struck him down instantly, the moment the party appeared; there were three or four of them; upon which the soldiers gravely turned round and walked off. I dare say there are not fifty men in this place who wouldn't click your card off a target a hundred and fifty yards away, at least. I have seen them, time after time, fire across a great ravine as wide as the ornamental ground in St. James's-park, and never miss the bull's-eye.

It is a horribly ungentlemanly thing to say here, though I *do* say it without the least reserve—but my sympathy is all with the radicals. I don't know any subject on which this indomitable people have so good a right to a strong feeling as Catholicity—if not as a religion, clearly as a means of social degradation. They know what it is. They live close to it. They have Italy beyond their mountains. They can compare the effect of the two systems at any time in their own valleys; and their dread of it, and their horror of the introduction of Catholic priests and emissaries into their towns, seems to me the most rational feeling in the world. Apart from this, you have no conception of the preposterous, insolent little aristocracy of Geneva: the most ridiculous caricature the fancy can suggest of what we know in England. I was talking to two famous gentlemen (very intelligent men) of that place, not long ago, who came over to invite me to a sort of reception there—which I declined. Really their talk about "the people" and "the masses", and the necessity they would shortly be under of shooting a few of them as an example for the rest, was a kind of monstrosity one might have heard at Genoa. The audacious insolence and contempt of the people by their newspapers, too, is quite absurd. It is difficult to believe that men of sense can be such donkeys politically. It was precisely such a state of things that brought about the change here. There was a most respectful petition presented on the Jesuit question, signed by its tens of thousands of small farmers; the regular peasants of the canton, all splendidly taught in public schools, and intellectually as well as physically a most remarkable body of labouring men. This document is treated by the gentlemanly party with the most sublime contempt, and the signatures are said to be the signatures of "the rabble". Upon which, each man of the rabble shoulders his rifle, and walks in upon a given day agreed upon among them to Lausanne; and the gentlemanly party walk out without striking a blow.

The Talfourds stayed two days, and I think they were very happy. He was in his best aspect; the manner so well known to us, not the less loveable for being laughable; and if you could have seen him going round and round the coach that brought them, as a preliminary to paying the voiturier to whom he couldn't speak, in a currency he didn't understand, you never would have forgotten it.

And now sir I will describe, modestly, tamely, literally, the visit to the small select circle which I promised should make your hair stand on end. In our hotel were Lady A, and Lady B, mother and daughter,[2] who came to the Peschiere shortly before we left it, and who have a deep admiration for your humble servant the inimitable B. They are both very clever. Lady B, extremely well-informed in languages, living and dead; books, and gossip; very pretty; with two little children, and not yet five and twenty. Lady A, plump, fresh, and rosy; matronly, but full of spirits and good looks. Nothing would serve them but we *must* dine with them; and accordingly, on Friday at six, we went down to their room. I knew them to be rather odd. For instance, I have known Lady A, *full dressed,* walk alone through the streets of Genoa, the squalid Italian bye streets, to the Governor's soirée; and announce herself at the palace of state, by knocking at the door. I have also met Lady B, full dressed, without any cap or bonnet, walking a mile to the opera, with all sorts of jingling jewels about her, beside a sedan chair in which sat enthroned her mama. Consequently, I was not surprised at such little sparkles in the conversation (from the young lady) as "Oh God what a sermon we had here, last Sunday!" "And did you ever read such infernal trash as Mrs. Gore's?"[3]—and the like. Still, but for Kate and Georgy (who were decidedly in the way, as we agreed afterwards), I should have thought it all very funny; and, as it was, I threw the ball back again, was mighty free and easy, made some rather broad jokes, and was highly applauded. "You smoke, don't you?" said the young lady, in a pause of this kind of conversation. "Yes," I said, "I generally take a cigar after dinner when I am alone." "I'll give you a good 'un," said she, "when we go up-stairs." Well, sir, in due course we went up-stairs, and there we were joined by an American lady residing in the same hotel, who looked like what we call in old England "a reg'lar Bunter"[4]—fluffy face (rouged); considerable development of figure; one groggy eye; blue satin dress made low with short sleeves, and shoes of the same. Also a daughter; face likewise fluffy; figure likewise developed; dress likewise low, with short sleeves, and shoes of the same; and one eye not yet actually groggy, but going to be. American lady married at sixteen; daughter sixteen now, often mistaken for sisters, &c. &c. &c. When that was over, Lady B brought out a cigar box, and gave me a cigar, made of negrohead she said, which would quell an elephant in six whiffs. The box was full of cigarettes—good large ones, made of pretty strong tobacco; I always smoke them here, and used to smoke them at Genoa, and I knew them well. When I lighted my cigar, Lady B lighted hers, at mine; leaned against the mantlepiece, in conversation with me; put out her stomach, folded her arms, and with her pretty face cocked up sideways and her cigarette smoking away like a Manchester cotton mill, laughed, and talked, and smoked, in the most gentlemanly manner I ever beheld. Lady A immediately lighted her cigar; American lady immediately lighted hers; and in five minutes the room was a cloud of smoke, with us four in the centre pulling away bravely, while American lady related stories of her "Hookah" up-stairs, and described different kinds of pipes. But even this was not all. For presently two Frenchmen came in, with whom, and the American lady, Lady B sat down to whist. The Frenchmen smoked of course (they were really modest gentlemen, and seemed dismayed), and Lady B played for the next hour or two with a cigar continually in her mouth—never out of it. She certainly smoked six or eight. Lady A gave in soon—I think she only did it out of vanity. American lady had been smoking all the morning. I took no more; and Lady B and the Frenchmen had it all to themselves.

Conceive this in a great hotel, with not only their own servants, but half a dozen waiters coming constantly in and out! I showed no atom of surprise; but I never *was* so surprised, so ridiculously taken aback, in my life; for in all my experience of "ladies" of one kind and another, I never saw a woman—not a basket woman or a gipsy—smoke, before!

I will write to Landor[5] as soon as I can possibly make time, but I really am so much at my desk perforce, and so full of work, whether I am there or elsewhere, between the Christmas book and Dombey, that it is the most difficult thing in the world for me to make up my mind to write a letter to anyone but you. I ought to have written to Macready. I wish you would tell him, with my love, how I am situated in respect of pen, ink, and paper. One of the Lausanne papers, treating of free trade, has been very copious lately in its mention of LORD GOBDEN. Fact; and I think it a good name.

1 Daniel O'Connell (1775–1847†), Irish nationalist leader, known as the Liberator.
2 Lady Pellew and Lady Walpole.
3 Caroline Gore (1799/1800–61†), prolific author of best-selling novels set in fashionable society.
4 'A woman who picks up rags about the street; and used, by way of contempt, for any low vulgar woman', *OED*.
5 Walter Savage Landor (1775–1864†), poet and author, lived in Italy for many years. CD met him 1840; thought to be the original for Boythorn in *BH*.

To John Forster, [4 NOVEMBER 1846, Rosemont]

I hope to finish the number by next Tuesday or Wednesday.[1] It is hard writing under these bird-of-passage circumstances, but I have no reason to complain, God knows, having come to no knot yet. . . . I hope you will like Mrs. Pipchin's establishment. It is from the life, and I was there—I don't suppose I was eight years old; but I remember it all as well, and certainly understood it as well, as I do now.[2] We should be devilish sharp in what we do to children. I thought of that passage in my small life, at Geneva. Shall I leave you my life in MS. when I die?[3] There are some things in it that would touch you very much, and that might go on the same shelf with the first volume of Holcroft's.[4]

1 i.e. No. 3.
2 Mrs Pipchin is thought to be based on Mrs Elizabeth Roylance, with whom the Dickenses lodged after leaving the Marshalsea prison in 1824.
3 An early reference to the autobiographical fragment, the basis for the early chapters of *DC*; see below, to Forster, 10 July 1849.
4 Thomas Holcroft (1745–1809†); his account of his early hardships form book I of his *Memoirs*.

To John Forster, [6 DECEMBER 1846, Paris]

It is extraordinary what nonsense English people talk, write, and believe, about foreign countries. The Swiss (so much decried) will do anything for you, if you are frank and civil; they are attentive and punctual in all their dealings; and may be relied upon as steadily as the English. The Parisian workpeople and smaller shopkeepers are more like (and unlike) Americans than I could have supposed possible. To the American indifference and carelessness, they add a procrastination and want of the least heed about keeping a promise or being exact, which is certainly not surpassed in Naples. They have the American semi-sentimental independence too, and none of the American vigour or purpose. If they ever get free trade in France (as I suppose they will, one day), these parts of the population must, for years and years, be ruined. They couldn't get the means of existence, in competition with the English workmen. Their inferior manual dexterity, their lazy habits, perfect unreliability, and habitual insubordination, would ruin them in any such contest, instantly. They are fit for nothing but soldiering—and so far, I believe, the successors in the policy of your friend Napoleon have reason on their side. Eh bien, mon ami, quand vous venez à Paris, nous nous mettrons à quatre épingles, et nous verrons toutes les merveilles de la cité, et vous en jugerez. God bless me, I beg your pardon! It comes so natural.

Here am I, writing letters, and delivering opinions, politico-economical and otherwise, as if there were no undone number, and no undone Dick! Well. Così va il mondo (God bless me! Italian! I beg your pardon)—and one must keep one's spirits up, if possible, even under Dombey pressure. Paul, I shall slaughter at the end of number five. His school ought to be pretty good, but I haven't been able to dash at it freely, yet. However, I have avoided unnecessary dialogue so far, to avoid overwriting;[1] and all I *have* written is point.

1 i.e writing too many pages for the number.

To Amelia Fillonneau,[1] 18 JANUARY 1847

48, Rue de Courcelles. | Eighteenth January, 1847

My Dear Mrs. F.

I send you, on the other side, the tremendous document which will make you for ninety years (I hope) a beautiful Punchmaker in more senses than one.

I shall be delighted to dine with you on Thursday. Mr. Forster says amen. Commend me to your Lord, and believe me (with respectful compliments to Lord Chesterfield) always

Faithfully yours,
CHARLES DICKENS

TO MAKE THREE PINTS OF PUNCH[2]

Peel into a very strong common basin (which may be broken, in case of accident, without damage to the owner's peace or pocket) the rinds of three lemons, cut very thin, and with as little as possible of the white coating between the peel and the fruit, attached. Add a double-handfull of lump sugar (good measure), a pint of good old rum, and a large wine-glass full of brandy—if it be not a large claret glass, say two. Set this on fire, by filling a warm silver spoon with the spirit, lighting the contents at a wax taper, and pouring them gently in. Let it burn three or four minutes at least, stirring it from time to time. Then extinguish it by covering the basin with a tray, which will immediately put out the flame. Then squeeze in the juice of the three lemons, and add a quart of *boiling* water. Stir the whole well, cover it up for five minutes, and stir again.

At this crisis (having skimmed off the lemon pips with a spoon) you may taste. If not sweet enough, add sugar to your liking, but observe that it will be a *little* sweeter presently. Pour the whole into a jug, tie a leather or coarse cloth over the top, so as to exclude the air completely, and stand it in a hot oven ten minutes, or on a hot stove one quarter of an hour. Keep it until it comes to table in a warm place near the fire, but not too hot. If it be intended to stand three or four hours, take half the lemon-peel out, or it will acquire a bitter taste.

The same punch allowed to grow cool by degrees, and then iced, is delicious. It requires less sugar when made for this purpose. If you wish to produce it bright, strain it into bottles through silk.

These proportions and directions will, of course, apply to any quantity.

1 Henry Austin's sister.
2 Cf. Mr Micawber's practical demonstration, *DC* ch. 28.

To Hablot K. Browne, 10 MARCH 1847

1 Chester Place, Regents Park. Tenth March 1847.

My Dear Browne. I can't get into my own house, having come home before my time; and am living here, until my Devonshire Terrace tenant performs that perfectly unintelligible ceremony which is called, in the vulgar, walking his chalks.[1]

The occasion of my coming home, makes me very late with my number, which I have only begun this morning. Otherwise you should have been "fed" sooner. My eldest boy's illness will excuse me, I hope.[2]

The first subject which I am now going to give, is very important to the book. *I should like to see your sketch of it, if possible.*[3]

I should premise that I want to make the Major, who is the incarnation of selfishness and small revenge, a kind of comic Mephistophelean power in the book; and the No. begins with the departure of Mr Dombey and the Major on that trip for change of air and scene, which is prepared for in the last Number. They go to Leamington, where you and I were once. In the Library, the Major introduces Mr. Dombey to a certain lady, whom, as I wish to foreshadow, dimly, said Dombey may come to marry in due season. She is about thirty—not a day more—handsome, though haughty-looking—good figure—well dressed—showy—and desirable. Quite a lady in appearance, with something of a proud indifference about her, suggestive of a spark of the Devil within. Was married young. Husband dead. Goes about with an old mother who rouges, and who lives upon the reputation of a diamond necklace and her family.—Wants a husband. Flies at none but high game, and couldn't marry anybody not rich—Mother affects cordiality and heart, and is the essence of sordid calculation—Mother usually shoved about in a Bath chair by a Page who has rather outgrown and out-shoved his strength, and who butts at it behind, like a Ram, while his mistress steers herself languidly by a handle in front—Nothing the matter with her to prevent her walking, only was once sketched (when a Beauty) reclining in a Barouche, and having outlived the beauty and the barouche too, still holds on to the attitude, as becoming her uncommonly. Mother is in this machine, in the Sketch. Daughter has a parasol.

The Major presents them to Mr. Dombey, gloating within himself over what may come of it, and over the discomfiture of Miss Tox. Mr. Dombey (in deep mourning) bows solemnly. Daughter bends. The Native in attendance, bearing a camp-stool and the Major's great coat. Native evidently afraid of the Major and his thick cane. If you like it better, the scene may be in the street or in a green lane. But a great deal will come of it: and I want the Major to express that, as much as possible in his apoplectico-Mephistophelean observation of the scene, and in his share in it.

Lettering.

Major Bagstock is delighted to have that opportunity.

1 Taking his departure (slang).
2 Charley had scarlet fever.
3 The first illustration for *D&S* ch. 20, No. 7. The numerous insertions and minor alterations in this letter show CD's concern that Browne should be faithful to him in detail and spirit.

To Hablot K. Browne, 15 MARCH 1847

1 Chester Place | Monday Night Fifteenth March 1847.

My Dear Browne. The sketch is admirable—the women *quite perfect*. I cannot tell you how much I like the younger one. There are one or two points, however, which I must ask you to alter. They are capital in themselves, and I speak solely for the Story.

First—I grieve to write it—that Native—who is so prodigiously good as he is—must be in European Costume. He may wear ear-rings, and look outlandish, and be dark brown, but his fashion must be of Moses, Mosesy—I don't mean old testament Moses, but him of the Minories.

Secondly, if you *can* make the Major older, and with a larger face—do.

That's all. Never mind the Pump Room now, unless you have found the Sketch, as we may have that another time. I shall propoge[1] to you, a Trip to Leamington together. We might go one day and return the next.

I wish you *had* been at poor Hall's funeral,[2]—and I am sure they would have been glad. They seem to have had a delicacy in asking anyone not of the family, lest it should be disagreeable. I went myself, only after communicating with Chapman, and telling him that I wished to pay that last mark of respect, if it did not interfere with their arrangements. He lies in the Highgate Cemetery, which is beautiful. He had a good little wife, if ever a man had; and their accounts of her tending of him at the last, are deeply affecting. Is it not a curious coincidence, remembering our connexion afterwards, that I bought the Magazine in which the first thing I ever wrote was published—from poor Hall's hands?[3]—I have been thinking all day of that, and of that time when the Queen went into the City, and we drank Claret (it was in their earlier days) in the Counting-house. You remember?

Charley, thank God, better and better every hour. Don't mind sending me the Second Sketch. It is so late. Ever Faithfully my dear Browne—CD.

1 Word used by the nurse Mrs Gamp in *MC*.
2 William Hall, of Chapman and Hall.
3 'A Dinner at Poplar Walk', published in the *Monthly Magazine*, Dec. 1833.

To Mrs Charles Wilson,[1] 25 MARCH 1847

London Twenty Fifth March 1847.

Respected Madam.

I have read your letter with the pleasure and interest which a communication so frank and agreeable could scarcely fail to awaken in any breast.

Let me assure you, in reply, that I have a great respect for the exertions of Father Matthew[2] and the advocates of Temperance in general, and that I believe them to have been productive of unspeakable good amongst Drunkards. But I do not—because I cannot, with such perceptions as I have of what is reasonable and what is unreasonable—go along with those excellent persons in confounding the use of anything with its abuse or in denying any man the cheerful enjoyment of a glass of wine, or beer, or spirits and water, because his neighbour is prone to make a Beast of himself by irrational excess in those things. I know nothing whatever allowed us for use and capable of abuse (as everything without us and within us is) that might not be denied to moderate people, and made a sinful enjoyment, on the same terms.

I have no doubt whatever that the warm stuff in the jug at Bob Cratchit's Christmas dinner, had a very pleasant effect on the simple party.[3] I am certain that if I had been at Mr. Fezziwig's ball, I should have taken a little Negus—and possibly not a little beer—and been none the worse for it, in heart or head. I am very sure that the working people of this country have not too many household enjoyments; and I could not, in my fancy, or in actual deed, deprive them of this one when it is innocently shared. Neither do I see why I should deny it to myself.

Dear Madam, there are two sides to this question. If I were so disposed, I could shew, I believe, where and how the proscription of the use of these refreshments, leads to their abuse in a very striking manner. But I would endeavour, in my poor way, to teach people to use such goods of life, cheerfully and thankfully, and not to abuse them. I am not sure but that this is the higher lesson, and that the principle will last the longer in the better ages of the World.

At any rate there will be the record of a certain Marriage Feast in Galilee and of a certain supper where a cup was filled with Wine and not with water, to bear it company.[4]

May you ever be as happy as you are now, and may I never have a less sincere and truthful correspondent!

> Madam | Faithfully Yours
> CHARLES DICKENS

1 Wife of railway director Charles Wilson.
2 Theobald Mathew (1790–1856†), Capuchin friar and temperance campaigner. He conducted missions across Ireland, claiming in 1842 that 5 million people had taken the pledge of abstinence. He visited England 1843–4.
3 The references in this paragraph are to *CC*. CD took this line of moderation to the many correspondents who wanted to enlist his support for total abstinence.
4 See New Testament, John 2: 1–11, and Mark 14: 22–5.

To *Mary Dickens*, 4 AUGUST 1847

Broadstairs, Wednesday, August 4th, 1847.

My Dearest Mamey,

I am delighted to hear that you are going to improve in your spelling, because nobody can write properly without spelling well. But I know you will learn whatever you are taught, because you are always good, industrious, and attentive. That is what I always say of my Mamey.

The note you sent me this morning is a very nice one, and the spelling is beautiful.

> Always, my dear Mamey,
> Your affectionate Papa.

To Thomas Mitton, 8 AUGUST 1847

Broadstairs | Sunday Eighth August 1847.

My Dear Mitton

I should have sent you those newspapers which crossed your letter, sooner; but a Dispatch box of mine containing them, was lost upon the railway coming home, and not recovered here, until last Friday.

The success was brilliant, and you can imagine nothing like the reception they gave me at both places[1]—standing up as one person, and shouting incessantly for a good ten minutes. The whole company acted excellently—I do not think any of them could have done better. It was hard work of course, for we were at it all day. But, at night, a very beautiful scene indeed—the Theatres being both large and crammed to the roof with people in full dress, who "took" everything in a manner I never saw equalled. We received nine hundred pounds, odd! But the expences are large, by reason of the charges incurred for the dropped Covent Garden Benefit.

I intend turning this to account once a year, and trying to shame the English Government, by giving as much every year to the reduced professors of Art, Literature, and Science, as the whole Civil List gives, on account of Great Britain. I have a scheme in my head for the purpose.[2]

So I hope you will, one of these days see that Two o'Clock in the Morning,[3] which, though I say it as shouldn't, is the best done thing, from beginning to end, and the drollest, you ever saw. The people laughed so, at it, at Manchester—as the grave Court did at the St. James's—that it was impossible to keep a grave face, and all but impossible to go on. I never heard or saw such laughing in a theatre. The people were drooping over the fronts of the boxes like fruit. And the carpenters and people behind, who were attending to the machinery of the scene (of which there is a good deal) had the most ridiculous tears rolling down their faces all the time.

I couldn't stand upon my legs on the Thursday after the Liverpool night: having been upon them, in the Theatre, fourteen hours—and the same at Manchester—and having danced, like a Madman on the Tuesday night. I was obliged to stay at Liverpool all Thursday, to rest. Before acting on the Wednesday night, I had a mustard poultice on my throat—being hoarse—and ate a bushel of anchovies, without bread or anything else, in the course of the evening, to keep my voice going! the oldest and best theatrical recipe.

Nothing could have been more complete. It amply repaid all trouble, and was perfectly splendid.

We have quite got over the whooping cough, thank God. I propose staying here, until the end of September. Let me hear where you go, and how you get on. I'll pay Roper.[4] I may possibly call upon you on Tuesday next, but don't wait in, as it is very uncertain.

Faithfully Ever
CD.

1 CD's amateur company performed in Manchester and Liverpool.
2 CD had just drafted a proposal for 'The Provident Union of Literature, Science and Art': a mutual insurance scheme for writers and artists, and forerunner of the Guild of Literature and Art.
3 The interlude by Charles Mathews; CD took the part of Mr Snobbington.
4 Probably William Roper, assistant secretary of the Artists' General Benevolent Institution.

To David Laing,[1] 2 SEPTEMBER 1847

Broadstairs, Kent | Second September 1847

My Dear Sir

My objection to the Governesses Institution, is increased every year. I think that canvassing,[2] one of the social vices of this time; and am ashamed of possessing a vote, when I find so many reduced ladies driven to the necessity of seeking it in vain. It appears to me that there is an amount of degradation and humiliating solicitation imposed upon the candidates which is very poorly paid for, even in a successful instance, and which we are not justified in inflicting upon any class of persons, however willing they may be to undergo it. This is an objection, and, as I have said, a continually increasing one, which applies, in my mind, to many of the charities of the day; but it applies particularly to the Governesses Institution, by reason of the education and rightful social position of the objects of its care, which render it especially desirable that such an Institution should be foremost to set a good example in this respect, and to establish some other mode of election.

When anything of this kind attains a preposterous height, it is sure to stagger and fall; and I am convinced that a very few annual returns of a Governesses Institution contest, must startle a great many supporters of what is in its design so good and generous, and set them thinking whether they do not seem to be buying for themselves the greatest possible amount of bustle and excitement that can be got for so many guineas, rather than providing, calmly and quietly, for decayed Governesses.

I know how much you have the real object at heart, and I cannot forbear, for the second time, observing to you where I think it is going astray; being well assured that we both wish for the same end, though we may differ—if we *do* differ—about the means of attaining it.

A pretty intimate acquaintance with our prisons, sharpens my perception of the case you so feelingly and truthfully describe. I have seen hundreds upon hundreds, thousands upon thousands, like it. Nothing will set such wrongs right, but the beginning to deal with these unhappy creatures before they go to Jail—but the barring of the Jail Door outside, quite as carefully as within. Is it not extraordinary that with Christianity nearly two thousand years old, we, who profess and call ourselves Christians, should be so far from the very beginning of justice and mercy? Indeed you have good reason to write so earnestly (and *not* "tediously") of the wickedness and foolishness of our social arrangements. I have been glad to read your letter.

My Dear Sir | Faithfully Yours
CHARLES DICKENS

1 Revd David Laing (1800–60), chaplain to the Middlesex Hospital, later a founder of the Playground and General Recreation Society.
2 Candidates for assistance competed for subscribers' votes: a system followed by many charities and preserved by the Governesses until 1938.

To *Angela Burdett Coutts*, 28 OCTOBER 1847

Devonshire Terrace | Thursday Night | Twenty Eighth October 1847

My Dear Miss Coutts.

I am in a state of great anxiety to talk to you about your "Home"[1] (that is the name I propose to give it) with which I have been very busy for some time, and which will be ready for the reception of its inmates, please God, on Saturday fortnight. I have a perfect confidence in your approving of the details, but it would be most interesting to me to talk them over with you.

You have so long overstayed your time, that I begin to think you must be keeping out of the way to preserve that spell unbroken. I send this to Stratton Street by the post, on the chance of its finding you somewhere.

I cannot tell you how much cause I have seen, and see daily, during the preparation of this place, to admire the goodness and devotion of Mr. Chesterton, whose time is always at our command, and whose interest in the design cannot be surpassed.

There are two objects (promising, I hope) recently discharged from his prison, who are giving the best proof of the sincerity of their desire to come to us, by remaining in the prison—prison clothed and fed—until we are enabled to take them. Which I think is an affecting and encouraging circumstance, as they knew on the evening when their time was up, that some of their old companions were waiting at the gate to bear them away. There is another girl—only seventeen— born of drunken parents, ill used from her cradle, plundered of her clothes that they might be sold for liquor, and sent to evil courses for their gain, to whom we are giving a few shillings now and then (her discharge took place some weeks ago, and they could not keep her in the prison too) until we are ready to take her. She comes to Mr. Chesterton at stated times, clean, decent, and quiet, and apparently quite altered. We have now eight, and I have as much confidence in five of them, as one *can* have in the beginning of anything so new. As we go on, I sincerely trust and believe you will do more good than your most sanguine expectations picture now.

We were at Mr. Tracey's to day to look for some others. There is a young woman there, who has more feeling—who shews more at least—than I have seen in any of them, but some points in her wretched history remain to be examined. I have taken some pains to find out the dispositions and natures of every individual we take; and I think I know them pretty well, and may be able to give the matron some useful foreknowledge of them, and to exercise some personal influence with them in case of need. A most extraordinary and mysterious study it is, but interesting and touching in the extreme.

I think it well to say to you that I have avoided Macconochie's ideas,[2] as they hardly seemed (or I fancied so) to meet with your full approval, and as they were perhaps unsuited to so small an establishment. The design is simply, as you and I agreed, to appeal to them by means of affectionate kindness and trustfulness,—but firmly too. To improve them by education and example—establish habits of the most rigid order, punctuality, and neatness—but to make as great a variety in their daily lives as their daily lives will admit of—and to render them an innocently cheerful Family while they live together there. On the cheerfulness and kindness all our hopes rest.

I am very anxious about Mr. Tracey's chaplain. But if I go on entering into all my points of anxiety and interest, I shall never leave off. Therefore I will only say that I hope you will write to me as soon as you come home, and give me an opportunity of unburdening my mind.

You must not see the house until it is quite ready. The bedsteads will not be put up for ten days, and there will be some trifling matters to get in after that. The dresses and linen are bought and making. The Superintendant's rooms are furnished, and she is living there.

I still remain in the hope that you will come with me to Mr. Chesterton's, where there is nothing to shock you but the sight of women in captivity—and where there is very much to gratify you in the humanity with which they are treated—for unless you see them now, you never can sufficiently feel what you will have done for those who turn out well.

We found it necessary that there should be some appeal for Mr. Chesterton to read to them, and then give them to read in their Cells. I wrote the enclosed for the purpose, and he found it affect them very heavily indeed.

Dear Miss Coutts | Most Faithfully Yours

CD.

P.S. I forgot to mention in reference to the Bishop of London that I shall be happy to call upon him when he is in town, if you please.

---

1 Urania Cottage, which opened in November.
2 His elaborate system of marks and rewards; later adopted in modified form.

Dickens's Letter To Fallen Women[1]

You will see, on beginning to read this letter, that it is not addressed to you by name. But I address it to a woman—a very young woman still—who was born to be happy, and has lived miserably; who has no prospect before her but sorrow, or behind her but a wasted youth; who, if she has ever been a mother, has felt shame, instead of pride, in her own unhappy child.

You are such a person, or this letter would not be put into your hands. If you have ever wished (I know you must have done so, sometimes) for a chance of rising out of your sad life, and having friends, a quiet home, means of being useful to yourself and others, peace of mind, self-respect, everything you have lost, pray read it attentively, and reflect upon it afterwards. I am going to offer you, not the chance but the certainty of all these blessings, if you will exert yourself to deserve them. And do not think that I write to you as if I felt myself very much above you, or wished to hurt your feelings by reminding you of the situation in which you are placed. GOD forbid! I mean nothing but kindness to you, and I write as if you were my sister.

Think, for a moment, what your present situation is. Think how impossible it is that it ever can be better if you continue to live as you have lived, and how certain it is that it must be worse. You know what the streets are; you know how cruel the companions that you find there, are; you know the vices practised there, and to what wretched consequences they bring you, even while you are young. Shunned by decent people, marked out from all other kinds of women as you walk along, avoided by the very children, hunted by the police, imprisoned, and only set free to be imprisoned over and over again—reading this very letter in a common jail—you have, already, dismal experience of the truth. But, to grow old in such a way of life, and among such company—to escape an early death from terrible disease, or your own maddened hand, and arrive at old age in such a course—will be an aggravation of every misery that you know now, which words cannot describe. Imagine for yourself the bed on which you, then an object terrible to look at, will lie down to die. Imagine all the long, long years of shame, want, crime, and ruin, that will rise before you. And by that dreadful day, and by the Judgment that will follow it, and by the recollection you are certain to have then, when it is too late, of the offer that is made to you now, when it is NOT too late, I implore you to think of it, and weigh it well!

There is a lady in this town, who, from the windows of her house, has seen such as you going past at night, and has felt her heart bleed at the sight. She is what is called a great lady; but she has looked after you with compassion, as being of her own sex and nature; and the thought of such fallen women has troubled her in her bed. She has resolved to open, at her own expense, a place of refuge very near London, for a small number of females, who, without such help, are lost for ever: and to make it A HOME for them. In this Home they will be taught all household work that would be useful to them in a home of their own, and enable them to make it comfortable and happy. In this Home, which stands in a pleasant country lane, and where each may have her little flower-garden, if she pleases, they will be treated with the greatest kindness; will lead an active, cheerful, healthy life; will learn many things it is profitable and good to know; and, being entirely removed from all who have any knowledge of their past career, will begin life afresh, and be able to win a good name and character. And because it is not the lady's wish that these young women should be shut out from the world, after they have repented and have learned how to do their duty there, and because it *is* her wish and object that they may be restored to society—a comfort to themselves and it—they will be supplied with every means, when some time shall have elapsed, and their conduct shall have fully proved their earnestness and reformation, to go abroad, where, in a distant country, they may become the faithful wives of honest men,[2] and live and die in peace.

I have been told that those who see you daily in this place, believe that there are virtuous inclinations lingering within you, and that you may be reclaimed. I offer the Home I have described in these few words, to you.

But, consider well before you accept it. As you are to pass from the gate of this Prison to a perfectly new life, where all the means of happiness from which you are now shut out, are opened brightly to you, so remember, on the other hand, that you must have the strength to leave behind you, all old habits. You must resolve to set a watch upon yourself, and to be firm in your control over yourself, and to restrain yourself; to be patient, gentle, persevering, and good-tempered. Above all things, to be truthful in every word you speak. Do this, and all the rest is easy. But you must solemnly remember that if you enter this Home without such constant resolutions, you will occupy, unworthily and uselessly, the place of some other unhappy girl, now wandering and lost; and that her ruin, no less than your own, will be upon your head, before Almighty God, who knows the secrets of our breasts, and Christ, who died upon the Cross, to save us.

In case there should be anything you wish to know, or any question you would like to ask, about this Home, you have only to say so, and every information shall be given to you. Whether you accept it or reject it, think of it. If you awake in the silence and solitude of night, think of it then. If any remembrance ever comes into your mind of any time when you were innocent and very different, think of it then. If you should be softened by a moment's recollection of any tenderness or affection you have ever felt, or that has ever been shown to you, or of any kind word that has ever been spoken to you, think of it then. If ever your poor heart is moved to feel, truly, what you might have been, and what you are, oh think of it then, and consider what you may be yet!

> Believe me that I am, indeed,
> YOUR FRIEND.

1 Untitled printed leaflet, enclosed in the previous letter to Miss Coutts.
2 Miss Coutts questioned this, but CD insisted; in *DC* the prostitute Martha Endell marries, while Little Em'ly remains single.

To John Forster, [21 DECEMBER 1847]

I am thoroughly delighted that you like what I sent. I enclose designs. Shadow-plate, poor. But I think Mr. Dombey admirable.[1] One of the prettiest things in the book ought to be at the end of the chapter I am writing now. But in Florence's marriage, and in her subsequent return to her father, I see a brilliant opportunity.

. . . Note from Jeffrey this morning, who won't believe (positively refuses) that Edith is Carker's mistress.[2] What do you think of a kind of inverted Maid's Tragedy, and a tremendous scene of her undeceiving Carker, and giving him to know that she never meant that?

1 The two plates for No. 16 (chs. 49–51), published Jan. 1848, were 'The Shadow in the little parlor' and 'Mr Dombey and the World'.

2 CD noted in the number-plan for No. 17, 'Edith *not* his mistress'; this allowed him to let her live, though he had considered her death, possibly by suicide. In Beaumont and Fletcher's *The Maid's Tragedy* Evadne first rejects her newly wedded husband out of loyalty to the king, whose mistress she had been, and then returns to him after stabbing the king. Evadne is rejected and kills herself. The 'Maid' Aspatia is betrayed and kills herself; in Macready's and Sheridan Knowles's adaptation *The Bridal*, which CD probably knew better, she survives.

To Angela Burdett Coutts, 24 DECEMBER 1847

Devonshire Terrace | Twenty fourth December 1847

My Dear Miss Coutts,

A thousand thanks for the noble turkey. I thought it was an infant, sent here by mistake, when it was brought in. It looked so like a fine baby.

I shall see you to-day, as I proposed yesterday. On Monday morning I go to Glasgow, but I shall be in Shepherd's Bush[1] again, please God, on that day week. I was there last night.

Very faithfully yours,

C.D.

1 London W, location of Urania Cottage.

To William Thackeray,[1] 9 JANUARY 1848

Devonshire Terrace, | Sunday Ninth January 1848.

My Dear Thackeray,

I need not tell you that I have been delighted—and cut tender, as it were to the very heart—by your generous letter.[2] You would never have written it if you had not known how truly and heartily I should feel it. I will only say the spirit in which I read it, was worthy of the spirit in which you wrote it, and that I think there is nothing in the world or out of it to which I am so sensitive as the least mark of such a manly and gallant regard.

I *do* sometimes please myself with thinking that my success has opened the way for good writers. And of this, I am quite sure now, and hope I shall be when I die— that in all my social doings I am mindful of this honour and dignity and always try to do something towards the quiet assertion of their right place. I am always possessed with the hope of leaving the position of literary men in England, something better and more independent than I found it.

There's a wild and egotistical fancy for you! See what it is to get into my confidence so thoroughly!

It is curious, about Punch, that I was so strongly impressed by the absurdity and injustice of my being left out of those imitations,[3] that I several times said at home here I would write to you and urge the merits of the case. But I never made up my mind to do so, for I feared you might misunderstand me.

I will tell you now, candidly, that I did not admire the design—but I think it is a great pity to take advantage of the means our calling gives us with such accursed readiness, of at all depreciating or vulgarizing each other—but this seems to me to be one of the main reasons why we are generally more divided among ourselves than artists who have not those means at their command—and that I thought your power thrown away on that series, however happily executed. So now I have made a clean breast too, and have nothing more to confess but that I am saving up the perusal of Vanity Fair[4] until I shall have done Dombey and that I cried most bitterly over your affecting picture of that cock-boat manned by babies, and shall never forget it.[5]

Kate says that whomsoever you bring on the 26th. will be warmly welcomed. We don't go in for grandeur on the occasion, and I am bent on a prodigious country dance at about the small hours.

Believe me my dear fellow I am very proud of your letter and very happy in its receipt. If I were to pursue the subject, I should come out in a style that would be full of all sorts of faults not insincerity. You have given me a new reason (if I wanted any) for interest in all you do, and for gratification in your progress afterwards: and though I did not write about Harness[6] with the least grain of ill humour, I think of him now as if he had done me a great service in occasioning me to write at all.

Affectionately yours,
CHARLES DICKENS.

1 William Makepeace Thackeray (1811–63†), novelist and early contributor to *Punch*. First met CD 1836; they moved in the same literary circles and were friendly but not always easy with each other, perhaps due to their different class backgrounds (Thackeray went to public school and Cambridge).
2 Not discovered, but clearly praising *D&S*.
3 Thackeray's series, *'Punch's Prize Novelists'*, began 3 Apr. 1847 with a parody of Bulwer Lytton; CD was not included.
4 No. 13 (chs. 43–6) published 1 Jan.
5 'Travels in London. The Curate's Walk', *Punch*, 27 Nov. 1847, describes the hard life of a widowed charwoman's three very small daughters, all thrifty, hard-working, and cheerful.

6 William Harness (1790–1869†), clergyman, literary scholar, and comic writer; one of the group to whom CD read *TC* in 1844.

To Hans Christian Andersen,[1] [?LATE JANUARY 1848]

A Thousand thanks, my dear Andersen, for your kind and dearly-prized remembrance of me in your Christmas book.[2] I am very proud of it, and feel deeply honored by it, and I cannot tell you how much I esteem so generous a mark of recollection from a man of such genius as you possess.

Your book made my Christmas fireside, happier. We were all charmed with it. The little boy, and the old man, and the pewter soldier, are my particular favorites. I read that story[3] over and over again, with the most unspeakable delight.

I was in Edinburgh a few weeks ago, where I saw some of your friends, who talked much about you. Come over to England again, soon! But whatever you do, don't leave off writing, for we cannot afford to lose any of your thoughts. They are too purely and simply beautiful to be kept in your own head.

We have long since come back from that sea-shore where I said Adieu to you, and are in our own house again. Mrs. Dickens says I am to give you her love. So says her sister. So say all my children. And as we are all in the same mind, I beg you to receive mine into the bargain, as the love of your true and admiring friend

CHARLES DICKENS

1 Hans Christian Andersen (1805–75), Danish author and poet, noted for his tales and fairy stories, which were meant for both adults and children. CD met him in 1847.
2 *A Christmas Greeting to my English Friends*, 1847, dedicated to CD.
3 One of the new tales, now known in England as 'The Tin Soldier'.

To William Thackeray, 30 MARCH 1848

Devonshire Terrace | Thirtieth March 1848.

My Dear Thackeray.
I purpose holding a solemn dinner here, on Tuesday the 11th. of April, to celebrate the conclusion of a certain immortal book.[1] Hour, half past six. It couldn't be done without you. Therefore, book it cher citoyen!—

Ever Faithfully Yours
CHARLES DICKENS

1 The other guests at the 'Dombey dinner' (CD's customary celebration at the end of a novel) were Macready, Forster, Beard, Lemon, Jerdan, Browne, D'Orsay, Ainsworth, Hogarth, Burnett, Evans, and Stone.

To *Augustus Tracey*, 8 APRIL 1848

H.M.S. Devonshire | Eighth April 1848

My Dear Admiral,

Keep your weather eye on that there Lion figure-head o' yourn, o' Monday, for in case I hoist my pennant aboard o' the Chartist Flagship,[1] I'm damned if I don't pour in a broadside on you (in answer to your'n) and rake you fore and aft, you swab!

So no more at present from—CHARLES DICKENS

his ⋎ mark

1 The Chartist leader Feargus O'Connor called a grand Chartist National Convention for Monday, 10 Apr. CD had some sympathy with the Chartists, and recognized that Tracey, as a prison governor (and ex- naval officer), would be on the other side.

To *Fanny Burnett*,[1] 3 MAY 1848

Devonshire Terrace | Wednesday Night | Third May 1848

My dear Fanny

All that I hear both from you and from Burnett of your illness, only convinces me that rest is the one great thing you want—I am confident that the benefit of that and cheerful society of old friends and relations will set you up again. And let me most affectionately & earnestly conjure you for the love of your Husband and Children and in the name of God and all the blessings we cannot ask from him unless we do our humble part to secure them—to look that fact steadily in the face and rest at all risks. There is nothing wanting but to make up your mind. *Doubt* is the anxiety and torture of a slow disease—*Decision* the sharp tearing out of a Tooth & there an end. It needs decision to determine not to work—make that resolution & you will begin to grow better. It is not in reason to expect that you should be better in such a short lived Holiday as you have had. It is next to impossible. Are you in any debt? I am sensible of the delicacy of Burnett in telling you that the trifle I was ready with & am ready with was yours in case of your changing your residence. But it is yours for rest. If you decide to take a Holiday and will calmly arrange in the best way you can to do so—I will send you a Hundred Pounds whenever you say the word—I do not think Manchester is healthy for you I confess. But all that can be considered at leisure.

Rest now & get a mind at ease. I am quite sure although I know how much fortitude and energy you have that you are worn out. There are times with me after mental excitement and toil when such a circumstance as the suicide of your Neighbour would become a dreadful idea that I could not shake off.

I have had sufferings of that sort sometime the oppression of which has been horrible. I am the better able to say that I know you want rest. Pray take it.

There is no Doctor on Earth so certain as the sinking within you. It is a friendly monitor in which there is nothing alarming—if you will only heed it. In any little local difficulty of arrangement with any Schoolmistresses or such like about your lessons—I will come down and see any body for you and arrange any thing with a readiness that I cannot & need not describe.

But do, do, do, decide to stop. Do not get worse when you may under God so easily get better.

I hope you will write me very soon more decisively. I shall be at Birmingham in any case most likely about the end of this month and shall certainly then come on to Manchester to see you. But don't stop for that.

Let me convey something of the earnestness I feel to you. Pray listen to my tender & heartfelt advice.—I write before going to Bed. I meant to say much more but cannot make up my mind to wait till tomorrow.

> In haste | Affectionately yours
> CHARLES DICKENS

1 CD's elder sister, suffering from consumption. Letter copied from CD's original.

To John Forster, [5 JULY 1848]

A change took place in poor Fanny about the middle of the day yesterday, which took me out there last night. Her cough suddenly ceased almost, and, strange to say, she immediately became aware of her hopeless state; to which she resigned herself, after an hour's unrest and struggle, with extraordinary sweetness and constancy. The irritability passed, and all hope faded away; though only two nights before, she had been planning for "after Christmas". She is greatly changed. I had a long interview with her to-day, alone; and when she had expressed some wishes about the funeral, and her being buried in unconsecrated ground,[1] I asked her whether she had any care or anxiety in the world. She said No, none. It was hard to die at such a time of life, but she had no alarm whatever in the prospect of the change; felt sure we should meet again in a better world; and although they had said she might rally for a time, did not really wish it. She said she was quite calm and happy, relied upon the mediation of Christ, and had no terror at all. She had worked very hard, even when ill; but believed that was in her nature, and neither regretted nor complained of it. Burnett had been always very good to her; they had never quarrelled; she was sorry to think of his going back to such a lonely home; and was distressed about her children, but not painfully so. She showed me how thin and worn she was; spoke about an invention she had heard of that she would like to have tried, for the deformed child's back;[2] called to my remembrance all our sister Letitia's patience and steadiness; and, though she shed tears sometimes, clearly impressed upon me that her mind was made up, and at rest. I asked her very often, if she could ever recall anything that she could leave to my doing, to put it down, or mention it to somebody if I was not there; and she said she would, but she firmly believed that there was nothing—nothing. Her husband being young, she said, and her children infants, she could not help thinking sometimes, that it would be very long in the course of nature before they were reunited; but she knew that was a mere human fancy, and could have no reality after she was dead. Such an affecting exhibition of strength and tenderness, in all that early decay, is quite indescribable. I need not tell you how it moved me. I cannot look round upon the dear children here, without some misgiving that this sad disease will not perish out of our blood with her; but I am sure I have no selfishness in the thought, and God knows how small the world looks to one who comes out of such a sick-room on a bright summer day. I don't know why I write this before going to bed. I only know that in the very pity and grief of my heart, I feel as if it were doing something.

1 Fanny and her husband were Dissenters. She died 2 Sept.
2 Her 8-year-old son Henry, thought to be the model for Paul Dombey.

To John Leech, 23 OCTOBER 1848

Devonshire Terrace. | Monday Twenty Third October | 1848.

My Dear Leech.

There is rather a good Britannia Saloon Bill, out, announcing a gentleman with a wooden leg to dance the Highland Fling. There is a portrait of him in the bill, with his wooden leg highly ornamented with rosettes.

It appears to me that this demands our attention. Egg[1] says he would like to go with us, and that if you will send him round a note, propoging an evening and a time for calling on him, he will, with yearnings, respond. Therefore if you'll send me one line, mentioning what evening this week you'll both call here—say at 7—I will be (as you know I always am) to the fore at the appointed time.

Ever Faithfully
CD.

1 Augustus Egg (1816–63†), genre and history painter. Met CD through Stone in 1847 and became a stalwart of the amateur theatricals.

To Angela Burdett Coutts, [?LATE 1848]

Devonshire Terrace | Thursday Evg.

My Dear Miss Coutts.

I am always for the promptest measures—and I suppose made you laugh by my ferocity.

I could call on you tomorrow afternoon at a quarter past four. If I don't hear from you, I will come then.

> Faithfully Yours always
> CHARLES DICKENS

To The Earl of Carlisle, 2 JANUARY 1849

Devonshire Terrace | Second January 1849.

My Dear Lord Carlisle.

I *must* tell you what pleasure I have had in the receipt of your pleasantest of letters, and how highly I esteem your affectionate frankness.

Here follows my defence.

William Swidger's catchword,[1] I give up. The temptation to intemperance in that wise, in a little book, where it is very difficult to mark the individuality of the characters, is great. We were merry about it here, too, because it is taken from a servant of ours, who invariably gives me that reply—and the more profoundly ignorant he is of what I speak of, the more earnest he makes it.

As the inventor of this sort of story, I may be allowed to plead that I think a little dreaminess and vagueness essential to its effect. I am greatly mistaken if the points that *do* tell, as they stand, would not be weakened without it. But the introduction of such a quality into any of my longer books, is what I never thought of in the remotest manner, and is something that I contemplate with a perfect shock. If it be there, it can only be because of my having taken great pains and thought about the subject in all its lights and shades. I shall set a close watch upon myself in future.

The process of my mind in the construction of such a picture as the opening one of twilight, is one incessant process of *rejection*. I bring it down to that, by working at it very slowly, and with infinite pains—rejecting things, day after day, as they come into my thoughts, and whipping the cream of them. But the heaping up of that quantity of shadows, I hold to be absolutely necessary, as a preparation to the appearance of the dark shadow of the Chemist. People will take anything for granted, in the Arabian Nights or the Persian Tales, but they won't walk out of Oxford Street, or the Market place of a county town, directly into the presence of a Phantom, albeit an allegorical one. And I believe it to be as essential that they come at that spectre through such a preparation of gathering gloom and darkness, as it would be for them to go through some such ordeal, in reality, before they could get up a private Ghost of their own.

—As the Counsel for the Prisoner says—"That is my case my Lud."

Mrs. Dickens can't understand why you should expect to be treated as Johnny was by Mr. Tetterby,[2] except on the principle of Mr. Tetterby's having boxed the ears of the wrong boy. It is a very just view of the case, I think.

I know you will be glad to hear that the little book has been a wonderful success. And I know you will believe me when I add that your earnestness and cordiality are stored away in my breast, among the most cherished associations connected with it.

> Dear Lord Carlisle | Yours ever faithfully
> CHARLES DICKENS

1 In *The Haunted Man*: 'That's what I always say, sir', and variants of this.
2 i.e. scolded. Mr Tetterby unjustly boxes Johnny's ears in *The Haunted Man* ch. 2.

To John Forster, [26 FEBRUARY 1849]

I wish you would look over carefully the titles now enclosed, and tell me to which you most incline. You will see that they give up *Mag* altogether, and refer exclusively to one name—that which I last sent you. I doubt whether I could, on the whole, get a better name.

1. *The Copperfield Disclosures.* Being the personal history, experience, and observation, of Mr. David Copperfield the Younger, of Blunderstone House.
2. *The Copperfield Records.* Being the personal history, experience, and observation, of Mr. David Copperfield the Younger, of Copperfield Cottage.
3. *The Last Living Speech and Confession of David Copperfield Junior,* of Blunderstone Lodge, who was never executed at the Old Bailey. Being his personal history found among his papers.
4. *The Copperfield Survey of the World as it Rolled.* Being the personal history, experience, and observation of David Copperfield the Younger, of Blunderstone Rookery.
7. *The Last Will and Testament of Mr. David Copperfield.* Being his personal history left as a legacy.
6. *Copperfield, Complete.* Being the whole personal history and experience of Mr. David Copperfield of Blunderstone House, which he never meant to be published on any account.

Or, the opening words of No. 6 might be *Copperfield's Entire;*[1] and *The Copperfield Confessions* might open Nos. 1 and 2. Now, WHAT SAY YOU?

1 A play on 'entire beer'.

To Mary Dickens, 27 FEBRUARY 1849

Devonshire Terrace | Tuesday Night, Feb. 27th, 1849.

My Dearest Mamey,

I am not engaged on the evening of your birthday. But even if I had an engagement of the most particular kind, I should excuse myself from keeping it, so that I might have the pleasure of celebrating at home, and among my children, the day that gave me such a dear and good daughter as you.

Ever affectionately yours
[CHARLES DICKENS]

To Mark Lemon,[1] 25 JUNE 1849

Devonshire Terrace, Monday, June 25th, 1849.

My Dear Lemon,

I am very unwilling to deny Charley the pleasure you so kindly offer him. But as it is just the close of the half-year when they are getting together all the half-year's work—and as that day's pleasure would weaken the next day's duty, I think I must be "more like an ancient Roman than a—"[2] Sparkler, and that it will be wisest in me to say nothing about it.

Get a clean pocket-handkerchief ready for the close of "Copperfield" No. 3; "simple and quiet, but very natural and touching."—*Evening Bore.*

Ever affectionately
[CHARLES DICKENS]

1 Mark Lemon (1809–70†), playwright and editor of *Punch* magazine 1841–70. Met CD in 1843 and formed a firm friendship which foundered in 1858 but was re-established in 1867.
2 Cf. *Hamlet*, v. ii. 333.

To John Forster, [10 JULY 1849]

Telling Forster that in accordance with the plan they had discussed he had introduced a great part of his MS[1] *into the fourth number of* Copperfield. I really think I have done it ingeniously, and with a very complicated interweaving of truth and fiction. Vous verrez. I am getting on like a house afire in point of health, and ditto ditto in point of number.

1 The fragment of autobiography, providing the substance for *DC* chs. 10–12.

To Frederick Evans, 25 SEPTEMBER 1849

Bonchurch, Tuesday Twenty Fifth September | 1849.

My Dear Evans.

This letter is really addressed both to you and Lemon—to whom Leech is anxious I should write.¹ As I promised yesterday to repeat my report to you, I write as *to* you to day, and will write to Lemon (at Whitefriars) tomorrow.

Leech continued pretty much the same until early yesterday evening, when he became worse; and, complaining afresh of the pain in his head, had leeches on again—mustard poultices to the back of his neck—a mustard bath to his feet—and bread-poultices on the leech-bites. I was there from 8 until ½ past 10, and observing the terrible restlessness of his condition, and knowing the utter impossibility of his getting better, and the moral certainty of his becoming worse, unless he could fall asleep, suggested that it might be well to mesmerize him. As neither he nor Mrs. Leech were anything but anxious that it should be done, on my assurance that it could not possibly do him any harm, we arranged that he should give some slight composing medicine of the Doctor's, a fair trial, and, if it did not succeed send to me. That they might do so, easily, I left John there, and came home to bed. At ½ past 2 this morning he knocked me up, and I went there. His restlessness had become most distressing, and it was quite impossible to get him to maintain any one position for five minutes. He was more like a ship in distress, in a sea of bedclothes, than anything else. In the difficulty of getting at him, and of doing the thing with any reasonable effect, at first, in a dark room, it was more than half an hour before I could so far tranquillize him (by the magnetism I mean) as to keep him composed, awake for five minutes together. Then, that effect began, and he said he felt comfortable and happy. As the clock struck four, he asked me (in the odd way, common to all people under that influence) what it meant by striking *twice*—and in a few minutes fell fast asleep, breathing deeply and regularly, and neither snoring nor starting. With one short interval of waking (less than a quarter of an hour) he slept an hour and thirty five minutes, during which a gentle perspiration came out upon his skin, and his face lost a very unpromising anxiety it had worn, and became quiet and perfectly peaceful. At the end of the sleep (the first he has had since he has been ill) as he expressed himself much refreshed, and took some breakfast in good spirits and with a relish, and as it was broad day, and there was no reason for his sleeping again, unless naturally, until tonight, I did not repeat the use of the agency, and came home at 7 o'Clock. I have seen him for two hours since. The doctor pronounces him greatly better (the said doctor was despondent and uneasy to me, last evening), and is much pleased with the improvement. To prevent talk about it, we have agreed not to tell him, the Doctor, of the thing—at all events for the present—though I understand he is favorable to Magnetism. I shall sleep there tonight, and I have little doubt, please God, that restlessness, which is the only thing to dread, can be kept off.

He is to have a whiting for his dinner.

Mrs. Leech has been out for a little to day—it is a most beautiful day—and has bathed in the sea, and so got freshened. She is in great spirits at the improvement, and was much astonished in the night when we talked across him as if he had been a Woolpack. His Eyes are not intolerant of light, he is not in pain, and he is quite cheerful. I am in great hopes that the improvement will continue. I have no doubt it will, if he can get rest tonight.

I am rather stupid, and write drowsily. Best remembrances from all.

Faithfully Yours always

CD.

1 The Leeches were holidaying with the Dickenses on the Isle of Wight. John Leech was knocked over by a wave and 'very ill with congestion of the brain', CD to Forster 24 Sept.

To John Forster, [7 OCTOBER 1849, Broadstairs]

I do great injustice to my floating ideas (pretty speedily and comfortably settling down into orderly arrangement) by saying anything about the Periodical now: but my notion is a weekly journal,[1] price either three-halfpence or two-pence, matter in part original and in part selected, and always having, if possible, a little good poetry. . . . Upon the selected matter, I have particular notions. One is, that it should always be *a subject*. For example, a history of Piracy; in connexion with which there is a vast deal of extraordinary, romantic, and almost unknown matter. A history of Knight-errantry, and the wild old notion of the Sangreal.[2] A history of Savages, showing the singular respects in which all savages are like each other; and those in which civilised men, under circumstances of difficulty, soonest become like savages. A history of remarkable characters, good and bad, *in* history; to assist the reader's judgment in his observation of men, and in his estimates of the truth of many characters in fiction. All these things, and fifty others that I have already thought of, would be compilations; through the whole of which the general intellect and purpose of the paper should run, and in which there would be scarcely less interest than in the original matter. The original matter to be essays, reviews, letters, theatrical criticisms, &c, &c, as amusing as possible, but all distinctly and boldly going to what in one's own view ought to be the spirit of the people and the time. . . . Now to bind all this together, and to get a character established as it were which any of the writers may maintain without difficulty, I want to suppose a certain SHADOW, which may go into any place, by sunlight, moonlight, starlight, firelight, candlelight, and be in all homes, and all nooks and corners, and be supposed to be cognisant of everything, and go everywhere, without the least difficulty. Which may be in the Theatre, the Palace, the House of Commons, the Prisons, the Unions,[3] the Churches, on the Railroad, on the Sea, abroad and at home: a kind of semi-omniscient, omnipresent, intangible creature. I don't think it would do to call the paper THE SHADOW: but I want something tacked to that title, to express the notion of its being a cheerful, useful, and always welcome Shadow. I want to open the first number with this Shadow's account of himself and his family. I want to have all the correspondence addressed to him. I want him to issue his warnings from time to time, that he is going to fall on such and such a subject; or to expose such and such a piece of humbug; or that he may be expected shortly in such and such a place. I want the compiled part of the paper to express the idea of this Shadow's having been in libraries, and among the books referred to. I want him to loom as a fanciful thing all over London; and to get up a general notion of "What will the Shadow say about this, I wonder? What will the Shadow say about that? Is the Shadow here?" and so forth. Do you understand? . . . I have an enormous difficulty in expressing what I mean, in this stage of the business; but I think the importance of the idea is, that once stated on paper, there is no difficulty in keeping it up. That it presents an odd, unsubstantial, whimsical, new thing: a sort of previously unthought-of Power going about. That it will concentrate into one focus all that is done in the paper. That it sets up a creature which isn't the Spectator, and isn't Isaac Bickerstaff,[4] and isn't anything of that kind: but in which people will be perfectly willing to believe, and which is just mysterious and quaint enough to have a sort of charm for their imagination, while it will represent common-sense and humanity. I want to express in the title, and in the grasp of the idea to express also, that it is the Thing at everybody's elbow, and in everybody's footsteps. At the window, by the fire, in the street, in the house, from infancy to old age, everyone's inseparable companion. . . . Now do you make anything out of this? which I let off as if I were a bladder full of it, and you had punctured me. I have not breathed the idea to any one; but I have a lively hope that it *is* an idea, and that out of it the whole scheme may be hammered.

1 The first issue of *HW* appeared on 30 Mar. 1850, price 2*d*. CD edited it and its successor, *AYR*, until his death. His idea of 'the Shadow' was dropped.
2 Pursuit of the Holy Grail.
3 i.e. the workhouses.
4 Pseudonym used by the satirist Jonathan Swift, and by Richard Steele when he launched the *Tatler*.

To John Leech, 9 OCTOBER 1849

Hotel Ballard,[1] Broadstairs sur Mer | Tuesday Night Ninth October 1849.

My Dear Leech.

I am quite delighted to receive such brilliant accounts of you, under your own hand and seal. I am well pleased too to learn that you have some idea of coming down here. You cannot think how delightful and fresh the place is (when it's fine) and how good the walks are. Room there is plenty, and to spare. I don't think there is any one in the hotel but ourselves, and I am sure we could not be more comfortable. So I hope you really will come, and give Ballard a turn.

As to him, he is a more decided and hopeless Maniac in point of contradiction, than he ever was. The last summer seems to have ripened him thoroughly. He won't let me have an opinion of my own, and bruises me (as Maclise would say) and dances on my body every day at dinner. Here is a specimen.

Scene, Our room. Time, halfpast 5. P.M. Kate, Georgina, and Inimitable, seated at dinner. In attendance—Ballard, and the amiable Waiter (the latter, decidedly the most affectionate and soft hearted man in the world.)

Inimitable (taking Punch) And how's Miss Collin going on, Ballard?

Ballard. Oh, well Sir, she ain't going on at all—not what can be called going on Sir, you know.

Inimitable (after being a little put down, and slightly recovering). Is she going off at all? Is she going to be married?

Ballard. No Sir, not much of that.

Inimitable. No, I suppose not? (*Smiles*)

Ballard (quickly) Not but what she's been very near it Sir once or twice—and is now, in deed—but I never believe a thing you know Sir till its done Sir.

(*The ladies laugh.*)

Georgina (here you must suppose the imitation) But she drinks, don't she Mr. Ballard.

Ballard. Oh dear no Miss!

Inimitable (to Georgina fiercely). What the Devil are you so fond of disparaging people for? Drinks! Who ever heard of her drinking! What a damned extraordinary thing it is, that you can't hold your tongue!—*I* never heard of her drinking (*to Ballard*) nor anybody else.

Ballard (with a smile of pity) Oh everybody *here,* has heard of it Sir—and knows it well—but we don't see these things in Broadstairs Sir, and make it a rule among ourselves never to mention 'em you know Sir. It's best not.

Inimitable (much affected by this Christian axiom) You're quite right Ballard. Nobody need know anything about it.

Ballard. Oh! They can't help knowing all about it Sir.

Inimitable (disconcerted). Why?

Ballard. Why, you see Sir when you come to be picked up in the street, four times in one winter, it gets talked about, you know. It gets to be the talk of the whole place, and who can wonder at it!

(Exit Ballard with dish-cover. Waiter takes round punch, and Scene closes).

I *think* I shall remain here until I have done the No., which will probably be about the 19th. or 20th. I am glad to find that you miss me, for I miss you too, and look forward to all sorts of snug evenings and other interchanges of friendship, in London, this next winter.

Kate and Georgy, Mamey and Katey, unite with me in loves, to you and Mrs. Leech. We all hope that if you come, she will come too, and maybe we might all return together?

> Ever My Dear Leech | Heartily Yours
> CHARLES DICKENS

1 James Ballard was the proprietor of the Albion Hotel, Broadstairs.

To William Brown,[1] 6 NOVEMBER 1849

Devonshire Terrace | Tuesday Night, Sixth November 1849.

My Dear Sir

We had a Committee at the Home today, when we transacted the usual business, and I paid all the bills. Mr. Chesterton, Mr. Illingworth, and Mr. Tennant were there with me.

I made them acquainted with the contents of the Bishop's letter from Adelaide,[2] which made upon all of them, as it had previously done upon me, an impression of heavy disappointment and great vexation. God send we may do better with some of the others! (I must claim, once more, to have been never a believer in Goldsmith.[3] And I think the Bishop's emphasizing marriage as their only chance of reclamation, most important. That idea I have steadily had in view, always.)

We found that Isabella Gordon was endeavouring to make a party in the house against Mrs. Morson[4] and Mrs. Macartney—was disturbing the general peace again—and intended coming to us with complaints. We investigated them with the utmost care, confronted her with Mrs. Morson, and were convinced that her whole story was utterly false and malicious. We ordered her to her room while we considered the subject, and she danced upstairs before Mrs. Morson, holding her skirts like a lady at a ball.

We were all of opinion that the authority of the place *must* be upheld—especially after the receipt of such news from abroad as the bishop's letter put us in possession of—and that however repugnant to our own feelings it might be, our duty to Miss Coutts and her beneficent undertaking *must* be discharged, and could only be discharged in one way. We therefore had her down again some time afterwards, and, to her utter bewilderment and amazement and that of the whole house, dismissed her.

Hannah Myers, who was unquestionably in concert with her, we spoke to in like manner, and confronted with both ladies. Her whole statement was evidently false, and her malignity against them (for the time) very intense and passionate. We informed her that after such conduct she could have no marks whatever for a week, and that she would, on the first repetition of such behaviour, be inexorably dismissed. She was not in the least prepared for this, and was quite as much amazed as the other.

A girl of the name of Sesina, lately come from Mr. Tracey's, and who I am persuaded is the pertest, vainest, (preposterous as the word seems in such a connexion) and most deceitful little Minx in this town—I never saw such a draggled piece of fringe upon the skirts of all that is bad—was the third party. I gave this young lady to understand, in the plainest and most emphatic words, that she appeared to us to misunderstand the place—and its object. That she must thoroughly change her whole feelings and demeanour, and put on a very different character, and conduct herself towards both the superintendents as a new creature altogether, if she had the least hope of remaining. My impression is that she will *not* remain; and I have no doubt, after taking her history and observing her closely while she tried to gloze[5] it, that it will be much better for us if she goes away.

It was five o'Clock, and dark, when we had got to this. As it was quite impossible to say what Isabella Gordon might or might not do if she were left alone with them, Mr. Chesterton and I remained there, until she went away. As she had no clothes she departed, of necessity, in those she had on, and in one of the rough shawls. We gave her half a crown to get a night's lodging, and directed her to a certain charity where she is *sure* to be taken in if she chooses, and if she means to work. Her going away, was a most pitiable sight. They all cried bitterly (Mrs. Morson and Mrs. Macartney included) and Rachael Bradley held to her skirts as she went out at the door, and implored us to let her stay and to give her one more trial—sobbing and weeping terribly. The girl herself, now that it had really come to this, cried, and hung down her head, and when she got out at the door, stopped and leaned against the house for a minute or two before she went to the gate—in a most miserable and wretched state. As it was impossible to relent, with any hope of doing good, we could not do so. We passed her in the lane, afterwards, going slowly away, and wiping her face with her shawl. A more forlorn and hopeless thing altogether, I never saw.

It has made a great impression on the rest, unquestionably. How long it may last, Heaven knows. As I know you will report this, all, to Miss Coutts I do not write to her about it,—the rather as I am in a dull state myself, just before going to bed, with the whole of the sad picture in my mind. Pray convey my best remembrances to Miss Coutts, and to Mrs. Brown.

I am glad to receive your hopeful and interesting account of Paris. I have heard here that the Legitimist party are plotting darkly in the desperate hope of setting on the Throne another of that ill-fated and incapable House. You see no signs of that, I suppose?

Faithfully Yours always
CHARLES DICKENS

---

1 Dr William Brown, who was married to Miss Coutts's former governess Hannah Meredith, served on the committee to oversee Urania Cottage; he attended the inmates in his medical capacity.

2 Miss Coutts had endowed the bishopric at Adelaide: the first bishop was Augustus Short, charged with overseeing the welfare of the emigrants from Urania Cottage. In June 1849 he sent poor reports on the first group to arrive.

3 Martha Goldsmith came to Urania Cottage in 1848 from the London Magdalen Hospital in Blackfriars, founded 1758 'for the reception of penitent prostitutes'.

4 Georgiana Morson, matron of Urania Cottage 1849–54; Mrs Macartney was her assistant.

5 Explain away.

To Mary Tayler, 6 NOVEMBER 1849

1 Devonshire Terrace | York Gate Regents Park | Sixth November 1849.

I am uncertain whether the correspondent to whom I address these few words be a gentleman or lady—and, if the latter, whether she be married or single. As the fault is not mine, I trust I need not apologize for the superscription of this letter.

In my opinion the Street Punch is one of those extravagant reliefs from the realities of life which would lose its hold upon the people if it were made moral and instructive. I regard it as quite harmless in its influence, and as an outrageous joke which no one in existence would think of regarding as an incentive to any course of action, or a model for any kind of conduct. It is possible, I think, that one secret source of the pleasure very generally derived from this performance, as from the more boisterous parts of a Christmas Pantomime, is the satisfaction the spectator feels in the circumstance that likenesses of men and women can be so knocked about, without any pain or suffering.

In countries where Punch is still a censor of the follies of the day, his influence is not beneficial. In the most popular Theatre in Naples, that is still his character every day and night; and Naples is perhaps the wickedest City upon earth.

CHARLES DICKENS

To William Brown, 7 NOVEMBER 1849

Devonshire Terrace. | Wednesday Seventh November 1849.

My Dear Sir

As a sequel to my letter of last night, I write to let you know that at halfpast eight this morning Mrs. Morson came here in a fly to tell me that little Sesina had been very insolent last night, and had been ordered to her own room; and that this morning she positively refused to get up, or to return any answer whatever, to any of the remonstrances that were made to her. In consequence of her behaviour they had kept the gardener in the house all night—a precaution at which I could not help laughing, when I thought of its object being a little dumpy atom of a girl whose head may be somewhere on a level with Mrs. Macartney's waist.

I directed Mrs. Morson to go back, give her her own clothes, and tell her she was to dress herself, and leave the place directly; or that when I came, in half an hour, if I found her still in bed, or found her there at all, I should send for a policeman and give her in custody for being there without our consent and making a disturbance. On receipt of this message she parleyed a little, and, after making a slight pretence of being ill, threw her nightcap to one end of the room and her nightgown to the other, and proceeded, very leisurely, to dress herself. On coming down stairs, she objected that she couldn't go away in the rain, on which she was told that she had better sit in the long room then, 'till I came. Declining this offer, she walked off. I met her in the lane, taking her departure. Before she went, she told Mrs. Morson "that she know'd Miss Coutts's address, and would write her a good long letter, telling her what treatment was had there." I passed her afterwards, walking in a jaunty way up Notting Hill, and refreshing herself with an occasional contemplation of the shop windows.

All the rest were very quiet, and Hannah Myers was very much subdued.[1] My belief is that this Sesina will join Isabella Gordon somewhere, today. I think she would corrupt a Nunnery in a fortnight.

Faithfully Yours always
CHARLES DICKENS

1 Hannah Myers absconded from Urania Cottage in Mar. 1850; she was soon back in prison.

To The Editor of The Times, 13 NOVEMBER 1849

Devonshire-terrace, Tuesday, Nov. 13.

Sir,

I was a witness of the execution at Horsemonger-lane this morning.[1] I went there with the intention of observing the crowd gathered to behold it, and I had excellent opportunities of doing so, at intervals all through the night, and continuously from daybreak until after the spectacle was over.

I do not address you on the subject with any intention of discussing the abstract question of capital punishment, or any of the arguments of its opponents or advocates. I simply wish to turn this dreadful experience to some account for the general good, by taking the readiest and most public means of adverting to an intimation given by Sir G. Grey in the last session of Parliament, that the Government might be induced to give its support to a measure making the infliction of capital punishment a private solemnity within the prison walls (with such guarantees for the last sentence of the law being inexorably and surely administered as should be satisfactory to the public at large), and of most earnestly beseeching Sir G. Grey, as a solemn duty which he owes to society, and a responsibility which he cannot for ever put away, to originate such a legislative change himself.

I believe that a sight so inconceivably awful as the wickedness and levity of the immense crowd collected at that execution this morning could be imagined by no man, and could be presented in no heathen land under the sun. The horrors of the gibbet and of the crime which brought the wretched murderers to it, faded in my mind before the atrocious bearing, looks and language, of the assembled spectators. When I came upon the scene at midnight, the *shrillness* of the cries and howls that were raised from time to time, denoting that they came from a concourse of boys and girls already assembled in the best places, made my blood run cold. As the night went on, screeching, and laughing, and yelling in strong chorus of parodies on Negro melodies, with substitutions of "Mrs. Manning" for "Susannah," and the like, were added to these. When the day dawned, thieves, low prostitutes, ruffians and vagabonds of every kind, flocked on to the ground, with every variety of offensive and foul behaviour. Fightings, faintings, whistlings, imitations of Punch, brutal jokes, tumultuous demonstrations of indecent delight when swooning women were dragged out of the crowd by the police with their dresses disordered, gave a new zest to the general entertainment. When the sun rose brightly—as it did—it gilded thousands upon thousands of upturned faces, so inexpressibly odious in their brutal mirth or callousness, that a man had cause to feel ashamed of the shape he wore, and to shrink from himself, as fashioned in the image of the Devil. When the two miserable creatures who attracted all this ghastly sight about them were turned quivering into the air, there was no more emotion, no more pity, no more thought that two immortal souls had gone to judgment, no more restraint in any of the previous obscenities, than if the name of Christ had never been heard in this world, and there were no belief among men but that they perished like the beasts.

I have seen, habitually, some of the worst sources of general contamination and corruption in this country, and I think there are not many phases of London life that could surprise me. I am solemnly convinced that nothing that ingenuity could devise to be done in this city, in the same compass of time, could work such ruin as one public execution, and I stand astounded and appalled by the wickedness it exhibits. I do not believe that any community can prosper where such a scene of horror and demoralization as was enacted this morning outside Horsemonger-lane Gaol is presented at the very doors of good citizens, and is passed by, unknown or forgotten. And when, in our prayers and thanksgivings for the season, we are humbly expressing before God our desire to remove the moral evils of the land, I would ask your readers to consider whether it is not a time to think of this one, and to root it out.

I am, Sir, your faithful servant,
CHARLES DICKENS.

---

1 Frederick and Maria Manning were found guilty of murdering her lover, and hanged together on 13 Nov. According to *The Times* of 14 Nov., more than 30,000 people were present. Maria Manning is thought to have inspired Mademoiselle Hortense in *BH*.

To John Forster, [20 NOVEMBER 1849]

Copperfield done after two days' very hard work indeed; and I think a smashing number.[1] His first dissipation I hope will be found worthy of attention, as a piece of grotesque truth.

1 No. 8, chs. 22–4.

To Jane Seymour Hill,[1] 18 DECEMBER 1849

Devonshire Terrace | Tuesday Morng. eighteenth Decr. 1849

Madam.

I am most exceedingly and unfeignedly sorry to receive your Letter and to have been the unfortunate occasion of giving you a moment's distress. I am bound to admit that in the character to which I take it for granted you refer, I have yielded to several little recollections of your general manner but I assure you that the original of a great portion of that character is well known to me and to several friends of mine and is wholly removed from you and a very different person. Indeed I never represent an individual but always a combination of individuals in one. To avoid giving offence, when I was conscious of remembering you—as where the person is represented as using a chair for a table & so forth—I was most careful (as I considered) to keep the calling,[2] domestic circumstances &c of the character quite clear of yours and I assure you that I had no idea of mixing you up with it further than by a whimsical shadowy possibility of association that I thought might be even amusing and serviceable to you rather than the reverse.

As to personal appearances, I have been for years in the habit of meeting in the streets some one unknown to me by name or pursuit, whom it resembles almost if not quite as much as it resembles you. If I had the least thought of presenting you personally in my book I could have had your portrait drawn any morning in the week and put there. Pray consider all these things and do not make yourself unhappy.

I should be most truly pained if you were to remain under the impression that you have any cause of complaint against me or that I have done you any injury however innocently. I am so sincere in this believe me that rather than you should pass another of those sleepless nights of which you write to me or go another morning tearfully to your daily work, I would alter the whole design of the character and remove it, in its progress, from the possibility of that bad construction at which you hint.[3]

I am quite serious in this. I do not mean it to be a very good character now, but I will make it so, and oblige the Reader to hold it in a pleasant remembrance—if that will give you any relief from this—by me quite unexpected and unforeseen distress.

Faithfully yr
CHARLES DICKENS

---

1 Mrs Jane Seymour Hill, manicurist and chiropodist, and a near neighbour of CD's. She was greatly distressed by what she and others were convinced was the portrait of her as Miss Mowcher, who had just been introduced in *DC* ch. 22., as 'a pursy dwarf, of about forty or forty-five, with a very large head and face'.

2 Though Miss Mowcher is also a chiropodist, her attentions to Steerforth in ch. 22 are to his hair, and her offers to David are to improve his eyebrows and whiskers.

3 This CD clearly did. Her visit to David in ch. 32 reverses the earlier impression; in ch. 61 she helps to arrest Littimer, and is 'cheered right home to her lodgings'.

To *William de Cerjat*, 29 DECEMBER 1849

Devonshire Terrace. | Saturday Twenty Ninth December 1849.

My Dear Cerjat.

I received your letter at breakfast-time this morning, with a pleasure my eloquence is unable to express, and your modesty unable to conceive. It is so delightful to be remembered at this time of the year, in your house where we have been so happy, and in dear old Lausanne that we always hope to see again, that I can't help pushing away the first page of Copperfield No.10—now staring at me with what I may literally call a *blank* aspect—and plunging energetically into this reply.

What a strange coincidence that is, about Blunderstone House! Of all the odd things of that kind, I have ever known (and their name is Legion) I think it is the oddest. I went down into that part of the country on the 7th. of January last year, when I was meditating the story; and chose Blunderstone for the sound of its name. I had previously observed much of what you say about the poor girls. In all you suggest with so much feeling of their return to virtue being cruelly cut off, I concur with a sore heart. I have been turning it over in my mind for some time, and hope, in the history of Little Em'ly (who *must* fall—there is no hope for her)[1] to put it before the thoughts of people, in a new and pathetic way, and perhaps to do some good. You will be glad to hear, I know, that Copperfield is a great success. I think it is better liked than any of my other books.[2]

We had a most delightful time at Watson's (for both of them we have preserved and strengthened a real affection) and were the gayest of the gay. There was a Miss Boyle staying in the house who is an excellent Amateur Actress,[3] and she and I got up some scenes from the School for Scandal, and from Nickleby, with immense success. We played in the old hall, with the Audience filled up and running over with servants. The entertainments concluded with feats of legerdemain (for the performance of which I have a pretty good apparatus, collected at divers times and in divers places) and we then fell to country dances of a most frantic description, and danced all night. We often spoke of you and Mrs. Cerjat, and of Haldimand, and wished you were all there. Watson and I have some fifty times "registered a vow" (like O'Connell) to come to Lausanne together, and have even settled in what month and week. Something or other has always interposed to prevent us; but I hope, please God, most certainly to see it again, when my labors-Copperfieldian shall have terminated.

You have no idea what that hanging of the Mannings really was. The conduct of the people was so indescribably frightful, that I felt, for some time afterwards, almost as if I were living in a city of Devils. I feel, at this hour, as if I never could go near the place again. My letters[4] have made a great to-do, and led to a great agitation of the subject; but I have not a confident belief in any change being made, mainly because the total abolitionists are utterly reckless and dishonest (generally speaking) and would play the deuce with any such proposition in Parliament, unless it were strongly supported by the Government—which it certainly would not be: the Whig motto (*in* office) being *"laissez aller"*. I think Peel[5] might do it, if he came in. Two points have occurred to me, as being a good commentary on the objections to my idea. The first is, that a most terrific uproar was made, when the hanging-processions were abolished, and the ceremony shrunk from Tyburn to the Prison Door. The second is, that at this very time, under the British Govt.—in New South Wales— executions take place *within the prison Walls,* with decidedly improved results. (I am waiting to explode this fact, on the first man of mark who gives me the opportunity.)

Unlike you, we have had no marriages or givings in marriage, here. We might have had, but a certain young lady whom you know, is hard to please.[6] The children are all well, thank God! Charley is going to Eton, the week after next, and has passed a first rate examination. Kate is quite well, and unites with me and Georgina, in loves to you and Mrs. Cerjat, and Haldimand—whom I would give a good deal (tell him) to have several hours contradiction of, at his own table. Good Heaven, how obstinate we would both be! I see him leaning back in his chair, with his right forefinger out, and saying "Good God!" in reply to some position of mine—and then laughing.

All in a minute, a feeling comes over me, as if you and I were still walking, smoking cigars, outside the Inn at Martigny—the piano sounding inside, and Lady Mary Taylour singing. I look into my garden (which is covered with snow) rather dolefully, but take heart again, and look brightly forward to another expedition to the Great St. Bernard, when Mrs. Cerjat and I shall laugh as I fancy I have never laughed since, in one of those one-sided Cars—when somebody's bed at the Convent (was it yours or Watsons?) shall break down again—and when we shall again learn from Haldimand, in a little dingy Cabaret[7] at lunch-time, how to secure a door in travelling (do you remember?) by balancing a chair against it, on its two hind legs!

I do hope that we may all come together again, once more, while there is a head of hair left among us, and in that hope remain my Dear Cerjat Your faithful friend

C.D.

1 The news of her elopement with Steerforth comes in ch. 31, which CD was about to start writing.
2 CD referred to it as his 'favourite child' in his 1869 preface.
3 Mary Boyle (1810–90†), writer. Distant cousin of Lavinia Watson; acted with CD's amateur company and became friendly with him. He described her as 'the very best actress I ever saw, off the stage—and immeasurably better than a great many I have seen on it' (to Edward Bulwer Lytton, 3 Sept. 1850).
4 To *The Times,* 13 and 17 Nov.
5 Sir Robert Peel (1788–1850†), Conservative prime minister 1834–5 and 1841–6.
6 Obviously Georgina.
7 Tavern.

To Elizabeth Gaskell,[1] 31 JANUARY 1850

Devonshire Terrace | Thirty First January 1850.

My Dear Mrs. Gaskell

You may perhaps have seen an announcement in the papers, of my intention to start a new cheap weekly journal of general literature?

I do not know what your literary vows of temperance or abstinence may be, but as I *do* honestly know that there is no living English writer whose aid I would desire to enlist, in preference to the authoress of Mary Barton (a book that most profoundly affected and impressed me) I venture to ask you whether you can give me any hope that you will write a *short* tale, or any number of tales, for the projected pages.

No writer's name will be used—neither my own, nor any others—every paper will be published without any signature; and all will seem to express the general mind and purpose of the Journal, which is, the raising up of those that are down, and the general improvement of our social condition. I should set a value on your help, which your modesty can hardly imagine; and I am perfectly sure that the least result of your reflection or observation in respect of the life around you, would attract attention and do good.

Of course I regard your time as valuable, and consider it so, when I ask you if you could devote any of it to this purpose.

If you could, and would prefer to speak to me on the subject, I should be very glad indeed to come to Manchester for a few hours, and explain anything you might wish to know. My unaffected and great admiration of your book, makes me very earnest in all relating to you.

Forgive my troubling you, for this reason, and believe me ever

Faithfully Yours
CHARLES DICKENS

Mrs. Dickens and her sister send their love. I should like to know what you have done with your protegée.[2]

1 Elizabeth Gaskell (1810–65†), novelist. Her first novel, *Mary Barton: A Story of Manchester Life*, was published Oct. 1848. CD invited her to dinner in Mar. 1849, probably their first meeting. She was the first of many authors CD invited to contribute to his as yet unnamed journal.
2 Gaskell wrote to CD on 8 Jan. for help with emigration arrangements for a 16-year-old girl in prison for theft and prostitution.

To Angela Burdett Coutts, 4 MARCH 1850

Devonshire Terrace | Fourth March 1850.

My Dear Miss Coutts.

The Colonial letters are certainly discouraging;[1] but less so, having the girls here, than if we had sent them out.

I return Sir W Napier's letter. It is a very good and characteristic one, and has interested me very much.

I dream of Mrs. Chisholm,[2] and her housekeeping. The dirty faces of her children are my continual companions. I forgot to tell you that she asked me if it were true that the girls at Shepherd's Bush *"had Pianos"*. I shall always regret that I didn't answer yes—each girl a grand, down stairs—and a cottage in her bedroom—besides a small guitar in the wash-house.

Ever Faithfully Yours
CHARLES DICKENS

1 i.e. reports on the young women from Urania Cottage who had emigrated.
2 Caroline Chisholm (1808–77†), immigration administrator, pioneer in aiding emigrants to Australia. CD visited her in Islington for 'A Bundle of Emigrants' Letters', an article for the first issue of *HW*. She is thought to have inspired Mrs Jellyby in *BH*.

To *William Bradbury*, 14 MARCH 1850

148 Kings Road, Brighton | Fourteenth March 1850.

My Dear Bradbury
"Positively for this occasion only", I think the proposed change in the Preliminary Word, *good*. The title now looks excellent.[1] I really think it is an extraordinary production; and if the Public be not satisfied, I don't know what they would have. *I* never read such a Number of anything else.

And here's a man for you!—They sent me today the proposed No. 2, in a list of articles. The amazing undersigned feels a little uncomfortable at a want of Household tenderness in it. So he puts away Copperfield, at which he has been working like a Steam Engine—writes (he thinks) exactly the kind of thing to supply the deficiency[2]—and sends it off, by this post, to Forster!

What an amazing man!

Ever Yours | CD.

My love to Evans.
P.S. All pieces of plate to be addressed, 1 Devonshire Terrace.

1 The title, 'A Preliminary Word', runs across both columns of the first page of *HW*; thereafter, the title of the first article was confined to the left-hand column.
2 'A Child's Dream of a Star', *HW*, 6 Apr. 1850.

To *Elizabeth Gaskell*, 14 MARCH 1850

Brighton, 148 Kings Road | Fourteenth March 1850.

My Dear Mrs. Gaskell
Will you address your answer to this, to Devonshire Terrace, and write *by return*?
I am strongly of opinion that as Lizzie[1] is not to die, she ought to put that child in Susan's own arms, and not to lay it down at the door. Observe!—The more forcibly

and strongly and affectingly, you exhibit her mother's love for her, the more cruel you will make this crime of desertion in her. The sentiment which animates the mother, will have been done violence to by the daughter; and you cannot set up the one, without pulling down the other.

The slightest alteration will suffice to set this right. If you will make it, in your answer, I should prefer it to *our* doing it; but rely upon it, it will do Lizzie an immense service,—and I am sure you would do anything to serve her! I am quite confident of its removing an objection otherwise certain to suggest itself—and the better you write, the stronger it is. I can't tell you how earnestly I feel it.

> Dear Mrs. Gaskell | Faithfully Yours always
> CHARLES DICKENS

1 Gaskell's story 'Lizzie Leigh' was serialized in the first three numbers of *HW*. Susan looks after Lizzie's illegitimate child; Gaskell made the changes CD suggested.

To *William H. Wills*,[1] 29 MARCH 1850

Devonshire Terrace | Twenty Ninth March 1850.

My Dear Wills.

I have sent a note to you just now, in Wellington Street. I suppose you'll get it before you get this?

I really can't *promise* to be comic. Indeed your note puts me out a little, for I had just sat down to begin "It will last my time".[2]—I will shake my head a little, and see if I can shake a more comic substitute out of it.

The first part of Miss Martineau's Story is in Greening's hands. It is heavy.

As to *two* comic articles, or two any sort of articles, out of me, that's the intensest extreme of nogoism.

> Faithfully CD.

1 William Henry Wills, 'Harry' (1810–80†), journalist and journal editor. Contributor to *Punch* since 1841, assistant editor for *Chambers's Journal* (Edinburgh). He worked for CD on the *Daily News* and became assistant editor of *HW* and later *AYR*; their offices were in Wellington Street, London WC. He was devoted to CD.
2 The refrain of CD's dark and prophetic 'A December Vision', *HW*, 14 Dec. 1850.

To *Daniel Maclise*, 1 APRIL 1850

Devonshire Terrace | Monday First April 1850.

My Dear Mac. I don't know where you got to, last night. The young lady was *not* interesting, and I was after you in three or four minutes.

I have written to Forster that you will meet him at the Rainbow today, *at halfpast five*. I don't think I shall come, having my eye on tomorrow.

> Affecy. always
> CD.

To Reginald Mason,[1] 20 APRIL 1850

Office of Household Words | Twentieth April 1850.

Dear Sir

I must ask you to forgive me for having, in the pressure of occupations that carry me into quite another region, forgotten your papers (though I remembered you) until I blushed to receive your reminder.

I have read them carefully. They seem to me to want purpose, and to stop short of any decided point of interest. They are not violent or unnatural—the Virginian family for example, might have existed just as you describe them; which is not in itself any reason for putting them into print—but they come to nothing. The mere circumstance of a Slave Dealer wanting to buy a slave, and his master refusing to sell him, is not enough. To make that dramatic (I don't mean in the Theatrical sense, but as a piece of art) the slave should be in doubt about his destiny, and the master should draw the Slave-Dealer out, by asking questions, as if he were undecided. Then, the landlord should have something about him, in his way of thinking and expressing himself, *like* a landlord, and a collector of curiosities. And the good-natured gambler ought to have something about *him,* expressive of *his* character and pursuits. It is not enough to say that they were this, or that. They must shew it for themselves, and have it in their grain. Then, they would act on one another, and would act for themselves whether the author liked it or no. As it is, there is not enough reason for your writing about them, because they do nothing and work out nothing.

I promised to tell you the truth. And this is the truth, as I feel it.

> Faithfully Yours
> CHARLES DICKENS

---

1 R. H. Mason, author of *Pictures of Life in Mexico with Etchings by the Author,* 1852. CD frequently replied at some length to would-be contributors to *HW,* explaining the reasons for his rejection or request for changes.

To Daniel Maclise, 21 APRIL 1850

Devonshire Terrace | Sunday Twenty First April, 1850.

My Dear Mac. Blossommy,[1] Forster, Ainsworth,[2] I, (and I hope Stanny) propose to dine at the Trafalgar, Greenwich, on Wednesday at 6, to talk over a projected small club, to dine together now and then. Can you leave your executional duties[3]—say at 4 (when Forster and I would be waiting in Wellington Street for you), and come? Say yes. Its a poor heart which *never* rejoices!

Ever Affectionately
CD.

1 Nickname for Robert Bell (1800–67†), journalist and writer.
2 William Harrison Ainsworth (1805–1882†), novelist and magazine editor. He had great success with his 'Newgate Novels' in the 1830s. Introduced CD to Forster and Cruikshank.
3 Maclise was judging paintings submitted for the Summer Exhibition.

To John Forster, [7 MAY 1850]

I am extremely sorry to hear about Fox.[1] Shall call to enquire, as I come by to the Temple. And will call on you (taking the chance of finding you) on my way to that Seat of Boredom. I wrote my paper for H.W. yesterday, and have begun Copperfield this morning. Still undecided about Dora, but MUST decide to-day.[2] La difficulté d'écrire l'Anglais m'est extrêmement ennuyeuse. Ah, mon Dieu! si l'on pourrait toujours écrire cette belle langue de France! Monsieur Rogere! Ah! qu'il est homme d'esprit, homme de génie, homme des lettres! Monsieur Landore! Ah qu'il parle Français—pas parfaitement comme un ange—un peu (peut-être) comme un diable! Mais il est bon garçon—sérieusement, il est un de la vraie noblesse de la nature. Votre tout dévoué, CHARLES. À Monsieur Monsieur Fos-tere.

1 William Johnson Fox (1786–1864†), preacher and politician; present at TC reading in 1844. He had slipped and fallen on leaving Forster's rooms the previous evening.
2 i.e. about her early death (Forster, 536–7).

To Henry Austin, 12 MAY 1850

Devonshire Terrace | Sunday Twelfth May, 1850.

My Dear Henry
    The Sanitary fellows are such terrible people, and give such short notice! The Meeting was originally to have been on Monday Week; then they change it to

Monday.¹ Now, on Monday I really *can't* go. My work (as you may suppose) is very hard just now; and at this time of the Month, I *must* get air and exercise in the evening—and think. It is not the time it would take that is of importance, but the putting of myself out. If I get fierce and antagonistic about burials, I can't go back to Copperfield for hours and hours. This is really the sort of condition on which I hold my inventive powers; and I can't get rid of it.

I am sincerely anxious to serve the cause, and am doing it all the good I can, by side-blows in the Household Words—in the compilation, the "Narrative" too. You will see next week, that I have turned a paper called "The Begging Letter Writer", to sanitary purposes. I will. [ ]² gaps and trapdoors of advocacy, that open unexpectedly when I have my hands (and head) full of other work.

I shall be very glad to have the High-Pressure notes.³ Will you dine in Wellington Street on Saturday.

1 The meeting of the Metropolitan Sanitary Association on 13 May in support of the Metropolitan Interments Bill; many undertakers were present and rushed the platform. See CD, 'From the Raven in the Happy Family', *HW*, 8 June 1850.
2 The cutting away of ending and signature has removed about forty-five words here.
3 Austin championed the high pressure system for London's water supply.

To Jacob Bell,¹ [12] MAY 1850

Devonshire Terrace | Eleventh May, 1850. Sunday

My Dear Sir

I have thought a great deal about that woman, the Wardswoman in the Itch Ward, who was crying about the dead child. If anything useful can be done for her, I should like to do it. Will you bear this in mind, in confidence, and if you can put me in the way of helping her, do me the kindness of telling me how it can be best done? I am not afraid to ask you, because I have an inward assurance that you will understand me?

Without identifying the Workhouse, I have written a fanciful kind of description of our Walk, which you will find at page 204 of the enclosed proof. Will you return it to me, whenever you may have had leisure to read it? I hope it will not remind you, disagreeably, of this day Week.

Faithfully Yours
CHARLES DICKENS

1 Jacob Bell (1800–59†), philanthropist and founder of the Pharmaceutical Society, shortly to enter Parliament as MP for St Albans. For CD's account of their visit to Marylebone Workhouse see 'A Walk in a Workhouse', *HW*, 25 May 1850.

To Michael Faraday,[1] 28 MAY 1850

Devonshire Terrace | Twenty Eighth May, 1850.

Dear Sir

I take the liberty of addressing you as if I knew you personally; trusting that I may venture to assume that you will excuse that freedom.

It has occurred to me that it would be extremely beneficial to a large class of the public, to have some account of your late lectures on the breakfast-table,[2] and of those you addressed, last year, to children. I should be exceedingly glad to have some papers in reference to them, published in my new enterprize "Household Words". May I ask you whether it would be agreeable to you,—and, if so, whether you would favor me with the loan of your notes of those Lectures for perusal?

I am sensible that you may have reasons of your own, for reserving the subject to yourself. In that case, I beg to assure you that I would on no account approach it.

With great respect and esteem, I remain Dear Sir

Your faithful Servant
CHARLES DICKENS

1 Michael Faraday (1791–1867†), scientist, discoverer of electromagnetic induction. Director of the Laboratory at the Royal Institution, where he created the Friday evening lectures to popularize science, and the Christmas lectures for children.
2 His course of six lectures, Apr.–June 1850, 'On some points of domestic philosophy—a fire, a candle, a lamp, a chimney, a kettle, ashes'. Faraday lent his notes, which led to two *HW* articles, 'The Chemistry of a Candle' (3 Aug. 1850) and 'The Mysteries of a Tea-Kettle' (16 Nov. 1850).

To Catherine Dickens, 17 AUGUST 1850

Broadstairs | Saturday Night | 17th. August 1850

My Dearest Kate,

Although I am writing at one table and Georgy at another in the same room, I have no idea what she is writing to you, so, if there should be any repetition between us, it is not my fault or hers. Upon the whole, I think the baby rather a failure down here.[1] Charley was the most struck last night as connecting it with you. Sydney I think has been the most reflective on the subject to-day. He was playing the piano after dinner while I was reading and suddenly left off with, "I say Pa, can Dora talk?" On my replying No, he seemed to think that weak on her part and put the question, "Is she tall?" In answer to this I measured off about a quarter of a yard on the table and said she was about that size. He gave her up after that and except suggesting that Mrs.Gobson's little girl's name must be Dora too, said no more on the subject. He is in great force. Frank is so handsome that he is quite a sight to behold; they all look wonderfully well.

The house is excellent. We were in mighty confusion last night and this morning getting it to rights, but it is now quite orderly and is full of sweet air, sea views and comfort. I was not successful in getting to work to-day but I hope to resume tomorrow. Without you we shall be quite incomplete and a great blank everywhere.

I suppose Georgy will have told you the Broadstairs news—how the place is full—how little Miss Baldwin[2] is the sworn friend of Mamey & Katey—how Miss Collin[3] still wears the pink gown a little more washed—how Barnes had a paralytic stroke (which came on without notice when he was going up in the steamer the other day and now lies speechless in London). I see by bills on the walls hereabouts that a maniac by the name of Gill (Fanny Vining's husband very possibly)[4] has the Margate Theatre and there are two new houses in Broadstairs.

I will not attempt to tell you, my love, how delighted I have been to receive such good tidings of you, and what relief and happiness we felt last night in coming down to think that it was over, and that we had left you so well. I thank God most heartily. Of course I shall see you next week as soon as I can possibly finish the No. concerning which I am rather low and penitent to-night, but shall brush up, I have no doubt, to-morrow. I have arranged to write in the Drawing Room. I tried Georgina's room, but the Preventive men[5] looked at me, and you know what a settler that would be to the most retiring of writers. Take every care of yourself and don't let them coddle you or weaken you by too much conventionality. I think of you all day. You will not be able to write before I see you I suppose, but when you can write I know you will. God bless you my darling,

Ever most affly yours,
CHARLES DICKENS

1 Dora, born 16 Aug.
2 Daughter of Edward Baldwin, the editor and proprietor of the *Morning Herald*, on which Thomas Beard was a reporter.
3 Miss Collins was the bathing-machine woman. David Barnes was a house agent and bath proprietor.
4 Fanny Elizabeth Vining (d. 1869†), acted with Macready and Charles Kean; married to Charles Gill, actor and theatre manager.
5 Coastguard officers employed to prevent smuggling.

To Catherine Dickens, 21 AUGUST 1850

Broadstairs | Wednesday Night | Twenty First August, 1850.

My Dearest Kate.

I received your letter with the utmost delight this morning, and never thought your handwriting so good.

Even now, I am uncertain of my movements, for, after another splitting day, I have still Dora to kill—I mean the Copperfield Dora—and cannot make certain how long it will take to do. But if I could manage it before dinner tomorrow, I should come up by the Express train tomorrow night, arriving at home between 11 and 12. This is not for your information (as you will have shut up shop then), but for Annes,[1] that she may make my bed in the night-nursery where I can have air. If I can't come tomorrow, I shall come on Friday, when I have a good deal before me at the H.W. office. I shall not come back until Saturday morning in any case. And of course come when I may, I shall come straight home.

Ever my Dearest | Most affectionately

(John waiting for the Post, with his mouth open, like a Post office in itself)

CD.

1 Catherine's maid.

To *Catherine Dickens*, 3 SEPTEMBER 1850

Broadstairs | Tuesday Third September | 1850.

My Dearest Kate.

I enclose a few lines from Georgy, and write these to say that I purpose being home at some time on Thursday, but I cannot say precisely when, as it depends on what work I do tomorrow. Yesterday, Charles Knight, White, Forster, Charley, and I, walked to Richborough Castle and back. Knight dined with us afterwards, and the Whites, the Bicknells, and Mrs. Gibson came in, in the evening and played Vingt et un. Forster was in a tip top state of amiability, but I think I never heard him *half so loud.* (!) He really, after the heat of the walk, so disordered me that by no process I could possibly try, could I get to sleep afterwards. At last, I gave it up as a bad job, and walked about the house 'till 5—paying Georgina a visit, and getting her up for company. I was just as I was that night at Geneva. But I tumbled out again at half past 7 this morning, and tumbled into the sea.

Having no news, I must tell you a story of Sydney. The children, Georgy, and I, were out in the garden on Sunday evening (by the bye, I made a beautiful passage down, and got to Margate a few minutes after one) when I asked Sydney if he would go to the Railroad and see if Forster was coming. As he answered very boldly, Yes, I opened the garden gate. Upon which he set off, alone, as fast as his legs would carry him; and being pursued, was not overtaken until he was through the Lawn House Archway, when he was still going on at full speed—I can't conceive where. Being brought back in triumph, he made a number of fictitious starts, for the sake of being overtaken again, and we made a regular game of it. At last when he and Ally had run away,—instead of running after them, we came into the garden, shut the gate, and crouched down on the ground. Presently, we heard them come back and say to each other with some alarm, "Why, the gate's shut, and they are all gone!" Ally began in a dismayed way to cry out, but the Phenomonon, shouting "Open the gate!" sent an enormous stone flying into the garden (among our heads) by way of alarming the establishment. I thought it a wonderful piece of character, shewing great readiness of resource. He would have fired a perfect battery of stones—or very likely have broken the pantry window, I think—if we hadn't let him in.

They are all in great force, and send their loves. They are all much excited with the expectation of receiving you on Friday—and would start me off to fetch you, now, if I would go.

Our train on Friday will be halfpast 12. I have spoken to Georgy about the partridges, and hope we may find some.

Ever my Dearest Kate | Most affectionately Yours
CHARLES DICKENS

To John Forster, [15 SEPTEMBER 1850]

I have been tremendously at work these two days; eight hours at a stretch yesterday, and six hours and a half to-day, with the Ham and Steerforth chapter,[1] which has completely knocked me over—utterly defeated me!

1 Ch. 55, the climax of *DC*.

To John Forster, [21 OCTOBER 1850]

I am within three pages of the shore; and am strangely divided, as usual in such cases, between sorrow and joy. Oh, my dear Forster, if I were to say half of what Copperfield makes me feel to-night, how strangely, even to you, I should be turned inside-out! I seem to be sending some part of myself into the Shadowy World.

To Lord John Russell, 18 DECEMBER 1850

Devonshire Terrace. | Wednesday Eighteenth December | 1850.

My Dear Lord.

Allow me to thank you for your ready and kind reply to my note, and to put you in possession of the exact state of Mr. John Poole's case.

He is 64 years of age. He is in a prematurely shattered state, and perfectly unable to write. He is very anxious to do so, and has (to my certain knowledge) tried hard; but the achievement of the most ordinary sentence in a letter, is a work of infinite labor to him. If he could even have compiled skilfully, I could have put the means of living without present anxiety, in his way, through employment on "Household Words", but no sort of capacity for any description of Literature is left in him. He has proved this, over and over again, in a very agony of fruitless endeavour to do Something. He is the author of a great number of Dramatic Pieces—many of them, such as Paul Pry, and Turning the Tables, of high repute—but wrote for the Theatres under bad managers, and was always poorly paid. His Magazine Writings are very numerous too, and his "Little Pedlington" is a famous piece of observation of English Life and Character; but these compositions were spread over a great many years—were always produced slowly and with difficulty—and never afforded him more than the means of living on from month to month. For some few years past, he has been living on a fifth story in a house in the Rue Neuve Luxembourg in Paris (on the proceeds of an Amateur Theatrical Performance for his benefit, of which I undertook the management and stewardship and which I have dispensed to him half yearly); and such is the nervous affection, of his hands particularly, that, when I have seen him there, trembling and staggering over a small wood fire, it has been a marvel to me, knowing him to live quite alone, how he ever got into, or out of, his clothes. To the best of my belief, he has no relative whomsoever. He must either have starved, or gone to the workhouse (and I have little doubt that he would have done the former) but for the funds I have doled out to him,—which were exhausted before you generously assisted him from the Queen's Bounty. He has no resource of any kind. Of that, I am perfectly sure. In the sunny time of the day, he puts a melancholy little hat on one side of his head, and, with a little stick under his arm, goes hitching himself about the Boulevards; but for any power he has of earning a livelihood he might as well be dead. For three years, I have been in the constant expectation of receiving a letter from the Portress of the house, to say that his ashes, and those of his wood fire—both of a very shrunken description—had been found lying together on the hearth. But he has lived on; and, for a few hours every day, has so concealed his real condition, out of doors, that many French Authors and Actors (who treat him with deference as an English man of letters) would stand amazed to know what I now tell you. I have endeavoured to put him before you precisely as he is, and neither to exaggerate his claims, nor to invest him with any interest that does not attach to him. He has lived in Paris, to make the least of his poverty, and the most of his means. Mr. Justice Talfourd, Mr. Hardwick the Police Magistrate, Mr. Forster the Editor of the Examiner, and I, are (I think) his only English friends. We all know him, just as I have described him.

I do not think he would hold a small pension very long—I need not add that he sorely needs it—and I do not doubt that the Public are well-acquainted with his name and works.

With every apology I can offer for troubling you at this length,

I am My Dear Lord | Your very faithful and obliged Servant
CHARLES DICKENS[1]

1 Lord John Russell was prime minister at this time. His immediate response was to award Poole, who outlived CD, a Civil List pension of £100 p.a. (which CD took responsibility for sending to Poole).

To Fanny M. Lomax, 1 JANUARY 1851

1 Devonshire Terrace | York Gate, Regents Park | First January 1851.

My young friend

I beg to thank you for your book, and to assure you that I have read it with pleasure, as the reflection of a young, earnest, and truthful heart.

But—these terrible buts!—I am bound in honesty to advise you, not to dream of venturing (except for pleasure-voyages) on the great sea of literature. The public have no concern with anything connected with your aspirations, save their results. What is very good to be "written" between the ages of twelve and fifteen, may not be so good to be published. My advice to you, is—dont venture on that aforesaid sea, out of sight of home. I fear you may be shipwrecked.

Very faithfully Yours
CHARLES DICKENS

To Edward Bulwer Lytton, 5 JANUARY 1851

Devonshire Terrace | Sunday Night | Fifth January 1851.

My Dear Bulwer

I am so sorry to have missed you!—I had gone down to Forster, Comedy in hand.[1]

I think it *most admirable.* Full of character, strong in interest, rich in capital situations, and *certain to go nobly.* You know how highly I thought of Money,[2] but I sincerely think these three acts finer. I did not think of the slight suggestions you make, but I said, en passant, that perhaps the drunken scene might do better, on the stage, a little concentrated. I don't believe it would require even that, with the leading-up which you propose. I cannot say too much of the Comedy, to express what I think and feel concerning it. And I look at it too, remember, with the yellow eye of an actor!! I should have taken to it (need I say so!) con amore in any case, but I should have been jealous of your reputation, exactly as I appreciate your generosity. If I had a misgiving of ten lines, I should have scrupulously mentioned it.

Stone[3] will look the Duke capitally; and I will answer for his being got into doing it, *very well.* Looking down the perspective of a few winter evenings here, I am confident about him. Forster will be thoroughly sound and real. Lemon is so surpassingly sensible and trustworthy on the stage that I don't think any actor could touch his part as he will. And I hope you will have opportunities of testing the accuracy of this prediction. Egg ought to do the author, to absolute perfection. As to Jerrold—there he stands, in the play! I would propose Leech (well made up) for Easy. He is a good name; and I see nothing else for him.

This brings me to my own part. If we had any one, or could get any one, for Wilmot, I could do (I think) something so near your meaning, in Sir Gilbert, that I let him go with a pang. Assumption has charms for me—I hardly know for how many wild reasons—so delightful, that I feel a loss of O I can't say what exquisite foolery, when I lose a chance of being some one, in voice &c not at all like myself. But—I speak quite freely, knowing you will not mistake me—I know, from experience, that we could find nobody to hold the play together, in Wilmot, if I didn't do it. I think I could touch the gallant, generous, careless, pretence—with the real man at the bottom of it—so as to take the audience with him from the first scene. I am quite sure I understand your meaning. And I am absolutely certain that as Jerrold, Forster, and Stone, come in, I could, as a mere little bit of mechanics, present them better, by doing that part, and paying as much attention to their points[4] as my own, than another Amateur Actor could. Therefore I throw up my cap for Wilmot, and do hereby devote myself to him, heart and head.[5]

I ought to tell you that in a play we once rehearsed and never played (but rehearsed several times and very carefully) I saw Lemon do a piece of reality, with a rugged pathos in it, which I felt, as I stood on the stage with him, to be extraordinarily good. In the serious part of Sir Gilbert, he will surprise you. And he has an intuitive discrimination in such things, which will just keep the suspicious part from being too droll in the outset—which will just shew a glimpse of something in the depths of it.

The moment I come back to town (within a fortnight, please God) I will ascertain from Forster where you are. Then I will propose to you that we call our Company together—agree upon our general plan of action—and that you and I immediately begin to see, and book, our Vice Presidents &c. Further, I think we ought to see about the Queen. I would suggest our playing first, about three weeks before the opening of the Exhibition,[6] in order that it may be the town-talk, before the Country people and Foreigners come. Macready thinks with me that a very large sum of money may be got in London.

I propose (for cheapness, and many other considerations) to make a Theatre expressly for the purpose, which we can put up and take down, say in the Hanover Square Rooms, and move into the country. As Watson wanted something of a Theatre made for his forthcoming Little Go,[7] I have made it a sort of Model of what I mean, and shall be able to test its working powers before I see you. Many things that, for portability, were to be avoided in Mr. Hewitt's theatre, I have replaced with less expensive and weighty contrivances.

In Re Tucker[8]

I have looked carefully over the bill. It appears very large, but I had not come far short of that amount in my mind. An immensity was done to every lamp of any consequence, in your house, with the best workmanship, in the shortest time. They were all wrong, and Mr. Payne did not spare the opportunity—nor could it really have been spared. Mind! *I saw* the men at work. It is not pretended, observe, that 32 chimneys were broken; but that certain of that number were supplied to your lamps, and certain others to the Theatre's. Now, as to the former, I assuredly did see the men (having my eye upon them) fitting such glasses to your lamps; and as to the latter, I know there were a good many broken. It always happens in a Theatre—even with gas, which is more handy and manageable—and the rollers of the scenes, and the heat, broke a good many to my knowledge. I don't think the man would exaggerate the quantity of oil consumed (which could be so very easily estimated to a certainty) and the quality was made, with my sanction, very good, in order that there might be no smell. If it were my case—considering that the work was undeniably well done, and very cheerfully done under difficulties, and that it extended by degrees all over your house—I should not dispute the bill, as one applying to a special occasion. But I want to impress two considerations upon you in saying this. First, that it is not a part of what you once called my "large way", because I oblige my other half to be very careful in all such matters, concerning which we hold solemn weekly councils when I consider it my bounden duty to break a chair or so, as a frugal demonstration. Secondly, that I should not have the least shadow of uncomfortable feeling as regards Mr. Tucker, if you *did* dispute the bill.

Now my dear Bulwer I have come to the small hours, and am writing alone here, as if *I* were writing something to do what your Comedy will. At such a time, the temptation is strong upon me to say a great deal more, but I will only say this—in mercy to you—that I do devoutly believe that this plan,[9] carried, will entirely change the status of the Literary Man in England, and make a revolution in his position which no Government, no Power on earth but his own, could ever effect. I have implicit confidence in the scheme—so splendidly begun—if we carry it out with a stedfast energy. I have a strong conviction that we hold in our hands the peace and honor of men of letters for centuries to come, and that you are destined to be their best and most enduring benefactor.

Oh what a procession of new years might walk out of all this, after we are very dusty!

Ever Yours faithfully
CD

I have forgotten something. I suggest this title.

Knowing the World.
Or
Not so bad as we seem.[10]

1 Bulwer Lytton's new play, to be performed by CD's amateur company.
2 Bulwer Lytton's comedy, produced in 1840 by Macready.
3 Frank Stone (1800–59†), artist. Close friend of CD, having met 1838–9. Illustrated *The Haunted Man*, 1848. Lived at Tavistock House before CD did, then moved next door.
4 Points: 'theatrical technique', *OED*.

5 CD played Lord Wilmot, described on the Devonshire House Playbill for 16 May 1851 as 'A Young Man at the Head of the Mode more than a century ago'.
6 The Great Exhibition in Hyde Park was opened by the Queen on 1 May and closed 11 Oct. It attracted 6 million visitors.
7 i.e. introduction to acting (metaphor from Cambridge University examinations).
8 Thomas Tucker had provided lamps for CD's amateur theatricals at Knebworth, Bulwer Lytton's home, in Nov.
9 For the Guild of Literature and Art, to help authors and artists in need. Land was donated at Knebworth by Bulwer Lytton and some houses built. *BH* is dedicated 'to my companions in the Guild of Literature and Art'.
10 *Not So Bad as We Seem; or, Many Sides to a Character* was the title Bulwer Lytton chose for the new play.

To *Thomas Stone,*[1] 2 FEBRUARY 1851

Devonshire Terrace. | Sunday Second February 1851.

Dear Sir

I take the liberty of offering a few remarks to you in reference to your paper on Dreams. If I venture to say that I think it may be made a little more original, and a little less recapitulative of the usual stories in the books, it is because I have read something on the subject, and have long observed it with the greatest attention and interest.

In the first place I would suggest that the influence of the day's occurrences, and of recent events, is by no means so great (generally speaking) as is usually supposed. I rather think there is a kind of conventional philosophy and belief, on this head. My own dreams are usually of twenty years ago. I often blend my present position with them; but very confusedly; whereas my life of twenty years ago is very distinctly represented. I have been married fourteen years, and have nine children, but I do not remember that I ever, on any occasion, dreamed of myself as being invested with those responsibilities, or surrounded by those relations. This would be so remarkable if it were an idiosyncrasy that I have asked many intelligent and observant men, whether they found their dreams usually of the same retrospective character. Many have thought not, at first; but on consideration have strongly confirmed my own experience. Ladies, affectionately and happily married, have often recalled, when I have made the same remark in conversation, that while they were engaged— though their thoughts were naturally much set on their engagement—they never dreamed of their lovers. I should say the chances were a thousand to one against anybody's dreaming of the subject closely occupying the waking mind—except— and this I wish particularly to suggest to you—in a sort of allegorical manner. For example. If I have been perplexed during the day, in bringing out the incidents of a story as I wish, I find that I dream at night—never by any chance, of the story itself—but perhaps of trying to shut a door that *will* fly open—or to screw something tight that *will* be loose—or to drive a horse on some very important journey, who unaccountably becomes a dog, and can't be urged along—or to find my way out of a series of chambers that appears to have no end. I sometimes think that the origin of all fable and Allegory—the very first conception of such fictions—may be referable to this class of dreams.

Did you ever hear of any person who, by trying and resolving to fix the mind on any subject, could dream of it—or who did not, under such circumstances, dream preposterously wide of the mark? When dreams *can* be directly traced to any incidents of recent occurrence, it appears to me that the incidents are usually of the most insignificant character—such as made no impression, of which we were conscious, at the time—such as present themselves again, in the wildest eccentricity.—Like Macnish's friend, with the stone, and the wooden leg, and the building.[2] The obvious convenience and effect of making the dreams of heroes and heroines bear on the great themes of a story as illustrated by their late experiences, seem to me to have led the Poets away from the truth, on this head—and to have established the conventional belief from which I differ.

Recurring dreams which come back almost as certainly as the night—an unhealthy and morbid species of these visions—should be particularly noticed. Secrecy on the part of the dreamer, as to these illusions, has a remarkable tendency to perpetuate them. I once underwent great affliction in the loss of a very dear young friend. For a year, I dreamed of her, every night—sometimes as living, sometimes as dead, never in any terrible or shocking aspect. As she had been my wife's sister, and had died suddenly in our house, I forbore to allude to these dreams—kept them wholly to myself. At the end of the year, I lay down to sleep, in an Inn on a wild Yorkshire Moor, covered with snow. As I looked out of the window on the bleak winter prospect before I undressed, I wondered within myself whether the subject would follow me here. It did. Writing home next morning, I mentioned the circumstance, cheerfully, as being curious. The subject immediately departed out of my dreams, and years passed before it returned. Then, I was living in Italy, and it was All Souls' Night, and people were going about with Bells, calling on the Inhabitants to pray for the dead.—Which I have no doubt I had some sense of, in my sleep; and so flew back to the Dead.

The assistance supposed to be sometimes furnished, in sleep, towards the solution of Problems, or invention of things that had baffled the waking mind, I take to be the result of a sudden vigorous effect of the refreshed intellect in waking. But language has a great part in dreams. I think, on waking, the head is usually full of words.

—The sudden picture of a whole life, in a certain stage of drowning, I cannot but consider an indisputable phenomonon. In Captain Beaufort's case, it has been most remarkably and minutely stated by himself.[3] I think I remember a similar description, in the autobiographical part of the life of Mathews the comedian. I have also received it from the lips of persons who have been saved. That others have been saved, who have not experienced the same sensations, is a fact that does not disprove these stories. Without enquiring whether these latter people may have been drowned enough, or drowned too much, I think we have sufficient evidence on which to found the conclusion that this remarkable mental feature *has* presented itself in drowning accidents, and in no other class of accidents.

Are dreams so very various and different, as you suppose? Or is there, taking into consideration our vast differences in point of mental and physical constitution, a remarkable sameness in them? Surely, it is an extremely unusual circumstance to hear any narration of a dream that does violence to our dreaming experience or enlarges it very much. And how many dreams are common to us all, from the Queen to the Costermonger! We all fall off that Tower—we all skim above the ground at a great pace and can't keep on it—we all say "this *must be* a dream, because I was in this strange, low-roofed, beam-obstructed place, once before, and it turned out to be a dream"—we all take unheard-of trouble to go to the Theatre and never get in—or to go to a Feast, which can't be eaten or drunk—or to read letters, placards, or books, that no study will render legible—or to break some Thraldom or other, from which we can't escape—or we all confound the living with the dead, and all frequently have a knowledge or suspicion that we are doing it—we all astonish ourselves by telling ourselves, in a dialogue with ourselves, the most astonishing and terrific secrets—we all go to public places in our night dresses, and are horribly disconcerted, lest the company should observe it.

—And this appears to me, to suggest another very curious point—the occasional endeavour to correct our delusions, made by some waking and reasoning faculty of the brain. For, it is to be observed that we *are,* actually, in our night dress at the time. I suspect that a man who lay down in his clothes under a hedge, or on a ship's deck, would not have, and could not have, this very common kind of dream. It has no connexion with our being cold, for it constantly presents itself to people warm in bed. I cannot help thinking that this observant and corrective speck of the brain suggests to you, "my good fellow how *can* you be in this crowd, when you *know* you are in your shirt?" It is not strong enough to dispel the vision, but is just strong enough to present this inconsistency.

If you think any of these random remarks worth your consideration, I should be happy to appoint a time for discussing the subject still further with you. I shall be happy to insert the paper, as it stands, if you prefer it—but in that case I should desire to pursue it with my own hints of experience and opinion—and if we could agree, we might dispatch the subject in one paper.[4]

Faithfully Yours
CHARLES DICKENS

1 Thomas Stone, MD, doctor and writer. He had contributed five articles to *HW* before 'Dreams', 8 Mar. 1851.

2 Robert MacNish (1802–37†), physician and author of *The Philosophy of Sleep* (1830), in which he illustrates his argument that dreams are the re-embodiment of former thoughts, with the example of a dream in which, while walking by the Great Canal in Glasgow, he fails to throw a large stone to a certain spot. A friend with two wooden legs (he had in fact only one) then throws the stone beyond the spot without difficulty.

3 Francis Beaufort (1774–1857†), naval officer and hydrographer. Saved from drowning in Portsmouth harbour, he described his thoughts travelling backwards in a panoramic review.

4 Stone adopted many of CD's suggestions in the published version of the article.

To Mary Boyle, 21 FEBRUARY 1851

Devonshire Terrace | Friday Night. Late. | Twenty First February 1851.

My Dear Miss Boyle.

I have devoted a couple of hours this evening to going very carefully over your paper (which I had read before), and to endeavouring to bring it closer, and to lighten it, and to give it that sort of compactness which a habit of composition, and of disciplining one's thoughts like a regiment, and of studying the art of putting each soldier into his right place, may have gradually taught me to think necessary. I hope, when you see it in print, you will not be alarmed by my use of the pruning-knife. I have tried to exercise it with the utmost delicacy and discretion, and to suggest to you, especially towards the end, how this sort of writing (regard being had to the size of the journal in which it appears) requires to be compressed, and is made pleasanter by compression. This all reads very solemnly, but only because I want you to read it (I mean the article) with as loving an eye, as I have truly tried to touch it with a loving and gentle hand.

I propose to call it *My Mahogany Friend.*[1] The other name is too long, and I think not attractive. Until I go to the office tomorrow, and see what is actually in hand, I am not certain of the No. in which it will appear, but Georgy shall write on Monday and tell you. We are always a fortnight in advance of the public, or the mechanical work could not be done.

I think there are many things in it that are *very pretty.* The Katie part, is particularly well done. If I don't say more, it is because I have a heavy sense, in all cases, of the responsibility of encouraging any one to enter on that thorny track where the prizes are so few, and the blanks so many—where–

But I won't write you a sermon. With the fire going out, and the first shadows of a new story hovering in a ghostly way about me[2] (as they usually begin to do, when I have finished an old one) I am in danger of doing the heavy business, and becoming a heavy guardian or something of that sort instead of the light and airy Joe.[3]

So good night, and believe that you may always trust me, and never find a grim expression (towards you) in any hat I wear.

Ever Yours CD.

1 It appeared under that title in *HW*, 8 Mar. 1851: episodes in a country family as told to the narrator by his 'mahogany friend', the family's hatstand.
2 The beginning of *BH*.
3 CD had played opposite Mary in Dion Boucicault and Charles Mathews's comedy *Used Up*, at Rockingham Castle on 15 Jan. CD was a blasé baronet disguised as Joe the ploughboy; Augustus Egg's picture of him in this part is in the Charles Dickens Museum.

To *William Macready*, 27 FEBRUARY 1851

Devonshire Terrace | Twenty Seventh February | 1851.

My Dear Macready

Forster told me today, that you wish Tennyson's Sonnet to be read, after your health is given on Saturday.[1]

I am perfectly certain that *it would not do,* at that time. I am quite convinced that the audience would not receive it, under those exciting circumstances, as it ought to be received. If *I* had to read it, I would on no account undertake to do so, at that period, in a great room crowded with a dense company. I have an instinctive assurance that it would fail. Being with Bulwer this morning, I communicated your wish to him; and he immediately felt as I do. I could enter into many reasons which induce me to form this opinion. But I believe you have that confidence in me, that I may spare you the statement of them.

I want to know one thing from you. As I shall be obliged to be at the London Tavern in the afternoon of tomorrow, Friday (I write, observe, on Thursday Night) I shall be much helped in the arrangements if you will send me your answer by a messenger (addressed *here*) on the receipt of this. Which would you prefer? That Auld Lang Syne should be sung *after* your health is given and *before* you return thanks—or, after you have spoken?

I cannot forbear a word about last night.[2] I think I have told you sometimes, my much-loved friend, how, when I was a mere boy, I was one of your faithful and devoted adherents in the Pit—I believe as true a member of that true host of followers as it has ever boasted. As I improved myself and was improved by favoring circumstances in mind and fortune, I only became the more earnest (if it were possible) in my study of you. No light portion of my life arose before me when the great vision to which I am beholden, in I don't know how great a degree, or for how much,—who does?— faded so nobly from my bodily eyes last night. And if I were to try to tell you what I felt—of regret for its being past for ever—and of joy in the thought that you could never take your leave of *me* but in God's own time—I should only blot this paper with some drops that would certainly not be of ink, and give very faint expression to very strong emotions.

What is all this in writing! It is only some sort of relief to my full heart, and shews very very little of it to you—but that's something, so I let it go.

Ever My Dearest Macready | Your most affectionate friend

CD.

My very flourish departs from me for the moment.

1 At the Farewell Dinner for Macready. Forster's reading of Tennyson's sonnet 'Farewell, Macready, since to-night we part' was received with much applause, according to *The Times,* 3 Mar.
2 Macready played Macbeth for his farewell performance.

To *Catherine Dickens*, 25 MARCH 1851[1]

Office | Tuesday Night Twenty Fifth March | 1851.

My Dearest Kate. I have been greatly hurried and shocked today. Mr. Davy came here this morning, to say that he thought it impossible my father could live many hours. He was in that state from active disease (of the bladder) which he had mentioned to nobody, that mortification and delirium, terminating in speedy death, seemed unavoidable. Mr. Wade was called in, who instantly performed (without chloroform) the most terrible operation known in surgery, as the only chance of saving him. He bore it with astonishing fortitude, and I saw him directly afterwards—his room, a slaughter house of blood. He was wonderfully cheerful and strong-hearted. The danger is that the wounds will slough and he will fall into a low fever—but the strength of his constitution may save him. I have been about, to get what is necessary for him, and write with such a shaking hand that I cannot write plainly.

You shall hear more at length by tomorrow's post. I hope to get down on Thursday. All this goes to my side directly, and I feel as if I had been struck there by a leaden bludgeon.

Children all blooming. Love to Georgy.

Ever affectionately
CD.[2]

1 Catherine was at Malvern (Worcestershire) for the 'cold water cure' for nervous diseases.
2 John Dickens died 31 Mar.

To *William H. Wills*, 3 APRIL 1851

Devonshire Terrace, Thursday Morning, April 3rd, 1851.

My Dear Wills,

I took my threatened walk last night, but it yielded little but generalities.

However, I thought of something for *to-night*, that I think will make a splendid paper. I have an idea that it might be connected with the gas paper (making gas a great agent in an effective police), and made one of the articles. This is it: "A Night in a Station-House".[1] If you would go down to our friend Mr. Yardley, at Scotland Yard, and get a letter or order to the acting chief authority at that station-house in Bow Street, to enable us to hear the charges, observe the internal economy of the station-house all night, go round to the cells with the visiting policeman, etc., I would stay there, say from twelve to-night to four or five in the morning. We might have a "night-cap", a fire, and some tea at the office hard by. If you could conveniently borrow an hour or two from the night we could both go. If not, I would go alone.

It would make a wonderful good paper at a most appropriate time, when the back slums of London are going to be invaded by all sorts of strangers.[2]

You needn't exactly say that *I* was going *in propriâ*[3] (unless it were necessary), and, of course, you wouldn't say that I propose to-night, because I am so worn by the sad arrangements in which I am engaged, and by what led to them,[4] that I cannot take my natural rest. But to-morrow night we go to the gas-works. I might not be so disposed for this station-house observation as I shall be to-night for a long time, and I see a most singular and admirable chance for us in the descriptive way, not to be lost.

Therefore, if you will arrange the thing before I come down at four this afternoon, any of the Scotland Yard people will do it, I should think; if our friend by any accident should not be there, I will go into it.

If they should recommend any other station-house as better for the purpose, or would think it better for us to go to more than one under the guidance of some trustworthy man, of course we will pay any man and do as they recommend. But I think one topping station-house would be best.

Faithfully ever

[CD.]

P.S.—I write from my bed.

1 It became 'The Metropolitan Protectives' by CD and Wills, *HW*, 26 Apr. 1851.
2 i.e. shortly before the Great Exhibition.
3 i.e. *in propria persona*, in person.
4 His father's death.

To *Catherine Dickens*, 15 APRIL 1851

Devonshire Terrace | Tuesday Morning | Fifteenth April 1851.

My dearest Kate.

Now observe. You must read this letter, very slowly and carefully. If you have hurried on thus far without quite understanding (apprehending some bad news), I rely on your turning back, and reading again.

Little Dora, without being in the least pain, is suddenly stricken ill.[1] She awoke out of a sleep, and was seen, in one moment, to be very ill. Mind! I will not deceive you. I think her *very* ill.

There is nothing in her appearance but perfect rest. You would suppose her quietly asleep. But I am sure she is very ill, and I cannot encourage myself with much hope of her recovery. I do not—why should I say I do, to you my dear!—I do not think her recovery at all likely.

I do not like to leave home, I can do nothing here, but I think it right to stay here. You will not like to be away, I know, and I cannot reconcile it to myself to keep you away. Forster with his usual affection for us comes down to bring you this letter and to bring you home. But I cannot close it without putting the strongest entreaty and injunction upon you to come home with perfect composure—to remember what I have often told you, that we never can expect to be exempt, as to our many children, from the afflictions of other parents—and that if—*if*—when you come, I should even have to say to you "our little baby is dead", you are to do your duty to the rest, and to shew yourself worthy of the great trust you hold in them.

If you will only read this, steadily, I have a perfect confidence in your doing what is right.

Ever affectionately
CHARLES DICKENS

1 Eight-month-old Dora died the previous evening, during the General Theatrical Fund Dinner. Catherine was still in Malvern.

To Messrs Brookes & Sons,[1] 25 APRIL 1851

Devonshire Terrace, London | Friday Night | Twenty Fifth April 1851.

My Dear Sirs.

I am most truly obliged to you for your elegant present and its accompanying letter. The beautiful production of your Manufactory is enhanced in value to an extent which your modesty can scarcely imagine by your manner of sending it to me. I accept it with the greatest gratification, and, I hope, in no uncongenial spirit.

The introduction of your name in the story, is one of those remarkable coincidences that defy all calculation. I had no idea that I was taking a liberty with any existing firm; and why I added Sheffield to Brookes[2] (of all the towns in England) I have no kind of knowledge. It came into my head as I wrote, just as any other name and address might have done if I had been diverting the attention of a real child.

As I wish to continue on such pleasant terms with you, and as I remember an old superstition concerning the severance of friendship with knives, and the absolute necessity of offering some trifle in exchange, I shall beg you to do me the favor of accepting my own copy of Copperfield, which, as coming from the shelves in my study will perhaps have an interest for you that another copy might not possess.

I will send it tomorrow, and I remain with many thanks and all good wishes,

Yours faithfully and obliged
CHARLES DICKENS

1 John Brookes, 16 Mulberry Street, Sheffield. Manufacturer of Fine Penknives, Razors etc. They sent CD a case of cutlery.
2 In *DC* ch. 2 Mr Murdstone refers to David as 'Brooks of Sheffield'.

To Edward Bulwer Lytton, 9 MAY 1851

Devonshire Terrace | Friday Ninth May 1851.

My Dear Bulwer.

After some few days' reflection, I decide on troubling you with this note, because we ought to leave nothing undone that can ensure our success at Devonshire House, so far as success *can* be ensured.

I think you may not be unprepared for it.—That misfortune of your life whom I need not name,[1] has addressed a letter to the Duke. It would be perfectly unimportant of course, but that she expresses some intention of attending as an Orange girl, and distributing some effusions among the company. Now this, of course, is simply preposterous, but the *possibility* crosses my mind of a ticket being transferred (after being obtained either in some other real name or in a feigned one) and so of her being present among the Company. This is preventible to an absolute certainty, if I can have some one at my disposal who knows her. I do not know how to get such a person without communicating with you, and therefore I make known to you what I should otherwise have utterly dismissed. For I feel that I ought not to set the delicacy I naturally feel on such a point, against the remotest chance of anything happening before the Queen that would pain you. I should be merely sparing myself, at the price of all friendship and duty.

Mr. Wills, who is exceedingly discreet and entirely in my confidence, would place such a person in the hall, and carefully instruct him. He would be there himself, besides. I have already sent for Inspector Field[2] of the Detective Police (who is used in all sorts of delicate matters, and is quite devoted to me) and have told him that I shall wish him to come with Wills, in plain clothes, and remain in the Hall all night. Upon the least hint that this person coming in was not to go up, he would very respectfully shew the way in a wrong direction, and say not a word until he had conducted the lady out of all hearing. Any of the Detective men will do anything for me, and, with your approval, I would have one or two more outside, to see that the people in the carriages were not interfered with. But nothing can, by possibility, go wrong, with the precaution I have already taken, if you can give me such a person as I have described. I am half inclined to smile at the remoteness of the chance against which I propose this guard but, on consideration, I think it so expedient, though a most extreme one, that I write.

And pray do not connect me involuntarily with the subject, or hold it in your thoughts a moment after you have empowered me (if you think it right to do so), to take these steps.

Ever Faithfully Yours

CD

1 Rosina Bulwer Lytton (1802–82†), novelist, estranged from her husband since 1836. Denied access to her children and pursued by creditors, she aimed to publicize her grievances and discredit the performance by CD's players, in front of the Queen at Devonshire House.

2 CD drew on Field's experiences in three articles for *HW*: 'A Detective Police Party' (27 July 1850), 'Three Detective Anecdotes' (14 Sept. 1850), 'On Duty with Inspector Field' (14 June 1851).

To *Lavinia Watson*, 11 JULY 1851

Broadstairs, Kent. | Eleventh July 1851.

My Dear Mrs. Watson.

I am so desperately indignant with you for writing me that short apology for a note, and pretending to suppose that under any circumstances I could fail to read with interest anything *you* wrote to me, that I have more than half a mind to inflict a regular letter upon you.—If I were not the gentlest of men, I should do it!

Poor dear Haldimand.[1] I have thought of him so often. That kind of decay is so inexpressibly affecting and piteous to me that I have no words to express my compassion and sorrow. When I was at Abbotsford, I saw in a vile glass case the last clothes Scott wore. Among them an old white hat, which seemed to be tumbled and bent and broken by the uneasy, purposeless wandering hither and thither of his heavy head. It so embodied Lockhart's[2] pathetic description of him when he tried to write, and laid down his pen and cried, that it associated itself in my mind with broken powers and mental weakness from that hour. I fancy Haldimand in such another, going listlessly about that beautiful place; and remembering the happy hours we have passed with him, and his goodness and truth, I think what a dream we live in until it seems for the moment the saddest dream that ever was dreamed.

Pray tell us if you hear more of him. We really loved him.

To go to the opposite side of life for a relief, let me tell you that a week or so ago, I took Charley and three of his schoolfellows down the river, gipseying. I secured the services of Charley's godfather[3] (an old friend of mine and a noble fellow with boys), and we went down to Slough accompanied by two immense hampers from Fortnum and Mason's, on (I believe) the wettest morning ever seen out of the tropics. It cleared before we got to Slough, but the boys (who had got up at 4: we being due at 11) had horrible misgivings that we might not come. In consequence of which, we saw them looking into the carriages before us, all face. They seemed to have no bodies whatever, but to be all face; their countenances lengthened to that surprising extent. When they saw us, their faces shut up, as if they were put on strong springs, and their waistcoats developed themselves in the usual places. When the first hamper came out of the luggage-van, I was conscious of their dancing behind the Guard. And when the second came out—with bottles in it—they all stood wildly on one leg. We then got a couple of flies to drive to the boathouse. I put them in the first, but they couldn't sit still a moment, and were perpetually flying up and down, like the toy-figures in the sham snuff boxes. In this order we went to "Tom Brown's the tailor's" where they all dressed in aquatic costume—and then to the boathouse where they all cried in shrill chorus for "Mahogany"—a gentleman so called by reason of his sunburnt complexion, and a waterman by profession. (He was likewise called, during the day, "Hog", and "Hogany", and seemed to be conscious of no proper-name whatever). We embarked—the sun shining now—in a galley with a striped awning, which I had ordered for the purpose, and all rowing hard went down the river. We dined in a field. What I suffered for fear those boys should get drunk—the struggles I underwent in a contest of feeling between hospitality and prudence—must ever remain untold. I feel, even now, old with the anxiety of that tremendous hour. They were very good, however. The speech of one became thick, and his eyes too like the lobster's to be comfortable, but only temporarily. He recovered, and I suppose outlived the Salad he took. I have heard nothing to the contrary, and I imagine I should have been implicated on the Inquest if there had been one. We had tea and rashers of bacon at a public house, and came home, the last five or six miles, in a prodigious thunderstorm. This was the great success of the day, which they certainly enjoyed more than anything else. The dinner had been great, and Mahogany had informed them, after a bottle of light champagne, that he never would come up the river "with ginger-beer company", any more. But the getting so completely wet through was the culminating point of the entertainments. You never in your life beheld such objects as they were—and their perfect unconsciousness that it was at all advisable to go home and change, or that there was anything to prevent their standing at the Station two mortal hours to see me off, was wonderful. As to getting them to their Dames' with any sort of sense that they were damp, I abandoned the idea. I thought it a success when they went down the street as airily as if they were just up and newly dressed—though they really looked as if you could have rubbed them to rags with a touch, like saturated curlpaper.

I am sorry you have not been able to see our Play, which I suppose you won't see now, for I take it you are not going on Monday the 21st.—our last night in town? It is worth seeing—not for the getting up (which modesty forbids me to approve) but for the little bijou it is, in the scenery, dresses, and appointments. They are such as never can be got together again, because such men as Stanfield, Roberts, Grieve, Haghe, Egg, and others, never can be again combined in such a work. Everything has been done at its best, from all sorts of authorities, and it is really very beautiful to look at.

I find I am "used up"[4] by the Exhibition. I don't say "there's nothing in it"—there's too much. I have only been twice. So many things bewildered me. I have a natural horror of sights, and the fusion of so many sights in one has not decreased it. I am not sure that I have seen anything but the Fountain—and perhaps the Amazon. It is a dreadful thing to be obliged to be false, but when anybody says "have you seen—?" I say "Yes," because if I don't, I know he'll explain it—and I can't bear that. Miss Coutts took all her Schools one day.[5] One School was composed of a hundred "Infants"—who got among the horses' legs, in crossing to the main entrance from the Kensington Gate, and came walking out from between the wheels of coaches, undisturbed in mind. They were clinging to horses, I am told, all over the Park. When they were collected and added up by the frantic monitors, they were all right. They were then regaled with cake &c. and went tottering and staring all over the place—the greater part wetting their forefingers, and drawing a wavy pattern over every accessible object. One Infant strayed. He was not missed. Ninety and nine were taken home, supposed to be the whole collection, but this particular Infant went to Hammersmith. He was found by the Police at night, going round and round the Turnpike—which he still supposed to be a part of the Exhibition. He had the same opinion of the police. Also of Hammersmith Workhouse, where he passed the night. When his mother came for him in the morning he asked when it would be over? It was a Great Exhibition, he said, but he thought it long.

As I begin to have a foreboding that you will think the same of this act of vengeance of mine, this present letter, I shall make an end of it, with my heartiest and most loving remembrances to Watson. I should have liked him of all things to have been in the Eton Expedition tell him, and to have heard a song (by the bye I have forgotten that) sung in the thunderstorm, solos by Charley, chorus by the friends, describing the career of a Booby who was plucked[6] at College; every verse ending—

> I don't care a fig what the people may think,
> But what WILL the Governor say!

—which was shouted with a deferential jollity towards myself, as a Governor who had that day done a creditable action, and proved himself worthy of all confidence.

> With love to the boys and girls | Ever Dear Mrs. Watson
> | Most Sincerely | Yours
> CHARLES DICKENS

1 William Haldimand (1784–1862†), philanthropist. One of the circle CD joined at Lausanne in 1846.
2 John Lockhart (1794–1854†), writer and literary editor, best known for his biography of Walter Scott. George Hogarth introduced him to Scott's eldest daughter, whom he married. CD met him 1837.
3 Thomas Beard. Charley was at Eton.
4 Reference to the play CD had acted in at Lavinia Watson's house, Rockingham Castle.
5 Her boys' and girls' schools at St Stephen's, Westminster.
6 Failed his examinations.

To Charles Knight, 27 JULY 1851

Broadstairs, Kent. | Sunday Twenty Seventh July 1851.

My Dear Knight.

A most excellent Shadow![1] I have sent it up to the Printer, and Wills is to send you a Proof. Will you look carefully at all the earlier part, where the use of the past tense instead of the present, a little hurts the picturesque effect? I understand each phase of the thing to be *always a thing present, before the mind's eye*—a shadow passing before it. Whatever is done, must be *doing*. Is it not so? For example. If I did the Shadow of Robinson Crusoe, I should not say he *was* a boy at Hull, where his father lectured him against going to sea and so forth—but he *is* a boy at Hull—there he is, in that particular Shadow, eternally a boy at Hull—his life to me is a series of Shadows, but there is no "was" in the case. If I choose to go to his manhood, I can.

If I choose to go to his boyhood, I can. These shadows dont change as realities do. No phase of his existence passes away, if I choose to bring it to this unsubstantial and delightful life, the only death of which, to me, is *my* death—and then he is immortal to unnumbered thousands. If I am right, will you look at the proof (through the first third or half of the Paper,) and see whether the Factor comes before us in that way? If not, it is merely the alteration of the verb here and there that is required.

You say you are coming down to look for a place, next week. Now Jerrold *says* he is coming on Thursday by the cheap Express at ½ past 12, to return with me for the Play, early on Monday Morning. Can't you make that a holiday too? I have promised him our only spare bed, but we'll find you a bed hard by, and shall be delighted "to eat and drink you"—as an American once wrote to me. We will make expeditions to Herne Bay—Canterbury—where not?—and drink deep draughts of fresh air. Come! They are beginning to cut the corn. You will never see the Country so pretty. If you stay in Town these days, you'll do nothing—I feel convinced you won't buy the Memoirs of a Man of Quality!²—Say you'll come?

Ever affecy

CD

---

1 'The Shadow of Margery Paston', *HW*, 9 Aug. 1851; the second of seven 'Shadows' Knight contributed to *HW*.

2 Jacob Tonson, played by Knight in *Not So Bad as We Seem*, wished to buy scandalous fictional memoirs for blackmail purposes.

To Henry Austin, 7 SEPTEMBER 1851

Broadstairs | Sunday Seventh September | 1851.

My Dear Henry. I am in that state of mind which you may (once) have seen described in the newspapers, as "bordering on distraction"—the house given up to me,¹ the fine weather going on (soon to break, I dare say), the Painting season oozing away, my new book waiting to be born, and

NO WORKMEN ON THE PREMISES

along of my not hearing from you!! I have torn all my hair off, and constantly beat my unoffending family.

Wild notions have occurred to me of sending in my own Plumber to do the Drains. Then I remember that you have probably written to prepare *your* man, and restrain my audacious hand. Then Stone presents himself, with a most exasperatingly mysterious visage, and says that a Rat has appeared in the Kitchen, and it's his opinion (Stone's—not the Rat's) that the Drains "want compo-ing"²—for the use of which explicit language, I could fell him without remorse. In my horrible desire to "compo" everything, the very postman becomes my enemy because he brings no letter from you, and, in short, I don't see what's to become of me unless I hear from you tomorrow. Which I have not the least expectation of doing.

Going over the house again, I have materially altered the plans—abandoned conservatory and front balcony—decided to make Stone's Painting Room the drawing room (it is nearly six inches higher than the room below) to carry the entrance passage right through the house to a back door leading to the garden, and so reduce the once-intended drawing room, now school-room, to a manageable size—making a door of communication between the new drawing room and the study. Curtains and Carpets, on a scale of awful splendor and magnitude are already in preparation, and still—still—

NO WORKMEN ON THE PREMISES.

To pursue this theme is madness. Where are you? When are you coming home? Where is *the* man who is to do the work? Does he know that an army of artificers must be turned in at once, and the whole thing finished out of hand? O rescue me from my present condition. Come up to the scratch, I entreat and implore you!

I send this to Laetitia, to forward.

Being, as you well know why,
Completely floored by N.W.I.

Sleep

I hope you may be able to read this. My state of mind does not admit of coherence.

Ever affectionately
CD.

P.S. NO WORKMEN ON THE PREMISES!
Ha! Ha! ha! (I am laughing demoniacally)

---

1 CD had taken the 45-year lease for Tavistock House in Tavistock Square, previously Frank Stone's house. CD's brother-in-law Henry Austin was supervising the renovations.
2 i.e. cementing.

To John Forster, [?LATE SEPTEMBER 1851]

I very nearly packed up a portmanteau and went away, the day before yesterday, into the mountains of Switzerland, alone! Still the victim of an intolerable restlessness, I shouldn't be at all surprised if I wrote to you one of these mornings from under Mont Blanc. I sit down between whiles to think of a new story, and, as it begins to grow, such a torment of a desire to be anywhere but where I am; and to be going I don't know where, I don't know why; takes hold of me, that it is like being *driven away.* If I had had a passport, I sincerely believe I should have gone to Switzerland the night before last. I should have remembered our engagement—say, at Paris, and have come back for it; but should probably have left by the next express train.

To Henry Austin, 14 OCTOBER 1851

Broadstairs, Kent. | Tuesday Evening | Fourteenth October 1851.

My Dear Henry

So far from my being tired of your handwriting, my anguish is the apprehension that you will be found (by trusty messengers) lying on your back on the office-floor, exhausted by the contemplation of mine.

I have not the least objection to curtains (water-proof) in lieu of partition, on the following conditions—always entirely subject to your approval.

I append an elegant drawing

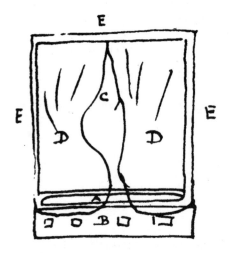

REFERENCE TO ELEGANT DRAWING

A. The Warm Bath
B. Wooden front, masking warm bath
C. Wooden back against Wall
D. Light, cheerful-colored water proof curtains, extending the whole width of Warm Bath, and capable of being drawn close for shower

Same being hung on rings and rod appended to

Centre E. E, E, E, supposed to be a wooden frame (as narrow as you please) enclosing bath and bath-space altogether.—Shower supposed to fall behind Curtains, from between the intersecting point E, and the point C.

You understand???

I don't care for the possibility of a Tepid Shower. But what I want is, *a Cold Shower of the best quality, always charged to an unlimited extent,* so that I have but to pull the string, and take any shower of cold water I choose. If the Redoubtable thinks this more certainly attainable by means of his separate tank I dont object to it in the least. But this is what has become a positive necessary of life to me. And without any disparagement to the Warm Bath, this, in perfection, it is my first object to secure.

I now leave it, with the most entire confidence, to you.

DRAWING ROOM.

Let us have (in the papering) paneled patterns in the wider spaces of the bow. You recollect its being left doubtful whether they should be plain or no? But I am now clear that they had better be ornamented, *in case* of the Curtains revealing those spaces at any time.

STUDY

I suppose the Bewildered Pantechnicon[1] will sketch out the bookcases on the Wall, to facilitate the paper-hanging in the two designs—larger pattern (you recollect?) in the shewn Wall; smaller behind the books.

ORNAMENTS ROUND LAMPS—ON CEILING

Yes, in the Hall. No, in the Schoolroom.

19 & ½[2]

I enclose his consent. I suppose it will cost very little—not merely to "whiten" the side of his[3]

1 CD's nickname for one of the workmen.
2 William Jackes, owner of 19½ Tavistock Square.
3 Second sheet of letter missing.

To Elizabeth Gaskell, [4] DECEMBER 1851

Tavistock House | Thursday Afternoon Fifth Decr. | 1851.

My Dear Mrs Gaskell

I write in great haste to tell you that Mr. Wills in the utmost consternation has brought me your letter just received (4 o'Clock) and that it is *too late* to recall your tale.[1] I was so delighted with it that I put it first in the No. (not hearing of any objection to my proposed alteration[2] by return of Post) and the No. is now made up and in the Printer's hands. I cannot possibly take the Tale out—it has departed from me.

I am truly concerned for this, but I hope you will not blame me for what I have done in perfect good faith. Any recollection of me from your pen, cannot (as I think you know) be otherwise than truly gratifying to me; but with my name on every page of Household Words there would be—or at least I should feel—an impropriety in so mentioning myself. I was particular, in changing the author, to make it Hoods *Poems* in the most important place—I mean where the Captain is killed—and I hope and trust that the substitution will not be any serious drawback to the paper, in any eyes but yours. I would do anything rather than cause you a minute's vexation arising out of what has given me so much pleasure, and I sincerely beseech you to think better of it, and not to fancy that any shade has been thrown on your charming writing, by the unfortunate but innocent

CHARLES DICKENS

I write at a Gallop, not to lose another Post.

1 'Our Society at Cranford', *HW*, 13 Dec. 1851; the first of the eight stories published as *Cranford*, 1853.
2 CD substituted 'Hood's Own' for *PP*, as the book whose merits Captain Brown proclaimed above Samuel Johnson's *Rasselas* at Miss Jenkyns's party; and made him read 'Hood's *Poems*' when he was killed by the train. For the one-vol. edn., 1853, Gaskell restored *PP*.

To Frederick Evans, 16 DECEMBER 1851

Tavistock House | Tuesday Sixteenth December 1851.

My Dear Evans
I declare before God that your men are enough to drive me mad! After all the trouble and care I have taken with that Xmas No. I open it now, and find in the second page—in my own article—"therefore we commit his body to the *Dark*"—for Deep—which was never wrong until now.[1] I don't believe there is a beastly unstamped newspaper in London in which such a flagrant and unpardonable mistake would be made. I am so disgusted by it, that I throw down my pen in an absolute despair, and could as soon paint an historical picture as go on writing.

Faithfully Yours always
CD.

1 In 'What Christmas is, as we grow Older', *HW*, Christmas 1851.

To Elizabeth Gaskell, 21 DECEMBER 1851

Tavistock House | Sunday Twenty First December 1851

My Dear Mrs. Gaskell
If you were not the most suspicious of women, always looking for soft sawder[1] in the purest metal of praise, I should call your paper delightful, and touched in the

tenderest and most delicate manner. Being what you are, I confine myself to the observation that I have called it "A Love-Affair at Cranford", and sent it off to the Printer.[2]

Faithfully Yours Ever
CHARLES DICKENS

We have just bought a neat little dinner service of pure gold for common use. It is very neat & quiet.[3]

1 i.e. flattery (*OED*).
2 The second of the eight Cranford stories, *HW*, 3 Jan. 1852.
3 A running joke about the splendours of Tavistock House.

To John Forster, [?9 MARCH 1852]

My Highgate journey yesterday was a sad one. Sad to think how all journeys tend that way. I went up to the cemetery to look for a piece of ground. In no hope of a Government bill, and in a foolish dislike to leaving the little child[1] shut up in a vault there, I think of pitching a tent under the sky. . . . Nothing has taken place here: but I believe, every hour, that it must next hour.[2] Wild ideas are upon me of going to Paris—Rouen—Switzerland—somewhere—and writing the remaining two-thirds of the next No. aloft in some queer inn room. I have been hanging over it, and have got restless. Want a change I think. Stupid. We were at 30,000[3] when I last heard. . . . I am sorry to say that after all kinds of evasions, I am obliged to dine at Lansdowne House to-morrow. But maybe the affair will come off to-night and give me an excuse! I enclose proofs of No. 2. Browne has done Skimpole, and helped to make him singularly unlike the great original.[4] Look it over, and say what occurs to you. . . . Don't you think Mrs. Gaskell charming? With one ill-considered thing that looks like a want of natural perception, I think it masterly.[5]

1 CD's daughter Dora.
2 Catherine's confinement.
3 Sales of *BH*, No. 1.
4 Leigh Hunt, who was tall and slender, unlike the tubby, round-faced Skimpole in *BH*.
5 In 'Memory at Cranford', *HW*, 13 Mar., young Peter Jenkyns parades in the garden dressed in his prim sister Deborah's clothes, carrying a pillow for a baby.

To John Forster, [18 MARCH 1852]

I have again gone over every part of it very carefully, and I think I have made it much less like.[1] I have also changed Leonard to Harold. I have no right to give Hunt pain, and I am so bent upon not doing it that I wish you would look at all the proof once more, and indicate any particular place in which you feel it particularly like. Whereupon I will alter that place.

1 i.e. Skimpole's resemblance to Leigh Hunt.

To *Georgiana Morson*, 26 MARCH 1852

Tavistock House | Twenty Sixth March | 1852

Dear Mrs. Morson

Yes.

Faithfully Yours
CHARLES DICKENS

To *William H. Wills*, 29 APRIL 1852

Tavistock House | Twenty Ninth April, 1852

My Dear Wills.

We forgot to speak, yesterday, about the begging letters. I send with this a black surtout.[1] That and £2 will be sufficient I think for the Rathbone Place man.

£2 for Macpherson, the Orphan

£1 for the Needlewoman.

And after this, I really must pull up. For I have no funds but my own, in hand or in reversion; and I get these letters by hundreds[2]—not counting those that *you* get.

Ever Faithfully
CD.

1 Man's overcoat.
2 A constant vexation: see CD's article 'The Begging-Letter Writer', *HW*, 18 May 1850.

To *John Gladding,*[1] 9 JUNE 1852

Tavistock House | Ninth June 1852

Sir.

I owe you many thanks for your obliging letter, and sincerely thank you for the confidence you repose in me.

But, being at present, fully occupied, I have no intention whatever of offering myself as a Candidate at the next election and prefer to be as useful as I can in my own way.

Very faithfully Yours
CHARLES DICKENS

1 Parliamentary agent for the Radical party. From 1841 onwards CD received many invitations to stand for Parliament, which he always declined.

To Henry Christopherson,[1] 9 JULY 1852

Tavistock House, Tavistock Square | Ninth July 1852

Sir.

I have received your letter of yesterday's date and shall content myself with a brief reply.

There was a long time during which benevolent societies were spending immense sums on missions abroad, when there was no such thing as a Ragged School in England, or any kind of associated endeavour to penetrate to those horrible domestic depths in which such schools are now to be found; and where they were, to my most certain knowledge, neither placed nor discovered by the Society for the propagation of the gospel in foreign parts.

If you think the balance between the home mission and the foreign mission justly held in the present time—I do not. I abstain from drawing the strange comparison that might be drawn, between the sums even now expended on foreign missions, and the sums expended in endeavours to remove the darkest ignorance and degradation from our very doors, because I have some respect for mistakes that may be founded in a sincere wish to do good. But, I present a general suggestion of the still-existing anomaly (in such a paragraph as that which offends you) in the hope of inducing some people to reflect on this matter, and to adjust the balance more correctly. I am decidedly of opinion that the two works, the home and the foreign, are *not* conducted with an equal hand; and that the home claim is by far the stronger and the more pressing of the two.

Indeed, I have very grave doubts whether a great commercial country holding communication with all parts of the world, can better christianise the benighted portions of it than by the bestowal of its wealth and energy on the making of good Christians at home and on the utter removal of neglected and untaught childhood from its streets, before it wanders elsewhere. For, if it steadily persist in this work, working downward to the lowest, the travellers of all grades whom it sends abroad, will be good, exemplary, practical missionaries, instead of undoers of what the best professed missionaries can do.

These are my opinions, founded, I believe, on some knowledge of facts and some observation. If I could be scared out of them, let me add in all good humour, by such easily-impressed words as "Anti-christian" or "irreligious", I should think that I deserved them in their real signification.

I have referred in vain to page 312 of Household Words for the sneer to which you call my attention.[2] Nor have I, I assure you, the least idea where else it is to be found.

I am Sir | Your faithful Servant

CHARLES DICKENS

1 A Congregational minister, who criticized ch. 16 of *BH*, querying 'Are such boys as Jo neglected?'
2 Probably a reference to G. A. Sala's 'Dumbledowndreary' (*HW*, 19 June), which mocked the annual meetings of religious and philanthropic societies at Exeter Hall.

To Harriet Beecher Stowe,[1] 17 JULY 1852

Tavistock House, London, | July 17, 1852.

Dear Madam,

I have read your book with the deepest interest and sympathy, and admire, more than I can express to you, both the generous feeling which inspired it, and the admirable power with which it is executed.

If I might suggest a fault in what has so charmed me, it would be that you go too far and seek to prove too much. The wrongs and atrocities of slavery are, God knows! case enough. I doubt there being any warrant for making out the African race to be a great race, or for supposing the future destinies of the world to lie in that direction; and I think this extreme championship likely to repel some useful sympathy and support.

Your book is worthy of any head and any heart that ever inspired a book. I am much your debtor, and I thank you most fervently and sincerely.

CHARLES DICKENS

1 Harriet Beecher Stowe (1811–96; *ANB*), author. Her very successful anti-slavery novel *Uncle Tom's Cabin* was serialized in the *National Era* June 1851–Apr. 1852; 1st English edn. Apr. 1852. She sent a copy to CD.

To Lavinia Watson, 5 AUGUST 1852

10 Camden Crescent, Dover | Fifth August 1852

My dear, dear Mrs. Watson.

I cannot bear to be silent longer,[1] though I know full well—no one better I think—how your love for him, and your trust in God, and your love for your children, will have come to the help of such a nature as yours and whispered better things than any friendship can, however faithful and affectionate.

We held him so close in our hearts—all of us here—and have been so happy with him, and so used to say how good he was, and what a gentle, generous, noble spirit he had, and how he shone out among commoner men as something so real and genuine and full of every kind of worthiness that it has often brought the tears into my eyes to talk of him—we have been so accustomed to do this, when we looked forward to years of unchanged intercourse, that now, when everything but Truth goes down into the dust, those recollections which make the sword so sharp pour balm into the wound. And if it be a consolation to us to know the virtues of his character, and the reasons that we had for loving him, O how much greater is your comfort who were so devoted to him and were the happiness of his life!

We have thought of you every day and every hour. We think of you now, in the dear old house, and know how right it is, for his dear children's sake, that you should have bravely set up your rest in the place consecrated by their father's memory, and within the same summer-shadows that fall upon his grave. We try to look on, through a few years, and to see the children brightening it, and George a comfort and a pride and an honor to you; and although it *is* hard to think of what we have lost, we know how something of it will be restored by your example and endeavours, and the blessing that will descend upon them. We know how the time will come when some reflection of that cordial, unaffected, most affectionate Presence which we never can forget, and never would forget if we could—such is God's great mercy—will shine out of your boy's eyes upon you, his best friend and his last consoler, and fill the void there is now.

May God who has received into his rest through this affliction as good a man as ever I can know and love and mourn for on this earth, be good to you, dear friend, through these coming years! May all those compassionate and hopeful lessons of the great teacher who shed Divine tears for the dead bring their full comfort to you! I have no fear of that. My confidence is certainty.

I cannot write what I wish—I had so many things to say—I seem to have said none. It is so with the remembrances we send. I cannot put them into words.

If you should ever set up a record in the little church, I would try to word it simply, and God knows out of the fullness of my heart, if you should think it well.

My Dear friend,

> Yours with the truest affection and sympathy
> CHARLES DICKENS

---

1 The Hon. Richard Watson died abroad 24 July. CD's offer to compose the wording for his memorial was not taken up.

To John Forster, [?19–21 SEPTEMBER 1852]

Ah me! ah me! This tremendous sickle certainly does cut deep into the surrounding corn, when one's own small blade has ripened.[1] But *this* is all a Dream, may be, and death will wake us.[2]

1　Watson, Count D'Orsay, and Mrs Macready had all died within the last seven weeks.
2　Cf. Shelley, *Adonais*: 'He is not dead, he doth not sleep | He has awakened from the dream of life.'

To Angela Burdett Coutts, 23 SEPTEMBER 1852

Dover, Thursday Twenty Third September | 1852

My Dear Miss Coutts.

The whole Public seems to me to have gone mad about the funeral of the Duke of Wellington.[1] I think it a grievous thing—a relapse into semi-barbarous practices—an almost ludicrous contrast to the calm good sense and example of responsibility set by the Queen Dowager[2]—a pernicious corruption of the popular mind, just beginning to awaken from the long dream of inconsistencies, monstrosities, horrors and ruinous expences, that has beset all classes of society in connexion with Death—and a folly sure to miss its object and to be soon attended by a strong reaction on the memory of the illustrious man so *mis*respected.

But to say anything about it now, or to hope to leaven with any grain of sense such a mass of wrong-doing, would be utterly useless. Afterwards, I shall try to present the sense of the case in Household Words. At present, I think I might as well whistle to the sea.

I quite concur with you as to Mr. Stone and the Westminster project.[3] The survey is actively going on. Do you think you can let me know, by Tuesday, whether you will go to Shepherd's Bush on Wednesday? If not, a note to the Household Words Office on Wednesday forenoon will do as well. I shall be there, at 11.

Ever Dear Miss Coutts | Most Faithfully Yours
CHARLES DICKENS

1　The Duke of Wellington (1769–1852†), army officer, prime minister, and national hero, died 14 Sept. Towards the end of his life he enjoyed a warm friendship with Miss Coutts.
2　Queen Adelaide, widow of William IV, died Dec. 1849; in his 'Court Ceremonies', *The Examiner*, 15 Dec. 1849, CD quotes with approval from her will: 'I request to have as private and quiet a funeral as possible.'
3　A housing improvement scheme.

To Elizabeth Gaskell, 6 NOVEMBER 1852

Tavistock House | Sixth November 1852

My Dear Mrs. Gaskell.

A very fine ghost-story indeed. Nobly told, and wonderfully managed.[1]

But it strikes me (fresh from the reading) that it would be very new and very awful, if, when the narrator goes down into the parlor on that last occasion, she took up her sleeping charge in her arms, and carried it down—if the child awoke when the noises began—if they all heard the noises—but *only the child* saw the spectral figures, except that they all see the phantom child.* I think the real child crying out what it is she sees, and describing the phantom child as shewing it all to her as it were, and Miss Furnivall then falling palsy-stricken, would be a very terrific end.[2]

What do you say to this? If you don't quite and entirely approve, it shall stand as it does. If you do quite and entirely approve, shall I make the necessary alteration in the last two MS pages, or will you?

It is a grand story, and the very thing for the Xmas No.

> In great haste Ever Faithfully Yours
> CD.

(* The real child in a kind of wildness to get at it all the time, and held by the nurse.)

1 'The Old Nurse's Story', *HW*, Extra Christmas No.
2 Gaskell did not make this change to the ending.

To Angela Burdett Coutts, 19 NOVEMBER 1852

Tavistock House | Friday Ninteenth November | 1852

My Dear Miss Coutts.

First, about the Home.

Shall I write to the woman at Boxley near Maidstone whose letter you enclosed to me in your last?

It has been necessary to discharge Stallion[1] who turned out to be a ferocious temper, and probably would have done some serious damage to somebody if she had remained. Little Willis from the Ragged School having tried her hand at the Key and Bible business[2] (in bed and in the dark, knowing it to be wrong) I told Mrs. Morson that unless she behaved very well, she should have no Marks for a month. After a day or two I went out, and she requested to see me, and said—I wish you could have seen her come in diplomatically to make terms with the establishment— "O! Without her marks, she found she couldn't do her work agreeable to herself"—

"If you do it agreeable to us", said I, "that'll do".—"O! But" she said "I could wish not to have my marks took away".—"Exactly so," said I. "That's quite right; and the only way to get them back again, is to do as well as you can".—"Ho! But if she didn't have 'em giv' up at once, she could wish fur to go".—"Very well", said I. "You shall go tomorrow morning."

Both these dismissals had a very good effect in the house, particularly on the new girl from Mr. À Beckett: who was a little dubious, and to whom I speak very seriously, telling her that if she once got outside the gate we knew, better than she might think for now, what she would give, if she could, to come back. Mr. Tracey, having sent Stallion, discharged her. She had no clothes of her own, and, it being a very wet day, they gave her an old but decent bonnet and shawl—which she immediately threw away in the Lane. To provide for such a case again, I told Mrs. Morson to buy at a slopseller's, the commonest and ugliest and coarsest (but still clean and whole) woman's dress that she could possibly purchase, and invariably to keep such a thing by her. It occurs to me that they will be very beneficially astonished when we have occasion to bring it out.

All the rest doing very well, and no complaints.

I cannot by any means find out the truth about Kelly's soup-kitchen, because it is not in action. But it was certainly found that the Soup Kitchen and Hospice in Leicester Square had an effect directly the reverse of that which he predicts, and assembled the sturdy vagrants from all quarters. His convictions on the subject are so extraordinary, that I would strongly advise you to do nothing yet, but to let me keep my eye a little while upon the place. With that view, I retain the letter. I can hardly compass the possibility of its having the anticipated result, but we will fairly see.

In the matter of Household Narrative,[3] I think, on looking back to the previous numbers, that there is nothing to be done, as to the Duke's Memory, beyond a general account of the Funeral Ceremony—unless there be anything that you would *like* to add about his character. If you will send me anything, of course I will take care to append it in the right place. I came home yesterday in time to write an article for the next No. of Household *Words*—which I had kept open for the purpose, and which is now at press, of necessity—objecting to the whole State Funeral, and shewing why. I will send you a proof—tomorrow night, I hope—thinking you may like to read it.[4]

The Military part of the show, was very fine. If it had been an ordinary Funeral of a great commander, it might have been impressive. I suppose for forms of ugliness, horrible combinations of color, hideous motion, and general failure, there never was such a work achieved as the Car.

It will be a great satisfaction to us, to know that Mrs. Brown keeps well. I have been so busy, leading up to the great turning idea of the Bleak House story,[5] that I have lived this last week or ten days in a perpetual scald and boil.

With kindest regards

Ever Dear Miss Coutts | Most Faithfully Yours
CHARLES DICKENS

1 Urania Cottage inmate; possibly a nickname.
2 The superstition whereby a girl put a key in the Bible at the Book of Ruth to find out her future husband's name. She would recite the alphabet and wait for the Bible to move at the significant initial letter.
3 The *Household Narrative of Current Events*, news summaries compiled by CD's father-in-law George Hogarth and published monthly.
4 'Trading in Death', 27 Nov.
5 One of CD's memoranda for this No. (chs. 30–2) is 'Connect Esther & Jo? *Yes*'.

To *Wilkie Collins*,[1] 20 DECEMBER 1852

Tavistock House | Monday Twentieth December | 1852

My dear Collins.

If I did not know that you are likely to have a forbearing remembrance of my occupations, I should be full of remorse for not having sooner thanked you for Basil.

Not to play the Sage or the critic (neither of which parts, I hope, is at all in my line) but to say what is the friendly truth, I may assure you that I have read the book with very great interest, and with a very thorough conviction that you have a call to this same art of fiction. I think the probabilities here and there require a little more respect than you are disposed to shew them, and I have no doubt that the Prefatory letter would have been better away; on the ground that a book (of all things) should speak for, and explain, itself. But the story contains admirable writing, and many clear evidences of a very delicate discrimination of character. It is delightful to find throughout that you have taken great pains with it besides, and have "gone at it" with a perfect knowledge of the jolter-headedness of the conceited idiots who suppose that volumes are to be tossed off like pancakes, and that any writing can be done without the utmost application, the greatest patience, and the steadiest energy, of which the writer is capable.

For all these reasons, I have made Basil's acquaintance with great gratification, and entertain a high respect for him. And I hope that I shall become intimate with many worthy descendants of his, who are yet in the limbo of creatures waiting to be born.

> Always faithfully Yours
> CHARLES DICKENS

P.S.

I am open to any proposal to go anywhere any day or days this week. Fresh air and change, in any amount, I am ready for. If I could only find an idle man (this is a general observation) he would find the warmest recognition in this direction.

1 William Wilkie Collins (1824–89†), writer. Met CD through Augustus Egg in 1851 and acted in his amateur company. He became, according to Forster, one of CD's 'dearest and most valued friends' (Forster, 520). Prolific contributor to both *HW* and *AYR* (in which *The Woman in White*, *No Name*, and *The Moonstone* appeared). *Basil: A Story of Modern Life* (1852) was his first novel of contemporary life.

To Mary Boyle, 25 DECEMBER 1852

Tavistock Farm | Christmas Day 1852

My own darling Mary.[1]

No end of merry Christmases and Happy New Years to you my gal!

Missis being out I don't wait for her to write respecting of the young woman as you proposes for to make me acquainted with[2] but my dear Mary I doe assure you that there an't a many young women as I should so much like fur to know as *her* which You will I hope my own tell her that much from him as is still yourn and knowing as you ant no cause to be jealous for all that I am certain beforehand as I shall a Door her O Mary wen you come to read the last chapter of the next number of Bleak House[3] I think my ever dear as you will say as him what we knows on as done a pretty womanly thing as the sex will like and as will make a sweet pint for to turn the story on my heart alive for such you are and so no more at present but yourn in Sir Rodger dee Coverley and reels as long as we can bear it and say to that young woman my always Imbraceable Mary as I hopes To dance with her much for I do A preciate on her and likeways my Rosy Posy for such it is well known you ever must be and let me see the man as says no to it and it will be the worse for is Ed and so I tell him candid i have had cast I on pillers put undersneath the dancing room which will prevent you and her from falling intoe the Kitching my ever blue ming Mary

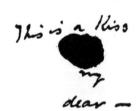

1 CD falls into the Joe the ploughboy role he had played opposite Mary in *Used Up.*
2 Eleanor Boyle, wife of Mary's cousin, was starting out as an artist.
3 i.e. ch. 35.

To Clarkson Stanfield,[1] 2 JANUARY 1853

H. M. S. Tavistock | 2nd. January 1853

Yoho old Salt!—Neptun' ahoy!—You don't forget, messmet, as you was to meet Dick Sparkler[2] and Mark Porpuss[3] on the fok'sle of the good ship Owsell Words Wednesday next ½ past 4? Not you, for when did Stanfell ever pass his word to go anywheers and not come! Well. Belay my heart of oak, belay. Come alongside the Tavistock same day and hour, 'stead of Owsell Words. Hail your shipmets, and they'll drop over the side and jine you, like two new shillings a droppin into the Purser's pocket. Damn all loblolly boys and swabs, and give *me* the lad with the tarry trousers which shines to me like di'mings bright!

1 Nautical slang and jokes characterize CD's letters to Stanfield, who had been at sea as a young man.
2 CD himself.
3 Mark Lemon, Uncle Porpoise to the Dickens children.

To Angela Burdett Coutts, 7 JANUARY 1853

OFFICE OF HOUSEHOLD WORDS | Friday Seventh January 1853

My Dear Miss Coutts.

I have been down to this Saint Mark's District[1] today, as a reasonably bad day on which to see it at its worst, and have looked well over it. It is intensely poor in some parts; and chiefly supported by river, wharf, and dock, employment; and by some lead mills. In one corner is a spot called Hickman's Folly (a Folly it is much to be regretted Hickman ever committed), which looks like the last hopeless climax of everything poor and filthy. There is a public house in it, with the odd sign of the Ship Aground, but it is wonderfully appropriate, for everything seems to have got aground there—never to be got off any more until the whole globe is stopped in its rolling and shivered. No more road than in an American swamp—odious sheds for horses, and donkeys, and vagrants, and rubbish, in front of the parlor windows— wooden houses like horrible old packing cases full of fever for a countless number of years. In a broken down gallery at the back of a row of these, there was a wan child looking over at a starved old white horse who was making a meal of oyster shells. The sun was going down and flaring out like an angry fire at the child— and the child, and I, and the pale horse, stared at one another in silence for some five minutes as if we were so many figures in a dismal allegory. I went round to look at the front of the house, but the windows were all broken and the door was shut up as tight as anything so dismantled could be. God knows when anybody will go in to the child, but I suppose it's looking over still—with a little wiry head of hair, as pale as the horse, all sticking up on its head—and an old weazen face—

and two bony hands holding on to the rail of the gallery, with little fingers like convulsed skewers.

I have no doubt that there would be innumerable claimants upon any little fund sent to the Incumbents,[2] but that may be said with equal truth of twenty places in a breath. There are no better sort of residents whatever—and never have been as I take it; which would account for the smallness of the sum in hand for purposes of charity. I am afraid it is not a promising place in which to try such an experiment as we have so much discussed. There is no lack of little houses to let, but there is no large space of ground; and I think the place too bad to attempt to make an Oasis in. It would be of no use to touch a limb of Hickman—his whole body is infected, and would spoil the mended part. An act of parliament would be necessary to clear the place. (There *may* be some such power in existence, for I observed the "Bermondsey Improvement" announced like an official thing on a church wall). Jacob's Island[3] adjoins Hickman's Folly, and I see that the ditch I described in Oliver Twist has since been filled up. If you would like to see the place, I shall be glad to shew it to you any afternoon. Or I will see the Incumbent if you desire it.

I cannot make out the money account in detail, because you have Charley's bill,[4] and I forget the precise amount. I however enclose the sum in compound addition duly drawn up, and it only wants that Item and its results to be complete.

I would have given any thing that you had seen my Birmingham people yesterday, for I don't think it possible to imagine such a scene quite accurately![5] I have promised at the end of the year, if all go well, to read the Christmas Carol to the Town Hall full of working people (the Salver and diamond ring were not confined to that class); and if there were any hope of your seeing them then, I think I could assure you of one of the most remarkable sights that this country could produce.

I asked the Mayor about the church experiment you mentioned. He said it had failed—had not been required or warranted, as he considered, by the local circumstances—and was being gradually abandoned. I had not the opportunity of asking the same question of Archdeacon Sandford; for he sat at some distance from me at the public dinner there was—and he made such a speech about a certain Writer's books by the bye, that I think you must have heard the cheering at Mivart's[6]—but the Mayor was quite confident, and spoke of the thing as a matter of fact.

With best regards to Mrs. Brown | Ever Dear Miss Coutts

Most Faithfully Yours

CD.

1 A slum parish in the borough of Southwark, where Miss Coutts was planning a housing project.
2 i.e. vicars or curates of local churches.
3 Scene of *OT* ch. 50.
4 Miss Coutts paid Charley's school fees at Eton.
5 A banquet, at which CD spoke, and was presented with a silver-gilt salver and diamond ring, subscribed for by shilling contributions.
6 Now Claridge's Hotel.

To J. B. Cardale,[1] 22 JANUARY 1853

Tavistock House | Twenty Second January 1853

My Dear Sir,

I saw your baker's man this morning using the corner just outside our gates into the Square, for his private purposes—very objectionable under my windows, and not agreeable to any of us. I spoke to him on the subject, and told him that I knew you would sanction no such conduct. He was *very impertinent,* and I gave him the information that I should let you know it; also that I should, on all our behalfs, give him into custody under the Police Act if I saw him do it again. He was rather urgent to know what I should do "if I was him",—which involved a flight of imagination into which I didn't follow him.

Faithfully yours,
CHARLES DICKENS[2]

1 CD's next-door neighbour.
2 On 26 June CD wrote to Cardale, 'Pray return the five shillings to the poor man', who had paid it to Cardale as the usual fine for this offence.

To John Elliotson,[1] 7 FEBRUARY 1853

Tavistock House | Seventh February 1853.

My Dear Elliotson

I am very truly obliged to you for the loan of your remarkable and learned lecture on Spontaneous Combustion;[2] and I am not a little pleased to find myself fortified by such high authority. Before writing that chapter of Bleak House,[3] I had looked up all the more famous cases you quote (as I dare say you divined in reading the description); but three or four of those you incidentally mention—two of them in 1820—are new to me. And your explanation is so beautifully clear, that I could particularly desire to refer to it several times before I come to the last No. and the Preface.

May I keep it carefully by me until the Summer? I can warrant myself most reliable in all matters connected with the preservation of papers, and should have it under my hand at any time. Or shall I return it to you, first copying it?—which I do not like to do without your permission.

It is inconceivable to me how people can reject such evidence, supported by so much familiar knowledge, and such reasonable analogy. But I suppose the long and short of it, is, that they don't know, and don't want to know, any thing about the matter.

Ever Faithfully Yours
CHARLES DICKENS

1 John Elliotson MD (1791–1868†), physician and mesmerist. Credited with introducing the stethoscope to England and founder of the London Phrenological Society. In the 1830s he caused controversy by mesmerizing young women, and was dismissed from his post at University College. He was patronized by CD, who met him in 1838, and was CD's family doctor for many years.

2 Not among Elliotson's published writings. CD seems to have requested his help in rebutting Lewes's criticism, in the *Leader* 11 Dec. 1852, of Krook's death by spontaneous combustion in *BH* ch. 32.

3 Ch. 33, the inquest on Krook, in which the long paragraph citing 'authorities' was inserted to dispute Lewes's claim that spontaneous combustion was 'scientific error'.

To George Lewes, 25 FEBRUARY 1853

Private
Tavistock House | Twenty Fifth February 1853.

My Dear Lewes.

Liebig[1] is a great man, deserving of all possible respect, and receiving no greater deference from any one than from me. But I cannot set his opinion—his mere opinion and argument—against full scientific evidence of a fact. That evidence appears to me to exist, on the subject of what is called (rightly or wrongly) spontaneous combustion. If I take anything on evidence, I must take that. I have the greatest regard for, and admiration of, Owen.[2] But if I had such evidence of the existence of a Sea Serpent as I have of cases similar to Krook's, I could not for a moment set even his ingenious argument against such human experience.

In the beginning you rather hastily (and not quite, I think in all good humour, with that consideration which your knowledge of me might have justified) assumed that I knew nothing at all about the question—had no kind of sense of my responsibility—and had taken no trouble to discriminate between truth and falsehood. Now the object of my note is simply to assure you that when I thought of the incident—which came into my mind, as having that analogy in it which is suggested at the end of the chapter[3]—I looked into a number of books with great care, expressly to learn what the truth was. I examined the subject as a Judge might have done. And without laying down any law upon the case, I placed the evidence impartially before myself, the Jury, as I will place it before you.

Into the argument it appears to me quite unnecessary, with such evidence, to enter. No one can suppose that such a death comes of any normal or natural condition of the body. No one can know what astonishing change has taken place *in* the body when it arrives at that pass; because the body is in the main destroyed. The difficulty of consuming a human body by ordinary fire (which is enormous) exaggerates beyond all bounds the impossibility of accounting for the deaths of this catalogue of people[4] by any ordinary means. I know very well that phosphuretted hydrogen gas will burn when it is almost surrounded by water. I also know that this gas is not usually formed in human beings, and I likewise know that of every human being so many pounds of water form a component part. But I know that before such a death can take place, there must be a stupendous disturbance of the usual functions of the body; and to tell me that if the gas were not there, and the water were all there, or other usual proportions and balances were preserved, the body could not be consumed, is merely to tell me in other words that if I be always quite well, I shall never die; or that if I retain the sight of both eyes, I cannot possibly be blind.

The question is a question of evidence. Have people been found almost consumed, when there were no external agencies by which they could have been reduced to that state? If so, have there usually (not without exception, but usually) been pervading circumstances of age, sex, or previous habits, or all three, suggesting the presence of pretty uniform conditions, essential to the extraordinary law (extraordinary, that is to say, within our small experience) governing such cases?

Refer to an article by Pierre Aime Lair in the Journal de Physique, or to the sixth Volume of the Philosophical Transactions where it is presented in another article by Alexander Tilloch. You will there find a number of cases—all of women in the decline of life. Refer to the Annual Register for 1773 for the case of Mary Clues—a woman of fifty, and a drunkard. To the transactions of the Royal Society of London for the case of Grace Pitt—a woman of sixty: not stated to be a drunkard, but not likely to have been a lady of very temperate habits, as she got out of bed every night to smoke a pipe, and had drunk an immense quantity of spirits within a few hours of her death. Refer to Le Cat for the case of Madame Millet who got drunk every day. He lived in the house, and minutely states the case. And besides his being a man of very high scientific and medical reputation, there was a certain M. Chretien, a surgeon, *who examined what remained of the body on the spot where it was consumed*, and gave his evidence in detail before the Tribunal of Justice that found the woman's husband guilty of her murder; though a High Court of Appeal, expressly on the ground that it was a case of spontaneous combustion and on the irresistible strength of the evidence, acquitted him. Refer to the Life of Bianchini prebendary of Verona to observe that the overpowering evidence of the death by these means of the Contessa Baudi (a most exact and minute account of the smallest particulars of which case he drew up with judicial precision and formality) quite devoted him to the theme afterwards: so important did it appear to him in Medical Jurisprudence, and so strong was his apprehension that its not being credited might lead to the conviction of innocent persons. This old lady was not a drunkard, but had been in the habit of bathing in great quantities of Camphor. Refer to the Journal de Medicine Vol LIX, for the case of a woman at Aix (a little drunken old woman), also minutely reported by M. Rocas, a surgeon who saw the cindery body and the room before they were disturbed. Dr. McCormac of Belfast (formerly a student at the Hotel Dieu in Paris) wrote to me, a few days since, "Dupuytren whose experience in burns was immense, was wont indeed, to consider the burns from human combustion, by some termed spontaneous, as a sixth form of burns". I could refer you to more cases, but these are enough. And throughout them there is apparent, not only the same general set of circumstances before death, but the same general appearances afterwards. Opinions on the subject, supporting me, and opinions of great practical men, I could give you by the score. But I lay them all aside, even those of the best lecturers and writers on Medical Jurisprudence (though those I might fairly impress, as being founded on the evidence); but the evidence is enough for me; and so far from making any qualifying statement in the Preface to Bleak House I can only say that I have read your ingenious letters with much pleasure—that I champion no hypothetical explanation of the fact—but that I take the fact upon the testimony, which I considered quite impartially and with no preconceived opinion.[5]

Ever My Dear Lewes | Faithfully Yours
CHARLES DICKENS

1 An eminent German chemist. Lewes contested the science of spontaneous combustion in two further open letters (*Leader*, 5 and 12 Feb.).

2 Richard Owen (1804–92†), prominent scientific figure, member of the 1847 Royal Commission on Public Health. He wrote for *HW*, and became friendly with CD. Lewes had cited him as an authority.

3 See final paragraph of *BH* ch. 32.

4 i.e. drunkards, who were thought by believers in spontaneous combustion to be inflammable, because saturated with alcohol which generated 'phosphuretted hydrogen'.

5 CD returned to the defence of spontaneous combustion in his preface to *BH*, Aug. 1853.

To Thomas Dixon,[1] 4 APRIL 1853

Tavistock House London | Fourth April, 1853.

Dear Sir

I am quite distressed, I assure you, that my note should have given you a moment's uneasiness. I do not recollect its terms, but it was one of many, and my correspondence is so very large that my business notes are necessarily brief. You may be perfectly certain that nothing in your communication to me required the least apology, or was received in any other spirit than one of friendliness and interest. Trust me I must be greatly changed, before I can resent the remembrance of "a tired mechanic after his day's labor", or his confidence in me. I cannot remember how I led you to a conclusion so painful to me, but I think the fault must somehow have been mine, and I am very sorry for it.

Faithfully Yours
CHARLES DICKENS

1 Almost certainly the cork cutter from Sunderland who corresponded with Ruskin and other writers.

To John Forster, 26 JUNE [1853, Boulogne]

26th of June.

O the rain here yesterday! A great sea-fog rolling in, a strong wind blowing, and the rain coming down in torrents all day long. . . . This house is on a great hill-side, backed up by woods of young trees. It faces the Haute Ville with the ramparts and the unfinished cathedral—which capital object is exactly opposite the windows. On the slope in front, going steep down to the right, all Boulogne is piled and jumbled about in a very picturesque manner. The view is charming—closed in at last by the tops of swelling hills; and the door is within ten minutes of the post office, and within quarter of an hour of the sea. The garden is made in terraces up the hillside, like an Italian garden; the top walks being in the before-mentioned woods. The best part of it begins at the level of the house, and goes up at the back, a couple of hundred feet perhaps. There are at present thousands of roses all about the house, and no end of other flowers. There are five great summer-houses, and (I think) fifteen fountains— not one of which (according to the invariable French custom) ever plays. The house is a doll's house of many rooms. It is one story high, with eight and thirty steps up and down—tribune wise[1]—to the front door: the noblest French demonstration I have ever seen I think. It is a double house; and as there are only four windows and a pigeon-hole to be beheld in front, you would suppose it to contain about four rooms. Being built on the hillside, the top story of the house at the back—there are two stories there—opens on the level of another garden. On the ground floor there is a very pretty hall, almost all glass; a little dining-room opening on a beautiful conservatory, which is also looked into through a great transparent glass in a mirror-frame over the chimney-piece, just as in Paxton's room at Chatsworth; a spare bed-room, two little drawing-rooms opening into one another, the family bed-rooms, a bath-room, a glass corridor, an open yard, and a kind of kitchen with a machinery of stoves and boilers. Above, there are eight tiny bed-rooms all opening on one great room in the roof, originally intended for a billiard-room. In the basement there is an admirable kitchen with every conceivable requisite in it, a noble cellar, first-rate man's room and pantry; coach-house, stable, coal-store and wood-store; and in the garden is a pavilion, containing an excellent spare bed-room on the ground floor. The getting-up of these places, the looking-glasses, clocks, little stoves, all manner of fittings, must be seen to be appreciated. The conservatory is full of choice flowers and perfectly beautiful.

But the landlord—M. Beaucourt—is wonderful. Everybody here has two surnames (I cannot conceive why), and M. Beaucourt, as he is always called, is by rights M. Beaucourt-Mutuel. He is a portly jolly fellow with a fine open face; lives on the hill behind, just outside the top of the garden; and was a linen draper in the town, where he still has a shop, but is supposed to have mortgaged his business and to be in difficulties—all along of this place, which he has planted with his own hands; which he cultivates all day; and which he never on any consideration speaks of but as "the Property". He is extraordinarily popular in Boulogne (the people in the shops invariably brightening up at the mention of his name, and congratulating us on being his tenants), and really seems to deserve it. He is such a liberal fellow that I can't bear to ask him for anything, since he instantly supplies it whatever it is. The things he has done in respect of unreasonable bed-steads and washing-stands, I blush to think of. I observed the other day in one of the side gardens—there are gardens at each side of the house too—a place where I thought the Comic Countryman[2] must infallibly trip over, and make a little descent of a dozen feet. So I said "M. Beaucourt"—who instantly pulled off his cap and stood bareheaded—"there are some spare pieces of wood lying by the cow-house, if you would have the kindness to have one laid across here I think it would be safer." "Ah, mon Dieu sir," said M. Beaucourt, "it must be iron. This is not a portion of the property where you would like to see wood." "But iron is so expensive," said I, "and it really is not worth while—" "Sir, pardon me a thousand times," said M. Beaucourt, "it shall be iron. Assuredly and perfectly it shall be iron." "Then M. Beaucourt," said I, "I shall be glad to pay a moiety of the cost." "Sir," said M. Beaucourt, "Never!" Then to change the subject, he slided from his firmness and gravity into a graceful conversational tone, and said, "In the moonlight last night, the flowers on the property appeared, O heaven, to be *bathing themselves in the sky*. You like the property?" "M. Beaucourt," said I, "I am enchanted with it; I am more than satisfied with everything." "And I sir," said M. Beaucourt, laying his cap upon his breast, and kissing his hand—" "I equally!" Yesterday two blacksmiths came for a day's work, and put up a good solid handsome bit of iron-railing, mortised into the stone parapet. . . . If the extraordinary things in the house defy description, the amazing phenomena in the gardens never could have been dreamed of by anybody but a Frenchman bent upon one idea. Besides a portrait of the house in the dining-room, there is a plan of the property in the hall. It looks about the size of Ireland; and to every one of the extraordinary objects there is a reference with some portentous name. There are fifty-one such references, including the Cottage of Tom Thumb, the Bridge of Austerlitz, the Bridge of Jena, the Hermitage, the Bower of the Old Guard, the Labyrinth (I have no idea which is which); and there is guidance to every room in the house, as if it were a place on that stupendous scale that without such a clue you must infallibly lose your way, and perhaps perish of starvation between bedroom and bedroom.

Provisions are scarcely as cheap as I expected, though very different from London: besides which, a pound weight here, is a pound and a quarter English. So that meat at 7d. a pound, is actually a fourth less. A capital dish of asparagus costs us about fivepence; a fowl, one and threepence; a duck a few halfpence more; a dish of fish, about a shilling. The very best wine at tenpence that I ever drank—I used to get it very good for the same money in Genoa, but not so good. The common people very engaging and obliging.

1 As if leading to platform or bishop's throne.
2 Edward Bulwer Lytton Dickens, aged fifteen months.

To *William H. Wills*, 5 AUGUST 1853

Boulogne | Friday Evening, Fifth August, 1853

My Dear Wills,

I am too much occupied with the conclusion of "Bleak House"—just getting fairly into it—to go, with a pen, over the No[1] without delaying it. I therefore send the corrections of the "Child's History" chapter enclosed, and, without returning the proof in a parcel, will herein note my objections.

In the first place the No. is an awfully and solemnly heavy one—and, if you have any kind of means to that end by you, must really be lightened. I read it last night, and had a Nightmare. I doubt if anything so heavy (except stewed lead) could possibly be taken, before going to bed.

1st. "Justice to Bears".The name won't do. We have already had "Justice to the Hyaena". "BROTHER BRUIN" would be a capital name, I think—thus introduced:

"The bear symbolises savage and primitive equality, and is therefore the aversion of the aristocracy." Such is the clue to ursine facts, according to Passional Zoology, which subject, and M. Toussenel's treatment of it, we now resume. It would appear that Mr. Sneak, in "The Mayor of Garratt",[2] had much reason in him when he addressed the rough personage of the piece as Brother Bruin. Was he not a Bear and a Brother?

"Here again"—M. Toussenel exclaims—"is another"—[3]

Then read the proof—you, W. H. W.—with an eye to this fact—that it wants to be made clearer all the way through, that it is M. Toussenel who is speaking, and not *H. W.* conducted by C. D.

Secondly, the first stage to Australia.There is a forlorn attempt at humour about the Deputy Inspector General (page 584) that cannot be too ferociously decapitated. Pray have nothing about a detective in that connection; it looks like weakly and palely hanging on Mr. Bucket. Damn "here they are" at page 585—and dele it too. "And the onus of the idea task strangles every newly born smile that struggles for existence"—at page 584 again—strike out with a pen of iron. Look at the whole paper.

If the "Glimpse of Dublin" be not by Allingham, strike it out. If it be, hold it over.

"Gore House"[4] is very poor. Page 591, first column. Stop at the Graces, and dele the rest of that paragraph. It is Skimpole, you know—the whole passage. I couldn't write it more like him.

I have forgotten "Licensed to Juggle". Look to the slang talk of it, and don't let "Ya" stand for "You."

The "Stereoscope" is dreadfully literal. Some fancy must be got into the No. if John writes an article for it himself (I mean our John:[5] not Forster). I should have thought the greater part of it written by McCulloch,[6] edited by Rintoul.[7]

I am going out for a walk, after a punishing day's work.

Ever faithfully,

C. D.

P.S.—Brighten it, brighten it, brighten it!

1 i.e revising and correcting the proofs of the current number of *HW*, 20 Aug., as was his habitual practice. This letter is typical of many.
2 Jerry Sneak, the submissive husband in Samuel Foote's comedy, 1763.
3 This was the opening of the article, as published.
4 By Leigh Hunt.
5 CD's servant John Thompson, now working at the *HW* office.
6 John McCulloch (1789–1864†), political economist; CD was thinking of his encyclopedic works such as *A Descriptive and Statistical Account of the British Empire*, 2 vols., 1837.
7 Stephen Rintoul (1787–1858†), founder and editor of the *Spectator*; noted for his exact journalism.

To The Editor of The Times, 18 SEPTEMBER 1853

Boulogne | Eighteenth September 1853.

To The Editor of The Times

Sir.

I observe two statements from a country paper, copied into your columns of Saturday last, and therefore made important. They represent me as having availed myself of the experiences of that excellent Police Officer, Mr. Inspector Field, in *Bleak House*, and also as having undertaken to write the said excellent officer's biography.[1] Allow me to assure you that amidst all the news in the Times, I found nothing more entirely and completely new to me than these two pieces of intelligence.

Your faithful Servant
CHARLES DICKENS

1 An article in *The Times* of 17 Sept., extracted from the *Bath Chronicle*, claimed that CD 'has made much use of Mr. Field's experiences in Inspector Bucket of *Bleak House*, and is, we understand, engaged in writing his life which, it would seem, has been replete with adventures'.

To *Lavinia Watson*, 21 SEPTEMBER 1853

Boulogne Wednesday Twenty First September 1853.

My Dear Mrs. Watson.

The Courier was unfortunately engaged. He offered to recommend another, but I had several applicants and begged Mr. Wills to hold a grand review at the Household Words office, and select the man who is to bring me down as his victim. I am extremely sorry the man you recommend was not to be had. I should have been delighted to take him.

—Skimpole. I must not forget Skimpole—Of whom I will now proceed to speak as if I had only read him, and had not written him. I suppose he is the most exact portrait that ever was painted in words![1] I have very seldom, if ever, done such a thing. But the likeness is astonishing. I don't think he could possibly be more like himself. It is so awfully true, that I make a bargain with myself "never to do so, any more". There is not an atom of exaggeration or suppression. It is an absolute reproduction of a real man. Of course I have been careful to keep the outward figure away from the fact; but in all else it is the Life itself. This in confidential reply to your enquiry.

I am finishing the Child's History and clearing the way through Household Words in general before I go upon my trip. I forget whether I told you that Mr. Egg the painter, and Mr. Collins, are going with me.

The other day I was in town. In case you should not have heard of the condition of that Deserted Village, I think it worth mentioning. All the streets of any note were unpaved, mountains high, and all the Omnibuses were sliding down alleys and looking into the upper windows of small houses. At eleven o'Clock one morning, I was positively *alone* in Bond Street. I went to one of my tailors, and he was at Brighton. A smutty faced woman among some gorgeous regimentals half finished, had not the least idea when he would be back. I went to another of my tailor's, and he was in an upper room, with open windows and surrounded by mignionette boxes, playing the piano in the bosom of his family. I went to my hosier's, and two of the least presentable of the "young men" of that elegant establishment, were playing at draughts in the back shop. (Likewise I beheld a porter pot hastily concealed under a Turkish dressing gown of a golden pattern). I then went wandering about to look for some ingenious portmanteau; and near the corner of St. James's street, saw a solitary Being sitting in a trunk shop, absorbed in a book which on closer inspection I found to be Bleak House. I thought this looked well, and went in. And he really was more interested in seeing me when he knew who I was, than any face I had seen in any house—every house I knew, being occupied by painters—including my own. I went to the Athenæum that same night, to get my dinner, and it was shut up for repairs. I went home late, and had forgotten the Key, and was locked out.

Preparations were made here, about 6 weeks ago, to receive the Emperor[2] who is not come yet. As they chiefly consisted of triumphal arches made in green boughs which have utterly withered, the town seems to be expressing its loyalty through the extraordinary medium of tea leaves. Meanwhile our countrymen (deluded over in the first excitement) go about staring at these arrangements, with a personal injury upon them which is most ridiculous. And they *will* persist in speaking an unknown tongue to the French people, who *will* speak English to them.

Kate and Georgina send their kindest loves. We are all quite well. Going to drop two small boys here, at school with a former Eton Tutor highly recommended to me. Charley was heard of, a day or two ago. He says his professor "is very shortsighted, always in green spectacles, always drinking weak beer, always smoking a pipe, and always at work". The last qualification seems to appear to Charley the most astonishing one.

> Ever My Dear Mrs. Watson Most affectionately Yours
>
> CD.

1 i.e. of Leigh Hunt.
2 Napoleon III, who became Emperor of France in 1852.

To *Catherine Dickens*, 20 and 21 OCTOBER 1853

Hotel de Londres, | Thursday Night Twentieth October 1853.

My Dearest Kate. We came here[1] last night after a very long journey over very bad roads, from Geneva, and leave here (for Martigny, by the Tete Noire) at 6 tomorrow morning. Next morning early we mean to try the Simplon.

After breakfast today we ascended to the Mer de Glace—wonderfully different at this time of the year from when we saw it—a great portion of the ascent being deeply covered with Snow, and the climbing very difficult. Regardless of my mule I walked up and walked down again, to the great admiration of the guides who pronounced me "an Intrepid". The little house at the top being closed for the winter, and Edward having forgotten to carry any brandy, we had nothing to drink at the top—which was a considerable disappointment to the Inimitable, who was steaming with perspiration from head to foot. But we made a fire in the snow with some sticks, and after a not too comfortable rest came down again. It took a long time—from 10 to 3.

The appearance of Chamounix at this time of the year, is very remarkable. The travellers are over for the season, the Inns are generally shut up, all the people who can afford it are moving off to Geneva, the snow is low on the mountains, and the general desolation and grandeur extraordinarily fine. I wanted to pass by the Col de Balme,[2] but the snow lies too deep upon it.

You would have been quite delighted if you could have seen the warmth of our old Lausanne friends, and the heartiness with which they crowded down on a fearfully bad morning to see us off. We passed the night at the Ecu de Geneve, in the rooms over our old rooms—at that time (the day before yesterday) occupied by the

Queen of the French (ex I mean) and Prince Joinville and his family. I think I did not tell you, apropos of Lausanne, that Dor³ is married again, and is Prefet of the town and one of its greatest nobs.

Tell Sydney that all the way here from Geneva and up to the Sea of Ice this morning, I wore his knitting: which was very comfortable indeed. I mean to wear it on the long mule journey to Martigny tomorrow.

We get on extremely well. Egg sometimes wants trifles of accommodation—in a place like this, for instance—which could hardly be got in Paris, and Collins sometimes wants to give people too little for their trouble. But a word puts it all right in a moment. Edward continues as before. He had never been here, and I took him up to the Mer de Glace this morning and had a Mule for him.

I shall leave this open, as usual, to add a word or two on our arrival at Martigny, as I should gain nothing by posting it here. We have had an amusingly absurd incident this afternoon. When we came home, I saw added to the hotel—our old hotel, and I am now writing in the room where we once dined at the table d'hote—some baths, cold and hot, down on the margin of the torrent below. This induced us to order three hot baths. Thereupon, the keys of the bath rooms were found with immense difficulty, women ran backwards and forwards across the bridge, men bore in great quantities of wood, a horrible furnace was lighted, and a smoke was raised which filled the whole Valley. This began at half past three, and we congratulated each other on the distinction we should probably acquire by being the cause of the conflagration of the whole village. We sat by the fire until half past five (dinner time) and still no baths. Then Edward came up to say that the water was as yet only "tippit"—which we suppose to be tepid—but that by half past 8 it would be in a noble state. Ever since, the smoke has poured forth in enormous volume, and the furnace has blazed, and the women have gone and come over the bridge, and piles of wood have been carried in, but we observe a general avoidance of us by the establishment which still looks like failure. We have had a capital dinner, the dessert whereof is now on the table. Soup, beefsteak admirably cooked, boiled fowl and rice, roast leg of Chamois, roast leg of mutton, and a pudding served in a blaze of rum. When we arrived, at nearly seven last night, all the linen in the house, newly washed, was piled in the sitting room—all the curtains were taken down—and all the chairs piled bottom upwards. They cleared away as much as they could, directly, and had even got the curtains up again at breakfast this morning.

I am looking forward to letters at Genoa, though I doubt if we shall get there (supposing all things right at the Simplon) before Monday night or Tuesday morning. I found here last night what Forster would call "Mr. Smith's" Story of Mont Blanc,⁴ and took it to bed to read. It is extremely well and unaffectedly done. You would be interested in it. I am obliged to leave off to go to the fire and warm myself, for where I am sitting it is very cold. Collins (with his short legs stretched out as far as they will go) is reading, and Egg writing in a marvellous Diary of an aggravatingly small size and unearthly shape, concerning the materials of which he remembers nothing, but is perpetually asking Collins as I write, about the names of places where we have been, signs of hotels we have put up at, and so forth—which Collins with his face all awry, blowing old snuff down one nostril and taking new snuff up the other, delivers oracularly.

Martigny Friday afternoon Twenty First October. Safely arrived here after a most delightful day, without a cloud. I walked the whole way. The Scenery most beautifully presented. We are in the Hotel where our old St. Bernard party assembled. Love to Georgina, and to Mamey and Katey, and Sydney and Harry, and the Plornishghenter[5] of the many merits. I should like to see you all, very much indeed. Ever affecy. CD.

1 Chamonix. CD, Wilkie Collins, and Augustus Egg travelled with Edward Kaub as courier.
2 The much more precipitous mountain pass by which he, Catherine, and Georgina had gone to Chamonix in July 1846.
3 CD's landlord at Rosemont in 1846.
4 Albert Smith's *The Story of Mont Blanc*, 1853, was based on his popular lecture, first given at the Egyptian Hall, Piccadilly.
5 Nickname for CD's youngest son Edward, later shortened to Plorn.

To Georgina Hogarth, 25 OCTOBER 1853[1]

Hotel de la Villa, Milan | Tuesday Twenty Fifth October 1853.

My Dear Georgy.

First of all, the main thing I have to tell you, is, that the word describing a sparkling wine—the word synonymous with Mousseaux—which I vaguely remembered at Boulogne but could not recal, turned up at Domo D'Ossala, the very first Italian place we stayed at. As follows:

INIMITABLE (To Waiter). C'e un vino che vido scritto sulla carta, "Vino d'Asti". C'e il vecchio vino che ho spesse volte bevuto—un vino come champagne—non e vero?

WAITER (To Inimitable) Si Signore. Un vino bianco, Italiano—un vino *spumante*.

INIMITABLE (apart)—Ecco la parola! L'ho trovato!

The next thing you will be interested in hearing of, is the progress of the emulative moustaches of the two other members of the Triumvirate. They are more distressing, more comic, more sparse and meagre, more straggling, wandering, wiry, stubbly, formless—more given to wandering into strange places and sprouting up noses and dribbling under chins—than anything in that nature ever produced, as I believe, since the Flood. Collins has taken to wiping his (which are like the Plornishghenter's eyebrows) at dinner; and Egg's are not near his nose, but begin at the corners of his mouth, like those of the Witches in Macbeth. I have suffered so much from the contemplation of these terrific objects from grey dawn to night in little carriages, that this morning, finding myself with a good looking glass, and a good light, I seized my best razor, and, as a great example, shaved off the whole of the Newgate fringe from under my chin! The moustache remains, and now looks enormous; but the beard I have sacrificed as a dread warning to competitors—which

I am bound to add does not produce the least effect; they merely observing with complacency that "it looks much better so".

I have walked to that extent in Switzerland (walked over the Simplon on Sunday, as an addition to the other feats) that one pair of the new strong shoes has gone to be mended this morning, and the other is in but a poor way; the snow having played the Mischief with them. I saw the deaf dumb and blind youth at Lausanne on the morning of my departure. Tremendous efforts were made by Hertzel,[2] to impress him with an idea of me and the associations belonging to me. It seemed in my eyes quite a failure, and I very much doubt if he had the least perception of his old acquaintance. Meanwhile he was always (according to his old custom) muttering strange eager sounds like "Town" and "Down" and "Mown"—which Townshend,[3] in a most ludicrous manner, wrested into an irrepressible desire on the poor fellow's part to articulate his name. As he evidently had no more idea of Townshend than of any lamp post in London it was so extraordinarily absurd that I laughed disgracefully and could not be stopped. The interview terminated by Townshend's buying every object down in that dismal little place where we used to see the boy at work—he perpetually coming back again for that purpose (when we were wild to get away, lest we should lose the boat) and saying, in the oddest french "Combien cette chose-là?—Oh!—Voulez-vous donc avoir la bonté d'envoyer cet objet chez-moi?—Et cet autre objet—combien?—Oh!—Vrai-ment!—Voulez-vous donc envoyez—cet objet—aussi—chez moi—Mon loisir"—We forced him out at last, and I left ten francs to be spent in cigars for my old friend. If I had taken one with me, I think I would have established the association more successfully than his master. The similarly afflicted child, the little girl, whom we saw there, was discharged after some trial as an Idiot, and was hardly remembered when I asked after her.

On the Swiss side of the Simplon, we slept at the beastliest little town, in the wildest kind of house, where some fifty cats tumbled into the corridor outside our bedrooms all at once in the middle of the night—whether through the roof or not, I don't know; for it was dark when we got up—and made such a horrible and terrific noise that we started out of our beds in a panic. I strongly objected to opening the door lest they should get into the room and tear at us; but Edward opened his, and laid about him until he dispersed them. At Domo d'Ossola we had three immense bedrooms (Egg's bed twelve feet wide!) and a Sala of imperceptible extent in the dim light of two candles and a wood fire; but were very well and very cheaply entertained. Here, we are, as you know, housed in the greatest comfort.

We continue to get on very well indeed together, though I am rather confirmed in general suspicions I have long entertained that other men in general (and Collins in particular) spit and snort rather more than I have ever found it necessary to do—particularly in the early part of the day. We really do admirably. I lose no opportunity of inculcating the lesson that it is of no use to be out of temper in travelling, and it is very seldom wanted for any of us. Egg is an excellent fellow and full of good qualities—I am sure a generous and staunch man at heart. He is not above the average, intellectually; but I believe he is, in a good and honorable nature.

I shall send Catherine from Genoa a list of the places where letters will find me. I shall hope to hear from you too, and shall be very glad indeed to do so. No more at present. Ever most affectionately CD.

1 On this day CD also wrote long letters to Catherine Dickens and Angela Burdett Coutts.
2 Hertzel was the director of the institution for blind people which CD had visited seven years earlier.
3 CD's friend Chauncy Hare Townshend, then living in Lausanne.

To Georgina Hogarth, 13 NOVEMBER 1853

Rome, Sunday Night, Nov. 13th, 1853.

My dearest Georgy,

We arrived here yesterday afternoon, at between three and four. On sending to the post-office this morning, I received your pleasant little letter, and one from Miss Coutts, who is still at Paris. But to my amazement there was none from Catherine! You mention her writing, and I cannot but suppose that your two letters must have been posted together. However, I received none from her, and I have all manner of doubts respecting the plainness of its direction.[1] They will not produce the letters here as at Genoa, but persist in looking them out at the post-office for you. I shall send again to-morrow, and every day until Friday, when we leave here. If I find no letter from her *to-morrow*, I shall write to her nevertheless by that post which brings this, so that you may both hear from me together.

One night, at Naples, Edward came in, open-mouthed, to the table d'hôte where we were dining with the Tennents, to announce "The Marchese Garofalo". I at first thought it must be the little parrot-marquess who was once your escort from Genoa; but I found him to be a man (married to an Englishwoman) whom we used to meet at Ridgway's. He was very glad to see me, and I afterwards met him at dinner at Mr. Lowther's,[2] our chargé d'affaires. Mr. Lowther was at the Rockingham play, and is a very agreeable fellow. We had an exceedingly pleasant dinner of eight, preparatory to which I was near having the ridiculous adventure of not being able to find the house and coming back dinnerless. I went in an open carriage from the hotel in all state, and the coachman, to my surprise, pulled up at the end of the Chiaja. "Behold the house," says he, "of Il Signor Larthoor!"—at the same time pointing with his whip into the seventh heaven, where the early stars were shining. "But the Signor Larthoor," returns the Inimitable darling, "lives at Pausilippo." "It is true," says the coachman (still pointing to the evening star), "but he lives high up the Salita Sant' Antonio, where no carriage ever yet ascended, and that is the house" (evening star as aforesaid), "and one must go on foot. Behold the Salita Sant' Antonio!" I went up it, a mile and a half I should think. I got into the strangest places, among the wildest Neapolitans—kitchens, washing-places, archways, stables, vineyards—was baited by dogs, answered in profoundly unintelligible Neapolitan, from behind lonely locked doors, in cracked female voices, quaking with fear; could hear of no such Englishman or any Englishman. By-and-by I came upon a Polenta-shop in the clouds, where an old Frenchman, with an umbrella like a faded tropical leaf (it had not rained for six weeks) was staring at nothing at all, with a snuff-box in his hand. To him I appealed concerning the Signor Larthoor. "Sir," said he, with the sweetest politeness, "can you speak French?" "Sir," said I, "a little." "Sir," said he, "I presume the Signor Loothere"—you will observe that he changed the name according to the custom of his country—"is an Englishman." I admitted that he was the victim of circumstances and had that misfortune. "Sir," said he, "one word more. *Has* he a servant with a wooden leg?" "Great Heaven, sir," said I, "how do I know! I should think not, but it is possible." "It is always," said the Frenchman, "possible. Almost all the things of the world are always possible." "Sir," said I—you may imagine my condition and dismal sense of my own absurdity, by this time—"that is true." He then took an immense pinch of snuff, wiped the dust off his umbrella, led me to an arch commanding a wonderful view of the bay of Naples, and pointed deep into the earth from which I had mounted. "Below there, near the lamp, one finds an Englishman, with a servant with a wooden leg. It is always possible that he is the Signor Loothere." I had been asked at six, and it was now getting on for seven. I went down again in a state of perspiration and misery not to be described, and without the faintest hope of finding the place. But as I was going down to the lamp, I saw the strangest staircase up a dark corner, with a man in a white-waistcoat (evidently hired) standing on the top of it, fuming. I dashed in at a venture, found it was the place, made the most of the whole story, and was indescribably popular. The best of it was, that as nobody ever did find the place, he had put a servant at the bottom of the Salita, to "wait for an English gentleman." The servant (as he presently pleaded), deceived by the moustache, had allowed the English gentleman to pass unchallenged.

The night before we left Naples we were at the San Carlo, where, with the Verdi rage of our old Genoa time, they were again doing the "Trovatore".[3] It seemed rubbish on the whole to me, but was very fairly done. I think "La [Penco]", the prima donna, will soon be a great hit in London. She is a very remarkable singer and a fine actress, to the best of my judgment on such premises. There seems to be no opera here, at present. There was a Festa in St. Peter's to-day, and the Pope passed to the Cathedral in state. We were all there.

We leave here, please God, on Friday morning, and post to Florence in three days and a half. We came here by Vetturino. Upon the whole, the roadside inns are greatly improved since our time. Half-past three and half-past four have been, however, our usual times of rising on the road.

I was in my old place at the Coliseum this morning, and it was as grand as ever. With that exception the ruined part of Rome—the real original Rome—looks smaller than my remembrance made it. It is the only place on which I have yet found that effect. We are in the old hotel.

You are going to Bonchurch I suppose? will be there, perhaps, when this letter reaches you? I shall be pleased to think of you as at home again, and making the commodious family mansion look natural and home-like. I don't like to think of my room without anybody to peep into it now and then. Here is a world of travelling arrangements for me to settle, and here are Collins and Egg looking sideways at me with an occasional imploring glance as beseeching me to settle it. So I leave off. Good-night.

Ever, my dearest Georgy, | Most affectionately yours

[CD]

1 Catherine's letter arrived next morning. CD replied immediately, warmly, and at great length, but commented that he was 'rather surprised that I got it [her letter] at all, for I do assure you that the illegibility of my name on the address would endanger it at any Foreign post office. How any frenchman or Italian could ever make out the first necessary condition—that my name begins with a D—I cannot imagine. I apprehend that it had been laid aside in positive despair. However, here it is, and most welcome it is with all its contents.'

2 William Lowther (1821–1912), brother of the 3rd Earl of Lonsdale and secretary of legation, Naples. The Lowther family home was in Rutland, near Rockingham Castle, home of CD's friends the Watsons, where CD had acted in 1851.

3 Verdi's opera *Il Trovatore*, first performed in Rome, Jan. 1853, and an instant success.

To John Forster, [?17–20 NOVEMBER 1853, Rome]

He had heard when first in Genoa that the finest Marionetti were in Rome; and now, after great difficulty, he discovered the company in a sort of stable attached to a decayed palace. It was a wet night, and there was no audience but a party of French officers and ourselves. We all sat together. I never saw anything more amazing than the performance—altogether only an hour long, but managed by as many as ten people, for we saw them all go behind, at the ringing of a bell. The saving of a young lady by a good fairy from the machinations of an enchanter, coupled with the comic business of her servant Pulcinella (the Roman Punch) formed the plot of the first piece. A scolding old peasant woman, who always leaned forward to scold and put her hands in the pockets of her apron, was incredibly natural. Pulcinella, so airy, so merry, so lifelike, so graceful, he was irresistible. To see him carrying an umbrella over his mistress's head in a storm, talking to a prodigious giant whom he met in the forest, and going to bed with a pony, were things never to be forgotten. And so delicate are the hands of the people who move them, that every puppet was an Italian, and did exactly what an Italian does. If he pointed at any object, if he saluted anybody, if he laughed, if he cried, he did it as never Englishman did it since Britain first at Heaven's command arose—arose—arose, &c.[1] There was a ballet afterwards, on the same scale, and we really came away quite enchanted with the delicate drollery of the thing. French officers more than ditto.

1 From 'Rule Britannia'.

To Catherine Dickens, 5 DECEMBER 1853

Turin, Monday Fifth December 1853.

My Dearest Catherine. We arrived here on Saturday afternoon, having made capital progress from Parma (it being hard frosty weather) and having also had the good fortune of just catching a train for this place, at Alessandria. De la Rue, through his agents the bankers here, had (as he promised in Genoa) taken every possible precaution for our getting on to Lyons. I arranged long ago, to leave here tomorrow; and I found the whole Courier's carriage which carries the Mail, and which is very difficult to be got, punctually secured for us. So we start from here over the Mont Cenis, tomorrow afternoon at 5 o'Clock and go straight through to Lyons. I cannot ascertain here about the boat up the Saone, or about the times of the trains from Chalons to Paris; but we are engaged to dine with Miss Coutts on Saturday, and, unless you hear to the contrary, I shall come home by *the Tidal Train from Paris on Sunday Morning*. Wills will tell you at what hour it comes in at London Bridge on that day, and when the carriage should be there to meet me. I *may* write to say that I shall come on Monday instead; but I do not think this at all likely, to the best of my present means of judging.

It is extremely cold, but Turin is a charming place—gay, bright, busy, and crowded with Inhabitants. There is a large and most beautiful Theatre, where we saw the Prophete last night—not well sung (except Viardot's part, by Madame Stoltz)[1] but admirably put upon the stage, and done by an immense number of people. The handsomest streets and squares I ever saw, are in this place. And the great range of Alps, now covered with snow, overhanging it, are most splendid to behold.

I have many arrangements to manage, and the Abercombys to call upon, and many letters to write; and therefore—being happily so near home as to time—must make this but a short epistle. I am anxious to close it with putting something to you, very seriously and affectionately, which I think deserves your particular attention.

Nine years have gone away since we were in Genoa. Whatever looked large in that little place may be supposed in such a time to have shrunk to its reasonable and natural proportions. You know my life too, and my character, and what has had its part in making them successful; and the more you see of me, the better perhaps you may understand that the intense pursuit of any idea that takes complete possession of me, is one of the qualities that makes me different—sometimes for good; sometimes I dare say for evil—from other men. Whatever made you unhappy in the Genoa time had no other root, beginning, middle, or end, than whatever has made you proud and honored in your married life, and given you station better than rank, and surrounded you with many enviable things. This is the plain truth, and here I leave it.

But since the time when you constrained me to make that painful declaration of your state of mind to the De la Rue's,[2] I have been, in all the correspondence I have ever had with him, deeply impressed by the delicacy and gratitude which has invariably restrained him from the least allusion to it, and has always led him to references to you and the children which none but a generous and affectionate man could possibly have been so natural and so instinctively manly in. I come back to Genoa after that long time, and find her, with all the change upon her of those many years of suffering—and all the weariness of attendance, night and day, upon her foolish sick mother who wears out everybody near her body and soul—alluding in the same manner to you—easily, gratefully, and full of interest—from the first moment of my setting eyes upon her, to her sending some brooches Egg and Collins had commissioned her to buy, yesterday, and begging to be recalled to Mamey's and Katey's remembrance, and to send her love to you and Georgina. Now I am perfectly clear that your position beside these people is not a good one, is not an amiable one, a generous one—is not worthy of you at all. And I see that you have it in your power to set it right at once by writing her a note to say that you have heard from me, with interest, of her sufferings and her cheerfulness—that you couldn't receive her messages of remembrance without a desire to respond to them—and that if you should ever be thrown together again by any circumstances, you hope it will be for a friendly association without any sort of shadow upon it. Understand above all things, that I do not ask you to do this, or want you to do this.[3] I shall never ask whether you have done it or not, and shall never approach the subject from this hour. My part in it was settled when we were in Switzerland, and there an end. But I am confident that if you could do this without any secret reservation in your own mind, you would do an unquestionably upright thing, and would place yourself on a far better station in your own eyes, at one time or other. And I am absolutely confident that they both deserve it, and would both be very sensitive to it. But I most earnestly repeat, for all that, that it would be utterly valueless and contemptible if it were done through a grain of any other influence than that of your own heart, reflecting on what I have written here.

I wonder whether you will have done the study mantelpiece by Sunday morning!—I hope so. Understand that if I come on Sunday, I will not write again. My best love to the darlings. I take Charley to be now on his way from Leipzig—and if I may judge of his weather by ours, he will have a mighty cold journey of it. Looking forward to *meeting* you so soon, Ever My Dearest Catherine Most affectionately Yours

CD.

1 Meyerbeer created the part of Fides in *Le Prophete* for Pauline Viardot. She was a close friend of George Sand. CD admired her, they met in 1855.
2 CD wrote to Emile de la Rue in Apr. 1846 that he could not persuade Catherine to return to Genoa, a reference to her resentment at his obsession with Mme de la Rue's nervous illness. (For CD's mesmerism of her see above, 15 and 27 Jan. 1845.)
3 Catherine did write, but the letter has not survived.

To Mark Lemon, 24 DECEMBER 1853

Tavistock House | Christmas Eve 1853.

My Dear Mark

A merry Christmas and a happy New Year to you and yours!

Will you give me a call on Monday Morning, to arrange with me (for Ireland,[1] whom I dare say you will be kind enough to see when I am at Birmingham) about the little Theatre?[2]—I have got in some capital old Stager dodges and scraps of music—and I think it will be very pretty and droll. Really very good.

Betty,[3] my dear Sir, is—I say it emphatically—an Actress!!!

Ever Affectionately
CD.

1 Thomas Ireland, of the Adelphi Theatre, who made the properties for the Tavistock House theatre.
2 The schoolroom at Tavistock House. The Dickens and Lemon children performed Fielding's *Tom Thumb* on 6 Jan. 1854; CD and Lemon also took part.
3 Betty Lemon, aged 9.

To Angela Burdett Coutts, 4 JANUARY 1854

Tavistock House | Wednesday Fourth January | 1854.

My Dear Miss Coutts

I was the Committee yesterday, and, it being the close of the year, send you the book.[1]

Rhena Pollard, that girl from Petworth jail, had been (as is supposed) the companion of the girl who ran away last Sunday, and had, in a most inveterately audacious manner, threatened Mrs. Morson that she would leave—had pretended indeed, that she waited for the Committee day, as a kind of obliging favor on her part. Accordingly I summoned Mrs. Morson when the girl appeared in her turn, and said "Mrs. Morson this is the girl who wants to go, I believe"—"Yes."—"Take her at her word. It is getting dark now, but, immediately after breakfast tomorrow morning, shut the gate upon her for ever." I think the girl was more taken by surprise, and more seized with consternation, than anybody I have ever seen in that place. She begged and prayed—was obliged to be taken out of the room—went into the long room, and, *before all the rest,* entreated and besought Mrs. Morson to intercede for her—and broke into the most forlorn and dismal lamentations. I told Mrs. Morson to give her no hope or relief all night—to have the rough dress down and air it in the long room—and this morning, if the girl again besought her in the same way *before all the others,* to pause and send to me. This she did. I wrote back a letter, which I arranged with her yesterday that she should read to them all. I put the case in the strongest and plainest manner possible, and said that you supported that Home, to save young women who desired to be saved and who knew the misery and degradation out of which they were taken—that it was *not* the place for those who audaciously slighted the shelter of the only roof interposed between them and the great black world of Crime and Shame—and that I *would not,* nor would any of the gentlemen who assisted you in its management allow its blessings to be thus grossly trifled with. As it was the great forgiving Christmas time, she was to give this girl one more trial; but only on the condition that if she ever repeated her threat in any way, she was to be instantly discharged. Also that all the rest were to understand that your consent had been obtained to this principle being in all cases severely and firmly carried out. We pitied such deluded creatures, and knew the remorse that always came upon them as soon as they were outside the gate; but the greatest object of our pity was the miserable girl in the streets who really would try hard to do well if she could get into the Home, and whose place was unjustly occupied by such a girl as this.

Both in words yesterday and in the letter to day, I was as emphatic as I could possibly be. I think you will approve of the wretched young creature's having one more chance in this bitter weather—but in a just remembrance of what is due to the Home and its Supporter, I could not have given it to her, if she had been other than a stranger in London, and an utterly friendless speck in the world.

Snow two feet deep in the streets today!

> Dear Miss Coutts | Ever Most Faithfully Yours
> CD.[2]

1 Probably the account book.
2 Rhena Pollard remained at Urania Cottage until 1855, and subsequently emigrated to Canada.

To *Lavinia Watson*, 13 JANUARY 1854

Tavistock House. | Thirteenth January 1854. | Friday.

My Dear Mrs. Watson.

On the very day after I sent the Christmas No. to Rockingham, I heard of your being at Brighton. I should have sent another there, but that I had a misgiving I might seem to be making too much of it. For, when I thought of the probability of the Rockingham copy going on to Brighton, and pictured to myself the advent of two of those very large envelopes at once at Junction House at breakfast time, a sort of comic modesty overcame me.

I was heartily pleased with the Birmingham Audience, which was a very fine one.[1] I never saw, nor do I suppose anybody ever did, such an interesting scene as the Working-people's night. There were two thousand five hundred of them there; and a more delicately observant audience it is impossible to imagine. They lost nothing, misinterpreted nothing, followed everything closely, laughed and cried with most delightful earnestness, and animated me to that extent that I felt as if we were all bodily going up into the clouds together. It is an enormous place for the purpose; but I had considered all that, carefully, and—I believe— made the most distant person hear, as well as if I had been reading in my own room. I was a little doubtful before I began on the first night whether it was quite practicable to conceal the requisite effort; but I soon had the satisfaction of finding that it was, and that we were all going on together, in the first page, as easily, to all appearance, as if we had been sitting round the fire.

I am obliged to go out on Monday at 5, and to dine out; but I will be at home at any time before that hour that you may appoint. You say you are only going to stay one night in Town; but if you could stay two, and would dine with us alone on Tuesday, *that* is the plan that we should all like best. Let me have one word from you by post on Monday Morning.

Few things that I saw when I was away, took my fancy so much as the Electric Telegraph piercing like a Sunbeam right through the cruel old heart of the Coliseum at Rome. And on the summit of the Alps among the eternal ice and snow, there it was still, with its posts sustained against the sweeping mountain winds by clusters of great beams—to say nothing of its being at the bottom of the Sea as we crossed the Channel.

With kindest loves | Ever My Dear Mrs. Watson | Most Faithfully Yours
CHARLES DICKENS

1 For CD's first public readings of his work; at this time benefit performances for good causes.

To John Forster, [20 JANUARY 1854]

I wish you would look at the enclosed titles for the H.W. story, between this and two o'clock or so, when I will call. It is my usual day, you observe, on which I have jotted them down—Friday! It seems to me that there are three very good ones among them. I should like to know whether you hit upon the same.

1. According to Cocker. 2. Prove it. 3. Stubborn Things. 4. Mr. Gradgrind's Facts. 5. The Grindstone. 6. Hard Times. 7. Two and Two are Four. 8. Something Tangible. 9. Our Hard-headed Friend. 10. Rust and Dust. 11. Simple Arithmetic. 12. A Matter of Calculation. 13. A Mere Question of Figures. 14. The Gradgrind Philosophy.

To Mark Lemon, 20 FEBRUARY 1854

Tavistock House | Monday Twentieth February 1854

My Dear Mark

Will you note down and send me any slang terms among tumblers and Circus-people, that you can call to mind? I have noted down some—I want them in my new story—but it is very probable that you will recall several which I have not got.

Ever affectionately

CD.

To John Forster, [?FEBRUARY 1854]

The difficulty of the space is CRUSHING. Nobody can have an idea of it who has not had an experience of patient fiction-writing with some elbow-room always, and open places in perspective. In this form, with any kind of regard to the current number,[1] there is absolutely no such thing.

1 According to Forster, CD wrote this complaint 'after a few weeks' trial' at producing the weekly Nos. of *HT* (Forster, 565).

To James White,[1] 7 MARCH 1854

Tavistock House, Tuesday, March 7th, 1854.

My dear White,

I am tardy in answering your letter; but "Hard Times", and an immense amount of enforced correspondence, are my excuse. To you a sufficient one, I know.

As I should judge from outward and visible appearances, I have exactly as much chance of seeing the Russian fleet reviewed by the Czar as I have of seeing the English fleet reviewed by the Queen.

"Club Law" made me laugh very much when I went over it in the proof yesterday. It is most capitally done, and not (as I feared it might be) too directly. It is in the next number but one.[2]

Mrs. Crowe[3] has gone stark mad—and stark naked—on the spirit-rapping imposition. She was found t'other day in the street, clothed only in her chastity, a pocket-handkerchief and a visiting card. She had been informed, it appeared, by the spirits, that if she went out in that trim she would be invisible. She is now in a madhouse, and, I fear, hopelessly insane.[4] One of the curious manifestations of her disorder is that she can bear nothing black. There is a terrific business to be done, even when they are obliged to put coals on her fire.

Bulwer has a thing called a Psycho-grapher, which writes at the dictation of spirits. It delivered itself, a few nights ago, of this extraordinarily lucid message:

X. Y. Z!

upon which it was gravely explained by the true believers that "the spirits were out of temper about something." Said Bulwer had a great party on Sunday, when it was rumoured "a count was going to raise the dead." I stayed till the ghostly hour, but the rumour was unfounded, for neither count nor plebeian came up to the spiritual scratch. It is really inexplicable to me that a man of his calibre can be run away with by such small deer.

À propos of spiritual messages comes in Georgina, and, hearing that I am writing to you, delivers the following enigma to be conveyed to Mrs. White:

"Wyon of the Mint lives *at* the Mint."[5]

Feeling my brain going after this, I only trust it with loves from all to all.

Ever faithfully
[CHARLES DICKENS]

1 Revd James White (1803–62†); writer, and frequent contributor to *HW*. Met CD about 1845 and they became friends.
2 *HW*, 18 Mar. 1854: a satirical sketch by White on joining London clubs.
3 Catherine Crowe (1790–1872†), novelist and writer on the supernatural. Contributed to *HW* 1850–2. CD's sceptical review of her *The Night Side of Nature; or, Ghosts and Ghost Seers*, appeared in *The Examiner*, 26 Feb. 1848.
4 She was committed briefly to Hanwell Asylum.
5 Leonard Wyon (1826–75†), chief engraver at the Royal Mint.

To Elizabeth Gaskell, 21 APRIL 1854

Tavistock House | Twenty First April 1854

My Dear Mrs. Gaskell

I safely received the paper from Mr. Shaen—welcomed it with three cheers—and instantly dispatched it to the printer, who has it in hand now.

I have no intention of striking.[1] The monstrous claims at domination made by a certain class of manufacturers, and the extent to which the way is made easy for working men to slide down into discontent under such hands, are within my scheme; but I am not going to strike. So don't be afraid of me. But I wish you would look at the story yourself, and judge where and how near I seem to be approaching what you have in your mind. The first two months of it will shew that.

I will "make my will" on the first favorable occasion. We were playing games last night, and were fearfully clever.

With kind regards to Mr. Gaskell

> Always My Dear Mrs. Gaskell | Faithfully Yours
> CHARLES DICKENS

1 In *HT*. Gaskell's *North and South* began serialization in *HW*, 2 Sept., and featured a strike.

To Henry Cole,[1] 17 JUNE 1854

Tavistock House | Seventeenth June 1854

Dear Mr. Cole.

Although I date from here, I have in fact retreated to Boulogne to pass the summer in the society of your friend Mr. Gradgrind and others, free from the disturbances of London. Otherwise, very readily responding to your good humour, I should have lost no time in calling on Mr. Redgrave.[2]

I often say to Mr. Gradgrind that there is reason and good intention in much that he does—in fact, in all that he does—but that he over-does it. Perhaps by dint of his going his way and my going mine, we shall meet at last at some halfway house where there are flowers on the carpets,[3] and a little standing-room for Queen Mab's Chariot[4] among the Steam Engines.

> Faithfully Yours
> CHARLES DICKENS

1 Henry Cole (1808–82†), civil servant; on the council of the Society for the Encouragement of Arts, Manufactures, and Commerce, helped organize the Great Exhibition. His relations with CD were friendly, but he protested about the caricature of himself as the 'third gentleman' in *HT* ch. 2.
2 Richard Redgrave (1804–88†), artist and arts administrator. Held posts at the Government School of Design (later the Royal College of Art).
3 An allusion to the third gentleman's question to the schoolchildren in *HT* ch. 2.
4 Cf. *Romeo and Juliet*, I. iv. 53 and 67.

To Elizabeth Gaskell, [15] and 17 JUNE 1854

Tavistock House | Thursday Evening Sixteenth June | 1854

My Dear Mrs. Gaskell.

I have read the MS[1] you have had the kindness to send me, with all possible attention and care. I have shut myself up for the purpose, and allowed nothing to divide my thoughts. It opens an admirable story, is full of character and power, has a strong suspended interest in it (the end of which, I don't in the least foresee), and has the very best marks of your hand upon it. If I had had more to read, I certainly could not have stopped, but must have read on.

Now, addressing myself to the consideration of its being published in weekly portions, let me endeavour to shew you as distinctly as I can, the divisions into which it must fall. According to the best of my judgment and experience, if it were divided in any other way—reference being always had to the weekly space available for the purpose in Household Words—it would be mortally injured.

I would end No. 1—With the announcement of Mr. Lennox at the parsonage

I would end No. 2—with Mr. Hale's announcement to Margaret, that Milton-Northern is the place they are going to. This No. therefore would contain Lennox's proposal, and the father's communication to his daughter of his leaving the church.

I would end No. 3—With their fixing on the watering-place as their temporary sojourn.

I would end No. 4—With Margaret's sitting down at night in their new house, to read Edith's letter. This No. therefore, would contain the account of Milton, and the new house, and the Mill Owner's first visit.

I would end No. 5—With the Mill-Owner's leaving the house after the tea-visit. This No. therefore would contain the introduction of his mother, and also of the working father and daughter—the Higgins family.

I would end No. 6—With Margaret leaving their dwelling, after the interview with Bessy when she is lying down.

These Nos. would sometimes require to be again divided into two chapters, and would sometimes want a word or two of conclusion. If you could be content to leave this to me, I could make those arrangements of the text without much difficulty. The only place where I do not see my way, and where the story—always with a special eye to this form of publication—seems to me to flag unmanageably, without an amount of excision that I dare scarcely hint at, is between Nos. 2 and 3, where the Dialogue is long—is on a difficult and dangerous subject[2]—and where, to bring the murder out at once, I think there is a necessity for fusing two Nos. into one. This is the only difficult place in the whole 114 sides of foolscap.

As nearly as I can calculate, *about* 18 sides of your writing would make a weekly No. On *about* this calculation, the MS I have, would divide at the good points I have mentioned, and pretty equally. I do not apologize to you for laying so much stress on the necessity of its dividing well, because I am bound to put before you my perfect conviction that if it did not, the story would be wasted—would miss its effect as it went on—*and would not recover it when published complete*. The last consideration is strong with me, because it is based on my long comparison of the advantages and disadvantages of the periodical form of appearance.

I hope these remarks will not confuse you, but you will come out tolerably clear after a second reading, and will convey to you the means of looking at your whole story from the weekly point of view. It cannot, I repeat, be disregarded without injury to the book. All the MS that I have—with the exception I have mentioned and allowing a very reasonable margin indeed for a little compression here and there—might have been expressly written to meet the exigencies of the case.

Saturday Seventeenth June.

That my calculations might be accurate, I thought it well to stop my note and send eighteen of your sides to the Printer's (I took them out at random) to be calculated. Their estimate exactly accords with mine. I have therefore no doubt of its correctness.

Is there anything else that I can tell you, or anything else you want to ask me? Pray do not entertain the idea that you can give me any trouble I shall not be delighted to encounter.

My address is,

Villa du Camp de droite
Boulogne Sur Mer

—where I shall be anxious to hear from you that you comprehend this long dull story of mine. That you may the more easily do so, I will make it no longer.

Have you thought of a name?[3] I cannot suggest one without knowing more of the story. Then perhaps I might hit upon a good title if you did not.

Ever My Dear Mrs. Gaskell | Faithfully Yours
CHARLES DICKENS

P.S. I have never thanked you for Mr. Gaskell's lectures,[4] which I have read with uncommon pleasure. They are so sagacious and unaffected, and tell so much that is interesting.

1 Corresponding to the first seven Nos. of *North and South*, to be serialized in *HW* weekly from 2 Sept. The first three Nos. end as CD suggests.

2 Mr Hale's explanation to Margaret about leaving the Church of England occupies more than half of ch. 4.

3 Gaskell's original title was *Margaret Hale*, after the heroine. On 17 Dec. 1854 she wrote to CD: 'I think a better title than N. & S. would have been "Death & Variations". There are 5 deaths, each beautifully suited to the character of the individual': *The Letters of Mrs Gaskell*, ed. J. A. V. Chapple and A. Pollard (Manchester: Manchester University Press, 1966), 324.

4 William Gaskell's *Two Lectures on the Lancashire Dialect*, 1854. Problems with dividing Elizabeth Gaskell's MSS persisted. CD complained to Wills when trying to deal with her story 'Half a Life-Time Ago': 'Mrs. Gaskell, fearful—fearful. If I were Mr. G. O Heaven how I would beat her!' (11 Sept. 1855).

To Thomas Carlyle, 13 JULY 1854

Villa du Camp de droite, Boulogne | Thursday Evening Thirteenth July 1854

My Dear Carlyle

I am going, next month, to publish in One Volume a story now coming out in Household Words, called Hard Times. I have constructed it patiently, with a view to its publication altogether in a compact cheap form. It contains what I do devoutly hope will shake some people in a terrible mistake of these days, when so presented. I know it contains nothing in which you do not think with me, for nò man knows your books better than I. I want to put in the first page of it, that it is inscribed to Thomas Carlyle. May I?[1]

Another thing. We are living here, in a queer, airy, lonely French house on the top of a windy hill—quite aloof from all Hunters of Lions before the Lord[2] (or the Devil), and yet as fresh and natural a place as ever you saw, within 7 hours of London Bridge. Can you give me anything in the way of that plain burly hope that alone condescends to come out of you, that you and Mrs. Carlyle could come and pass a week with us in September? If you tell me Yes, she and Mrs. Dickens shall be a Commission to settle the rest, and so my love to her and you.

Affectionately Yours
CHARLES DICKENS

P.S. I wouldn't flourish to you, if it were not the nature of me.[3]

1 The dedication is: 'Inscribed | To | THOMAS CARLYLE.'
2 Echoing Genesis 10: 9 'Even as Nimrod the mighty hunter before the Lord'.
3 Referring to CD's habitual flamboyant signature, and knowing Carlyle's scorn of pretentiousness.

To John Forster, [?29 SEPTEMBER 1854]

I have had dreadful thoughts of getting away somewhere altogether by myself. If I could have managed it, I think possibly I might have gone to the Pyreennees (you know what I mean that word for, so I won't re-write it) for six months! I have put the idea into the perspective of six months, but have not abandoned it. I have visions of living for half a year or so, in all sorts of inaccessible places, and opening a new book therein. A floating idea of going up above the snow-line in Switzerland, and living in some astonishing convent,[1] hovers about me. If Household Words could be got into a good train, in short, I don't know in what strange place, or at what remote elevation above the level of the sea, I might fall to work next. *Restlessness*, you will say. Whatever it is, it is always driving me, and I cannot help it. I have rested nine or ten weeks, and sometimes feel as if it had been a year—though I had the strangest nervous miseries before I stopped. If I couldn't walk fast and far, I should just explode and perish.

1 Like the Great St Bernard monastery, visited by CD in 1846 and used in *LD* bk. 2, ch. 1.

To *Leigh Hunt*, [?EARLY NOVEMBER 1854]

Separate in your own mind what you see of yourself from what other people tell you that they see.[1] As it has given you so much pain, I take it at its worst, and say I am deeply sorry, and that I feel I did wrong in doing it. I should otherwise have taken it at its best, and ridden off upon what I strongly feel to be the truth, that there is nothing in it that *should* have given you pain. Everyone in writing must speak from points of his experience, and so I of mine with you: but when I have felt it was going too close I stopped myself, and the most blotted parts of my MS. are those in which I have been striving hard to make the impression I was writing from, *un*like you. The diary-writing I took from Haydon,[2] not from you. I now first learn from yourself that you ever set anything to music, and I could not have copied *that* from you. The character is not you, for there are traits in it common to fifty thousand people besides, and I did not fancy you would ever recognize it. Under similar disguises my own father and mother are in my books, and you might as well see your likeness in Micawber.

1   i.e. Hunt's likeness to Skimpole, which was widely recognized.
2   CD relates Skimpole's unpleasant diary (*BH* ch. 61) to the historical painter Benjamin Haydon, who had committed suicide in 1846.

To *Angela Burdett Coutts*, 17 NOVEMBER 1854

I received the following letter,[1] from a Correspondent quite unknown to me, while I was at Boulogne. I think, in the beginning of October.

On my return to town, I wrote to the young man, representing to him that I had scarcely any hope of helping him in so difficult a matter, but that I was unwilling to seem to slight so peculiar a confidence, and that I would speak with him on the subject, if he would call on the following Sunday at a certain hour. That was, Sunday the 29th.of October.

At the appointed time, he came. I found him a very quiet, youthful-looking young man of two or three and twenty, with the appearance of being much younger. He was very becomingly and suitably dressed, in black; and his manner and his whole account of himself were in perfect accordance with his letter. He cried, at several points of our conversation: but he sat in my room with his back to the light, and always made an effort to hide it, and was evidently relieved when I appeared not to notice it.

To make the least of the wretched story, I will only set down here that the person with whom his sister lived so long, was engaged in commerce, and was ruined. The sister seems to have done a great deal for him, in the management of his house and accounts, and some of his relations declared, when he fell into difficulties, "that she was the only true friend he had". He was quite reduced to poverty when they parted, and he is far away now and lost sight of, altogether. She has known nothing about him these many years.

She had only one course of life open to her then, and she has pursued it ever since.

She has a child; a little girl of two years old, to whom she is devoted. Although she is what she is, in the very house to which this brother goes home every night of his life, he has an unbounded respect and love for her, which presents one of the strangest and most bewildering spectacles I ever saw within my remembrance.

She educated her younger sister, who is a Nursery-Governess.[2] The mother (with whom they had a miserable home) is living, and has a small situation in Kensington Workhouse. The young man said he had no consideration for his mother and no love for her. That this elder sister of his had been such a mother to him, always, as he thought few boys had; and that the gratitude and affection with which she had inspired him and his younger sister, "couldn't be described". There is no doubt of this being true. I really had a difficulty in collecting myself to understand that in the tremendous circumstances of their daily existence, she has not fallen in this brother's *respect*.

He represented her as two or three and thirty; as having acquired no accomplishments; but as having had a good plain education, and being a good housekeeper. He said, she loved her child in the most passionate manner imaginable.

When the break-up took place, it was impossible for the young man to continue under his articles, because he was then unable to support himself without a Salary—which, while articled, he was not to receive. His articles were cancelled, therefore (no part of the premium being returned), and he obtained a situation as Architectural Draughtsman—which he holds now—at One pound fifteen per week. This class of people have no rise or advance, he says; but are at last, what they are at first. If he could make enough to keep his sister and her child he would be heartily thankful, and they would joyfully maintain home together, and he would ask no help. He had tried all sorts of things in despair. He had written, only a week or two ago, to Mr. Wigan of the Olympic Theatre, applying for a situation to take checks at the door of an evening, to eke out his income. There was nothing he wouldn't do, to change his sister's life. Not that it had corrupted her—if I would only see her, I should know, before I had spoken to her five minutes, what a nature she had. (And so he began to sob, and said she was the best—the kindest—the least selfish—I don't know what.)

To try how the shock of a separation they had evidently never thought of, would affect him, I asked him if she had ever thought of being sent abroad—to the Cape—to America—to Australia? He was quite stunned by the idea of parting from her, and asked me, Oh Mr. Dickens, did I consider how the natural ties between them must have been strengthened by this time! I said what I have said so many times to the Home[3] people, and I urged him to consider that if (as he had said) she would do anything for her child's sake, she would do that thing on occasion, hard as I admitted it to be. He didn't know, he answered. He believed she would do almost anything—but she had never thought of this—she was almost as fond of him as he was of her—he couldn't hastily pledge her to such a separation as she had never had in her thoughts. "Ask her", said I. He was going out, and came back, and said "Mr. Dickens, I know it would be utterly in vain to ask her to leave her child behind her"—"No one would propose that", said I. "Let us suppose that she was to take it with her."

This is all I know, as yet. I have not replied, nor have I seen her. I will do both, if you feel interested, and I don't disguise that I hope you do. But I have told the story very coldly, in comparison with the impression, it has made upon me. I asked the young man whether there was any one who could speak of his sister besides himself and herself? He replied "Dr. Lavis of Westminster had attended her, was interested in her (he felt sure), and would know the truth of what he had told". This Dr. Lavis is the medical attendant at Tracey's prison, and I know him very well.

I cannot be right, without seeing the girl, of course; but I think that if anything could be done for her, or for her brother, here, it would seem that they had a better chance together than apart.

If you wish to pursue the case, I would first see the Doctor—then her. In any case I cannot let it rest; for the position of this brother—his perception of his sister's disgrace, and undiminished admiration of her, and the confidence he has grown up in, of her being something good, and never to be mentioned without tenderness and deference—is a romance at once so astonishing and yet so intelligible as I never had the boldness to think of.

I made up my mind not to tell you all this, if I had any reason to doubt the strength of their sincerity. On Wednesday—having done nothing but keep quiet in the meanwhile—I received the two following letters.[4]

1 From Frederick Maynard, previously articled to an architect in Russell Square.
2 According to the Revd William Tennant, 'a milliner alas! of damaged reputation'.
3 Urania Cottage.
4 Letters from Frederick Maynard and his sister Caroline Thompson to CD, and from the Revd William Tennant to Miss Coutts are reprinted appendix to Pilgrim 7. CD met Caroline Thompson and arranged for her to run a lodging house. Later he helped her to emigrate to Canada with her brother and daughter.

To John Forster, [3 and 4 FEBRUARY 1855]

I am hourly strengthened in my old belief, that our political aristocracy and our tuft-hunting[1] are the death of England. In all this business I don't see a gleam of hope.[2] As to the popular spirit, it has come to be so entirely separated from the Parliament and Government, and so perfectly apathetic about them both, that I seriously think it a most portentous sign.

You will hear of me in Paris, probably next Sunday, and I *may* go on to Bordeaux. Have general ideas of emigrating in the summer to the mountain-ground between France and Spain. Am altogether in a dishevelled state of mind—motes of new books in the dirty air, miseries of older growth threatening to close upon me. Why is it, that as with poor David, a sense comes always crushing on me now, when I fall into low spirits, as of one happiness I have missed in life, and one friend and companion I have never made?[3]

1 'One who meanly or obsequiously courts the acquaintance of persons of rank and title', *OED*.
2 The crisis in government brought on by criticisms of the conduct of the Crimean War.
3 Cf. 'a vague unhappy loss or want of something', *DC* ch. 35; a similar phrase is repeated in chs. 44, 48, 58, and 62. CD was currently reading *DC* in order to construct a version for a public reading.

To *William H. Wills,* 9 FEBRUARY 1855

OFFICE OF HOUSEHOLD WORDS, | Friday Ninth February 1855

My Dear Wills.

I want to alter our arrangements tomorrow, and put you to some inconvenience.

When I was at Gravesend t'other day,[1] I saw, at Gads Hill—just opposite to the Hermitage where your charmer Miss Lynn[2] used to live—a little Freehold to be sold. The spot and the very house are literally "a dream of my childhood", and I should like to look at it before I go to Paris. With that purpose I must go to Strood by the North Kent at a 1/4 past 10 tomorrow morning. And I want you, strongly booted, to go with me! (I have the particulars from the Agent.)

Can you?—Let me know. If you can, can you manage so that we can take the Proofs with us? If you can't, will you bring them to Tavistock House at dinner time tomorrow, ½ past 5. Forster will dine with us, but no one else.

I am uncertain of your being in town tonight, but I send John up with this.

Ever Faithfully
CD

1 On 7 Feb., during his birthday ramble.
2 Eliza Lynn Linton (1822–98†), journalist and novelist, met CD in 1849. A valued contributor to HW and AYR, although CD remarked to Wills, 'I don't know how it is but she gets so near the sexual side of things as to be a little dangerous to us at times,' 6 Oct. 1854.

To *Maria Winter,*[1] 10 FEBRUARY 1855

Tavistock House | Saturday Tenth February 1855.

My Dear Mrs. Winter.

I constantly receive hundreds of letters, in great varieties of writing all perfectly strange to me, and (as you may suppose) have no particular interest in the faces of such general epistles. As I was reading by my fire last night, a handfull of notes was laid down on my table. I looked them over, and, recognizing the writing of no private friend, let them lie there, and went back to my book. But I found my mind curiously disturbed, and wandering away through so many years to such early times of my life, that I was quite perplexed to account for it. There was nothing in what I had been reading or immediately thinking about, to awaken such a train of thought, and at last it came into my head that it must have been suggested by something in the look of one of those letters. So I turned them over again,—and suddenly the remembrance of your hand, came upon me with an influence that I cannot express to you. Three or four and twenty years vanished like a dream, and I opened it with the touch of my young friend David Copperfield when he was in love.

There was something so busy and pleasant in your letter—so true and cheerful and frank and affectionate—that I read on with perfect delight until I came to your mention of your two little girls. In the unsettled state of my thoughts, the existence of these dear children appeared such a prodigious phaenomonon, that I was inclined to suspect myself of being out of my mind, until it occurred to me that perhaps I had nine children of my own! Then the three or four and twenty years began to rearrange themselves in a long procession between me and the changeless Past, and I could not help considering what strange stuff all our little stories are made of.

Believe me, you cannnot more tenderly remember our old days and our old friends than I do. I hardly ever go into the City, but I walk up an odd little court at the back of the Mansion House, and come out by the corner of Lombard Street. Hundreds of times as I have passed the church there—on my way to and from the Sea, the Continent, and where not—I invariably associate it with somebody (God knows who) having told me that poor Anne[2] was buried there. If you would like to examine me in the name of a good-looking Cornish servant you used to have (I suppose she has twenty-nine great grandchildren now, and walks with a stick), you will find my knowledge on the point correct, though it was a monstrous name too. I forget nothing of those times. They are just as still and plain and clear, as if I had never been in a crowd since and I had never seen or heard my own name out of my own house. What should I be worth, or what would labour and success be worth, if it were otherwise!

Your letter is more touching to me from its good and gentle association with the state of Spring in which I was either much more wise or much more foolish than I am now—I never know which to think it—than I could tell you if I tried for a week. I will not try at all. I heartily respond to it, and shall be charmed to have a long talk with you, and most cordially glad to see you, after all this length of time.

I am going to Paris tomorrow morning, but I purpose being back within a fortnight. When I return, Mrs. Dickens will come to you, to arrange a day for our seeing you and Mr. Winter (to whom I beg to be remembered) quietly to dinner. We will have no intruder or foreign creature on any pretence whatever, in order that we may set in, without any restraint, for a tremendous gossip.

Mary Anne Leigh[3] we saw at Broadstairs about fifty years ago. Mrs. Dickens and her sister, who read all the marriages in all the papers, shrieked to me when the announcement of hers appeared, what did I think of *that*? I calmly replied that I thought it was time. I should have been more excited if I had known of the old gentleman with seven thousand a year, uncountable grown up children, and no English grammar.

My mother has a strong objection to being considered in the least old, and usually appears here on Christmas Day in a juvenile cap which takes an immense time in the putting on. The Fates seem to have made up their minds that I shall never see your Father when he comes this way. David Lloyd[4] is altogether an Imposter—not having in the least changed (that I could make out when I saw him at the London Tavern), since what I suppose to have been the year 1770 when I found you three on Cornhill with your poor mother, going to St. Mary Axe to order mysterious dresses—which afterwards turned out to be Wedding garments. That was in the remote period when you all wore green cloaks, cut (in my remembrance) very round, and which I am resolved to believe were made of Merino. I escorted you with native gallantry to the Dress Maker's door, and your mother, seized with an apprehension—groundless, upon my honor—that I might come in, said emphatically, "And now Mr. Dickin"— which she always used to call me—"we'll wish *you* good morning!"

When I was writing the word Paris just now, I remembered that my existence was once entirely uprooted and my whole Being blighted, by the Angel of my soul being sent there to finish her education![5] If I can discharge any little commission for you or bring home anything for the darlings whom I cannot yet believe to be anything but a delusion of yours, pray employ me. I shall be at the Hotel Meurice—locked up when within, as my only defence against my country and the United States—but a most punctual and reliable functionary if you will give me any employment.

My Dear Mrs. Winter I have been much moved by your letter; and the pleasure it has given me has some little sorrowful ingredient in it. In the strife and struggle of this great world where most of us lose each other so strangely, it is impossible to be spoken to out of the old times without a softened emotion. You so belong to the days when the qualities that have done me most good since, were growing in my boyish heart that I cannot end my answer to you lightly. The associations my memory has with you, make your letter more—I want a word—invest it with a more immediate address to me—than such a letter could have from anybody else. Mr. Winter will not mind that. We are all sailing away to the sea, and have a pleasure in thinking of the river we are upon, when it was very narrow and little. Faithfully Your friend

CHARLES DICKENS

1 Formerly Maria Beadnell, CD's first love (see above 1831–3), now married to Henry Winter, a saw-mill manager. CD implies that he has not seen Maria since 1833, but he seems to have visited her with Catherine and Georgina in 1846, the year after her marriage. See Michael Slater, *Dickens and Women* (London: J. M. Dent, 1983), ch. 4.
2 Maria's sister, who married CD's friend Henry Kolle 1833; she died 1836.
3 A friend of Maria's (see above 7 Mar. 1831 and 14–17 May 1833), who made trouble between CD and Maria. She married in 1854.
4 Married Maria's sister Margaret 1831.
5 Maria was sent to France in 1832 to remove her from CD; cf. Mr Spenlow's proposal to send Dora abroad again, *DC* ch. 38.

To Maria Winter, 15 FEBRUARY 1855

Hôtel Meurice, Paris | Thursday Fifteenth February 1855.

My Dear Mrs. Winter. (I had half a mind when I dipped my pen in the ink, to address you by your old natural Christian name.)

The snow lies so deep on the Northern Railway, and the Posts have been so interrupted in consequence, that your charming note arrived here only this morning. I reply by return of post, with a general idea that Sarah will come to Finsbury Place with a basket and a face of good-humoured compassion, and carry the letter away, and leave me as desolate as she used to do.

I get the heartache again when I read your commission, written in the hand which I find now to be not in the least changed, and yet it is a great pleasure to be entrusted with it, and to have that share in your gentler remembrances which I cannot find it still my privilege to have, without a stirring of the old fancies. I need not tell you that it shall be executed to the letter—with as much interest as I once matched a little pair of gloves for you which I recollect were blue ones. (I wonder whether people generally wore blue gloves when I was nineteen, or whether it was only you!) I am very very sorry you mistrusted me in not writing before your little girl was born; but I hope now you know me better you will teach her, one day, to tell her children, in times to come when they may have some interest in wondering about it, that I loved her mother with the most extraordinary earnestness when I was a boy.

I have always believed since, and always shall to the last, that there never was such a faithful and devoted poor fellow as I was. Whatever of fancy, romance, energy, passion, aspiration and determination belong to me, I never have separated and never shall separate from the hard hearted little woman—you—whom it is nothing to say I would have died for, with the greatest alacrity! I never can think, and I never seem to observe, that other young people are in such desperate earnest, or set so much, so long, upon one absorbing hope. It is a matter of perfect certainty to me that I began to fight my way out of poverty and obscurity, with one perpetual idea of you. This is so fixed in my knowledge that to the hour when I opened your letter last Friday night, I have never heard anybody addressed by your name or spoken of by your name, without a start. The sound of it has always filled me with a kind of pity and respect for the deep truth that I had, in my silly hobbledehoyhood, to bestow upon one creature who represented the whole world to me. I have never been so good a man since, as I was when you made me wretchedly happy. I shall never be half so good a fellow any more.

This is all so strange now, both to think of, and to say, after every change that has come about; but I think, when you ask me to write to you, you are not unprepared for what it is so natural to me to recal, and will not be displeased to read it. I fancy,— though you may not have thought in the old time how manfully I loved you—that you may have seen in one of my books a faithful reflection of the passion I had for you, and may have thought that it was something to have been loved so well, and may have seen in little bits of "Dora" touches of your old self sometimes, and a grace here and there that may be revived in your little girls, years hence, for the bewilderment of some other young lover—though he will never be as terribly in earnest as I and David Copperfield were. People used to say to me how pretty all that was, and how fanciful it was, and how elevated it was above the little foolish loves of very young men and women. But they little thought what reason I had to know it was true and nothing more nor less.

These are things that I have locked up in my own breast, and that I never thought to bring out any more. But when I find myself writing to you again "all to your self", how can I forbear to let as much light in upon them as will shew you that they are there still! If the most innocent, the most ardent, and the most disinterested days of my life had you for their Sun—as indeed they had—and if I know that the Dream I lived in did me good, refined my heart, and made me patient and persevering, and if the Dream were all of you—as God knows it was—how can I receive a confidence from you, and return it, and make a feint of blotting all this out!

As I have said, I fancy that you know all about it quite as well as I do, however. I have a strong belief—there is no harm in adding hope to that—that perhaps you have once or twice laid down that book, and thought "How dearly that boy must have loved me, and how vividly this man remembers it!"

I shall be here until Tuesday or Wednesday. If the snow allows this letter to come to you in the meantime, perhaps it would allow one to come to me "all to myself", if you were to try it. A number of recollections came into my head when I began, and I meant to have gone through a string of them and to have asked you if they lived in your mind too. But they all belong to the one I have indulged in—half pleasantly, half painfully—and are all swallowed up in that,—so let them go.

My Dear Mrs. Winter | Ever affectionately Yours

CHARLES DICKENS

I wonder what has become of a bundle of letters I sent you back once (according to order) tied with a blue ribbon, of the color of the gloves.[1]

---

1 See above, 18 Mar. 1833.

To Maria Winter, 22 FEBRUARY 1855

Tavistock House | Thursday Twenty Second February 1855

My Dear Maria.

The old writing is so plain to *me*, that I have read your letter with great ease (though it is just a little crossed), and have not lost a word of it. I was obliged to leave Paris on Tuesday Morning before the Post came in; but I took such precautions to prevent the possibility of any mischance, that the letter came close behind me. I arrived at home last night, and it followed me this morning. No one but myself has the slightest knowledge of my correspondence, I may add in this place. I could be nowhere addressed with stricter privacy or in more absolute confidence than at my own house.

Ah! Though it is so late to read in the old hand what I never read before, I have read it with great emotion, and with the old tenderness softened to a more sorrowful remembrance than I could easily tell you. How it all happened as it did, we shall never know on this side of Time; but if you had ever told me then what you tell me now, I know myself well enough to be thoroughly assured that the simple truth and energy which were in my love would have overcome everything. I remember well that long after I came of age—I say long; well! It seemed long then—I wrote to you for the last time of all, with a dawn upon me of some sensible idea that we were changing into man and woman, saying Would you forget our little differences and separations and let us begin again? You answered me very coldly and reproachfully,—and so I went my way.

But nobody can ever know with what a sad heart I resigned you, or after what struggles and what a conflict. My entire devotion to you, and the wasted tenderness of those hard years which I have ever since half loved half dreaded to recall, made so deep an impression on me that I refer to it a habit of suppression which now belongs to me, which I know is no part of my original nature, but which makes me chary of shewing my affections, even to my children, except when they are very young. A few years ago (just before Copperfield) I began to write my life, intending the Manuscript to be found among my papers when its subject should be concluded. But as I began to approach within sight of that part of it, I lost courage and burned the rest. I have never blamed you at all, but I have believed until now that you never had the stake in that serious game which I had.

All this mist passes away before your earnest words; and when I find myself to have been in your mind at that thoughtful crisis in your life which you so unaffectedly and feelingly describe, I am quite subdued and strangely enlightened. When poor Fanny died (I think she always knew that I never could bear to hear of you as of any common person) we were out of town, and I never heard of your having been in Devonshire Terrace—least of all in my room! I never heard of you in association with that time, until I read your letter to day. I could not, however—really *could not*—at any time within these nineteen years, have been so unmindful of my old truth, and have so set my old passion aside, as to talk to you like a person in any ordinary relation towards me. And this I think is the main reason on my side why the few opportunities that there have been of our seeing one another again, have died out.

All this again you have changed and set right—at once so courageously, so delicately and gently, that you open the way to a confidence between us which still once more, in perfect innocence and good faith, may be between ourselves alone. All that you propose, I accept with my whole heart. Whom can you ever trust if it be not your old lover! Lady Olliffe asked me in Paris the other day (we are, in our way, confidential you must know) whether it was really true that I used to love Maria Beadnell so very, very, very much? I told her that there was no woman in the world, and there were very few men, who could ever imagine how much.

You are always the same in my remembrance. When you say you are "toothless, fat, old, and ugly" (which I don't believe), I fly away to the house in Lombard Street which is pulled down, as if it were necessary that the very bricks and mortar should go the way of my airy castles, and see you in a sort of raspberry colored dress with a little black trimming at the top—black velvet it seems to be made of—cut into vandykes[1]—an immense number of vandykes—with my boyish heart pinned like a captured butterfly on every one of them. I have never seen a girl play the harp, from that day to this, but my attention has been instantly arrested, and that drawing room has stood before me so plainly that I could write a most accurate description of it. I remember that there used to be a tendency in your eyebrows to join together; and sometimes in the most unlikely places—in Scotland, America, Italy—on the stateliest occasions and the most unceremonious—when I have been talking to a strange face and have observed even such a slight association as this in it, I have suddenly been carried away at the rate of a thousand miles a second, and have thought "Maria Beadnell!" When we were falling off from each other, I came from the House of Commons many a night at two or three o'Clock in the morning, only to wander past the place you were asleep in. And I have gone over that ground within these twelve months, hoping it was not ungrateful to consider whether any reputation the world can bestow, is repayment to a man for the loss of such a vision of his youth as mine. You ask me to treasure what you tell me, in my heart of hearts. O see what I have cherished there, through all this [ ]² time and all these changes!

In the course of Saturday I will write to you at Artillery Place, sending the little brooches and telling you when Catherine will come—not forgetting the little Niece, though I don't expect her to remind me of Somebody or Anybody. And now to what I have reserved for the last.

I am a dangerous man to be seen with, for so many people know me. At St. Paul's, the Dean and the whole chapter know me. In Paternoster Row³ of all places, the very tiles and chimney pots know me. At first I a little hesitated whether or no to advise you to forego that interview or suggest another—principally because what would be very natural and probable a fortnight hence, seems scarcely so probable now. Still I should very much like to see you before we meet when others are by—I feel it as it were, so necessary to our being at ease—and unless I hear from you to the contrary, you may expect to encounter a stranger whom you may suspect to be the right person if he wears a moustache. You would not like better to call here on Sunday, asking first for Catherine and then for me? It is almost a positive certainty that there will be no one here but I, between 3 and 4. I make this suggestion, knowing what odd coincidences take place in streets, when they are not wanted to happen; though I know them to be so unlikely, that I should not think of such a thing if any one but you were concerned. If you think you would not like to come here, make no change. I will come there.

I cannot trust myself to begin afresh, or I should have *my* remembrances of our separation, and think yours hard to me. I remember poor Anne writing to me once, (in answer to some burst of low-spirited madness of mine), and saying "My dear Charles, I really cannot understand Maria, or venture to take the responsibility of saying what the state of her affections is"—and she added, I recollect, God bless her, a long quotation about Patience and Time.⁴ Well, well. It was not to be, until Patience and Time should bring us round together thus—

Remember. I accept all with my whole soul, and reciprocate all.

Ever Your Affectionate friend
CHARLES DICKENS

1 Deeply cut or scalloped edges on the collar of a dress.
2 Word illegible through damage.
3 Near St Paul's, mainly publishers' premises; Maria Winter may have suggested places for a 'chance' meeting. The Winters dined at Tavistock House on 27 Feb.
4 Recalled in Julia Mills's journal entries in *DC* ch. 38.

To Augustus Tracey, 24 FEBRUARY 1855

Tavistock House | Twenty Fourth February 1855

My Dear Tracey

I have just come home from Paris and found your letter on my table—for which, many thanks!

The drying-closet for Scutari is being made.[1] I have been greatly prepossessed by Mr. Jeakes.

Faithfully Yours always
CHARLES DICKENS

If I can get to the Athenæum from another engagement on Monday, I will not forget your request.

---

1 For drying clothes at the chief military hospital in the Crimea: laundry was reported as grossly inadequate before Florence Nightingale's efforts. The closet was paid for by Angela Burdett Coutts and made by William Jeakes, a mechanical engineer 'ingenious in his trade', CD to Miss Coutts, 21 Jan. 1855.

To John Forster, [?EARLY MARCH 1855]

I don't quite apprehend what you mean by my over-rating the strength of the feeling of five-and-twenty years ago. If you mean of my own feeling, and will only think what the desperate intensity of my nature is, and that this began when I was Charley's age; that it excluded every other idea from my mind for four years, at a time of life when four years are equal to four times four; and that I went at it with a determination to overcome all the difficulties, which fairly lifted me up into that newspaper life, and floated me away over a hundred men's heads: then you are wrong, because nothing can exaggerate that. I have positively stood amazed at myself ever since!—And so I suffered, and so worked, and so beat and hammered away at the maddest romances that ever got into any boy's head and stayed there, that to see the mere cause of it all, now, loosens my hold upon myself. Without for a moment sincerely believing that it would have been better if we had never got separated, I cannot see the occasion of so much emotion as I should see anyone else. No one can imagine in the most distant degree what pain the recollection gave me in Copperfield. And, just as I can never open that book as I open any other book, I cannot see the face (even at four-and-forty), or hear the voice, without going wandering away over the ashes of all that youth and hope in the wildest manner.

To *Wilkie Collins,* 4 MARCH 1855

Tavistock House | Sunday Fourth March 1855

My Dear Collins.

I have to report another failure on the part of our friend Williams,[1] last night. He so confounded an enlightened British Audience at the Standard Theatre on the subject of Antony and Cleopatra, that I clearly saw them wondering towards the end of the Fourth Act, when the play was going to begin.

A man much heavier than Mark (in the actual scale, I mean), and about twenty years older, played Cæsar. When he came on with a Map of London—pretending it was a scroll and making believe to read it—and said, "He calls me Boy"[2]—a howl of derision arose from the Audience which you probably heard in the Park, without knowing what occasioned it. All the smaller characters, having their speeches much upon their minds, came in and let them off without the slightest reference to cues. And Miss Glyn, in some entirely new conception of her art, "read" her part like a Patter song—several lines on end with the rapidity of Charles Mathews, and then one very long word. It was very brightly and creditably got up, but (as I have said) Williams did not carry the Audience and I don't think the Sixty Pounds a week will be got back by the Manager.

You will have the goodness to picture me to yourself—alone—in profound solitude—in an abyss of despair—ensconced in a small Managerial Private Box in the very centre of the House—frightfully sleepy (I had a dirty steak in the City first, and I think they must have put Laudanum into the Harvey's sauce), and played at, point blank, by the entire strength of the Company. The terrors in which I constantly woke up, and found myself detected, you will imagine. The gentle Glyn on being called for, heaved her snowy bosom straight at me, and the box keeper informed me that the Manager who brought her on would "have the honor of stepping round directly." I sneaked away in the most craven and dastardly manner, and made an utterly false representation that I was coming back again.

If you will give me one glass of hot gin and water on Thursday or Friday Evening, I will come up at about 8* o'Clock with a cigar in my pocket, and inspect the Hospital.[3] I am afraid this relaxing weather will tell a little faintly on your medicine, but I hope you will soon begin to see land beyond the Hunterian Ocean.[4]

I have been writing and planning and making notes over an immense number of little bits of paper[5] and I never can write legibly under such circumstances.

Always Cordially Yours

CD.

* Intended for EIGHT

1 Stage director of Sadler's Wells.
2 *Antony and Cleopatra*, IV. i. 1.
3 i.e. Collins's sick room.
4 Alluding to the surgeon and anatomist John Hunter (1728–93).
5 The beginnings of *LD*.

To Mark Lemon, 5 MARCH 1855

Tavistock House | Monday Fifth March 1855

My Dear Mark

It's not today. Its this day week. What are you up to?

I am engaged to dine with Hardwick the Magistrate, today. But if anybody was to come round and particularly propose—in short, anything—down a Railroad or anywhere—I am in a Spring humour and might be false to him.

Ever affecy.

CD.

To Mark Lemon, 5 MARCH 1855

Tavistock House | Monday Fifth March 1855

My Dear Mark.

I will expect you here, from and after 3.

Ever affecy.

CD.

To Elisha Morgan,[1] [19 MARCH] 1855

1855.

Dear Friend,

I am always delighted to hear from you. Your genial earnestness does me good to think of. And every day of my life I feel more and more that to be thoroughly in earnest is everything, and to be anything short of it is nothing. You see what we have been doing to our valiant soldiers. You see what miserable humbugs we are. And because we have got involved in meshes of aristocratic red tape to our unspeakable confusion, loss, and sorrow, the gentlemen who have been so kind as to ruin us are going to give us a day of humiliation and fasting the day after to-morrow.[2] I am sick and sour to think of such things at this age of the world. . . . I am in the first stage of a new book, which consists in going round and round the idea, as you see a bird in his cage go about and about his sugar before he touches it.

Always most cordially yours

[CHARLES DICKENS]

1 Captain Elisha Ely Morgan (?1805–64) of the American merchant service; CD met him in 1841 and had a
high regard for him. Morgan sent cigars from America to CD and other English friends.
2 A royal proclamation of 28 Feb. ordered a day of 'Solemn Fast, Humiliation and Prayer' on 21 Mar.
Correspondents in *The Times* suggested that the government should be fasting rather than the people.

To *Maria Winter*, 3 APRIL 1855

Tuesday Third April, 1855

My Dear Maria.

Going down to Ashford this day week, already with a bad cold, I increased it so much by getting into the intense heat consequent upon a reading of three hours[1] and then coming up in the night (which I was obliged to do, having business in town next morning), that I was very unwell all the week, and on Friday night was so completely knocked up that I came home at 9 o'Clock to bed. A necessity is upon me now—as at most times—of wandering about in my own wild way, to think. I could no more resist this on Sunday or yesterday, than a man can dispense with food, or a horse can help himself from being driven. I hold my inventive capacity on the stern condition that it must master my whole life, often have complete possession of me, make its own demands upon me, and, sometimes for months together, put everything else away from me. If I had not known long ago that my place could never be held, unless I were at any moment ready to devote myself to it entirely, I should have dropped out of it very soon. All this I can hardly expect you to understand—or the restlessness and waywardness of an author's mind. You have never seen it before you, or lived with it, or had occasion to think or care about it, and you cannot have the necessary consideration for it. "It is only half an hour"—"it is only an afternoon"—"it is only an evening"—people say to me over and over again—but they don't know that it is impossible to command one's self sometimes to any stipulated and set disposal of five minutes—or that the mere consciousness of an engagement will sometimes worry a whole day. These are the penalties paid for writing books. Whoever is devoted to an Art must be content to deliver himself wholly up to it, and to find his recompense in it. I am grieved if you suspect me of not wanting to see you; but I can't help it; I must go my way, whether or no.

I thought you would understand that in sending the card for the box, I sent an assurance that there was nothing amiss.[2] I am pleased to find that you were all so much interested with the play. My ladies say that the first part is too painful and wants relief. I have been going to see it a dozen times, but have never seen it yet, and never may. Madame Celeste is injured thereby (you see how unreasonable people are!) and says in the Green Room, with a very tight cheek, "M. Dickens est artiste! Mais il n'a jamais vu Janet Pride!"

It is like a breath of fresh spring air to know that that unfortunate Baby of yours is out of her one close room and has about half a pint of very doubtful air per day. I could only have become her Godfather on the condition that she had 500 gallons of open air at any rate, every day of her life. And you would soon see a rose or two in the face of my other little friend, Ella, if you opened all your doors and windows throughout the whole of all fine weather, from morning to night.

I am going off, I don't know where or how far, to ponder about I don't know what. Sometimes I am half in the mood to set off for France, sometimes I think I will go and walk about on the sea shore for three or four months, sometimes I look towards the Pyrenees, sometimes Switzerland. I made a compact with a great Spanish authority last week, and vowed I would go to Spain. Two days afterwards, Layard and I agreed to go to Constantinople when Parliament rises. Tomorrow I shall probably discuss with somebody else, the idea of going to Greenland or the North Pole. The end of all this, most likely, will be, that I shall shut myself up in some out of the way place I have never yet thought of, and go desperately to work there.

Once upon a time I didn't do such things, you say. No. But I have done them through a good many years now, and they have become myself and my life.

Ever affectionately

CD.

1 *CC*, read for the benefit of the South-Eastern Railway Mechanics' Institution.
2 CD had given Maria a box for the performance of Dion Boucicault's *Janet Pride* on 29 Mar., but feared he himself would be 'waylaid by Household Words'. It seems he was, and that Maria had complained.

To *Austen Layard*,[1] 10 APRIL 1855

Tavistock House | Tuesday Tenth April, 1855

My Dear Layard

I shall of course observe the strictest silence, at present, in reference to your resolutions.[2] It will be a most acceptable occupation to me, to go over them with you; and I have not a doubt of their producing a strong effect out of doors.[3]

There is nothing in the present time at once so galling and so alarming to me as the alienation of the people from their own public affairs. I have no difficulty in understanding it. They have had so little to do with the Game through all these years of Parliamentary Reform, that they have sullenly laid down their cards and taken to looking on. The Players who are left at the table do not see beyond it—conceive that the gain and loss and all the interest of the play are in their hands—and will never be wiser until they and the table and the lights and the money are all overturned together. And I believe the discontent to be so much the worse for smouldering instead of blazing openly, that it is extremely like the general mind of France before the breaking out of the first Revolution, and is in danger of being turned by any one of a thousand accidents—a bad harvest—the last straw too much of aristocratic insolence or incapacity—a defeat abroad—a mere chance at home—into such a Devil of a conflagration as has never been beheld since.

Meanwhile, all our English Tufthunting, Toad Eating, and other manifestations of accursed Gentility—to say nothing of Palmerston's,[4] Graham's, Wood's, Sidney Herbert's and the Lord knows who's defiances of the proven Truth before six hundred and fifty men[5]—*are* expressing themselves every day. So, every day the disgusted millions with this unnatural gloom and calm upon them, are confirmed and hardened in the very worst of moods. Finally, round all this is an atmosphere of poverty, hunger, and ignorant desperation, of the mere existence of which, perhaps not one man in a thousand of those not actually enveloped in it, through the whole extent of this country, has the least idea.

It seems to me an absolute impossibility to direct the spirit of the people at this pass, until it shews itself. If they would begin to bestir themselves in the vigorous national manner—if they would appear in Political Unions—array themselves peacefully, but in vast numbers, against a system that they know to be rotten altogether—make themselves heard like the Sea, all round this Island—I for one should be in such a movement, heart and soul, and should think it a duty of the plainest kind to go along with it (and try to guide it), by all possible means. But you can no more help a people who do not help themselves, than you can help a man who does not help himself. And until the people can be got up from the lethargy which is an awful symptom of the advanced state of their disease, I know of nothing that can be done beyond keeping their wrongs continually before them.

I shall hope to see you soon after you come back. Your speeches at Aberdeen are most admirable, manful, and earnest. I would have such speeches at every market cross, and in every town hall, and among all sorts and conditions of men—up in the very balloons, and down in the very diving-bells.

Ever Cordially Yours
CD.

1 Austen Layard (1817–94†), excavator of Nineveh and Liberal politician. Spearheaded the campaign against the government's incompetent handling of the Crimean War. First met CD *c*.1851.
2 The basis for the Administrative Reform Association, one of the few political movements CD supported.
3 i.e. outside Parliament.
4 Prime minister since 13 Feb. Sir James Graham, Sir Charles Wood, and Sidney Herbert all held political offices.
5 i.e. the House of Commons.

To Frank Smedley,[1] 8 MAY 1855

Tavistock House | Eighth May 1855, Tuesday.

My Dear Sir
I have read the enclosed with much interest, and greatly admire the point and brevity with which it is written. It is unaffected and spirited, and altogether worthy of its subject.

But I cannot reconcile it to my heart, to publish these details so soon after Miss Brontë's death.[2] For anything I know, they might be saddening and painful to her husband; and I am not at all clear that I have any right to them. I have a particular objection to that kind of interest in a great mind, which prompts a visitor to take "a good look" at the mortal habiliments in which it is arrayed, and afterwards to catalogue them like an auctioneer. I have no sympathy whatever, with the staring curiosity that it gratifies.

And beyond the husband, and even the father, of this lady, I cannot help going to herself. It seems that she would have shrunk from this account of her trials; and that such as she wanted given, she has given herself;[3] and that for the present there is enough said about them.

The subject does not present itself to you in this light. I quite understand; nor do I seek to convert you to my opinions. I state them plainly, merely as my sole reason for not retaining the paper.

I perfectly remember our meeting at Mr. Stanfield's, and have read your note with much pleasure. It is a high gratification to me, I assure you, to be received (in my books) into such companionship as you describe.

Faithfully Yours
CHARLES DICKENS

1 Frank Smedley (1818–64†), novelist and magazine editor. His article 'A Few Words about "Jane Eyre"', *Sharpe's Magazine* (June 1855), led to Patrick Brontë's invitation to Elizabeth Gaskell to write *The Life of Charlotte Brontë*.
2 Charlotte Brontë died 31 Mar.
3 CD seems to be referring to Brontë's 1848 preface to *Jane Eyre*.

To Clarkson Stanfield, 20 MAY 1855

Tavistock House | Sunday Twentieth May 1855

My Dear Stanny
I have a little Lark in contemplation, if you will help it to fly.
Collins has done a Melo Drama (a regular old-style Melo Drama),[1] in which there is a very good notion. I am going to act it, as an experiment, in the childrens' Theatre here—I, Mark,[2] Collins, Egg, and my daughter Mary, the whole dram: pers:—our families and yours, the whole Audience; for I want to make the stage large, and shouldn't have room for above five and twenty spectators. Now, there is only one scene in the piece, and that—my Tarry Lad—is the inside of a Lighthouse. Will you come and paint it for us one night, and we'll all turn to and help? It is a mere wall of course, but Mark and I have sworn that you must do it.[3]

If you will say yes, I should like to have the tiny flats[4] made, after you have looked at the place and not before. On Wednesday in this week I am good for a steak and the Play, if you will make your own appointment here; or any day next week except Thursday. Write me a line in reply.

We mean to burst on an astonished World with the Melo Drama, without any note of preparation. So don't say a syllable to Forster, if you should happen to see him.

Ever affectionately Yours
CD.

1 *The Lighthouse*, performed at Tavistock House 16, 18, and 19 June.
2 Mark Lemon.
3 Stanfield designed the interior and painted a frontdrop showing the lighthouse in a storm.
4 Wooden frames covered with canvas, for the scenery.

To John Forster, [19 AUGUST 1855]

As to the story I am in the second number,[1] and last night and this morning had half a mind to begin again, and work in what I have done, afterwards. *It occurred to him that, by making the fellow-travellers at once known to each other, he missed an effect.* It struck me that it would be a new thing to show people coming together, in a chance way, as fellow-travellers, and being in the same place, ignorant of one another, as happens in life; and to connect them afterwards, and to make the waiting for that connection a part of the interest.

1 *LD* bk. 1, chs. 5–8.

To Lavinia Watson, 16 SEPTEMBER 1855

Folkestone, Sunday Sixteenth September 1855

My Dear Mrs. Watson.
This will be a short letter, but I hope not unwelcome. If you knew how often I write to you—in intention—I don't know where you would find room for the correspondence.

Catherine tells me that you want to know the name of my new book. I cannot bear that you should know it from anyone but me. It will not be made public until the end of October; the title is,

NOBODY'S FAULT.[1]

Keep it as the apple of your eye—an expressive form of speech, though I have not the least idea of what it means.

Next, I wish to tell you that I have appointed to read at Peterboro', on Tuesday the 18th. of December. I have told the Dean that I cannot accept his hospitality, and that I am going with Mr. Wills to the Inn. Therefore I shall be absolutely at your disposal, and shall be more than disappointed if you don't stay with us. As the time approaches, will you let me know your arrangements, and whether Mr. Wills can bespeak any rooms for you in arranging for me? Georgy will give you our address in Paris as soon as we shall have settled there. We shall leave here, I think, in rather less than a month from this time.

You know my state of mind, as well as I do—indeed, if you don't know it much better, it is not the state of mind I take it to be. How I work, how I walk, how I shut myself up, how I roll down hills and climb up cliffs, how the new story is everywhere—heaving in the sea, flying with the clouds, blowing in the wind—how I settle to nothing, and wonder (in the old way) at my own incomprehensibility. I am getting on pretty well—have done the first two numbers—and am just now beginning the third; which egotistical announcements I make to you, because I know you will be interested in them.

All the house send their kindest loves. I think of inserting an advertisement in the Times, offering to submit the Plornishghenter to public competition; I to receive £50,000 if such another boy cannot be found; and to pay £5 (my fortune) if he can.

Ever My Dear Mrs. Watson
Affectionately Yours
CHARLES DICKENS

1 Only with the Number Plan for No. 4 did CD settle on *Little Dorrit* as his title.

To John Forster, 16 SEPTEMBER 1855 [Folkestone]

I am going to read for them here, on the 5th of next month, and have answered in the last fortnight thirty applications to do the like all over England, Ireland, and Scotland. Fancy my having to come from Paris in December to do this, at Peterborough, Birmingham, and Sheffield—old promises.

I am just now getting to work on number three;[1] sometimes enthusiastic, more often dull enough. There is an enormous outlay in the Father of the Marshalsea chapter, in the way of getting a great lot of matter into a small space. I am not quite resolved, but I have a great idea of overwhelming that family with wealth. Their condition would be very curious. I can make Dorrit[2] very strong in the story, I hope.

1 LD bk. 1, chs. 9–11, includes ch. 10, 'Containing the Whole Science of Government', on the Circumlocution Office. CD wrote to Wilkie Collins on 30 Sept.: 'I have almost finished No. 3, in which I have relieved my indignant soul with a scarifier,' and to Forster on 30 Jan. 1856: 'I have a grim pleasure upon me to-night in thinking that the Circumlocution Office sees the light, and in wondering what effect it will make.'

2 i.e. Amy, still called 'Dorrit', not 'Little Dorrit' in the MS at this stage.

To Prospective Contributors to Household Words Christmas Number,[1] [EARLY OCTOBER 1855]

A traveller who finds himself the only person staying at an Inn on Christmas Day, is at his wits' end what to do with himself; the rather as he is of a timid and reserved character, and, being shut up in his solitary sitting-room, doesn't well know how to come out of it and speak to anybody. The general idea of the Number is, that he overcomes this feeling—finds out the stories of the different people belonging to the Inn—or some curious experience that each has had—and writes down what he discovers.

Both for the sake of a variety between this No. and previous Christmas numbers, and also for the preservation of the idea, it is necessary that the stories should *not* be in the first person, but should be turned as if this traveller were recording them. Thus the Headings will not be The Waiter's Story, the Cook's Story, The Chambermaid's Story, &c, but simply The Waiter—The Cook—The Chambermaid—and under each head the traveller himself is supposed to tell whatever he heard from, or fancied about, or found out about, that particular person. Thus the person to whom the story belongs may be described, if necessary, as pretty or ugly—of such an age—of such a bringing up—and what is related about him or her may have happened at that Inn, or at another Inn, or at no Inn; and may belong to that person's present condition in life, or to some previous condition in life—and not only to himself or herself, but (if necessary) to other persons encountered in life.

1 A draft of the letter sent out to solicit contributions for the Christmas Number, a practice CD adopted for some years.

To Mark Lemon, 7 JANUARY 1856

49, Champs Elysees, Paris, Monday, Jan. 7th, 1856.

My dear Mark,

I want to know how "Jack and the Beanstalk"[1] goes. I have a notion from a notice—a favourable notice, however—which I saw in *Galignani*, that Webster has let down the comic business.

In a piece at the Ambigu, called the "Rentrée à Paris," a mere scene in honour of the return of the troops from the Crimea the other day, there is a novelty which I think it worth letting you know of, as it is easily available, either for a serious or a comic interest—the introduction of a supposed electric telegraph. The scene is the railway terminus at Paris, with the electric telegraph office on the prompt side, and the clerks *with their backs to the audience*—much more real than if they were, as they infallibly would be, staring about the house—working the needles; and the little bell perpetually ringing. There are assembled to greet the soldiers, all the easily and naturally imagined elements of interest—old veteran fathers, young children, agonised mothers, sisters and brothers, girl lovers—each impatient to know of his or her own object of solicitude. Enter to these a certain marquis, full of sympathy for all, who says "My friends, I am one of you. My brother has no commission yet. He is a common soldier. I wait for him as well as all brothers and sisters here wait for *their* brothers. Tell me whom you are expecting." Then they all tell him. Then he goes into the telegraph-office, and sends a message down the line to know how long the troops will be. Bell rings. Answer handed out on slip of paper. "Delay on the line. Troops will not arrive for a quarter of an hour." General disappointment. "But we have this brave electric telegraph, my friends," says the marquis. "Give me your little messages, and I'll send them off." General rush round the marquis. Exclamations: "How's Henri?" "My love to Georges;" "Has Guillaume forgotten Elise?" "Is my son wounded?" "Is my brother promoted?" etc. etc. Marquis composes tumult. Sends message—such a regiment, such a company—"Elise's love to Georges." Little bell rings, slip of paper handed out—"Georges in ten minutes will embrace his Elise. Sends her a thousand kisses." Marquis sends message—such a regiment, such a company—"Is my son wounded?" Little bell rings. Slip of paper handed out—"No. He has not yet upon him those marks of bravery in the glorious service of his country which his dear old father bears" (father being lamed and invalided). Last of all, the widowed mother. Marquis sends message—such a regiment, such a company—"Is my only son safe?" Little bell rings. Slip of paper handed out—"He was first upon the heights of Alma." General cheer. Bell rings again, another slip of paper handed out. "He was made a sergeant at Inkermann." Another cheer. Bell rings again, another slip of paper handed out. "He was made colour-sergeant at Sebastopol." Another cheer. Bell rings again, another slip of paper handed out. "He was the first man who leaped with the French banner on the Malakhoff tower." Tremendous cheer. Bell rings again, another slip of paper handed out. "But he was struck down there by a musket-ball, and—Troops have proceeded. Will arive in half a minute after this." Mother abandons all hope; general commiseration; troops rush in, down a platform; son only wounded, and embraces her.

As I have said, and as you will see, this is available for any purpose. But done with equal distinction and rapidity, it is a tremendous effect, and got by the simplest means in the world. There is nothing in the piece, but it was impossible not to be moved and excited by the telegraph part of it.

I hope you have seen something of Stanny, and have been to pantomimes with him, and have drunk to the absent Dick. I miss you, my dear old boy, at the play, woefully, and miss the walk home, and the partings at the corner of Tavistock Square. And when I go by myself, I come home stewing "Little Dorrit" in my head; and the best part of *my* play is (or ought to be) in Gordon Street.[2]

I have written to Beaucourt about taking that breezy house— a little improved— for the summer, and I hope you and yours will come there often and stay there long. My present idea, if nothing should arise to unroot me sooner, is to stay here until the middle of May, then plant the family at Boulogne, and come with Catherine and

Georgy home for two or three weeks. When I shall next run across I don't know, but I suppose next month.

We are up to our knees in mud here. Literally in vehement despair, I walked down the avenue outside the Barrière de l'Etoile here yesterday, and went straight on among the trees. I came back with top-boots of mud on. Nothing will cleanse the streets. Numbers of men and women are for ever scooping and sweeping in them, and they are always one lake of yellow mud. All my trousers go to the tailor's every day, and are ravelled out at the heels every night. Washing is awful.

Tell Mrs. Lemon, with my love, that I have bought her some Eau d'Or,[3] in grateful remembrance of her knowing what it is, and crushing the tyrant of her existence by resolutely refusing to be put down when that monster would have silenced her. You may imagine the loves and messages that are now being poured in upon me by all of them, so I will give none of them; though I am pretending to be very scrupulous about it, and am looking (I have no doubt) as if I were writing them down with the greatest care.

Ever affectionately

[CD]

1 The pantomime written by Lemon and staged at the Adelphi Theatre, where Benjamin Webster (1798–1882†) was actor-manager.

2 Lemon lived at No. 11, close to Tavistock House.

3 The French equivalent of Danziger Goldwasser, a liqueur made with aniseed and caraway. In *NN* ch. 51, it is offered to Newman Noggs by Arthur Gride, who likes it 'on account of its name'.

To Angela Burdett Coutts, 9 FEBRUARY 1856

Household Words Office | Saturday Ninth February 1856

My Dear Miss Coutts.

First, as to Teignmouth,[1] Wills knows it very well. The soil is a red loam, and not naturally damp. But the town itself stands in a rent or gash made among great hills, by the mouth of the river, and is certainly moist and low—decidedly *not* advisable for your purpose I should say. On the other hand, if the house should not be in Teignmouth or in the valley of the river, but should be on the bold hills which rise about it, then the objection to it would be removed. The whole question turns upon the exact position of the house. If it be on the hills, good. If it be in the valley, bad. If it be in neither the one place nor the other, rather dubious.

Secondly, as to Wills himself. I have communicated to him the result of our conversation yesterday, and he is "gratified beyond expression".[2] He says he considers it most generous, and is extremely anxious that I should express his sense of it to you in the most earnest and emphatic words I can employ.

Thirdly, as to Gad's Hill Place—which is the name of my house. If you mean in your kind note, the refusal of it *now,* I am sorry to say that it is not now available. As I told Mrs. Brown yesterday, the Rector lives in it, and has lived in it for some years; and the object Wills and I have in view in going down there directly, is to ask him how and when it will suit his convenience to come out—as of course I wish to treat him with all handsome consideration. It is not now a furnished house, but my object is, as soon as I shall have got rid of the tenant, to make it clean and pretty in the papering and painting way, and then to furnish it in the most comfortable and cosey manner, and let it by the month whenever I can. Whenever I cannot, I shall use it for myself and make it a change for Charley from Saturday to Monday. When all this is done, I shall have a delight in taking you down to see it which I shall not try here to express; and if you should like it so well as to think of ever occupying it as a little easy change, I shall be far more attached to the spot than ever. I think you will be very much pleased with it. It is old-fashioned, plain, and comfortable. On the summit of Gad's Hill, with a noble prospect at the side and behind, looking down into the Valley of the Medway. Lord Darnley's Park of Cobham (a beautiful place with a noble walk through a wood) is close by it; and Rochester is within a mile or two. It is only an hour and a quarter from London by the Railway. To crown all, the sign of the Sir John Falstaff is over the way, and I used to look at it as a wonderful Mansion (which God knows it is not), when I was a very odd little child with the first faint shadows of all my books, in my head—I suppose.

Mr. Austin surveyed it for me, and was greatly struck by it. Large sums of money have been expended on it (for such a small place) at various times, and he found everything about the garden and so forth, in the best order. There is a very pretty garden, and a Shrubbery on the other side of the high road, at which the house looks. When I exhibit it to you with all my contrivances accomplished—of course some of them will be wonderfully ingenious—I will tell you what I paid for it.

With love to Mrs. Brown, who is looking immensely better.

Ever Dear Miss Coutts | Yours most faithfully and affecy.

CD.

1 On the Devon coast; Miss Coutts was thinking of renting a house there.
2 After William Brown's death in Oct. 1855, Miss Coutts needed aministrative help with her philanthropic enterprises. CD first offered his own services ('consider whether a daily messenger with a Dispatch Box could not put me in possession of all such business', 16 Nov. 1855), and then suggested Wills.

To *William Macready*, 22 MARCH 1856

49 Champs Elysées, Paris | Saturday March Twenty Second, 1856

My Dear Macready

I want you—you being quite well again, as I trust you are, and resolute to come to Paris—so to arrange your order of March as to let me know beforehand when you will come and how long you will stay. We owe Scribe[1] and his wife a dinner, and I should like to pay the debt when you are with us. Ary Scheffer[2] too, would be delighted to see you again. If I could arrange for a certain day, I would secure them. We cannot afford (you and I, I mean) to keep much company, because we shall want to look in at a Theatre or so, I dare say!—

It would suit my work best, if I could keep myself clear until Monday the 7th. of April. But in case that day should be too late for the beginning of your brief visit, with a reference to any other engagements you have in contemplation, then fix an earlier one, and I will make Little Dorrit curtsey to it. My recent visit to London and my having only just now come back, have thrown me a little behind-hand; but I hope to come up with a wet sail in a few days.

You should have seen the ruins of Covent Garden Theatre![3]—I went in, the moment I got to London—four days after the fire. Although the audience part, and the stage, were so tremendously burnt out that there was not a piece of wood half the size of a Lucifer Match, for the eye to rest on—though nothing whatever remained but bricks and smelted iron, lying on a great black desert—the Theatre still looked so wonderfully like its old self grown Gigantic, that I never saw so strange a sight. The wall dividing the Front from the stage still remained, and the iron pass-doors stood ajar, in an impossible and inaccessible frame. The arches that supported the stage were there, and the arches that supported the pit; and on the centre of the latter, lay something like a Titanic grape-vine that a hurricane had pulled up by the roots, twisted, and flung down there. This was the great chandelier. Gye[4] had kept the men's wardrobe at the top of the house, over the great entrance staircase. When the roof fell in, it came down bodily, and all that part of the ruin was like an old babylonic pavement—bright rags tesselating the black ground—sometimes in pieces so large that I could make out the dresses in the Trovatore.

I should run on for a couple of hours if I were to describe the spectacle as I saw it. Wherefore I will immediately muzzle myself. All here unite in kindest loves to dear Miss Macready,[5] to Katie, Lillie, Benvenuta, my Godson, and the noble Johnny. We are charmed to hear such happy accounts of Willie and Ned, and send our loving remembrances to them in the next letters.

All Parisian Novelties you shall see and hear for yourself.

Ever My Dearest Macready | Your Affectionate friend
CHARLES DICKENS

Mr. F's Aunt sends her defiant respects.[6]

---

1 Augustin Eugène Scribe (1791–1861), French dramatist and librettist.

2 Ary Scheffer (1795–1858), artist; born in Holland; studied and worked in Paris from 1811. He was finishing his portrait of CD at this time.

3 Burnt on 5 Mar. while sub-let to J. H. Anderson, conjuror, 'The Wizard of the North'.

4 Frederick Gye (1810–78†), businessman, opera-manager, and director of the Royal Italian Opera, Covent Garden.

5 Macready's sister; the rest are his children.

6 This eccentric and belligerent character first appeared in *LD* bk. I, ch. 13, published 29 Feb.

To John Forster, [?29–30 MARCH 1856]

Of Little Dorrit, *No. VI, he wrote* I had the general idea of the Society business before the Sadleir affair,[1] but I shaped Mr. Merdle himself out of that precious rascality. Society, the Circumlocution Office, and Mr. Gowan, are of course three parts of one idea and design. Mr. Merdle's complaint, which you find in the end to be fraud and forgery, came into my mind as the last drop in the silver cream-jug on Hampstead-heath. I shall beg, when you have read the present number, to inquire whether you consider "Bar" an instance, in reference to K F, of a suggested likeness in not many touches?[2]

1 John Sadleir (1813–56†), politician and swindler. Poisoned himself on Hampstead Heath on 16 Feb. by drinking prussic acid from a silver cream-jug. His long history of forgery and fraudulent share-dealing was soon revealed, and caused a sensation.
2 K F is Sir Fitzroy Kelly (1796–1880†), barrister and Conservative MP; he would have been recognizable and Forster has reversed his initials to disguise his identity.

To John Forster, [7 APRIL 1856]

There are some things in Flora in number seven[1] that seem to me to be extraordinarily droll, with something serious at the bottom of them after all. Ah, well! was there *not* something very serious in it once?[2] I am glad to think of being in the country with the long summer mornings as I approach number ten,[3] where I have finally resolved to make Dorrit rich. It should be a very fine point in the story. . . . Nothing in Flora made me laugh so much as the confusion of ideas between gout flying upwards, and its soaring with Mr. F—— to another sphere.

1 Bk. 1, chs. 23–5, published 31 May. Forster was reading proofs.
2 His love for Maria Beadnell.
3 Bk. 1, chs. 33–6.

To John Forster, [13 APRIL 1856]

It fills me with pity to think of him[1] away in that lonely Sherborne place. I have always felt of myself that I must, please God, die in harness, but I have never felt it more strongly than in looking at, and thinking of, him. However strange it is to be never at rest, and never satisfied, and ever trying after something that is never reached, and to be always laden with plot and plan and care and worry, how clear it is that it must be, and that one is driven by an irresisitible might until the journey is worked out! It is much better to go on and fret, than to stop and fret. As to repose— for some men there's no such thing in this life. The foregoing has the appearance of a small sermon; but it is so often in my head in these days that it cannot help coming out. The old days—the old days! Shall I ever, I wonder, get the frame of mind back as it used to be then? Something of it perhaps—but never quite as it used to be. I find that the skeleton in my domestic closet is becoming a pretty big one.

1 Macready, who had retired to Sherborne in Dorset.

To *Wilkie Collins*, 22 APRIL 1856

Champs Elysées | Tuesday Twenty-Second April, 1856

My Dear Collins.

I have been quite taken aback by your account of your alarming seizure; and have only become reassured again, firstly by the good fortune of your having left here and got so near your Doctor; secondly, by your hopefulness of now making head in the right direction. On the third or fourth I purpose being in town, and I need not say that I shall forthwith come to look after my old Patient.

On Sunday, to my infinite amazement, Townshend appeared. He has changed his plans, and is staying in Paris a week, before going to Town for a couple of months. He dined here on Sunday, and placidly ate and drank in the most vigorous manner, and mildly laid out a terrific perspective of projects for carrying me off to the Theatre every night. But in the morning he found himself with dawnings of Bronchitis, and is now luxuriously laid up in lavender at his Hotel—confining himself entirely to precious stones,[1] chicken, and fragrant wines qualified with iced waters.

Last Friday, I took Mrs. Dickens, Georgina, and Mary and Katey, to dine at the Trois freres. Mrs. Dickens nearly killed herself, but the others hardly did that justice to the dinner that I had expected. We then Sir went off to the Français; to see Comme il vous plaira[2] which is a kind of Theatrical Representation that I think might be got up, with great completeness, by the Patients in the Asylum for Idiots. Dreariness is no word for it, vacancy is no word for it, gammon is no word for it, there *is* no word for it. Nobody has anything to do, but to sit upon as many grey stones as he can. When Jacques had sat upon seventy seven stones and forty two roots of trees (which was at the end of the second act), we came away. He had by that time been made violent love to by Celia, had shewn himself in every phase of his existence to be utterly unknown to Shakespeare, had made the speech about the Seven Ages out of its right place and apropos of nothing on earth, and had in all respects conducted himself like a brutalized, benighted, and besotted Beast.

A wonderful dinner at Girardin's[3] last Monday, with only one new (but appropriate) feature in it. When we went into the drawing room after the banquet, which had terminated in a flower pot out of a ballet being set before every guest, piled to the brim with the ruddiest fresh strawberries, he asked me if I would come into another room (a chamber of no account—rather like the last Scene in Gustavus) and smoke a Cigar? On my replying yes, he opened, with a key attached to his watch chain, a species of mahogany Cave, which appeared to me to extend under the Champs Elysées, and in which were piled about four hundred thousand inestimable and unattainable Cigars, in bundles or bales of about a thousand each.

Yesterday I dined at the booksellers with the body of Translators engaged on my new Edition—one of them a lady—young and pretty. (I hope by the bye, judging from the questions which they asked me and which I asked them, that it will be really well done.) Among them was an extremely able old Savant who occasionally expressed himself in a foreign tongue which I supposed to be Russian (I thought he had something to do with the Congress perhaps), but which my host told me when I came away, was English! We wallowed in an odd sort of dinner which would have been splashy[4] if it hadn't been too sticky. Salmon appeared late in the evening, and unforeseen creatures of the lobster species strayed in after the pudding. It was very hospitable and good natured though, and we all got on in the friendliest way. Please to imagine me, for three mortal hours, incessantly holding forth to the translators, and, among other things, addressing them in a neat and appropriate (French) speech. I came home quite light-headed.

On Saturday night, I paid three francs at the door of that place where we saw the wrestling, and went in, at 11 o-Clock, to a Ball. Much the same as our own National Argyll Rooms.[5] Some pretty faces, but all of two classes—wicked and coldly calculating, or haggard and wretched in their worn beauty. Among the latter, was a woman of thirty or so, in an Indian shawl, who never stirred from a seat in a corner all the time I was there. Handsome, regardless, brooding, and yet with some nobler qualities in her forehead. I mean to walk about tonight, and look for her. I didn't speak to her there, but I have a fancy that I should like to know more about her. Never shall, I suppose.

Franconi's[6] I have been to again, of course. Nowhere else. I finished "that" No. as soon as Macready went away, and have done something for Household Words next week, called Proposals for a National Jest Book,[7] that I take rather kindly to. The first blank page of Little Dorrit No. 8 now eyes me on this desk with a pressing curiosity. It will get nothing out of me to day, I distinctly perceive.

Townshend's Henri,[8] and Bully (the dog) have just been here—came in with a message at the double dash. Bully disconcerts me a good deal. He dined here on Sunday with his master, and got a young family of puppies out of each of the doors, fell into indecent transports with the claw of the round table, and was madly in love with Townshend's boots. All of which, Townshend seems to have no idea of, but merely says "Bul-ly!" when he is on his hind-legs like the sign of a public house. If he dines here again, I mean to have a trifle of camphor ready for him, and to try whether it has the effect upon him that it is said to have upon the Monks (with which piece of scientific knowledge I taunt Stanfield when we go out together).

That swearing of the Academy Carpenters is the best thing of its kind I ever heard of. I suppose the oath to be administered by little Knight. It's my belief that the stout Porter now no more, wouldn't have taken it.—Our cook's going. Says she an't strong enought for Boo Lone.[9] I don't know what there is particularly trying in that climate.—The Nice little Nurse who goes into all manner of shops without knowing one word of French, took some Lace to be mended the other day, and the Shopkeeper impressed with the idea that she had come to sell it, *would* give her money; with which she returned weeping, believing it (until explanation ensued) to be the price of shame. All send kindest regard. Ever Faithfully

CD.

1 Of which Townshend had a major collection, bequeathed to the V&A.
2 *As You Like It*.
3 Émile de Girardin (1802–81), writer, journalist, and politician.
4 Ostentatious (slang).
5 In London, a notorious place of entertainment frequented by prostitutes and their clients.
6 The Franconi family and their troupe staged magnificent horse-riding entertainments.
7 *HW*, 3 May, a satirical piece calling for the publication of a Jest-Book containing 'rich materials' from parliamentary debates etc.
8 His manservant.
9 i.e. Boulogne.

To *Wilkie Collins,* 6 JUNE 1856

Tavistock House | Sixth June 1856

My Dear Collins

I have never seen anything about myself in Print, which has much correctness in it—any biographical account of myself, I mean. I do not supply such particulars when I am asked for them by editors and compilers, simply because I am asked for them every day. If you want to prime Forgues[1] you may tell him without fear of being wrong, That I was born at Portsmouth on the 7th. of February 1812. That my father was in the Navy Pay office. That I was taken by him to Chatham when I was very young, and lived and was educated there till I was—12 or 13, I suppose. That I was then put to a school near London, where (as at the other place) I distinguished myself like a Brick. That I was put in the office of a Solicitor, a friend of my father's, and didn't much like it, and after a couple of years (as well as I can remember) applied myself with a celestial or diabolical energy to the study of such things as would qualify me to be a first-rate Parliamentary Reporter— at that time a calling pursued by many clever men who were young at the Bar. That I made my debut in the Gallery (at about 18, I suppose), engaged on a Voluminous publication no longer in existence, called The Mirror of Parliament. That when the Morning Chronicle was purchased by Sir John Easthope and acquired a large circulation I was engaged there, and that I remained there until I had begun to publish Pickwick; when I found myself in a condition to relinquish that part of my labors. That I left the reputation behind me of being the best and most rapid Reporter ever known, and that I could do anything in that way under any sort of circumstances—and often did. (I dare say I am at this present writing, the best Short Hand Writer in the World.)

That I began, without any interest or introduction of any kind, to write fugitive pieces for the old Monthly Magazine, when I was in the Gallery for the Mirror of

Parliament. That my faculty for descriptive writing was seized upon, the moment I joined the Morning Chronicle, and that I was liberally paid there, and handsomely acknowledged, and wrote the greater part of the short descriptive "Sketches by Boz" in that paper. That I had been a writer when I was a mere Baby, and always an Actor from the same age.

That I married the daughter of a Writer to the Signet in Edinburgh who was the great friend and assistant of Scott, and who first made Lockhart known to him.

And That here I am.

Finally, if you want any dates of publication of books, tell Wills and he'll get them for you.

This is the first time I ever set down even these particulars, and, glancing them over, I feel like a Wild Beast in a Caravan, describing himself in the keeper's absence.

With my kindest regard to Mrs. Glutch.[2]

Ever Faithfully
CD.

I made a Speech last night at the London Tavern,[3] at the end of which all the Company sat holding their napkins to their eyes with one hand, and putting the other into their pockets. A hundred people or so, contributed Nine Hundred Pounds, then and there.

1 Paul Émile Durand Forgues (1813–83), journalist and critic; he wrote a biographical sketch of CD in the Paris weekly journal *L'Ami de la maison*.
2 The name Collins gave to his landlady in 'My London Lodgings', *HW*, 14 June 1856.
3 At the first anniversary dinner of the Royal Hospital for Incurables.

To John Forster, [22 JUNE 1856, Boulogne]

I have had a story[1] to hack and hew into some form for Household Words this morning, which has taken me four hours of close attention. And I am perfectly addled by its horrible want of continuity after all, and the dreadful spectacle I have made of the proofs—which look like an inky fishing-net.

Replying to some questions about an English family,[2] *put to Beaucourt by CD one day, he had only enlarged on their sacrifices and self-denials.* "Ah, that family, unfortunate!", he had answered. "And you, Monsieur Beaucourt", I said to him, "you are unfortunate too, God knows!" Upon which he said in the pleasantest way in the world, "Ah, Monsieur Dickens, thank you, don't speak of it!"—And backed himself down the avenue with his cap in his hand, as if he were going to back himself straight into the evening star, without the ceremony of dying first. I never did see such a gentle, kind heart.

1 Mrs J. C. Bateman's 'Eric Walderthorn'.
2 The impoverished Revd Richard Cattermole (George's brother) and his family were tenants of Beaucourt's.

To John Forster, [15 AUGUST 1856, Boulogne]

Writing of the limitations placed upon the artist in England. Similarly I have always a fine feeling of the honest state into which we have got, when some smooth gentleman says to me or to some one else when I am by, how odd it is that the hero of an English book is always uninteresting—too good—too natural, &c. I am continually hearing this of Scott from English people here, who pass their lives with Balzac and Sand. But O my smooth friend, what a shining impostor you must think yourself and what an ass you must think me, when you suppose that by putting a brazen face upon it you can blot out of my knowledge the fact that this same unnatural young gentleman (if to be decent is to be necessarily unnatural), whom you meet in those other books and in mine, *must be* presented to you in that unnatural aspect by reason of your morality, and is not to have, I will not say any of the indecencies you like, but not even any of the experiences, trials, perplexities, and confusions inseparable from the making or unmaking of all men!

To Hablot K. Browne, 8 NOVEMBER 1856

Tavistock House | Saturday Eighth November, 1856.

My Dear Browne.
  All right. Please keep Clennam, always, as agreeable and well-looking as possible.[1] He is very good in the Flintwinch scene here. Mrs. Clennam's expression, capital.
  Letterings below.[2]

Ever Faithfully CD.

1 CD is looking at sketches for the two plates in No. 13, bk. 2, chs. 9 and 10.
2 Cut off.

To Catherine Dickens, 8 NOVEMBER 1856

Tavistock House | Saturday Eighth November 1856.[1]

My Dearest Catherine
  I must make very short work of this letter, for I have been writing hard all day (being now engaged on the Xmas No. of Household Words) and only leave off as the darkness begins.
  The Rehearsal[2] came off last night, and the progress was satisfactory. Especially, considering that Lemon had the Rheumatism in his jaw, and that Berger[3] had such a cold as to be wrapped up like a Stage Coachman, and screened in with the Print-Screen.

The only two bits of news, are, that the Half year's balance of Household Words is very indifferent indeed, and that I don't think the Cook will do. She seems too sulky a woman to tolerate in a house where the other servants deserve anything but mortification of spirit.

Shrieks of amazement and delight today, proclaimed the return of Cobbler,[4] looking wonderfully fat and well. Immediately afterwards, he ran away again— and then it was discovered that it was not Cobbler at all, but a dog very like him, belonging to the Adelphi Theatre, who had come up with a Carpenter.

My best love to dear Macready, and Miss Macready, and Katie, and the dear little girls, and Henry my godson, and Johnny. Tell Macready that if he doesn't come to the Play, I shall join the Tory ranks in Politics immediately afterwards, and become one of whatsoever religious denomination most requires me, in the words of Miggs "to hate and despise my feller creeters, as every practicable Christian should."[5] Tell him I have not yet settled the exact church I shall favor, there being so many of this kind.

All well, and all send loves. I went over Forster's house a day or two ago, which is very pretty indeed, and very excellently done.

Ever affectionately
CD.

1 The last extant letter from CD to Catherine before their separation.
2 For *The Frozen Deep*, play written by Wilkie Collins in collaboration with CD, and performed at Tavistock House.
3 Francesco Berger (1834–1933†), pianist, composer, and music administrator. Friendly with CD and Collins, he composed the music for *The Frozen Deep*.
4 A dog entrusted to CD by a cobbler in Boulogne and brought back to London, where he ran away.
5 Cf. Miggs's protestation, *BR* ch. 13.

To Angela Burdett Coutts, 15 NOVEMBER 1856

Tavistock House | Saturday Fifteenth November | 1856.

My Dear Miss Coutts

I return Derry.[1] I have no doubt it's a capital article, but it's a mortal dull color. Color these people always want, and color (as allied to fancy), I would always give them. In these cast-iron and mechanical days, I think even such a garnish to the dish of their monotonous and hard lives, of unspeakable importance. One color, and that of the earth earthy, is too much with them early and late. Derry might just as well break out into a stripe, or put forth a bud, or even burst into a full blown flower. Who is Derry that he is to make quakers of us all, whether we will or no!

You will immediately hear from Mr. Wills, with all the information you want, drawn fresh from the fountain head.

At Shepherd's Bush on Wednesday, all were in excellent order. Mr. Dyer and I represented the august Committee. It was very pleasant to see Louisa Cooper,[2] nicely dressed and looking very well to do, sitting with Mrs. Macartney in the Long Room. She brought me for a present, the most hideous Ostrich's Egg ever laid— wrought all over with frightful devices, the most tasteful of which represents Queen Victoria (with her crown on) standing on the top of a Church, receiving professions of affection from a British Seaman.

How long are you going to stay in Devonshire? And don't you mean to come to town at Christmas Time? I always want to know, and you never will tell me.

With kind regard to Mrs. Brown,

Ever Dear Miss Coutts | Most Faithfully Yours
CHARLES DICKENS

I re-open this to say that I have just received the enclosed from Mr. Macready, who is very anxious indeed that you should have it. Would you like Mr. Wills to see the boy,[3] and give him a suit of clothes?

1 Drab cotton material which Miss Coutts was proposing for clothes for Urania Cottage inmates. She thought an interest in dress was a strong temptation to working-class girls.
2 Louisa Cooper arrived at Urania Cottage Apr. 1853, emigrated to Cape Town Oct. 1854, but returned July 1856. She was engaged, but unable to marry until her fiancé found a gardener's place as a married man.
3 Probably the son of the actress and theatre manager Mary Amelia Warner (1804–54†). On her death Miss Coutts offered to pay her daughter's school fees and Macready those of her son.

To Hablot K. Browne, 6 DECEMBER 1856

Tavistock House | Saturday Sixth December 1856.

My Dear Browne

Don't have Lord Decimus's hand put out, because that looks condescending; and I want him to be upright, stiff, unmixable with mere mortality.[1]

Mrs. Plornish is too old, and Cavalletto a leetle bit too furious and wanting in stealthiness.

Faithfully Always
CD.

1 CD is commenting on Browne's sketches. The changes he wanted were all made in the plates for No. 14 (bk. 2, chs. 12 and 13), published Dec. 1831.

To *Frederick Dickens*, 12 DECEMBER 1856

Tavistock House | Friday December Twelfth | 1856.

My Dear Frederick

I am very sorry to receive your letter; not only on account of the position it makes known to me, but because it forces me to write a very plain answer.

I have already done more for you than most dispassionate persons would consider right or reasonable in itself.[1] But, considered with any fair reference to the great expences I have sustained for other relations, it becomes little else than monstrous. The possibility of your having any further assistance from me, is absolutely and finally past.

Affectionately Yours
CHARLES DICKENS

1 CD had paid his brother's debts in 1848 and 1850, and stood security for a loan in 1850.

To *William Macready*, 13 DECEMBER 1856

Tavistock House | Saturday Evening | Thirteenth December 1856.

My Dearest Macready.

We shall be charmed to squeeze Willie's friend in[1]—and it shall be done, by some undiscovered power of compression, on the Second Night—Thursday the 14th. Will you make our compliments to his Honor the Deputy Fiscal,[2] present him with the enclosed bill, and tell him we shall be cordially glad to see him? I hope to entrust him with a special shake of the hand, to be forwarded to our dear boy (if a hoary Sage like myself may venture on that expression), by the next Mail.

I would have proposed the first night, but that is too full.

You may faintly imagine, my venerable friend, the occupation of these also-grey hairs, between Golden Marys,[3] Little Dorrits, Household Wordses, four stage-carpenters entirely boarding on the premises, a carpenter's shop erected in the back-garden, size always boiling over on all the lower fires, Stanfield perpetually elevated on planks and splashing himself from head to foot, Telbin[4] requiring impossibilities of swart gasmen, and a legion of prowling nondescripts ever slinking in and out. Calm amidst the wrack, your aged friend glides away on the Dorrit stream, forgetting the uproar for a stretch of hours—refreshes himself with a ten or twelve miles walk—pitches himself head-foremost into foaming rehearsals—placidly emerges for Editorial purposes—smokes over buckets of distemper with Mr. Stanfield aforesaid—again calmly floats upon the Dorrit waters.

One piece of News I have, that I think you will be pleased to hear. Lord Gardner has married Miss Fortescue,⁵ and they are living quietly and very happily.

With my best love to Miss Macready, and to all the rest,

Ever My Dear Macready | Most affectionately Yours
CHARLES DICKENS

1 To *The Frozen Deep*, a play written by Wilkie Collins in collaboration with CD, performed at Tavistock House.
2 No doubt refers to a friend of Macready's son Willie, who had been in Ceylon since 1854. The bill is presumably a playbill for *The Frozen Deep*.
3 The Christmas story for *HW*.
4 William Telbin (1813–73), theatrical scene-painter.
5 The actress Julia Fortescue already had five children by Lord Gardner.

To Robert Davies,¹ 24 DECEMBER 1856

Tavistock House | Christmas Eve, 1856.

My Dear Sir

I beg to thank you for your very acceptable letter—not the less gratifying to me, because I am myself the writer of "The Wreck"² in the Christmas Number to which you refer.

There cannot be many men, I believe, who have a more humble veneration for the New Testament or a more profound conviction of its all-sufficiency than I have. If I am ever (as you tell me I am) mistaken on this subject, it is because I discountenance all obtrusive professions of, and tradings in, Religion, as one of the main causes of real Christianity's having been retarded in this world; and because my observation of life induces me to hold in unspeakable dread and horror, those unseemly squabbles about the Letter, which drive the Spirit out of hundreds of thousands.

Faithfully Yours
CHARLES DICKENS

1 Revd Robert Henry Davies (1821–1908), vicar of the Old Church, Chelsea.
2 'The Wreck of the Golden Mary' by CD with stories by five others.

To John Forster, [?9 FEBRUARY 1857]

I don't see the practicability of making the History of a Self-Tormentor, with which I took great pains, a written narrative.¹ But I do see the possibility of making it a chapter by itself, which might enable me to dispense with the necessity of the turned commas. Do you think that would be better? I have no doubt that a great part of Fielding's reason for the introduced story, and Smollett's also, was, that it is sometimes really impossible to present, in a full book, the idea it contains (which yet it may be on all accounts desirable to present), without supposing the reader to be possessed of almost as much romantic allowance as would put him on a level with the writer. In Miss Wade I had an idea, which I thought a new one, of making the introduced story so fit into surroundings impossible of separation from the main story, as to make the blood of the book circulate through both. But I can only suppose, from what you say, that I have not exactly succeeded in this.

1 CD planned to have the equivalent of eight printed pages spoken by Miss Wade to Clennam (bk. 2, ch. 21); see *Little Dorrit*, ed. Harvey Peter Sucksmith (Oxford: Clarendon Press, 1979), xxxvi.

To Hablot K. Browne, 10 FEBRUARY 1857

Tavistock House | Tuesday Tenth February 1857

My Dear Browne.

In the dinner scene,[1] it is highly important that Mr. Dorrit should not be too comic. He is too comic now. He is described in the text as "shedding tears", and what he imperatively wants, is an expression doing less violence in the reader's mind to what is going to happen to him, and much more in accordance with that serious end which is so close before him. Pray do not neglect this change.

Ever Faithfully
CD.

Over
LETTERING FOR THE SUBJECTS.
An unexpected After-Dinner Speech.
The Night.

1 CD is commenting on the sketches for No. 16 (bk. 2, ch. 19), published 28 Feb.

To John Forster, [?13 FEBRUARY 1857]

I have been (by mere accident) seeing the serpents fed to-day, with the live birds, rabbits, and guinea pigs—a sight so very horrible that I cannot get rid of the impression, and am, at this present, imagining serpents coming up the legs of the table, with their infernal flat heads, and their tongues like the Devil's tail (evidently taken from that model, in the magic lanterns and other such popular representations), elongated for dinner. I saw one small serpent, whose father was asleep, go up to a guinea pig (white and yellow, and with a gentle eye—every hair upon him erect with horror); corkscrew himself on the tip of his tail; open a mouth which couldn't have swallowed the guinea pig's nose; dilate a throat which wouldn't have made him a stocking; and show him what his father meant to do with him when he came out of that ill-looking Hookah into which he had resolved himself. The guinea pig backed against the side of the cage—said "I know it, I know it!"—and his eye glared and his coat turned wiry, as he made the remark. Five small sparrows crouching together in a little trench at the back of the cage, peeped over the brim of it, all the time; and when they saw the guinea pig give it up, and the young serpent go away looking at him over about two yards and a quarter of shoulder, struggled which should get into the innermost angle and be seized last. Everyone of them then hid his eyes in another's breast, and then they all shook together like dry leaves—as I daresay they may be doing now, for old Hookah was as dull as laudanum. . . . Please to imagine two small serpents, one beginning on the tail of a white mouse, and one on the head, and each pulling his own way, and the mouse very much alive all the time, with the middle of him madly writhing.

To John Forster, [?5 APRIL 1857]

I was ludicrously foiled here[1] the other night in a resolution I have kept for twenty years not to know of any attack upon myself, by stumbling, before I could pick myself up, on a short extract in the Globe from Blackwood's Magazine, informing me that Little Dorrit is "Twaddle." I was sufficiently put out by it to be angry with myself for being such a fool, and then pleased with myself for having so long been constant to a good resolution.

1 CD seems to have been writing from one of his clubs. *The Globe* and *Blackwood's* both criticized *LD*; *Blackwood's* described Mr Dorrit and Mrs General as talking 'twaddle'.

To L. Mackenzie, 18 APRIL 1857

Tavistock House | Eighteenth April, 1857

Sir.

Allow me to thank you for your note. It gives me the first intelligence of a coincidence which I shall examine with interest when the completion of the labor I am at present engaged on shall leave me more leisure that I have just now. I do not know Mrs. Opie's[1] story in the least; nor have I her books in my library to settle its place in her works. I have observed Miss Wade in real life (as I dare say Mrs. Opie observed her gentleman), and know the character to be true in every respect. It quite fascinated me in its singular anatomy and I devoted great pains to it in the little narrative. I observe it to be out of the familiar experience of most people and that they regard it with an incredulous kind of astonishment,—though in reality it is often before them.

Faithfully Yours
CHARLES DICKENS

1 Amelia Opie (1769–1853†), novelist and poet; popular and well respected in 1800s and 1810s.

To Emily Jolly, 30 MAY 1857

Tavistock House, Saturday Morning, 30th May, 1857.

Dear Madam,

I read your story, with all possible attention, last night.¹ I cannot tell you with what reluctance I write to you respecting it, for my opinion of it is *not* favourable, although I perceive your heart in it, and great strength.

Pray understand that I claim no infallibility. I merely express my own honest opinion, formed against my earnest desire. I do not lay it down as law for others, though, of course, I believe that many others would come to the same conclusion. It appears to me that the story is one that cannot possibly be told within the compass to which you have limited yourself. The three principal people are, every one of them, in the wrong with the reader, and you cannot put any of them right, without making the story extend over a longer space of time, and without anatomising the souls of the actors more slowly and carefully. Nothing would justify the departure of Alice, but her having some strong reason to believe that in taking that step, *she saved her lover.* In your intentions as to that lover's transfer of his affections to Eleanor, I descry a striking truth; but I think it confusedly wrought out, and all but certain to fail in expressing itself. Eleanor, I regard as forced and overstrained. The natural result is, that she carries a train of anti-climax after her. I particularly notice this at the point when she thinks she is going to be drowned.

The whole idea of the story is sufficiently difficult to require the most exact truth and the greatest knowledge and skill in the colouring throughout. In this respect I have no doubt of its being extremely defective. The people do not talk as such people would; and the little subtle touches of description which, by making the country house and the general scene real, would give an air of reality to the people (much to be desired) are altogether wanting. The more you set yourself to the illustration of your heroine's passionate nature, the more indispensable this attendant atmosphere of truth becomes. It would, in a manner, oblige the reader to believe in her. Whereas, for ever exploding like a great firework without any background, she glares and wheels and hisses, and goes out, and has lighted nothing.

Lastly, I fear she is too convulsive from beginning to end. Pray reconsider, from this point of view, her brow, and her eyes, and her drawing herself up to her full height, and her being a perfumed presence, and her floating into rooms, also her asking people how they dare, and the like, on small provocation. When she hears her music being played, I think she is particularly objectionable.

I have a strong belief that if you keep this story by you three or four years, you will form an opinion of it not greatly differing from mine. There is so much good in it, so much reflection, so much passion and earnestness, that, if my judgment be right, I feel sure you will come over to it. On the other hand, I do not think that its publication, as it stands, would do you service, or be agreeable to you hereafter.

I have no means of knowing whether you are patient in the pursuit of this art; but I am inclined to think that you are not, and that you do not discipline yourself enough. When one is impelled to write this or that, one has still to consider: "How much of this will tell for what I mean? How much of it is my own wild emotion and superfluous energy—how much remains that is truly belonging to this ideal character and these ideal circumstances?" It is in the laborious struggle to make this distinction, and in the determination to try for it, that the road to the correction of faults lies. (Perhaps I may remark, in support of the sincerity with which I write this, that I am an impatient and impulsive person myself, but that it has been for many years the constant effort of my life to practise at my desk what I preach to you.)

I should not have written so much, or so plainly, but for your last letter to me. It seems to demand that I should be strictly true with you, and I am so in this letter, without any reservation either way.

Very faithfully yours
[CHARLES DICKENS]

1 Jolly's 'A Wife's Story' and 'The Sisters' were published in *HW* in Sept. 1855 and Jan. 1856. CD rejected at least three more stories but accepted 'An Experience' for *AYR*; see below 6 Aug. 1869.

To Daniel Maclise, 8 JULY 1857

Tavistock House | Eighth July, 1857

My Dear Maclise

We may cry quits. I cannot possibly have given you more pleasure through Richard Wardour,[1] than you have given me through your appreciation of it. In that perpetual struggle after an expression of the Truth, which is at once the pleasure and the pain of the lives of workers in the Arts, the interest of such a character to me is that it enables me, as it were, *to write a book in company* instead of in my own solitary room, and to feel its effect coming freshly back upon me from the reader. With such a reader as you to send it back, it is a most fascinating exercise. I could blow off my superfluous fierceness, in nothing so curious to me.

I shall take you at your word! When we have done, I shall send you the book[2] to annotate.

You should have seen the Company's appreciation of *your* appreciation, when I told them of it. You really would have felt pleased with their thorough knowledge of its worth.

The Queen was undoubtedly wonderfully taken.[3] I had a letter on Sunday, of the most unofficial and uncourtly character. She sent for me after the Play, but I beg to be excused from presenting myself in any dress but my own.

When will you come down to Gad's Hill?

Ever Faithfully

CD.

1 CD's part in *The Frozen Deep*.
2 i.e. the prompt-book, but no illustrations by Maclise survive.
3 Queen Victoria and her guests attended a private performance of *The Frozen Deep* on 4 July.

To Edmund Yates,[1] 19 JULY 1857

Tavistock House | Sunday Nineteenth July, 1857

My Dear Yates.

Although I date this as above, I really write it from Southampton (dont notice this fact in your reply, for I shall be in town on Wednesday). I have come here on an errand which will grow familiar to you before you know that Time has flapped his wings over your head. Like me, you will find those babies grow to be young men, before you are quite sure they are born. Like me, you will have great teeth drawn with a wrench, and will only then know that you ever cut them. I am here to send Walter away over what they call in Green Bush Melodramas[2] "the Big Drink" and I dont at all know this day how he comes to be mine, or I, his.

I don't write to say this—or to say how, seeing Charley and he going aboard the Ship before me just now, I suddenly came into possession of a photograph of my own back at 16 and 20, and also into a suspicion that I had doubled the last age. I merely write to mention that Telbin and his wife are going down to Gad's Hill with us, about mid-day next Sunday, and that if you and Mrs. Yates will come too, we shall be delighted to have you. We can give you a bed, and you can be in town (if you have such a savage necessity) by 20 minutes before 10 on Monday morning.

I was very much pleased (as I had reason to be) with your account of the Play in the Daily News. I thank you heartily.[3]

Faithfully Yours

CHARLES DICKENS

It is now half-past 5 by Greenwich time—whatever that is—I never did know and never shall. Wills, I believe, knows all about it.

1 Edmund Yates (1831–94†), journalist and novelist, and son of actors Frederick and Eizabeth Yates. CD was godfather to one of his twin sons, and tried to intercede on Yates's behalf with Thackeray in 1858, leading to the estrangement between CD and Thackeray.
2 So called after Buckstone's highly popular play *The Green Bushes*, first performed at the Adelphi 1845. CD's son Walter sailed for India on 20 July.
3 Rest of letter cut away.

To *William Jerdan*,[1] 21 JULY 1857

Gad's Hill, Higham, by Rochester | Tuesday Twenty First July, 1857

My Dear Jerdan

In addition to the whirl and fatigue of the Jerrold Remembrance matter,[2] I have been at Southampton these two days, embarking my second boy for India. The poor fellow steamed away yesterday, and I have a day's rest on the grass here, to think whether the best definition of man may not be, after all, that he is (for his sins) a parting and farewell-taking animal.

I have not the means of reference at hand, but I think I may say I am *sure* that the brief contribution has been published—that both the brief contributions have been published.[3]

Andersen went to Paris, to go thence to Dresden and thence home, last Wednesday morning. I took him over to Maidstone, and booked him for Folkestone. He had been here, five weeks. He had spoken of you with much regard, and, I understood or fancied, had seen you. But whenever he got to London, he got into wild entanglements of Cabs and Sherry, and never seemed to get out of them again until he came back here, and cut out paper into all sorts of patterns, and gathered the strangest little nosegays in the woods. His unintelligible vocabulary was marvellous. In French or Italian, he was Peter the Wild Boy— in English, the Deaf and Dumb Asylum. My eldest boy swears that the ear of man cannot recognize his German; and his translatress declares to Bentley that he can't speak Danish!

One day he came home to Tavistock House, apparently suffering from corns that had ripened in two hours. It turned out that a Cab Driver had brought him from the City, by way of the new unfinished thoroughfare through Clerkenwell. Satisfied that the Cabman was bent on robbery and murder, he had put his watch and money into his boots—together with a Bradshaw, a pocket book, a pair of scissors, a penknife, a book or two, a few letters of introduction, and some other miscellaneous property.

These are all the particulars I am in a condition to report. He received a good many letters—lost (I should say) a good many more—and was for the most part utterly conglomerated—with a general impression that everything was going to clear itself up, "tomorrow".

Ever Faithfully
CHARLES DICKENS

1 William Jerdan (1782–1869†), journalist and editor of the *Literary Gazette*; founder member of the Royal Society of Literature. Had known CD since 1836. Became a friend of Hans Christian Andersen.
2 Douglas Jerrold had died suddenly in June. A memorial committee, chaired by CD, organized events to raise money for his family, against their wishes.
3 By Jerdan in *HW*, 10 Jan. 1857 and 11 Apr. 1857.

To *William Macready*, 3 AUGUST 1857

Gad's Hill Place, Higham, by Rochester | Monday Third August 1857

My Dearest Macready

I write to you in reference to your last note, as soon as I can positively know our final movements in the Jerrold matter.

We are going to wind up by acting at Manchester (on solemn requisition) on the evenings of Friday and Saturday, the 21st. and 22nd. (Actresses substituted for the girls, of course.)[1] We shall have to leave here on the morning of the 20th. You thought of coming on the 16th. Can't you make it a day or two earlier, so as to be with us a whole week? Decide and pronounce. Again—cannot you bring Katey with you? Decide and pronounce thereupon, also.

I read at Manchester last Friday. As many thousand people were there, as you like to name. The collection of Pictures in the Exhibition[2] is wonderful. And the power with which the modern English School asserts itself, is a very gratifying and delightful thing to behold. The care for the common people, in the provision made for their comfort and refreshment, is also admirable, and worthy of all commendation. But they want more amusement, and particularly (as it strikes me) *something in motion,* though it were only a twisting fountain. The thing is too still, after their lives of machinery, and Art fires over their heads in consequence.

I hope you have seen my tussle with the Edinburgh.[3] I saw the chance last Friday week, as I was going down to read the Carol in St. Martin's Hall. Instantly turned to, then and there, and wrote half the article. Flew out of bed early next morning, and finished it by Noon. Went down to Gallery of Illustration (we acted there that night), did the day's business, corrected the proof in Polar costume in dressingroom, broke up two numbers of Household Words to get it out directly, played in Frozen Deep and Uncle John,[4] presided at Supper of company, made no end of speeches, went home and gave in completely for four hours, then got sound asleep, and next day was as fresh as—you used to be in the far off days of your lusty Youth.

All here send kindest love to your dear good sister and all the house.

Ever and ever affectionately. CD.

1 Frances Ternan (1802–73†), actress, performed in *The Frozen Deep* at Manchester, as did her three actress daughters. Maria Ternan took over the part of the heroine Clara Burnham from Mamie Dickens. Ellen Lawless Ternan (1839–1914†), known as Nelly; had a small part in *The Frozen Deep*. CD's relationship with her continued until his death.
2 The Manchester Art Treasures Exhibition, opened 5 May.
3 CD's article 'Curious Misprint in the Edinburgh Review' (*HW*, 1 Aug.) refutes James Fitzjames Stephen's attack on *LD* in 'The Licence of Modern Novelists' (*Edinburgh Review*, July 1857).
4 A farce by John Buckstone.

To *Georgina Hogarth*, 7 AUGUST 1857

Tavistock House | Friday Morning Seventh August | 1857

My Dearest Georgy

I have had an excellent night (a little opiate in the medicine), and have had no return whatever of the distress of yesterday morning. Come to me at the Garrick, in a Cab, at ½ past 8.

Ever Affectionately
CD.

To *Wilkie Collins*, 29 AUGUST 1857

Tavistock House | Saturday Twenty Ninth August | 1857

My Dear Collins.

Partly in the grim despair and restlessness of this subsidence from excitement,[1] and partly for the sake of Household Words, I want to cast about whether you and I can go anywhere—take any tour—see any thing—whereon we could write something together. Have you any idea, tending to any place in the world? Will you rattle your head and see if there is any pebble in it which we could wander away and play at Marbles with? We want something for Household Words, and I want to escape from myself. For, when I *do* start up and stare myself seedily in the face, as happens to be my case at present, my blankness is inconceivable—indescribable— my misery, amazing.

I shall be in town on Monday. Shall we talk then? Shall we talk at Gad's hill? *What shall we do?* As I close this, I am on my way back by train.

Ever Faithfully

CD.

1 The public performances of *The Frozen Deep.* CD had contributed only one article to *HW* since June, which caused a drop in circulation.

To Hans Christian Andersen, 2 SEPTEMBER 1857

Gad's Hill Place, Higham, by Rochester | Wednesday Second September 1857

My Dear Andersen.

I have been away from here—at Manchester—which is the cause of this slow and late reply to your two welcome letters.

You are in your own home again by this time; happy to see its familiar face, I do not doubt; and happy in being received with open arms by all good Danish men, women, and children.

Everything here, goes on as usual. Baby (too large for his name, this long while!) calls "Aunty" all over the house, and the dogs come dancing about us and go running down the green lanes before us, as they used to do when you were here. But the days are shorter, and the evenings darker, and when we go up to the Monument to see the Sunset, we are obliged to go directly after dinner, and it gets dark while we are up there, and as we pass the grim dog who rattles his chain, we can hardly see his dim old eyes as we feed him with biscuit. The workmen who have been digging in that well in the Stable Yard so long, have found a great spring of clear bright water, and they got rather drunk when they found it (not with the water, but with some Gin I gave them), and then they packed up their tools and went away, and now the big dog and the Raven have all that place to themselves. The corn-fields that were golden when you were here, are ploughed up brown; the hops are being picked; the leaves on the trees are just beginning to turn; and the rain is falling as I write—very sadly—very steadily.

We have just closed our labors in remembrance of poor Jerrold, and have raised for his widow and daughter, Two Thousand Pounds. On Monday I am going away (with Collins) for a fortnight or so, into odd corners of England, to write some descriptions for Household Words. When I come back, I shall find them dining here by lamplight. And when I come back, I will write to you again.

I never meet any of the friends whom you saw here, but they always say "How's Andersen—Where's Andersen"—and I draw imaginary pictures of where you are, and declare that you desired to be heartily remembered to them. They are always pleased to be told this. I told old Jerdan so, the other day, when he wrote to me asking when he was to come and see you!—

All the house send you their kind regard. Baby says you shall not be put out of window when you come back. I have read To Be or Not To Be,[1] and think it a very fine book—full of a good purpose admirably wrought out—a book in every way worthy of its great author.

Ever My Dear Andersen | Affectionately Your friend
CHARLES DICKENS

---

1 By Andersen, a mixture of novel and religious tract.

To John Forster, [?3 SEPTEMBER 1857]

Your letter of yesterday was so kind and hearty, and sounded so gently the many chords we have touched together, that I cannot leave it unanswered, though I have not much (to any purpose) to say. My reference to "confidences" was merely to the relief of saying a word of what has long been pent up in my mind. Poor Catherine and I are not made for each other, and there is no help for it. It is not only that she makes me uneasy and unhappy, but that I make her so too—and much more so. She is exactly what you know, in the way of being amiable and complying; but we are strangely ill-assorted for the bond there is between us. God knows she would have been a thousand times happier if she had married another kind of man, and that her avoidance of this destiny would have been at least equally good for us both. I am often cut to the heart by thinking what a pity it is, for her own sake, that I ever fell in her way; and if I were sick or disabled to-morrow, I know how sorry she would be, and how deeply grieved myself, to think how we had lost each other. But exactly the same incompatibility would arise, the moment I was well again; and nothing on earth could make her understand me, or suit us to each other. Her temperament will not go with mine. It mattered not so much when we had only ourselves to consider, but reasons have been growing since which make it all but hopeless that we should even try to struggle on. What is now befalling me I have seen steadily coming, ever since the days you remember when Mary was born; and I know too well that you cannot, and no one can, help me. Why I have even written I hardly know; but it is a miserable sort of comfort that you should be clearly aware how matters stand. The mere mention of the fact, without any complaint or blame of any sort, is a relief to my present state of spirits—and I can get this only from you, because I can speak of it to no one else.

To Angela Burdett Coutts, 5 SEPTEMBER 1857

Gad's Hill Place | Saturday Fifth September 1857

My Dear Miss Coutts
  I think I would head the paper
          An independent and useful career for young women of the
                          Middle Classes.[1]
— such a heading as that, something to that effect, arrests the attention directly. So
much Boredom, and Red Tape, and what I may call Kayshuttleworry[2] are associated
with the word "Education", that I fear it might repel readers.

The paper itself is very good indeed. Very plain, very easily remembered, very
direct to the purpose.

Apprehensive, like Mrs. Brown, of the moist valleys, I have decided on a foray
into the bleak fells of Cumberland. So the idle apprentices go to Carlisle on Monday.[3]

Sometimes of late, when I have been very much excited by the crying of two
thousand people over the grave of Richard Wardour, new ideas for a story have
come into my head as I lay on the ground, with surprising force and brilliancy. Last
night, being quiet here, I noted them down in a little book I keep. When I went into
the dining room and mentioned what I had been doing, they all called out *"Friday!"*
I was born on a Friday, and it is a most astonishing coincidence that I have never in
my life, whatever projects I may have determined on, otherwise—never begun a
book, or begun any thing of interest to me, or done any thing of importance to me,
but it was on a Friday. I am certain to be brought round to Friday. It *must* have been
on a Friday that I first dined with you at Mr. Marjoribanks's!

Mentioning Richard Wardour,—perhaps Mr. Wills has not told you how much
impressed I was at Manchester by the womanly tenderness of a very gentle and
good little girl who acted Mary's part. She came to see the Play beforehand at the
Gallery of Illustration, and when we rehearsed it, she said "I am afraid, Mr. Dickens,
I shall never be able to bear it; it affected me so much when I saw it, that I hope you
will excuse my trembling this morning, for I am afraid of myself." At night when
she came out of the cave and Wardour recognized her, I never saw any thing like
the distress and agitation of her face—a very good little pale face, with large black
eyes;—it had a natural emotion in it (though it was turned away from the audience)
which was quite a study of expression. But when she had to kneel over Wardour
dying, and be taken leave of, the tears streamed out of her eyes into his mouth, down
his beard, all over his rags—down his arms as he held her by the hair. At the same
time she sobbed as if she were breaking her heart, and was quite convulsed with
grief. It was of no use for the compassionate Wardour to whisper "My dear child, it
will be over in two minutes—there is nothing the matter—don't be so distressed!"
She could only sob out, "O! It's so sad, O it's so sad!' and set Mr. Lemon (the softest
hearted of men) crying too. By the time the Curtain fell, we were all crying together,
and then her mother and sister used to come and put her in a chair and comfort her,

before taking her away to be dressed for the Farce. I told her on the last night that I was sure she had one of the most genuine and feeling hearts in the world; and I don't think I ever saw any thing more prettily simple and unaffected. Yet I remember her on the stage, a little child, and I dare say she was born in a country theatre.

Very pleasant to know, I submit to you and Mrs. Brown? And if you ever see, at Kean's or elsewhere, Miss Maria Ternan, that is the young lady.

Dear Miss Coutts | Ever most Faithfully & affecy. Yours
CHARLES DICKENS

1 Miss Coutts's paper, now lost, probably relates to her *Summary Account of Prizes for Common Things*, 1856, emphasizing the importance of domestic subjects in teacher-training.

2 Sir James Kay-Shuttleworth (1804–77†), civil servant and influential educationist; thought to be among the targets of CD's satire in *HT* ch. 2.

3 From 7 to 21 Sept. CD and Collins visited Cumberland, Lancaster, and Doncaster; see 'The Lazy Tour of Two Idle Apprentices', *HW*, 3–31 Oct.

To John Forster, [5 SEPTEMBER 1857, Gad's Hill]

To the most part of what you say—Amen! You are not so tolerant as perhaps you might be of the wayward and unsettled feeling which is part (I suppose) of the tenure on which one holds an imaginative life, and which I have, as you ought to know well, often only kept down by riding over it like a dragoon—but let that go by. I make no maudlin complaint. I agree with you as to the very possible incidents, even not less bearable than mine, that might and must often occur to the married condition when it is entered into very young. I am always deeply sensible of the wonderful exercise I have of life and its highest sensations, and have said to myself for years, and have honestly and truly felt, This is the drawback to such a career, and is not to be complained of. I say it and feel it now as strongly as ever I did; and, as I told you in my last, I do not with that view put all this forward. But the years have not made it easier to bear for either of us; and, for her sake as well as mine, the wish will force itself upon me that something might be done. I know too well it is impossible. There is the fact, and that is all one can say. Nor are you to suppose that I disguise from myself what might be urged on the other side. I claim no immunity from blame. There is plenty of fault on my side, I dare say, in the way of a thousand uncertainties, caprices, and difficulties of disposition; but only one thing will alter all that, and that is, the end which alters everything.

Hop-picking is going on, and people sleep in the garden, and breathe in at the keyhole of the house door. I have been amazed, before this year, by the number of miserable lean wretches, hardly able to crawl, who go hop-picking. I find it is a superstition that the dust of the newly picked hop, falling freshly into the throat, is a cure for consumption. So the poor creatures drag themselves along the roads, and sleep under wet hedges, and get cured soon and finally.

What do you think of my paying for this place, by reviving that old idea of some Readings from my books. I am very strongly tempted. Think of it.[1]

1 Forster opposed CD's proposal to read for personal gain rather than charitable causes.

To Anne Cornelius,[1] 11 OCTOBER 1857

Gad's Hill Place | Sunday Eleventh October 1857

My Dear Anne

I want some little changes made in the arrangement of my dressing-room and the Bathroom. And as I would rather not have them talked about by comparative strangers, I shall be much obliged to you, my old friend, if you will see them completed before you leave Tavistock House.

I wish to make the Bathroom my washing-room also. It will be therefore necessary to carry into the Bathroom, to remain there, the two washing-stands from my Dressing-Room. Then, to get rid altogether, of the chest of drawers in the Dressing-Room I want the recess of the doorway between the Dressing-Room and Mrs. Dickens's room, fitted with plain white deal shelves, and closed in with a plain light deal door, painted white. Rudkin can do this—or Lillie,[2] being in the house, can do it if he likes. The sooner it is done, the better.

My wardrobe will then stand where the chest of Drawers stands now, and a small iron bedstead will go behind the door, with its side against the wall, as you enter the Dressing-Room; its head towards the stairs, and its foot towards the window. I have ordered the bedstead and bedding, and they will be sent to Tavistock House to you. The chest of drawers shall come down here, when the van comes down to bring our luggage home at the end of the month.

They all send their love.

Ever Faithfully Yours
[CHARLES DICKENS]

1 Formerly Anne Brown, Catherine Dickens's maid.
2 Benjamin Lillie, plumber and painter.

To John Forster, [?EARLY OCTOBER 1857]

Too late to say, put the curb on, and don't rush at hills—the wrong man to say it to. I have now no relief but in action. I am become incapable of rest. I am quite confident I should rust, break, and die, if I spared myself. Much better to die, doing. What I am in that way, nature made me first, and my way of life has of late, alas! confirmed. I must accept the drawback—since it is one—with the powers I have; and I must hold upon the tenure prescribed to me.

To Emile de la Rue, 23 OCTOBER 1857

OFFICE OF HOUSEHOLD WORDS, | Friday Twenty Third October 1857

My Dear De la Rue.

I cannot tell you how delighted I have been to receive your budget of news, or with what interest I have read, and re-read, your letter. I hope you really will produce yourself at Tavistock House before the year is out, and that my dear old patient will appear there before the next year is out. Both of you shall have the heartiest welcome that the Inimitable's house and its inmates can give. Believe that, and take it from my heart to both of yours!—

Between ourselves (I beckon Madame De la Rue nearer with my fore-finger, and whisper this with a serio-comic smile), I don't get on better in these later times with a certain poor lady you know of, than I did in the earlier Peschiere days. Much worse. Much worse! Neither do the children, elder or younger. Neither can she get on with herself, or be any thing but unhappy. (She has been excruciatingly jealous of, and has obtained positive proofs of my being on the most confidential terms with, at least Fifteen Thousand Women of various conditions in life, every condition in life, since we left Genoa. Please to respect me for this vast experience.) What we should do, or what the Girls would be, without Georgy, I cannot imagine. She is the active spirit of the house, and the children dote upon her. Enough of this. We put the Skeleton away in the cupboard, and very few people, comparatively, know of its existence.

—Not Albert Smith,[1] for one, I dare say! I thought you would be pleased with him, and rather chuckled when I sent him to you. He is a very good, kind fellow, under certain oddities of manner, and has a most hearty recollection of his intercourse with you. Only yesterday (he being now at home again), he wrote me a letter, asking me when we should go to some place about Town and dine, and then stroll to the Theatre "and talk about the De la Rues and Genoa"? I appointed tomorrow night, so we shall overhaul you at a great rate.

My visual ray[2] has been lately dwelling on the wilds of Cumberland and Yorkshire, where whole towns have turned out (as in duty bound) to greet the Inimitable and offer him homage. One night at Doncaster I was at the Theatre, where I had been behaving excessively ill in the way of gaping and rubbing my head wearily, from 7 to 11, without the slightest idea that anybody knew me; and I was slouching out at the fall of the Curtain, with my hands in my pockets and a general expression upon me of total want of dignity, when the Pit suddenly got up without the slightest warning, and cried out "Three cheers for Charles Dickens Esquire!" Thereupon all the house took it up, the actors came back and joined in the demonstration, and I was obliged instantaneously to convert myself into a most affable, interesting, and beaming personage. (I was a little troubled in my mind by not having that other waistcoat on, but made a very splendid appearance, all things considered.)

Why did they know nothing of the Hindoo character? Why? Do you ask why? Because it was the system to know nothing of anything; and to believe that England, while doing nothing, was doing everything. There are Thousands of Asses now— and Asses in power: which is the worst of it—who will hold this faith—if one could dignify such idiotcy by the name—until they have done for all of us. It is not three years since there were Indian Princes here; and in the rush after *them,* that baser side of the genteel character which would go Tuft-Hunting after the Devil was exhibited in a most astounding degree. Again and again, I have said to Ladies, spirited enough and handsome enough and clever enough to have known better (*not* of the 15,000, please to observe!), "what on earth do you see in those men to go mad about? You know faces, when they are not brown; you know common expressions when they are not under turbans; Look at the dogs—low, treacherous, murderous, tigerous villains who despise you while you pay court to them, and who would rend you to pieces at half an hour's notice." I suppose a greater mistake was never committed in the world, than this wretched Lord Canning's[3] maudlin proclamation about mercy. It would have been bad enough, if the Hindoos lived in the Strand here, and had the ideas of London vagabonds; but, addressed to the Oriental character, it is hideously absurd and dangerous. I wish I were Commander in Chief over there! I would address that Oriental character which must be powerfully spoken to, in something like the following placard, which should be vigorously translated into all native dialects, "I, The Inimitable, holding this office of mine, and firmly believing that I hold it by the permission of Heaven and not by the appointment of Satan, have the honor to inform you Hindoo gentry that it is my intention, with all possible avoidance of unnecessary cruelty and with all merciful swiftness of execution, to exterminate the Race from the face of the earth, which disfigured the earth with the late abominable atrocities."

Poor Charley Gibbs, poor dear Gibbs. Give him my Love, and tell him everything that is cheery and friendly from me. And poor Browne[4]—the man cast in the same mould as myself—the man formed (as he said) to be my twin brother! Broken his rib! Why the wrong rib? Why not break Mrs. Browne! I have hope of his recovery, poor fellow, if he can only be got to take it into his head that somebody wants him to die. His constitutional obstinacy will then most certainly prevent his doing it.

Perhaps I may see you in Genoa, before I won't say you—but at all events before Madame De la Rue—shall come to London. There are times when I think—really think—of coming, en garçon, and staying Weeks in the dear old City. It *may* be a castle in the air—a house in Spain—it *may* turn out to be an idea with a solid foundation.

I met Thompson one day, about two months ago. He told me they were living in the country, about 30 or 40 miles from London. We have been at a house I have in Kent, all the summer, and I have heard no more of them—except that I believe he has been much troubled by his two sisters at Jersey, who get into all manner of Debt, and look to him to be got out.

Wilkie Collins has just come in, and begs me to send his kindest regard to you and Madame. All at home would send their loves, if they knew me to be writing.

Adieu! | Ever and Ever Affectionately
CHARLES DICKENS

1 Albert Smith (1816–60†), author, public lecturer, and mountaineer. CD gave him a letter of introduction to de la Rue.
2 A reference to CD's mesmerism and an old joke, adapting a quotation from Milton.
3 Charles Canning (1812–62†), governor-general and first viceroy of India. The British press attacked Canning for not punishing the sepoys (Indians in the British Army) in units not actively involved in the Indian Mutiny.
4 Timothy Yeats Brown (1789–1858), British consul at Genoa.

To Lavinia Watson, 7 DECEMBER 1857

Tavistock House, London. W.C. | Seventh December, 1857

My Dear Mrs. Watson. I cannot tell you how interested and pleased I have been by the receipt of your letter, or how delightful it is to me to picture you among those beautiful objects, enjoying the life, change, and movement, you must have so drearily wanted at Rockingham. I had been speaking about you to Georgina, over and over again. She had just been telling me that Mary Boyle had spoken of you as being abroad—I had been saying what a good thing that was—and we had set in for a long train of remembrance, in my room one night, while your letter was making its way to me.

You want an egotistical reply from me, and you shall have it. I have been very busy with the Xmas Number of Household Words,¹ in which I have endeavoured to commemorate the foremost of the great English qualities shewn in India, without laying the scene there, or making any vulgar association with real events or calamities. I believe it is rather a remarkable production, and will make a great noise. I should send it with this, but for the uncertainty of its ever getting to you. It is published to day. It is all one story. The Second Chapter by Wilkie Collins; all the rest of it by me.

It leaves me—as my Art always finds me and always leaves me—the most restless of created Beings. I am the modern embodiment of the old Enchanters, whose Familiars tore them to pieces. I weary of rest, and have no satisfaction but in fatigue. Realities and idealities are always comparing themselves together before me, and I don't like the Realities except when they are unattainable—*then*, I like them of all things. I wish I had been born in the days of Ogres and Dragon-guarded Castles. I wish an Ogre with seven heads (and no particular evidence of brains in the whole lot of them) had taken the Princess whom I adore—you have no idea how intensely

I love her!—to his stronghold on the top of a high series of Mountains, and there tied her up by the hair. Nothing would suit me half so well this day, as climbing after her, sword in hand, and either winning her or being killed.—*There's* a state of mind for you, in 1857.

All last summer I had a transitory satisfaction in rending the very heart out of my body by doing that Richard Wardour part. It was a good thing to have a couple of thousand people all rigid and frozen together, in the palm of one's hand—as at Manchester—and to see the hardened Carpenters at the sides crying and trembling at it night after night. Which reminds me of a pretty little story about it. We engaged for Manchester, a young lady from Kean's Theatre—Miss Maria Ternan—born on the stage, and inured to it from the days when she was the little child in Pizarro. She had been brought to the Gallery of Illustration in town, to see the Play; and when she came on to me in the Morning at Manchester, I said, "Why my dear, how cold your hand is, and what a tremble you are in! This won't do at night."—"Oh Mr. Dickens", she said, "I am so afraid I can't bear it, that I hope you'll be very gentle with me this morning. I cried so much when I saw it, that I have a dread of it, and I don't know what to do." She had to take my head up as I was dying, and to put it in her lap, and give me her face to hold between my two hands. All of which I shewed her elaborately (as Mary had done it before), that morning. When we came to that point at night, her tears fell down my face, down my beard (excuse my mentioning that hateful appendage), down my ragged dress—poured all over me like Rain, so that it was as much as I could do to speak for them. I whispered to her, "My dear child, it will be over in two minutes. Pray compose yourself."—"It's no comfort to me that it will be soon over", she answered. "Oh it is so sad, it is so dreadfully sad. Oh don't die! Give me time, give me a little time! Don't take leave of me in this terrible way—pray, pray, pray!!" Whereupon Lemon, the softest-hearted of men, began to cry too, and then they all went at it together. I think I never saw such a pretty little genuine emotion in my life. And if you had seen the poor little thing, when the Curtain fell, put in a chair behind it—with her mother and sister taking care of her—and your humble servant drying her eyes and administering Sherry (in Rags so horrible that they would scarcely hold together), and the people in front all blowing their noses, and our own people behind standing about in corners and getting themselves right again, you would have remembered it for a long, long time.

Our Indian boy[2] was at Dum-Dum (which means a school of musketry, some 6 miles from Calcutta) when last heard of, but expected to be sent up the country in a few days. Where or why, I don't know; for he belongs to the Bengal Army, which is virtually extinct. He likes the country and the life, of all things, and is quite happy. My usual fortune of falling in with strange people, attended me, by the bye, when I took him down to Southampton. A very strange fellow got into our Railway Carriage, and took such an immense fancy to me, that I couldn't shake him off. He went out in the same ship—died of delirium tremens, within three days of their leaving Southampton—and had no luggage whatever, with him, but 3 shirts and 240 Sovereigns.

I am going to read, twice this month. On the 15th. at Coventry, and on the 22nd. at Rochester. On the 19th. of January I am going to read at Bristol, and, in April, at Edinburgh. After that, if I bind myself to any more promises, I'll—but I won't forswear myself; I *shall* bind myself, I know, in weakly amiable moments.

I hope the badly-stuffed Horse continues to conduct himself as if he were better stuffed? I have taken to Dogs lately, and, when I am at Gad's Hill, go out attended by tall Prowlers that are the terror of the neighbourhood. Six or eight weeks ago, I performed my celebrated feat of getting out of bed at 2 in the morning, and walking down there from Tavistock House—over 30 miles—through the dead night. I had been very much put-out; and I thought, "After all, it would be better to be up and doing something, than lying here." So I got up, and did that.

Poor Stafford![3] I had seen him pretty often, and had made an engagement with him to go down to Chatham, and talk with some of the poor wounded men from the Crimea, to whom he had been very kind. I believe that he was really beloved among them and had been exceedingly good to them. Inquests may come to contrary conclusions five hundred times over, but I make bold to give *my* verdict—"Murdered by the Doctor."

There is a Legend current here, that to pay the Postage of this letter would be to insure its non-delivery, so I have told my servant *not* to pay it. Is it egotistical enough? If not, what DO you want? Kindest loves and remembrances from all. And from no one in the world can they come to you more fervently, my dear Mrs Watson, than from your Ever affectionate friend

CHARLES DICKENS

I am afraid Spencer Lyttelton[4] is not mending his ways.

1 'The Perils of Certain English Prisoners', CD's response to the Indian Mutiny.
2 Walter had been in India since Aug. 1857, at first in the 26th Native Infantry Regt., then in the 42nd Highlanders.
3 Augustus Stafford O'Brien Stafford (1812–57), MP and actor in CD's amateur theatricals.
4 The Hon. Spencer Lyttelton (1818–81), Mrs Watson's cousin; with CD in Paris in Feb. 1851.

To George Eliot,[1] 18 JANUARY 1858

Tavistock House, London. W. C. | Monday Eighteenth January 1858

My Dear Sir

I have been so strongly affected by the two first tales in the book you have had the kindness to send me through Messrs. Blackwood, that I hope you will excuse my writing to you to express my admiration of their extraordinary merit. The exquisite truth and delicacy, both of the humour and the pathos of those stories, I have never seen the like of; and they have impressed me in a manner that I should find it very difficult to describe to you, if I had the impertinence to try.

In addressing these few words of thankfulness, to the creator of the sad fortunes of Mr. Amos Barton, and the sad love-story of Mr. Gilfil, I am (I presume) bound to adopt the name that it pleases that excellent writer to assume. I can suggest no better one; but I should have been strongly disposed, if I had been left to my own devices, to address the said writer as a woman. I have observed what seem to me to be such womanly touches, in those moving fictions, that the assurance on the title-page is insufficient to satisfy me, even now. If they originated with no woman, I believe that no man ever before had the art of making himself, mentally, so like a woman, since the world began.

You will not suppose that I have any vulgar wish to fathom your secret. I mention the point as one of great interest to me—not of mere curiosity. If it should ever suit your convenience and inclination, to shew me the face of the man or woman who has written so charmingly, it will be a very memorable occasion to me. If otherwise, I shall always hold that impalpable personage in loving attachment and respect, and shall yield myself up to all future utterances from the same source, with a perfect confidence in their making me wiser and better.

Your obliged and faithful Servant, | and admirer
CHARLES DICKENS

1 George Eliot, pseudonym of Marian Evans (1819–80†), novelist. Reviewer and editor of the *Westminster Review*, 1851–4, through which she met CD's friend George Lewes; from 1854 they lived together as man and wife. *Scenes of Clerical Life,* her first work of fiction, was published in *Blackwood's Magazine*, Jan.–Nov. 1857, in book form 1858.

To John Forster, [15 MARCH 1858]

What do you think of this name for my story—*Buried Alive*? Does it seem too grim? Or, *The Thread of Gold*?[1] Or, *The Doctor of Beauvais*?

1 'The Golden Thread' is the title of bk. 2 of *TTC*.

To Frederick Evans, 16 MARCH 1858

TAVISTOCK HOUSE, | TAVISTOCK SQUARE, LONDON. W.C.
Tuesday March Sixteenth 1858

My Dear Evans.

I want you to consider this letter as being strictly private and confidential between you and me. I am anxious to have your soundest opinion on the point it refers to you, and I shall give it great weight—though I do not, of course, pledge myself to be bound by it.

The Reading idea that I had, some time ago, sticks to me. Let me read where I will, an effect is produced which seems to belong to nothing else; and the number of people who want to come, cannot by any means be got in. I have in my mind this project:—

After reading in London on the 15th. of next month for the Benefit of the childrens' Hospital, to announce by advertisement (what is quite true), that I cannot answer the applications that are made to me, so numerous are they, and that compliance with ever so few of them is in any reason impossible. That therefore I have resolved upon a course of Readings both in town and country, and that those in London will take place at St. Martins Hall on certain evenings—four or six Thursdays—through May, and just into June.

Then, in August, September, and October, in the Eastern Counties, the West of England, Lancashire, Yorkshire, and Scotland, I should read from 35 to 40 times. At each place where there was a great success, I should myself announce that I should come back, on the turn of Christmas, to read a new Christmas Story written for the purpose (and which I should first read in London). Unless I am gigantically mistaken,—by March or April *a very large sum of money* would be cleared—and Ireland would be still untouched; not to speak of America, where I believe I could make (if I could resolve to go there) ten thousand pounds.

Now, the question I want your opinion on, is this:—Assuming these hopes to be well-grounded, would such an use of the personal (I may almost say affectionate) relations which subsist between me and the public, and make my standing with them very peculiar, at all affect my position with them as a writer? Would it be likely to have any influence on my next book? If it had any influence at all, would it be likely to be of a weakening or a strengthening kind?

(It is not to the purpose of this point, to remark that I should confide the whole of the Business arrangements to Arthur Smith.[1] I merely mention it, that you may have the whole case).

> Ever Faithfully
> CHARLES DICKENS

1 Arthur Smith (1825–61), Albert Smith's brother; managed CD's reading tours.

To *Wilkie Collins*, 21 MARCH 1858

TAVISTOCK HOUSE, | TAVISTOCK SQUARE, LONDON. W.C.
Sunday Twenty First March 1858

My Dear Wilkie
    I too had intended to come to the enclosed subject—and I too forgot it.
    You (or somebody else) will find the cheque crossed to Coutts's!

All day yesterday I was pursuing the Reading idea. Forster seems to me to be extraordinarily irrational about it. (I have a misgiving sometimes, that his money must have got into his head.)[1] I propounded it to Miss Coutts, who might have been expected to be dismayed, but *was not,* in the least. I am no further on my road to a decision, than that I resolve I will decide within 7 days from this date. Could you possibly believe that Forster asked me what I thought of consulting (on the Literary-position question)

F.L.A.D.G.A.T.E.[2]

!

The Doncaster unhappiness remains so strong upon me that I can't write, and (waking) can't rest, one minute. I have never known a moment's peace or content, since the last night of the Frozen Deep. I do suppose that there never was a Man so seized and rended by one Spirit. In this condition, though nothing can alter or soften it, I have a turning notion that the mere physical effort and change of the Readings would be good, as another means of bearing it.

—I suppose it is the penalty I pay for having written all these red-backed books[3] upon my shelves—?

Ever Faithfully
CD.

1 In 1856 Forster married a widow of considerable wealth.
2 Probably Frank Fladgate (1799–1892), barrister, close friend of Thackeray, and member of the Garrick Club.
3 CD's own copies of his first editions were specially bound in half-crimson morocco.

To Edmund Yates, 28 APRIL 1858

TAVISTOCK HOUSE, | TAVISTOCK SQUARE, LONDON. W.C.
Wednesday Twenty Eighth April, 1858

My Dear Yates

I send you an Orthopaedic shield, to defend your manly bosom from the pens of the enemy.[1]

For a good many years, I have suffered a great deal from Charities, but never anything like what I suffer now. The amount of correspondence they inflict upon me, is really incredible. But this is nothing. Benevolent men get behind the piers of the gates, lying in wait for my going out; and when I peep shrinkingly from my study-windows, I see their pot-bellied shadows projected on the gravel. Benevolent bullies drive up in Hansom Cabs (with engraved portraits of their benevolent Institutions hanging over the aprons, like banners on their outward walls),[2] and stay so long at the door, that their horses deposit beehives of excellent manure all over the front court. Benevolent Area-Sneaks[3] get lost in the kitchens, and are found to impede the circulation of the knife-cleaning Machine. My man has been heard to say (at the Burton Arms) "that if it was a wicious place, well and good—*that* an't door-work; but that wen all the Christian wirtues is always a shoulderin and a helberin on you in the All, a tryin to git past you and cut upstairs into Master's room, wy no wages as you couldn't name, wouldn't make it up to you."

Persecuted Ever

CD.

1 At a friend's request, Yates had asked CD to take the chair at a dinner in support of the Orthopaedic Hospital; he did not do so.
2 Cf. *Macbeth*, v. v. 1.
3 Thieves who get into a house through the basement area.

To *Angela Burdett Coutts*, 9 MAY 1858

Sunday Ninth May, 1858

My Dear Miss Coutts,

You have been too near and dear a friend to me for many years, and I am bound to you by too many ties of grateful and affectionate regard, to admit of my any longer keeping silence to you on a sad domestic topic. I believe you are not quite unprepared for what I am going to say, and will, in the main, have anticipated it.

I believe my marriage has been for years and years as miserable a one as ever was made. I believe that no two people were ever created, with such an impossibility of interest, sympathy, confidence, sentiment, tender union of any kind between them, as there is between my wife and me. It is an immense misfortune to her—it is an immense misfortune to me—but Nature has put an insurmountable barrier between us, which never in this world can be thrown down.

You know me too well to suppose that I have the faintest thought of influencing you on either side. I merely mention a fact which may induce you to pity us both, when I tell you that she is the only person I have ever known with whom I could not get on somehow or other, and in communicating with whom I could not find some way to some kind of interest. You know that I have the many impulsive faults which often belong to my impulsive way of life and exercise of fancy; but I am very patient and considerate at heart, and would have beaten out a path to a better journey's end than we have come to, if I could.

We have been virtually separated for a long time. We must put a wider space between us now, than can be found in one house.

If the children loved her, or ever had loved her, this severance would have been a far easier thing than it is. But she has never attached one of them to herself, never played with them in their infancy, never attracted their confidence as they have grown older, never presented herself before them in the aspect of a mother.[1] I have seen them fall off from her in a natural—not *un*natural—progress of estrangement, and at this moment I believe that Mary and Katey (whose dispositions are of the gentlest and most affectionate conceivable) harden into stone figures of girls when they can be got to go near her, and have their hearts shut up in her presence as if they closed by some horrid spring.

No one can understand this, but Georgina who has seen it grow from year to year, and who is the best, the most unselfish, and the most devoted of human Creatures. Her sister Mary, who died suddenly and who lived with us before her, understood it as well though in the first months of our marriage. It is her misery to live in some fatal atmosphere which slays every one to whom she should be dearest. It is my misery that no one can ever understand the truth in its full force, or know what a blighted and wasted life my married life has been.

Forster is trying what he can, to arrange matters with her mother. But I know that the mother herself could not live with her. I am perfectly sure that her younger sister and her brother could not live with her. An old servant of ours[2] is the only hope I see, as she took care of her, like a poor child, for sixteen years. But she is married now, and I doubt her being afraid that the companionship would wear her to death. Macready used to get on better with her than anyone else, and sometimes I have a fancy that she may think of him and his sister. To suggest them to her would be to inspire her with an instant determination never to go near them.

In the mean time I have come for a time to the office, to leave her Mother free to do what she can at home, towards the getting of her away to some happier mode of existence if possible. They all know that I will do anything for her comfort, and spend anything upon her.

It is a relief to me to have written this to you. Don't think the worse of me; don't think the worse of her. I am firmly persuaded that it is not within the compass of her character and faculties, to be other than she is. If she had married another sort of man, she might however have done better. I think she has always felt herself at the disadvantage of groping blindly about me and never touching me, and so has fallen into the most miserable weaknesses and jealousies. Her mind has, at times, been certainly confused besides.

All this is for Mrs. Brown no less than for you. Put a kind construction on it, and hold me in the old place in your regard.

> Ever Dear Miss Coutts | Yours faithfully and affectionately
> CHARLES DICKENS

---

1 There seems to be no foundation for this charge.
2 Anne Cornelius, formerly Brown.

The *'Violated Letter'*, 25 MAY 1858[1]

Tavistock house, Tavistock Square | London, W.C.
Tuesday, May 25th, 1858.

Mrs. Dickens and I have lived unhappily together for many years. Hardly any one who has known us intimately can fail to have known that we are, in all respects of character and temperament, wonderfully unsuited to each other. I suppose that no two people, not vicious in themselves, ever were joined together, who had a greater difficulty in understanding one another, or who had less in common. An attached woman servant (more friend to both of us than a servant), who lived with us sixteen years, and is now married, and who was, and still is, in Mrs. Dickens's confidence and in mine, who had the closest familiar experience of this unhappiness, in London, in the country, in France, in Italy, wherever we have been, year after year, month after month, week after week, day after day, will bear testimony to this.

Nothing has, on many occasions, stood between us and a separation but Mrs. Dickens's sister, Georgina Hogarth. From the age of fifteen, she has devoted herself to our home and our children. She has been their playmate, nurse, instructress, friend, protectress, adviser and companion. In the manly consideration toward Mrs. Dickens which I owe to my wife, I will merely remark of her that the peculiarity of her character has thrown all the children on someone else. I do not know—I cannot by any stretch of fancy imagine—what would have become of them but for this aunt, who has grown up with them, to whom they are devoted, and who has sacrificed the best part of her youth and life to them.

She has remonstrated, reasoned, suffered and toiled, again and again to prevent a separation between Mrs. Dickens and me. Mrs. Dickens has often expressed to her her sense of her affectionate care and devotion in her home—never more strongly than within the last twelve months.

For some years past Mrs. Dickens has been in the habit of representing to me that it would be better for her to go away and live apart; that her always increasing estrangement made a mental disorder under which she sometimes labours—more, that she felt herself unfit for the life she had to lead as my wife and that she would be better far away. I have uniformly replied that we must bear our misfortune, and fight the fight out to the end; that the children were the first consideration, and that I feared they must bind us together "in appearance".

At length, within these three weeks, it was suggested to me by Forster that even for their sakes, it would surely be better to reconstruct and rearrange their unhappy home. I empowered him to treat with Mrs. Dickens, as the friend of both of us for one and twenty years. Mrs. Dickens wished to add on her part, Mark Lemon, and did so.[2] On Saturday last Lemon wrote to Forster that Mrs. Dickens "gratefully and thankfully accepted" the terms I proposed to her.

Of the pecuniary part of them, I will only say that I believe they are as generous as if Mrs. Dickens were a lady of distinction, and I a man of fortune. The remaining parts of them are easily described—my eldest boy to live with Mrs. Dickens and take care of her; my eldest girl to keep my house; both my girls and all my children but the eldest one, to live with me, in the continued companionship of their aunt Georgina, for whom they have all the tenderest affection that I have ever seen among young people, and who has a higher claim (as I have often declared for many years) upon my affection, respect and gratitude than anybody in the world.

I hope that no one who may become acquainted with what I write here, can possibly be so cruel and unjust, as to put any misconstruction on our separation, so far. My elder children all understand it perfectly, and all accept it as inevitable. There is not a shadow of doubt or concealment among us—my eldest son and I are one, as to it all.

Two wicked persons who should have spoken very differently of me,[3] in consideration of earned respect and gratitude, have (as I am told, and indeed to my personal knowledge) coupled with this separation the name of a young lady for whom I have a great attachment and regard. I will not repeat her name—I honour it too much. Upon my soul and honour, there is not on this earth a more virtuous and spotless creature than this young lady. I know her to be innocent and pure, and as good as my own dear daughters. Further, I am sure quite that Mrs. Dickens, having received this assurance from me, must now believe it, in the respect I know her to have for me, and in the perfect confidence I know her, in her better moments to repose in my truthfulness.

On this head, again, there is not a shadow of doubt or concealment between my children and me. All is open and plain among us, as though we were brothers and sisters. They are perfectly certain that I would not deceive them, and the confidence among us is without a fear.

C.D.

1 CD gave this written statement to Arthur Smith who was organizing his reading tour and assailed by rumours. CD authorized Smith to show it 'to any one who wishes to do me right, or to any one who may have been misled into doing me wrong', 25 May. He later claimed to be 'exceedingly pained' when this 'private and personal communication . . . found its way into some of the London papers, extracted from an American paper', CD to his solicitor Frederic Ouvry, 5 Sept. It is not known how it got into the American press; CD described it to Collins as 'evidently a private document of mine, violated in America and sent home here', 6 Sept. It subsequently became known as the 'violated letter'.

2 CD's breach with Lemon no doubt partly stemmed from Lemon's acting for Catherine and becoming one of her trustees.

3 i.e. Catherine's mother, and her sister Helen.

To Catherine Dickens, 4 JUNE 1858

TAVISTOCK HOUSE, | TAVISTOCK SQUARE, LONDON. W.C.
Friday Fourth June 1858

Dear Catherine.

I will not write a word as to any *causes* that have made it necessary for me to publish the enclosed in Household Words.[1] Whoever there may be among the living, whom I will never forgive alive or dead,[2] I earnestly hope that all unkindness is over between you and me.

But as you are referred to in the article, I think you ought to see it. You have only to say to Wills (who kindly brings it to you), that you do not object to the allusion.[3]

CHARLES DICKENS

1 'Personal' filled the front page of *HW*, 12 June. It alludes to 'some domestic trouble of mine, of long-standing' now 'amicably composed', and ends by 'solemnly declar[ing] . . . both in my own name and in my wife's name—that all the lately whispered rumours . . . are abominably false'.
2 Catherine's mother and her sister Helen.
3 Catherine raised no objection; but, after giving Wills her consent, she sent the statement to her solicitor, who attempted, unsuccessfully, to have its publication postponed.

To Edmund Yates, 8 JUNE 1858

TAVISTOCK HOUSE, | TAVISTOCK SQUARE, LONDON. W.C.
Tuesday Eighth June 1858

My Dear Edmund

Of course I can have nothing to say to this,[1] but that I deeply feel it. If you could know how much I have felt within this last month, and what a sense of Wrong has been upon me, and what a strain and struggle I have lived under, you would see that my heart is so jagged and rent and out of shape, that it does not this day leave me hand enough to shape these words.

Ever Faithfully
CD.

1 Presumably a letter sympathizing with CD.

To Frederick Evans, 22 JULY 1858

GAD'S HILL PLACE, | HIGHAM BY ROCHESTER, KENT.
Thursday July Twenty-Second 1858

Dear Sir,

I have had stern occasion to impress upon my children that their father's name is their best possession and that it would indeed be trifled with and wasted by him, if, either through himself or through them, he held any terms with those who have been false to it, in the only great need and under the only great wrong it has ever known. You know very well, why (with hard distress of mind and bitter disappointment), I have been forced to include you in this class. I have no more to say.[1]

[CHARLES DICKENS]

P.S.—Your letter reached me, only yesterday.

1 Bradbury & Evans had not printed CD's 'Personal' statement of 7 June in *Punch*, despite his appeal to his fellow-journalists 'to lend their aid to the dissemination of my present words'. He never met Evans socially again.

To Wilkie Collins, 11 AUGUST 1858

Swan Hotel, Worcester | Wednesday Evening | Eleventh August | 1858

My Dear Wilkie

I have just now toned down the capital Unknown Public article,[1] a little, here and there. Not because I dispute its positions, but because there are some things (true enough), that it would not be generous in me, as a novelist and a periodical editor, to put too prominently forward. You will not find it essentially changed, anywhere.

Your letter gave me great pleasure, as all letters that you write me are sure to do. But the mysterious addresses, O misconstructive one, merely refer to places where Arthur Smith did not know aforehand the names of the best Hotels. As to that furtive and Don Giovanni purpose at which you hint—that may be all very well for *your* violent vigor, or that of the companions with whom you may have travelled continentally, or the Caliphs Haroon Alraschid with whom you have unbent metropolitanly;[2] but Anchorites who read themselves red hot every night are chaste as Diana (I suppose *she* was by the bye, but I find I don't quite believe it when I write her name).

We have done exceedingly well since we have been out—with this remarkable (and pleasant) incident; that wherever I read twice, the turn-away is invariably on the second occasion. They don't quite understand beforehand what it is, I think, and expect a man to be sitting down in some corner, droning away like a mild bagpipe. In that large room at Clifton, for instance, the people were perfectly taken off their legs by the Chimes—started—looked at each other—started again—looked at me—and then burst into a storm of applause. I think the best audiences I have yet had, were at Exeter and Plymouth. At Exeter, the best I have ever seen. At Plymouth, I read three times. Twice in one day. A better morning audience for Little Dombey, could not be. And the Boots at night, was a shout all through.

I cannot deny that I shall be heartily glad when it is all over, and that I miss the thoughtfulness of my quiet room and desk. But perhaps it is best for me not to have it just now, and to wear and toss my Storm away—or as much of it as will ever calm down while the water rolls—in this restless manner.

Arthur Smith knows I am writing to you, and sends his kindest regard. He is all usefulness and service. I never could have done it without him.—Should have left the unredeemed Bills on the walls, and taken flight.

This is a stupid letter, but I write it before dressing to read; and you know what a brute I am at such times.

> Ever Affectionately
>
> CD.

P.S. I miss Richard Wardour's dress, and always want to put it on. I would rather, by a great deal, act. Apropos of which, I think I have a very fine notion of a part. It shall be yours.

1 Collins's article on novel readers, *HW*, 21 Aug.
2 In the 'Adventure of Haroon Al Rusheed', *The Arabian Nights' Entertainments* (1811), the Caliph Haroon and his Grand Vizier travel round his capital disguised as foreign merchants.

To *Angela Burdett Coutts*, 23 AUGUST 1858

Morrison's Hotel, Dublin | Monday Twenty Third August. 1858.

My Dear Miss Coutts.

I shall address this to Mr. Wills, as I am not certain where you may be. I passed through Bangor last Saturday night at midnight, and wondered whether you were there.

My dear friend, I quite understand and appreciate your feeling that there must be no reservation between us, and that we must not have a skeleton in a closet, and make belief it is not there. But I must not enter on the wretched subject, upon false pretences. I must not do what would make my dear girls out to be a sort of phænomona, and what would make my own relations with Mrs. Dickens, incomprehensible. Since we spoke of her before, she has caused me unspeakable agony of mind; and I must plainly put before you what I know to be true, and what nothing shall induce me to affect to doubt. She does not—and she never did—care for the children; and the children do not—and they never did—care for her. The little play that is acted in your Drawing-room is not the truth, and the less the children play it, the better for themselves, because they know it is not the truth. (If I stood before you at this moment and told you what difficulty we have to get Frank, for instance, to go near his mother, or keep near his mother, you would stand amazed.) As to Mrs. Dickens's "simplicity" in speaking of me and my doings, O my dear Miss Coutts do I not know that the weak hand that never could help or serve my name in the least, has struck at it—in conjunction with the wickedest people, whom I have loaded with benefits! I want to communicate with her no more. I want to forgive her and forget her.

I could not begin a course of references to her, without recording, as between you and me, what I know to be true. It would be monstrous to myself, and to the children also. From Walter away in India, to Little Plornish at Gad's Hill there is a grim knowledge among them, as familiar to them as their knowledge of Day light that what I now write, is the plain bare fact. She has always disconcerted them; they have always disconcerted her; and she is glad to be rid of them, and they are glad to be rid of her. No more of it here.

The country expedition has been doing extremely well. The expenses are large (including Mr. Smith's share, about 50 per cent), but the returns come out handsomely. At Liverpool last week, I read 4 times. The audiences amounted to about 6,300 people. My clear profit, after all deductions, was £260.9.0. What we are going to do here, I don't know. The Dublin audience are accustomed to do nothing in the way of taking places, until the last moment, or until they actually "take them" by walking in at the Doors. We are therefore quite in the Dark. I read the Carol here—the Chimes tomorrow—Little Dombey on Wednesday morning—and the Poor Traveller &c on Thursday evening. We had a five hours passage from Holyhead in the night of Saturday, and it was very, very, nasty.

I am greatly surprised by this place. It is very much larger than I had supposed, and very much more populous and busy. Upon the whole it is no shabbier than London is, and the people seem to enjoy themselves more than the London people do. The old town of Edinburgh is a thousand times more squalid than the bye places I have seen in Dublin; and I have wandered about it for 6 or 8 hours in all directions. It may be presumed that it has greatly improved of late years. There are far fewer spirit shops than I have been used to see in great cities. And even Donnybrook Fair (which is on now, though sought to be abolished) is less disagreeable than Chalk Farm; and I have seen numbers of common people buying the most innocent and *un*life-like of Dolls there, for their little children.

Among my English audiences, I have had more clergymen than I ever saw in my life before. It is very curious to see how many people in black come to Little Dombey. And when it is over they almost uniformly go away as if the child were really Dead— with a hush upon them. They certainly laugh more at the Boots' story of the Little Elopement,[1] than at anything else; and I notice that they sit with their heads on one side, and an expression of playful pity on their faces—as if they saw the tiny boy and girl. Which is tender and pleasant, I think? The Chimes is always a surprise. They fall into it with a start, and look at me in the strangest way before they begin to applaud. The Cratchit family in the Carol are always a delight. And they always visibly lie in wait for Tiny Tim. The little books sell extraordinarily well. Besides being in every bookshop window in every place, my men alone will sell from 6 to 12 dozen in a night. I think I have now told you every bit of egotism I can screw out of myself. But I know that you and Mrs. Brown (to whom I send my love) will be interested in these scraps.

I shall hope to find another letter from you, somewhere, soon, telling me how you both are, and whether you have found any place to breathe in. Then I will report further of my proceedings. Ever Dear Miss Coutts, Yours affecy. & faithfully

CD.

1 In 'The Boots at the Holly-Tree Inn', Cobbs, the Boots, tells the story of the little boy and girl who 'elope' with the intention of marrying at Gretna Green.

To *William H. Wills*, 25 OCTOBER 1858

TAVISTOCK HOUSE, | TAVISTOCK SQUARE, LONDON. W.C.
Monday Night Twenty Fifth October | 1858

My Dear Wills

Since I left you tonight, I have heard of a case of such extraordinary, and (apparently) dangerous and unwarrantable conduct in a Policeman, that I shall take it as a great kindness if you will go to Yardley in Scotland Yard when you know the facts for yourself, and ask him to enquire what it means.

I am quite sure that if the circumstances as they stand were stated in the Times, there would be a most prodigious public uproar.

Before you wait upon Yardley, saying that you know the young ladies and can answer for them and for their being in all things most irreproachable in themselves and most respectably connected in all ways, and that you want to know what the Devil the mystery means—see the young ladies and get the particulars from them.

No. 31 Berners Street Oxford Street, is the address of the young ladies, and the young ladies are Miss Maria and Miss Ellen Ternan, both of whom you know. You are to understand, between you and me, that I have sent the eldest sister to Italy, to complete a musical education— that Mrs. Ternan is gone with her, to see her comfortably established in Florence; and that our two little friends are left together, in the meanwhile, in the family lodgings.[1] Observe that they don't live about in furnished lodgings, but have their own furniture. They have not been many weeks in their present address, and I strongly advised Mrs. Ternan to move from their last one, which I thought unwholesome.

Can you call and see them between 3 and 5 tomorrow (Tuesday)? They will expect you, unless you write to the contrary. If you can't go, will you write and make another appointment.

(N.B. Maria is a good deal looked after.² And my suspicion is, that the Policeman in question has been suborned to find out all about their domesticity by some "Swell". If so, there can be no doubt that the man ought to be dismissed.)

They will tell you his No. They don't seem so clear about his letter, but that is no matter. The division on duty in Berners Street, is of course ascertainable by Scotland Yard authorities.

Ever Faithfully

CD.

1 They were both acting: Maria at the Strand, Nelly in walk-on parts at the Haymarket.
2 i.e. has many admirers.

*To Blanchard Jerrold,*¹ 26 NOVEMBER 1858.

It is not likely that I can furnish you with any new particulars of interest concerning your lamented father. Such details of his life and early struggles as I have often heard from himself, are better known to you than to me; and my praises of him can make no new sound in your ears.

But, as you wish me to note down for you, my last remembrance and experience of him, I proceed to do so. It is natural that my thoughts should first rush back (as they instantly do) to the days when he began to be known to me, and to the many happy hours I afterwards passed in his society.

Few of his friends, I think, can have had more favorable opportunities of knowing him, in his gentlest and most affectionate aspect, than I have had. He was one of the gentlest and most affectionate of men. I remember very well that when I first saw him, in or about the year 1835—when I went into his sick room in St. Michael's Grove Brompton, and found him propped up in a great chair, bright-eyed, and eager and quick in spirit, but very lame in body—he gave me an impression of tenderness. It never became dissociated from him. There was nothing cynical or sour in his heart, as I knew it. In the company of children and young people, he was particularly happy, and shewed to extraordinary advantage. He never was so gay, so sweet-tempered, so pleasing, and so pleased as there. Among my own children, I have observed this many and many a time. When they and I came home from Italy in 1845, your father went to Brussels to meet us—in company with our friends, *Mr. Forster* and *Mr. Maclise*. We all travelled together, about Belgium for a little while, and all came home together. He was the delight of the children all the time, and they were his delight. He was in his most brilliant spirits, and I doubt if he were ever more humorous in his life. But the most enduring impression that he left upon us who were grown up— and we have, all, often spoken of it since— was that *Jerrold*, in his amiable capacity of being easily pleased, in his freshness, in his good-nature, in his cordiality, and in the unrestrained openness of his heart, had quite captivated us.

Of his generosity I had a proof, within these two or three years, which it saddens me to think of now. There had been an estrangement between us[2]—not on any personal subject, and not involving an angry word— and a good many months had passed without my once seeing him in the street, when it fell out that we dined, each with his own separate party, in the strangers' room of a club. Our chairs were almost back to back, and I took mine after he was seated and at dinner. I said not a word (I am sorry to remember) and did not look that way. Before we had sat so, long, he openly wheeled his chair round, stretched out both his hands in a most engaging manner, and said aloud, with a bright and loving face that I can see as I write to you—"For God's sake, let us be friends again! Life's not long enough for this!"

On Sunday, May 31st, 1857, I had an appointment to meet him at the Gallery of Illustration, in Regent Street. We had been advising our friend, Mr. Russell,[3] in the condensation of his lectures on the war in the Crimea, and we had engaged with him to go over the last of the series there at one o'clock that day. Arriving some minutes before the time, I found your father sitting alone in the hall. "There must be some mistake," he said: no one else was there; the place was locked up; he had tried all the doors; and he had been waiting there a quarter of an hour by himself. I sat down by him in a niche in the staircase, and he told me that he had been very unwell for three or four days. A window in his study had been newly painted, and the smell of the paint (he thought it must be that) had filled him with nausea and turned him sick, and he felt quite weak and giddy through not having been able to retain any food. He was a little subdued at first and out of spirits; but we sat there half-an-hour, talking, and when we came out together he was quite himself.

In the shadow I had not observed him closely; but when we got into the sunshine of the streets, I saw that he looked ill. We were both engaged to dine with Mr. Russell at Greenwich, and I thought him so ill then that I advised him not to go, but to let me take him, or send him, home in a cab. He complained, however, of having turned so weak—we had now strolled as far as Leicester Square—that he was fearful he might faint in the Cab, unless I could get him some restorative, and unless he could "keep it down". I deliberated for a moment whether to turn back to the Athenaeum, where I could have got a little brandy for him, or to take him on into Covent Garden for the purpose; meanwhile, he stood leaning against the rails of the enclosure, looking for the moment, very ill indeed. Finally, we walked on to Covent Garden, and before we had gone fifty yards he was very much better. On our way Mr. Russell joined us. He was then better still, and walked between us, unassisted. I got him a hard biscuit and a little weak cold brandy and water, and begged him by all means to try to eat. He broke up and ate the greater part of the biscuit, and then was much refreshed and comforted by the brandy; he said that he felt the sickness was overcome at last, and that he was quite a new man; it would do him good to have a few quiet hours in the air, and he would go with us to Greenwich. I still tried to dissuade him, but he was by this time bent upon it, and his natural color had returned, and he was very hopeful and confident.

We strolled through the Temple on our way to a boat and I have a lively recollection of him stamping about Elm Tree Court, with his hat in one hand and the other pushing his hair back, laughing in his heartiest manner at a ridiculous remembrance we had in common, which I had presented in some exaggerated light to divert him. We found our boat, and went down the river, and looked at the Leviathan[4] which was building, and talked all the way. It was a bright day, and as soon as we reached Greenwich we got an open carriage and went out for a drive about Shooter's Hill. In the carriage, Mr. Russell read us his Lecture, and we discussed it with great interest; we planned out the ground of Inkermann, on the heath, and your father was very earnest indeed. The subject held us so, that we were graver than usual; but he broke out at intervals in the same hilarious way as in the Temple, and he over and over again said to me with great satisfaction, how happy he was, that he had "quite got over that Paint."

The dinner-party was a large one, and I did not sit near him at table. But he and I arranged before we went in to dinner that he was only to eat of some simple dish that we agreed upon, and was only to drink sherry and water. We broke up very early, and before I went away with *Mr. Leech*, who was to take me to London, I went round to Jerrold, for whom some one else had a seat in a carriage, and put my hand upon his shoulder, asking him how he was? He turned round to shew me the glass beside him, with a little wine and water in it: "I have kept to the prescription; it has answered as well as this morning's, my dear old boy; I have quite got over the paint, and I am perfectly well." He was really elated by the relief of having recovered, and was as quietly happy as I ever saw him. We exchanged "God bless you !" and shook hands.

I went down to Gad's Hill next morning, where he was to write to me after a little while, appointing his own time for coming to see me there. A week afterwards, another passenger in the Railway carriage in which I was on my way to London Bridge, opened his morning paper, and said "Douglas Jerrold is dead!"

1 William Blanchard Jerrold (1826–84†), journalist and playwright. Son of Douglas Jerrold, he wrote for *HW* and *AYR*, and published a biography of his father in 1859.

2 Perhaps due to their disagreement over capital punishment, which Jerrold thought should be abolished, while CD advocated only the abolition of public executions. Or perhaps because Jerrold had withdrawn from a CD amateur production at short notice. CD complained to Bulwer Lytton: 'Jerrold—who never in his life was true to Anything—has deserted us! When the walls of Manchester and Liverpool had been for days covered with bills announcing him for next week in his part!' (4 Feb. 1852). See Michael Slater, *Douglas Jerrold, 1803–1857* (London: Gerald Duckworth & Co, 2002), 181–2.

3 William Russell (1820–1907†), journalist. His reports on the Crimean War for *The Times* aroused public indignation.

4 Afterwards called the *Great Eastern*, the iron sailing steam ship designed by Isambard Kingdom Brunel and launched 1858. Far larger than any previous ship, she attracted much interest.

To John Forster, [24 JANUARY 1859]

Don't you think this is a good name and quotation? I have been quite delighted to get hold of it for our title.

HOUSEHOLD HARMONY.

"At last by notes of Household Harmony."—*Shakespeare.*[1]

1 *3 Henry VI*, IV. vi. 14. Following his break with Evans over the separation with Catherine, CD decided to shut down *HW*. He was planning to publish a new weekly journal, to start at the end of April with the first part of *TTC*.

To John Forster, [?25 JANUARY 1859]

He was at first reluctant even to admit the objection.[1] I am afraid we must not be too particular about the possibility of personal references and applications: otherwise it is manifest that I never can write another book. I could not invent a story of any sort, it is quite plain, incapable of being twisted into some such nonsensical shape. It would be wholly impossible to turn one through half a dozen chapters.

1 To the title for the new journal, proposed above.

To Frank Beard,[1] 25 JUNE 1859

OFFICE OF ALL THE YEAR ROUND, | Saturday Twenty Fifth June 1859

My Dear Frank Beard

My bachelor state has engendered a small malady[2] on which I want to see you. I am at Gad's Hill for the summer, but have come up this morning on purpose. Will you let me know at what time to day it will be convenient to you to call here, and also at what time you leave home; so that IF the former should be incompatible with my train, I may come up to you at once.

Faithfully Yours always
CHARLES DICKENS

1 Francis Beard, FRCS (1814–93), Thomas Beard's younger brother, and from Feb. 1859 CD's regular family doctor.
2 Perhaps a sexually transmitted disease.

To George Eliot, 10 JULY 1859

GAD'S HILL PLACE, | HIGHAM BY ROCHESTER, KENT.
Sunday Tenth July, 1859

My Dear Madam.

I have received your letter[1] here this morning, with the greatest interest and pleasure. It is unnecessary for me to add, that I have received it in confidence.

Believe me, when I wrote to you on the subject of the Scenes of Clerical Life, I did nothing but relieve my mind, very inadequately, of the strong feelings of admiration with which you had filled it. Wherever I went, I said the same things. It was a rare and genuine delight to me, to become acquainted in the spirit with so noble a writer; and it would have been hardly less difficult to me, to repress myself for good and all, than to repress my admiration of such genius.

This opportunity of writing to you, relieves me from a difficulty in which I have felt myself to be placed ever since you sent me Adam Bede, and for my extrication from which, I have always trusted to the result that has come—for I have always had the vanity to believe that I should one day hear from you as a real individual woman.

I had no means of acknowledging the receipt of that book, but through Blackwood, and knowing at that time what changes I was going to make in my publishing arrangements, I had a great delicacy in suggesting to the Scotch-Publishing-Mind, through any after-splicing of this and that together, that I had been waylaying you! Confident that you could not doubt my enthusiasm after I had read the book, I therefore resolved not to write to George Elliot, but to wait until I could write to you in person, whoever you might be.

Adam Bede has taken its place among the actual experiences and endurances of my life. Every high quality that was in the former book, is in that, with a World of Power added thereunto. The conception of Hetty's character is so extraordinarily subtle and true, that I laid the book down fifty times, to shut my eyes and think about it. I know nothing so skilful, determined, and uncompromising. The whole country life that the story is set in, is so real, and so droll and genuine, and yet so selected and polished by Art, that I cannot praise it enough to you. And that part of the book which follow's Hetty's trial (and which I have observed to be not as widely understood as the rest), affected me far more than any other, and exalted my sympathy with the writer to its utmost height. You must not suppose that I am writing this to *you*. I have been saying it over and over again, here and elsewhere, until I feel in a ludicrously apologetic state for repeating myself on this paper.

I cannot close this note without touching on two heads. Firstly (Blackwood not now being the medium of communication), if you should ever have the freedom and inclination to be a fellow labourer with me, it would yield me a pleasure that I have never known yet and can never know otherwise; and no channel that even you could command, should be so profitable as to yourself. Secondly, I hope you will let me come to see you when we are all in or near London again, and tell you—as a curiosity—my reasons for the faith that was in me that you were a woman, and for the absolute and never-doubting confidence with which I have waved all men away from Adam Bede, and nailed my colors to the Mast, with "Eve" upon them.

A word of remembrance and regard to Lewes—and of congratulation—that I know he will feel and understand as I do.

My Dear Madam | Your faithful
CHARLES DICKENS

1 Her positive reply to an invitation to contribute her next story to *AYR*. She later declined: 'We have written to Dickens saying that *Time* is an insurmountable obstacle to his proposition as he puts it.' George Eliot's Journal, 18 Nov. 1859, quoted in Gordon Haight: *George Eliot: A Biography* (Oxford: Oxford University Press, 1968), 311.

To *Wilkie Collins*, 6 OCTOBER 1859

GAD'S HILL PLACE, | HIGHAM BY ROCHESTER, KENT.
Thursday Sixth October 1859

My Dear Wilkie

I do not positively say that the point you put, might not have been done in your manner; but I have a very strong conviction that it would have been overdone in that manner—too elaborately trapped, baited, and prepared—in the main, anticipated and its interest wasted. This is quite apart from the peculiarity of the Doctor's[1] character, as affected by his imprisonment; which of itself would—to my way of thinking— render it quite out of the question to put the reader inside of him before the proper time, in respect of matters that were dim to himself through being, in a diseased way, morbidly shunned by him. I think the business of Art is to lay all that ground carefully, but with the care that conceals itself—to shew, by a backward light, what everything has been working to—but only to SUGGEST, until the fulfilment comes. These are the ways of Providence—of which ways, all Art is but a little imitation.

"Could it have been done at all, in the way I suggest, to advantage?" is your question. I don't see the way, and I never have seen the way, is my answer. I cannot imagine it that way, without imagining the reader wearied, and the expectation wire-drawn.[2]

I am very glad you like it so much. It has greatly moved and excited me in the doing, and Heaven knows I have done my best and have believed in it.

Ever affecy.
CD.

1 Dr Manette, in *TTC*.
2 Collins, having now read at least bk. 3, ch. 10, apparently thought the connection of Dr Manette with Darnay as a St Evrémonde could have been indicated much earlier.

To Thomas Carlyle, 30 OCTOBER 1859

GAD'S HILL PLACE, | HIGHAM BY ROCHESTER, KENT.
Sunday Thirtieth October, 1859

My Dear Carlyle.

Forster is here, and has given me your message concerning the Tale of Two Cities—which has heartily delighted me. It will be published some three weeks hence in one dose, after having occasioned me the utmost misery by being presented in the "tea-spoon-full" form.[1] Nevertheless I should like you to read what remains of it, before the Many-Headed does, and I therefore take heart to overwhelm you with the enclosed proofs. They are not long, and don't need to be returned. They go on to the end from the current No. and they include the current No. in case you should not have seen it.

I have said in the Preface to the complete Tale (said Preface is not here, because I have no Proof of it), "that all the references to the condition of the French people, however slight, are from trustworthy authorities; and that it has been one of my hopes to add something to the popular and picturesque means of understanding that terrible time, though no one can hope to add anything to the philosophy of Mr. Carlyle's wonderful book."[2]

With love from my daughters and Georgy to Mrs. Carlyle and you, I am ever my Dear Carlyle

Your affectionate
CHARLES DICKENS

1 'Teaspoons' was Carlyle's name for the weekly Nos., which were generally one or two chapters.
2 Carlyle's *The French Revolution* (1837). CD took his advice on which books to borrow from the London Library.

To Mary Boyle, 8 DECEMBER 1859

TAVISTOCK HOUSE, | TAVISTOCK SQUARE, LONDON. W.C.
Thursday Night, Eighth December 1859

My Dear Mary.

I really cannot tell you how truly and tenderly I feel your letter, and how gratified I am by its contents. Your truth and attachment are always so precious to me that I cannot get my heart out on my sleeve, to shew it you. It is like a child, and, at the sound of some familiar voices, "goes and hides".

You know what an affection I have for Mrs. Watson, and how happy it made me to see her again—younger, much, than when I first knew her in Switzerland.

The Mormon joke, excellent—Even to me, who (if I had been the examined boy) might have been more frightfully heretical than either of the unmarried young gentlemen.

Yes, Mary dear; I must say that I like my Carton. And I have a faint idea sometimes, that if I had acted him, I could have done something with his life and death.

God bless you always! | Ever Affectionately Yours
CHARLES DICKENS

To *Wilkie Collins*, 7 JANUARY 1860

TAVISTOCK HOUSE, | TAVISTOCK SQUARE, LONDON. W.C.
Saturday Night Seventh January 1860

My Dear Wilkie

I have read this book,[1] with great care and attention. There cannot be a doubt that it is a very great advance on all your former writing, and most especially in respect of tenderness. In character, it is excellent. Mr. Fairlie as good as the lawyer, and the lawyer as good as he; Mrs. Vesey and Miss Halcombe in their different ways, equally meritorious. Sir Percival also, is most skilfully shewn; though I doubt (you see what small points I come to) whether any man ever shewed uneasiness by hand or foot, without being forced by nature to shew it in his face too. The story is very interesting, and the writing of it admirable.

I seem to have noticed, here and there, that the great pains you take express themselves a trifle too much; and you know that I always contest your disposition to give an audience credit for nothing—which necessarily involves the forcing of points on their attention—and which I have always observed them to resent when they find it out—as they always will and do. But on turning to the book again, I find it difficult to take out an instance of this. It rather belongs to your habits of thought, and manner of going about the work. Perhaps I express my meaning best when I say that the three people who write the narratives in these proofs, have a DISSECTIVE property in common, which is essentially not theirs but yours; and that my own effort would be to strike more of what is got, *that way,* out of them by collision with one another, and by the working of the story.

You know what an interest I have felt in your powers from the beginning of our friendship, and how very high I rate them: *I* know that this is an admirable book, and that it grips the difficulties of the weekly portion and throws them, in masterly style. No one else could do it, half so well. I have stopped in every chapter to notice some instance of ingenuity, or some happy turn of writing; and I am absolutely certain that you never did half so well yourself.

So go on and prosper, and let me see some more when you have enough (for your own satisfaction), to shew me! I think of coming in to back you up, if I can get an idea for my series of gossiping papers.[2] One of these days, please God, we may do a story together; I have very odd half-formed notions—in a mist—of something that might be done that way.

Ever affecy.

CD.

1 *The Woman in White*, published *AYR*, Nov. 1859–Aug. 1860.
2 *The Uncommercial Traveller*.

To *Angela Burdett Coutts*, 5 APRIL 1860

TAVISTOCK HOUSE, | TAVISTOCK SQUARE, LONDON. W.C.
Thursday Fifth April 1860

My Dear Miss Coutts,

I cannot be easy under the chance of *seeming*, through the silence of a week or two, to debate within myself of the possibility of what your affectionate kindness suggested yesterday.[1] In the last two years, I have been stabbed too often and too deep, not to have a settled knowledge of the wounded place.

It is simply impossible that such a thing can be. That figure is out of my life for evermore (except to darken it), and my desire is, Never to see it again.

Ever yours affectionately and faithfully
CHARLES DICKENS

1 She seems to have offered to help reconcile CD and Catherine, but the couple did not meet after the separation. Catherine and Miss Coutts remained friendly.

To *Angela Burdett Coutts*, 8 APRIL 1860

GAD'S HILL PLACE, | HIGHAM BY ROCHESTER, KENT.
Easter Sunday Eighth April, 1860.

My Dear Miss Coutts.

Don't be afraid of my hand-writing, for I hope I can write you a few reassuring words, this blessed morning.—I believe I am exactly what I always have been; quite as hopeful, cheerful, and active, as I ever was. I am not so weak or wicked as to visit any small unhappiness of my own, upon the world in which I live. I know very well, it is just as it was. As to my art, I have as great a delight in it as the most enthusiastic of my readers; and the sense of my trust and responsibility in that wise, is always upon me when I take pen in hand. If *I* were soured, I should still try to sweeten the lives and fancies of others; but I am not—not at all.

Neither do I ever complain, or ever touch that subject. What I have written to you respecting it, I have written merely because I wished you to understand me thoroughly.

Lastly, I do not suppose myself blameless, but in this thing as in all others know, every day more and more, how much I stand in need of the highest of all charity and mercy. All I claim for myself, is, that when I was very young, I made a miserable mistake, and that the wretched consequences which might naturally have been expected from it, have resulted from it. That is all.

Do not think you failed to express yourself to me. You expressed—emphatically—*yourself*, and what more could I have, or what could I more earnestly feel?

Charley is here, and has gained a colour in a dozen hours. I hope you may not have read The Tale of Two Cities, for I have entrusted your copy to his care.

Ever My Dear friend
CD.

To Edward Bulwer Lytton, 5 JUNE 1860

Gad's Hill, Tuesday, June 5th, 1860.

My Dear Bulwer Lytton,

I am very much interested and gratified by your letter concerning "A Tale of Two Cities." I do not quite agree with you on two points, but that is no deduction from my pleasure.

In the first place, although the surrender of the feudal privileges (on a motion seconded by a nobleman of great rank) was the occasion of a sentimental scene, I see no reason to doubt, but on the contrary, many reasons to believe, that some of these privileges had been used to the frightful oppression of the peasant, quite as near to the time of the Revolution as the doctor's narrative, which, you will remember, dates long before the Terror. And surely when the new philosophy was the talk of the salons and the slang of the hour, it is not unreasonable or unallowable to suppose a nobleman wedded to the old cruel ideas, and representing the time going out, as his nephew represents the time coming in; as to the condition of the peasant in France generally at that day, I take it that if anything be certain on earth it is certain that it was intolerable. No *ex post facto* enquiries and provings by figures will hold water, surely, against the tremendous testimony of men living at the time.

There is a curious book printed at Amsterdam, written to make out no case whatever, and tiresome enough in its literal dictionary-like minuteness, scattered up and down the pages of which is full authority for my marquis. This is "Mercier's Tableau de Paris." Rousseau is the authority for the peasant's shutting up his house when he had a bit of meat. The tax-taker was the authority for the wretched creature's impoverishment.

I am not clear, and I never have been clear, respecting that canon of fiction which forbids the interposition of accident in such a case as Madame Defarge's death. Where the accident is inseparable from the passion and emotion of the character, where it is strictly consistent with the whole design, and arises out of some culminating proceeding on the part of the character which the whole story has led up to, it seems to me to become, as it were, an act of divine justice. And when I use Miss Pross (though this is quite another question) to bring about that catastrophe, I have the positive intention of making that half-comic intervention a part of the desperate woman's failure, and of opposing that mean death—instead of a desperate one in the streets, which she wouldn't have minded—to the dignity of Carton's wrong or right; this *was* the design, and seemed to be in the fitness of things.

Now, as to the reading. I am sorry to say that it is out of the question this season. I have had an attack of rheumatism—quite a stranger to me—which remains hovering about my left side, after having doubled me up in the back, and which would disable me from standing for two hours. I have given up all dinners and town engagements, and come to my little Falstaff House here, sensible of the necessity of country training all through the summer. Smith would have proposed any appointment to see you on the subject, but he has been dreadfully ill with tic. Whenever I read in London, I will gladly put a night aside for your purpose, and we will plot to connect your name with it, and give it some speciality. But this could not be before Christmas time, as I should not be able to read sooner, for in the hot weather it would be useless. Let me hear from you about this when you have considered it. It would greatly diminish the expenses, remember.

Ever affectionately and faithfully
[CHARLES DICKENS]

To Frances Dickinson,[1] 19 AUGUST 1860

GAD'S HILL PLACE, | HIGHAM BY ROCHESTER, KENT
Sunday Nineteenth August, 1860

My Dear Mrs. Dickinson.

Pray don't suppose me unmindful of your confidence, or slow, from inclination, to respond to it. I have been involved in great anxiety and worry by the unexpected death of my poor brother Alfred. He had had no opportunity of providing for his family—died worth nothing—and has left a widow and five children—you may suppose to whom. Day after day I have been scheming and contriving for them, and I am still doing so, and I have schemed myself into broken rest and low spirits. My mother, who was also left to me when my father died (I never had anything left to me but relations), is in the strangest state of mind from senile decay: and the impossibility of getting her to understand what is the matter, combined with her desire to be got up in sables like a female Hamlet, illumines the dreary scene with a ghastly absurdity that is the chief relief I can find in it.

Well! Life is a fight and must be fought out. Not new, but true, and I don't complain of it.

Your friend Robert Bell, having become Gentleman Usher in the spiritual establishment of Mrs. Milner Gibson, has been writing a portentous account of Spirit Rapping and Table Leaping, in the Cornhill Magazine.² My opinion of the whole party is, that it is a combination of addle-headed persons, Toadies, and Humbugs.

Wilkie has finished his White Woman (if he had done with his flesh-coloured one,³ I should mention that too), and is in great force. Charley and his bride⁴ remain—at Calais! Having left here with ideas of going to Switzerland, they have naturally remained at Calais ever since. Katie writes that they think of remaining "abroad", a long time. That general definition seems to express all they know of their intentions. She really looked wonderfully pretty on the day of her marriage, and her appearance produced an immense effect on the beholders. Not the least pleasant part of it was Mary's pride in it. I had tried to keep it very quiet, but all the neighbouring country turned out in the most bewildering manner, and the people of the village strewed flowers in the churchyard, and erected triumphal arches, and fired guns, and came to look at the breakfast, and made a regular day of it. One very funny thing was, the entrance into church of the few friends whom I had caused to be brought down straight from town by Special Train. They didn't know whether they were to look melancholy, beaming, or maudlin; and their uncertainty struck me as so uncommonly droll, that I was obliged to hide my reverend parental countenance in my hand on the altar Railing. There was no misery of any kind—not even speechifying—and the whole was a great success—*So far.*

I may congratulate you on the distribution of your daughters, present and prospective,⁵ over the face of the earth. Of course the Australian daughter will marry Tom Tiddler, and give you golden grandchildren.

What to say to your account of yourself, I don't know. Profoundly true, I do know, and therefore tremendously difficult to remark upon. But, calmly now, is it worse than you expected? At least is it not pretty much what you expected on the day when you were sitting here, in this room where I write? It seems to me that since then you have gradually built up a little castle that never had any foundations. Am I right in that? And are you quite sure that what you are disposed to resent as indifference, is not the stealing apathy of advanced age? Under other circumstances—say in your humble servant, for example—it would be affronting or idiotic; but not in these, I think? I am inclined to think, on this ground alone, that you are better apart. As the foregathering was of your seeking and not his may it not be that he thinks so too, and has my reason for thinking so? As to yourself I might be very moral in my admonitions and didactic remarks—but you are a woman—and I am a man—and we should both know better, even if I were. There is no doubt that your position is a trying one, and that is the honest truth. But would it not be more trying still, if you were more pursued, sought out, and hovered about?

This is not a letter; this is only an explanation why I cannot write a letter. Even while I have been writing this, I have had black figures, little and big,[6] coming in and wistfully questioning me about what is to be done in this wise or that. (They are at present lodged in a farm house near here).

I shall be glad to know that you have received this, and that, bad as it was, it was better than nothing.

Kindest remembrances from Mary and Georgy.

Ever My Dear Mrs. Dickinson | Faithfully Yours
CD.

1 Frances Dickinson, 1820–98, miscellaneous writer, introduced to CD by Wilkie Collins, and acted in *The Frozen Deep*. Her first marriage, by which she had four daughters, ended in divorce.
2 July 1860.
3 His mistress, Caroline Graves.
4 Charles Collins (1828–73†), painter and writer, and Wilkie's younger brother; he married CD's daughter Katey on 17 July.
5 Frances Dickinson was about to marry Gilbert Elliot, Dean of Bristol, who had two daughters, and was twenty years older than she.
6 Alfred's widow and children.

To John Forster, 4 OCTOBER 1860

GAD'S HILL PLACE, | HIGHAM BY ROCHESTER, KENT,
Thursday, Oct. 4th, 1860.

My Dear Forster,

It would be a great pleasure to me to come to you, an immense pleasure, and to sniff the sea I love (from the shore); but I fear I must come down one morning and come back at night. I will tell you why.

Last week I got to work on the new story. I had previously very carefully considered the state and prospects of All the Year Round,[1] and, the more I considered them, the less hope I saw of being able to get back, *now*, to the profit of a separate publication in the old 20 numbers. However I worked on, knowing that what I was doing would run into another groove; and I called a council of war at the office on Tuesday. It was perfectly clear that the one thing to be done was, for me to strike in. I have therefore decided to begin the story as of the length of the Tale of Two Cities on the first of December—begin publishing, that is. I must make the most I can out of the book. You shall have the first two or three weekly parts to-morrow. The name is GREAT EXPECTATIONS. I think a good name?

Now the preparations to get ahead, combined with the absolute necessity of my giving a good deal of time to the Christmas number, will tie me to the grindstone pretty tightly. It will be just as much as I can hope to do. Therefore, what I had hoped would be a few days at Eastbourne diminish to a few hours.

I took the Admiral[2] down to Portsmouth. Every maritime person in the town knew him. He seemed to know every boy on board the Britannia, and was a tremendous favourite evidently. It was very characteristic of him that they good-naturedly helped him, he being so very small, into his hammock at night. But he couldn't rest in it on these terms, and got out again to learn the right way of getting in independently. Official report stated that "after a few spills, he succeeded perfectly, and went to sleep." He is perfectly happy on board, takes tea with the captain, leads choruses on Saturday nights, and has an immense marine for a servant.

I saw Edmund Yates at the office, and he told me that during all his mother's wanderings of mind, which were almost incessant at last, she never once went back to the old Adelphi days until she was just dying, when he heard her say, in great perplexity: "I can *not* get the words."

Best love to Mrs. Forster.

Ever, my dear Forster, affectionately
[CHARLES DICKENS]

1 *AYR* was losing sales. The current serialized novel, Charles Lever's *A Day's Ride*, did not, CD told Lever, '*take hold*' with subscribers.
2 CD's son Sydney.

To John Forster, [EARLY OCTOBER 1860]

The book will be written in the first person throughout, and during these first three weekly numbers you will find the hero to be a boy-child, like David. Then he will be an apprentice. You will not have to complain of the want of humour as in The Tale of Two Cities. I have made the opening, I hope, in its general effect exceedingly droll. I have put a child and a good-natured foolish man, in relations that seem to me very funny. Of course I have got in the pivot on which the story will turn too—and which indeed, as you will remember, was the grotesque tragi-comic conception that first encouraged me.[1] To be quite sure I had fallen into no unconscious repetitions, I read David Copperfield again the other day, and was affected by it to a degree you would hardly believe.

1 Mentioned to Forster in mid-Sept., possibly concerning Pip and Magwitch. CD wrote to Mary Boyle after five weekly Nos. had been published: 'Pray read Great Expectations. I think it is very droll. It is a very great success, and seems universally liked—I suppose because it opens funnily and with an interest too' (28 Dec. 1860).

To Esther Nash,[1] 5 MARCH 1861

3 Hanover Terrace, Regents Park | Tuesday Fifth March 1861.

My Dear Esther.

I am exceedingly sorry that you should suppose my silence to have been occasioned by any thing but constant occupation and one or two concurrent causes of procrastination—as for instance, my having been in town (alone at the office) unwell, from the 26th. of December until nearly the end of January—and then my having been house-hunting until we fixed ourselves here, in a really delightful house, until Midsummer. My story is a perpetual employment of my time and thoughts, as I have a great deal to condense into a short space. And the letters I *must* write, are so many that the letters I would like to write, often go to the wall—instead of the post. This is the truth, the whole truth, and nothing but the truth.

You don't want me to say how sorry I am to hear of the illness of your daughters, or how I sympathize with you in that distress and anxiety away out yonder. You want me to exchange news with you, and I go on to do it.

Katie and her husband have come home; but how long they may remain at home is unknown to the writer of these presents as it probably is to themselves. Katie looks extremely well, and they seem to get on together admirably. Charley is at work upon a book describing their journey, with illustrations by himself.[2] I ardently wish he were painting, instead; but of course I don't say so. There are no "Great Expectations" of perspective Collinses. Which I think a blessed thing, though again I don't say so. Old Mrs. Collins dined here last Sunday week, and contradicted everybody upon every subject for five hours and a half, and was invariably Pig-headed and wrong. So I was very glad when she tied her head up in a bundle and took it home,—though again I didn't say so.

Wilkie is in a potential and popular state, and is beginning to think of a new book, looming some eight or ten months ahead. He has made his rooms in Harley Street, very handsome and comfortable. We never speak of the (female) skeleton in that house,[3] and I therefore have not the least idea of the state of his mind on that subject. I hope it does not run in any matrimonial groove. I can imagine similar cases in which that end is well and wisely put to the difficulty. But I can *not* imagine any good coming of such an end in this instance.

I am just as I was when I last saw you, except for being busier; almost absorbed. I am going to read at St. James's Hall, three times in this month; and I shall probably go into the country for that purpose in October, November, and December. Arthur Smith manages for me, of course. He told me of a curious special instance of the changes of Life and Death. There came to him the other day, a long letter written from China by Bowlby[4]—the Times correspondent, afterwards killed there—to Albert. Albert was dead when it was written,[5] and Bowlby was dead when it arrived!

The madness of the English world is at present revolving round "Essays and Reviews"[6]—a collection of writings by some eminent men in orders, respecting the heresy whereof there is mighty bluster and balderdash. The Bishops are wonderful to consider in their holdings forth upon the subject. I suspect there are an odd few thousands of people in this country, beginning to think with a little doubtful amazement, that whenever that wonderful Institution shews itself, it is always aggressive and abusive. Here are the holy creatures pitching their right reverend mud about in all directions, but not a lawn sleeve fluttered when the poor law broke down in the frost and the people (more meritorious of the poor) were starving to death.[7] The world moves very slowly, after all, and I sometimes feel as grim as—Richard Wardour sitting on the chest in the midst of it.

My son Charley has just come home from China, and is seeking for a mercantile partnership, and, when he finds it, will probably marry the daughter of Mr. Evans the printer[8]— the very last person on earth whom I could desire so to honor me. But it is not his fault, for they have been engaged since they were mere children. It is sure not to answer—if my authority on such a subject can be accepted.

Mary is as she was, and Georgina of course. We do very well indeed together, and live in peace. Gad's Hill has been very much improved since you were there. It looked very pretty yesterday when we were down there, even with the house abandoned and all its hair in papers, and a shrill North wind howling and raging at it fiercely.

This is all the news I have outside my story, and I know that if I lay this sheet of paper by, one single hour, and wait to think of more, I shall never send it. So I send this no-letter rather than none at all, and entreat you to put me back in my old place in your heart, as one whose regard for you cannot be capricious.

Ever affectionately Yours

CD.

Kindest regard from Mary and Georgina.

1　Née Esther Elton. Her father, the actor Edward Elton, died in 1843 leaving six daughters and one son. CD organized benefit performances on their behalf, and interested himself in Esther's training and career as a teacher. 'I honor Esther very much. Her conduct has been gallant and true, throughout,' wrote CD (23 Dec. 1845). She taught at the National School in Mitcham, Surrey, and in 1849 married James Nash, also a teacher there. From 1854 onwards he ran a school for English boys in Nice, France.

2　*A Cruise upon Wheels*, 1863.

3　Caroline Graves.

4　Thomas Bowlby (1817–60†), journalist; captured and imprisoned in Aug. and died 22 Sept. 1860.

5　Albert Smith died 23 May 1860.

6　A volume of essays on Christianity published 1860. Very controversial; the essayists were dubbed 'The Seven Against Christ'.

7　The suffering was particularly bad among the dock-labourers and wharfmen of East London, unemployed through stoppage of river traffic on the Thames.

8　Charley married Bessie Evans 19 Nov. 1861. CD, having quarrelled irrevocably with Frederick Evans, did not attend the wedding.

To John Forster, [?MID-APRIL 1861]

It is a pity that the third portion[1] cannot be read all at once, because its purpose would be much more apparent; and the pity is the greater, because the general turn and tone of the working out and winding up, will be away from all such things as they conventionally go. But what must be, must be. As to the planning out from week to week, nobody can imagine what the difficulty is, without trying. But, as in all such cases, when it is overcome the pleasure is proportionate. Two months more will see me through it, I trust. All the iron is in the fire, and I have "only" to beat it out.

1 The last stage of Pip's expectations, beginning in ch. 40, after Magwitch's return.

To Wilkie Collins, 23 JUNE 1861

GAD'S HILL PLACE, | HIGHAM BY ROCHESTER, KENT
Sunday Twenty Third June 1861.

My Dear Wilkie. We will arrange our Xmas No. please God, under the shade of the Oak Trees.

I shall remain in town on the Thursday, and will return with you on the Friday. We can settle our Train when we meet on Wednesday.

As yet, I have hardly got into the enjoyment of thorough laziness. Bulwer was so very anxious that I should alter the end of Great Expectations—the extreme end, I mean, after Biddy and Joe are done with—and stated his reasons so well, that I have resumed the wheel, and taken another turn at it. Upon the whole I think it is for the better. You shall see the change when we meet.[1]

The country is most charming, and this place very pretty. I am sorry to hear that the hot East winds have taken such a devastating blow into No. 12 Harley Street. They have been rather surprising, if any thing in weather can be said to surprise.

I don't know whether anything remarkable comes off in the air today; but the blue bottles (there are 9 in this room) are all banging their heads against the windowglass, in the most astonishing manner. I think there must be some competitive examination somewhere, and these 9 have been rejected.

Ever affy,
CD.

P.S. I reopen this, to state that the most madly despondent blue bottle has committed suicide, and fallen dead on the carpet.

1 The original version ended with a casual meeting between Pip and Estella, who is now remarried.

To *Edward Bulwer Lytton*, 24 JUNE 1861

GAD'S HILL PLACE, | HIGHAM BY ROCHESTER, KENT.
Monday Twenty Fourth June 1861.

My Dear Bulwer Lytton. I send you enclosed, the whole of the concluding weekly
No. of Great Expectations,[1] in order that you may the more readily understand
where I have made the change.

My difficulty was, to avoid doing too much. My tendency—when I began to
unwind the thread that I thought I had wound for ever—was to labour it, and get
out of proportion.

So I have done it in as few words as possible;[2] and I hope you will like the alteration
that is entirely due to you.

It would give us great pleasure if you would come down to this small parsonage
and see us. I would ask Mr. Baylis[3] and no one else. French should have an appropriate
nook for the pipe sticks. Could you come on Friday the 5th. of July, or Saturday the
6th? Or if that time would not suit you, will you tell me generally how your time lies
spread out before you.

I was so heartily glad to be with you at Knebworth, that it would be delightful
to me to have a quiet visit from you. Write me a line, concerning the dates herein
suggested.

Ever Cordially
CD.

1 Chs. 58 and 59, pub. *AYR*, 3 Aug. 1861.
2 The revised ending is *c*.1,000 words, as against *c*.300 words of the original one.
3 Thomas Baylis (1795–1875), collector of antiques, and close friend of Bulwer Lytton.

To *Benjamin Webster*, 9 SEPTEMBER 1861

GAD'S HILL PLACE, | HIGHAM BY ROCHESTER, KENT.
Monday Ninth September 1861.

My Dear Webster

I have received a letter here this afternoon by the day post, from Mrs. Ternan
(whose address is 2 Houghton Place Ampthill Square), telling me that you are
making some prospective changes in your company, and asking me if I would object
to recommend to you one of her daughters, Miss Maria Ternan. I cannot possibly
object to do so, on any other ground than unwillingness to give you trouble, for
I have a high opinion of the young lady and take a strong interest in herself and
her family. It is likely enough that you know what she can do—how that she is
accomplished and attractive, well used to the stage, sings prettily, and is favorably

known to London Audiences. If you should be undecided between two applicants of equal pretensions (counting this young lady as one), I should be heartily glad if you would turn the scale in my direction— as I am sure you would in any such case.[1]

Always Faithfully Yours
CHARLES DICKENS

1 Boucicault's *The Coleen Bawn* was having a long run at the Adelphi. Maria was not taken on.

To John Forster, [?6 OCTOBER 1861]

There was a very touching thing in the Chapel.[1] When the body was to be taken up and carried to the grave, there stepped out, instead of the undertaker's men with their hideous paraphernalia, the men who had always been with the two brothers at the Egyptian Hall;[2] and they, in their plain, decent, own mourning clothes, carried the poor fellow away. Also, standing among the gravestones, dressed in black, I noticed every kind of person who had ever had to do with him—from our own gas man and doorkeepers and billstickers, up to Johnson the printer and that class of man. The father and Albert and he now lie together, and the grave, I suppose, will be no more disturbed. I wrote a little inscription for the stone and it is quite full.

1 At the funeral of Arthur Smith, who had organized CD's reading tours.
2 Where Albert Smith gave his public entertainments, managed by his brother Arthur.

To Mary Dickens, 23 NOVEMBER 1861

Queen's Head, Newcastle-on-Tyne, | Saturday, Nov. 23rd, 1861.

[My Dearest Mamie]

A most tremendous hall here last night; something almost terrible in the cram. A fearful thing might have happened. Suddenly, when they were all very still over Smike, my gas batten came down, and it looked as if the room was falling. There were three great galleries crammed to the roof, and a high steep flight of stairs, and a panic must have destroyed numbers of people. A lady in the front row of stalls screamed, and ran out wildly towards me, and for one instant there was a terrible wave in the crowd. I addressed that lady laughing (for I knew she was in sight of everybody there), and called out as if it happened every night, "There's nothing the matter, I assure you; don't be alarmed; pray sit down;" and she sat down directly, and there was a thunder of applause. It took some few minutes to mend, and I looked on with my hands in my pockets; for I think if I had turned my back for a moment there might still have been a move. My people were dreadfully alarmed, Boycett[1] in particular, who I suppose had some notion that the whole place might have taken fire.

"But there stood the master," he did me the honour to say afterwards, in addressing the rest, "as cool as ever I see him a-lounging at a railway station." A telegram from Berry at Edinburgh yesterday evening, to say that he had got the bills, and that they would all be up and dispersed yesterday evening under his own eyes. So no time was lost in setting things as right as they can be set. He has now gone on to Glasgow.

Ever affectionately

[CD]

P.S. Duty to Mrs. Bouncer.[2]

1 In charge of the gas.
2 Mamie's dog.

To Georgina Hogarth, 3 DECEMBER 1861

Carrick's Royal Hotel, Glasgow, Tuesday, Dec. 3rd, 1861.

I send you by this post another *Scotsman*. From a paragraph in it, a letter, and an advertisement, you may be able to form some dim guess of the scene at Edinburgh last night. Such a pouring of hundreds into a place already full to the throat, such indescribable confusion, such a rending and tearing of dresses, and yet such a scene of good humour on the whole. I never saw the faintest approach to it. While I addressed the crowd in the room, Gordon addressed the crowd in the street. Fifty frantic men got up in all parts of the hall and addressed me all at once. Other frantic men made speeches to the walls. The whole Blackwood family were borne in on the top of a wave, and landed with their faces against the front of the platform. I read with the platform crammed with people. I got them to lie down upon it, and it was like some impossible tableau or gigantic picnic; one pretty girl in full dress lying on her side all night, holding on to one of the legs of my table. It was the most extraordinary sight. And yet from the moment I began to the moment of my leaving off, they never missed a point, and they ended with a burst of cheers.

The confusion was decidedly owing to the local agents. But I think it may have been a little heightened by Headland's[1] way of sending them the tickets to sell in the first instance.

Now, as I must read again in Edinburgh on Saturday night, your travelling arrangements are affected. So observe carefully (you and Mamie) all that I am going to say. It appears to me that the best course will be for you to come to *Edinburgh* on Saturday; taking the fast train from the Great Northern station at nine in the morning. This would bring you to the Waterloo at Edinburgh, at about nine or so at night, and I should be home at ten. We could then have a quiet Sunday in Edinburgh, and go over to Carlisle on the Monday morning.

The expenditure of lungs and spirits was (as you may suppose) rather great last night, and to sleep well was out of the question; I am therefore rather fagged to-day. And as the hall in which I read to-night is a large one, I must make my letter a short one.

My people were torn to ribbons last night. They have not a hat among them, and scarcely a coat.

Give my love to Mamie. To her question, "Will there be war with America?" I answer, "Yes;" I fear the North to be utterly mad, and war to be unavoidable.[2]

---

1 Thomas Headland, Arthur Smith's successor.
2 Two Confederate emissaries to Britain and France had just been taken off the British packet boat *Trent*, which had been captured by an American navy ship. The British saw this as a violation of the law of the sea, and only when President Lincoln agreed to release the men did the talk of war subside.

To David Macrae,[1] [1861]

I have so strong an objection to *mere* professions of religion, and to the audacious interposition of vain and ignorant men between the sublime simplicity of the New Testament and the general human mind to which our Saviour addressed it, that I urge that objection as strongly and as positively as I can. In my experience, true practical Christianity has been very much obstructed by the conceit against which I protest. . . . With a deep sense of my great responsibility always upon me when I exercise my art, one of my most constant and most earnest endeavours has been to exhibit in all my good people some faint reflections of the teachings of our great Master, and unostentatiously to lead the reader up to those teachings as the great source of all moral goodness. All my strongest illustrations are derived from the New Testament: all my social abuses are shown as departures from its spirit; all my good people are humble, charitable, faithful, and forgiving. Over and over again, I claim them in express words as disciples of the Founder of our religion; but I must admit that to a man (or woman) they all arise and wash their faces, and do not appear unto men to fast. Furthermore, I devised a new kind of book for Christmas years ago[2] (which has since been imitated all over England, France, and America), absolutely impossible, I think, to be separated from the exemplification of the Christian virtues and the inculcation of the Christian precepts. In every one of those books there is an express text preached on, and the text is always taken from the lips of Christ.

---

1 Revd David Macrae (1837–1907), United Presbyterian minister, later deposed for 'heresy'; wrote books supporting temperance. CD is answering Macrae's criticism that while portraying 'hypocrites as they deserved, he had not, on the other side, given us amongst his good people, any specimens of earnest Christianity to show that Christian profession may be marked and yet sincere'.
2 The five Christmas Books.

To *William H. Wills,* 2 JANUARY 1862

At The Birmingham Station
Thursday Second January 1862

My Dear Wills.

Being stranded here for an hour, on my way from Leamington to Cheltenham, I write to you.

Firstly to reciprocate all your cordial and affectionate wishes for the New Year, and to express my earnest hope that we may go on through many years to come, as we have gone on through many years that are gone. And I think we can say that we doubt whether any two men can have gone on more happily and smoothly, or with greater trust and confidence in one another.[1]

Secondly: As the Proofs[2] reached me yesterday at Leamington where I had a double day, I was not able to look at them. I have eyed them on the Railway to day, but necessarily in a cursory way. Look to the Russian paper for clearness. In Robert Lytton's poem—at the end—the word "both" is used as applied to several things. The word "all", with a slight alteration in the pointing, will express what he means.

Keep articles which *will* have the first person singular, inveterately, as wide asunder as you can.

Birmingham is in a very depressed state, with very few of its trades at work. Nevertheless we did extremely well here. At Leamington yesterday, immense. Copperfield in the morning absolutely stunned the people: and at Nickleby and the Trial[3] at night, they roared and roared until I think they must have shaken all the air in Warwickshire.

Faithfully Ever
CD.

1 This paragraph was endorsed by Wills: 'It would gratify me to see this passage in print. The whole is worthy publishing, I think.'
2 Of *AYR*, 18 Jan.
3 From *PP*.

To *Georgina Hogarth,* 8 JANUARY 1862

Torquay | Wednesday Eighth January 1862

My Dearest Georgy. I feel that if I had not been reading, still I never could have borne the marriage,[1] and should have excused myself somehow. As I have told Mamie, I *could not* write to Clara (Mamie wished me) in my consciousness of the dismal absurdity of my congratulating her upon her doing what I did once with such brilliant success.

As to Blackwood,[2] I think I told you that I saw him three times in Edinburgh, and always extremely drunk. Your estimate of him I take to be quite correct.

Wills's account of that base fellow "about London"[3] is really highly humourous and entertaining. It seems to be the most miserable and pitiable failure conceivable. Pursuant to agreement, I send Wills's report by this post to Forster. But if you see Wills at the office, I beg you to insist on his giving you his first-rate description.

You know, I think, that I was very averse to going to Plymouth, and would not have gone there again but for poor Arthur. We had one good night, and one bad one.[4] But on the bad one (last night) I read Copperfield, and positively enthralled the people. It was a most overpowering effect, and poor Andrew[5] came behind the screen, after the storm, and cried in the best and manliest manner. Also there were two or three lines of his shipmates and other sailors, and they were extraordinarily affected. But its culminating effect was on Macready at Cheltenham. You know that he is not too prone to praise what comes at all in his own way; but when I got home after Copperfield, I found him quite unable to speak, and able to do nothing but square his dear old jaw all on one side, and roll his eyes (half closed), like Jackson's picture of him. And when I said something light about it, he returned "No—er—Dickens! I swear to Heaven that as a piece of passion and playfulness—er—indescribably mixed up together, it does—er—No, really Dickens!—amaze me as profoundly as it moves me. But as a piece of Art—and you know—er—that I—No Dickens! By God!—have seen the best Art in a great time—it is incomprehensible to me. How it is got at— er—how it is done—er—how one man can—well! It lays me on my—er—back, and it is of no use talking about it!"—With which, he put his hand upon my breast, and pulled out his pocket handkerchief, and I felt as if I were doing somebody to his Werner.[6] Katie by the bye is a wonderful audience, and has a great fund of wild feeling in her. You are not to suppose that Butty is fragile, for she is a fine handsome girl, with a face of great power and character. But I fear she is too much of a woman for her years. Johnny not at all unlike Plorn.

We are now in the region of small rooms, and therefore this trip will not be as profitable as the long one. I have not yet seen the room here, but imagine it to be very small. Exeter, I know; and that is small also. I am very much used up, on the whole, for I cannot bear this moist warm climate. It would kill me very soon. And I have now got to the point of taking so much out of myself with Copperfield, that I might as well do Richard Wardour.

Headland I can only describe as damned aggravating. Yet I cannot blow him up, though I found, this day, on the cards for this place, exactly the same mistakes as I corrected at Norwich. Didn't I always say he would get his money from Hullah? I have got Hullah into such a corner at last, by steadily refusing to let him get away from the point, that he *must* pay—and *will*.

Umphrey[7] is doing well, and is going to read the declamatory part of Athalie at a private performance at his own house. But it cannot be done without Edland (Extall says), who is to perpetrate some infernal bass.

You have now, my dearest Georgy, the fullest extent of my tidings. This is a very pretty place—a compound of Hastings, Tunbridge Wells, and little bits of the hills about Naples—but I met four Respirators[8] as I came up from the Station, and three pale curates without them who seemed in a bad way.

—Frightful intelligence has just been brought in by Boycett concerning the small size of the room. I have terrified Block[9] by sending him to look at it, and swearing that if it's too small, I will go away to Exeter.

Ever Your most affectionate

CD.

1 i.e. gone to the wedding of his friend James White's daughter Clara, at Bonchurch that day.
2 Perhaps William Blackwood (1836–1912), who became a partner in the firm in 1862.
3 Mark Lemon and his series of lectures about London and its past.
4 In financial terms.
5 Andrew Gordon, lieutenant RN; son of CD's old friend John Gordon; they met in Scotland in 1841.
6 In Byron's play; one of Macready's greatest successes. The following references are to Macready's children. CD had hoped for Clarkson Stanfield's company too, and wrote to him, 'Lord! If you could manage to join me there [at Macready's], what enormous delight it would give him, and what pleasure it would give to all of us Three to be together again!' 10 Dec. 1861.
7 Humphrey and Hextall were members of the reading staff.
8 i.e. people wearing devices covering the mouth and nose, in order to inhale warmed air.
9 Blockhead, i.e. Headland.

To Thomas Baylis, 1 FEBRUARY 1862

GAD'S HILL PLACE, | HIGHAM BY ROCHESTER, KENT.
Saturday First February 1862

My Dear Mr. Baylis

I have just come home from a long series of Readings in the country. Finding your note, I write to you at once, or you might do me the wrong of supposing me unmindful of it and you.

I do not quite understand from your note, whether the two papers you mention are at the office or not. If they be, I shall have them on Wednesday from Wills. But in reference to the first one, I am bound to say that I cannot take any part whatever in reference to the Memorial to Prince Albert. With a sufficient respect for the deceased gentleman, and all loyalty and attachment towards the Queen, I have been so very much shocked by the rampant toadyism that has been given to the four winds on that subject and by the blatant speeches that have been made respecting it, that the refuge of my soul is Silence.

I hope the Green Park may not be inseparable from the Theme?

Faithfully Yours always

CD

To Herbert Lawrence, 27 FEBRUARY 1862

OFFICE OF ALL THE YEAR ROUND, | Thursday Twenty Seventh February 1862

Sir

Your letter is a very difficult one to answer. I should wish to make my reply acceptable to you, but I must not compromise what I have some reason to suppose to be the truth.

Because I suppose it to be the truth, and not because I seek to discourage you, I am bound to tell you that the circumstance of your having written "a poem of three hundred lines in an evening", or "as much in eight hours as would make fourteen printed columns of All The Year Round", is not at all favourable to your pretensions. After some slight experience of the pains and patience inseparable from authorship, I believe you to be labouring under a very complete, though not very uncommon, mistake.

Therefore I can but give you the assurance that whatever is offered for acceptance here is honestly read, and that if there be the slightest ray of hope in it, it comes before me; but not otherwise.

Yours
CHARLES DICKENS

To John Forster, [JUNE 1862]

I must entreat you, to pause for an instant, and go back to what you know of my childish days, and to ask yourself whether it is natural that something of the character formed in me then, and lost under happier circumstances, should have reappeared in the last five years. The never-to-be-forgotten misery of that old time bred a certain shrinking sensitiveness in a certain ill-clad, ill-fed child, that I have found come back in the never-to-be-forgotten misery of this later time.

To Wilkie Collins, 20 SEPTEMBER 1862

OFFICE OF ALL THE YEAR ROUND, | Saturday Twentieth September 1862

My Dear Wilkie

I have gone through the Second Volume[1] at a Sitting, and I find it *wonderfully fine*. It goes on with an ever-rising power and force in it, that fill me with admiration. It is as far before and beyond The Woman in White, as *that* was beyond the wretched common level of fiction-writing. There are some touches in the Captain, which no one but a born (and cultivated) Writer could get near—could draw within hail of. And the originality of Mrs. Wragge, without compromise of her probability, involves a really great achievement. But they are all admirable; Mr. Noel Vanstone and the house-keeper, both in their way as meritorious as the rest; Magdalen wrought out with truth, energy, sentiment, and passion, of the very first water.

I cannot tell you with what a strange dash of pride, as well as pleasure, I read the great results of your hard work. Because, as you know, I was certain from the Basil days, that you were the Writer who would come ahead of all the Field—being the only one who combined invention and power, both humourous and pathetic, with that invincible determination to work, and that profound conviction that nothing of worth is to be done without work, of which triflers and feigners have no conception.

I send the books back, by South Eastern Railway today.

There is one slight slip, occurring more than once, which you have not corrected. Magdalen "laid down", and I think some one else "laid down". It is clear that she must either lay herself down, or lie down. To lay is a verb active, and to lie down is a verb neuter. Consequently she lay down, or laid herself down.

It would be a very great pleasure to me if I could get to you once again at Broadstairs, but I fear it is not at all likely. I forget how long you stay there. Will you tell me? We purpose going to Paris on the 20th of October. I have half a mind to read in Paris when I *am* there; but this is as yet an unformed object in my thoughts.

You will not be able, I suppose, to do any little thing for the Xmas No.? I have done the introduction and Conclusion, and will send them you bye and bye, when the Printer shall have (thus Wills) "dealt with them". They are done in the character of a Waiter, and I think are very droll. The leading idea admits of any kind of contribution, and does not require it to be in any way whatever accounted for. Besides having this advantage, it is a comic defiance of the difficulty of a Xmas No. with an unexpected end to it. The name (between ourselves) is *Somebody's Luggage*.

Georgina keeps better, though she is very weak. She has been reading the book with the deepest interest, and sends her love and all my admiration—and really was so pleased to see how strongly I felt about it, that I think you would have been pleased to see *her*.

I have some rather miserable anxieties which I must impart one of these days when I come to you or you come to me. I shall fight out of them, I dare say: being not easily beaten—but they have gathered and gathered.

Leech dined here yesterday, Impromptu, and he, Georgy, and I, went to the Adelphi. Where Benjamin[2] did some of the most amazingly inconsistent and bad things I ever saw, in a piece called One Touch of Nature—spoilt by his own hand from some French drama. Among other brilliant hits, he called his young Daughter—scene, the neighbourhood of Long Acre—"Madame", and was perpetually in a mental stagger between me, and himself, and some Frenchman whom he had seen do the part.

Wills sends kind regard.

Ever My Dear Wilkie | Affectionately Yours

CD.

---

1 Of Collins's *No Name*, serialized in *AYR* Mar. 1862–Jan. 1863; published in 3 vols. 1862.
2 Webster.

To *Wilkie Collins,* 14 OCTOBER 1862

GAD'S HILL PLACE, | HIGHAM BY ROCHESTER, KENT.
Tuesday Night, Fourteenth October, 1862

My Dear Wilkie.

Frank Beard has been here this evening—of course since I posted my this-day's letter to you—and has told me how you are not at all well,[1] and how he has given you something which he hopes and believes will bring you round.[2] It is not to convey this insignificant piece of intelligence, or to tell you how anxious I am that you should come up with a wet sheet and a following sail[3] (as we say at sea—when we are not sick) that I write. It is, simply, to say what follows: which I hope may save you some mental uneasiness. For I was stricken ill when I was doing Bleak House, and I shall not easily forget what I suffered under the fear of not being able to come up to time.

Dismiss that fear (if you have it) altogether from your mind. Write to me at Paris, at any moment, and say you are unequal to your work, and want me, and I will come to London straight and do your work. I am quite confident that, with your notes and a few words of explanation, I could take it up at any time and do it. Absurdly unnecessary to say that it would be a make-shift! but I could do it, at a pinch, so like you as that no one should find out the difference. Don't make much of this offer in your mind—it is nothing—except to ease it. If you should want help, I am as safe as the Bank. The trouble would be nothing to me, and the triumph of overcoming a difficulty—great. Think it a Xmas No., an Idle apprentice, a Lighthouse, a Frozen Deep.[4] I am as ready as in any of those cases to strike in and hammer the hot iron out.

You won't want me.[5] You will be well (and thankless!) in no time. But here I am. And I hope that the knowledge may be a comfort to you. Call me, and I come.

As Beard always has a sense of medical responsibility, and says anything about a patient in confidence, I have merely remarked here that "Wilkie is out of sorts". Charley (who is here with Katie) has no other cue from me.

Ever affecy
CD.

1　Collins was suffering from chronic gout; CD's letter earlier that day contained a detailed analysis of the latest proofs of *No Name*.
2　Probably laudanum, on which Collins increasingly relied.
3　Misquotation of Alan Cunningham's 'A Wet Sheet and a Flowing Sea' (*The Songs of Scotland, Ancient and Modern*, 1825).
4　On all of which they had collaborated.
5　He did not.

To Charles Lever,[1] 4 NOVEMBER 1862

Paris. rue du Faubourg St. Honoré, 27 | Tuesday Fourth November 1862

My Dear Lever

Behold my address here, until just before Xmas. In respect of Chapman and Hall, refer all your business to me: resting fully assured that I will accept your part in it whenever it comes, and will do my best with it.

Indeed I suppose (this in answer to yours) that few men are more restless than I am, and that few sleep in more strange beds and dine at more new cooks' shops. But sundry ties and troubles confine my present oscillations to between this place and England—and I fear the South and I are separated by months at least.

As to contributions—decidely yes! always rejoiced to have them!

Paris is more amazing than ever, and the Genius of the Lamp is always building Palaces in the night.—But he charges for them in the article of rent, in a manner altogether Parisian and not in the least Arabian.

The last time I was here as a resident, I went to the Theatres with Scribe; and the last time but one, Victor Hugo[2] had the most fantastic of apartments, and stood in the midst of it, a little fine-featured fiery-eyed gallant fellow. Now, Scribe is in Pere la Chaise,[3] and the fantastic apartment is in the Channel Islands and Victor Hugo is an old photograph in the shops, with a quenched eye and a stubbly beard and no likeness to anyone I ever saw.

My Dear Lever | Ever affectionately Yours
CHARLES DICKENS

1 Charles Lever (1806–72†), novelist, had early success with *The Confessions of Harry Lorrequer* 1837–40. Friendly with CD from the 1840s.
2 Victor Hugo (1802–85), French novelist and playwright, met CD in 1847. His apartment was 6 Place Royale, now the Victor Hugo Museum. From 1852 he lived in exile in the Channel Islands.
3 The oldest and largest extramural cemetery in Paris.

To Thomas Beard, 4 NOVEMBER 1862

Paris. rue du Faubourg St. Honoré, 27 | Fourth November, 1862

My Dear Beard

Mary, Georgina, and I, are here until just before Christmas Day.

I am going to ask you rather a startling, staggering question. Hold up, therefore!

If I were to decide to go and read in Australia,[1] how stand your inclination and spirits for going with me? Outside term of absence, a year. Period of departure, May or June. Overland journey both ways. The journey and climate are said to be wonderful restorers. The work would be, seconding the Inimitable in the ring, delivering him at the scratch in fine condition, keeping off the crowd, polishing him up when at all punished, and checking the local accounts. The Arthur Smith class of arrangements would necessarily have to be made by the Colonial sharer, and my bottle-holder would merely in all things represent me. A servant should go, to valet both of us, and make washing and dressing easy.

Observe. I don't in the least know that I shall go. But supposing I *did* re-open the question with the Australian people, and supposing the negociations *did* proceed to the going point, and supposing you *did* like the notion of what such a trip would ensure you free of all expense, do you feel equal to it? There are not six men in the world, I would go with—and I don't know the other five!

I cannot too strongly put to you when I come bursting at you with this surprising question, the extreme uncertainty in which the matter stands. But I am wavering between reading in Australia, and writing a book at home; that, in strict confidence, is the whole truth. If I were to go to Australia, I would not let myself out, but would go with my own capital and on my own account. The man who came over to bid for me, has gone back. "Shall I write out to him and ask him on what terms he will become my agent?" is the question that revives in my mind. I may not write at all. I may write, and his reply may be such that it will come to nothing three months hence. But constantly disturbed and dazzled by the great chances that seem to lie waiting over there, I am restless—and this mark of confidence in my old comrade is the very first form my restlessness has shaped out for itself.

I parted with the bidder thus:— "I cannot go now, I don't know that I ever *can* go, and therefore terms are not in question. But if I can ever make up my mind to go, I will certainly communicate with your Melbourne House." (He opened the business with me by producing a letter of credit for £10,000.)

Write me a word when you get your breath again.

> Startlingly always
> THE INIMITABLE

1 CD wrote to Forster on 28 June: 'A man from Australia is in London ready to pay £10,000 for eight months there.' This was Felix Spiers, of Spiers & Pond, caterers and orginal leaseholders of the Theatre Royal Café, Melbourne. In 1861 they brought out the first English cricket team to Australia.

To Clarkson Stanfield, 18 DECEMBER 1862

Paris, rue du Faubourg St. Honoré, 27 | Thursday Eighteenth December, 1862

My Dear Stanny.

I cannot tell you what concern your letter has given me, or how distressed I am by your describing yourself as suffering so much pain. Since I have been wandering about, I have always had the idea—founded, I imagine, on some vague purpose you had when you were at Gad's Hill—that you too were travelling in search of picturesque things. And now I am amazed to be told under your own hand (very plain and steady it looks though, mind you!) that you have been ill three mortal months.[1] Poor dear fellow!

Your letter—sent on here—crossed me. I was telegraphed to England, most unexpectedly, to do what service I could in aid of a friend who sorely needed help at his right hand.[2] The moment I had done what I could—and the business hurried me here and there, in a quite distracting manner—I came back here, where Mary and Georgina had been left behind, and were anxiously expecting me. I think Davie[3] must have been mistaken in his impression that I was in London when he spoke of me. It is as likely as not, that he derived it from my signature on the wrapper of the Christmas Number—which signature is a lithograph, several years old.

But we are coming back to Gad's Hill for Christmas, and on the Monday after Christmas Day, please God, I will come to town and to the Green Hill[4] to see you. About mid-day I will come, as the time most likely to be the best. Towards the middle of January I am going to read gratuitously, at our Embassy here, for a Charity. But I shall be at home during the whole interval. I arrived here again, only last night.

My dear dear fellow, I hope and pray that you have times of ease, and that the "shade better" of which you tell me in your note has become a bright light better, and that you will soon be—literally—on your legs again—with your "tarry trousers" on them, and all complete. I send you at this good time of the year, as at all times good or bad, my most affectionate and earnest love, and do most earnestly, in the great seasonable name in which we both trust and hope, assure you that I have never for a single day in all these years been otherwise than your affectionate and true friend. If we at all misunderstood one another in a passing time that is gone, it was without a touch of coldness or unkindness on my side. More than one of our friends could testify that to the question "What is the matter between you and Stanny?" I replied, "I don't know; I only know that I love him, just as I always did and always shall."

God bless you, my dear Stanny. There cannot be in this world a heart more affectionately and faithfully yours than this that beats in me.

Your attached old friend,
DICK

---

1 Stanfield suffered ill-health during the last ten years of his life.
2 Dr John Elliotson.
3 David Roberts (1796–1864†), artist. Met CD through Stanfield, and painted scenery for CD's amateur theatricals 1851–2.
4 Stanfield's home, in Hampstead.

To *Frederick Lehmann,*[1] 8 JANUARY [1863]

OFFICE OF ALL THE YEAR ROUND, | Thursday Eighth January 1862

My Dear Lehmann. I am exceedingly obliged to you for your kind letter;—more so than I could easily express. My difficulty is this: I am afraid to keep my boys about London. You see Frank is already here[2] and I am afraid of their spoiling one another. Hence my desire to get Alfred away from home. Advantageous as his name is to him in some respects, I have always a misgiving that, with the ease and resources of home added, and London added too, it may be disadvantageous. If I could get him abroad therefore, I should prefer it much.

He already knows French almost as well as English. His childhood and early schooling were French throughout.

On the whole perhaps I had best not trouble you by bringing him to your offices until we have spoken together; towards which end I will call on you in Nicholas Lane tomorrow between 12 and 1—alone.

> Faithfully Yours always
> CHARLES DICKENS

1 Augustus Frederick Lehmann (1826–91), a businessman from Hamburg and an excellent musician. He married Mrs Wills's niece Nina, and was a close friend of CD, Browning, and Wilkie Collins.
2 Working in the *AYR* office.

To *William Macready,* 19 FEBRUARY 1863

OFFICE OF ALL THE YEAR ROUND, | Thursday Nineteenth February 1863

My Dearest Macready

I have just come back from Paris, where the Readings—Copperfield—Dombey and Trial—and Carol and Trial—have made a sensation which modesty (my natural modesty) renders it impossible for me to describe. You know what a noble audience the Paris audience is! They are at their very noblest with me.

I was very much concerned by hearing hurriedly from Georgy that you were ill. But when I came home at night, she shewed me Katie's letter, and that set me up again. Ah! you have the best of companions and nurses,[1] and can afford to be ill now and then, for the happiness of being so brought through it.—But don't do it again yet awhile, for all that.

Legouvé[2] (whom you remember in Paris as writing for the Ristori[3]) was anxious that I should bring you the enclosed. A manly and generous effort, I think? Regnier desired to be warmly remembered to you. He has been losing money in speculation, but looks just as of yore.

Paris generally is about as wicked and extravagant as in the days of the Regency. Madame Viardot in the Orphée, most splendid. An opera of Faust,[4] a very sad and noble rendering of that sad and noble story. Stage management remarkable for some admirable—and really poetical—effects of light. In the more striking situations, Mephistopheles surrounded by an infernal red atmosphere of his own. Marguerite by a pale blue mournful light. The two never blending. After Marguerite has taken the jewels placed in her way in the garden, a weird evening draws on, and the bloom fades from the flowers, and the leaves of the trees droop and lose their fresh green, and mournful shadows over-hang her chamber-window which was innocently bright and gay at first. I couldn't bear it, and gave in completely.

Fechter[5] doing wonders over the way here, with a picturesque French drama. Miss Kate Terry, in a small part in it, perfectly charming. You may remember her making a noise, years ago, doing a boy at an Inn in the Courier of Lyons? She has a tender love-scene in this piece, which is a really beautiful and artistic thing. I saw her do it at about 3 in the morning of the day when the Theatre opened, surrounded by shavings and carpenters, and (of course) with that inevitable Hammer going; and I told Fechter "that is the very best piece of womanly tenderness I have ever seen on the stage, and you'll find that no Audience can miss it." It is a comfort to add that it was instantly seized upon, and is much talked of.

Stanfield was very very ill for some months; then suddenly picked up, and is really rosy and jovial again. Going to see him when he was very despondent, I told him the story of Fechter's piece (then in rehearsal) with appropriate action: fighting a duel with the washing-stand, defying the bedstead, and saving the life of the sofa-cushion. This so kindled his old theatrical ardor, that I think he turned the corner on the spot.

With love to Mrs. Macready, and Katie, and (be still my heart!) Benvenuta, and the exiled Johnny (not too attentive at school, I hope?) and the personally-unknown young Parr, ever My Dearest Macready

Your most affectionate
CHARLES DICKENS

---

1 Macready's second wife, whom he married in 1860.

2 Ernest Legouvé (1807–1903), French dramatist and essayist, gave CD a copy of his verse pamphlet *Un souvenir de Manin*, 1858, for Macready.

3 Adelaide Ristori (1822–1906), Italian actress, played in Italy until 1855, then throughout Europe.

4 By Gounod.

5 Charles Fechter (1822–79†), actor. Began his career in Paris but moved to England and performed in English from 1860s. CD greatly admired his acting (especially his Hamlet), and they became good friends.

To Thomas Carlyle, 13 APRIL 1863

GAD'S HILL PLACE, | HIGHAM BY ROCHESTER, KENT.
Monday Thirteenth April 1863.

My Dear Carlyle.

I should be very glad if you would come to one of my Readings one night. I think if you would come some evening when I read the Trial from Pickwick, you would find a healthy suggestion of an abuse or two, that sets people thinking in the right direction.

Georgina being all but quite well now, I look for that long-delayed visit from you and Mrs. Carlyle, this coming summer. This is really a pleasant place, and as good a little house to work in—or to do what you like in—as you will find anywhere. I am always reading you faithfully, and trying to go your way.

Affectionately Yours ever
CHARLES DICKENS

To John Forster, [30 MAY 1863]

Here is a curious case at first-hand. On Thursday night in last week, being at the office here, I dreamed that I saw a lady in a red shawl with her back towards me (whom I supposed to be E.)[1] On her turning round I found that I didn't know her, and she said 'I am Miss Napier.' All the time I was dressing next morning, I thought— What a preposterous thing to have so very distinct a dream about nothing! and why Miss Napier? for I never heard of any Miss Napier. That same Friday night, I read. After the reading, came into my retiring-room, Mary Boyle and her brother, and *the* Lady in the red shawl whom they present as 'Miss Napier'! These are all the circumstances, exactly told.

1 Ellen Ternan (Nelly).

To Joseph Ellis,[1] 4 JULY 1863

GAD'S HILL PLACE, | HIGHAM BY ROCHESTER, KENT.
Saturday Fourth July. 1863.

Dear Mr. Ellis

I think it very possible that you may know of something I want to find. And in any case I feel sure that you will not mind my troubling you.

All my boys have been at large schools, from Eton downward. But my youngest boy, now about 12, does not take to a large school. He is a good amiable boy, and sufficiently clever, but, in consequence of having passed his childhood at home among grown people, he finds himself confused and troubled in a great boy-crowd. He entreats me to place him somewhere where there are six or a dozen pupils, and where he could remain when he grew older and more advanced.

It is immensely difficult to find a good and kind Master who confines his attention to a few pupils, and receives them in his own home. Do you happen to know of any such gentleman—a clergyman or otherwise—at Brighton? You know, I have no doubt, what kind of education I seek for my boy;—that I want him to be well taught, but not worn out or over-crammed, and to be trained in the spirit of the Time.

> Faithfully Yours
> CHARLES DICKENS

1 Manager of the Bedford Hotel Brighton, and a leading spirit in the Brighton Literary Society.

To Eliza Davis,[1] 10 JULY 1863

GAD'S HILL PLACE, | HIGHAM BY ROCHESTER, KENT.
Friday Tenth July, 1863.

Dear Madam.

I hope you will excuse this tardy reply to your letter. It is often impossible for me by any means to keep pace with my correspondents.

I must take leave to say that if there be any general feeling on the part of the intelligent Jewish people, that I have done them what you describe as "a great wrong", they are a far less sensible, a far less just, and a far less good tempered, people than I have always supposed them to be. Fagin in Oliver Twist is a Jew, because it unfortunately was true of the time to which that story refers, that that class of criminal almost invariably *was* a Jew. But surely no sensible man or woman of your persuasion can fail to observe—firstly, that all the rest of the wicked dramatis personae are Christians; and secondly, that he is called "The Jew", not because of his religion, but because of his race. If I were to write a story, in which I pursued a Frenchman or a Spaniard as "The Roman Catholic", I should do a very indecent and unjustifiable thing but I make mention of Fagin as the Jew, because he is one of the Jewish people, and because it conveys that kind of idea of him, which I should give my readers of a Chinaman by calling him a Chinese.

The enclosed is quite a nominal subscription towards the good object in which you are interested, but I hope it may serve to shew you that I have no feeling towards the Jewish people but a friendly one. I always speak well of them, whether in public, or in private, and bear my testimony (as I ought to do) to their perfect good faith in such transactions as I have ever had with them. And in my "Child's History of England", I have lost no opportunity of setting forth their cruel persecution in old times.[2] Dear Madam

Faithfully Yours
CHARLES DICKENS

1 Eliza Davis's husband bought the lease of Tavistock House from CD in 1860. Mrs Davis wrote to CD on 22 June asking for a donation for a convalescent home for the Jewish poor, also to accuse him of encouraging, through Fagin, 'a vile prejudice against the despised Hebrew'.
2 In ch. 14 he refers to King John's 'oppressing and torturing of the unhappy Jews'.

To *John Bennet*, 14 SEPTEMBER 1863

GAD'S HILL PLACE, | HIGHAM BY ROCHESTER, KENT
Monday Night, Fourteenth September, 1863

My Dear Sir,
    Since my hall clock[1] was sent to your establishment to be cleaned it has gone (as indeed it always had) perfectly well, but has struck the hours with great reluctance, and after enduring internal agonies of a most distressing nature, it has now ceased striking altogether. Though a happy release for the clock, this is not convenient to the household. If you can send down any confidential person with whom the clock can confer, I think it may have something on its works that it would be glad to make a clean breast of.

Faithfully yours,
[CHARLES DICKENS]

1 Now in the Charles Dickens Museum.

To *Wilkie Collins*, 25 JANUARY 1864

GAD'S HILL PLACE, | HIGHAM BY ROCHESTER, KENT.
Monday Twenty Fifth January 1864.

My Dear Wilkie.
    I am horribly behind hand in answering your welcome letter;[1] but I have been so busy, and have had the house so full for Xmas and the New Year, and have had so much to see to—and to pay for—in getting Frank out to India, that I have not been

able to settle down to a regular long letter.—Which I mean this to be, but which it may not turn out to be, after all.

First, I will answer your enquiries about the Xmas No.[2] and the new book. The Xmas No. has been the greatest success of all; has shot ahead of last year; has sold about 220,000; and has made the name of Mrs. Lirriper so swiftly and domestically famous as never was. I had a very strong belief in her when I wrote about her, finding that she made a great effect upon me; but she certainly has gone beyond my hopes. (Probably you know nothing about her? which is a very unpleasant consideration). Of the new book, I have done the two first Nos, and am now beginning the third.[3] It is a combination of drollery with romance which requires a deal of pains and a perfect throwing away of points that might be amplified; but I hope it is *very good*. I confess, in short, that I think it is. Strange to say I felt at first quite dazed in getting back to the large canvas and the big brushes; and even now, I have a sensation as of acting at the San Carlo[4] after Tavistock House, which I could hardly have supposed would have come upon so old a stager.

You will have read about poor Thackeray's death—sudden, and yet not sudden, for he had long been alarmingly ill. At the solicitation of Mr. Smith and some of his friends, I have done what I would most gladly have excused myself from doing, if I felt I could—written a couple of pages about him in what was his own Magazine.[5]

Therein I have tried—so far as I could, with his mother and children before me—to avoid the fulsome and injudicious trash that has been written about him in the papers, and delicately to suggest the two points in his character as a literary man that were bad for the literary cause. Happily (I suppose) you can have no idea of the vile stuff that has been written: the scribes particularly dwelling on his having been "a gentleman", "a great gentleman", and the like—as if the rest of us were of the tinker tribe; and also on his wonderful gift of putting all people and all companies at their ease; at their perfect repose, enjoyment, and genial ease—which is much as if they should praise me, being dead, for having always lived with my wife. Of course the natural result is, that everybody else begins to disparage the poor fellow, and that people who would have beslavered him living, begin to bespatter him dead.

The Forsters have got into their new house which has instantly taken them both by the throat, chest, and nose, and caused them excruciating torments. Yet it is impossible to persuade Forster (because he has settled it otherwise) that the walls are not wet. I asked him if they were dry, why they were not going to be papered for 12 months? At which he made pensive and abstracted references to totally different subjects. I don't know what it may come out like, when it is papered and carpeted and furnished in apple-pie order; but at present (we dined there the other day) it is something between a government office and a hospital. And *they* look as if they were put in at Six and Sixpence a week to take care of it. It has every blessing in it that can emanate from Cubitt's, and yet I would rather have Leech's house.

We think of taking a place in town next month, and remaining until June. Whether we can get any place for simply enormous terms, is not yet at all clear. Reade[6] was down here for New Year's Day, and is going to furnish two houses in May Fair, for season-letting. But somehow I think I would rather not have him for a landlord. He told Georgina as an illustration of the various kinds of knowledge sifted into Hard Cash, that before beginning it, he had, expressly for the purpose "read five hundred books, and examined forty five witnesses"!

Wills is in his usual force, but his brother seems to have struck into the road down which the poor sister went. George Russell[7] has been down here, to impart frightful conspiracies against the peace of mind of the Garrick. I have joined the gloomy band, and have been duly sworn to Sir Charles-Taylor-extermination.[8] We meet, disguised, in the dead of night, in the Cloisters of Westminster Abbey. Palgrave Simpson I saw at the Athenaeum last Tuesday, with the stuff on his moustache (which smells of Tonquin bean) coming off, and sticking to the paper he was reading. He was very nice, as he always is, and asked for news of you. Charles Ward I saw at Coutts's last Thursday, coming towards me with his back confidentially bent, and a letter from you in his hand. Our charming and capable little cook is going away, because her health is bad. Alfred[9] is doing wonderfully well in the City, and is posted into a very responsible place, over four Senior heads, and will probably go out to China within a year. Beard is made Court Newsman, am truly happy to say (it is worth full four hundred a year), and is going to take the old Guild Chambers to live in, and is delightfully picked up by sunshine. Frank Beard, I fear, does not improve in worldly circumstances, or in a judicious handling of the circumstances that do come in his way. A.Y.R. was rather dropped by Reade, but has remained stationary since he finished. When you come back, in the early vegetable Covent Garden time, the mutton shall be punished and the Rosy drained in the halls of AYR aforesaid.

Concerning the Italian experiment,[10] De la Rue is more hopeful than you. He and his bank are closely leagued with the powers at Turin, and he had long been devoted to Cavour; but he gave me the strongest assurances (with illustrations) of the fusion between place and place, and of the blending of small mutually antagonistic characters, into one national character, progressing cheeringly and certainly. Of course there must be discouragements and discrepancies in the first struggles of a country previously so degraded and enslaved. And the time, as yet, has been very very short.

I should like to have a day with you at the Coliseum, and on the Appian Way, and among the tombs, and with the Orvieto.[11] But Rome and I are wide asunder, physically, as well as morally. I should like to see the Butler[12] contemplating the gory horrors on the walls of St. Stefano Rotondo, and also the models on the steps of the Trinita del Monte. I wonder whether the dramatic stable where we saw the Marionetti[13] still receives the Roman public. And Lord! when I think of you in that hotel, how I think of poor dear Egg in the long front drawing room giving on the Piazza, posting up that wonderful necromantic volume which we never shall see opened!

The Shakespeare Committee[14] (of which I am ashamed, and which I have never attended) is tumbling to pieces. The best thing it could possibly do. The original author of The Ticket of Leave Man,[15] accompanied by Theodore Martin and Shirley Brooks Esquires, has retired on defeat of a motion for "an endowed Shakespeare

Theatre". Of which, conceive the hideous dreariness! I wonder whether its wicked, not to take to the notion of penal servitude to Shakespeare for life. If the love of the wretch who cannot take to this, be conveyable, without contamination to the Butler, please present it. Likewise, kind remembrances to the Missis, from the Venerable Grand Parient—who has no room for my signature

Ever my Dear Wilkie | Affecy. Yours

CD.

1 From Rome.
2 'Mrs. Lirriper's Lodgings'.
3 *OMF* began monthly publication on 30 Apr. CD's two previous novels had been published in weekly instalments.
4 The grand theatre in Naples.
5 'In Memoriam', *Cornhill Magazine*, Feb. 1864.
6 Charles Reade (1814–84†), novelist and playwright. Fellow of Magdalen College, Oxford, from 1835, a stalwart of the Garrick Club, and great admirer of CD. His novel *Hard Cash* (1863) is about mental hospitals.
7 George Russell (1828–98), barrister and recorder of Wokingham; friendly with CD from early 1860s.
8 Sir Charles Taylor, the manager of the Garrick Club.
9 CD's fourth son, emigrated to Australia 1865.
10 The unification of Italy into one nation.
11 Italian white wine.
12 CD's nickname for Caroline Graves's daughter Harriet.
13 See above, 17–20 Nov. 1853.
14 National Shakespeare Committee formed to celebrate the tercentenary of Shakespeare's birth (Apr. 1864). CD, Tennyson, and Bulwer Lyttton were among the vice presidents.
15 Tom Taylor (1817–80†), playwright and comic writer.

To Angela Burdett Coutts, 12 FEBRUARY 1864

57 Gloucester Place, Hyde Park Gardens | Friday Twelfth February 1864

My Dear Miss Coutts.

I have taken this house until June, to be in town when my book is preparing and begins to come out.

I cannot tell you my Dearest Friend—and I know I need not—with what feelings I received your affectionate letter this morning, or how dearly I prize it. Let me give you briefly, the circumstances of poor Walter's death.

He had always been in debt, poor boy, and I never could make out how, except that I suppose the Regiment to have been ill looked after by the Colonel. When Charley was in India the two brothers were together for a fortnight, and Charley paid, as he supposed, everything. Yet before he got back to England, there was more to pay. This led in course of time to Walter's writing to me to say that his difficulties had led to his being placed low on the list for a Company (though he had never failed in exactness in his duty on any occasion), and that he had put his name down for home service. I wrote to him urging the folly of that proceeding and its reduction of his Income, and pointed out to him that although I was very sorry, I was not angry, and that he must now, as a matter of common reason and justice to his other brothers, live upon his own means. Thereupon he wrote to Mary, saying that he had made up his mind to write home no more, "until he was out of debt". So nothing was heard of him for many months. Mary then got—this last Autumn—a short note from him to the effect that he was not well, and would presently write again. Then, about the turn of Christmas, she had another short note from him to say that he had not said how ill he was when he last wrote, for fear of alarming us, but that he had been very ill indeed, and was now packing up to go to Calcutta to be certified by a medical board there, and sent home on sick leave. He said he was "so weak that he could hardly crawl," but otherwise was much better; and he was in joyful expectation of seeing Gad's Hill again. He arrived at Calcutta, from the Station where his regiment was, on the 27th. of December. He was consigned by the Regimental Doctor to the Officers' Hospital there, which is a very fine place. On the last day of the old year at a quarter past 5 in the afternoon he was talking to the other patients about his arrangements for coming home, when he became excited, coughed violently, had a great gush of blood from the mouth, and fell dead;—all this, in a few seconds. It was then found that there was extensive and perfectly incurable aneurism of the Aorta, which had burst. I could have wished it had pleased God to let him see his home again; but I think he would have died at the door.

The immediate cause of his death, his sisters and Charley and I, keep to ourselves; both because his Aunt has the same disorder, and because we observe strong traces of it in one of his brothers. Another of his brothers, Frank, I sent out to Calcutta on the 20th. of December. He would hear of his brother's death, on touching the shore.

Do not think me unimpressed by certain words in your letter concerning forgiveness and tenderness when I say that I do not claim to have any thing to forgive—that if I had, I hope and believe I would forgive freely—but that a page in my life which once had writing on it, has become absolutely blank, and that it is not in my power to pretend that it has a solitary word upon it.

I am beyond measure interested beforehand, by what you are to tell me.' Pray write it as soon as you can. Do not suppose, that I am unfit to pursue it. I am at work, though in a rather dull slow way for the moment.

On the last night of the old Year I was acting charades with all the children. I had made something to carry, as the Goddess of Discord; and it came into my head as it stood against the wall while I was dressing, that it was like the dismal things that are carried at Funerals. I took a pair of scissors and cut away a quantity of black calico that was upon it, to remove this likeness. But while I was using it, I noticed that its *shadow* on the wall still had that resemblance, though the thing itself had not. And when I went to bed, it was in my bedroom, and still looked so like, that I took it to pieces before I went to sleep. All this would have been exactly the same, if poor Walter had not died that night. And examining my own mind closely, since I received the news, I recall that at Thackeray's funeral I had sat looking at that very object of which I was reminded. See how easily a marvellours story may be made.

I enclose a line for Mrs. Brown, and am Ever My Dear friend

Your affectionate and grateful
CHARLES DICKENS

---

1 Presumably her campaign for extending national education to villages, begun by her in Devon.

To Marcus Stone,[1] 23 FEBRUARY 1864

57 Glo'ster Place, Hyde Park Gardens | Tuesday Twenty Third February 1864

My Dear Marcus

I think the design for the cover, *excellent,* and do not doubt its coming out to perfection. The slight alteration I am going to suggest, originates in a business consideration not to be overlooked.

The word "Our" in the title, must be out in the open, like Mutual Friend; making the Title three distinct long lines—"Our" as big as "Mutual Friend". This will give you too much design at the bottom. I would therefore take out the Dustman, and put the Wegg and Boffin composition (which is capital), in its place. I don't want Mr. Inspector or the Murder Reward bill, because those points are sufficiently indicated in the River at the top. Therefore you can have an indication of the Dustman, in Mr. Inspector's place. Note, that the Dustman's face should be droll, and not horrible. Twemlow's elbow will still go out of the frame as it does now, and the same with Lizzie's skirts on the opposite side. With these changes, work away!

I have done the St. Andrew Street place,[2] and have made it the last Chapter of the 2nd. No.[3] I will send you a proof when I get it. It is very like, with an imaginary man and an imaginary place in the story.

Affecy always
CD.

---

1 Marcus Stone (1840–1921), son of CD's friend Frank Stone. CD had employed him as an illustrator for the Library edition of his works; he was now illustrating *OMF*.

2 Mr Venus's shop.

3 Bk. 1, ch. 7.

To a Chimney-Sweep, 15 MARCH 1864

GAD'S HILL PLACE, HIGHAM BY ROCHESTER, KENT.
15th March 1864

Dear Sir,

Since you last swept my study chimney it has developed some peculiar eccentricities. Smoke has indeed proceeded from the cowl that surmounts it, but it has seemingly been undergoing internal agonies of a most distressing nature, and pours forth disastrous volumes of swarthy vapour into the apartment wherein I habitually labour. Although a comforting relief probably to the chimney, this is not altogether convenient to me. If you can send a confidential sub-sweep, with whom the chimney can engage in social intercourse, it might be induced to disclose the cause of the departure from its normal functions.

Faithfully yours
[CHARLES DICKENS]

To Michael Bass,[1] [?EARLY MAY 1864]

Sir,

Your undersigned correspondents are desirous to offer you their hearty thanks for your introduction into the House of Commons of a Bill for the Suppression of Street Music; and they beg to assure you that, in the various ways open to them, they will, out of Parliament, do their utmost to support you in your endeavour to abolish that intolerable nuisance.

Your correspondents are, all, professors and practitioners of one or other of the arts or sciences. In their devotion to their pursuits—tending to the peace and comfort of mankind—they are daily interrupted, harassed, worried, wearied, driven nearly mad, by street musicians. They are even made especial objects of persecution by brazen performers on brazen instruments, beaters of drums, grinders of organs, bangers of banjos, clashers of cymbals, worriers of fiddles, and bellowers of ballads; for, no sooner does it become known to those producers of horrible sounds that any of your correspondents have particular need of quiet in their own houses, than the said houses are beleaguered by discordant hosts seeking to be bought off.

Your correspondents represent to you that these pecuniary speculations in the misery they endure are far more destructive to their spirits than their pockets; and that some of them, not absolutely tied to London by their avocations, have actually fled into the country for refuge from this unmerited persecution—which is none the less grievous or hard to bear, because it is absurd.

Your grateful correspondents take the liberty to suggest to you that, although a Parliamentary debate undoubtedly requires great delicacy in the handling, their avocations require at least as much, and that it would highly conduce towards the success of your proposed enactments, if you prevail on its opponents to consent to state their objections to it, assailed on all sides by the frightful noises in despite of which your correspondents have to gain their bread.

CHARLES DICKENS[2]

1 Michael Bass (1799–1884†), brewer, philanthropist, and Liberal MP for Derby.
2 The twenty-seven other signatories included Tennyson, Millais, Carlyle, and Collins. The Street Music (Metropolis) Bill received the Royal Assent on 25 July.

To *Marcus Stone*, 5 MAY 1864

57 Glo'ster Place | Thursday Night Fifth May 1864

My Dear Marcus.
The lady on the sands,[1] to be got up, as to her being un peu passée; but still to be well-looking—engaging looking when she chooses.
Mrs. Boffin, as I judge of her from the sketch, very good indeed. I want Boffins oddity, without being at all blinked,[2] to be an oddity of a very honest kind, that people will like.

Faithfully ever
CD.

1 Mrs Alfred Lammle; 'The Happy Pair', *OMF*, bk. 1, ch. 10.
2 Evaded.

To *The Editors of* The Gad's Hill Gazette,[1] [EARLY AUGUST 1864]

Gentlemen,
Ingratitude being one of the worst vices of the human heart, it is with considerable pain I notice that it is stalking rampant in the hearts of so many of your subscribers.
In a spirited leader in your last issue you have justly rebuked the grumblers who have ventured to find fault with the admirable type in which The Gad's Hill Gazette is ever printed. Permit me, however, to say that it is unwise to offer to return the money of those sordid grumblers who would cavil at the caligraphy of your admirable journal. If they do not like it they can leave it alone. For myself, I honestly confess that its perusal over my Saturday morning meal affords me intense gratification. There is a terseness and vigour in its leaders

perfectly marvellous, while the news that it contains is always of the lightest and most healthy description, serving to counteract the injurious effects of a heavy breakfast.

The editor of a public journal is a public man, and consequently becomes public property. He is pleased to bask in the sunshine of a people's applause, and must face the winter of their discontent[2] when it bursts around him. But be not discouraged. You at least have the satisfaction of knowing that your efforts are appreciated by the intelligent, and as for the others—why—having secured their money, you can afford to dispense with their patronage.

WELL WISHER.

1 A news-sheet issued by the four Dickens boys at home in the holidays, between 1862 and 1866. Originally handwritten, then printed on a small press given to them by Wills. Issued at 2*d.* for 4 pages, it had over 100 subscribers, mainly CD's friends.
2 Cf. *Richard III*, I. i.1.

To Marcus Stone, 29 SEPTEMBER 1864

GAD'S HILL PLACE, | HIGHAM BY ROCHESTER, KENT
Thursday Twenty Ninth September 1864

My Dear Marcus. This is the kind of man.[1] The Doll's dressmaker is immensely better than she was. I think she should now come extremely well. A weird sharpness not without beauty, is the thing I want.

Affecy. always
CD.

1 Fascination Fledgeby or Riah, as they come onto the roof to find Lizzie and Jenny Wren, *OMF* bk. 2, ch. 5.

To Christopher Cay,[1] 7 NOVEMBER 1864

GAD'S HILL PLACE, | HIGHAM BY ROCHESTER, KENT.
Monday Seventh November 1864

Dear Sir

Mrs. Cay having mentioned to my sister in law that you would be glad to compare notes with me on likely means of ensuring audibility in reading to a congregation, I very readily offer you a few slight words of suggestion out of my own practice and experience.

The main point is difficult to express, and will have, I am sensible, a very odd appearance on this paper.—If you could form a habit of finding your voice, *lower down*—in other words, of reading more from the chest and less from the throat—you would find yourself immensely relieved, and your voice greatly strengthened. When you experience any little distress or difficulty now, I think it is in the throat; and I think that is, because the strain is in the wrong place. If you make the trial, reading aloud alone, of placing your hand on your chest, and trying as it were to originate your voice behind the hand, you will probably soon find a capacity in it almost new to you, while the ease of speaking will be correspondingly increased.

I should have supposed your perfectly unaffected reading of the Lessons to be generally audible throughout the Church. If it be not so, it may pretty surely be made so, by addressing the last persons in the building and by being always watchful and careful not to drop the voice towards the close of a sentence or a verse, but rather to sustain and prolong the distinctness of the concluding words. Always supposing the words to be well separated and never run into one another, I believe that a very moderate voice, observing this method, may be heard with ease and pleasure in a large place, when a very powerful voice, neglecting it, might be quite ineffective. The habit of reading *down-hill,*—or dropping the voice as the sentence proceeds,—is so extremely common, that perhaps even if Mrs. Cay were to happen to read a few pages to you by the fireside, you would detect yourself asking what this or that lost word towards the close of a sentence was. Imagine how fatal the fault must be to distinctness, when there are listeners at various removed distances.

I should be even more diffident than I am in offering these simple hints, if I had not habitually acted on them, with the result that I am said to be always heard.

To be of the least service to you would be a real gratification to me. With which sincere assurance I am Dear Sir

Faithfully Yours
CHARLES DICKENS

1 Revd Christopher Cay, curate in charge of St John's Church, Higham, which CD attended.

To Eneas Sweetland Dallas,[1] 12 NOVEMBER 1864

OFFICE OF ALL THE YEAR ROUND,
Saturday Evening Twelfth November 1864

My Dear Dallas.
I have taken my people into council on the subject of poor dear Leech,[2] but quite in vain. We agree that there is really nothing to tell but what is quite of private and familiar life. All our near intercourse of many years in the confidence of Autumn holidays by the sea, resolve themselves into this phase. All the little jokes we humoured, and exaggerated, originated in things quite apart from the public and

the key to which would be wanting. A little incident specially like one class of his drawings, is the only exception—for that reason solely—that I can call to mind. He was very fond of a boy of mine³ (an extraordinarily small boy) of a great spirit, who is a Midshipman in the Queen's Navy; and whenever this boy came home from a Cruise, he and Leech, and never anybody else, used to go out in great state, and dine at the Garrick, and go to the play, and finish in an exemplary way with kidneys and harmony. On the first of these occasions the officer came out so frightfully small, that Leech told us afterwards he was filled with horror when he saw him eating his dinner at the Garrick with a large knife. On the other hand he felt that to suggest a small knife to an officer and a gentleman would be an unpardonable affront. So after meditating for some time, he felt that his course was, to object to the Club-knives as enormous and gigantic—to remonstrate with the servant on their huge proportions—and with a grim dissatisfaction to demand small ones. After which, he and the officer messed with great satisfaction, and agreed that things in general were running too large in England.

Ever Yours
CHARLES DICKENS

If this note be a little behind its time, my occupation of "making up" the Xmas No. is the plea in excuse. For the same reason I cannot write plainly, and can hardly write at all.

1 Eneas Sweetland Dallas (1828–79†), writer and critic, on the staff of *The Times* for many years. CD was so pleased by Dallas's review of *OMF* in *The Times* (29 Nov. 1865) that he gave him the manuscript of the novel.
2 Leech died 29 Oct. Dallas was writing his obituary in the *Cornhill.*
3 Sydney.

*To Samuel Hole,*¹ 20 DECEMBER 1864

GAD'S HILL | HIGHAM BY ROCHESTER, KENT | Tuesday, December 20, 1864

My Dear Sir,
I am very much interested in your letter, for the love of our departed friend, for the promise it holds out of a good record of his life and work, and for the remembrance of a very pathetic voice, which I heard at his grave.
There is not in my possession one single note of his writing. A year or two ago, shocked by the misuse of the private letters of public men, which I constantly observed, I destroyed a very large and very rare mass of correspondence. It was not done without pain, you may believe, but, the first reluctance conquered, I have steadily abided by my determination to keep no letters by me, and to consign all such papers to the fire. I therefore fear that I can render you no help at all. All that I could

tell you of Leech you know, even (probably) to the circumstance that for several years we always went to the seaside together in the autumn, and lived, through the autumn months, in constant daily association.

Your reference to my books is truly gratifying to me, and I hope this sad occasion may be the means of bringing us into personal relations, which may not lessen your pleasure in them.

Believe me, dear sir, very faithfully yours,
CHARLES DICKENS

1 Revd Samuel Hole (1819–1904†), dean of Rochester and horticulturalist. A close friend of Leech, he was collecting material for a biography of him. He took the funeral service for Leech and read the prayers at his graveside.

To *Ralph Bernal Osborne*,[1] 20 MAY 1865

16 Somers Place | Saturday Twentieth May 1865

Dear Bernal Osborne

My name is not set to the petition in favor of Locke's bill,[2] because I never petition if I can possibly help it.

On principle I am for free-trade in popular amusements, and in practice I believe that the conversion of the Musical Halls into Theatres would do a great deal of good. It would take the Theatrical "trade" out of a few hands, would give increased employment and gains to a great number of struggling people, and would bring into a wholesome competition with ill-conducted Theatres that have gradually brought themselves down some enterprising men with capital at their disposal, and a good knowledge of the public. The sure consequence of a great success of a theatrical kind on the part of one of these, would be the want of more room in front for the accomodation of the audience; and the sure tendency of that would be, the removal of the tables on which the eatables and drinkables are set, and the substitution of more seats. Why the eating and drinking, however, should be supposed to be so objectionable, I cannot imagine. In these places at present there is the most rigid enforcement of order, without any distinction of class. I am always looking about, and have never seen drunkenness in a Music-Hall. As to loose women, I know no means of keeping them out of chapels, if they choose to go there. It is quite a mistake to suppose (as some of your fellow M.P.s do) that they are invited to Music Halls or placed on the Free List there. No such thing. If they go there, they must conduct themselves like the rest of the Audience; and you will see as many men with their wives and daughters at a Music Hall—at least as many—as in the most bumptiously virtuous assembly going.

I observe in society that the Argyll rooms in Windmill Street Haymarket, is legislatively supposed to be a Music Hall. It is nothing of the sort, and was expressly established as a kind of resort that *must* exist somewhere in a great city.

The managers don't want to be stirred up in their activity and stirred down in their prices, and that is the whole secret of their opposition. Moreover they have been complaining, as against the Music Halls, for a long time, that they, the managers, can't get singing chambermaids and the like, because the Music Halls take them away—that is to say, give them better pay and more durable engagements. I know of many such small people who are supporting relations and friends out of number by being respectably engaged and respectably paid at Music Halls.

The Britannia at Hoxton is an immense Theatre, beautifully constructed, having immense audiences all through the year, the great body composed of the very commonest people. I have seen the gradual transformation of that place from a "Saloon" to a fine Theatre. That the character of the entertainments has risen as the transformation has progressed, I know beyond all doubt.

> Faithfully yours
> CHARLES DICKENS

1 Ralph Bernal Osborne (1808–82†), Liberal politician, supporter of free trade; a forceful and witty speaker.
2 The Theatres and Music Hall Bill proposed that music halls be empowered to perform, at the least, 'burlettas, interludes, and melodramas', and to have the same right as licensed theatres to sell wine and beer.

To John Forster, [?END MAY 1865]

Work and worry, without exercise, would soon make an end of me. If I were not going away now, I should break down. No one knows as I know to-day how near to it I have been.

To Frank Beard, 10 JUNE 1865

OFFICE OF ALL THE YEAR ROUND, | Saturday Tenth June 1865

My Dear Frank Beard

I was in the terrible accident yesterday,[1] and worked some hours among the dying and dead.

I was in the carriage that did not go down, but hung in the air over the side of the broken bridge. I was not touched—scarcely shaken. But the terrific nature of the scene makes me think that I should be the better for a gentle composing draught or two.

I must away to Gad's directly to quiet their minds. John[2] would get made and would bring down, any prescription you might let him have here. Don't come down to Gad's, yourself, unless you can stay all night and be comfortable. In that case, do.

Ever Yours
CD.

(I can't sign my flourish to day!)[3]

1 This letter to his doctor was among the first that CD wrote after the Staplehurst railway accident. CD was returning from France with Nelly Ternan and her mother on the tidal express from Folkestone. The foreman of the platelayers repairing the track checked the wrong timetable for the express, and rails on the bridge over the river Beult had been temporarily removed. Ten people were killed and fourteen badly injured. Nelly suffered injuries to her arm and shoulder.
2 John Thompson, CD's manservant.
3 He did a flourish under his initials, but a shaky one.

To Catherine Dickens, 11 JUNE 1865

GAD'S HILL PLACE, | HIGHAM BY ROCHESTER, KENT.
Sunday Eleventh June 1865

Dear Catherine

I thank you for your letter.

I was in the carriage that did not go over the bridge, but which caught on one side and hung suspended over the ruined parapet. I am shaken, but not by that shock. Two or three hours work afterwards among the dead and dying surrounded by terrific sights, render my hand unsteady.

Affectionately
CHARLES DICKENS

To The Head Station Master, Charing Cross, 12 JUNE 1865

GAD'S HILL PLACE, | HIGHAM BY ROCHESTER, KENT.
Monday Twelfth June 1865

Dear Sir

A lady who was in the carriage with me in the terrible accident on Friday, lost, in the struggle of being got out of the carriage, a gold watch-chain with a smaller gold watch chain attached, a bundle of charms, a gold watch-key, and a gold seal engraved "Ellen".

I promised the lady to make her loss known at headquarters, in case these trinkets should be found. Will you have the kindness to note this application.

The carriage was the first class carriage which was dragged aslant, but did not go over, being caught upon the turn. The Engine broke from it before, and the rest of the train broke from it behind and went down into the stream below.

I mention these particulars to make the lady's case plain. I would have spoken to you instead of writing, but that I am shaken;—not by the beating of the carriage, but by the work afterwards of getting out the dying and dead.

Faithfully Yours
CHARLES DICKENS

To *Thomas Mitton*, 13 JUNE 1865

GAD'S HILL PLACE, | HIGHAM BY ROCHESTER, KENT.
Tuesday, Thirteenth June 1865

My Dear Mitton. I should have written to you yesterday or the day before, if I had been quite up to writing. I am a *little* shaken, not by the beating and dragging of the carriage in which I was, but by the hard work afterwards in getting out the dying and dead, which was most horrible.

I was in the only carriage that did not go over into the stream. It was caught upon the turn by some of the ruin of the bridge, and hung suspended and balanced in an apparently impossible manner. Two ladies were my fellow passengers; an old one, and a young one. This is exactly what passed:—you may judge from it the precise length of the suspense. Suddenly we were off the rail and beating the ground as the car of a half emptied balloon might. The old lady cried out "My God!" and the young one screamed. I caught hold of them both (the old lady sat opposite, and the young one on my left), and said: "We can't help ourselves, but we can be quiet and composed. Pray don't cry out." The old lady immediately answered, "Thank you. Rely upon me. Upon my soul, I will be quiet." The young lady said in a frantic way, "Let us join hands and die friends." We were then all tilted down together in a corner of the carriage, and stopped. I said to them thereupon: "You may be sure nothing worse can happen. Our danger *must* be over. Will you remain here without stirring, while I get out of the window?" They both answered quite collectedly, "Yes," and I got out without the least notion what had happened. Fortunately I got out with great caution and stood upon the step. Looking down, I saw the bridge gone and nothing below me but the line of rail. Some people in the two other compartments were madly trying to plunge out at window, and had no idea that there was an open swampy field 15 feet down below them and nothing else! The two guards (one with his face cut) were running up and down on the down side of the bridge (which was not torn up) quite wildly. I called out to them "Look at me. Do stop an instant and look at me, and tell me whether you don't know me." One of them answered "We know you very well, Mr. Dickens." "Then," I said, "my good fellow for God's sake give me your key, and send one of those labourers here, and I'll empty this carriage."—We did it quite safely, by means of a plank or two and when it was done I saw all the rest of the train except the two baggage cars down in the stream. I got into the carriage again for my brandy flask, took off my travelling hat for a basin, climbed down the brickwork, and filled my hat with water. Suddenly I came upon a staggering man covered with blood (I think he must have been flung clean out of his carriage) with such a frightful cut across the skull that I couldn't bear to look at him. I poured some water over his face, and gave him some to drink, and gave him some brandy, and laid him down on the grass, and he said "I am gone" and died afterwards. Then I stumbled over a lady lying on her back against a little pollard tree, with the blood streaming over her face (which was lead color) in a number of distinct little streams from the head. I asked her if she could swallow a little brandy, and she just nodded, and I gave her some and left her for somebody else. The next time I passed her, she was dead. Then a man examined at the Inquest yesterday (who evidently had not the least remembrance of what really passed) came running up to me and implored me to help him find his wife, who was afterwards found dead. No imagination can conceive the ruin of the carriages, or the extraordinary weights under which the people were lying, or the complications into which they were twisted up among iron and wood, and mud and water.

I don't want to be examined at the Inquest, and I don't want to write about it. It could do no good either way, and I could only seem to speak about myself, which, of course I would rather not do. I am keeping very quiet here. I have a—I don't know what to call it—constitutional (I suppose) presence of mind, and was not in the least fluttered at the time. I instantly remembered that I had the MS. of a No.[1] with me, and clambered back into the carriage for it. But in writing these scanty words of recollection I feel the shake and am obliged to stop.

Ever faithfully,
C.D.

1 *OMF* No. 16 (bk. 4, chs. 1–4) for Aug. 1865.

To John Thompson, 25 JUNE 1865

Gad's Hill Place | 25th June 1865

Dr. John,

Take Miss Ellen tomorrow morning, a little basket of fresh fruit, a jar of clotted cream from Tuckers,[1] and a chicken, a pair of pigeons, or some nice little bird. Also on Wednesday morning, and on Friday morning, take her some other things of the same sort—making a little variety each day.

1 William Tucker & Sons, 'poulterers and dealers in game . . . and Devonshire clotted cream', 287 Strand.

To John Forster, [EARLY JULY 1865]

Fancy! fancy my having under-written number sixteen by two and a half pages—a thing I have not done since Pickwick!

To Marcus Stone, 29 AUGUST 1865

GAD'S HILL PLACE, | HIGHAM BY ROCHESTER, KENT
Tuesday Twenty Ninth August 1865

My Dear Marcus.

By this same post I return you the sketches for No. 18,[1] with the Lettering attached.

I think the Frontispiece to the Second Volume should be the Dustyard with the three mounds, and Mr. Boffin digging up the Dutch Bottle, and Venus restraining Wegg's ardor to get at him. Or Mr. Boffin might be coming down with the bottle, and Venus might be dragging Wegg out of the way, as described.

I hope to send you the complete proofs of Nos. 19 and 20[2] next week. There will be 3 other illustrations to choose from them, you know.

Affecy.
CD.

1 *OMF* bk. 4, chs. 8–11.
2 The final double No.

To John Brackenbury,[1] 18 SEPTEMBER 1865

GAD'S HILL PLACE, | HIGHAM BY ROCHESTER, KENT
Monday Eighteenth September 1865

My Dear Sir

Before returning to school just now, Harry spoke to me and told me that he did not wish to enter the Indian Civil Service. I told him in reply that many of us have many duties to discharge in life which we do not wish to undertake, and that we must do the best we can to earn our respective livings and make our way. I also clearly pointed out to him that I bear as heavy a train as can well be attached to any one working man, and that I could by no means afford to send a son to College who went there for any other purpose than to work hard, and to gain distinction. So we came to this point:—that I would write to you, and beg you, between this and Christmas, to tell me whether you believe that he really will be worth sending to Cambridge, and really has the qualities and habits essential to marked success there. And that if you should be of this opinion, he should study accordingly. And that if you should not be of this opinion, he should decidedly go up for the Indian Civil Service Examination.

Will you kindly, at your leisure and convenience, give me the result of your observation of him, before the next holiday time? I fear his name is too notorious to help him, unless he can very strongly help himself;—I mean that in competing in a great race, he would have to justify some higher expectation than would attach to the son of a private gentleman, or would virtually fail, and had far better be out of the lists.

Believe me always My Dear Sir | Faithfully Yours
CHARLES DICKENS

1 Revd John Brackenbury, Headmaster of Wimbledon School, which trained boys for Indian cadetships and the British Army artillery and engineers. Henry was 16 at this time. He became a successful lawyer.

To Percy Fitzgerald,[1] 23 SEPTEMBER 1865

OFFICE OF ALL THE YEAR ROUND, | Saturday Twenty Third September [1865]

My Dear FitzGerald

I cannot thank you too much for Sultan.[2] He is a noble fellow, has fallen into the ways of the family with a grace and dignity that denote the gentleman, and came down to the Railway a day or two since to welcome me home (it was our first meeting) with a profound absence of interest in my individual opinion of him which captivated me completely. I am going home to day to take him about the country, and improve his acquaintance. You will find a perfect understanding between us, I hope, when you next come to Gad's Hill. (He has only swallowed Bouncer[3] once, and temporarily.)

Your hint that you were getting on with your story and liked it, was more than golden intelligence to me in foreign parts. The intensity of the heat, both in Paris and in the Provinces, was such that I found nothing else so refreshing in the course of my rambles.

I hope you have not forgotten the Mimmery[4] at South Mims, and that when you next find yourself as near it as London, you will come to Gad's Hill instead.

With many more thanks for the Dog than any sheet of paper could hold.

Believe me ever | Very faithfully Yours
[CHARLES DICKENS]

1 Percy Fitzgerald (1831–1925), Irish novelist, and prolific contributor to *HW*. First president of the Dickens Fellowship.
2 Described by his donor as 'a magnificent Spanish mastiff', by the Pilgrim editors as 'an Irish bloodhound', and by CD as 'a splendid dog, as big as an average lioness' (4 Sept. 1866); CD grew particularly fond of him.
3 Mamie's white Pomeranian.
4 According to Fitzgerald, CD's joke-name for the home of the poet laureate, Alfred Austin.

To *Frederick Lehmann*,[1] 7 NOVEMBER 1865

OFFICE OF ALL THE YEAR ROUND, | Tuesday Seventh November 1865

My Dear Lehmann
    The recipe for one dog's allowance, is this:

    2 pints oatmeal
    1 pint Barley Meal
    1 pound Mangel Wurzel

boiled together, and then mixed with pot-liquor, which is poured over it. If there be no pot liquor in the house, a sheep's head will make it very well. Any bones that happen to be about, may be put into the mixture, for the exercise of the dog's teeth. Its effect upon the body and spirits of the creature is quite surprising. I have my dogs fed, once a day, always at the same hour.
    I am sorry to say that I cannot take my pleasure tomorrow, having to "make up" the Xmas No. with the printer. Always a tough job.

Ever Yours
CHARLES DICKENS

1 Lehmann had just given CD a Newfoundland dog, sent from America.

To *Edward Bulwer Lytton*, [?28 NOVEMBER 1865]

I cannot tell you, how highly I prize your letter,[1] or with what pride and pleasure it inspires me. Nor do I for a moment question its criticism (if objection so generous and easy may be called by that hard name) otherwise than on this ground—that I work slowly and with great care, and never give way to my invention recklessly, but constantly restrain it; and that I think it is my infirmity to fancy or perceive relations in things which are not apparent generally. Also, I have such an inexpressible enjoyment of what I see in a droll light, that I dare say I pet it as if it were a spoilt child. This is all I have to offer in arrest of judgment.

1 Clearly praising *OMF*.

To *William de Cerjat*, 30 NOVEMBER 1865

GAD'S HILL PLACE, | HIGHAM BY ROCHESTER, KENT
Thirtieth November, 1865

My Dear Cerjat,

Having achieved my book and my Christmas number, and having shaken myself after two years' work, I send you my annual greeting. How are you? Asthmatic, I know you will reply; but as my poor father (who was asthmatic, too, and the jolliest of men) used philosophically to say, "one must have something wrong, I suppose, and I like to know what it is."

In England we are groaning under the brigandage of the butcher, which is being carried to that height that I think I foresee resistance on the part of the middle-class, and some combination in perspective for abolishing the middleman, whensoever he turns up (which is everywhere) between producer and consumer. The cattle plague is the butcher's stalking-horse, and it is unquestionably worse than it was; but seeing that the great majority of creatures lost or destroyed have been cows, and likewise that the rise in butchers' meat bears no reasonable proportion to the market prices of the beasts, one comes to the conclusion that the public is done. The commission[1] has ended very weakly and ineffectually, as such things in England rather frequently do; and everybody writes to *The Times,*and nobody does anything else.

If the Americans don't embroil us in a war before long it will not be their fault. What with their swagger and bombast, what with their claims for indemnification,[2] what with Ireland and Fenianism,[3] and what with Canada,[4] I have strong apprehensions. With a settled animosity towards the French usurper, I believe him to have always been sound in his desire to divide the States against themselves,[5] and that we were unsound and wrong in "letting I dare not wait upon I would."[6] The Jamaica insurrection[7] is another hopeful piece of business. That platform-sympathy with the black—or the native, or the devil—afar off, and that platform indifference to our own countrymen at enormous odds in the midst of bloodshed and savagery, makes me stark wild. Only the other day, here was a meeting of jawbones of asses at Manchester, to censure the Jamaica Governor for his manner of putting down the insurrection! So we are badgered about New Zealanders[8] and Hottentots,[9] as if they were identical with men in clean shirts at Camberwell, and were to be bound by pen and ink accordingly. So Exeter Hall holds us in mortal submission to missionaries, who (Livingstone[10] always excepted) are perfect nuisances, and leave every place worse than they found it.

Of all the many evidences that are visible of our being ill-governed, no one is so remarkable to me as our ignorance of what is going on under our Government. What will future generations think of that enormous Indian Mutiny being ripened without suspicion, until whole regiments arose and killed their officers? A week ago, red tape, half-bouncing and half pooh-poohing what it bounced at, would have scouted the idea of a Dublin jail not being able to hold a political prisoner.[11] But for the blacks in Jamaica being over-impatient and before their time, the whites might have been exterminated, without a previous hint or suspicion that there was anything amiss. *Laissez aller*, and Britons never, never, never!——

Meantime, if your honour were in London, you would see a great embankment rising high and dry out of the Thames on the Middlesex shore, from Westminster Bridge to Blackfriars.[12] A really fine work, and really getting on. Moreover, a great system of drainage. Another really fine work, and likewise really getting on. Lastly, a muddle of railways in all directions possible and impossible, with no general public scheme, no general public supervision, enormous waste of money, no fix-able responsibility, no accountability but under Lord Campbell's Act.[13] I think of that accident in which I was preserved. Before the most furious and notable train in the four-and-twenty hours, the head of a gang of workmen takes up the rails. That train changes its time every day as the tide changes, and that head workman is not provided by the railway company with any clock or watch! Lord Shaftesbury wrote to me to ask me what I thought of an obligation on railway companies to put strong walls to all bridges and viaducts. I told him, of course, that the force of such a shock would carry away anything that any company could set up, and I added: "Ask the minister what *he* thinks about the votes of the railway interest in the House of Commons, and about his being afraid to lay a finger on it with an eye to his majority."

I seem to be grumbling, but I am in the best of humours. All goes well with me and mine, thank God.

Last night my gardener came upon a man in the garden and fired. The man returned the compliment by kicking him in the groin and causing him great pain. I set off, with a great mastiff-bloodhound I have, in pursuit. Couldn't find the evil-doer, but had the greatest difficulty in preventing the dog from tearing two policemen down. They were coming towards us with professional mystery, and he was in the air on his way to the throat of an eminently respectable constable when I caught him.

My daughter Mary and her aunt Georgina sent kindest regard and remembrance. Katey and her husband are going to try London this winter, but I rather doubt (for they are both delicate) their being able to weather it out.

It has been blowing here tremendously for a fortnight but to-day is like a spring day, and plenty of roses are growing over the labourers' cottages. The *Great Eastern* lies at her moorings beyond the window where I write these words; looks very dull and unpromising. A dark column of smoke from Chatham Dockyard, where the iron shipbuilding is in progress, has a greater significance in it, I fancy.

Believe me, my Dear Cerjat, | Ever Faithfully Yours

[CHARLES DICKENS]

1 A Royal Commission to investigate the cattle plague.
2 For destruction of civilian property during the Civil War by the SS *Alabama* and other Confederate cruisers built in Britain.
3 The Fenian Brotherhood, founded 1858 to win the support of Irish settlers in America for its goal of an Irish Republic.
4 The framework for uniting the British colonies in North America within a federation was being negotiated.
5 In fact Napoleon III had consistently refused to recognize the independence of the Confederate States throughout the War.
6 *Macbeth*, I. vii. 44.
7 Governor Edward Eyre proclaimed martial law and imposed harsh reprisals after an insurrection by ex-slave workers. Initial approval in England of Eyre's prompt action gave way to widespread denunciation of his severity; he was subsequently dismissed. The case divided British intellectuals, with John Stuart Mill, Charles Darwin, and Thomas Huxley demanding Eyre's prosecution, and Carlyle, Ruskin, Tennyson, and CD defending him.
8 The Maori War had broken out in North Island in 1860, largely through resistance to compulsory land sales demanded by the New Zealand government.
9 Derogatory term for indigenous South Africans.
10 David Livingstone (1813–73†), missionary, explorer in Africa, and national hero.
11 The Fenian leader James Stephens had escaped from prison and fled to France.
12 The Victoria Embankment, built 1865–70 under the direction of Joseph Bazalgette.
13 The Act of 1846 which gave representatives of a person killed by the wrongful act or neglect of another the right to bring an action for damages.

To Georgina Hogarth, 9 FEBRUARY 1866

OFFICE OF ALL THE YEAR ROUND, | Friday Ninth February 1866

My Dearest Georgy.

I found your letter here when I came back on Wednesday evening, and was extremely glad to get it.

Frank Beard wrote me word that with such a pulse as I described, an examination of the heart was absolutely necessary, and that I had better make an appointment with him alone for the purpose. This I did. I was not at all disconcerted, for I knew well beforehand that the effect could not possibly be, without that one cause at the bottom of it. There seems to be degeneration of some functions of the heart. It does not contract as it should. So I have got a prescription of iron, quinine and digitalis, to set it a going, and send the blood more quickly through the system. If it should not seem to succeed, on a reasonable trial, I will then propose a consultation with someone else. Of course I am not so foolish as to suppose that all my work can have been achieved without *some* penalty, and I have noticed for some time a decided change in my buoyancy and hopefulness:—in other words, in my usual "tone".

I shall wait to see Beard again on Monday, and shall most probably come down that day. If I should not, I will telegraph after seeing him. Best love to Mamie.

Ever affectionately

CD.

To Jane Brookfield,[1] 20 FEBRUARY 1866

OFFICE OF ALL THE YEAR ROUND, | Tuesday Twentieth February 1866

My Dear Mrs. Brookfield

Having gone through your MS[2] (which I should have done sooner, but that I have not been very well), I write you these few following words about it. Firstly, with a limited reference to its unsuitability to these pages. Secondly, with a more enlarged reference to the merits of the story itself.

If you will take any part of it and cut it up (in fancy) into the small portions into which it would have to be divided here for only a month's supply, you will (I think) at once discover the impossibility of publishing it in weekly parts. The scheme of the chapters, the manner of introducing the people, the progress of the interest, the places in which the principal incidents fall, are all hopelessly against it. It would seem as though the story were never coming, and hardly ever moving. There must be a special design, to overcome that specially trying mode of publication; and I cannot better express the difficulty and labor of it than by asking you to turn over any two weekly Nos. of a Tale of Two Cities, or Great Expectations; or Bulwer's story, or Wilkie Collins's, or Reade's, or "At the Bar",[3] and notice how patiently and expressly the thing has to be planned for presentation in these fragments, and yet for afterwards fusing together as an uninterrupted whole.

Of the story itself, I honestly say that I think highly. The style is particularly easy and agreeable—infinitely above ordinary writing—and sometimes reminds me of Mrs. Inchbald at her best. The characters are remarkably well observed, and with a rare mixture of delicacy and truthfulness. I observe this particularly in the brother and sister, and in Mrs. Neville. But it strikes me that you constantly hurry your narrative (and yet without getting on) *by telling it, in a sort of impetuous breathless way, in your own person when the people should tell it and act it for themselves.* My notion always is, that when I have made the people to play out the play, it is, as it were, their business to do it, and not mine. Then, unless you really have led up to a great situation like Basil's death, you are bound in art to make more of it. Such a scene should form a chapter of itself. Impressed upon the reader's memory, it would go far to make the fortune of the book. Suppose yourself telling that affecting incident in a letter to a friend. Wouldn't you describe how you went through the life and stir of the streets and roads, to the sick-room? Wouldn't you say what kind of room it was, what time of day it was, whether it was sunlight, starlight, or moonlight? Wouldn't you have a strong impression on your mind of how you were received, when you first met the look of the dying man, what strange contrasts were about you and struck you? I don't want you, in a novel, to present *yourself* to tell such things, but I want the things to be there. You make no more of the situation than an index might, or a descriptive playbill might in giving a summary of the Tragedy under representation.

As a mere piece of mechanical workmanship, I think all your chapters should be shorter; that is to say, that they should be subdivided. Also, when you change from narrative to dialogue, or vice versâ you should make the transition more carefully. Also, taking the pains to sit down and recall the principal landmarks in your story, you should then make them far more elaborate and conspicuous than the rest. Even with these changes I do not believe that the story would attract the attention due to it, if it were published even in such monthly portions as the space of Fraser[4] would admit of. Even so brightened, it would not, to the best of my judgment, express itself piecemeal. It seems to me to be so constituted as to require to be read "off the reel." As a book in two volumes, I think it would have good claims to success, and good chances of obtaining success. But I suppose the polishing I have hinted at (not a meretricious adornment, but positively necessary to good work and good art) to have been first thoroughly administered.

Now don't hate me if you can help it.

Ever very faithfully yours
CHARLES DICKENS

The MS shall be delivered at your house tomorrow. And your petitioner again prays not to be &c.

1 Jane Brookfield (1821–96†), literary hostess and writer; she and her husband were close friends of Thackeray's. She published four novels.
2 Of her novel *Only George*, published by Chapman & Hall; she seems to have followed the advice CD gave her here.
3 All of these had appeared in *AYR*; 'At the Bar' was by Charles Collins.
4 *Fraser's Magazine.*

To Robert Browning,[1] 12 MARCH 1866

6, Southwick Place, Hyde Park | Monday, 12th March, 1866

My Dear Browning,

Will you dine here next Sunday at half-past six punctually, instead of with Forster? I am going to read Thirty times, in London and elsewhere, and as I am coming out with "Doctor Marigold", I had written to ask Forster to come on Sunday and hear me sketch him.[2] Forster says (with his own boldness) that he is sure it would not bore you to have that taste of his quality after dinner. I should be delighted if this should prove true. But I give warning that in that case I shall exact a promise from you to come to St. James's Hall one evening in April or May, and hear "David Copperfield", my own particular favourite.

Ever affectionately yours
[CHARLES DICKENS]

1 Robert Browning (1812–89†), poet; Forster was an early supporter of his work and became a good friend. In 1842 CD wrote enthusiastically to Forster about Browning's play *A Blot in the 'Scutcheon*.
2 i.e. Dr Marigold, at a private performance.

To Georgina Hogarth, 19 APRIL 1866

Edinburgh Thursday Nineteenth April | 1866

My Dearest Georgy

Before going over to Glasgow, I write to you—hurriedly, of course.

The house was more than twice better than any first night here previously. There was £90 in it. They were, as usual here, remarkably intelligent, and the Reading went *brilliantly*. I have not sent up any Newspapers, as they are generally so poorly written that you may know beforehand all the commonplaces that they will write. But the Scotsman has so pretty an article this morning, and (so far as I know) so true a one, that I will try to post it to you, either from here or Glasgow. John and Dolby[1] went over early, and Wills and I follow them at half past eleven.[2]

It is cold and wet here. We have laid half crown bets with Dolby that he will be assaulted to night at Glasgow. He has a surprising knowledge of what the receipts will be always, and wins half crowns every night. Chang[3] is living in this house. John (not knowing it) was rendered perfectly drivelling last night by meeting him on the stairs. The Tartar Dwarf[4] is always twining himself up stairs sideways, and drinks a bottle of whiskey per day, and is reported to be a surprising little villain.

I will write a line to Mamie tomorrow. My best love to her.

Ever My Dearest Georgy | Your most affectionate
CD.

1 George Dolby (1831–1900), managed CD's reading tours and went to America with him.
2 Some of the letter is missing.
3 Chang Woo Gow or Tu Sing (1847–95), a Chinese giant then touring the provinces.
4 The Chinese dwarf Chung Mow, frequently exhibited with Chang the giant.

To John Forster, [?25 APRIL 1866]

It was a terrible shock to me, and poor dear Carlyle has been in my mind ever since.[1] How often I have thought of the unfinished novel.[2] No one now to finish it. None of the writing women come near her at all.

1 Jane Carlyle died 21 Apr.
2 Which Jane Carlyle had described to CD at their last meeting, on 2 Apr. It was based on her observation of a house near her home in Chelsea.

To Thomas Carlyle, 30 MAY 1866

6 Southwick Place, Hyde Park W. | Wednesday Thirtieth May 1866

My Dear Carlyle.

I have not written to you from any part of the country where I have lately been employed (and I have been working hard in many parts), for a reason that I instinctively felt you would understand. Even now I touch one hand with mine in the spirit, hardly venturing to press it.

My dear friend my thoughts have been very much with you, for I truly love and honor you. To your great heart and mind, little can come out of mine but sympathy.—That has been with you from the first, and ever will be while I live.

Your truly affectionate friend
CHARLES DICKENS

To Thomas Adolphus Trollope,[1] 2 NOVEMBER 1866

GAD'S HILL PLACE, | HIGHAM BY ROCHESTER, KENT.
Friday Second November, 1866

My Dear Trollope.

I should have written immediately to congratulate you on your then approaching marriage, and to assure you of my most cordial and affectionate interest in all that nearly concerns you, but that I thought it best to wait until I should have seen Nelly and her mother on their return, and should have known from them how best to address you.

No friend that you have can be more truly attached to you than I am. I congratulate you with all my heart, and believe that your marriage will stand high upon the list of happy ones. As to your wife's winning a high reputation out of your house—if you care for that—it is not much, as an addition to the delights of love and peace and a suitable companion for life—I have not the least doubt of her power to make herself famous.

I little thought what an important Master of the Ceremonies I was, when I first presented the late Fanny Ternan to you. Bear me in your mind even as the unconscious instrument of your having given your best affections to a worthy object, and I shall be the best paid Master of the Ceremonies since Nash drove his coach and six through the streets of Bath.

> Faithfully Yours
> CHARLES DICKENS

1 Thomas Adolphus Trollope (1810–92†), historian and prolific writer; elder brother of Anthony Trollope. Married Nelly's sister Fanny as his second wife on 28 Oct.

To George Russell, 19 DECEMBER 1866

GAD'S HILL PLACE, | HIGHAM BY ROCHESTER, KENT.
Wednesday Nineteenth December 1866

My Dear George.

I think this notion far too crude and immature to go before the public yet.

I have no doubt that an enormous quantity of good food is wasted in this town, and that the habit of wasting it—this is an important consideration—engenders a vast amount of pilfering, lying, secret huckstering in petty spoil, and consequent deterioration of character among servants. Also I have no doubt that if such food were well recooked and well re-distributed among poor children, it would soon prove itself to be so much labour-stamina.

But the scale on which it is proposed to try the experiment in the beginning—the place in which it is proposed to try it—the sort of kitchen—the sort of dining Hall—the staff and its wages—the rent to be paid—the cost of the cooking apparatus to be erected—the hours at which meals can be had—all these things must be made subjects of accurate calculation and statement, before the public help can be got to any useful purpose. Then there would be the vantage-ground occupied: "For so much money, to be so spent, such a system can be fairly tried". And then I think the money could be got. Otherwise, no.

I see danger in the halfpenny. Thus. It would instantly multiply by an unknown figure, the number of little mendicants. The whole neighbourhood of the Scrap Kitchen would be thronged with children each begging for that halfpenny. The parents in the mass would never give the halfpenny. They would say "Go out and get it". Then the Police would bring the children up before the Magistrates, by the half dozen at a haul.

Again. To try the scheme—on any terms—in only one place, would be to swamp that place instantly, and to assemble in it from various quarters a crowd of famishing children (even supposing they were not beggars), who must be disappointed soon after the opening of the doors. And supposing that nearest the doors there are 500 little thieves, and on the outer skirts of that crowd 500 starving children who are not thieves (the most likely to be shouldered out), is the Scrap Kitchen to exhaust itself on the former, and leave the latter unfed?

Surely there must be some sort of enquiry established, or some principle of selection?

I think Chadwick[1] as likely a man as any, to meet these difficulties, and I should much like Dr. Stallard[2] to take his opinion.

Ever Faithfully
CHARLES DICKENS

---

1 Edwin Chadwick (1800–90†), civil servant and influential social reformer. Henry Austin served as secretary on the Royal Commission on the Sanitation of London, chaired by Chadwick in 1847.
2 Joshua Stallard, physician at St George's and St James's Dispensary, published *Workhouse Hospitals*, 1865. His 'Scrap Kitchen' scheme not traced.

To Unknown Correspondent, 27 DECEMBER 1866

Gad's Hill, Thursday 27th December, 1866

Dear Madam,

You make an absurd, though common mistake, in supposing that any human creature can help you to be an authoress, if you cannot become one in virtue of your own powers. I know nothing about "impenetrable barrier," "outsiders," and "charmed circles." I know that anyone who can write what is suitable to the requirements of my own journal—for instance—is a person I am heartily glad to discover, and do not very often find. And I believe this to be no rare case in periodical literature. I cannot undertake to advise you in the abstract, as I number my unknown correspondents by the hundred. But if you offer anything to me for insertion in "All the Year Round," you may be sure that it will be honestly read, and that it will be judged by no test but its own merits and adaptability to those pages.

But I am bound to add that I do not regard successful fiction as a thing to be achieved in "leisure moments".

Faithfully yours
[CHARLES DICKENS]

To Georgina Hogarth, 24 JANUARY 1867

Hen and Chickens, Birmingham | Thursday Twenty Fourth Jany. 1867

My Dearest Georgy.

I forget to whom I wrote last:—whether to you or to Mary. But as I think my last was to Mary, I send this to you.

At Chester we read in a snowstorm, and a fall of ice. I think it was the worst weather I ever saw. Nevertheless we had £66 in the house, and the people were enthusiastic. At Wolverhampton last night (the thaw had thoroughly set in, and it rained heavily) we had £78. We had not intended to go back there, but have arranged to do so, on the day after Ash Wednesday. Last night I was again heavily beaten. We came on here after the Reading (it is only a ride of forty minutes), and it was as much as I could do to hold out the journey. But I was not faint, as at Liverpool. I was only exhausted. I am all right this morning; and tonight, as you know, I have a rest.

The enclosed key is the key of the drawers of my writing table at Gads. In the left hand top-drawer is a bunch of keys, one of which has a bone-label attached to it. That key is the key of the nest of drawers on the top of the stand with the looking-glass door, between the new window and the large window. In one of those drawers (I think the second or third from the bottom) are several of the bound books of my Readings. TWO of them are Nicholas Nickleby. I want those TWO NICKLEBYS sent up to town, so that I may find them at the office on Monday. If you will copy these instructions for Matilda, she cannot go wrong. Let her lock all up again, and return the key to you.

I trust that Charley Collins is better, and that Mamie is strong and well again. Yesterday I had a note from Katie, which seemed hopeful and encouraging.

With best love | Ever My Dearest Georgy | Your most affectionate

CD.

I see in "Fun"[1] this week, a very droll version of Fechter's play.[2] It is really not very wide of the truth.

---

[1] *Fun* was a weekly magazine founded in 1861 as a competitor to *Punch*, by actor and playwright H. J. Byron.

[2] *Rouge et noir*; Fechter's love of melodrama is particularly mocked.

To Robert Lytton,[1] 17 APRIL 1867

GAD'S HILL PLACE, | HIGHAM BY ROCHESTER, KENT.
Wednesday Seventeenth April 1867

My Dear Robert Lytton

It would have been really painful to me, if I had seen you and yours at a Reading of mine, in right of any other credentials than my own. Your appreciation has given me higher and purer gratification than your modesty can readily believe. When I first entered on this interpretation of myself (then quite strange in the public ear), I was sustained by the hope that I could drop into some hearts, some new expression of the meaning of my books, that would touch them in a new way. To this hour that purpose is so strong in me, and so real are my fictions to myself, that, after hundreds of nights, I come with a feeling of perfect freshness to that little red table, and laugh and cry with my hearers, as if I had never stood there before. You will know from this what a delight it is to be delicately understood, and why your earnest words cannot fail to move me.

I beg to send my love (if I may) to Mrs. Lytton. And my sister in law charges me with more kind regard than this paper will hold, both to you and her. Do believe me to be, as I am,

Your genuine admirer | And affectionate friend
CHARLES DICKENS

1 Edward Robert Bulwer Lytton, pseud. Owen Meredith (1831–91†), poet, later viceroy of India, son of Edward Bulwer Lytton.

To John Forster, [14 MAY 1867]

Last Monday evening I finished the 50 Readings with great success. You have no idea how I have worked at them. Finding it necessary; as their reputation widened, that they should be better than at first, I have *learnt them all,* so as to have no mechanical drawback in looking after the words. I have tested all the serious passion in them by everything I know; made the humorous points much more humorous; corrected my utterance of certain words; cultivated a self-possession not to be disturbed; and made myself master of the situation. Finishing with Dombey (which I had not read for a long time) I learnt that, like the rest; and did it to myself, often twice a day, with exactly the same pains as at night, over and over and over again.

I must close with an odd story of a Newfoundland dog. An immense black good-humoured Newfoundland dog. He came from Oxford and had lived all his life at a brewery. Instructions were given with him that if he were let out every morning alone, he would immediately find out the river; regularly take a swim; and gravely come home again. This he did with the greatest punctuality, but after a little while was observed to smell of beer. She was so sure that he smelt of beer that she resolved to watch him. Accordingly, he was seen to come back from his swim, round the usual corner, and to go up a flight of steps into a beer-shop. Being instantly followed, the beer-shop-keeper is seen to take down a pot (pewter pot), and is heard to say: "Well, old chap! Come for your beer as usual, have you?" Upon which he draws a pint and puts it down, and the dog drinks it. Being required to explain how this came to pass, the man says "Yes, ma'am, I know he's your dog, ma'am, but I didn't when he first come. He looked in ma'am—as a Brickmaker might—and then he come in— as a Brickmaker might—and he wagged his tail at the pots, and he giv'a sniff round, and conveyed to me as he was used to beer. So I draw'd him a drop, and he drunk it up. Next morning he come agen by the clock and I drawed him a pint, and ever since he has took his pint reglar!"

To *William H. Wills*, 6 JUNE 1867[1]

Thursday Sixth June 1867

My Dear Wills

I cannot tell you how warmly I feel your letter, or how deeply I appreciate the affection and regard in which it originates. I thank you for it with all my heart.

You will not suppose that I make light of any of your misgivings if I present the other side of the question. Every objection that you make, strongly impresses me, and will be revolved in my mind again and again.

When I went to America in '42, I was so much younger, but (I think) very much weaker too. I had had a painful surgical operation performed, shortly before going out, and had had the labour from week to week of Master Humphrey's Clock. My life in the States was a life of continual speech-making (quite as laborious as Reading), and I was less patient and more irritable then, than I am now. My idea of a course of Readings in America, is, that it would involve far less travelling than you suppose— that the large first class towns would absorb the whole course—and that the receipts would be very much larger than your Estimate. Unless the demand for the Readings is ENORMOUSLY EXAGGERATED ON ALL HANDS, there is considerable reason for this view of the case. And I can hardly think that all the Speculators who beset me, and all the private correspondents who urge me, are in a conspiracy or under a common delusion.

I also believe that an immense impulse would be given to the C. D. Edition[2] by my going out.

If you were to work out the question of Reading profits here, with Dolby, you would find that it would take years to get £10,000. To get that sum in a heap so soon is an immense consideration to me—my wife's income to pay—a very expensive position to hold—and my boys with a curse of limpness on them. You don't know what it is to look round the table and see reflected from every seat at it (where they sit) some horribly well remembered expression of inadaptability to anything.

I shall never rest much while my faculties last, and (if I know myself) have a certain something in me that would still be active in rusting and corroding me, if I flattered myself that it was in repose. On the other hand, I think that my habit of easy self-abstraction and withdrawal into fancies, has always refreshed and strengthened me in short intervals wonderfully. I always seem to myself to have rested far more than I have worked; and I do really believe that I have some exceptional faculty of accumulating young feelings in short pauses, which obliterates a quantity of wear and tear.

My worldly circumstances (such a family considered) are very good. I don't want money. All my possessions are free, and in the best order. Still, at 55 or 56, the likelihood of making a very great addition to one's capital in half a year, is an immense consideration. I repeat the phrase because there *should* be something large, to set against the objections.

The Patient,[3] I acknowledge to be the gigantic difficulty. But you know I don't like to give in before a difficulty, if it can be beaten.

I dine with Forster to day to talk it over. I have no doubt he will urge most of your objections, and particularly the last—though American friends and correspondents he has, have undoubtedly staggered him more than I ever knew him to be staggered, on the money question. Be assured that no one can present any argument to me, which will weigh more heavily with me than your kind words; and that, whatever comes of my present state of abeyance, I shall never forget your letter or cease to be grateful for it.

Ever My Dear Wills | Faithfully
CD.

1 On writing paper headed with Ellen Ternan's monogram.
2 The Charles Dickens edn. 21 vols, published by Chapman & Hall, 1867–75, with some additions, running headlines, revisions, and some new prefaces by CD.
3 CD referred to Nelly in this way after the Staplehurst accident.

To *William H. Wills*, 28 JUNE 1867

OFFICE OF ALL THE YEAR ROUND, | Friday Twenty Eighth June 1867

My Dear Wills.

No doubt Eliza Fenning[1] will come down to Gad's. I will return her by post to you. I did not mean to negative her. Merely raised my eyebrows at a subject so well known.

I am glad you see a certain unlikeness to any thing, in the American story;[2] and I hope that when you see it complete, you will think still better of it. Upon myself, it has made the strangest impression of reality and originality!! And I feel as if I had read something (by somebody else) which I should never get out of my mind!!! The main idea of the narrator's position towards the other people, was the idea I *had* for my next novel in A. Y. R. But it is very curious that I did not in the least see how to begin his state of mind, until I walked into Hoghton Towers[3] one bright April day with Dolby.

Faithfully Ever

CD.

1　A kitchen-maid executed for murder in 1815, and the subject of one of Walter Thornbury's 'Old Stories Re-told' for *AYR*.

2　CD's story, 'George Silverman's Explanation', first published in the *Atlantic Monthly*, Jan.–Mar. 1868.

3　In Lancashire, half-ruined at this time.

To Frances Elliot,[1] 4 JULY [1867]

GAD'S HILL PLACE, | HIGHAM BY ROCHESTER, KENT.
Thursday Fourth July, 1866.

My Dear F.

I am really troubled by the receipt of your tidings of the Dean. Don't even think rashly of the matter. It will assume a softer aspect in a little while. Don't think of it so as to give it, in your own eyes, any one fixed color. You see you *must* allow something for her being his daughter, just as you claim something for your own daughters.

The "magic circle" consists of but one member.[2] I don't in the least care for Mrs. T. T. except that her share in the story is (as far as *I* am concerned) a remembrance impossible to swallow. Therefore, and for the magic sake, I scrupulously try to do her justice, and not to see her—out of my path—with a jaundiced vision.

I feel your affectionate letter truly and deeply, but it would be inexpressibly painful to N to think that you knew the history. She has no suspicion that your assertion of your friend against the opposite powers,[3] ever brought you to the knowledge of it. She would not believe that you could see her with my eyes, or know her with my mind. Such a presentation is impossible. It would distress her for the rest of her life. I thank you none the less, but it is quite out of the question. If she could bear that, she could not have the pride and self reliance which (mingled with the gentlest nature) has borne her, alone, through so much.

If I decide to go to America, it will not be within my means to form a determination until the middle or latter end of September. I am going to send Mr. Dolby out, early next month, and he will come back to me with his report before I arrive at a conclusion. Whensoever you can come here, I shall be heartily pleased to fix a time with you. Of course you will be very strictly on your guard, if you see Tom Trollope—or his wife—or both—to make no reference to me which either can piece into any thing. She is infinitely sharper than the Serpent's Tooth. Mind that.

Ever affectionately
CD.

---

1 Frances Elliot, formerly Dickinson, confided in CD about her marriage difficulties. In 1869 he acted as adviser and mediator. Letter misdated by CD.
2 i.e. Nelly, the 'magic circle' being the Ternan family; Mrs T. T. is Nelly's sister Fanny.
3 Perhaps objectors to Trollope's marriage, on the grounds that he was marrying a former child-actress.

To Bertha Stone,[1] 27 JULY 1867

GAD'S HILL PLACE, | HIGHAM BY ROCHESTER, KENT
Saturday Twenty Seventh July 1867

My Dear Bertha

I have devoted a morning's leisure to going very carefully over your story—to piecing it together—to filling up the cracks, and smoothing the joints and hinges— and to giving it an air of novelty at the end; also a little suggestion of playfulness and happiness. I call it (for these last reasons):

GUESS!

In its present shape, I am not afraid to venture it in All The Year Round.[2] You shall have it in proof, as soon as it is all printed. You must prepare yourself for finding it greatly cut. But I hope it may serve as a not useless pattern for you to work by, another time.

My Love to Marcus, who I hope is getting well. Tell him the Gad's doesn't know itself without him.

Ever affectionately Yours
CHARLES DICKENS

---

1 Frank Stone's youngest daughter.
2 Published under this title, *AYR*, 24 Aug. 1867.

To *Wilkie Collins*, 23 AUGUST 1867

GAD'S HILL PLACE, | HIGHAM BY ROCHESTER, KENT.
Friday Twenty Third August 1867

My Dear Wilkie,

I have done the overture,[1] but I don't write to make *that* feeble report.

I have a general idea which I hope will supply the kind of interest we want. Let us arrange to culminate in a wintry flight and pursuit across the Alps. Let us be obliged to go over—say the Simplon Pass—under lonely circumstances, and against warnings. Let us get into all the horrors and dangers of such an adventure under the most terrific circumstances, either escaping from, or trying to overtake (the latter, the better, I think) some one, on escaping from, or overtaking, whom, the love, prosperity and Nemesis of the story depend. There we can get Ghostly interest, picturesque interest, breathless interest of time and circumstance, and force the design up to any powerful climax we please. If you will keep this in your mind as I will in mine—urging the story towards it as we go along—we shall get a very Avalanche of power out of it, and thunder it down on the readers' heads.

Ever affecy.

CD.

1 The opening chapter of 'No Thoroughfare', which CD and Collins were writing together for the Christmas No. of *AYR*, and afterwards as a stage play.

Memorandum to William H. Wills, [EARLY NOVEMBER 1867]

A.Y.R.

Remember that no reference, however slight is to be made to America in any article whatever, unless by myself.

Remember that the same remark applies to the subject of the Fenians.

Remember that a Poem by Mrs. Cowden Clarke is accepted for the ordinary current No. at Christmas time.

Remember that a narrative from official documents of the Webster Murder case, is to come in from Sir James Emerson Tennent.

JOHN POOLE.

His address is 8, Fitzroy Place, Kentish Town. He will be very thankful if you will sometimes give him a call as you go by on Holly Lodge affairs.[1] He has six envelopes addressed to you at the office, in my writing, with "John Poole" in the corner. This is in case of his wanting any looking after. He is to have £25 sent to him on the 24th of

December, and £25 on the 25th of March. *In case of his death I have £25 of his money in my hands for funeral expenses.*

LETTERS.

Any that may come to Gad's Hill will be forwarded to you to open and dispose of. Similarly, open all letters addressed to me that may come here.

PLORN

After the Christmas Holidays is to go to a Sheep-Farmer for a few months. He, or his tutor, or Mary, or Georgina, will ask you to settle that matter. I suppose that through Sidney and his Agricultural Hall connexion[2] we can know reasonably well whether any suggested person and terms would be likely to act well; or could find out the right person and terms, if none were suggested.

NELLY[3]

If she needs any help will come to you, or if she changes her address, you will immediately let me know if she changes. Until then it will be Villa Trollope, à Ricorboli, Firenze, Italy

Villa Trollope | à Ricorboli | Firenze | Italy

On the day after my arrival out I will send you a short Telegram at the office. Please copy its exact words, (as they will have a special meaning for her), and post them to her as above by the very next post after receiving my telegram. And also let Gad's Hill know—and let Forster know—what the telegram is.

MRS. SCOTT AND MRS. KELLY AND MRS. ALLISON[4]

Mrs. Scott is to be paid One Pound every Saturday, down in the office; beginning this next Saturday, the day of my leaving Liverpool. Mrs. Mary Kelly, 21 Leigh Street, Charles Street, Manchester, is to have a P.O. order for £1 every Saturday. Mrs. Allison, at Mrs. Spreights, Kirkgate, Wakefield, Ditto.

FORSTER:

has an ample Power of Attorney from me, in case you should want any legal authority to act in my name. For he knows Nelly as you do, and will do anything for her, if you want anything done

MY PRIVATE ACCOUNT AT COUTTS'S:

is subject, in my absence, to the joint cheques of Mary and Georgina.

---

1 i.e. Miss Coutts's.

2 Samuel Sidney (1813–83†), writer on agriculture and emigration, author of the popular *Book of the Horse* (1873); secretary of the Agricultural Hall Co.

3 Heavily inked out, this paragraph was retrieved through infra-red photography by John D. Gordan, curator of the Berg Collection at the New York Public Library. See Ada Nesbit, *Dickens and Ellen Ternan* (Berkeley and Los Angeles: University of California Press, 1952), 52.

4 Wives of the staff organizing his American readings.

To *William H. Wills,* 22 NOVEMBER 1867

THE ELECTRIC AND INTERNATIONAL TELEGRAPH COMPANY.

The following Message has been received at G. D. Station.
22.11.1867
FROM
Dickens
TO
Wills Twenty six Wellington St. Strand—Ldn—Safe & well expect good letter full of Hope.[1]

---

1 The code for the telegram, arranged between CD and Nelly, and discovered by Ada Nisbet in CD's 1867 pocket Diary, was as follows: 'Tel: all well means | *you come* | Tel: safe and well, means | *you don't come* | To Wills. Who sends the Te. on to | Villa Trollope | fuori la porta S' Niccolo | Florence', Nisbet, 54.

To *Charles Dickens Jnr,* 30 NOVEMBER and 3 DECEMBER 1867

Parker House, Boston, U.S., | Saturday, Nov. 30th, 1867.

My Dear Charley,
You will have heard before now how fortunate I was on my voyage, and how I was not sick for a moment. These screws are tremendous ships for carrying on, and for rolling, and their vibration is rather distressing. But my little cabin, being for'ard of the machinery, was in the best part of the vessel, and I had as much air in it, night and day, as I chose. The saloon being kept absolutely without air, I mostly dined in my own den, in spite of my being allotted the post of honour on the right hand of the captain.

The tickets for the first four readings here (the only readings announced) were all sold immediately, and many are now re-selling at a large premium. The tickets for the first four readings in New York (the only readings announced there also) were on sale yesterday, and were all sold in a few hours. The receipts are very large indeed; but engagements of any kind and every kind I steadily refuse, being resolved to take what is to be taken myself. Dolby is nearly worked off his legs, is now at New York, and goes backwards and forwards between this place and that (about the distance from London to Liverpool, though they take nine hours to do it) incessantly. Nothing can exceed his energy and good humour, and he is extremely popular everywhere. My great desire is to avoid much travelling, and to try to get the people to come to me, instead of my going to them. If I can effect this to any moderate extent, I shall be saved a great deal of knocking about. My original purpose was not to go to Canada at all; but Canada is so up in arms on the subject that I think I shall be obliged to take it at last. In that case I should work round to Halifax, Nova Scotia, and then take the packet for home.

As they don't seem (Americans who have heard me on their travels excepted) to have the least idea here of what the readings are like, and as they are accustomed to mere readings out of a book, I am inclined to think the excitement will increase when I shall have begun. Everybody is very kind and considerate, and I have a number of old friends here, at the Bar and connected with the University. I am now negotiating to bring out the dramatic version of "No Thoroughfare" at New York. It is quite upon the cards that it may turn up trumps.

I was interrupted in that place by a call from my old secretary in the States, Mr. Putnam. It was quite affecting to see his delight in meeting his old master again. And when I told him that Anne[1] was married, and that I had (unacknowledged) grandchildren, he laughed and cried together. I suppose you don't remember Longfellow, though he remembers you in a black velvet frock very well. He is now white-haired and white-bearded, but remarkably handsome. He still lives in his old house, where his beautiful wife was burnt to death. I dined with him the other day, and could not get the terrific scene out of my imagination. She was in a blaze in an instant, rushed into his arms with a wild cry, and never spoke afterwards.

My love to Bessie, and to Mekitty,[2] and all the babbies.[3] I will lay this by until Tuesday morning, and then add a final line to it.

Ever, my dear Charley, your affectionate Father
[CHARLES DICKENS]

1 Catherine's maid.
2 Nickname of Charley's eldest daughter, Mary Angela (1862–1948).
3 Ethel Kate (1864–1936); Charles Walter (1865–1923), and Sydney Margaret (b. 1866). CD instructed his grandchildren to address him as 'Wenerables'.

To *William. H. Wills*, 10 and 11 DECEMBER 1867

Westminster [Hotel], Irving Place, New York City
Tuesday Evening Tenth December 1867

My Dear Wills

Enclosed is another letter for my dear girl, to your usual care and exactness. By this same post you will receive some New York papers from Dolby. Will you take care to send her the Tribune?

It is absolutely impossible that we could have made a more brilliant success than we made here last night. The reception was splendid, the audience bright and perceptive. I believe that I never read so well since I began, and the general delight was most enthusiastic. And *now* I may tell you that before I came away, I received at the office by two or three Mails from here, various letters about Danger, Anti

Dickens feeling, Anti English feeling, New York rowdyism, and I don't know what else. As I was in for coming, I resolved to say no word about it to anyone. Nor did I, until I came off from the Trial last night, when I told Dolby.

This Hotel is quieter than Mivart's in Brook Street! It is quite as comfortable, and the French cuisine is immeasurably better. I go in and out by a side door and a little staircase that leads straight to my bedroom. The platform absorbs my individuality, and I am very little troubled. We have on the first floor, a pretty drawing room, my bedroom, bath-room, W.C. & Scott's[1] bedroom. Dolby has his bedroom and another room in which to see his clients, on the floor above. There are Hotels (on the American principle) very near, with 500 bedrooms and I don't know how many boarders. This Hotel (on the Eurōpiăn[2] principle) is almost faultless, and is as singularly unlike your idea of an American Hotel as unlike can be. New York has grown out of my knowledge, and is enormous. Everything in it looks as if the order of nature were reversed, and everything grew newer every day, instead of older. The Room[3]—very much larger than its capacity of holding people—is about as trying as St. James's Hall. I am in capital health and voice—but my spirits flutter woefully towards a certain place at which you dined one day not long before I left, with the present writer and a third (most drearily missed) person.[4]

It has been intensely cold. But to day it has thawed, after a fall of snow. Nothing more to report at present, except my love to Mrs. Wills, and my affectionate and faithful regard to you.

CD.

Wednesday Morning
Copperfield and Bob[5] even a greater success last night than Carol and Trial on the night before. "Mr. Digguns", said the German Janitor (the invariable name for the Hall Keeper) "you are gread, mein herr. There is no ent to you!"—That was his parting salutation as he locked me out into a hard frost.—"Bedder and bedder"—he re-opened the door to add.—"Wot negst!"

1 CD's dresser.
2 Accented by CD to show American pronunciation.
3 The Steinway Hall.
4 i.e. Nelly.
5 'Mr Bob Sawyer's Party' from *PP*.

To John Forster, [14 JANUARY 1868, Philadelphia]

I see *great changes* for the better, socially. Politically, no. England governed by the Marylebone vestry[1] and the penny papers, and England as she would be after years of such governing; is what I make of *that*. Socially, the change in manners is remarkable. There is much greater politeness and forbearance in all ways . . . On the other hand there are still provincial oddities wonderfully quizzical; and the newspapers are constantly expressing the popular amazement at "Mr. Dickens's extraordinary composure." They seem to take it ill that I don't stagger on to the platform overpowered by the spectacle before me, and the national greatness. They are all so accustomed to do public things with a flourish of trumpets, that the notion of my coming in to read without somebody first flying up and delivering an "Oration" about me, and flying down again and leading me in, is so very unaccountable to them, that sometimes they have no idea until I open my lips that it can possibly be Charles Dickens.

The Irish element is acquiring such enormous influence in New York city, that when I think of it, and see the large Roman Catholic cathedral rising there,[2] it seems unfair to stigmatise as "American" other monstrous things that one also sees. But the general corruption in respect of the local funds appears to be stupendous, and there is an alarming thing as to some of the courts of law which I am afraid is native-born. A case came under my notice the other day in which it was perfectly plain, from what was said to me by a person interested in resisting an injunction, that his first proceeding had been to "look up the Judge." . . . Last night here in Philadelphia (my first night), a very impressible and responsive audience were so astounded by my simply walking in and opening my book that I wondered what was the matter. They evidently thought that there ought to have been a flourish, and Dolby sent in to prepare for me. With them it is the simplicity of the operation that raises wonder. With the newspapers "Mr. Dickens's extraordinary composure" is not reasoned out as being necessary to the art of the thing, but is sensitively watched with a lurking doubt whether it may not imply disparagement of the audience. Both these things strike me as drolly expressive.

I think it reasonable to expect that as I go westward, I shall find the old manners going on before me, and may tread upon their skirts mayhap. But so far, I have had no more intrusion or boredom than I have when I lead the same life in England. I write this in an immense hotel, but I am as much at peace in my own rooms, and am left as wholly undisturbed, as if I were at the Station Hotel in York. I have now read in New York city to 40,000 people, and am quite as well known in the streets there as I am in London. People will turn back, turn again and face me, and have a look at me, or will say to one another "Look here! Dickens coming!" But no one ever stops me or addresses me. Sitting reading in the carriage outside the New York post-office while one of the staff was stamping the letters inside, I became conscious that a few people who had been looking at the turn-out had discovered me within. On my peeping out good-humouredly, one of them (I should say a merchant's book-keeper) stepped up to the door, took off his hat, and said in a frank way: "Mr. Dickens, I should very much like to have the honour of shaking hands with you"—and, that done, presented two others. Nothing could be more quiet or less intrusive. In the railway cars, if I see anybody who clearly wants to speak to me, I usually anticipate the wish by speaking myself. If I am standing on the brake outside (to avoid the intolerable stove), people getting down will say with a smile: "As I am taking my departure,

Mr. Dickens, and can't trouble you for more than a moment, I should like to take you by the hand sir." And so we shake hands and go our ways. . . . Of course many of my impressions come through the readings. Thus I find the people lighter and more humorous than formerly; and there must be a great deal of innocent imagination among every class, or they never could pet with such extraordinary pleasure as they do, the Boots' story of the elopement of the two little children. They seem to see the children; and the women set up a shrill undercurrent of half-pity and half-pleasure that is quite affecting. To-night's reading is my 26th; but as all the Philadelphia tickets for four more are sold, as well as four at Brooklyn, you must assume that I am at— say—my 35th reading. I have remitted to Coutts's in English gold £10,000 odd; and I roughly calculate that on this number Dolby will have another thousand pounds profit to pay me. These figures are of course between ourselves, at present; but are they not magnificent? The expenses, always recollect, are enormous. On the other hand we never have occasion to print a bill of any sort (bill-printing and posting are great charges at home); and have just now sold off £90 worth of bill-paper, provided beforehand, as a wholly useless incumbrance.

The work is very severe. There is now no chance of my being rid of this American catarrh until I embark for England. It is very distressing. It likewise happens, not seldom, that I am so dead beat when I come off that they lay me down on a sofa after I have been washed and dressed, and I lie there, extremely faint, for a quarter of an hour. In that time I rally and come right.

1 i.e. local parish powers.
2 St Patrick's Cathedral, Fifth Avenue.

To John Forster, [4 FEBRUARY 1868, Washington]

I am going to-morrow to see the President,[1] who has sent to me twice. I dined with Charles Sumner[2] last Sunday, against my rule; and as I had stipulated for no party, Mr. Secretary Stanton[3] was the only other guest, besides his own secretary. Stanton is a man with a very remarkable memory, and extraordinarily familiar with my books. . . . He and Sumner having been the first two public men at the dying President's[4] bedside, and having remained with him until he breathed his last, we fell into a very interesting conversation after dinner, when, each of them giving his own narrative separately, the usual discrepancies about details of time were observable. Then Mr. Stanton told me a curious little story which will form the remainder of this short letter.

On the afternoon of the day on which the President was shot, there was a cabinet council at which he presided. Mr. Stanton, being at the time commander-in-chief of the Northern troops that were concentrated about here, arrived rather late. Indeed they were waiting for him, and on his entering the room, the President broke off in something he was saying, and remarked: "Let us proceed to business, gentlemen." Mr. Stanton then noticed, with great surprise, that the President sat with an air of dignity in his chair instead of lolling about it in the most ungainly attitudes, as his invariable custom was; and that instead of telling irrelevant or questionable stories, he was grave and calm, and quite a different man. Mr. Stanton, on leaving the council with the Attorney-General, said to him, "That is the most satisfactory cabinet meeting I have attended for many a long day! What an extraordinary change in Mr. Lincoln!" The Attorney-General replied, "We all saw it, before you came in. While we were waiting for you, he said, with his chin down on his breast, 'Gentlemen, something very extraordinary is going to happen, and that very soon.' To which the Attorney-General had observed, 'Something good, sir, I hope?' when the President answered very gravely: 'I don't know; I don't know. But it will happen, and shortly too!' As they were all impressed by his manner, the Attorney-General took him up again: 'Have you received any information, sir, not yet disclosed to us?' 'No,' answered the President: 'but I have had a dream. And I have now had the same dream three times. Once, on the night preceding the Battle of Bull Run. Once, on the night preceding' such another (naming a battle also not favourable to the North). His chin sank on his breast again, and he sat reflecting. 'Might one ask the nature of this dream, sir?' said the Attorney-General. 'Well,' replied the President, without lifting his head or changing his attitude, 'I am on a great broad rolling river—and I am in a boat—and I drift—and I drift!—but this is not business'—suddenly raising his face and looking round the table as Mr. Stanton entered, 'let us proceed to business, gentlemen.'" Mr. Stanton and the Attorney-General said, as they walked on together, it would be curious to notice whether anything ensued on this; and they agreed to notice. He was shot that night.

1 Andrew Johnson.
2 Charles Sumner (1811–74; *ANB*), politician and abolitionist.
3 Edwin Stanton (1814–69; *ANB*), Secretary of State for War since 1862.
4 President Abraham Lincoln, shot dead at the theatre by John Wilkes Booth on 14 Apr. 1865.

To Sarah Palfrey,[1] 4 APRIL 1868

Boston | 4th April 1868

Convey yourself back to London by the agency of that powerful Locomotive, your imagination, and walk through the centre avenue of Covent Garden Market from West to East:—that is to say, with your back towards the church, and your face towards Drury Lane Theatre. Keep straight on along the side of the Theatre, and about halfway down, on the left side of the way, behind the houses, is a closely hemmed-in grave yard—happily long disused and closed by the Law. I do not remember that the grave-yard is accessible from the street now, but when I was a boy it was to be got at by a low covered passage under a house, and was guarded by a rusty iron gate. In that churchyard I long afterwards buried the "Nemo" of Bleak House.[2]

This important piece of information is in redemption of a pledge I gave you in Halifax Harbour walking the deck of the Cuba one bright cold morning in last November.

1 Sarah Palfrey (1823–1914), philanthropist and miscellaneous writer.
2 The burial ground of St Martin's-in-the-Fields, at the corner of Drury Lane and Russell St.

To Mary Dickens, 7 APRIL 1868

Boston, Tuesday, April 7th, 1868

I not only read last Friday, when I was doubtful of being able to do so, but read as I never did before, and astonished the audience quite as much as myself. You never saw or heard such a scene of excitement.

Longfellow and all the Cambridge men urged me to give in. I have been very near doing so, but feel stronger to-day. I cannot tell whether the catarrh may have done me any lasting injury in the lungs or other breathing organs, until I shall have rested and got home. I hope and believe not. Consider the weather. There have been two snowstorms since I wrote last, and to-day the town is blotted out in a ceaseless whirl of snow and wind.

I cannot eat (to anything like the ordinary extent), and have established this system: At seven in the morning, in bed, a tumbler of new cream and two tablespoonsful of rum. At twelve, a sherry cobbler and a biscuit. At three (dinner time), a pint of champagne. At five minutes to eight, an egg beaten up with a glass of sherry. Between the parts, the strongest beef tea that can be made, drunk hot. At a quarter-past ten, soup, and anything to drink that I can fancy. I don't eat more than half a pound of solid food in the whole four-and-twenty hours, if so much.

If I hold out, as I hope to do, I shall be greatly pressed in leaving here and getting over to New York before next Saturday's mail from there. Do not, therefore, *if all be well*, expect to hear from me by Saturday's mail, but look for my last letter from America by the mail of the following Wednesday, the 15th. *Be sure* that you shall hear, however, by Saturday's mail, if I should knock up as to reading. I am tremendously "beat", but I feel really and unaffectedly so much stronger to-day, both in my body and hopes, that I am much encouraged. I have a fancy that I turned my worst time last night.

Dolby is as tender as a woman and as watchful as a doctor. He never leaves me during the reading now, but sits at the side of the platform and keeps his eye upon me all the time. Ditto George, the gasman, steadiest and most reliable man I ever employed. I am the more hopeful of my not having to relinquish a reading, because last night was "Copperfield" and "Bob"—by a quarter of an hour the longest, and, in consideration of the storm, by very much the most trying. Yet I was far fresher afterwards than I have been these three weeks.

I have "Dombey" to do to-night, and must go through it carefully; so here ends my report. The personal affection of the people in this place is charming to the last.

To *Annie Fields*,[1] 25 MAY 1868

Gad's Hill, Higham by Rochester, Kent, | 25th May, 1868.

My Dear Mrs. Fields,

As you ask me about the dogs, I begin with them. When I came down first, I came to Gravesend, five miles off. The two Newfoundland dogs, coming to meet me with the usual carriage and the usual driver, and beholding me coming in my usual dress out at the usual door, it struck me that their recollection of my having been absent for any unusual time was at once cancelled. They behaved (they are both young dogs) exactly in their usual manner; coming behind the basket phaeton as we trotted along, and lifting their heads to have their ears pulled—a special attention which they receive from no one else. But when I drove into the stable-yard, Linda (the St. Bernard) was greatly excited; weeping profusely, and throwing herself on her back that she might caress my foot with her great fore-paws. Mamie's little dog, too, Mrs. Bouncer, barked in the greatest agitation on being called down and asked by Mamie, "Who is this?" and tore round and round me, like the dog in the Faust outlines.[2] You must know that all the farmers turned out on the road in their market-chaises to say, "Welcome home, sir!" and that all the houses along the road were dressed with flags; and that our servants, to cut out the rest, had dressed this house so that every brick of it was hidden. They had asked Mamie's permission to "ring the alarm-bell" (!) when master drove up, but Mamie, having some slight idea that that compliment might awaken master's sense of the ludicrous, had recommended bell abstinence. But on Sunday the village choir (which includes the bell-ringers) made amends. After some unusually brief pious reflections in the crowns of their hats at the end of the sermon, the ringers bolted out, and rang like mad until I got home. There had been a conspiracy among the villagers to take the horse out, if I had come to our own station, and draw me here. Mamie and Georgy had got wind of it and warned me.

Divers birds sing here all day, and the nightingales all night. The place is lovely, and in perfect order. I have put five mirrors in the Swiss châlet[3] (where I write) and they reflect and refract in all kinds of ways the leaves that are quivering at the windows, and the great fields of waving corn, and the sail-dotted river. My room is up among the branches of the trees; and the birds and the butterflies fly in and out, and the green branches shoot in, at the open windows, and the lights and shadows of the clouds come and go with the rest of the company. The scent of the flowers, and indeed of everything that is growing for miles and miles, is most delicious.

Dolby (who sends a world of messages) found his wife much better than he expected, and the children (wonderful to relate!) perfect. The little girl winds up her prayers every night with a special commendation to Heaven of me and the pony[4]— as if I must mount him to get there! I dine with Dolby (I was going to write "him", but found it would look as if I were going to dine with the pony) at Greenwich this very day, and if your ears do not burn from six to nine this evening, then the Atlantic is a non-conductor. We are already settling—think of this!—the details of my farewell course of readings. I am brown beyond belief, and cause the greatest disappointment in all quarters by looking so well. It is really wonderful what those fine days at sea did for me! My doctor was quite broken down in spirits when he saw me, for the first time since my return, last Saturday. "Good Lord!" he said, recoiling, "seven years younger!"

It is time I should explain the otherwise inexplicable enclosure. Will you tell Fields, with my love (I suppose he hasn't used *all* the pens yet?), that I think there is in Tremont Street a set of my books, sent out by Chapman, not arrived when I departed. Such set of the immortal works of our illustrious, etc., is designed for the gentleman to whom the enclosure is addressed. If T., F. and Co., will kindly forward the set (carriage paid) with the enclosure to Hamilton's address, I will invoke new blessings on their heads, and will get Dolby's little daughter to mention them nightly.

"No Thoroughfare" is very shortly coming out in Paris, where it is now in active rehearsal. It is still playing here, but without Fechter, who has been very ill. The doctor's dismissal of him to Paris, however, and his getting better there, enables him to get up the play there. He and Wilkie missed so many pieces of stage-effect here, that, unless I am quite satisfied with his report, I shall go over and try my stage-managerial hand at the Vaudeville Theatre. I particularly want the drugging and attempted robbing in the bedroom scene at the Swiss inn to be done to the sound of a waterfall rising and falling with the wind. Although in the very opening of that scene they speak of the waterfall and listen to it, nobody thought of its mysterious music. I could make it, with a good stage-carpenter, in an hour.

Is it not a curious thing that they want to make me a governor of the Foundling Hospital, because, since the Christmas number, they have had such an amazing access of visitors and money?[5]

My dear love to Fields once again. Same to you and him from Mamie and Georgie. I cannot tell you both how I miss you, or how overjoyed I should be to see you here.

> Ever, my dear Mrs. Fields, | Your most affectionate friend
>
> CD

1 Annie Fields (1834–1915; *ANB*), literary hostess and wife of James Fields (1817–81; *ANB*), CD's main American publisher, at Ticknor, Reed & Fields, and good friend.
2 Faust's dog, which turns into Mephistopheles, Goethe's *Faust*, part 1, sc. iii.
3 A gift from CD's friend Charles Fechter.
4 CD had given Dolby's wife a pony on the occasion of her son's birth.
5 The plot of 'No Thoroughfare' turns upon the Foundling Hospital.

To Joseph Parkinson,[1] 4 JUNE 1868

OFFICE OF ALL THE YEAR ROUND, | Thursday Fourth June 1868

My Dear Mr. Parkinson

There is a bill before Parliament (but I forget whose it is) for enabling a married woman to possess her own earnings.[2] I should much like to champion the sex—

reasonably—and to dwell upon the hardship inflicted by the present law on a woman who finds herself bound to a drunken, profligate, and spend-thrift husband—who is willing to support him—does so—but has her little savings bullied out of her, continually. The case is this:—The bill will not pass, we know very well; but would it not be wise and just to take any such opportunity of setting right some little item in the wrong that springs up under our laws of marriage and divorce? Grant what we are told by bishops, priests, and deacons about sanctity of marriage, indissolubility of marriage tie &c &c. Grant that such things *must be,* for the general good. Cannot we—and ought not we—in such a case as this, to help the weak and injured party? Reverse the case, and take a working man with a drunken woman saddled on him as long as he lives, who strips his house continually to buy drink. If he must not be able to divorce himself—for the general good—surely "the general good" should, in return, punish the woman.

Would you like to take this subject?[3]

Faithfully Yours Always
CHARLES DICKENS

1 Joseph Parkinson (1833–1908), civil servant, and regular contributor to *AYR*.
2 The Married Women's Property Bill, finally passed Aug. 1870.
3 He did, in 'Slaves of the Ring', *AYR*, 4 July 1868.

To Edward Dickens, [?26 SEPTEMBER 1868]

My Dearest Plorn,

I write this note to-day because your going away is much upon my mind,[1] and because I want you to have a few parting words from me to think of now and then at quiet times. I need not tell you that I love you dearly, and am very, very sorry in my heart to part with you. But this life is half made up of partings, and these pains must be borne. It is my comfort and my sincere conviction that you are going to try the life for which you are best fitted. I think its freedom and wildness more suited to you than any experiment in a study or office would ever have been; and without that training, you could have followed no other suitable occupation.

What you have always wanted until now has been a set, steady, constant purpose. I therefore exhort you to persevere in a thorough determination to do whatever you have to do as well as you can do it. I was not so old as you are now when I first had to win my food, and do it out of this determination, and I have never slackened in it since.

Never take a mean advantage of anyone in any transaction, and never be hard upon people who are in your power. Try to do to others, as you would have them do to you, and do not be discouraged if they fail sometimes. It is much better for you that they should fail in obeying the greatest rule laid down by our Saviour, than that you should.

I put a New Testament among your books, for the very same reasons, and with the very same hopes that made me write an easy account of it for you,[2] when you were a little child; because it is the best book that ever was or will be known in the world, and because it teaches you the best lessons by which any human creature who tries to be truthful and faithful to duty can possibly be guided. As your brothers have gone away, one by one, I have written to each such words as I am now writing to you, and have entreated them all to guide themselves by this book, putting aside the interpretations and inventions of man.

You will remember that you have never at home been wearied about religious observances or mere formalities. I have always been anxious not to weary my children with such things before they are old enough to form opinions respecting them. You will therefore understand the better that I now most solemnly impress upon you the truth and beauty of the Christian religion, as it came from Christ Himself, and the impossibility of your going far wrong if you humbly but heartily respect it.

Only one thing more on this head. The more we are in earnest as to feeling it, the less we are disposed to hold forth about it. Never abandon the wholesome practice of saying your own private prayers, night and morning. I have never abandoned it myself, and I know the comfort of it.

I hope you will always be able to say in after life, that you had a kind father. You cannot show your affection for him so well, or make him so happy, as by doing your duty.

> Your affectionate Father
> [CHARLES DICKENS]

1 Plorn left London on 26 Sept. for Australia. He was 16 years old.
2 *The Life of Our Lord*, see above, 28 June 1846.

To Henry Dickens, 15 OCTOBER 1868

Adelphi Hotel, Liverpool | Thursday Fifteenth October 1868

My Dear Harry.

I have your letter here this morning. I enclose you another cheque for £25, and I write to London by this post, ordering 3 Doz: Sherry, 2 Doz: Port, and 3 Doz: light claret to be sent down to you. And 6 bottles of brandy. I also enclose a cheque in favor of the Rev. F. L. Hopkins[1] for £5 . . 10 . . 0.

Now, observe attentively. We must have no shadow of debt. Square up everything whatsoever that it has been necessary to buy. Let not a farthing be outstanding on any account, when we begin together with your allowance. Be particular in the minutest detail.

I wish to have no secret from you in the relations we are to establish together, and I therefore send you Joe Chitty's[2] letter bodily. Reading it, you will know exactly what

I know, and will understand that I treat you with perfect confidence. It appears to me that an allowance of £250 a year will be handsome for all your wants, if I send you your wine. I mean this to include your tailor's bills as well as every other expence; and I strongly recommend you to buy nothing in Cambridge, and to take credit for nothing but the clothes with which your tailor provides you. As soon as you have got your furniture accounts in, let us wipe all these preliminary expences clean out, and I will then send you your first quarter. We will count in it, October, November, and December; and your second quarter will begin with the New Year. If you dislike, at first, taking charge of so large a sum as £62 . . 10 . . o you can have your money from me half quarterly.

You know how hard I work for what I get, and I think you know that I never had money help from any human creature after I was a child. You know that you are one of many heavy charges on me, and that I trust to your so exercising your abilities and improving the advantages of your past expensive education, as soon to diminish *this* charge. I say no more on that head.

Whatever you do, above all other things keep out of debt, and confide in me. If you ever find yourself on the verge of any perplexity or difficulty, come to me. You will never find me hard with you while you are manly and truthful.

As your brothers have gone away one by one, I have written to each of them what I am now going to write to you. You know that you have never been hampered with religious forms of restraint, and that with mere unmeaning forms I have no sympathy. But I most strongly and affectionately impress upon you the priceless value of the New Testament, and the study of that book as the one unfailing guide in Life. Deeply respecting it, and bowing down before the character of Our Saviour, as separated from the vain constructions and inventions of men, you cannot go very wrong and will always preserve at heart a true spirit of veneration and humility. Similarly, I impress upon you the habit of saying a Christian prayer every night and morning. These things have stood by me all through my life, and you remember that I tried to render the New Testament intelligible to you and loveable by you when you were a mere baby.

And so God bless you.

Ever Your affectionate Father
CHARLES DICKENS

1 Revd Frank Lawrence Hopkins, Fellow and Tutor of Trinity Hall, Cambridge, where Harry went, Oct. 1868.

2 Joseph Chitty (1828–99†); a barrister in Lincoln's Inn, he excelled at Oxford both academically and athletically. CD had asked his advice on Harry's allowance.

To John Forster, [?15 NOVEMBER 1868]

We might have agreed to differ about it very well,[1] because we only wanted to find out the truth if we could, and because it was quite understood that I wanted to leave behind me the recollection of something very passionate and dramatic, done with simple means, if the art would justify the theme.

1 i.e. the 'Sikes and Nancy' reading, referred to by CD as the 'Oliver Murder'; he gave a private reading on 14 Nov.

To *William Macready*, 19 NOVEMBER 1868

GAD'S HILL PLACE, | HIGHAM BY ROCHESTER, KENT.
Thursday Nineteenth November 1868

My Dearest Macready

I should have written to you much sooner, but that I have been waiting on from week to week while the Chappells were doubtful whether or no to take Cheltenham in the tour. The small size of the room was their objection, but I believe they have now resolved to take it in, at high prices. So I write at once, and will write again when I know more.

We are having the most astonishing houses, in London! It seems as though we could fill Saint Pauls.

On the fifth of January I am coming out with the Murder from Oliver Twist, which I have put together and got up with great pains and elaboration. It so horrified myself at last, that I got afraid of it, and tried it privately last Saturday upon about a hundred people at St. James's Hall. The verdict of ninety of them was: "It must be done." So it is going to be done. "Well," says Mrs. Keeley, drawing a very long and very tight breath after it was over: "the public have been wanting a sensation for a few years—and now they've got it!" How I wished for you on the Jury!

We are all well, except Charles Collins, who never will be well on this earth.[1] Katie, Mary, and Georgina, are all here, and all send best love to Mrs. Macready and to you. My work is very hard at present; but I don't mind that, having health and spirits—and not being across the Atlantic. I am away to Scotland before Christmas, and to Ireland afterwards, and shall not get done before the end of May.

Ever my Dearest Macready | Your most affectionate

CD.

1 He died in 1873 from stomach cancer.

To Mary Boyle, 6 JANUARY 1869

OFFICE OF ALL THE YEAR ROUND, | Wednesday Sixth January 1869

My Dear Mary

I was more affected than you could easily believe, by the sight of your gift lying on my dressing-table on the morning of the New Year. To be remembered in a friend's heart when it is sore, is a touching thing; and that, and the remembrance of the dead,[1] quite overpowered me: the one being inseparable from the other.

You may be sure that I shall attach a special interest and value to the beautiful present,[2] and shall wear it as a kind of charm. God bless you, and may we carry our friendship through many coming years!

My preparations for a certain Murder[3] that I had to do last night, have rendered me unfit for letter-writing these last few days, or you would have heard from me sooner. The crime being comfortably off my mind and the blood spilled, I am (like many of my fellow-criminals) in a highly edifying state to day.

Ever believe me | Your affectionate Friend
CHARLES DICKENS

1 Mary's brother Cavendish Spencer Boyle, died Nov 1868.
2 A waistcoat.
3 The 'Sikes and Nancy' reading.

To Mark Lemon, 16 APRIL 1869

Queen's Hotel, Leeds | Friday Sixteenth April, 1869

My Dear Lemon

I send you a hasty line to let you know that I have had your messages to day, and that I am heartily glad to know that you were but very slightly shaken by your "Railway accident". The phrase has had a dreadful significance to me, ever since the Staplehurst occasion. Be sure that you do right in being as quiet as you can. My watch (a chronometer) had palpitations six months afterwards, and I often wonder whether it would have escaped them if I had stopped it for rest.

Ever Faithfully
CHARLES DICKENS

To Thomas Adolphus Trollope, 6 MAY 1869

OFFICE OF ALL THE YEAR ROUND, | Thursday Sixth May 1869

My Dear Trollope

I am happy to reply to your kind and welcome letter that I hope I am all right. With too short a rest after the heavy American experience, I undoubtedly over-did the work of the Readings and the jar of continual Express Trains; the latter, incessant and extending over great distances; the former, greatly enhanced by the Murder from Oliver Twist, continually done with great passion and fury. All of a sudden (as it seemed) I became exhausted,—giddy, faint, and oddly uncertain of touch and tread. I asked my Doctor[1] (we were students together as boys) "What is this?" He immediately came to Preston to meet me, and said "It is a serious warning. I know it well. Leave off instantly, and come away with me." I didn't even read that night, but came away straight. Watson immediately endorsed the advice as thoroughly sound, and would not even let me finish the London Readings. The very day I rested, I began to recover myself. I am very rarely giddy even for a few moments—eat well, drink well, sleep soundly, and have almost recovered my usual face, they tell me. Probably I should have had a bad bout of it, but for being so promptly dealt with.

A thousand thanks for your kind tempting, but I must not travel. Through the summer and autumn I have promised to be as idle *as I can,* and to oscillate only between London and Gad's Hill. I am to be always in the air, but am to be as shy as possible of railway travelling.

I don't know whether Fanny has heard of poor Macready's having lost his eldest surviving daughter. She died on her passage home from Madeira (where she had been with a nurse, for her health) while Macready was waiting for her at Southampton. She was buried at sea in the early morning, and a majestic rainbow irradiated the place where the body dipped into the water. It had not happened when I saw Macready last at Cheltenham; but I knew from Mrs. Macready's look when he was not observing, that it would happen. He is dismally old, and infirm, and indistinct beyond belief. In talking with him, I could sometimes hardly believe that I had before me the grey ashes of the old fierce fire. His wife is really in all things the staff of his life. Yet he brightened up in talking of old times, and was very grimly interested in the Murder. When it was over, his jaw became square again, and he tried to say with energy: "Dickens —er—By Heavens I swear its—er—its—er—Two Macbeths!"

I saw your brother Anthony[2] at the Athenæum not long ago, who was in the act of reading a letter from you. He is a perfect cordial to me, whenever and wherever I see him, as the heartiest and best of fellows.

With kind regard | Ever My Dear Trollope

Most affectionately Yours
CHARLES DICKENS

1 Frank Beard.
2 Anthony Trollope (1815–82†), novelist; parodied CD as Mr Popular Sentiment in *The Warden* (1855).

To John Forster, [9 MAY 1869]

I see you have told, with what our friend[1] would have called *wonderful* accuracy, the little St. James's Square story, which a certain faithless wretch was to have related.

It was at a celebration of his birthday in the first of his Bath lodgings, 35, St. James's Square, that the fancy which took the form of Little Nell in The Curiosity Shop first dawned on the genius of its creator. No character in prose fiction was a greater favourite with Landor. He thought that, upon her, Juliet might for a moment have turned her eyes from Romeo, and that Desdemona might have taken her hairbreadth escapes to heart, so interesting and pathetic did she seem to him; and when, some years later, the circumstances I have named were recalled to him, he broke into one of those whimsical bursts of comical extravagance, out of which arose the fancy of Boythorn. With tremendous emphasis he confirmed the fact and added that he had never in his life regretted anything so much as having failed to carry out an intention he had formed respecting it; for he meant to have purchased that house, 35, St. James's Square, and then and there to have burned it to the ground, to the end that no meaner association should ever desecrate the birthplace of Nell. Then he would pause a little, become conscious of our sense of his absurdity, and break into a thundering peal of laughter.

1 i.e. Landor. Forster had sent CD an advance copy of his *Walter Savage Landor: A Biography*. CD had wanted to contribute this story himself, but was prevented by his departure for America.

To John Forster, [MID-JULY 1869]

What should you think of the idea of a story beginning in this way?—Two people, boy and girl, or very young, going apart from one another, pledged to be married after many years—at the end of the book. The interest to arise out of the tracing of their separate ways, and the impossibility of telling what will be done with that impending fate.[1]

1 The genesis of *ED*.

To John Forster, [6 AUGUST 1869]

I have a very remarkable story indeed for you to read.[1] It is in only two chapters. A thing never to melt into other stories in the mind, but always to keep itself apart.

I laid aside the fancy I told you of, and have a very curious and new idea for my new story[2] *of the murder of a nephew by his uncle, the originality of which was to consist in the review of the murderer's career by himself at the close, when its temptations were to be dwelt upon, as if, not he the culprit, but some other man, were the tempted. The last chapters were to be written in the condemned cell, to which his wickedness, all elaborately elicited from him as if told of another, had brought him.* Not a communicable idea (or the interest of the book would be gone), but a very strong one, though difficult to work.

1 'An Experience' by Emily Jolly, *AYR*, 14 and 21 Aug. 1869.
2 *ED*.

To *Arthur Ryland*,[1] 13 AUGUST 1869

GAD'S HILL PLACE, | HIGHAM BY ROCHESTER, KENT,
Friday, Aug 13th, 1869

My Dear Mr Ryland,
    Many thanks for your letter.
    I have very strong opinions on the subject of speechification, and hold that there is, everywhere, a vast amount too much of it. A sense of absurdity would be so strong upon me, if I got up at Birmingham to make a flourish on the advantages of education in the abstract for all sorts and conditions of men, that I should inevitably check myself and present a surprising incarnation of the soul of wit. But if I could interest myself in the practical usefulness of the particular institution; in the ways of life of the students; in their examples of perseverance and determination to get on; in their numbers, their favourite studies, the number of hours they must daily give to the work that must be done for a livelihood, before they can devote themselves to the acquisition of new knowledge, and so forth, then I could interest others. This is the kind of information I want.[2] Mere holding forth "I utterly detest, abominate, and abjure."[3]
    I fear I shall not be in London next week. But if you will kindly send me here, at your leisure, the roughest notes of such points as I have indicated, I shall be heartily obliged to you, and will take care of their falling into shape and order in my mind. Meantime I "make a note of"[4] Monday, 27th September, and of writing to you touching your kind offer of hospitality, three weeks before that date.
    I beg to send my kind regard to Mrs. and Miss Ryland, and am always,

Very faithfully yours
[CHARLES DICKENS]

1 Arthur Ryland (1807–77†), lawyer and local politician. Founded the Birmingham and Midland Institute, in aid of which CD gave readings in 1853.
2 For his speech, drawing on information given to him by Ryland; see *Speeches*, 398–407.
3 Cf. Deuteronomy 7: 26.
4 Cf. Captain Cuttle, in *D&S*.

To Henry Dickens, 20 AUGUST 1869

Office, Friday Twentieth August 1869

My Dear Harry

You must bear in mind that the new furnishing[1] was not necessary—really was not in the slightest degree necessary, considering the manner in which you had furnished those top rooms so very recently—and that if your fancies go before your means, you never will, or can, be out of debt. I must not admit the accuracy of your expression "the double furnishing *that I have had to do*"—as though it had been forced upon you—because there is simply no reason in it.

I enclose a cheque for £35.

Ever affectionately
CHARLES DICKENS

1 For his rooms at Gad's Hill.

To Sheridan Le Fanu,[1] 24 NOVEMBER 1869

GAD'S HILL PLACE, | HIGHAM BY ROCHESTER, KENT.
Wednesday Twenty Fourth November 1869

My Dear Sir

In reply to your obliging letter, I beg to assure you that I shall be truly glad to count upon you as a very frequent contributor.

Your sketch is very new, striking, and touching. It should make a remarkable story.[2]

Let me explain to you that I am now about to begin to publish in "All The Year Round" (at the end of each No.) a serial story by FitzGerald of about one good Volume in length.[3] A longer serial story being always in course of publication at the same time, and each No. containing only 24 pages, it is desirable that the rest of the matter should be always at such times, if possible, complete in itself. For the reason that the public have a natural tendency, having more than two serial stories to bear in mind at once, to jumble them all together, and do justice to none of them.

I think the enclosed letter will interest you, as showing how very admirably the story of "Green Tea"[4] was told. It is from the lady I mentioned to you in a note: who has, for thirty or forty years been the subject of far more horrible spectral illusions than have ever, within my knowledge, been placed on record.[5] She is an English lady married to a foreigner of good position, and long resident in an old Italian City:—its name you will see on the letter—Genoa. I became an intimate friend of her husband's when I was living in Genoa five and twenty years ago, and, seeing that she suffered most frightfully from tic (I knew of her having no other disorder, at that time), I confided to her husband that I had found myself to possess some rather exceptional power of Animal Magnetism (of which I had tested the efficacy in nervous disorders), and that I would gladly try her. She never developed any of the ordinarily-related phænomona, but after a month began to sleep at night— which she had not done for years—and to change, amazingly to her own mother, in appearance. She then disclosed to me that she was, and had long been, pursued by myriads of bloody phantoms of the most frightful aspect; and that, after becoming paler, they had all *veiled their faces*. From that time, wheresoever I travelled in Italy, she and her husband travelled with me, and every day I magnetized her; sometimes under olive trees, sometimes in Vineyards, sometimes in the travelling carriage, sometimes at wayside Inns during the mid-day halt. Her husband called me up to her, one night at Rome, when she was rolled into an apparently impossible ball, by tic in the brain, and I only knew where her head was by following her long hair to its source. Such a fit had always held her before, at least 30 hours, and it was so alarming to see that I had hardly any belief in myself with reference to it. But in half an hour she was peacefully and naturally asleep, and next morning was quite well.

When I left Italy that time, the spectres had departed. They returned by degrees as time went on, and have ever since been as bad as ever. She has tried other Magnetism, however, and has derived partial relief. When I went back to Genoa for a few days, a dozen years ago, I asked her should I magnetize her again? She replied that she *felt* the relief would be immediate; but that the agony of leaving it off so soon, would be so great, that she would rather suffer on.

She is, as you will see, a very brave woman, and has thoroughly considered her disorder. But her sufferings are unspeakable; and if you could write me a few lines giving her any such knowledge as she wants, you would do an action of equally unspeakable kindness.

My Dear Sir | Faithfully Yours always
CHARLES DICKENS

1 Sheridan Le Fanu (1814–73†), novelist, newspaper proprietor, magazine owner and editor.
2 *The Rose and the Key*, serialized *AYR*, Jan.–Sept. 1871.
3 'The Bridge of Sighs: A Yachting Story'.
4 By Le Fanu, serialized *AYR*, Oct.–Nov. 1869.
5 Augusta de la Rue.

To *William H. Wills*, 23 JANUARY 1870

5 Hyde Park Place, London W | Sunday Twenty Third Jany. 1870

My Dear Wills.

In the note I had from you about Nancy and Sikes, you seem to refer to some other note you had written me. Therefore I think it well merely to mention that I have received no other note.

I do not wonder at your not being up to the undertaking (even if you had had no cough) under the wearing circumstances. It was a very curious scene.[1] The actors and actresses (most of the latter looking very pretty) mustered in extraordinary force, and were a fine audience. I set myself to carrying out of themselves and their observation, those who were bent on watching how the effects were got:—and I believe I succeeded. Coming back to it again however, I feel it was madness ever to do it continuously. My ordinary pulse is 72, and it runs up under this effort to 112. Besides which, it takes me ten or twelve minutes to get my wind back at all: I being in the meantime like the man who lost the fight:—in fact, his express image. Frank Beard was in attendance to make divers experiments to report to Watson; and although, as you know, he stopped it instantly when he found me at Preston, he was very much astonished by the effects of the "Reading" on the Reader.

So I hope you may be able to come and hear it before it is silent for ever. It is done again on the evenings of the 1st. Feby, 15th. Feby, and 8th. March. I hope, now I have got over the mornings, that I may be able to work at my book. But up to this time the great preparation required in getting the subjects up again, and the twice a week besides, have almost exclusively occupied me.

I have something the matter with my right thumb, and Can't (as you see) write plainly. I sent a word to poor Robert Chambers, and I send my love to Mrs. Wills.

The patient[2] was in attendance and missed you. I was charged with all manner of good and kind remembrance.

Ever My Dear Wills | Affectionately Yours

CD.

1 The second of CD's special matinées for the theatrical professions, on 21 Jan. He read 'Boots' and 'Sikes and Nancy'.
2 Nelly.

To *Edward Bulwer Lytton,* 12 FEBRUARY 1870

5 Hyde Park Place W. | Saturday Twelfth Feby. 1870

My Dear Lytton
The move initiated by Murray and Longman in the enclosed (or rather accompanying) papers, is very important, and refers to one of the most preposterous robberies ever systematically committed.[1] I have so completely lost faith in the governing of my blessed country, "the dread and envy of them all",[2] that I do not believe it cares to remedy any injustice, so long as it can possibly leave it alone. Nevertheless I feel it right to go to this Meeting, just as I should feel it right to go a Station House if I were knocked down and robbed in the street. I wish you may think it well to come too. I understand it to be private, and merely to involve a delicate suggestion to the Supreme Powers that writers are not, ipso facto, felons, and that Rule Britannia

may be sung to any extent, without necessarily demanding the confiscation of their property.

Ever Yours
CHARLES DICKENS

1 The publishers Murray and Longman were supporting the repeal of the 1847 Imperial Copyright Act, which allowed foreign (mainly American) reprints of British copyright works into the Colonies.
2 From 'Rule Britannia'.

To Henry Dickens, 17 FEBRUARY 1870

5 Hyde Park Place W | Thursday Seventeenth February 1870

My Dear Harry
    I am extremely glad to hear that you have made a good start at the Union.[1] Take any amount of pains about it, open your mouth well and roundly, speak to the last person visible, and give yourself time.

Loves from all | Ever affectionately
CD

1 Harry was speaking in debates at the Cambridge Union.

To Arthur Helps,[1] 26 MARCH 1870

5 Hyde Park Place W. | Saturday Twenty Sixth March 1870

My Dear Helps
    The binder reports to me to day that he wants "another fortnight" for the completion of the set of my books which I have entrusted to him to bind for the Queen. Of course he must have it, or he will for ever believe that I spoilt his work by driving him.
    En attendant, I send you for Her Majesty the first No. of my new story which will not be published until next Thursday the 31st. Will you kindly forward it to the Queen with my loyal duty and devotion? If Her Majesty should ever be sufficiently interested in the tale to desire to know a little more of it in advance of her subjects, you know how proud I shall be to anticipate the publication.
    You will receive soon after this, a copy of your Godson's[2] most portable edition of his writings, for yourself. I hope you may like it, and, reversing and abbreviating the Catechism, "do one thing in his name":—read it.
    In the accompanying box is a bundle of those choice little cigars duly dried in the summer heat of Gad's Hill. If you continue to like them and will impress on

Mr. Carlin[3] that you confide in his supplying you as he supplies me, I think you will rarely get any worse.

Faithfully Yours ever
CHARLES DICKENS

1 Arthur Helps (1813–75†), public servant and author. Clerk to the Privy Council, and confidential adviser to Queen Victoria; he edited her books.
2 As CD termed himself to Helps, after his interview with the Queen on 9 Mar.
3 Thomas Carlin, cigar merchant, 189 Regent Street.

To John Forster, [29 APRIL 1870]

Like you at Ely, so I at Higham, had the shock of first reading at a railway station of the death of our old dear friend and companion.[1] What the shock would be, you know too well. It has been only after great difficulty, and after hardening and steeling myself to the subject by at once thinking of it and avoiding it in a strange way, that I have been able to get any command over it or over myself. If I feel at the time that I can be sure of the necessary composure, I shall make a little reference to it at the Academy to-morrow.[2] I suppose you won't be there.

It is very strange—you remember I suppose?—that the last time we spoke of him together, you said that we should one day hear that the wayward life into which he had fallen was over, and there an end of our knowledge of it.

1 Daniel Maclise, who had been virtually a recluse for the past five years.
2 CD paid tribute to him at the Royal Academy Dinner.

To Alfred Dickens, 20 MAY 1870

ATHENÆUM | Friday Night Twentieth May, 1870

My Dear Alfred

I have just time to tell you under my own hand that I invited Mr. Bear[1] to a dinner of such guests as he would naturally like to see, and that we took to him very much, and got on with him capitally.

I am doubtful whether Plorn is taking to Australia. Can you find out his real mind? I notice that he always writes as if his present life were the be-all and the end-all of his emigration, and as if I had no idea of you two becoming proprietors, and aspiring to the first positions in the Colony, without casting off the old connexion.

From Mr. Bear I had the best accounts of you. I told him that they did not surprise me, for I had unbounded faith in you. For which take my love and Blessing.

I fear that Sydney is much too far gone for recovery, and I begin to wish that he were honestly dead.[2]

They will have told you all the cheerfuler news here, and that I am hard at work. This is not a letter, so much as an assurance that I never think of you without hope and comfort.

Ever My Dear Alfred | Your affectionate Father
CHARLES DICKENS

1 The Hon. John Pinney Bear, Melbourne banker and member of the Legislative Council of Victoria.
2 He died in 1872.

To *Sheridan Le Fanu*, 26 MAY 1870

GAD'S HILL PLACE, | HIGHAM BY ROCHESTER, KENT.
Thursday Twenty Sixth May, 1870

My Dear Mr. Le Fanu

I have been very tardy in answering your letter, but a Neuralgic attack in the foot to which I am occasionally liable (it originated in over-walking in deep snow, and was revived by a hard winter in America), has caused me great pain, and has lamed me, and distracted my attention.

I quite agree with you that no story should be planned out too elaborately in detail beforehand, or the characters become mere puppets and will not act for themselves when the occasion arises. But your story[1] is so very slightly sketched in some of its most important stages, that I cannot yet see it as you see it, or feel its capacity as you feel it. I do not doubt, however, the strength of its leading ideas.

All I can clearly see, by way of suggestion, in the present imperfect state of my knowledge is, that the daughter's love-story should have begun before her intimacy with her unknown brother, and should be the express cause of her not being open with her mother as to her feeling towards him. This would prevent the very disagreeable suspicion on the reader's part (the reader being instructed on the subject), that she was in any danger of falling into tender relations towards her brother. I also think that if a love story on the part of the young man himself could be the mainspring of the mother's Nemesis, it would be strong and interesting.

It occurs to me, moreover, that you might weave into the innermost thread of the narrative with great point and advantage, such a character as this:—an Irish youth who is incapable of his own happiness or anybody elses, and attributes that incapacity—not to his own faults, but to his country's real or supposed wrongs. It seems to me that thus a most useful and striking mark might be set upon the time.

It will never be a trouble to me to be taken into council upon any refinement or enlargement of the idea that may present itself to your mind: indeed I shall highly esteem such a confidence on your part, and will do my best to be suggestive and helpful in reference to it.

> Believe me alys | Very faithfully Yours
> CHARLES DICKENS

1 *The Rose and the Key.*

To Messrs Pulvermacher & Co., 3 JUNE 1870

GAD'S HILL PLACE, | HIGHAM BY ROCHESTER, KENT

Friday Third June 1870

Mr. Charles Dickens sends his compliments to Messrs. Pulvermacher and Co. and begs to say that he wishes to try a voltaic band across his right foot, as a remedy against what he supposes to be Neuralgia there (originating in over-walking in deep snow), to which he is occasionally liable.

Mr. Dickens writes on the recommendation of Mrs. Bancroft, who assures him that she has derived great relief from a similar complaint from the use of one of these bands. If Messrs. Pulvermacher and Co. will be so good as send him one, he will remit a cheque for its cost by return of post, and will give it the fairest trial.

To John Makeham,[1] 8 JUNE 1870

GAD'S HILL PLACE, | HIGHAM BY ROCHESTER, KENT.
Wednesday Eighth June 1870

Dear Sir

It would be quite inconceivable to me—but for your letter—that any reasonable reader could possibly attach a scriptural reference to a passage in a book of mine, reproducing a much abused social figure of speech, impressed into all sorts of service, on all sorts of inappropriate occasions, without the faintest connexion of it with its original source.[2] I am truly shocked to find that any reader can make the mistake.

I have always striven in my writings to express veneration for the life and lessons of Our Saviour; because I feel it; and because I re-wrote that history for my children— every one of whom knew it from having it repeated to them, long before they could read, and almost as soon as they could speak.

But I have never made proclamation of this from the house tops.

Faithfully Yours
CHARLES DICKENS[3]

1 John Makeham, a clerk in the civil service, living at 27 Canonbury Villas, Islington, London N.
2 Used of Crisparkle in *ED* ch. 10: 'like the highly-popular lamb who has so long and unresistingly been led to the slaughter', CD's expansion of Isaiah 53: 7.
3 CD was writing letters on the afternoon of 8 June (see Forster, 851). He suffered a stroke that evening, and died the next day.

Select Bibliography

Editions of the Letters

The Letters of Charles Dickens, edited by his Sister-in-Law and his Eldest Daughter, 3 vols. (London: Chapman & Hall, 1880–2).

The Letters, Speeches, Plays and Poems of Charles Dickens, ed. Frederic Kitton (New York: The University Society, 1908).

The Letters of Charles Dickens, ed. Walter Dexter, 3 vols. (Bloomsbury: Nonesuch Press, 1938).

Selected Letters of Charles Dickens, ed. David Paroissien (London: Macmillan, 1985).

The British Academy Pilgrim Edition: The Letters of Charles Dickens, 12 vols. (Oxford: Clarendon Press):

Volume One, 1820–1839, ed. Madeline House and Graham Storey, 1965.

Volume Two, 1840–1841, ed. Madeline House and Graham Storey, 1969.

Volume Three, 1842–1843, ed. Madeline House, Graham Storey, and Kathleen Tillotson, 1974.

Volume Four, 1844–1846, ed. Kathleen Tillotson, 1977.

Volume Five, 1847–1849, ed. Graham Storey and K. J. Fielding, 1981.

Volume Six, 1850–1852, ed. Graham Storey, Kathleen Tillotson, and Nina Burgis, 1988.

Volume Seven, 1853–1855, ed. Graham Storey, Kathleen Tillotson, and Angus Easson, 1993.

Volume Eight, 1856–1858, ed. Graham Storey and Kathleen Tillotson, 1995.

Volume Nine, 1859–1861, ed. Graham Storey, 1997.

Volume Ten, 1862–1864, ed. Graham Storey, 1998.

Volume Eleven, 1865–1867, ed. Graham Storey, 1999.

Volume Twelve, 1868–1870, ed. Graham Storey, 2002.

Other Writing, Biography, and Relevant Criticism

Ackroyd, Peter, *Dickens* (London: Sinclair Stevenson, 1990).

Andrews, Malcolm, *Charles Dickens and his Performing Selves: Dickens and the Public Readings* (Oxford: Oxford University Press, 2006).

Bodenheimer, Rosemarie, *Knowing Dickens* (Ithaca, NY: Cornell University Press, 2007).

Collins, Philip (ed.), *Dickens: The Critical Heritage* (London: Routledge, 1971).

——(ed.), *Dickens, Interviews and Recollections*, 2 vols. (London: Macmillan, 1981).

Easson, Angus, 'Letters of Dickens', in Paul Schlicke (ed.), *Oxford Reader's Companion to Dickens* (Oxford: Oxford University Press, 1999), 327–31.

Fielding, K. J. (ed.), *The Speeches of Charles Dickens* (Oxford: Clarendon Press, 1960).

Forster, John, *The Life of Charles Dickens* (3 vols. 1872–4), ed. J. W. T. Ley (London: Cecil Palmer, 1928).

Hartley, Jenny, *Charles Dickens and the House of Fallen Women* (London: Methuen, 2008).

House, Humphry, 'A New Edition of Dickens's Letters', *The Listener*, 18 Oct. 1951, reprinted in *All in Due Time: The Collected Essays and Broadcast Talks of Humphry House* (London: Rupert Hart-Davis, 1955), 221–9.

Johnson, Edgar, *Charles Dickens: His Tragedy and Triumph*, 2 vols. (Boston: Little Brown, 1952).

Johnson, Edgar, 'The Art of Biography: An Interview with Edgar Johnson', *Dickens Studies Annual*, 8 (New York: AMS Press, 1980), 1–38.

Kaplan, Fred, *Dickens and Mesmerism* (Princeton: Princeton University Press, 1975).

Lohrli, Anne, *'Household Words': A Weekly Journal 1850–1859, Conducted by Charles Dickens* (Toronto: University of Toronto Press, 1973).

Oppenlander, Ella Ann, *Dickens' 'All the Year Round': Descriptive Index and Contributor List* (Troy, NY: Whitston Publishing Co., 1984).

Paroissien, David, ' "Faithfully Yours, Charles Dickens": The Epistolary Art of the Inimitable', in David Paroissien (ed.), *A Companion to Charles Dickens* (Oxford: Blackwell Publishing, 2008), 33–46.

Sanders, Andrew, *Authors in Context: Charles Dickens* (Oxford: Oxford World's Classics, 2003).

Slater, Michael, *Dickens and Women* (London: J. M. Dent, 1983).

——*Charles Dickens* (New Haven: Yale University Press, 2009).

——and Drew, John (eds.), *Dickens' Journalism*, 4 vols. (London: J. M. Dent, 1994–2000).

Tomalin, Claire, *The Invisible Woman: The Story of Nelly Ternan and Charles Dickens* (London: Viking, 1990).

——*Charles Dickens, A Life* (London: Viking, 2011).

Index